Essentials of
Contemporary
Advertising

William F. Arens
Stratimark Consulting

David H. Schaefer
Sacramento City College

 **McGraw-Hill**
Irwin

Boston   Burr Ridge, IL   Dubuque, IA   Madison, WI   New York   San Francisco   St. Louis
Bangkok   Bogotá   Caracas   Kuala Lumpur   Lisbon   London   Madrid   Mexico City
Milan   Montreal   New Delhi   Santiago   Seoul   Singapore   Sydney   Taipei   Toronto

 **McGraw-Hill
Irwin**

ESSENTIALS OF CONTEMPORARY ADVERTISING

Published by McGraw-Hill/Irwin, a business unit of The McGraw-Hill Companies, Inc. 1221 Avenue of the Americas, New York, NY, 10020. Copyright © 2007 by The McGraw-Hill Companies, Inc. All rights reserved. No part of this publication may be reproduced or distributed in any form or by any means, or stored in a database or retrieval system, without the prior written consent of The McGraw-Hill Companies, Inc., including, but not limited to, in any network or other electronic storage or transmission, or broadcast for distance learning.

Some ancillaries, including electronic and print components, may not be available to customers outside the United States.

This book is printed on acid-free paper.

2 3 4 5 6 7 8 9 0 CCI/CCI 0 9 8 7 6

ISBN-13:   978-0-07-313666-0
ISBN-10:   0-07-313666-2

Editorial director: *John E. Biernat*
Publisher: *Andy Winston*
Developmental editor I: *Anna M. Chan*
Executive marketing manager: *Trent Whatcott*
Producer, Media technology: *Janna Martin*
Senior project manager: *Laura Griffin*
Production supervisor: *Debra R. Sylvester*
Lead designer: *Matthew Baldwin*
Photo research coordinator: *Ira C. Roberts*
Photo researcher: *Mike Hruby*
Senior media project manager: *Susan Lombardi*
Cover/interior design: *Kiera Pohl*
Cover images: *©2005 Dell Computer Corporation. All rights reserved. ©2005 Oldemark, LLC. Reprinted with permission. ©British Airways plc 2005. © GettyImages*
Typeface: *10.5/12 Garamond*
Compositor: *Precision Graphics*
Printer: *Courier Kendallville*

Library of Congress Cataloging-in-Publication Data

Arens, William F.
    Essentials of contemporary advertising / William F. Arens, David H. Schaefer.
       p. cm.
    Includes bibliographical references and index.
    ISBN-13: 978-0-07-313666-0 (alk. paper)
    ISBN-10: 0-07-313666-2 (alk. paper)
      1. Advertising. I. Schaefer, David H. II. Title.
  HF5821.A74 2007
  659.1—dc22

                                                                    2005057672

www.mhhe.com

A mi esposa Olivia, con mucho cariño.
WFA

To the memory of my father, Klaus Schaefer, who laid the foundation for my marketing acumen; to my wife, Ellen, and my daughters, Kristen and Alison, who tolerated me working at the computer for the past eighteen months.
DHS

William F. Arens, President Stratimark Consulting

William F. Arens has spent his entire career in the advertising business, and after 35 years in the field he has literally done it all. As an undergraduate at Berkeley he worked part-time as a media rep for a San Francisco radio station, at the University of Paris he held a position in the Promotions Department for the Paris edition of *The New York Times,* and upon graduation from Whittier College, he began his career in earnest as a sales rep for various print media.

Within a few years, he changed tracks by taking an account management position at a large San Francisco-based high-tech advertising agency, where he rapidly rose to become the manager of their branch office in San Diego.

An entrepreneur at heart, Mr. Arens soon left that position to form his own agency with a partner, where he was both a principal and the chief creative officer. Specializing in business-to-business and financial accounts, that agency grew in stature and reputation over the years, accumulating many awards for creative excellence.

In 1975 he formed William F. Arens and Associates and began focusing on both national and international accounts. Among others, he did award-winning work for Banco Nacional de Mexico (Mexico's largest private bank), Gulfa Water (a bottled water brand in the United Arab Emirates), Bentley Bank (a diamond investment trust headquartered in the Cayman Islands), and Scripps Institute and Research Foundation (an internationally recognized health care institute in La Jolla, California).

A lifelong fascination with foreign languages propelled Mr. Arens into the field of multicultural advertising. In 1982 he formed one of the early Hispanic agencies, Arens & Guiterrez, as a joint venture between his agency and one of the largest in Mexico. Working with mainstream American Agencies, A&G created Spanish-language advertising for blue chip advertisers including McDonald's, General Mills, Sav-On Drugstores, and the California Lottery.

In 1989, Mr. Arens jumped to the client side when he bought a chain of quick-lube stores in San Diego. As chief marketing officer, Mr. Arens was responsible for all the firm's advertising and promotion. He oversaw the company's growth in daily revenue as it doubled and then tripled.

Currently, Mr. Arens heads Stratimark Consulting, which specializes in strategic integrated marketing communications consulting for clients in the health care field. At the same time, he travels and lectures extensively, visiting, among other countries, Russia and France regularly.

David H. Schaefer, Professor Sacramento City College

David H. Schaefer is a professor of Business and Marketing at Sacramento City College. He teaches introductory courses in business, marketing, advertising, customer service, and personal finance. He previously held an adjunct teaching position in the College of Business Administration at California State University, Sacramento.

He received his BA in Economics from the University of California, Santa Cruz and his Masters in Business from the Harvard Business School. He also spent six months as an intern on the President's Council of Economic Advisers, working under Chairman Paul McCracken.

Most of David Schaefer's career has been spent working in industry in marketing, advertising, and general management positions. He started his career in brand management at General Foods Corporation, marketing the Jell-O and Cool Whip brands. Then, during six years at Foote, Cone & Belding Advertising, as a vice president and management supervisor, he supervised accounts for the Clorox Corporation, Levi Strauss, and C&H Sugar. When Mount Zion Medical Center (San Francisco) recognized the need to market its services, he joined them as the vice president for Marketing and Planning and developed programs to promote the hospital's managed care services. He also served for several months as the hospital's CEO.

Mr. Schaefer has also provided his marketing skills in a number of small businesses. He founded a retail eyewear business and helped establish an automotive smog inspection service. Most recently he was the director of marketing and business development for Altaireyewear, a division of Vision Service Plan. In all of these positions he was responsible for developing marketing plans, advertising campaigns, and promotional programs.

His wife, Ellen, is also a marketer and the owner of Group Works, conducting qualitative research and facilitating meetings for businesses and not-for-profit organizations. Both of their daughters are currently attending the University of California.

Preface

Advertising is an ever-changing, creative discipline. The power of advertising is so remarkable in its ability to inspire, influence, and communicate that the study of advertising is more important today than ever before. It's important not just for students of business or journalism—who may be contemplating a career in the field—but also for students of sociology, psychology, political science, economics, history, language, science, or the arts. Many of these people will become creators of advertising; all will be lifetime consumers of it.

Essentials of Contemporary Advertising explores the core principles that drive advertising, using a concise and lively voice that goes beyond academic theory. Students in many short-format courses, some community college curricula, and other nontraditional learning programs may not have the time to successfully complete an exhaustive course in advertising. They are likely to be attending school while working part- or full-time. They may be exploring new majors or new careers. One introductory advertising course may be all they need to enhance their skills, or it might inspire them to take more advertising courses.

Our goal is to present advertising as it is actually practiced and make the fundamentals accessible and relevant to the student's "real life." Advertising should be taught as it really is—as a business, a marketing tool, a creative process, and a dynamic, hybrid discipline that draws upon various arts and sciences to influence our everyday lives. The study of advertising gives students, regardless of their major field of study, many valuable tools to use in any subsequent profession. It teaches them to think and plan strategically; gather and analyze primary and secondary research data; compute and evaluate alternative courses of action; cooperate with teams in developing creative solutions to problems; analyze competitive proposals; understand why people behave the way they do; express themselves and their ideas with clarity and simplicity; defend their points of view with others; appreciate and assess the quality of different creative endeavors; and use data to speak with knowledge, confidence, and conviction.

The spirit of advertising evokes enthusiasm and vital energy—our goal is to provide the tools so this energy can transcend to those studying advertising. Therein lies the key to this textbook—we want students to like it. We don't want them to be intimidated or overwhelmed. We do want them to be excited and inspired about the field of advertising. If we're successful, they will continue in their studies.

Organization

Essentials of Contemporary Advertising is divided into six parts. Part 1, "An Introduction to Advertising," looks at what advertising is today and how it has evolved (Chapter 1). Chapter 2 looks at the social and economic impact of advertising and the role of regulatory policies. Then, Chapter 3 gives an overview of the advertising industry and each of the key players in the business.

Part 2, "Understanding the Target Audience," first explores marketing segmentation and its role in the marketing mix in Chapter 4. Then, Chapter 5 looks at the communication process, consumer behavior, and the steps involved in consumer decision making.

In Part 3, "The Planning Process," the account planning function and how research improves advertising decision making are discussed in Chapter 6. The roles of strategic planning and brand positioning are discussed in Chapter 7.

Part 4, "The Creative Process," begins by explaining why a creative strategy is essential to the creation of great advertising and proceeds to explore the creative process (Chapter 8). Next, in Chapter 9 we explore how art and copy come together to form ads. And, in Chapter 10, we discuss the different processes for producing advertising for print, television, radio, and the Internet.

Part 5, "Reaching the Target Audience," analyzes the different channels of communication through which advertising messages are conveyed. We begin with print advertising (Chapter 11) and discuss television and radio advertising in Chapter 12. Next, we explore interactive media and direct mail (Chapter 13) before concluding the part with an examination of outdoor and supplementary media such as billboards, specialty advertising, and trade shows (Chapter 14).

In Part 6, "Integrating Marketing Communications Elements," we first look at the role of media planning and how it helps to accomplish the advertising objectives (Chapter 15). Next, Chapters 16 and 17 focus on integrated marketing communications and how other elements of the marketing mix can be combined with advertising to build effective relationships with customers.

Acknowledgments

Writing an advertising textbook would be nearly impossible without the assistance and cooperation of a legion of individuals and companies. We are therefore deeply indebted to many people and organizations on all sides of the advertising business (agencies, clients, media, and suppliers) and academia for their professional assistance and personal encouragement. These include, but are certainly not limited to, Joyce Harrington, John Wolfe, and Burtch Drake at the American Association of Advertising Agencies; Paula Alex and Linda McCreight at the Advertising Educational Foundation; Paula Veale at the Ad Council; Shawn O'Neill at New American Financial; Vonda LePage at Deutsch, New York; Roy Elvove at BBDO; David DeCecco at Pepsi-Cola Company; and Peter Farago at Farago & Partners.

We owe a tremendous thank-you to Susan Irwin at McCann-Erickson Worldwide for her many years of friendship and assistance. We are likewise very grateful to everybody at Saatchi & Saatchi Los Angeles, Tokyo, and New York, as well as Toyota Motor Sales U.S.A. for their invaluable assistance, openness, and cooperation in providing important material. We also thank Brannon Wait at Saatchi & Saatchi Chicago for his initiative in getting us together with the Saatchi people in the first place.

For our chapter on the scope of advertising, we are very grateful to our friends at Muse Cordero Chen & Partners for sharing their interesting work on the Honda Civic with us. A big thank you to Shelley Yamane, Wilky Lao, and Jo Muse.

The chapter on Internet advertising required extensive revisions and updating, and for his incredible contributions of time, knowledge, and material, we are indebted to John Keck, formerly senior VP/interactive media director at FCB San Francisco and to Christian Arens at Carat Interactive, Boston. Also, for the outstanding portfolio of layout styles in Chapter 9, thanks go to Tom Michael and Tabitha Ziegler at Market Design in Encinitas, CA.

For their warm, open, and gracious contributions of time, counsel, and materials, we extend our appreciation to all our Canadian friends, especially Paul Lavoie, Daniel Rabinowicz, and Ann Boldt at Taxi; Pierre Delagrave, Normand Chiasson, and Manon Caza at Cossette Communication-Marketing; Yves Gougoux at Publicis/BCP Stratégie Créativité; and Normand Grenier at Communications Grenier.

We are also grateful to our friends at the International Advertising Festival in Cannes for their cooperation and assistance in providing all the award winners for this book. We are especially appreciative of the efforts of Terry Savage, Amanda Benfel, and Monika Barrau. We are grateful for the tremendous personal assistance we've had the last two years at Cannes, first from the assistant video producer Severin Ledresseur and then from Elena Vorobyeva, most recently with Euro RSCG Mordapour, Moscow.

We must give special thanks to several longtime friends in the business whose contributions, continuous support, and wise counsel we value and appreciate immeasurably: Susan Irwin at McCann-Erickson; Jan Sneed at Grey Advertising; Rance Crain at *Advertising Age;* Jack Trout at Trout and Partners; Jorge Gutierrez Orvañanos at MerchanDesign, Guadalajara, Mexico; Brad Lynch, retired from the Ad Council; Jack Balousek, former president of Foote, Cone & Belding; and, of course, a good friend of many years, Al Ries at Ries & Ries.

Deadlines impact family life the worst. For their continued understanding and encouragement, we thank our children, William and Christian and Kristen and Alison, who over the years have paid the highest price for their dads to be teachers and authors. We also thank our wives, Olivia and Ellen, for their constancy, fortitude, and incredible patience.

Finally, we want to give special recognition to a very capable editorial assistant and research manager Sarah Steinberg. Her attention to detail, writing skills, and inimitable dry wit make her a pleasure to work with. We really appreciate the opportunity to work with her.

We also appreciate the skill and dedication of our publishing team at McGraw-Hill/Irwin. Thank you John Biernat, Andy Winston, Anna Chan, and Trent Whatcott. The McGraw-Hill/Irwin A-team also included Laura Griffin, Mike Hruby, Janna Martin, Debra Sylvester, Matthew Baldwin, Ira Roberts, and Sue Lombardi. For moral support and wise counsel when needed, thanks also to Jerry Saykes, Steve Patterson, and Gary Burke. A major thank-you to all of you for again finding the way to do the impossible. We appreciate your patience, dedication to excellence, and your friendship more than you can possibly know.

We also want to recognize and thank the American Academy of Advertising, the American Association for Education in Journalism and Mass Communications, and the American Marketing Association, three organizations whose publications and meetings provide a valuable forum for the exchange of ideas and for professional growth.

We are deeply grateful to the many instructors, professors, academic reviewers, and friends in academia who do the real heavy lifting through their ongoing research, writing, and teaching. Their creative ideas and critical insights were invaluable in the preparation of this book. These people include, but are certainly not limited to, Robyn Blakeman, The University of Tennessee, Knoxville; Lisa Bogaty, Pellissippi State Technical Community College; Tom Hayden, Northwestern University; Won Jang, University of Wisconsin-Eau Claire; Joseph Reihing, Nassau Community College; Daniel Ricica, Sinclair Community College; Patricia Rose, Florida International University; Eugene Secunda, New York University; Shallin Suber, Tri-County Technical College; and Stacy Strawn, Northeast Community College. Finally, we must acknowledge the personal contributions of Hugh Cannon of Wayne State University, a good and generous friend whose wise counsel and brilliant suggestions have enriched this book immeasurably.

To each and every one of you, we thank you. It's your contributions that make this thing work.

William F. Arens
David H. Schaefer

A Guide to
Essentials of Contemporary Advertising

chapter eleven

Print Advertising

Objectives

To examine how print advertising enhances the advertiser's media mix. Newspapers and magazines, with their unique qualities, can complement broadcast, direct mail, and other media. By using print wisely, advertisers can significantly increase the reach and impact of their campaigns and still stay within their budget.

After studying this chapter, you will be able to:

* **Explain** the advantages and disadvantages of magazine advertising.
* **Discuss** the various ways to analyze a magazine's circulation.
* **Describe** how newspapers are categorized.
* **Define** the major types of newspaper advertising.
* **Explain** the advantages and disadvantages of newspaper advertising.
* **Discuss** how rates are determined for print media.
* **Describe** the alternatives for print advertising in foreign markets.

For today's increasingly health-conscious public, the steak and egg meals of yesteryear have lost their appeal. Now, Americans count their calories meticulously, right down to a simple can of soda.

Given this changing attitude, the National Fluid Milk Processor Promotion Board faced a considerable dilemma. How could it reestablish milk as sufficiently savvy for the country's modern beverage consumer? Milk from the dairies of the heartland didn't have the panache sought by the majority of people. Fortunately, unlike many food marketers, the milk board held a trump card of superior nutritional value that it felt could complete a winning hand. What it needed was to educate the public about its special secret and overcome fears of what had become that most taboo "F word": fat.

Science (and nature) worked in the organization's favor. Nutritionists began publishing study after study that confirmed that most Americans did not receive enough calcium from their diet. And calcium is easily obtained through the consumption of milk. The National Institutes of Health (NIH) warned that without enough calcium, middle-age people (especially women) could suffer from the bone-degenerating disease osteoporosis. It reported that after the age of 11, no age group of females achieves even 75 percent of the recommended levels of calcium, and that only one out of three males receives the levels recommended for adults.[1] Armed with this information, the milk board set out to create a campaign that would spark public interest in its solution to this health problem.

The board hired Bozell Worldwide, an advertising agency well known for its print ads. The puzzle was to create a campaign that would resonate with the times, one that would create appeal for a new era of milk, and one that could be supported by the data from the NIH.

Opening Vignettes

Chapter-opening vignettes introduce each chapter, featuring an actual situation that illustrates a relevant concept in the study of advertising. Wherever possible, the opening story is then woven through the chapter to demonstrate how textbook concepts actually come to life in real-world situations.

Commercial Break 11–B

Innovations in Magazine Advertising

Magazines work closely with advertisers to develop new technologies for presenting ideas and products. From these efforts have come such innovations as fragrance strips, color strips, and pop-up ads.

Fragrance strips are a great favorite with perfume advertisers. With the Scentstrip, readers sample a scent by opening a sealed insert tucked into a magazine. Despite some consumer complaints, Scentstrips have been incredibly popular. Fragrances are useful for other products as well. For example, a Rolls-Royce ad in *Architectural Digest* carried a Scentstrip bearing the essence of leather.

Cosmetics manufacturers insert **color strip** samples of eye shadow, blush, lipstick, and other makeup that readers can try immediately. Color strips are expensive to produce, but many advertisers think they're worth it.

Another costly innovation is the **pop-up ad.** Corporate advertisers such as Honeywell and TransAmerica were among the first to try this eye-catching approach. Product ads, such as a pop-up for the Dodge Dakota, followed.

Other intriguing approaches include **3-D ads** (complete with 3-D glasses), **product samples** (facial tissues and paper towels), and unusual shapes and sizes for **preprinted inserts.** An ad for Sara Lee cheesecake used a single heavy-stock page with what appeared to be a bite taken out of a life-size cheesecake slice. A half-page insert for Gleem toothpaste featured a metallic graphic of a mirror with the slogan "Check your mirror."

Researchers are probing the possibilities of holograms and ads that talk. Already ads can sing—liquor companies included microchips that played Christmas carols in their December magazine ads, and ads for a cigarette brand played "Happy Birthday" on the brand's 75th anniversary.

Recently, Global Commerce Group invented the Web Decoder™, a transparent device made of clear polyester Mylar. The recipient is invited to interact with an image on a Web site. When the piece is positioned over the designated image, a hidden word, icon, or phrase is revealed. Advertisers can tailor the Web Decoder to their specific promotional needs, from cents-off coupons to instant-winner prizes.

Such innovative approaches not only attract readers' attention but also involve them in the experience by appealing to more than just the visual sense.

Applying the Breaks
What are some other products that could benefit from the use of these technological innovations?

Commercial Breaks

Active participation enhances learning, so the Commercial Break plays a significant role in many chapters. These unique sidebars to the world of advertising introduce students to topics of current interest or controversy and then involve them in the subject by posing questions (Applying the Breaks) that stimulate critical thinking.

Ethical Issues

Brand Niching May Cause Brand Switching

Advertisers recognize that offensive advertisements don't pay. They know that alienating or stereotyping minorities and other demographic groups causes serious controversy and bad PR for their clients. And, in addition to avoiding the negative effects, there are benefits to being politically correct in advertising: Hispanics, African Americans, Asian Americans, gays, and other minority groups are all sizable target markets with considerable buying power—so much buying power, in fact, that many marketing campaigns are designed specifically to appeal to these market sectors.

Unfortunately, even advertisements that are designed to be sensitive can sometimes backfire. During the 2000 Olympics, John Hancock Financial Services made a sudden revision to a commercial set to air during the events. In the spot, two women were shown together in an airport holding an Asian infant whom they presumably had just adopted. Although the ad never specifically identified the child's nationality, international adoption agencies pressured Hancock to amend the ad to avoid offending the Chinese government, which would be opposed to the evident homosexuality of the American parents. But Hancock was lucky—the ad was caught before it aired. This isn't always the case, and the results can be disastrous when a controversial ad is aired.

To counter recent accusations that they favored white clientele over their African American patrons, Denny's created some ads that attempted to resolve the issue—badly. The three-spot television campaign featured black customers being "welcomed back" to Denny's and having the time of their lives. However, 100 percent of the people Denny's "welcomed back" were black, affluent, well-dressed, and apparently aristocratic and successful. One would think that if they were going to solely feature African American customers in the ad, they would do so with a fair representation of the group. Instead of creating an ad that proved Denny's was racially unbiased, as intended, the company had displayed the same behavior it was trying to resolve. Although the company later worked to improve its image, the damage was done.

Not only businesses and retailers have these problems; not-for-profit and government organizations also have to watch their step. During the 2002 Super Bowl, the White House introduced a new series of antidrug public service announcements. The campaign tried to link the money spent on drugs to the funding of terrorist activities. Print and television ads in muted black-and-white traced teens' use of drugs for recreation through the supply chain back to tragic, violent episodes in drug-producing regions. To say that the guilt-trip method did not go over well with teenagers would be putting it mildly. Teens felt that the ads were deliberately manipulative and misrepresented the facts in an attempt to support President George W. Bush's war on terrorism. As a result, studies showed that, over time, teens exposed to the ads shifted to a significantly more "prodrug" attitude than those of kids who did not view the ads. In short, the ads fostered enough resentment among their target audience that teens deliberately defied the message being sent.

Advertising sensitivity is a difficult issue. What is politically correct enough? When is something too politically correct? And what should be done when a conflict cannot be avoided? Some groups simply cannot be targeted without excluding, and thereby offending, other groups. When this happens, a choice must be made, and it must be made carefully, with serious consideration of all potential consequences.

Ethical Issues in Advertising

Ethics play a vital role in the practice of advertising. The Ethical Issues features focus attention on the most critical social questions facing advertisers today. These include debates over puffery, advertising to children, comparative advertising, targeting ethnic minorities, consumer profiling, manipulating research results, creative plagiarism, sexually explicit content, and others.

Review Questions

1. How does the concept of shared characteristics relate to the market segmentation process?
2. How could you use VALS to develop the marketing strategy for a product of your choice?
3. How does the segmentation of business markets differ from that of consumer markets?
4. What is the most important factor to consider when determining the elements of the marketing mix?
5. What is the difference between a product and a product concept?
6. What are some examples of product positioning not discussed in this chapter?
7. What effect does the product life cycle have on the advertising a company uses?
8. What factors influence the price of a product?
9. How do the basic methods of distribution affect advertising?
10. What product characteristics encourage heavy advertising? Little advertising? Why?

Exploring Advertising

1. Find a print ad and identify the *utility* that is communicated in the ad. Does it address a functional need or a symbolic want? Describe that need or want.
2. Bring in or describe an advertisement that seems to be directed toward a specific target market. Describe what you perceive to be the targeted market segment. Define it using behavioristic, demographic, psychographic, and geographic variables.
3. Select a consumer product and describe what stage of the Product Life Cycle you believe it to be in. How would being in that stage affect the target market selected and the marketing mix used for this product or service?
4. Think of a product or service (not mentioned in this chapter) that is strongly positioned. Describe its positioning. Does its advertising differentiate it from other products with perceptible, hidden, or induced differences?
5. Go to the VALS Web site (www.sric-bi.com) and take the VALS Survey. Do you agree with the results? Do they correctly describe your segment? How would this information be useful to a marketer who was trying to target its product or service to you?

Exploring Advertising

Every chapter concludes with active learning exercises that provide students opportunities to apply what they just read to real-world situations. Instructors will find these activities extremely useful as homework assignments or in-class activities.

Checklist

Practical Checklists

Handy Checklists appear regularly throughout the text—they teach students how to handle a large volume of information and creatively convert this information into effective marketing communications. The Checklists can stimulate memory, organize thinking, and reinforce important concepts.

"Power to Move Forward" TV commercial
Following the shoot, the footage goes to the editing studios where music, voice-overs, special effects, and supers are all incorporated into the finished commercial. For the "Power to Move Forward" spot, treadmills, which had been placed under the talent and the vehicles to create a natural pacing, were removed during the postproduction stage.

With computer and videotape technology, editors [...] tape and add effects such as wipes and dissolves [...] director will spend many hours editing a commercial [...] be considerably less than what would be needed for f[...]

Many professionals still prefer film. The visual p[...] appears on one piece of celluloid (film) without the [...] or **supers** (words superimposed on the picture). The [...] bled on another piece of celluloid. This is the **work pr[...]** *rough cut* or *interlock*).

External sound is recorded next. The sound engine[...] and singers, as well as the announcer's voice-over nar[...] music may be bought and integrated into the comm[...] includes any sound effects, s[...] or doors slamming.

Once sound editing is co[...] the finished sound is com[...] completed visual celluloid, y[...] **lock.** The addition of optical [...] the **answer print.** This is the[...] approved, **dupes** (duplicate[...] delivery to the networks or T[...]

CONCEPT CHECK
Describe the important tasks that take place during each stage of the television commercial production process?

Built-in Learning Aids

Learning objectives, concept checks, bold key terms, chapter summaries, and review questions facilitate learning and allow students to check their understanding of the material. The concept checks and review questions may be assigned as homework to confirm comprehension.

Chapter Summary

The advertising business comprises four main groups: advertisers (clients), agencies, suppliers, and media. It employs a wide range of artists and businesspeople, sales reps and engineers, top executives, and clerical personnel.

There are four main categories of advertisers based on their geographic activities: local, regional, national, and transnational. Local advertising is placed by businesses in a particular city or county and aimed at customers in the same geographic area. It is important because most sales are made or lost in the local arena.

Regional advertisers operate in one or several states and market exclusively within that region. National advertisers operate in several regions or throughout the country and comprise the largest advertisers.

A large company's advertising department may be centralized or decentralized. Each structure has advantages and disadvantages. The centralized organization is the most typical and may be structured by product, subfunction of advertising, end user, or geography. Decentralized departments are typical of large, far-flung organizations with numerous divisions, subsidiaries, products, countries, regions, and/or brands.

Transnational advertisers face unique challenges. Their markets have different value systems, environments, and languages with customers of different purchasing abilities, habits, and motivations. Media that are customary in the United States may be unavailable or ineffective. Companies therefore often need different advertising strategies. To manage their advertising, transnational advertisers use an international, multinational, or global marketing structure.

Ad agencies are independent organizations of creative people and businesspeople who specialize in developing and preparing advertising plans, ads, and other promotional tools on behalf of their clients.

Key Terms

account executive (AE), 74
account planning, 75
account supervisor, 74
advertiser, 60
advertising agency, 60, 71
art directors, 76
art studios, 85
brand manager, 67
business-to-business agency, 73
centralized advertising department, 66
classified advertising, 62
cooperative (co-op) advertising, 63

copy, 76
copywriter, 76
creative boutique, 73
creative director, 76
decentralized system, 6[?]
departmental system, 7[?]
fee-commission combina[...]
foreign media, 70
full-service advertising a[...]
general consumer agenc[...]
global marketer, 69
group system, 78

media, 60, 85
media-buying service, 74
media commission, 79
multinational corporation, 68
national advertiser, 64
national agency, 72
printer, 85

product advertising, 62
production department, 76
production house, 85
regional advertiser, 63
regional agency, 72
research supplier, 85
retainer method, 80

sale advertising, 62
sales promotion department, 77
speculative presentation, 81
straight-fee method, 80
supplier, 60
traffic department, 77
Web design house, 85

Review Questions

1. Almost half of advertising dollars are spent on local advertising. Why is local advertising so important?
2. What are the three types of local advertising and what purposes do they serve?
3. Why do wholesalers and manufacturers provide co-op advertising funds and materials to local advertisers?
4. What services might a modern full-service advertising agency offer a large business-to-business advertiser?
5. What additional challenges are faced by companies that advertise internationally?

6. How do the media in other countries tend to differ from that which we are accustomed to in the United States?
7. Why do so many advertisers hire ad agencies?
8. In what ways does the role of an Account Planner differ from that of an Account Executive?
9. What are the most important things an advertiser should consider when selecting an agency?
10. What is the best way to compensate an agency? Explain your answer.

Exploring Advertising

1. Select the advertising agency position that is most appealing to you. Describe what educational background, work experience, skills, and personality might be most appropriate for that position. Search the Internet for recruitment ads for that position to confirm your answers.
2. Your agency is paid on a traditional 15 percent media commission. You purchase $300,000 in network TV time to run an ad for your client. How much will your client pay for the TV time? How much will the network receive? How much will the agency be paid?
   The ad you ran cost $30,000 to produce. Your agency charges a 17.65 percent markup for production costs. How much will your client pay for the production? How much will your agency receive?

3. Select an advertising agency that interests you. You may admire its campaigns or you might be interested in it as a possible employer. Write a review of the agency organization and philosophy including as much of the following information possible. Consider using the *Standard Directory of Advertising Agencies*, Web sites, annual reports, *Advertising Age*, and *Adweek* as sources.
   - Agency size: billings and number of employees
   - Corporate affiliation (part of a holding company?)
   - Locations of major offices
   - Top officers of the company
   - Key clients
   - Most notable campaigns
   - Brief agency history
   - Agency philosophy
   - What makes this agency unique?
   If you were an advertiser seeking an agency, why might this agency appeal to you? What if you were a job seeker?

Supplemental Teaching Aids

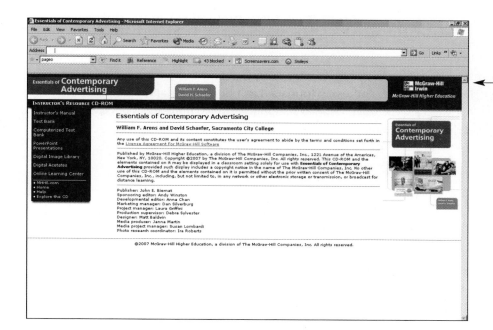

Instructor's Resource CD-ROM

This presentation CD-ROM allows instructors to easily create their own custom presentations using resources on the CD like the instructor's manual, PowerPoint slides, and digital art from the text.

Instructor's Manual

Prepared by Michael Weigold of the University of Florida, the Instructor's Manual contains learning objectives, teaching tips, lecture outlines, discussions of Commercial Breaks, Ethical Issues, and Exploring Advertising material, additional in-class exercises and homework assignments for students, Internet activities, and answers to end-of-chapter questions.

Test Bank and Computerized Test Bank

Created by Betty Pritchett of Kennesaw State University, the test bank has approximately 1,600 test questions, including true/false, multiple-choice, fill-in, short answer, and essay formats. Each question is also designated by knowledge type (fact, definition, application, comprehension, etc.) and includes a page reference to the text.

PowerPoint Presentations

Containing approximately 400 slides, full-color ads and exhibits from the text are featured throughout these PowerPoint presentations, created by Tracy Tuten Ryan of Virginia Commonwealth University. The comprehensive chapter presentations can easily be edited to meet the instructor's requirements.

NEW!
Interactive Advertising Simulation

Advertising Target Practice: Creating Solutions to Marketing Problems, a new Web-based tool, combines video and interactive material to allow students to explore the concepts and theories presented in the text as they relate to real-world practice. Each segment takes an in-depth look at a real advertising agency and their work on a real-world based campaign. Students will watch interviews, examine objectives of the campaign process, choose a strategy, and then create their own versions of the campaigns. This exciting new tool allows students to view video and then apply their own critical thinking to build a campaign.

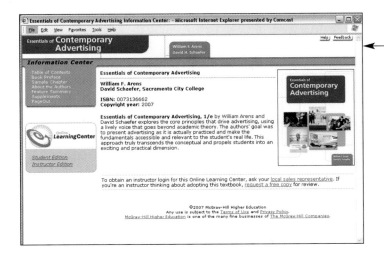

Online Learning Center

Students and instructors will find a multitude of helpful resources online at **www.mhhe.com/ arensessentials1e**. Student study tools include practice quizzes, video clips, a glossary of key terms, sample marketing and advertising plans, portfolios of outstanding creative work, and industry resources. The instructor's side includes downloadable versions of the Instructor's Manual, PowerPoint presentations, video clips, the Video Instructor's Manual, and a link to PageOut for access to test materials.

Brief Contents

Contents

Ethical Issues
Truth in Advertising: Fluffing and Puffing, 34

Commercial Break 2–A
Unfair and Deceptive Practices in Advertising, 45

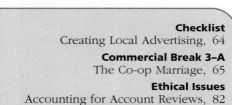

chapter nine   Creative Execution: Art and Copy   232

chapter ten   Producing Ads for Print, Electronic, and Digital Media   266

part 5   Reaching the Target Audience

chapter eleven   Print Advertising   294

chapter twelve   Electronic Media:
Television and Radio   320

part 6   Integrating Marketing Communications Elements

Essentials of
Contemporary Advertising

chapter one

Advertising Today and How We Got Here

Objectives

To define advertising and review its evolution. You will learn what advertising is and what it is not; the role advertising plays in business and our economy; how advertising evolved to the position it occupies today; and the impact that advertising has on our society.

After studying this chapter, you will be able to:

* **Define** advertising and differentiate it from other forms of marketing communications.

* **Explain** the role advertising plays in business and marketing.

* **Explain** the importance of advertising in a free market economy.

* **Discuss** how advertising evolved with the history of commerce.

* **Explore** the impact of advertising on society yesterday, today, and tomorrow.

NOW THIS
WON'T HURT A BIT.
THE CURIOUSLY STRONG MINTS

At the turn of the nineteenth century, a small confectionery firm in London created a recipe for an "exceptionally strong" lozenge intended to relieve intestinal discomfort.[1] The name of these miracle lozenges was Altoids, and although the reason for their consumption has changed from fighting stomach pains to combating bad breath, the tradition of taking a couple after meals has stayed the same.

Yet, contrary to its lengthy history, the success of Altoids as we know it today has been a recent occurrence—just over the past decade. There are several reasons for this. First, the brand's price was three times higher than competitive products. Second, it had achieved only very narrow distribution. Finally, it suffered from extremely low awareness due to virtually no advertising. As a result, Altoids faced very limited success before the mid-1990s.[2]

Following a series of mergers and acquisitions in the consumer products industry—which resulted in Altoids being owned by Callard & Broward-Suchard, a subsidiary of Kraft General Foods—change finally, and suddenly, came about. In 1995, Altoids launched its first major marketing campaign in its 215-year history. With a budget far below what its competitors were spending, Altoids and its ad agency, Leo Burnett Chicago, developed an advertising strategy that would prove to be deceivingly simple yet amazingly effective. According to its research, Altoids found that its customers tended to be young, urban, socially active, and culturally aware—but somewhat difficult to reach via conventional advertising media.

The solution: place advertisements outdoors, in locations nobody could miss—on billboards, in bus shelters, phone booths, and subway cars. Most importantly, the ads themselves were great—they were highly creative and just as simple as the media that carried them. Focusing on the product's unique, exceptionally strong flavor and its one-of-a-kind tin packaging, the ads generally featured an Altoids' signature tin, with a simple, humorous catch phrase at the bottom. The ads were indicative of the mint—simple, clean, and fresh. (For more Altoids ads, see the Portfolio Review on the *Essentials of Contemporary Advertising* Web site.)

Within a year, studies showed a substantial increase in brand awareness and consumption. Moreover, the brand jumped from number six in U.S. breath mint ranking to number one in 2001.[3]

The moral of this story is simple: good advertising can have a curiously strong effect on a brand's success. Success stories like this are what encourage companies and organizations in the United States to spend over $245 billion annually on advertising, and they will likely continue to spend even more in the future.[4]

Altoids: "Invented in 1780. Properly marketed 215 years later."[5]

What Is Advertising?

As a consumer, you are exposed to hundreds and maybe even thousands of commercial messages every day. They may appear in the form of billboards like the Altoids campaign, or in the form of newspaper ads, TV commercials, coupons, publicity, event sponsorships, telemarketing calls, or even e-mails. These are just a few of the many communication tools that companies and organizations use to initiate and maintain contact with their customers, clients, and prospects. You may simply refer to them all as "advertising." But, in fact, the correct term for these various tools is **marketing communications.** And advertising is just one type of marketing communications.

So, then, what is advertising?

At the beginning of the twentieth century, Albert Lasker, who today is generally regarded as the father of modern advertising, owned a prominent advertising agency, Lord & Thomas. At the time, he defined advertising as "salesmanship in print, driven by a reason why."[6] But that was long before the advent of radio, television, or the Internet. The nature and scope of the business world, and advertising, were quite limited. A century later, our planet is a far different place. The nature and needs of business have changed, and so have the concept and practice of advertising.

Today, definitions of advertising abound. Journalists, for example, might define it as a communication, public relations, or persuasion process; businesspeople see it as a marketing process; economists and sociologists tend to focus on its economic, societal, or ethical significance. And some consumers might define it simply as a nuisance. Each of these perspectives has some merit, but for now we'll use the following functional definition:

> **Advertising** is the structured and composed nonpersonal communication of information, usually paid for and usually persuasive in nature, about products (goods, services, and ideas) by identified sponsors through various media.

Let's take this definition apart and analyze its components. Advertising is, first of all, a type of *communication*. It is actually a very *structured* form of communication, employing both verbal and nonverbal elements that are *composed* to fill specific space and time formats determined by the sponsor.

Second, advertising is typically directed to groups of people rather than to individuals. It is therefore *nonpersonal,* or *mass communication.* These people could be **consumers,** who buy products like Altoids for their personal use. Or they might be businesspeople who would buy large quantities of Altoids for resale in their stores.

Most advertising is *paid* for by sponsors. GM, Wal-Mart, Coca-Cola, and your local fitness salon pay the newspaper or the radio or TV station to carry the ads you read, see, and hear. But some sponsors don't have to pay for their ads. The

American Red Cross, United Way, and American Cancer Society are among the many national organizations whose **public service announcements (PSAs)** are carried at no charge because of their nonprofit status. Likewise, a poster on a school bulletin board promoting a dance is not paid for, but it is still an ad—a structured, nonpersonal, persuasive communication.

Of course, most advertising is intended to be *persuasive*—to win converts to a product, service, or idea. Some ads, such as legal announcements, are intended merely to inform, not to persuade. But they are still ads because they satisfy all the other requirements of the definition.

In addition to promoting tangible **goods** such as oranges, oatmeal, and olive oil, advertising helps publicize the intangible **services** of bankers, beauticians, bike repair shops, bill collectors, and the telephone company. Increasingly, advertising is used to advocate a wide variety of **ideas,** whether economic, political, religious, or social. In this book the term **product** encompasses goods, services, and ideas.

An ad *identifies* its sponsor. This seems obvious. The sponsor wants to be identified, or why pay to advertise?

Finally, advertising reaches us through a channel of communication referred to as a **medium.** An advertising medium is any paid means used to present an ad to its target audience. Thus, we have radio advertising, television advertising, newspaper ads, and so on. When you tell somebody how good Altoids taste, that's sometimes called **word-of-mouth (WOM) advertising.** Although WOM is a communication medium, it's not an advertising medium. It's not structured, or openly sponsored, or paid for. Historically, advertisers have used the traditional **mass media** (the plural of medium)—radio, TV, newspapers, magazines, and billboards—to send their messages. But today technology enables advertising to reach us efficiently through a variety of addressable media (like direct mail) and interactive media (like the Internet). Advertisers also use an increasing variety of other nontraditional media such as shopping carts, blimps, and videocassettes to find their audience.

The vinyl that the image of the girl was printed on has been scorched using a blow torch to simulate the effect of badly burned skin.

Even nonprofits feel the squeeze to bring in revenue to operate. This New Zealand advocacy group won a Bronze Lion at Cannes for its creative use of billboard advertising to seek donations for establishing a nationwide burn center.

Describe the six components that define advertising.

CONCEPT CHECK

The Role of Advertising in Business

In Chapter 5, we will discuss in more detail how advertising communicates for the purpose of informing and persuading consumers, but first let's consider advertising's role in business. Every business organization performs a number of diverse activities. Management typically classifies these activities into three broad functional divisions:

- Operations (production/manufacturing)
- Finance/administration
- Marketing

Of all the business functions, marketing is the only one whose primary role is to bring in revenue. Without revenue, of course, a company cannot pay its employees' salaries or earn a profit. So marketing is very important.

What Is Marketing?

Over the years, the concept of marketing has evolved based on the supply of and demand for products. Because we need to understand marketing as it relates to *advertising,* we will use the American Marketing Association's definition:

> **Marketing** is an organizational function and a set of processes for creating, communicating, and delivering value to customers and for managing customer relationships in ways that benefit the organization and its stakeholders.[7]

We will devote all of Part 2 to the subject of marketing and consumer behavior. What's important to understand now is that marketing is a *set of processes*—a series of actions that take place sequentially—aimed at satisfying customer needs profitably. These processes are typically broken down into the 4 Ps of the **marketing mix:** developing *products, pricing* them strategically, distributing them so they are available to customers at appropriate *places,* and *promoting* them through sales and advertising activities (see Exhibit 1–1). The ultimate goal of the marketing process is to earn a profit for the firm by consummating the exchange of products or services with those customers who need or want them. And the role of advertising is to promote—to inform, persuade, and remind groups of customers, or markets, about the need-satisfying value of the company's goods and services.

Advertising and the Marketing Process

Advertising helps the organization achieve its marketing goals. So do market research, sales, and distribution. And these other marketing specialties all have an impact on the kind of advertising a company employs. An effective advertising specialist must have a broad understanding of the whole marketing process in order to know what type of advertising to use in a given situation.

Companies and organizations use many different types of advertising, depending on their particular marketing strategy. The marketing strategy will help determine who the targets of advertising should be, in what markets the advertising should appear, and what goals the advertising should accomplish. The advertising strategy, in turn, will refine the target audience and define what response the advertiser is seeking—what that audience should notice, think,

Exhibit 1–1

Advertising is just one of several activities that fall under the promotion component of the marketing mix.

and feel. We will discuss the development of marketing, advertising, and media strategies later in the text.

But first, we need to understand the economic dimension of advertising and how advertising has evolved as both an economic and a societal tool.

CONCEPT CHECK

What is the goal of marketing and what role does advertising play in achieving that goal?

Economics: The Growing Need for Advertising

Economics has driven the growth of advertising since its earliest beginnings and has made it one of the hallmarks of the free enterprise system. As English historian Raymond Williams said, "Advertising is the official art of capitalist society."[8]

Today, business—and advertising—are undergoing the most dramatic changes in history. To understand the nature of these changes and why they're taking place, we need to look at how advertising has evolved. We'll explain how the changing economic environment has influenced the evolution of advertising through the centuries. Then, in Chapter 2, we'll look at how advertising itself influences the economy and society and, as a result, is often an object of controversy and criticism.

Principles of Free Market Economics

Our economy is based on the notion of competition. While there is no such thing as *perfect competition,* there are four fundamental assumptions of free market economics that our market-driven society believes in and strives to achieve:

1. *Self-interest.* People and organizations tend to act in their own self-interest. By their very nature, people are acquisitive. They always want more—for less. Therefore, open competition between self-interested sellers advertising to self-interested buyers naturally leads to greater product availability at more competitive prices.

2. *Complete information.* Access by buyers and sellers to all information at all times about what products are available, at what quality, and at what prices leads to greater competition and lower prices for all. (This is why attorneys are now allowed to advertise.)

3. *Many buyers and sellers.* Having a wide range of sellers ensures that if one company does not meet customer needs, another will be available to capitalize on the situation by producing a more market-responsive product. Similarly, having a wide range of buyers ensures that sellers can find customers who are interested in the unique products they are able to produce at a fair price. (This is why we have antitrust laws.)

4. *Absence of externalities (social costs).* Sometimes the sale or consumption of products may benefit or harm other people who are not involved in the transaction and didn't pay for the product. In these cases, the government may use taxation and/or regulation to compensate for or eliminate the **externalities.** (This is why there are restrictions and requirements placed on tobacco advertisers.)

Now, given these basic assumptions, let's see how advertising fits into the scheme of a free market economy.

Functions and Effects of Advertising in a Free Economy

For any business, advertising may perform a variety of functions and, when executed correctly, its effects may be dramatic. To see how this works, let's go back to the beginnings of the Eastman Kodak Company.

When George Eastman first developed his plans for transparent roll film and subsequently the box camera, he realized he also had to think up a new, distinctive name for the company. Eastman explained, "I devised the name myself. The letter 'K' had been a favorite with me—it seems a strong, incisive sort of letter. It became a question of trying out a great number of combinations of letters that made words starting and ending with 'K.' The word 'Kodak' is the result." Once Eastman decided on a name he felt would distinguish his company and its products in the minds of consumers, he quickly registered the word "Kodak" as a trademark with the U.S. Patent and Trademark Office. Shortly thereafter, Eastman selected the distinctive yellow packaging that is now widely associated with Kodak throughout the world—an association that has become one of the company's more valued assets. This demonstrates one of the most basic functions of **branding** as well as advertising: *to identify products and to differentiate them from others.*

 def of branding

Once Eastman and his partners had named the product and the company, they began running ads to promote the Kodak camera, to tell people how it worked, and to publicize where they could get one. Here is another basic function of advertising: *to communicate information about the product, its features, and its place of sale.* (The functions and effects discussed here are listed in Exhibit 1–2.)

Prior to the introduction of Kodak film, photography had been the purview of dedicated professionals or wealthy amateurs. It was Eastman's intention to change that. Toward the turn of the twentieth century, Kodak's ad campaign sought to make the camera a part of daily life—something everyone could enjoy. Hence the introduction of the $1.00 Kodak Brownie camera and Kodak's ambitious ad campaign covering a wide variety of media. By June 1900, the magazines carrying Brownie advertisements reached a combined circulation of 6 million readers. The Brownie campaign, which lasted until the early 1960s, changed the perception of who could use a camera and the ease with which film could be developed. To us, this campaign demonstrates another function of advertising: *to induce consumers to try new products and to suggest reuse.*[9]

Over the past century, as the camera became an integral part of everyday life in the United States, Kodak conducted many simultaneous campaigns outside the country to increase global awareness as well. Through various activities, such as its sponsorship of the Olympic Games where it supplied free cameras and film to participating media personnel, Kodak succeeded in accomplishing yet another function of advertising: *to stimulate the distribution of a product*—in this case, on a global level.

Since the introduction of the first Kodak box camera in 1888, technology has dramatically changed the field of photography, and Kodak has been at the forefront of this progress. The result of these advances has been to make basic photography simpler and more accessible to the masses while improving the overall quality for both amateur and professional photographers alike. By effectively communicating the news of these advancements to its customers, Kodak achieved another of the most important functions of advertising: *to increase product use.*

In a free market economy, when one company starts to make significant profits, other companies immediately jump in to compete. Over the years, to battle the growing compet-

Exhibit 1–2

Functions and effects of advertising as a marketing tool.

- To identify products and differentiate them from others.
- To communicate information about the product, its features, and its place of sale.
- To induce consumers to try new products and to suggest reuse.
- To stimulate the distribution of a product.
- To increase product use.
- To build value, brand preference, and loyalty.
- To lower the overall cost of sales.

itive threat, Kodak has consistently funded ongoing marketing communications campaigns aimed at accomplishing yet another function of advertising: *to build value, brand preference, and loyalty.*

Today Kodak offers a myriad of products ranging from simple film roll cameras, to disposable cameras, to high-tech digital cameras, to printers and scanners, as well as its ubiquitous Kodak film processing service. Its advertising, though, such as its current campaign, "Share Moments. Share Life," has always strived to unify the products under a common voice and a common theme: quality, reliability, and trust.

For more than 100 years, the Eastman Kodak Company has used a variety of media to communicate advertising messages to very divergent audiences. Why? To achieve the most significant function of advertising: *to lower the cost of sales.* For the cost of reaching just one prospect through personal selling, companies can reach thousands of people through media advertising.

Now, considering this brief synopsis of Kodak history, how does Kodak's advertising fit with the basic assumptions of a free market economy? Has Kodak's advertising helped make photography available to more people at lower cost? Has it contributed important information to people? Has the freedom to advertise contributed to the competitive environment? What externalities might have had a positive or negative impact on Kodak's efforts to market photographic supplies?

> Describe the seven basic functions of advertising.

CONCEPT CHECK

Perhaps you can see from this one example how advertising contributes to a free economy. But if it's so good, then why is advertising considered a twentieth-century phenomenon? Why wasn't it developed and used for the last several thousand years of recorded history? Or was it?

To get a full sense of what advertising really is today, we need to understand where it has come from, how and why it grew to be so large, and what the forces are that drive it.

The Evolution of Advertising as an Economic Tool

Thousands of years ago, most people were engaged in hunting, herding, farming, or handicrafts. To make products, they used primitive hand tools. Humans devoted most of their efforts to meeting basic survival needs: food, clothing, shelter. They lived in small, isolated communities where artisans and farmers bartered products and services among themselves. Distribution was limited to how far vendors could walk and "advertising" to how loud they could shout. Because goods weren't produced in great quantity, there was no need for advertising to stimulate mass purchases. There were also no mass media available for possible advertisers to use. Notwithstanding, archaeologists have found evidence of advertising among the Babylonians dating back as far as 3000 BC (see Exhibit 1–3).

The Preindustrial Age

As the marketplace grew larger and became more complex, the demand for products increased, and the need for advertising slowly developed. At first, merchants hung carved signs in front of their shops so passersby could see what products were being offered. Most people couldn't read, so the signs often used symbols, such as a boot for a cobbler. This period was called the **preindustrial age,** and, for Western civilization, it extended from the beginning of recorded history to roughly the start of the nineteenth century.[10]

An early form of advertising. Until the advent of public schooling, most people couldn't read—so signs featured symbols of the goods or services for sale, such as the jerkin on this tailor's sign in Williamsburg, Virginia.

3000 BC–AD 499	AD 500–1599	1600–1799	1800–1899
3000 BC. Written advertisement offering "Whole gold coin" for runaway slave "Shem." **500 BC.** Political and trade graffiti on Pompeii walls. **AD 1.** First uppercase lettering appears on Greek buildings.	**1455.** First printed Bible. **1472.** First printed ad in English tacked on London church doors. **1544.** Claude Garamond, first "typefounder," perfects a roman typeface that bears his name and is still used today.	**1650.** First newspaper ad offers reward for stolen horses. **1662.** *London Gazette* offers first advertising supplement. **1704.** First ads in America published in the *Boston Newsletter.* **1729.** Ben Franklin is first to use "white space" and illustration in ads. **1785.** Widespread use of advertising and long print runs become possible.	**1841.** Volney B. Palmer becomes first "newspaper agent" (advertising agent) in America. **1844.** First magazine ad runs. **1869.** Francis W. Ayer founds ad agency bearing his father's name, N. W. Ayer & Sons, in Philadelphia. He initiates first "for commission" ad contract (1876), first market survey for an ad (1879), and first on-staff creative services (art in 1890, copywriting in 1892). **1888.** *Printers' Ink* is first U.S. publication for ad profession.

1900–1919	1920–1939	1940–1959	1960–1969
1900. Psychologists study the attention-getting and persuasive qualities of advertising. **1900.** Northwestern University is first to offer advertising as a discipline. **1903.** Scripps-McRae League of Newspapers appoints ad censor, rejects $500,000 in ads in first year. **1905.** First national ad plan is for the "Gillette Safety Razor." **1911.** First "truth in advertising" codes are established by what is now called the American Advertising Federation (AAF).	**1920s.** Albert Lasker, father of modern advertising, calls advertising "salesmanship in print." First ad testimonials by movie stars appear. Full-color printing is available in magazines. **1922.** First radio ad solves radio's need for financing. **1924.** N. W. Ayer produces first sponsored radio broadcast, the "Eveready Hour." **1930.** *Advertising Age* magazine is founded. **1938.** Wheeler-Lea amendments to FTC Act of 1938 grant FTC further power to curb false ad practices.	**1946.** America has 12 TV stations broadcasting to the public. **1947.** Lanham Trademark Act protects brand names and slogans. **1948.** 46 TV stations are operating and 300 others are awaiting FCC approval. **1950.** First political ads are used on TV by Gov. Dewey of New York. **1950s.** David Ogilvy's "Hathaway man" and "Commander Whitehead" become popular ad personae.	**1960s.** Doyle Dane Bernbach's "Think small" ad for American Volkswagen becomes one of the most famous ads of the decade, establishing a strong market position for the smallest European import. The agency's slogan for Avis, "We're only No. 2, so we try harder" is also very successful. New York's Madison Avenue becomes known worldwide as the center of the advertising world and features the best in advertising creativity.

1970–1979	1980–1989	1990–1999	2000–2005
1971. Armed services begin first advertising for the new "all-volunteer" military ("Be all that you can be in the Army"). **1972.** The *Ad Age* article "Positioning: The Battle for Your Mind" by Al Ries and Jack Trout details the strategy of positioning that dominates the 1970s. **1973.** Oil shortages begin period of "demarketing," ads aimed at slowing demand. **1970s (late).** Growth in self-indulgence, signified by popularity of self-fulfillment activities, spurs some agencies into making infomercials.	**1980s.** The "me" decade begins (baby boomers are indulgent but want social accountability). Ad agency megamergers take place worldwide. **1982.** First edition of *Contemporary Advertising* is published. **1984.** The Internet (government controlled since 1973) is turned over to the private sector. **1986.** *Marketing Warfare* by Al Ries and Jack Trout portrays marketing in terms of classic warfare manual written by General Clausewitz in 1831.	**1990s.** Early part of decade experiences recession. Marketers shift funds from advertising to sales promotion, leaving major agencies to fail or merge. **1994.** Media glut leads to market fragmentation; network TV is no longer sole medium for reaching total marketplace. Ad professions adopt integrated marketing communications (IMC) as the new strategy to build market relationships.	**2000.** The Internet is the fastest-growing new ad medium since TV, with 400 million users. Advertising is evolving into a two-way medium. **2005.** As the spread of personal video recorders and video on demand allows more television viewers to bypass advertisements, product placement is gaining favor. The number of placements on television shows doubles every quarter.

Exhibit 1–3

Timetable of advertising history.

During the preindustrial age, several important developments enabled the eventual birth of modern advertising. The Chinese invented paper and Europe had its first paper mill by 1275. In the 1440s, Johannes Gutenberg invented the printing press in Germany. The press was not only the most important development in the history of advertising, and indeed communication, but it also revolutionized the way people lived and worked.

Before the printing press, most people were illiterate. Only monks and scholars could read and write; the average person had to memorize important information and communicate orally. Because oral communication could not be substantiated, people lived without documentable facts. And because dialects varied from region to region, most news never traveled more than 50 miles.

The introduction of printing allowed facts to be established, substantiated, recorded, and transported. People no longer had to rely on their memories. Movable letters provided the flexibility to print in local dialects. The slow hand transcription of the monks gave way to more rapid, volume printing by a less select group. Some entrepreneurs bought printing presses, mounted them in wagons, and traveled from town to town, selling printing. This new technology made possible the first formats of advertising—posters, handbills, and signs—and, eventually, the first mass medium—the newspaper. In effect, the cry of the vendor could now be multiplied many times and heard beyond the immediate neighborhood.

In 1472, the first ad in English appeared: a handbill tacked on church doors in London announcing a prayer book for sale. Two hundred years later the first newspaper ad was published, offering a reward for the return of 12 stolen horses. Soon newspapers carried ads for coffee, chocolate, tea, real estate, medicines, and even personal ads. These early ads were still directed to a very limited number of people: the customers of the coffeehouses where most newspapers were read.

By the early 1700s, the world's population had grown to about 600 million people, and some major cities were big enough to support larger volumes of advertising. In fact, the greater volume caused a shift in advertising strategy. Samuel Johnson, the famous English literary figure, observed in 1758 that advertisements were now so numerous that they were "negligently perused" and that it had become necessary to gain attention "by magnificence of promise." This was the beginning of *puffery* in advertising.

In the American colonies, the *Boston Newsletter* began carrying ads in 1704. About 25 years later, Benjamin Franklin, the father of advertising art, made ads more readable by using large headlines and considerable white space. In fact, Franklin was the first American known to use illustrations in ads.

The Industrializing Age

In the mid-1700s, the Industrial Revolution began in England and by the early 1800s it had reached North America. Machinery began to replace animal power. By using machines to mass-produce goods with uniform quality, large companies increased their productivity. For the first time, it cost people less to buy a product than to make it themselves. As people left the farm to work in the city, mass urban markets began to emerge. This further fueled market development and the growth of advertising.

By the mid-1800s, the world's population had doubled to 1.2 billion. Suddenly, producers needed mass consumption to match the high levels of manufactured goods. Fortunately, breakthroughs in bulk transportation—the railroad and steamship—facilitated the sale and distribution of products beyond a manufacturer's local market. But with the need for mass consumption came the increasing need for

It wasn't until 1729 that Ben Franklin, innovator of advertising art, made ads more readable by using larger headlines, changing fonts, and adding art. This 1767 ad announces the availability of Stage Waggons to carry passengers from Powles Hook Ferry to Philadelphia.

In 1890, N. W. Ayer & Sons became the first agency to operate as agencies do today, planning, creating, and executing complete ad campaigns for advertisers. This 1899 Ayer ad for Uneeda biscuits (catch the play on words) was one of a series of popular ads of the times.

This full-page of advertising from an 1894 *Scientific American* (www.scientificamerican.com) is historically telling in that nearly all the ads have yet to develop any brand identity but merely sell unbranded commodities such as soap, paper, paint, or services.

mass marketing techniques such as advertising to inform new markets of the availability of products.

During this **industrializing age,** which lasted roughly until the end of World War I, manufacturers were principally concerned with production. The primary burden of marketing fell on the wholesalers, who knew the sources of supply, the providers of transportation, the market requirements, and how to arrange for product shipments to the appropriate locations. They used advertising primarily as an information vehicle, placing announcements in publications called *price currents* to let retailer customers know about the sources of supply and shipping schedules for the basic, unbranded commodities they carried. Advertising to consumers was the job of the local retailer and the large mail-order catalog companies like Montgomery Ward and Sears Roebuck. Only a few innovative manufacturers (mostly of patent medicines, soaps, tobacco products, and canned foods) foresaw the usefulness of mass media advertising to stimulate consumer demand for their products beyond their immediate market areas.

For Americans, the *profession* of advertising began when Volney B. Palmer set up business in Philadelphia in 1841. He contracted with newspapers for large volumes of advertising space at discount rates and then resold the space to advertisers at a higher rate. The advertisers usually prepared the ads themselves.

In 1869, at the ripe old age of 21, Francis Ayer formed an ad agency in Philadelphia and, to make it sound more credible, named it after his father. N. W. Ayer & Sons was the first agency to charge a commission based on the "net cost of space" and the first to conduct a formal market survey. In 1890, Ayer became the first ad agency to operate as agencies do today—planning, creating, and executing complete ad campaigns in exchange for media-paid commissions or fees from advertisers. In 1892, Ayer set up a copy department and hired the first full-time agency copywriter. For the next century, Ayer was considered the oldest agency in America, as well as one of its largest, until 2002 when it disappeared in a merger.

The technological advances of the Industrial Revolution enabled the greatest changes in advertising since the 1400s. Photography, introduced in 1839, added credibility and a new world of creativity. Now ads could show products, people, and places as they really were, rather than how an illustrator visualized them.

In the 1840s, some manufacturers began using magazine ads to reach the mass market and stimulate mass consumption. Magazines became an ideal medium because they provided national advertising and offered the best quality reproduction.

The telegraph, telephone, typewriter, phonograph, and later, motion pictures, all let people communicate as never before. With the development of the nationwide railroad system, the United States entered a period of spectacular economic growth. In 1896, when the federal government inaugurated rural free mail delivery, direct-mail advertising and mail-order selling flourished. Manufacturers now had an ever-increasing variety of products to sell and a new way to deliver their advertisements and products to the public.

With the advent of public schooling, the nation reached an unparalleled 90 percent literacy rate. Manufacturers gained a large reading public that could understand print ads. The United States thus entered the twentieth century as a great industrial state with a national marketing system propelled by advertising. With the end of World War I, the modern period in advertising emerged.

The Industrial Age

The **industrial age** started around the turn of the twentieth century and lasted well into the 1970s. It was a period marked by tremendous growth and maturation of the country's industrial base. As U.S. industry met the basic needs of most of the population, commodity markets became saturated. Fresh mass markets then developed for new brands of consumer luxury and convenience goods we refer to as **consumer packaged goods.**

During the industrializing age of the nineteenth century, wholesalers controlled the marketing process as they distributed the manufacturers' unbranded commodity products. When those markets became saturated, though, the wholesalers started playing one manufacturer off against another. This hurt manufacturers' profits dramatically, so they started looking for ways to wrest back control. The manufacturers changed their focus from a *production* orientation to a *sales* orientation. They dedicated themselves to new product development, strengthened their own sales forces, packaged and branded their products, and engaged in heavy national brand advertising. Early brands of this era included Wrigley's spearmint gum, Coca-Cola, Jell-O gelatin, Kellogg's Corn Flakes, and Campbell's soup.

In the 1920s, the United States was rich and powerful. As the war machine returned to peacetime production, society became consumption driven. The era of salesmanship had arrived and its bible was *Scientific Advertising,* written by the legendary copywriter Claude Hopkins at Albert Lasker's agency, Lord & Thomas. Published in 1923, it became a classic and was republished in 1950 and 1980. "Advertising has reached the status of a science," Hopkins proclaimed. "It is based on fixed principles." His principles outlawed humor, style, literary flair, and anything that might detract from his basic copy strategy of a preemptive product claim repeated loudly and often.[11]

Radio was born at about this same time and rapidly became the nation's primary means of mass communication and a powerful new advertising medium with great immediacy. World and national news now arrived direct from the scene, and a whole new array of family entertainment—music, drama, and sports—became possible. Suddenly, national advertisers could quickly reach huge audiences. In fact, the first radio shows were produced by their sponsors' ad agencies.

To differentiate their products from competitors, several manufacturers branded their products and advertised those brands aggressively. Wrigley's has been selling the same product, with the same brand name, for more than a century.

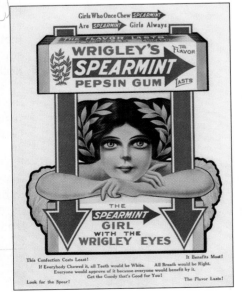

(handwritten margin note: turned to research after Depression)

On October 29, 1929, the stock market crashed, the Great Depression began, and advertising expenditures plummeted. In the face of consumer sales resistance and corporate budget cutting, the advertising industry needed to improve its effectiveness. It turned to research. Daniel Starch, A. C. Nielsen, and George Gallup had founded research groups to study consumer attitudes and preferences. By providing information on public opinion, the performance of ad messages, and sales of advertised products, these companies started a whole new business: the marketing research industry.

During this period, each brand sought to sell the public on its own special qualities. Wheaties became the "Breakfast of Champions" not because of its ingredients but because of its advertising. Manufacturers followed this strategy of **product differentiation** vigorously, seeking to portray their brands as different from and better than the competition by offering consumers quality, variety, and convenience.

The greatest expansion of any medium up to that time occurred with the introduction of television in 1941. After World War II, TV advertising grew rapidly, and in time achieved its current status as the largest advertising medium in terms of advertising revenues.

(handwritten margin note: Golden Era 1940 + 1950s)

During the postwar prosperity of the late 1940s and early 1950s, consumers tried to climb the social ladder by buying more and more modern products. Advertising entered its golden era. A creative revolution ensued in which ads focused on product features that implied social acceptance, style, luxury, and success. Giants in the field emerged—people such as Leo Burnett, David Ogilvy, and Bill Bernbach, who built their agencies from scratch and forever changed the way advertising was planned and created.[12]

Rosser Reeves of the Ted Bates Agency introduced the idea that every ad must point out the product's USP **(unique selling proposition)**—features that would differentiate it from competitive products. The USP was a logical extension of the Lasker and Hopkins "reason why" credo. But as the USP was used over and over, consumers started finding it difficult to see what was unique anymore.

Finally, as more and more imitative products showed up in the marketplace, all offering quality, variety, and convenience, the effectiveness of this strategy wore out. Companies turned to a new mantra: **market segmentation,** a process by which marketers searched for unique groups of people whose needs could be addressed through more specialized products. The image era of the 1960s was thus the natural culmination of the creative revolution. Advertising's emphasis shifted from product features to brand image or personality as advertisers sought to align their brands with particularly profitable market segments. Cadillac, for example, became the worldwide image of luxury, the consummate symbol of success, surpassed only by the aristocratic snootiness of Rolls-Royce.

But just as me-too product features killed the product differentiation era, me-too images eventually killed the market segmentation era. With increased competition, a new kind of advertising strategy evolved in the 1970s, where competitors' strengths became just as important as the advertiser's. Jack Trout and Al Ries trumpeted the arrival of the *positioning era.* They acknowledged the importance of product features and image, but they insisted that what really mattered was how the brand ranked against the competition in the consumer's mind—how it was positioned.

Positioning proved to be an effective way to separate a particular brand from its competitors by associating that brand with a particular set of customer needs that ranked high on the consumer's priority list. Thus, it became a more effective way to use product differentiation and market segmentation. The most famous American ads of the positioning era were Volkswagen ("Think small"), Avis ("We're #2"), and 7Up ("The uncola"). Product differentiation,

Hailed by Jack Trout and Al Ries as "the most famous ad of the 60s," this Volkswagen ad co-opted the "small" position in consumers' minds, giving VW (www.volkswagen.com) a leadership rank for many years.

In recent years, VW has attempted to recapture the style of its 60s advertising.

market segmentation, and positioning are all very important concepts to understand, so we will discuss them further in Chapter 4.

While this was all going on in the United States, across the Atlantic a new generation of advertising professionals had graduated from the training grounds of Procter & Gamble (P&G) and Colgate-Palmolive and were now teaching their international clients the secrets of mass marketing.

The Postindustrial Age

Beginning around 1980, the **postindustrial age** has been a period of cataclysmic change. For the first time, people became truly aware of the sensitive environment in which we live and became alarmed by our dependence on vital natural resources. During the acute energy shortages of the 1970s and 1980s, a new marketing term, **demarketing,** appeared. Producers of energy and energy-consuming goods started using advertising to *slow* the demand for their products. Ads asked people to refrain from operating washers and dryers during the day when the demand for electricity peaked. In time, demarketing became a more aggressive strategic tool for advertisers to use against competitors, political opponents, and social problems. For example, many organizations today actively seek to demarket the use of tobacco.

Then, following a period of unprecedented boom in the West and bust in the East, the Berlin Wall and the Iron Curtain came tumbling down. This finally ended the Cold War and with it the need for a defense-driven economy. Observing the huge, new, untapped markets in the former Warsaw Pact states,

Slow the demand

Demarketing is used not only to dampen the demand for products but also to encourage safe use of already ubiquitous ones. This Hutchison Essar Telecom (India) outdoor ad, a 2004 Cannes Bronze Lion winner, shows the dangers of driving while distracted by a mobile phone.

Western financiers and marketers rubbed their hands in glee. To expand their power globally, big multinational companies and their advertising agencies went on a binge, buying other big companies and creating a new word in the financial lexicon: *megamerger.*

By now European and Asian advertising had caught up with the United States. TV was suddenly the hot medium, and agencies focused on growth, acquisitions, and superior creative executions. For several years, Young & Rubicam in New York and Dentsu in Japan alternated as the largest advertising agency in the world. Then two brothers in London, Charles and Maurice Saatchi, started acquiring agencies globally. In rapid succession, a number of high-profile U.S. agencies disappeared under the Saatchi & Saatchi umbrella—big companies such as Ted Bates Worldwide and Dancer, Fitzgerald, Sample. Saatchi & Saatchi was suddenly the largest agency in the world. Then followed more buyouts as the big agencies from Europe, the United States, and Japan emulated the merger mania of their huge multinational clients. Names of agency founders disappeared from the doors, replaced by initials and acronyms: WPP Group, RSCG, TBWA, FCA, DDB Needham, and FCB, to mention just a few.[13]

Unfortunately, the euphoria of this period was short-lived. Sparked by unprecedented layoffs in the defense industries, the United States, as well as much of the world, fell into an economic recession. While it was technically short-lived, some regions of the country felt the effects of it from the late 1980s well into the mid-1990s. The mergers temporarily stopped, the business world sucked in its collective belt, and management turned to new theories of Total Quality Management (TQM), reengineering, and downsizing—theories aimed at cutting costs and increasing efficiency, all in the name of better customer service. Two related economic factors characterized the marketing world of this period: (1) the aging of traditional products, with a corresponding growth in competition, and (2) the growing affluence and sophistication of the consuming public, led by the huge baby-boomer generation.[14]

The most important factor was competition, intensified by lower trade barriers and growing international trade. As high profits lured imitators into the marketplace, each offering the most attractive product features at lower cost, consumers became the beneficiaries of more choices, higher quality, and lower prices. The priests of positioning, Al Ries and Jack Trout, foresaw this competitive struggle in the mid-1980s. They published *Marketing Warfare,* which portrayed marketing as a *war* that businesses must be prepared to wage. Marketers must take aim at their competitors and be prepared to defend their own turf from would-be attackers at all times.

On the demand side, newly affluent consumers concerned themselves more with the quality of their lives. With their basic commodity needs already met, the baby boomers were now interested in saving time and money to spend on more leisure-time activities or on products, services, and social causes that represented the kind of people they aspired to be.

By the mid-1980s, an avalanche of ads—especially in the toiletry and cosmetics industries—was aimed at the "me" generation ("L'Oreal. Because I'm worth it."). At the same time, the nation's largest industrial concerns spent millions of dollars on corporate advertising to extol their social consciousness and good citizenship for cleaning up after themselves and protecting the environment.

As the U.S. economy slowed, many companies were chasing too few consumer dollars. Clients trimmed their ad budgets, and many turned to more cost-effective **sales promotion** alternatives, such as coupons, direct mail, and direct marketing to build sales volume. By 1990, advertising had lost 25 percent of its share of the marketing budget to other forms of marketing communications.[15]

As the 1990s unfolded, this recession deepened. The traditional advertising industry found itself threatened on all sides and suffering from overpopulation.[16] Clients demanded better results from their promotional dollars; small, imaginative, upstart agencies competed for (and won) some big accounts that had never before been available to them; TV viewers appeared immune to conventional commercials; and an abundance of new media options based on new technologies promised to reinvent the very process of advertising. In three short years, the advertising agency business lost over 13,500 jobs. Major clients such as Coca-Cola defected from the big agencies, giving various portions of their business to specialists in small, regional creative shops and media-buying services. But the setback went far beyond the agency business. Throughout the media world, newspapers, magazines, and TV networks all lost advertising dollars. About 40 magazines went out of business during the two-year slump.[17]

By the mid-1990s, U.S. marketers had begun shifting dollars back from sales promotion to advertising to rebuild value in their brands. In 1994, ad budgets surged ahead by 8.1 percent to $150 billion nationally. And throughout the rest of the 1990s, ad spending increased about 7 percent every year until the year 2000, when U.S. advertisers spent $247.5 billion, a whopping 11.3 percent increase over the previous year.[18]

But then the bubble burst. In 2001, the combination of a mild recession, the collapse of the stock market, and the bust of the dot-coms all contributed to a record decline in advertising activity. On September 11 of that year, terrorists attacked the United States and suddenly all marketing and advertising seemed to stop—not just in the United States, but also around the world.[19] Spending in the United States declined 6.5 percent to $231 billion, and overseas spending dropped 8.6 percent to $210 billion.[20]

A year later, though, the economy seemed to be turning around and marketers were again starting to spend money on advertising. During 2003, U.S. advertising expenditures reached $245 billion, a near-complete recovery from the 2001 decline.[21] But hardly anybody thought the problems were over. Technology, evolving lifestyles, new fears over security, and the rising cost of reaching consumers had already changed the advertising business forever. With the explosion of the Internet, we had entered a new electronic frontier—what Tom

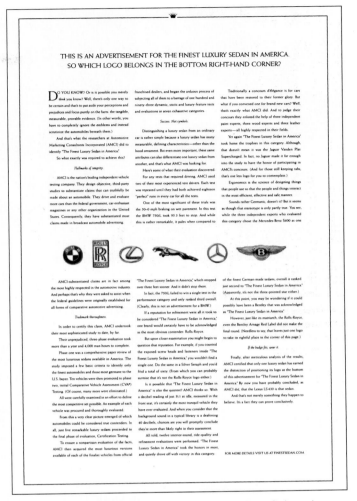

In highly competitive industries, a company may benefit by going head-to-head against the competition through marketing warfare. In this ad, for instance, Lexus (www.lexus.com) attempts to distinguish itself by providing the criteria used in ranking one of its models over its competitors' as "The Finest Luxury Sedan in America."

The recession of the early 90s slammed the advertising industry with over 13,500 layoffs. However, specialists in small, regional creative shops were able to snatch away some large accounts during this period and produce ads for established corporations. This Coca-Cola ad came from the clever minds at Creative Artists Agency in Hollywood (a talent agency).

Cuniff, VP/creative director at Lord, Dentsu & Partners, called "the second creative revolution."[22]

The Interactive Age: Looking at the Twenty-first Century

The explosion of new technologies in the last decade has affected advertising considerably. With cable TV and satellite receivers, viewers can watch channels devoted to single types of programming, such as straight news, home shopping, sports, or comedy. This shift transformed television from the most widespread of mass media to a more specialized, **narrowcasting** medium.[23] Now small companies and product marketers that appeal to a limited clientele can use TV to reach audiences with select interests.

A concurrent change that didn't please advertisers was the growing presence of VCRs and remote controls, which allow viewers to avoid commercials altogether by channel surfing during breaks or simply zipping through them when watching a previously recorded show. Advertisers and TV executives became even more upset with the introduction of PVRs **(personal video recorders)** like TiVo, which allow viewers to pause, fast-forward, and rewind live TV, store programming, and skip commercials altogether. To its credit, TiVo never promoted the ad-skipping feature to consumers, but it was no secret. Everybody knew.

Ironically, though, within a very short time, TiVo executives were courting marketers and agencies to join its charter advertiser program, which would let viewers opt in to a marketer's "advertainment" show. Best Buy bought in early and so did Sony Pictures, Lexus, Procter & Gamble, and Miller Brewing. One of the major features of TiVo is its ability to target potential customers and measure effectiveness

New technology has created new media. TiVo initially allowed viewers to pause, fast-forward, and rewind television shows. But it was not long until viewers could also save some shows to their PCs or burn them on DVDs. TiVo's Web site (www.tivo.com) demonstrates how TiVo works.

against that target. As *Advertising Age* pointed out, the Holy Grail to advertisers is a one-to-one relationship with consumers, and that becomes increasingly possible with permission-based, opt-in, and two-way interactions with viewers.[24]

Computer technology has also had a huge impact. Personal computers, the Internet, e-mail, and electronic bulletin boards give advertisers new media for reaching potential customers. Now even the smallest companies can maintain computer databases of customers' names to integrate their marketing campaigns.

What we are witnessing is an interactive revolution. Advertising is evolving into a two-way medium where consumers with PCs, Internet connections, CD-ROMs, and cable TV can choose which information they access and then spend time researching the product information they desire.[25] With interactivity, rather than zipping or zapping commercials, people actually seek them out. As we discuss in Chapter 13, this is a revolutionary way for advertisers to reach consumers. Agencies now have the opportunity to prove once again that advertising creativity is not about winning awards but about helping marketers *sell* things.[26]

Computer technology has had an enormous impact on the ability of companies to establish and maintain one-to-one relationships with their customers. Consumers can now seek out the advertising that provides the information they desire. Dell Computer capitalized on this technology early to become the world's largest supplier of personal computers.

Advertising has come a long way from the simple sign on the bootmaker's shop. Today it is a powerful device that announces the availability and location of products, describes their quality and value, imbues brands with personality, and simultaneously defines the personalities of the people who buy them while entertaining us. More than a reflection of society and its desires, advertising can start and end fads, trends, and credos—sometimes all by itself.[27]

The endless search for competitive advantage and efficiency has made advertising's journey in the last 100+ years fascinating. Now companies are realizing that their most important asset is not capital equipment, or research capability, or their line of products. In the heated competition of the global marketplace, their most important asset is their customer and the relationship they have with that person or organization. Protecting that asset has become the new marketing imperative for the twenty-first century. In an effort to do a better job of *relationship marketing,* companies are now learning that they must be consistent in both what they say and what they do. It's not enough to produce outstanding advertising anymore. They must integrate all their marketing communications with everything else they do, too. That's what *integrated marketing communications* really means. And that will present exciting new challenges to marketing and advertising professionals in the immediate future.

Identify the key developments that have taken place throughout history that have had an impact on the advertising industry.

CONCEPT CHECK

Society and Ethics: The Effects of Advertising

As a social force, advertising has been a major factor in improving the standard of living in the United States and around the world. By publicizing the material, social, and cultural opportunities of a free enterprise society, advertising has encouraged increased productivity by both management and labor.

With just a small amount of money, for instance, you can buy a car today. It may be secondhand, but from advertising you know it's available. If you earn more money, you can buy a new car or one with more luxury features. You can also make a statement about yourself as an individual with the vehicle you purchase. As with many products, advertising has created a personality for each automobile make and model on the market. You, as a free individual, have the opportunity to select the product that best matches your functional, financial, or social needs and aspirations.

Advertising serves other social needs besides simply stimulating sales. Newspapers, magazines, radio, television, and many Web sites all receive their primary income from advertising. This facilitates freedom of the press and promotes more complete information. Public service announcements by a number of advertising organizations also foster growth and understanding of important social issues and causes. The Red Cross, Community Chest, United Way, and other noncommercial organizations receive continuous financial support and volunteer assistance due in large part to the power of advertising.

However, advertising is certainly not without its shortcomings. Since its beginnings, the profession has had to struggle with issues of honesty and ethics. In fact, in the early 1900s, the advertising profession was forced to mend its ethical ways. Consumers suffered for years from unsubstantiated product claims, especially for patent medicines and health devices. The simmering resentment finally boiled over into a full-blown consumer movement, which led to government regulation and ultimately to industry efforts at self-regulation.

In 1906, Congress responded to public outrage by passing the Pure Food and Drug Act to protect the public's health and control drug advertising. In 1914, it passed the Federal Trade Commission Act to protect the public from unfair business practices, including misleading and deceptive advertising.

Advertising practitioners themselves formed groups to improve advertising effectiveness and promote professionalism and started vigilance committees to safeguard the integrity of the industry. The Association of National Advertisers (ANA), the American Advertising Federation (AAF), and the Better Business Bureau (BBB) are today's outgrowths of those early groups.

But in times of economic crisis, false and misleading advertising has invariably reappeared, perhaps out of advertiser desperation. During the Depression years, several best-selling books exposed the advertising industry as an unscrupulous exploiter of consumers, giving birth to a new consumer movement and further government regulation.

In a 1962 message to Congress, President Kennedy asserted, "If consumers are offered inferior products, if prices are exorbitant . . . if the consumer is unable to choose on an informed basis, then his dollar is wasted . . . and the national interest suffers." In his Bill for Consumer Rights, Kennedy gave the American consumer four basic rights, including the right "to be protected against fraudulent, deceitful or grossly misleading information, advertising, labeling, or other practices, and to be given the facts s/he needs to make an informed choice."

In the 1970s, a new American consumer movement grew out of the widespread disillusionment following the Kennedy assassination, the Vietnam War, the Watergate scandals, and the sudden shortage of vital natural resources—all communicated instantly to the world via new satellite technology. These issues fostered cynicism and distrust of the establishment and tradition, and gave rise to a new twist in moral consciousness. On the one hand, people justified their personal irresponsibility and self-indulgence in the name of self-fulfillment. On the other, they attacked corporate America's quest for self-fulfillment (profits) in the name of social accountability.

Today, corporate America has generally cleaned up the major inequities in advertising. But now attention has shifted to more subtle problems of puffery, advertising to children, the advertising of legal but unhealthful products, and advertising ethics. We believe ethics in advertising is such an important issue that we have included features on this topic throughout the text.

In short, advertising has had a pronounced effect on society as well as the economy. It has also fostered a host of social attitudes and laws that have dramatically affected advertising itself. We'll take a closer look at these issues in Chapter 2.

CONCEPT CHECK

What important benefits and issues has advertising contributed to our society?

Chapter Summary

As a tool of marketing communications, advertising is the structured and composed, nonpersonal communication of information. It is usually paid for and usually persuasive, about products, services, or ideas, by identified sponsors through various media.

Marketing is the process of planning and executing the conception, pricing, distribution, and promotion of ideas, goods, and services to create exchanges that satisfy the perceived needs, wants, and objectives of individuals and organizations. Advertising helps the organization achieve its marketing goals. An effective advertising specialist must have a broad understanding of the whole marketing process in order to know what type of advertising to use in a given situation.

Companies and organizations use many different types of advertising, depending on their particular marketing strategy. The marketing strategy will determine who the targets of advertising should be, in what regions the advertising should appear, what media should be used, and what purposes the advertising should accomplish.

In economic theory, there are four fundamental assumptions of free-market economics: self-interest, complete information, many buyers and sellers, and absence of externalities. Given these principles, there are a number of functions and effects of advertising in a free economy. It identifies and differentiates products; communicates information about them; induces nonusers to try products and users to repurchase them; stimulates products' distribution; increases product use; builds value, brand preference, and loyalty; and lowers the overall cost of sales.

The greatest impact on the evolution of advertising has been economic. In ancient times when most people could not read or write, there was little need for advertising. Marketers used symbols on signs to advertise their products. As the world expanded, urban populations soared, and manufacturing and communication technologies developed, as did advertising. Printing was the first major technology to affect advertising; cable TV and the Internet are the most recent.

With changing economies and increased competition, advertising has evolved from the preindustrial age through the industrializing and industrial ages to the postindustrial age. Since World War II, advertisers have used a variety of strategies, such as product differentiation, market segmentation, and positioning, to set their products apart. Recently the advertising industry experienced a period of retrenchment and reevaluation, but the future offers new opportunities for advertisers and agencies that can harness the interactive revolution and develop deep relationships with their customers.

As a social force, advertising has helped improve the standard of living, both in the United States and around the world. Advertising makes us aware of the availability of products, imbues products with personality, and enables us to communicate information about ourselves through the products we buy. Through its financial support, advertising also fosters the free press and the growth of many nonprofit organizations.

However, advertising has also been severely criticized over the years for its lack of honesty and ethics. This has given rise to numerous consumer movements and a plethora of laws that now regulate the practice of advertising.

Key Terms

advertising, 4
branding, 8
consumer packaged goods, 13
consumers, 4
demarketing, 15
externalities, 7
goods, 5
ideas, 5
industrial age, 13
industrializing age, 12

marketing, 6
marketing communications, 4
marketing mix, 6
market segmentation, 14
mass media, 5
medium, 5
narrowcasting, 18
personal video recorders, 18
positioning, 14

postindustrial age, 15
preindustrial age, 9
product, 5
product differentiation, 14
public service announcement (PSA), 5
sales promotion, 17
services, 5
unique selling proposition, 14
word of mouth (WOM) advertising, 5

Review Questions

1. How does advertising for the American Cancer Society compare with the standard definition of advertising?
2. What are the three major functional areas of business and which function is most closely related to advertising?
3. What are the four elements that comprise a company's marketing strategy and how do they affect the type of advertising a company uses?
4. What are the four fundamental assumptions of free market economics?
5. How does advertising lower the cost of sales?
6. What has been the most important influence on advertising in the postindustrial age?
7. What are three examples of companies or organizations that use a demarketing strategy?
8. What companies can you think of that are engaged in marketing warfare?
9. As a consumer, are you likely to save money buying at a store that doesn't advertise? Explain.
10. What is a company's most important asset and what must companies do to protect that asset?

Exploring Advertising

1. Collect or describe three examples of marketing communications. Explain why you would or would not consider each one to be an example of advertising.
2. Bring into class or describe an advertising example of demarketing. Explain why you think the advertiser would want to slow demand for a product.
3. Find a print ad that exemplifies several of the seven functions and effects of advertising. Describe how the ad addresses each one.

chapter two

The Economic, Social, and Regulatory Aspects of Advertising

Objectives

To identify and explain the economic, social, ethical, and legal issues advertisers must consider. The basic economic principles that guided the evolution of advertising also have social and legal effects. When they are violated, social issues arise and the government may take corrective measures. Society determines what is offensive, excessive, and irresponsible; government bodies determine what is deceptive and unfair. To be law-abiding, ethical, and socially responsible, as well as economically effective, advertisers must understand these issues.

After studying this chapter, you will be able to:

* **Discuss** the impact of advertising on the economy.

* **Debate** the validity of the various social criticisms of advertising.

* **Explain** the difference between social responsibility and ethics in advertising.

* **Describe** how government agencies regulate advertising to protect both consumers and competitors.

* **Discuss** the activities of nongovernment organizations in fighting fraudulent and deceptive advertising.

good example ✓

In their constant quest to attract consumers and associate products with "cool" or luxurious and hedonistic lifestyles, some advertisers have consistently pushed the boundaries of what is ethically and socially acceptable. American advertising has always embraced erotic suggestiveness while usually staying clear of full nudity and explicit sexuality. Campaigns that blur that distinction often arouse controversy and even protest.

For two decades, the most notorious purveyor of sensual "cool" was Calvin Klein—beginning in the late 1970s with the "nothing comes between me and my Calvin's" campaign featuring Brooke Shields and culminating in 1998's "kiddie-porn" controversy. Since the millennium, however, the mantle of "the most controversial advertiser" has passed from Klein to trendy teen retailer Abercrombie and Fitch (A&F).

A&F hired iconic 1980s fashion photographer Bruce Weber, who had been responsible for some of the steamier Calvin Klein images, as the principal photographer for the *A&F Quarterly,* a hybrid catalog and "lifestyle" magazine, known as a "magalog." The magazine originally featured pseudo-adult photographs of hunky, underdressed young adult men, but as it became increasingly popular in campus Greek culture, it began featuring under- and undressed women as well in increasingly suggestive sexual situations. The publication's articles, sexually explicit but often tongue-in-cheek, underscored this "sex and games" attitude. The explicit articles bred controversy, particularly as it was hard to see what they had to do with the clothing.

A feature article on alcohol consumption, called "Drinking 101," caught the attention of Mothers Against Drunk Driving, and the magazine's 1999 issue "Naughty or Nice" prompted Illinois Lieutenant Governor Corinne Wood to call for a boycott of the retailer for "peddling soft porn in the guise of a clothing catalog."[1] When controversy over the *Quarterly* broke out again in December 2003, this time over an article on group sex, the company finally reformatted the *Quarterly* and introduced a new publication for summer 2004, *A&F Magazine,* which focused exclusively on artistic photographs of models wearing A&F clothing.

The confusion of the soft-porn genre with conventional advertising seemed particularly distressing to conservative critics like the National Coalition for the Protection of Children and Families, who claim that the company uses "clothing to sell a sexual philosophy."[2] Especially since the target market is teens and young adults, the advertising is viewed as transgressing the proper place of marketing.

But as with the Calvin Klein ads, the impact of controversy on brand-name recognition is sometimes worth the risk to the corporate image: Abercrombie and Fitch's profits were up for the second quarter of 2004, and copies of the last issue of the *A&F Quarterly* fetch up to $100 on eBay.

And although the lifestyle depicted may not be popular with certain groups, the clothes themselves have achieved the status of uniform among preppy suburban youth.

In advertising, it seems generating controversy is a sure way to be seen.

The Many Controversies about Advertising

Advertising is one of the most visible activities of business. By inviting people to try their products, companies risk public criticism and attack if their advertising displeases or offends the audience or if their products don't measure up to the advertised promises. Proponents of advertising say it's therefore safer to buy advertised products because, when a company's name and reputation are on the line, it tries harder to fulfill its promises.

Advertising is both applauded and criticized not only for its role in selling products but also for its influence on the economy and on society. For years, critics have denigrated advertising for a wide range of sins—some real, some imagined.

Views of offensiveness vary a great deal from country to country. Clothing retailer Benetton uses the same ads all over the world, and sometimes the ads impinge on the customs and religious beliefs of certain countries. The intended message in this ad, poignantly called "A Kiss from God," is that love surmounts all conventional taboos. But the Italian Advertising Authority banned it. In areas where the influence of the church was less strong, the message was better understood. In England, for example, it won the Eurobest Award. And Sister Barbara of Alzey wrote to Benetton from Germany: "I think that this photo expresses a great deal of tenderness, serenity, and peace." Spend some time on Benetton's Web site (www.benetton.com) and see how the company uses its themeline, the United Colors of Benetton, to promote racial tolerance and peace among nations.

John O'Toole, the late chair of Foote, Cone & Belding and president of the American Association of Advertising Agencies, pointed out that many critics attack advertising because it *isn't something else.* Advertising isn't journalism, education, or entertainment—although it often performs the tasks of all three. But it shouldn't be judged by those standards. To go back to Albert Lasker's original definition, advertising is salesmanship in print. Sponsors advertise because they hope it will help them sell some product, service, or idea.[3]

Notwithstanding O'Toole's articulate defense, many controversies still swirl around the whole field of advertising. Some of them focus on advertising's *economic* role. For example, how does advertising affect the value of products? Does it cause higher or lower prices? Does it promote competition or discourage it? How does advertising affect overall consumer demand? What effect does it have on consumer choice and on the overall business cycle?

UNITED COLORS OF BENETTON.

Other controversies focus on the *societal* effects of advertising. For instance, does advertising make us more materialistic? Does it force us to buy things we don't need? Does it reach us subliminally in ways we can't control? How does it affect the art and culture of our society? Does advertising debase our language?

From these economic and social controversies, new questions arise regarding the responsibility for and control of advertising. What is the proper role for participants in the marketing process? How much latitude should marketers have in the kinds of products they promote and how they advertise them? And what about consumers? Don't they have some responsibility in the process? Finally, what is the proper role of government? What laws should we have to protect consumers? And what laws go too far and violate the marketer's freedom of speech?

These are important questions, and there are no simple answers. But debate is healthy. This chapter addresses some of the major questions and criticisms about advertising, both the pros and the cons, and delves into the regulatory methods used to remedy advertisers' abuses.

Recall from Chapter 1 the underlying principle of free-market economics—that a society is best served by empowering people to make their own decisions and act as free agents within a system characterized by four fundamental assumptions: *self-interest, many buyers and sellers, complete information,* and *absence of* **externalities** (social costs).

free enterprise

This fundamentally utilitarian framework, derived from the goal of society to promote behaviors that foster the greatest good for the most people, offers a system of economic activity—free enterprise—that has accomplished that goal better than any other economic system in history. This is why societies around the world are increasingly adopting free enterprise economics.

By using this framework for our discussion of advertising controversies, we have a basis for understanding how advertising may contribute to, or detract from, the basic goal of free enterprise: "the most good for the most people."

> **CONCEPT CHECK**
>
> Describe some of the economic and social controversies surrounding advertising.

The Economic Impact of Advertising

Advertising accounts for approximately 2.2 percent of the U.S. gross domestic product (GDP). In relation to the total U.S. economy, this percentage is small, but it's higher than in most countries. It amounts to a spending level of $876.59 for every person in the country—the highest per capita advertising spending in the world. As Marcel Bleustein-Blanchet, the father of modern French advertising, pointed out, it's no coincidence that the level of advertising investment in a country is directly proportional to its standard of living.[4] Exhibit 2–1 shows the level of spending in other countries around the world.

The economic effect of advertising is like the break shot in billiards or pool. The moment a company begins to advertise, it sets off a chain reaction of economic events, as shown in Exhibit 2–2. The extent of the chain reaction, although hard to predict, is related to the force of the shot and the economic environment in which it occurred. Let's consider the economic questions we posed earlier.

Effect on the Value of Products

Why do most people prefer Coca-Cola to some other cola? Why do some people prefer Calvin Klein underwear to some other unadvertised brand? Are the advertised products functionally better? Not necessarily. But, in the mind of the consumer, advertising has given these brands **added value.**

Exhibit 2–1

A country's level of ad spending
is typically proportional to its
standard of living (2005).

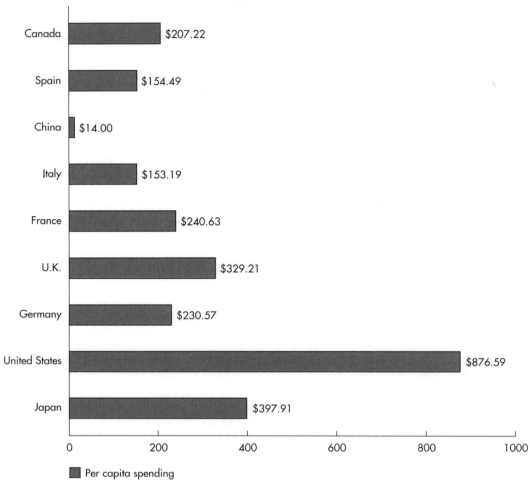

Per Capita Ad Spending (2005 in U.S. dollars)

Country	Per capita spending
Canada	$207.22
Spain	$154.49
China	$14.00
Italy	$153.19
France	$240.63
U.K.	$329.21
Germany	$230.57
United States	$876.59
Japan	$397.91

■ Per capita spending

Exhibit 2–2

The economic effect of advertising is
like the opening break shot in
billiards.

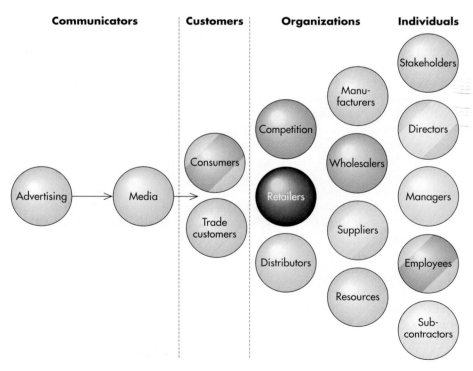

In the mid-1960s, a famous psychologist named Ernest Dichter asserted that a product's *image,* created in part by advertising and promotion, is *an inherent feature of the product itself.*[5] Subsequent studies showed that while an ad may not address a product's quality directly, the positive image conveyed by advertising may imply quality. Moreover, by simply making the product better known, advertising can make the product more desirable to the consumer. In these ways, advertising adds value to the brand.[6] That's why people pay more for Bufferin than an unadvertised brand displayed right next to it—even though all buffered aspirin, by law, is functionally the same.[7]

Advertising also adds value to a brand by educating customers about new uses for a product. Kleenex was originally advertised as a makeup remover, later as a disposable handkerchief. AT&T first promoted the telephone as a necessity and later as a convenience.

One advantage of the free market system is that consumers can choose the values they want in the products they buy. If, for example, low price is important, they can buy an inexpensive economy car. If status and luxury are important, they can buy a fancy sedan or racy sports car. Many of our wants are emotional, social, or psychological rather than functional. One way we communicate who we are (or want to be) is through the products we purchase and display. By associating the product with some desirable image, advertising offers people the opportunity to satisfy those psychic or symbolic wants and needs.

In terms of our economic framework, by adding value to products, advertising contributes to self-interest—for both the consumer and the advertiser. It also contributes to the number of sellers. That increases competition, which also serves the consumer's self-interest.

Effect on Prices

If advertising adds value to products, it follows that advertising also adds cost, right? And if companies stopped all that expensive advertising, products would cost less, right?

Wrong.

Some advertised products do cost more than unadvertised products, but the opposite is also true. Both the Federal Trade Commission and the Supreme Court have ruled that by encouraging competition, advertising has the effect of keeping prices down. This again serves the consumer's self-interest.

Sweeping statements about advertising's positive or negative effect on prices are likely to be too simplistic. We can make some important points, though.

- As one of the many costs of doing business, advertising is indeed paid for by the consumer who buys the product. In most product categories, though, the amount spent on advertising is usually very small compared with the total cost of the product.

- Advertising is one element of the mass-distribution system that enables many manufacturers to engage in mass production, which in turn lowers the unit cost of products. These savings can then be passed on to consumers in the form of lower prices. In this indirect way, advertising helps lower prices.

- In industries subject to government price regulation (agriculture, utilities), advertising has historically had no effect on prices. In the 1980s, though, the government deregulated many of these industries in an effort to restore free market pressures on prices. In these cases, advertising has affected price—usually downward, but not always.

Advertising often makes it possible for small businesses to compete effectively against large corporations. Anthony's Pizza's freedom to advertise allows this neighborhood pizza parlor to compete with the national chains.

- In retailing, price is a prominent element in many ads, so advertising tends to hold prices down. On the other hand, national manufacturers use advertising to stress features that make their brands better; in these cases advertising tends to support higher prices for their brands.

Effect on Competition

Some observers believe advertising actually restricts competition because small companies or industry newcomers can't compete with the immense advertising budgets of large firms.

It's true that intense competition does tend to reduce the number of businesses in an industry. However, some of the firms eliminated by competition may be those that served customers least effectively. In other cases, competition is reduced because of mergers and acquisitions.

High costs may inhibit the entry of new competitors in industries that spend heavily on advertising. In some markets, the original brands probably benefit greatly from this barrier. However, the investments needed for plants, machinery, and labor are of far greater significance. These are typically greater barriers to entry than advertising.

Advertising by big companies often has only a limited effect on small businesses because a single advertiser is rarely large enough to dominate the whole country. Regional oil companies, for example, compete very successfully with national oil companies on the local level. In fact, the freedom to advertise encourages more sellers to enter the market. And we've all seen nonadvertised store brands of food compete very effectively with nationally advertised brands on the same grocery shelves.

Effect on Consumer Demand

The question of advertising's effect on total consumer demand is extremely complex. Numerous studies show that promotional activity does affect aggregate consumption, but they disagree as to the extent of its influence. Many social and economic forces, including technological advances, the population's educational level, increases in population and income, and revolutionary changes in lifestyle, are more significant. For example, the demand for CD players, cellular phones, and personal computers expanded at a tremendous rate, thanks in part to advertising but more to favorable market conditions. At the same time, advertising hasn't reversed declining sales of such items as hats, fur coats, and manual typewriters.

Advertising can help get new products off the ground by giving more people more "complete information," thereby stimulating **primary demand**—demand for the entire product class. In declining markets, when the only information people want is price information, advertising can influence **selective demand**—demand for a particular brand. But the only effect it will have on primary demand is to slow the rate of decline. In growing markets, advertisers generally compete for shares of that growth. In mature, static, or declining markets, they compete for each other's shares.

Effect on Consumer Choice

For manufacturers, the best way to beat the competition is to make their product different. For example, look at the long list of car models, sizes, colors, and features designed to attract different buyers. And grocery shelves may carry more than 100 different brands of breakfast cereals—

DocuSystems is a local distributor of copiers in Vancouver. This clever label points out that a nonworking copier costs a lot of expensive, nonbillable time. This kind of ad promotes selective demand because it promotes a particular source for copiers rather than copiers in general.

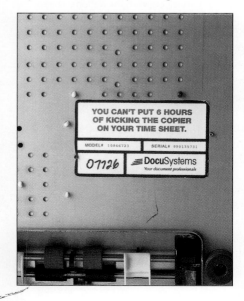

Handwritten margin note: Is it advertising a favorable market conditions the affect ↑ in Sales.

something for everybody. The freedom to advertise encourages businesses to create new brands and improve old ones. When one brand reaches market dominance, smaller brands may disappear for a time. But the moment a better product comes along and is advertised skillfully, the dominant brand loses out to the newer, better product. Once again, the freedom to advertise promotes the existence of more sellers, and that gives consumers wider choices.

Effect on the Business Cycle

The relationship between advertising and gross domestic product has long been debated. John Kenneth Galbraith, a perennial critic of advertising, concedes that by helping to maintain the flow of consumer demand (encouraging more buyers), advertising helps sustain employment and income. But he maintains that despite declines in the value of the dollar, the U.S. trade deficit persists because advertising and marketing activities create consumer preference for certain foreign products.[8]

Historically, when business cycles dip, companies cut advertising expenditures. That may help short-term profits, but studies prove that businesses that continue to invest in advertising during a recession are better able to protect, and sometimes build, market shares.[9] However, no study has shown that if everybody just kept advertising, a recessionary cycle would turn around. We conclude that when business cycles are up, advertising contributes to the increase. When business cycles are down, advertising may act as a stabilizing force by encouraging buyers to continue buying.

The Abundance Principle: The Economic Impact of Advertising in Perspective

To individual businesses such as Calvin Klein, the local car dealer, and the convenience store on the corner, advertising pays back more than it costs. If advertising didn't pay, no one would use it. And the various news and entertainment media that depend on advertising for financial support would go out of business.

Advertising costs less for the consumer than most people think. The cost of a bottle of Coke includes about a penny for advertising. And the $20,000 price tag on a new car usually includes a manufacturer's advertising cost of less than $400.

To the economy as a whole, the importance of advertising may best be demonstrated by the **abundance principle.** This states that in an economy that produces more goods and services than can be consumed, advertising serves two important purposes: It keeps consumers informed of their alternatives *(complete information),* and it allows companies to compete more effectively for consumer dollars *(self-interest).* In North America alone, the U.S. and Canadian economies produce an enormous selection of products. Most supermarkets carry more than 30,000 different items. Each automaker markets dozens of models. And many suppliers compete for the consumer dollar. This competition generally results in more and better products at similar or lower prices.

Advertising stimulates competition *(many buyers and sellers).* In countries where consumers have more income to spend after their physical needs are satisfied, advertising also stimulates innovation and new products. However, no amount of advertising can achieve long-term acceptance for products that do not meet consumer approval. Despite massive advertising expenditures, fewer than a dozen of the 50 best-known cars developed in the twentieth century are still sold today.

The most beautiful thing that ever happened to horsepower

1958 EDSEL

Despite extensive advertising efforts, some products, like the Edsel automobile, will fail simply because they do not meet the expectations of customers at that particular time. Many of the best-known cars developed in the twentieth century are no longer sold today. Ironically, the Edsel has since become a pricy collector's item for automobile aficionados.

Advertising stimulates competition.

CONCEPT CHECK

In what ways does advertising have an impact on our economy?

Advertising stimulates a healthy economy. It also helps create financially healthy consumers who are more informed, better educated, and more demanding. As a result, consumers now demand that manufacturers be held accountable for their advertising. This has led to an unprecedented level of social criticism and legal regulation, the subject of our next sections.

The Social Impact of Advertising

Because it's so visible, advertising gets criticized frequently, for both what it is and what it isn't. Many of the criticisms focus on the *style* of advertising, saying it's deceptive or manipulative. Other criticisms focus on the *social* or *environmental impact of advertising*. Let's look at some of these common criticisms of advertising, debunk some misconceptions, and examine the problems that do exist.

Deception in Advertising

One of the most common short-term arguments about advertising is that it is so frequently deceptive. If a product does not live up to its ads, dissatisfaction occurs—and in the long term that is as harmful to the advertiser as to the buyer.

For advertising to be effective, consumers must have confidence in it. So any kind of deception not only detracts from the complete information principle of free enterprise but also risks being self-defeating. Even meaningless (but legal) puffery might be taken literally and therefore become deceptive. **Puffery** refers to exaggerated, often subjective claims that can't necessarily be proven true or false, such as "the best," "premier," or "the only way to fly."

Under current advertising law, the only product claims—explicit or implied—that are considered deceptive are those that are *factually false* or convey a false impression and therefore have the potential to deceive or mislead reasonable people.[10] But puffery is excluded from this requirement because regulators maintain that reasonable people don't believe it anyway.

Puffery is rarely so literal as it is in this 2004 Cannes Bronze Lion winner from Jung von Matt (Germany) for Tabasco hot sauce. Although the peppery condiment won't actually cause corn kernels to pop off the cob, such puffery is not illegal because it is so unbelievable.

The fact is that advertising, by its very nature, is *not* complete information. It is biased in favor of the advertiser and the brand. People expect advertisers to be proud of their products and probably don't mind if they puff them a little. But when advertisers cross the line between simply giving their point of view and creating false expectations, that's when people begin to object. One problem is the difficulty of seeing the line, which may be drawn differently by different people. Papa John's Pizza no doubt thought it was just puffing when it advertised "Better ingredients. Better pizza." Pizza Hut saw it differently, though, and sued Papa John's for deceptive advertising. A U.S. District judge agreed and awarded Pizza Hut close to half a million dollars in damages. The judge then ordered Papa John's to stop using its "Better ingredients" slogan.[11] This decision was later overturned on appeal, but the case still goes to show that there are limits on what an advertiser can safely puff. For more on this story and on puffery, see "Ethical Issues: Truth in Advertising: Fluffing and Puffing" on page 34.

The Subliminal Advertising Myth

Wilson Bryan Key promotes the notion that, to seduce consumers, advertisers intentionally create ads with sexual messages hidden in the illustrations just below the **limen**—or the threshold of perception. He calls this **subliminal advertising.** His premise is that by embedding dirty words in the ice cubes in a liquor ad, for instance, advertisers can somehow make us want to buy the product. Over the years, many academic studies have completely debunked this theory.[12] In fact, to date no study has proved that such embedding exists or that it would have any effect if it did exist.[13] Unfortunately, by promulgating this fiction, Key has been able to sell many thousands of books; worse, he has propagated a generation of consumers who believe in the poppycock of subliminal advertising.

The nerve that Key has been able to touch, though, is important to discuss: the widespread fear that advertisers are messing with our heads—manipulating us psychologically, and without our consent, into buying things we don't want or need. This gets to the heart of the *complete information* principle because the criticism suggests that advertising does not give consumers information upon which to base rational decisions, but rather manipulates us through brainwashing. Consumers are, therefore, like captured prey, helpless in the jaws of marketing predators.

If you think about all the products you buy, how many involve a choice between different brands and different styles? And how many involve a decision based on price or convenience? Probably most. So how many of your purchases can you trace to having been helplessly manipulated? Probably none. You receive information from many different sources: friends and relatives, store displays, ads, packaging, and retail store clerks. At some point, you make a decision. In many cases, your decision is *not* to buy at all—to wait for either more information or more money. As always, the customer, acting in his or her own self-interest, is king.

Daffy's (www.daffys.com) uses tongue-in-cheek humor to take a stand against advertising puffery—inflated promises and claims often accompanied by inflated prices. Daffy's beckons smart consumers to shop where they can find the same quality goods with "no bull" price tags.

The Effect of Advertising on Our Value System

A related long-term argument, often voiced by certain professional critics—sociologists, journalists, consumer advocates, and government regulators—is that advertising degrades people's value systems by promoting a hedonistic, materialistic way of life. Advertising, they say, encourages us to buy more cars, more CDs, more clothing, and more junk we don't need. It is destroying the essence of our "citizen democracy," replacing it with a self-oriented consumer democracy.[14]

Critics claim advertising manipulates us into buying things by playing on our emotions and promising greater status, social acceptance, and sex appeal. It causes people to take up harmful habits, makes poor kids buy $170 sneakers, and tempts ordinary people to buy useless products in the vain attempt to emulate celebrity endorsers.[15] Again, they claim advertising is so powerful consumers are helpless to defend themselves against it.

Once again, this argument exaggerates the power of advertising. In fact, most Americans express a healthy skepticism toward it. One study showed that

Truth in Advertising: Fluffing and Puffing

Perhaps nothing characterizes advertising in the minds of most people more than the term puffery. In advertising, puffery means exaggerated commendation, or hype. The term comes from the Old English word *pyffan,* meaning "to blow in short gusts" or "to inflate; make proud or conceited." Puffery surely predates recorded history.

The Nature of Puffery

Regardless of its long heritage and current widespread use, we should question puffery's role in advertising. Inherently, puffery erodes advertising's credibility as a trustworthy messenger by lowering the public's belief in the advertising they see. People begin to question those who support and create such advertising—the advertisers, ad professionals, and ultimately the media that run such ads.

Defining Puffery

Regardless of the criticisms, puffery remains legal. And in the United States, it's relatively well defined by law.

In 1906, as part of the Uniform Sales Act (now called the Uniform Commercial Code), a seller's opinion (an element of puffery) cannot constitute the sole basis of a warranty to the customer; more information is required. In 1916, the law stipulated puffery as acceptable if it is "mere exaggeration" but illegal if it invents advantages and then "falsely asserts their existence." The buyer's state of mind entered the definition in 1941: "'Sales talk,' or 'puffing,' . . . is considered to be offered and understood as an expression of the seller's opinion only, which is to be discounted

as such by the buyer, and on which no *reasonable man* would rely." The Federal Trade Commission joined the dialogue in the late 1950s, confirming, "Puffery does not embrace misstatements of material facts."

As you can see, puffery's legal definition establishes that the characteristics puffed must, in fact, exist. The challenge is defining where puffing crosses over from exaggeration into falsehood and then to deception. Exaggeration is often the starting point of falsehood, but falsehood is not necessarily harmful or injurious—in fact, it may be playful and creative. Deception, however, is interpreted as being injurious to consumers and is therefore illegal.

Take, for example, the case with Papa John's International, who invested millions of dollars over the years in its "Better ingredients, Better pizza" advertising campaign. The vague and subjective claim might be considered puffery. But when it named its rival Pizza Hut in ads, the issue changed from mere puffery to comparison. And comparison advertising requires convincing substantiation; otherwise it may be considered deceptive.

In 1998, Pizza Hut filed a lawsuit in Dallas federal court against Papa John's, alleging that its campaign was "false, misleading, and deceptive," as defined by the Lanham Act. A Texas jury ruled in favor of Pizza Hut, charging that Papa John's "Better ingredients, Better pizza" campaign constituted deceptive advertising. Pizza Hut was awarded $467,619.75. Papa John's was ordered to remove its slogan from ads, pizza boxes, restaurant signage, and delivery trucks.

Later, the decision was reversed by the District Court of Appeals after Papa John's removed the references to Pizza Hut. But the point had still been made: Advertisers

only 17 percent of U.S. consumers see advertising as a source of information to help them decide what to buy.[16] Perhaps that's why more advertised products fail than succeed in the marketplace.

Still, this may be the most damning criticism of advertising because there's no question that advertisers do indeed spend millions trying to convince people their products will make them sexier, healthier, and more successful. The very amount of advertising we witness every day seems to suggest that every problem we have can be solved by the purchase of some product.

The Proliferation of Advertising

One of the most common long-term complaints about advertising is that there's just too much of it. In the United States alone, the average person may be exposed to 500 to 1,000 commercial messages a day. With so many products

have to be careful about the puffery claims they make—they no longer have free rein. Marketers need to be able to substantiate any claims that they make. An indirect comparison, or even the appearance of one, could render them liable.

The Use of Puffery

Common usage portrays puffery as praise for the item to be sold using subjective opinions, superlatives, exaggerations, and vagueness, and generally stating no specific facts. Ivan Preston, the leading scholar on the issue of puffery, has established six levels of puffery:

- Best (strongest claim): "Nestle's makes the very best chocolate."
- Best possible: "Nothing cleans stains better than Clorox bleach" or "Visa—It's everywhere you want to be."
- Better: "Advil just works better."
- Especially good: "Extraordinary elegance." (Coty)
- Good: "M'm, m'm good." (Campbell's soup)
- Subjective qualities (weakest claim): "There's a smile in every Hershey bar."

Puffery often takes the form of "nonproduct facts," information not specifically about the product and therefore not directly ascertainable as being truths, falsehoods, or deceptions specific to the product. Nonproduct facts are typically about consumers: their personalities, lifestyles, fears, anxieties. An example is the Army's positioning message, "Be all that you can be in the Army." The claim relies on the potential for what can happen to the ad's readers while they're in the Army. It doesn't actually promise any specific benefits such as improved physical fitness or more education. Thus, regardless of what actually happens to readers who join up, the claim is neither true nor false about the Army.

Puffery can also be "artful display," the visual presentation of a product. Although not well defined by law, visual exaggeration is ever present in ads to enhance moods, excite viewers, and more. The existence of professional models, for example, suggests that some individuals are more visually attractive than others. This factor makes them appealing. But does their appearance in an ad imply that owning the product will make the buyer more physically attractive? Although most prospective purchasers don't expect the product to improve their physical appearance, they might well become disappointed if the product failed to live up to the implied promise—the puffery—that it can improve their psychological self-image.

Judging Puffery

We live in exciting times. Populations are more literate, satellites and the Internet keep the world informed instantly, and modern technology speeds up the way we live and play. And part of the glitz of our modern life is puffery, adding pizzazz and stimulating our dreams.

But who should protect consumers from their love/hate relationship with puffery, especially when puffery crosses the line and becomes injurious? Who should evaluate puffery's ethics? The courts may, but only when a consumer challenges an advertiser. The actions and attitudes of the advertising profession can make a huge difference. If the First Amendment doesn't curtail them, the media can also affect the use and abuse of puffery.

competing for attention (more than 30,000 in the average supermarket), advertisers themselves worry about the negative impact of excessive advertising. According to a recent study by the American Association of Advertising Agencies, ad clutter is still on the rise. In 2002, the amount of nonprogram time ranged from a low of 16 minutes per hour in prime time to nearly 21 minutes per hour in daytime, a daypart that is particularly important to advertisers.[17] The networks add to the problem themselves by jamming every possible moment with promotions for their shows. Too much advertising creates an externality not only for consumers (nuisance), but for the advertisers themselves—the more commercials that hit the consumer's brain, the less effective paid advertising is. Conscious of this, Meredith Broadcasting Group cut 15 percent of its advertising inventory from local newscasts at its CBS-affiliate, WGNX Atlanta, and saw its household ratings go up 20 percent.[18] Higher ratings, of course, means they can charge more for their remaining commercial time. Hopefully, other stations will follow suit.

While the clutter problem is irksome to viewers and advertisers alike, most people tolerate it as the price for free TV, freedom of the press, and a high standard of living. However, with the proliferation of new media choices, this externality is only likely to get worse. Virtually every popular Web site is cluttered with advertising banners, and our e-mail boxes are flooded with advertising messages on a daily basis. While the Federal Communications Commission exercises no jurisdiction over the Internet, it did consider reinstating commercial time limits on television. But, as of now, the only limits currently in force relate to TV programming aimed at children 12 and under—advertising may not exceed 10.5 minutes per hour on weekends and 12 minutes per hour on weekdays.[19]

Clutter is not so evident in other countries. In France, for example, government-owned stations can carry no more than 12 minutes of commercials per hour. During movies there is only one 4-minute commercial break, although the government is considering changing that rule to allow two breaks.[20]

The Use of Stereotypes in Advertising

Advertising has long been criticized for insensitivity to minorities, women, immigrants, the disabled, the elderly, and a myriad of other groups—that is, for not being "politically correct."[21] This long-term argument also addresses externalities because the very presence of advertising affects the nature of our culture and environment, even when we do not want it.

Since the 1980s, national advertisers have become more sensitive to the concerns of minorities and women. Latinos, African Americans, Asians, Native Americans, and others are now usually portrayed favorably in ads, not only because of pressure from watchdog groups, but also because it's just good business; these consumers represent sizable target markets. Marilyn Kern-Foxworth, a Texas A&M professor and an expert on minorities in advertising, points out that positive role portrayal in some mainstream ads has had a positive effect on the self-esteem of African American youth.[22]

In national advertising, the image of women is also changing from their historic depiction as either subservient housewives or sex objects. This may be partially due to the increasing number of women in managerial and executive positions with both advertisers and agencies. By 2000, more than 60 percent of all women were participating in the workforce, with more than 20 million of them in managerial and professional careers.[23] Advertisers want to reach, not offend, this sizable market of upwardly mobile consumers. Some agencies now retain feminist consultants to review ads that may risk offending women.[24]

However, problems still exist, especially in local and regional advertising and in certain product categories such as beer and sports promotions. Many advertisers are just not aware of the externalities that their ads can create, and they may perpetuate male and female stereotypes without even realizing it.[25]

Other advertisers resort to **stereotypes** for convenience. All too often, women are still not represented accurately. And the minimal use of minorities in mainstream ads, both local and national, still smacks of tokenism. Observers hope that with increasing numbers of women and minorities joining the ranks of marketing and advertising professionals, and with continuing academic studies of minority and sex-role stereotyping, greater attention will be focused on these issues.

Offensiveness in Advertising

Offensiveness is another short-term style argument that also speaks to externalities. Many parents, for instance, were incensed at Calvin Klein's ads because they perceived them as pornographic, thereby causing a social cost that

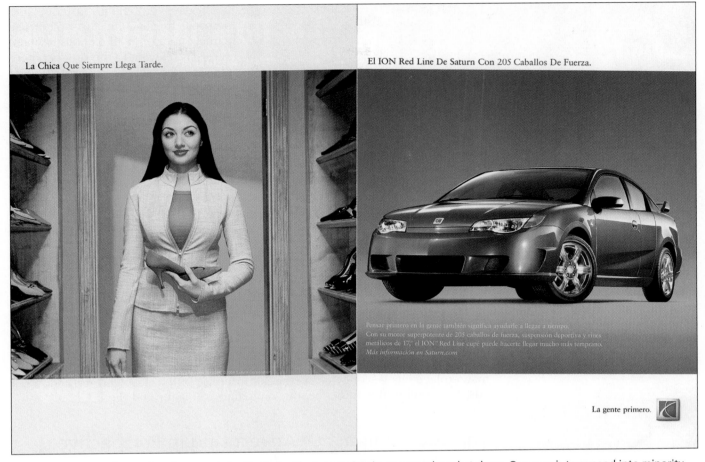

La Chica Que Siempre Llega Tarde.

El ION Red Line De Saturn Con 205 Caballos De Fuerza.

Pensar primero en la gente también significa ayudarle a llegar a tiempo.
Con su motor superpotente de 205 caballos de fuerza, suspensión deportiva y rines
metálicos de 17," el ION™ Red Line cupé puede hacerte llegar mucho más temprano.
Más información en Saturn.com

La gente primero.

With tightening markets, advertisers must double their efforts to maintain or expand market share. One way is to expand into minority communities, which have enormous buying power and offer a significant amount of market share. Minorities are now portrayed more favorably in ads, not only because of societal pressure, but because it's good for business.

extended well beyond the limited scope of merely selling clothes. More recently, Abercrombie & Fitch came under attack for showing nude and semi-nude models in the company's quarterly catalogs. The fact is, people just don't want their children exposed to messages that they deem immoral, offensive, or strictly adult-oriented.[26]

Taste, of course, is highly subjective: What is bad taste to some is perfectly acceptable to others. And tastes change. What is considered offensive today may not be so tomorrow. People were outraged when the first ad for underarm deodorant appeared in a 1927 *Ladies Home Journal;* today no one questions such ads. Yet, even with the AIDS scare, all the broadcast networks except Fox still restrict condom ads to local stations, and all forbid any talk of contraception.[27]

Taste is also geographic. A shockingly bloody ad for a small surfwear company in Sydney, Australia, showed a gutted shark lying on a dock. Protruding from its cut-open belly were a human skeleton and an intact pair of surfer shorts. The tagline: "Tough clothes by Kadu—Triple stitched. Strongest materials available. Homegrown and sewn." While we might consider that ad quite offensive in North America, it won the Grand Prix at the International Advertising Festival in Cannes, France. In Australia it received wide media coverage, since two surfers were killed by sharks while it was running. Rather than pulling the ad out of respect, the company reveled in its timeliness, and the local surfer set responded very favorably.[28]

www.abccookingstudio.com

IT'S TIME TO GO TO SCHOOL ABC

What is offensive to consumers is highly subjective and may vary geographically. What some people may consider in bad taste may be perfectly acceptable to others. OgilvyOne Worldwide created this ad for the ABC Cooking Studio in Thailand.

Today, grooming, fashion, and personal hygiene products often use partial nudity in their ads. Where nudity is relevant to the product, people are less likely to regard it as obscene or offensive—except, as in the case of Abercrombie & Fitch, when the advertising is targeting kids. In many European countries, in fact, nudity in commercials is commonplace. Even the usually staid Brits are starting to see women's breasts in TV commercials and posters.[29] Some industry observers predict that nudity in U.S. advertising will increase in the twenty-first century, but there will be fewer overt sexual scenes of the Abercrombie & Fitch style.[30]

Some consumers get so offended by both advertising and TV programming that they boycott sponsors' products.[31] Of course, they also have the option to just change the channel. Both of these are effective strategies for consumers because, ultimately, the marketplace has veto power. As the 2003 demise of the *A&F Quarterly* shows, if ads don't pull in the audience, the campaign will falter and die.

The Social Impact of Advertising in Perspective

Marketing professionals earnestly believe in the benefits that advertising brings to society. Advertising, they say, encourages the development and speeds the acceptance of new products and technologies. It fosters employment. It gives consumers and business customers a wider variety of choices. By encouraging mass production, it helps keep prices down. And it stimulates healthy competition between producers, which benefits all buyers.[32] Advertising, they point out, also promotes a higher standard of living; it pays for most of our news media and subsidizes the arts; it supports freedom of the press; and it provides a means to disseminate public information about important health and social issues.

Critics of advertising might agree with some of these points but certainly not all of them. For example, critics charge that rather than supporting a free press, advertising actually creates an externality that interferes with it. The media, they say, pander to national advertisers to attract the big ad dollars. In the process, they modify their editorial content to suit their corporate benefactors and consequently shirk their primary journalistic responsibility of presenting news in the public interest.[33]

In summary, we can conclude that while advertising may legitimately be criticized for offering less-than-complete information and, in some instances, for creating unwanted externalities, it should also be applauded when it contributes to the validity of the principles of free enterprise economics. In most cases, by being a rich information source (albeit not complete), advertising contributes to the existence of many buyers and sellers and, therefore, to the self-interest of both consumers and marketers.

CONCEPT CHECK

What are some of the criticisms that are leveled against advertising?

Social Responsibility and Advertising Ethics

When advertising violates one of the basic economic assumptions we've described, some corrective action is needed. As we'll discuss in the next section, numerous laws determine what advertisers can and cannot do, but they also allow a significant amount of leeway. That's where ethics and social responsibility come into play. An advertiser can act unethically or irresponsibly without breaking any laws. Beer and tobacco companies could sponsor rock concerts for college students, and a shoe company could market a basketball sneaker to urban youth as the "Run 'N Gun" brand. As Ivan Preston says, ethics begin where the law ends.[34]

Ethical advertising means doing what the advertiser and the advertiser's peers believe is morally right in a given situation. **Social responsibility** means doing what society views as best for the welfare of people in general or for a specific community of people. Together, ethics and social responsibility can be seen as the moral obligation of advertisers not to violate our basic economic assumptions, even when there is no legal obligation.

Without advertising, public service organizations would be unable to reach a mass audience to educate people about important health and social issues. Here, the Ad Council promotes awareness of the problems associated with learning disabilities.

Advertisers' Social Responsibility

The foundation of any human society is the amicable relationship among its members. Without harmony, a society will collapse. So all the institutions within a society have some responsibility for helping to maintain social harmony through proper stewardship of families and companies, exercise of honesty and integrity in all relationships, adherence to accepted ethical standards, willingness to assist various segments of the society, and the courtesy to respect the privacy of others.

Advertising plays an important role in developed countries. It influences a society's stability and growth. It helps secure large armies, creates entertainment events attracting hundreds of thousands of fans, and often affects the outcome of political elections. Such power places a burden of responsibility on those who sponsor, buy, create, produce, and sell advertising to maintain ethical standards that support the society and contribute to the economic system.

In the United States, for example, the advertising industry is part of a large business community. Like any good neighbor, it has responsibilities: to keep its property clean, participate in civic events, support local enterprises, and improve the community. U.S. advertising professionals have met these challenges by forming local advertising clubs, the American Advertising Federation (AAF), the American Association of Advertising Agencies (AAAA), and the Ad Council. These organizations provide thousands of hours and millions of dollars' worth of *pro bono* (free) work to charitable organizations and public agencies. They also provide scholarships and internships, contributions that serve the whole society. As we discuss later, they even regulate themselves fairly effectively.

Today's consumer is more sophisticated than ever about social issues like environmentalism. Leclerc addresses the issue of "plastic bag pollution" in a beautifully produced campaign, where it tells customers "No, Leclerc does not really want to be seen everywhere." Other ads in the series say, "There are some places we don't want to see our name," and "Some advertising we'll pass up willingly."

Non, E. Leclerc ne veut pas être présent partout.

Avec votre aide, mettons fin à la pollution par les sacs en plastique.

Ethics of Advertising

Philosophies of ethics span the centuries since Socrates. We can hardly do them justice here. But for practical purposes, let's consider three levels of ethical responsibility and apply them to advertising.

On one level, ethics comprise two interrelated components: the traditional actions taken by people in a society or community and the philosophical rules that society establishes to justify such past actions and decree future actions. These components create the primary rules of ethical behavior in the society and enable us to measure how far an individual or company (or advertiser) strays from the norm. Here, the individual's rights are subject to the standards of what is customary (and therefore proper) for the group.

Every individual also faces a second set of ethical issues: the attitudes, feelings, and beliefs that add up to a personal value system. When these two systems conflict, should the individual act on personal beliefs or on the obligation to serve the group and its policies? When the group or individuals cannot resolve an ethical dilemma, they must redefine the issue in dispute. Thus, the third level of ethics concerns singular ethical concepts such as good, bad, right, wrong, duty, integrity, and truth. Are these concepts absolute, universal, and binding? Or are they relative, dependent on situations and consequences? A person's moral and ethical philosophy, influenced by religion, society, and individual values, will determine their answer.

Most advertisers today strive to maintain fair ethical standards and practice socially responsible advertising. Ad agencies rarely force employees to work on accounts they morally oppose. Once a free-swinging, unchecked business, advertising is today a closely scrutinized and heavily regulated profession. Advertising's past shortcomings have created layer upon layer of laws, regulations, and regulatory bodies. Consumer groups, governments, special-interest groups, and even other advertisers now review, control, and modify advertising in order to create more *complete information* and reduce the impact of unwanted *externalities*.

CONCEPT CHECK

What are the social and ethical responsibilities of advertisers and what has the industry done to meet those responsibilities?

Current Regulatory Issues Affecting U.S. Advertisers

In recent years, both federal and state courts have made a number of significant rulings pertaining to advertising issues. The most important of these concern First Amendment rights and privacy rights. We'll discuss each of these, while paying special attention to the recent controversy surrounding tobacco advertising as well as the very sensitive issue of advertising to children.

Freedom of Commercial Speech

The Supreme Court historically distinguishes between "speech" and "commercial speech" (speech that promotes a commercial transaction). But decisions over the last two decades suggest that truthful commercial speech is also entitled to significant, if not full, protection under the First Amendment.

The trend started in 1976 when the Supreme Court held in *Virginia State Board of Pharmacy v. Virginia Citizens Consumer Council* that ads enjoy protection under the First Amendment as commercial speech.[35] The next year the Court declared that the ban by state bar associations on attorney advertising also violated the First Amendment. Now a third of all lawyers advertise, and a few states even permit client testimonials. In 1980 the Court used *Central Hudson Gas v. Public Service Commission* to test whether specific examples of commercial speech can be regulated.[36] The four-pronged *Central Hudson* test includes the following parts:

1. *Does the commercial speech at issue concern a lawful activity?* The ad in question must be for a legal product and must be free of misleading claims.

2. *Will the restriction of commercial speech serve the asserted government interest substantially?* The government must prove that the absence of regulation would have a substantial negative effect.

3. *Does the regulation directly advance the government interest asserted?* The government must be able to establish conclusively that cessation of the advertising would be effective in furthering the government's interest.

4. *Is the restriction no more than necessary to further the interest asserted?* The government would have to establish that there are no other means to accomplish the same end without restricting free speech.[37]

In 1982, the Supreme Court upheld an FTC order allowing physicians and dentists to advertise. Since then, advertising for medical and dental services has skyrocketed.

In 1993, the Supreme Court gave the advertising industry its biggest win in years. It said the Cincinnati City Council violated the First Amendment when it banned racks of advertising brochures from city streets for "aesthetic and safety reasons" while permitting newspaper vending machines.[38]

The issue of freedom of commercial speech is far from settled. Allowing greater freedom of commercial speech enhances the "government interests" of many buyers and sellers and complete information. But the additional interest of reducing externalities creates heated controversies surrounding issues like tobacco and alcohol advertising and advertising to children. These will likely continue for years to come.

The Tobacco Advertising Controversy

Take the case of cigarette advertising. While tobacco is a legal product, the harm created by smoking ends up killing or disabling more than half a million people annually and costing taxpayers billions of dollars every year in health costs—a major externality. To recover these costs, a number of states' attorneys general sued the tobacco industry. In 1998, they reached a historic settlement. It mandated significant reform on cigarette marketing activities and provided for the largest financial recovery in the nation's history. Because the industry had abused its freedom of commercial speech for so many years, the settlement called for sweeping changes in how, when, and where tobacco companies could advertise. Most importantly, the attorneys general sought to protect children from tobacco advertising. Thus, the settlement banned outdoor advertising posters (for example, on billboards, buses, and video arcades), sponsorship of events with a significant youth audience, as well as the use of cartoon characters in any tobacco advertising.[39]

For businesspeople who believe that freedom of commercial speech should be afforded equal protection under the First Amendment, the tobacco case is ominous. Many people are antismoking, antialcohol, antipornography, or antigun. But the "free speechers" believe it's a travesty of the First Amendment to selectively abridge any free speech, whether it's for any political, social, or religious idea or any legal, commercial product. They warn that this selective limitation of freedom of commercial speech threatens every legal business in America, especially because any limitation on the freedom to advertise automatically gives a huge, monopolistic advantage to those big brands that are already the category leaders.[40]

The Issue of Advertising to Children

Advertising to children presents different challenges. Kids are not sophisticated consumers. Their conceptions of self, time, and money are immature. As a result, they know very little about their desires, needs, and preferences—or how to use economic resources rationally to satisfy them. And the nature of children's conceptual ability makes it likely that child-oriented advertising can lead to false beliefs or highly improbable product expectations.

While most children and parents are still joint consumers, more and more children are becoming sole decision makers. To protect them, and their parents, both critics and defenders agree that advertisers should not intentionally deceive children. The central issue is how far advertisers should go to ensure that children are not misled by their ads.

To promote responsible children's advertising and to respond to public concerns, the Council of Better Business Bureaus established the *Children's Advertising Review Unit (CARU)*. The basic activity of CARU is the review and evaluation of child-directed advertising in all media. When children's advertising is found to be misleading, inaccurate, or inconsistent with the *Guidelines*, CARU seeks changes through voluntary cooperation of the advertisers.[41] For an overview of the basic principles underlying CARU's *Guidelines*, see Exhibit 2–3.

Exhibit 2–3

Children's Advertising Review Unit's guidelines for advertising to children.

Seven basic principles underlie CARU's guidelines for advertising to children under the age of 12:

1. Advertisers should always take into account the level of knowledge, sophistication, and maturity of the audience to which their message is primarily directed. Younger children have a limited capacity for evaluating the credibility of information they receive. They also may lack the ability to understand the nature of the information they provide. Advertisers, therefore, have a special responsibility to protect children from their own susceptibilities.

2. Realizing that children are imaginative and that make-believe play constitutes an important part of the growing up process, advertisers should exercise care not to exploit unfairly the imaginative quality of children. Unreasonable expectations of product quality or performance should not be stimulated either directly or indirectly by advertising.

3. Products and content that are inappropriate for use by children should not be advertised or promoted directly to children.

4. Recognizing that advertising may play an important part in educating a child, advertisers should communicate information in a truthful and accurate manner and in language understandable to young children with full recognition that the child may learn practices from advertising that can affect his or her health and well being.

5. Advertisers are urged to capitalize on the potential of advertising to influence behavior by developing advertising that, wherever possible, addresses itself to positive and beneficial social behavior such as friendship, kindness, honesty, justice, generosity, and respect for others.

6. Care should be taken to incorporate minority and other groups in advertising in order to present positive and prosocial roles and role models wherever possible. Social stereotyping and appeals to prejudice should be avoided.

7. Although many influences affect a child's personal and social development, it remains the prime responsibility of the parents to provide guidance for children. Advertisers should contribute to this parent–child relationship in a constructive manner.

In the developed world, other countries are far more strict than the United States about advertising to children. Sweden and Norway, for example, do not permit any television advertising to be directed toward children under 12, and no advertisements at all are allowed during children's programs. While the highest level of advertising to children is in Australia (an average of 34 ads per hour), that country allows no ads on programs aimed at preschool children.[42]

In the area of television advertising, the government and consumer groups play an important role at both the national and international levels to ensure that adequate consumer protection for children is maintained and strengthened where necessary.

Consumer Privacy

The second major regulatory issue facing advertisers is privacy. Today, most advertisers know it's illegal to use a person's likeness in an ad without the individual's permission. And since 1987, even using a celebrity lookalike (or soundalike) can violate that person's rights. The courts have also ruled that people's *privacy rights* continue even after their death.

Now, with the increased use of fax machines, cell phones, and the Internet, all of which can be used for advertising directly to prospects, the issue of **privacy rights** is again in the news. This time it's over people's right to protect their personal information. As we shall see in Chapter 13, privacy is an ethical issue as well as a legal one. It's also a practical issue: Prospective customers who find advertising faxes, telemarketing calls, and e-mails annoying and intrusive aren't likely to buy the offending company's products.

Internet users worry about people they don't know, and even businesses they do know, getting personal information about them. And their concern is not without reason. Many Web sites create profiles of their visitors to get data such as e-mail addresses, clothing sizes, or favorite books. Some sites also track users' Internet surfing habits, usually without their knowledge, to better target ads for products.

Naturally the dot-com companies would prefer to avoid government intervention and the layers of laws and regulations that this would bring. So it's in everybody's interest for self-regulation to work. Time will tell.

> Describe the major regulatory issues facing advertisers today and provide examples of each.
>
> CONCEPT CHECK

Federal Regulation of Advertising in North America

The U.S. government imposes strict controls on advertisers through laws, regulations, and judicial interpretations. Among the many federal agencies and departments that regulate advertising are the Federal Trade Commission, the Food and Drug Administration, the Federal Communications Commission, the Patent and Trademark Office, and the Library of Congress. Because their jurisdictions often overlap, advertisers may sometimes have difficulty complying with their regulations.

Canada has a similar maze of federal regulators. But the Canadian legal situation is considerably more complex than that in the United States due to the separate (but often concurrent) jurisdictions of paternalistic federal and provincial governments, the broad powers of government regulators, the vast array of self-regulatory codes, and the very nature of a bilingual and bicultural society. One simple example of this is the fact that all packages and labels must be printed in both English and French throughout Canada.[43]

When planning to advertise overseas, companies must be very cautious about the do's and don'ts of other countries. Typically, they retain the services of attorneys familiar with local laws. Many international law firms have Web sites that can be quickly located on the Internet. Hall Dickler, a law firm which specializes in advertising and marketing, refers its clients to GALA (www.gala-marketlaw.com), an international network of lawyers to which it belongs.

The U.S. Federal Trade Commission

In the United States, the *Federal Trade Commission (FTC)* is the major regulator of advertising for products sold in interstate commerce. Established by an act of Congress, the FTC has a mission of ensuring "that the nation's markets function competitively, and are vigorous, efficient, and free of undue restrictions."[44] The commission enforces a variety of federal antitrust and consumer protection laws and works to enhance the operation of the marketplace by eliminating acts or practices that are deceptive or unfair. In other words, it is the FTC's responsibility to maintain the existence of *many sellers* in the marketplace, strive to provide more *complete information* to consumers, and keep the marketing process as free of *externalities* as possible.

The FTC's job is complicated by the fact that the definitions of deceptive and unfair are controversial.

Defining Deception

The FTC defines **deceptive advertising** as any ad that contains a misrepresentation, omission, or any other practice that can mislead a significant number of reasonable consumers to their detriment. Proof that consumers were deceived is not required, and the representation may be either expressed or implied. The issue is whether the ad conveys a false impression—even if it is literally true.[45]

Take the case of the FTC against Office Depot, Buy.com, and Value America. According to the FTC, the companies engaged in deceptive practices in advertising "free" and "low-cost" personal computer (PC) systems because they failed to adequately disclose the true costs and important restrictions on the offers. The low cost of the PCs was tied to rebates that were conditioned on the purchase of long-term Internet service contracts.[46]

The FTC is a powerful regulator. The commission cracked down on Exxon and ordered a groundbreaking educational campaign to inform consumers that the right octane for most cars is regular octane, not the more expensive premium grade.[47] The FTC also looks at environmental claims such as biodegradable and recyclable. Commercial Break 2–A lists some common deceptive practices that have been found illegal by the courts.

Defining Unfairness

According to FTC policy, some ads that are not deceptive may still be considered unfair to consumers. **Unfair advertising** occurs when a consumer is "unjustifiably injured" or there is a "violation of public policy" (such as other government

Unfair and Deceptive Practices in Advertising

The courts have held that these acts constitute unfair or deceptive trade practices and are therefore illegal.

False Promises
Making an advertising promise that cannot be kept, such as "restores youth" or "prevents cancer." When Listerine claimed to prevent or reduce the impact of colds and sore throats, the FTC banned the campaign and required the company to run millions of dollars' worth of corrective ads.

Incomplete Description
Stating some but not all of a product's contents, such as advertising a "solid oak" desk without mentioning that only the top is solid oak and the rest is pine.

False and Misleading Comparisons
Making false comparisons, either explicitly or by implication, such as "Like Tylenol, Advil doesn't upset my stomach." That implies that Advil is equal in avoiding stomach upset, though in truth Tylenol is better. To some people, Advil's claim might even suggest that Tylenol upsets the stomach, which is also false.

Bait-and-Switch Offers
Advertising an item at an unusually low price to bring people into the store and then "switching" them to a higher-priced model by claiming that the advertised product is out of stock or poorly made.

Visual Distortions and False Demonstrations
Using trick photography or computer manipulation to enhance a product's appearance—for example, a TV commercial for a "giant steak" dinner special showing the steak on a miniature plate that makes it look extra large. In one classic case, General Motors and its window supplier, Libby Owens-Ford, rigged a demonstration to show how clear their windows were. The GM cars were photographed with the windows down, the competitor's car with the windows up—and Vaseline smeared on them.

False Testimonials
Implying that a product has the endorsement of a celebrity or an authority who is not a bona fide user, or implying that endorsers have a certain expertise that in fact they don't.

Partial Disclosure
Stating certain facts about the advertised product but omitting other material information. An example is claiming, "Kraft's Singles processed cheese slices are made from five ounces of milk," which give Singles more calcium than the imitators' products without mentioning that processing loses about two ounces of the milk.

Small-Print Qualifications
Making a statement in large print, such as Beneficial's "Instant Tax Refund," only to qualify or retract it in obscure, small, or unreadable type elsewhere in the ad: "If you qualify for one of our loans." To the FTC, if readers don't see the qualification, it's not there.

Applying the Breaks
Referring to the acts described above, describe or provide examples of unfair or deceptive practices you have seen in advertising.

statutes). In other words, unfair advertising is due to the inadequacy of *complete information* or some other *externality*. For example, practices considered unfair are claims made without prior substantiation, claims that exploit vulnerable groups such as children and the elderly, and cases where the consumer cannot make a valid choice because the advertiser omits important information about the product or about competing products mentioned in the ad.[48]

In one case, the FTC found that an automaker's failure to warn of a safety problem was not deceptive but was unfair. Advertising organizations have argued that the word "unfair" is so vague it can mean whatever any given individual wants it to. They have lobbied Congress to eliminate the FTC's power to prosecute on unfairness grounds, and Congress did pass a compromise bill requiring the FTC to show that (1) an alleged unfair practice involves substantial, unavoidable injury to consumers; (2) the injury is not reasonably avoidable by consumers themselves; and (3) the injury is not outweighed by benefits to consumers or competition.[49] This legislation suggests that in the future the FTC will have to balance on a far narrower beam in its effort to regulate unfairness.[50]

The purpose of comparative ads is to demonstrate the superiority of one product over another. Dy•Dee Wash takes the au natural marketing approach, with a cloth diaper service that is more environmentally friendly than the use of disposable diapers.

Advertising law requires that celebrity endorsers actually use the product. For example, this ad for Crest toothpaste features the beautiful smile of actress Vanessa Williams. Since the implication is that Crest helped her keep this "ageless smile," she would have to be an actual user of the product.

Comparative Advertising

Advertisers use **comparative advertising** to claim superiority to competitors in some aspect. In the United States, such ads are legal (and encouraged by the FTC) so long as the comparison is truthful. In fact, the FTC cracked down on the Arizona Automobile Dealers Association for restricting truthful, nondeceptive comparative price advertising among its members.[51]

The 1988 Trademark Law Revision Act closed a loophole in the Lanham Act, which governed comparison ads but did not mention misrepresenting another company's product. Under current law, any advertiser that misrepresents its own or another firm's goods, services, or activities is vulnerable to a civil action.

In addition to being truthful, comparative ads must compare some objectively measurable characteristic. And the greatest scrutiny must be given to the substantiation. Given the potential for sizable damages—up to millions of dollars—for faulty comparative advertising, the greatest care must be exercised in this area.[52]

Investigating Suspected Violations

If it receives complaints from consumers, competitors, or its own staff members who monitor ads in various media, the FTC may decide to investigate an advertiser. The agency has broad powers to pursue suspected violators and demand information from them. Typically, the FTC looks for three kinds of information: *substantiation, endorsements,* and *affirmative disclosures.*

If a suspected violator cites survey findings or scientific studies, the FTC may ask for **substantiation.** Advertisers are expected to have supporting data before running an ad, although the FTC sometimes allows postclaim evidence. The FTC does not solicit substantiation for ads it is not investigating.

The FTC also scrutinizes ads that contain questionable **endorsements** or **testimonials.** If a noncelebrity endorser is paid, the ad must disclose this onscreen.[53] The endorsers may not make claims the advertiser can't substantiate. Further, celebrity endorsers must actually use the product or service (if portrayed), and they can be held personally liable if they misrepresent it.[54]

Advertisers must make **affirmative disclosure** of their product's limitations or deficiencies: for example, EPA mileage ratings for cars, pesticide warnings, and statements that saccharin may be hazardous to one's health.

Remedies for Unfair or Deceptive Advertising

When the FTC determines that an ad is deceptive or unfair, it may take three courses of action: negotiate with the advertiser for a *consent decree,* issue a *cease-and-desist order,* and/or require *corrective advertising.*

A **consent decree** is a document the advertiser signs agreeing to stop the objectionable advertising without admitting any wrongdoing. Before signing, the advertiser can negotiate specific directives with the FTC that will govern future advertising claims.

If an advertiser won't sign a consent decree, the FTC may issue a **cease-and-desist order** prohibiting further use of the ad. Before the order is final, it is heard by an administrative law judge. Most advertisers sign the consent decree after the hearing and agree, without admitting guilt, to halt the advertising. Advertisers who violate either a consent decree or a cease-and-desist order can be fined up to $11,000 per showing of the offending ad.

The FTC may also require **corrective advertising** for some period of time to explain and correct offending ads. In 1999 the FTC ruled that pharmaceutical giant Novartis advertised without substantiation that its Doan's Pills brand was more effective against back pain than its rivals. Because the deceptive advertising had gone on for more than nine years, the FTC ordered Novartis to run $8 million worth of corrective advertising. The advertising was to include the statement: "Although Doan's is an effective pain reliever, there is no evidence that Doan's is more effective than other pain relievers for back pain." They also ordered Doan's to place the statement on their packaging for a year.[55]

In Canada, the laws are even tougher and the consequences stiffer. It's an offense for any public promotion to be "false or misleading in a material respect." It is not necessary that anyone be misled by the representation, only that it be false. An offense is a crime. If convicted, an advertiser or agency executive could go to jail for up to five years, pay a fine, or both.[56]

The Food and Drug Administration (FDA)

A division of the Department of Health and Human Services, the *Food and Drug Administration (FDA)* is authorized by Congress to enforce the Federal Food, Drug, and Cosmetic Act and several other health laws. The agency monitors the manufacture, import, transport, storage, and sale of over $1 trillion worth of products annually, which accounts for 25 cents of every dollar spent each year by American consumers. And they do so at a cost to the public of little more than a penny a day per person.[57]

It's the FDA's job to see that the food we eat is safe, the cosmetics we use won't hurt us, and the medicines and therapeutic devices we buy are safe and effective. With authority over the labeling, packaging, and branding of packaged foods and therapeutic devices, the FDA strives to give consumers *complete information* by ensuring that products are labeled truthfully with the information people need to use them properly. The FDA requires manufacturers to disclose all ingredients on product labels, in in-store product advertising, and in product literature. The label must accurately state the weight or volume of the contents. Labels on therapeutic devices must give clear instructions for use. The FDA can require warning statements on packages of hazardous products. It regulates "cents off" and other promotions on package labels and has jurisdiction over the use of words such as "giant" or "family" to describe package sizes.

When consumer-oriented drug ads became common in the mid-1980s, the FDA ruled that any ad for a brand-name drug must include all the information from the package insert.[58] That meant advertisers had to run lengthy commercials or use minuscule type in print ads. In 1997, the FDA changed that rule, allowing pharmaceutical companies to advertise their drugs on broadcast media as long as they mentioned any important possible side effects and directed people to their print ads, their Internet sites, or consumers' own doctors for more information.[59] The *Nutritional Labeling and Education Act (NLEA)*, which went into effect in 1994, gave the FDA additional muscle by setting stringent legal definitions for terms such as fresh, light, low fat, and reduced calories. It also sets standard serving sizes and requires labels to show food value for one serving alongside the total recommended daily value as established by the National Research Council.[60]

The first time the FDA took severe action against a prominent marketer over a labeling dispute, it seized 2,400 cases of Procter & Gamble's Citrus Hill Fresh Choice orange juice. Fresh Choice was made from concentrate, not fresh-squeezed juice as P&G claimed.[61] Due to increased FDA scrutiny, many advertisers are now more cautious about their health and nutritional claims.

revolution (selamectin)

Topical Parasiticide For Dogs and Cats

CAUTION:
U.S. Federal law restricts this drug to use by or on the order of a licensed veterinarian.

INDICATIONS:
Revolution kills adult fleas and prevents flea eggs from hatching for one month and is indicated for the prevention and control of flea infestations (Ctenocephalides felis), prevention of heartworm disease caused by Dirofilaria immitis, and the treatment and control of ear mite (Otodectes cynotis) infestations in dogs and cats. Revolution also is indicated for the treatment and control of sarcoptic mange (Sarcoptes scabiei) and for the control of tick (Dermacentor variabilis) infestations in dogs, and the treatment of intestinal hookworm (Ancylostoma tubaeforme) and roundworm (Toxocara cati) infections in cats. Revolution is recommended for use in dogs and cats six weeks of age and older.

WARNINGS:
Not for human use. Keep out of the reach of children.
May be irritating to skin and eyes. Wash hands after use and wash off any product in contact with the skin immediately with soap and water. If contact with eyes occurs, then flush eyes copiously with water. In case of ingestion by a human, contact a physician immediately. The material safety data sheet (MSDS) provides more detailed occupational safety information. For a copy of the MSDS or to report adverse reactions attributable to exposure to this product, call 1-800-366-5288.

Flammable—Keep away from heat, sparks, open flames or other sources of ignition.

PRECAUTIONS:
Use with caution in sick, debilitated or underweight animals (see SAFETY).
Prior to administration of Revolution, dogs should be tested for existing heartworm infections. At the discretion of the veterinarian, infected dogs should be treated to remove adult heartworms. Revolution is not effective against adult D. immitis and, while the number of circulating microfilariae may decrease following treatment, Revolution is not effective for microfilariae clearance.

Hypersensitivity reactions have not been observed in dogs with patent heartworm infections administered three times the recommended dose of Revolution. Higher doses were not tested.

ADVERSE REACTIONS:
Following treatment with Revolution, transient localized alopecia with or without inflammation at or near the site of application was observed in approximately 1% of 691 treated cats. Other signs observed rarely (≤0.5% of 1743 treated cats and dogs) included vomiting, loose stool or diarrhea with or without blood, anorexia, lethargy, salivation, tachypnea, and muscle tremors.

DOSAGE:
The recommended minimum dose is 2.7 mg selamectin per pound (6 mg/kg) of body weight.

Administer the entire contents of a single dose tube of Revolution topically in accordance with label directions. (See ADMINISTRATION for the recommended treatment intervals.)

For cats over 15 lbs use the appropriate combination of tubes.

For dogs over 85 lbs use the appropriate combination of tubes.
Recommended for use in animals 6 weeks of age and older.

ADMINISTRATION:
Firmly depress the cap to puncture the seal on the Revolution tube; then remove the cap to administer the product.

Part the hair on the back of the animal at the base of the neck in front of the shoulder blades until the skin is visible. Place the tip of the tube on the skin and squeeze the tube to empty its entire contents directly onto the skin in one spot. Do not massage the product into the skin. Due to alcohol content, do not apply to broken skin. Avoid contact between the product and fingers. Do not apply when the hair coat is wet. Bathing or shampooing the animal 2 or more hours after treatment will not reduce the effectiveness of Revolution. Stiff hair, clumping of hair, hair discoloration, or a slight powdery residue may be observed at the treatment site in some animals. These effects are temporary and do not affect the safety or effectiveness of the product. Discard empty tubes in your ordinary household refuse.

Flea Control in Dogs and Cats
For the prevention and control of flea infestations, Revolution should be administered at monthly intervals throughout the flea season, starting one month before fleas become active. In controlled laboratory studies >98% of fleas were killed within 36 hours. Results of clinical field studies using Revolution monthly demonstrated >90% control of flea infestations within 30 days of the first dose. Dogs and cats treated with Revolution, including those with pre-existing flea allergy dermatitis, showed improvement in clinical signs associated with fleas as a direct result of eliminating the fleas from the animals and their environment.

If the dog or cat is already infested with fleas when the first dose of Revolution is administered, adult fleas on the animal are killed and no viable fleas hatch from eggs after the first administration. However, an environmental infestation of fleas may persist for a short time after beginning treatment with Revolution because of the emergence of adult fleas from pupae.

Heartworm Prevention in Dogs and Cats
For the prevention of heartworm disease, Revolution must be administered on a monthly basis. Revolution may be administered year-round or at least within one month after the animal's first exposure to mosquitoes and monthly thereafter until the end of the mosquito season. The final dose must be given within one month after the last exposure to mosquitoes. If a dose is missed and a monthly interval between dosing is exceeded then immediate administration of Revolution and resumption of monthly dosing will minimize the opportunity for the development of adult heartworms. When replacing another heartworm preventive product in a heartworm disease prevention program, the first dose of Revolution must be given within a month of the last dose of the former medication.

At the discretion of the veterinarian, cats ≥6 months of age may be tested to determine the presence of existing heartworm infections before beginning treatment with Revolution. Cats already infected with adult heartworms can safely be given Revolution monthly to prevent further infections.

Ear Mite Treatment in Dogs and Cats
For the treatment of ear mite (O. cynotis) infestations in dogs and cats, Revolution should be administered once as a single topical dose. A second monthly dose may be required in some dogs. Monthly use of Revolution will control any subsequent ear mite infestations. In the clinical field trials ears were not cleaned, and many animals still had debris in their ears after the second dose. Cleansing of the infested ears is recommended to remove the debris.

Sarcoptic Mange Treatment in Dogs
For the treatment of sarcoptic mange (S. scabiei) in dogs, Revolution should be administered once as a single topical dose. A second monthly dose may be required in some dogs. Monthly use of Revolution will control any subsequent sarcoptic mange mite infestations. Because of the difficulty in finding sarcoptic mange mites on skin scrapings, effectiveness assessments also were based on resolution of clinical signs. Resolution of the pruritus associated with the mite infestations was observed in approximately 50% of the dogs 30 days after the first treatment and in approximately 90% of the dogs 30 days after the second monthly treatment.

Tick Control in Dogs
For the control of tick (Dermacentor variabilis) infestations in dogs, Revolution should be administered on a monthly basis. In heavy tick infestations, complete efficacy may not be achieved after the first dose. In these cases, one additional dose may be administered two weeks after the previous dose, with monthly dosing continued thereafter.

Nematode Treatment in Cats
For the treatment of intestinal hookworm (A. tubaeforme) and roundworm (T. cati) infections, Revolution should be applied once as a single topical dose.

NADA 141-152, Approved by FDA.

  Animal Health
Exton, PA 19341, USA
Div. of Pfizer Inc
NY, NY 10017

www.revolutionpet.com

To provide consumers with more complete information, the U.S. Food and Drug Administration regulates the content of pharmaceutical ads. It used to require that advertisers include all the information from the package insert in its TV ads. This necessitated lengthy commercials with minuscule copy. In 1997, the rule was changed, allowing pharmaceutical companies to advertise on TV and radio as long as they mentioned any important side effects and directed consumers to other sources for further information, such as their magazine ads or their Web site. Notice how this magazine ad for Animal Health's Revolution complies with the FDA's disclosure requirements.

The Federal Communications Commission (FCC)

The seven-member *Federal Communications Commission (FCC)* is an independent federal agency with jurisdiction over the radio, television, telephone, satellite and cable TV industries, and the Internet. The FCC is responsible for protecting the public interest and encouraging competition. Its control over broadcast advertising is actually *indirect,* stemming from its authority to license broadcasters (or take away their licenses). The FCC stringently controls the airing of obscenity and profanity, and it can restrict both the products advertised and the content of ads. For example, the FCC required stations to run commercials about the harmful effects of smoking even before Congress banned cigarette advertising on TV and radio.

In the 1980s, the FCC decided there were enough buyers and sellers that marketplace forces could adequately control broadcast media, so it deregulated both radio and TV stations. The FCC no longer limits commercial time or requires stations to maintain detailed program and commercial logs. However, stations still keep records of commercial broadcasts to assure advertisers they ran.

The FCC's visibility as an arbiter of broadcast decency increased immediately following Janet Jackson's "wardrobe malfunction," which exposed the singer's breast during the 2004 Super Bowl halftime show. A record

500,000 complaints were registered with the FCC. According to FCC rules, over-the-air television channels cannot air "obscene" material at any time. The FCC defines obscene material as describing sexual conduct "in a patently offensive way" and lacking "serious literary, artistic, political or scientific value." The FCC later levied a fine of $550,000 for the Super Bowl incident. Since then, the FCC has launched a crackdown on indecency, fining radio stations as much as $1.75 million for comments made on the air by Howard Stern and other radio personalities. Congress has also proposed increasing the maximum indecency fines. Television networks have begun taking preemptive action by implementing broadcast delays so censors can edit out anything deemed too racy.

Coca-Cola's trademark varies from country to country. But the overall look is retained through use of similar letterforms and style, even with different alphabets.

The Patent and Trademark Office and the Library of Congress

1. Arabic   5. Spanish
2. French   6. Chinese
3. Japanese 7. Hebrew
4. Thai   8. Polish

A basic role of government is to promote and protect the economic well-being *(self-interest)* of its citizens. One way the U.S. government does this is by promoting "the progress of science and useful arts, by securing for limited times to authors and inventors the exclusive right to their respective writings and discoveries"; in other words, by registering and protecting their citizens' **intellectual property.**[62]

Through the issuance of **patents,** the government provides incentives to invent, invest in, and disclose new technology worldwide. By registering trademarks and copyrights, the government helps businesses protect their investments, promote their goods and services, and safeguard consumers against confusion and deception in the marketplace *(complete information)*.

A trademark such as Coca-Cola, AT&T, or Levi's is a valuable asset. According to the Lanham Trademark Act (1947), a **trademark** is "any word, name, symbol, or device or any combination thereof adopted and used by a manufacturer or merchant to identify his goods and distinguish them from those manufactured or sold by others."

Patents and trademarks are registered with and protected by the *U.S. Patent and Trademark Office,* a bureau of the Department of Commerce. Ownership of a trademark may be designated in advertising or on a label, package, or letterhead by the word *Registered,* the symbol ®, or the symbol ™. If someone persists in using a trademark owned by another or confusingly similar to another's mark, the trademark owner can ask for a court order and sue for trademark infringement.

The Library of Congress protects all copyrighted material, including advertising, in the United States. A **copyright** is a form of protection provided to the authors of "original works of authorship," including literary, dramatic, musical, artistic, and certain other "intellectual works."[62a] A copyright issued to an individual grants the exclusive right to print, publish, or reproduce the protected material for the life of the copyright owner plus 70 years. If it is the work of corporate authorship, the term is the shorter of 95 years from publication or 120 years from creation.

With what aspects of advertising do federal regulatory agencies concern themselves?

CONCEPT CHECK

State and Local Regulation

Advertisers are also subject to state or local laws. Since the U.S. federal deregulation trend of the 1980s, state and local governments have taken a far more active role.

Regulation by State Governments

State legislation governing advertising is often based on the truth-in-advertising model statute developed in 1911 by *Printer's Ink,* for many years the major trade publication of the industry. The statute holds that any maker of an ad found to contain "untrue, deceptive, or misleading" material is guilty of a misdemeanor. Today 46 states (all except Arkansas, Delaware, Mississippi, and New Mexico) enforce laws patterned after this statute.

Different states have different regulations governing what can be advertised. Some states prohibit advertising for certain types of wine and liquor, and most states restrict the use of state flags in advertising.

This can present a major problem to national marketers. And in some cases, it actually hurts consumers. For example, many companies trying to conduct environmentally responsible marketing programs feel stymied by the different state laws governing packaging materials and recycling.[62b] In the tobacco case discussed earlier, the teaming of numerous state attorneys general proved a formidable foe for the giant tobacco industry. In the end, facing the prospect of an infinite number of lawsuits from individual states and even municipalities, the industry buckled under, agreeing to settle and pay the various states hundreds of billions of dollars.[63]

Regulation by Local Governments

Many cities and counties also have consumer protection agencies to enforce laws regulating local advertising practices. The chief function of these agencies is to protect local consumers against unfair and misleading practices by area merchants.

In one year alone, the Orange County, California, district attorney's office received more than 1,200 complaint letters from consumers about everything from dishonest mechanics and phony sale ads to a taco stand that skimped on the beef in its "macho" burrito.[64] In a case against Los Angeles–based Closet Factory, Inc., the DA collected $40,000 in fines to settle a false advertising suit. The company was charged with running newspaper ads that gave consumers a false sense of urgency regarding "sales" that actually never end. This type of advertising, known as a *continuous sale,* violates the state's Business and Professions Code. It also advertises a false percentage off the regular price. Since the sale is never really over, the sale price becomes the regular price.[65]

> **CONCEPT CHECK**
>
> With what aspects of advertising do state and local regulatory agencies concern themselves?

Nongovernment Regulation

Nongovernment organizations also issue advertising guidelines (see Exhibit 2–4). In fact, advertisers face considerable regulation by business-monitoring organizations, related trade associations, the media, consumer groups, and advertising agencies themselves.

The Board of Directors of the American Association of Advertising Agencies recognizes that when used truthfully and fairly, comparative advertising provides the consumer with needed and useful information.

However, extreme caution should be exercised. The use of comparative advertising, by its very nature, can distort facts and, by implication, convey to the consumer information that misrepresents the truth.

Therefore, the Board believes that comparative advertising should follow certain guidelines:

1. The intent and connotation of the ad should be to inform and never to discredit or unfairly attack competitors, competing products, or services.
2. When a competitive product is named, it should be one that exists in the marketplace as significant competition.
3. The competition should be fairly and properly identified but never in a manner or tone of voice that degrades the competitive product or service.
4. The advertising should compare related or similar properties or ingredients of the product, dimension to dimension, feature to feature.
5. The identification should be for honest comparison purposes and not simply to upgrade by association.
6. If a competitive test is conducted, it should be done by an objective testing source, preferably an independent one, so that there will be no doubt as to the veracity of the test.
7. In all cases the test should be supportive of all claims made in the advertising that are based on the test.
8. The advertising should never use partial results or stress insignificant differences to cause the consumer to draw an improper conclusion.
9. The property being compared should be significant in terms of value or usefulness of the product to the consumer.
10. Comparatives delivered through the use of testimonials should not imply that the testimonial is more than one individual's thought unless that individual represents a sample of the majority viewpoint.

Exhibit 2–4

American Association of Advertising Agencies policy statement and guidelines for comparative advertising.

The Better Business Bureau (BBB)

The largest of the U.S. business-monitoring organizations is the *Better Business Bureau (BBB)*, established in 1916. Funded by dues from more than 100,000 member companies, it operates primarily at the local level to protect consumers against fraudulent and deceptive advertising and sales practices. When local bureaus contact violators and ask them to revise their advertising, most comply.

The BBB's files on violators are open to the public. Records of violators who do not comply are sent to appropriate government agencies for further action. The BBB often works with local law enforcement agencies to prosecute advertisers guilty of fraud and misrepresentation. Each year, the BBB investigates thousands of ads for possible violations of truth and accuracy.

The National Advertising Review Council (NARC)

The *National Advertising Review Council (NARC)* was established in 1971 by the Council of Better Business Bureaus, the American Association of Advertising Agencies, the American Advertising Federation, and the Association of National Advertisers. Its primary purpose is to promote and enforce standards of truth, accuracy, taste, morality, and social responsibility in advertising. NARC is one of the most comprehensive and effective mechanisms for regulating American advertising. A U.S. district court judge noted in a 1985 case that its "speed, informality, and modest cost," as well as its expertise, give NARC special advantages over the court system in resolving advertising disputes.[66]

The NARC has two operating arms: the *National Advertising Division (NAD)* of the Council of Better Business Bureaus and the *National Advertising Review Board*

(NARB). The NAD monitors advertising practices and reviews complaints about advertising from consumers and consumer groups, brand competitors, local Better Business Bureaus, trade associations, and others. The appeals board for NAD decisions is the NARB, which consists of a chairperson and 70 volunteer members (39 national advertisers, 21 agency representatives, and 10 laypeople).

The case of the leather flight jacket shows how well the NAD process works. Neil Cooper LLC is a company that manufactures a leather jacket. In its print ads it claims that its A-2 leather flight jackets are the "official battle gear of U.S. Air Force Pilots." Avirex, Ltd., a competing company, complained to the NAD since the A-2 jacket currently being purchased by the Department of Defense and worn by U.S. pilots is the jacket manufactured by them, not Neil Cooper. Neil Cooper explained that, while it was not the current supplier, many pilots continued to buy from Neil Cooper directly because they preferred that product. Notwithstanding, the NAD sided with Avirex and recommended that Neil Cooper qualify its claims to make it clear that it is selling a reproduction of an authentic A-2 flight jacket rather than the current official jacket of the U.S. Air Force. Neil Cooper agreed.[67]

Regulation by the Media

Almost all media review ads and reject material they regard as objectionable, even if it isn't deceptive. Many people think the media are more effective regulators than the government.

Television

Of all media, the TV networks conduct the strictest review. Advertisers must submit all commercials intended for a network or affiliated station to its **broadcast standards department.** Many commercials (in script or storyboard form) are returned with suggestions for changes or greater substantiation. Some ads are rejected outright if they violate network policies.

The three major U.S. broadcast networks base their policies on the original National Association of Broadcasters Television Code. But network policies vary enough that it's difficult to prepare universally acceptable commercials. Cable networks and local stations tend to be much less stringent, as demonstrated by their acceptance of condom ads.

Radio

The 19 U.S. radio networks, unlike TV networks, supply only a small percentage of their affiliates' programming, so they have little or no say in what their affiliates advertise. A radio station is also less likely to return a script or tape for changes. Some stations, such as KLBJ in Austin, Texas, look mainly at whether the advertising is illegal, unethical, or immoral.[68] They don't want spots to offend listeners or detract from the rest of the programming.

Every radio station typically has its own unwritten guidelines. KDWB, a Minneapolis/St. Paul station with a large teenage audience, turned down a psychic who wanted to buy advertising time but did allow condom and other contraceptive ads.[69] KSDO in San Diego, a station with a business and information format, won't air commercials for X-rated movies or topless bars.[70]

Magazines

National magazines monitor all advertising, especially by new advertisers and for new products. Newer publications eager to sell space may not be so vigilant, but established magazines, such as *Time* and *Newsweek,* are highly scrupulous.

Many magazines will not accept advertising for certain types of products. The *New Yorker* won't run discount retail store advertising or ads for feminine hygiene or self-medication products. *Reader's Digest* won't accept tobacco ads.

Some magazines test every product before accepting the advertising. *Good Housekeeping* rejects ads if its tests don't substantiate the advertiser's claims. Products that pass are allowed to feature the Good Housekeeping "Seal of Approval," and the magazine will stand behind those products.

Newspapers

Newspapers also monitor and review advertising. Larger newspapers have clearance staffs who read every ad submitted; most smaller newspapers rely on the advertising manager, sales personnel, or proofreaders.

The advertising policies set forth in *Newspaper Rates & Data* specify, "No objectionable medical, personal, matrimonial, clairvoyant, or palmistry advertising accepted; no stock promotion or financial advertising, other than those securities of known value." Another rule prohibits ads that might easily be mistaken for regular reading material unless they feature the word *advertisement.*

One problem advertisers face is that newspapers' codes are far from uniform. Handgun ads may be prohibited by one newspaper, accepted by another if the guns are antique, and permitted by a third as long as the guns aren't automatic.

Feel the Intensity

HEAT-N-GLO
No one builds a better fire

To help consumers make informed decisions, *Good Housekeeping* magazine tests the products in their ads and provides a seal of approval to those advertisers, such as Heat-N-Glo, who substantiate their claims. This gives the consumer a more authoritative voice to listen to when trying to decide on purchases.

Regulation by Consumer Groups

Of all the regulatory forces governing advertising, consumer protection organizations have shown the greatest growth. Starting in the 1960s, the consumer movement became increasingly active in fighting fraudulent and deceptive advertising. Consumers demanded that products perform as advertised and that more product information be provided for people to compare and make better buying decisions. The consumer movement gave rise to **consumerism**, social action to dramatize the rights of the buying public. It is clear now that the U.S. consumer has the power to influence advertising practices dramatically.

Consumer advocate groups investigate advertising complaints received from the public and those that grow out of their own research. If a complaint is warranted, they ask the advertiser to halt the objectionable ad or practice. If the advertiser does not comply, they release publicity or criticism about the offense to the media and submit complaints with substantiating evidence to appropriate government agencies for further action. In some instances, they file a lawsuit to obtain a cease-and-desist order, a fine, or other penalty against the violator.

Today, with so many special-interest advocacy groups, even the most responsible advertisers feel challenged. To attract attention, advertising must be creative and stand out from competing noise. Yet advertisers fear attention from politically correct activists (the "PC police"). Calvin Klein ads were attacked by the Boycott Anorexic Marketing group. A Nike ad starring Porky Pig was protested by the National Stuttering Project in San Francisco. An animated public service spot from Aetna Insurance drew complaints from a witches' rights group.[71]

When the protests start flying, the ads usually get pulled. Steve Hayden, chair of BBDO Los Angeles, believes it would be possible to get any spot pulled with "about five letters that appear on the right stationery."[72] As Shelly Garcia noted in *Adweek,* "The way things are these days, nothing motivates middle managers like the need to avoid attention." She lamented the fact that "there are fewer and fewer opportunities to have any fun in advertising."[73]

Self-Regulation by Advertisers and Ad Agencies

Advertisers also regulate themselves. They have to. In today's competitive marketplace, consumer confidence is essential. Most large advertisers gather strong data to substantiate their claims. They maintain careful systems of advertising review to ensure that ads meet both their own standards and industry, media, and legal requirements.

Most ad agencies monitor their own practices. Professional advertising associations also oversee members' activities to prevent problems that might trigger government intervention. Advertising publications report issues and court actions to educate agencies and advertisers and warn them about possible legal infractions.

Although advertisers supply information about their product or service to their agencies, the agencies must research and verify product claims and comparative product data before using them in advertising. The media may require such documentation before accepting the advertising, and substantiation may be needed if government or consumer agencies challenge the claims.

Agencies can be held legally liable for fraudulent or misleading advertising claims. For this reason, most major advertising agencies have an in-house legal counsel and regularly submit their ads for review. If any aspect of the advertising is challenged, the agency asks its client to review the advertising and either confirm claims as truthful or replace unverified material.

Several associations monitor industrywide advertising practices. The *American Association of Advertising Agencies (AAAA)*, an association of the largest advertising agencies throughout the United States, controls agency practices by denying membership to any agency judged unethical. The *American Advertising Federation (AAF)* helped to establish the FTC, and its early vigilance committees were the forerunners of the Better Business Bureau. The *AAF Advertising Principles of American Business*, adopted in 1984, define standards for truthful and responsible advertising (see Exhibit 2–5). The *Association of National Advertisers (ANA)* comprises 400 major manufacturing and service companies that are clients of member agencies of the AAAA. These companies pledge to uphold the ANA code of advertising ethics.

CONCEPT CHECK

What nongovernmental groups are concerned with the regulation of advertising and what types of issues do they examine?

Exhibit 2–5

Advertising Principles of American Business of the American Advertising Federation (AAF).

1. *Truth.* Advertising shall tell the truth, and shall reveal significant facts, the omission of which would mislead the public.

2. *Substantiation.* Advertising claims shall be substantiated by evidence in possession of the advertiser and the advertising agency prior to making such claims.

3. *Comparisons.* Advertising shall refrain from making false, misleading, or unsubstantiated statements or claims about a competitor or his products or services.

4. *Bait advertising.* Advertising shall not offer products or services for sale unless such offer constitutes a bona fide effort to sell the advertised products or services and is not a device to switch consumers to other goods or services, usually higher priced.

5. *Guarantees and warranties.* Advertising of guarantees and warranties shall be explicit, with sufficient information to apprise consumers of their principal terms and limitations or, when space or time restrictions preclude such disclosures, the advertisement shall clearly reveal where the full text of the guarantee or warranty can be examined before purchase.

6. *Price claims.* Advertising shall avoid price claims that are false or misleading, or savings claims that do not offer provable savings.

7. *Testimonials.* Advertising containing testimonials shall be limited to those of competent witnesses who are reflecting a real and honest opinion or experience.

8. *Taste and decency.* Advertising shall be free of statements, illustrations, or implications that are offensive to good taste or public decency.

Government Restraints on International Advertisers

Now that advertising has become global, many campaigns use similar themes and even the same ads across frontiers. But foreign governments often regulate advertising considerably more than either the United States or Canada. And while Europe has moved toward uniformity in marketing activities, the laws governing advertising remain largely national.[74] So advertisers need to keep up with the changing legal environments of the countries in which they advertise.

Foreign governments are frequently more authoritarian. Some governments not only regulate what ads say, show, or do; they often impose severe restrictions or outright bans on advertising specific products. The Swedes ban advertising to children on television. The Greeks ban toy advertising before 10:00 p.m. Throughout Europe, broadcast advertising for tobacco products is prohibited, and liquor ads are sharply restricted, especially in France.[75]

Many countries prohibit puffery superlatives. In Germany, for example, advertisers may use only scientifically provable superlatives. McCann-Erickson once had to retranslate the old Coca-Cola slogan, "Refreshes you best," because it implied a leadership position that was unprovable. The agency substituted "Refreshes you right" in Germany. In Austria, however, which typically follows Germany's lead in advertising law, the original line would be permissible.[76]

Many European countries also ban coupons, premiums, free tie-in offers, and the like. Companies may advertise price cuts only during "official sales periods," and advertisers often need government approval before publishing a sale ad. Across Europe, advertising on television must be clearly recognizable and kept separate from other programming. Paid *product placements* in programs, therefore, are typically prohibited.[77]

In international advertising, the only solution to this morass of potential legal problems is to retain a good local lawyer who specializes in advertising law.

> Describe some of the ways in which the regulation of international advertisers differs from that in the United States or Canada.

CONCEPT CHECK

The Ethical and Legal Aspects of Advertising in Perspective

Unquestionably, advertising offers considerable benefits to marketers and consumers alike. However, there's also no disputing that advertising has been and still is too often misused. As *Adweek* editor Andrew Jaffe says, the industry should do all it can to "raise its standards and try to drive out that which is misleading, untruthful, or downright tasteless and irresponsible." Otherwise, he warns, the pressure to regulate even more will become overwhelming.[78]

Advertising apologists point out that of all the advertising reviewed by the Federal Trade Commission in a typical year, 97 percent is found to be satisfactory.[79] In the end, advertisers and consumers need to work together to ensure that advertising is used intelligently, ethically, and responsibly for the benefit of all.

Chapter Summary

As one of the most visible activities of business, advertising is both lauded and criticized for the role it plays in selling products and influencing society. Advertising is often considered the trigger on a country's mass-distribution system, enabling manufacturers to produce the products people want in high volume, at low prices, and with standardized quality. People may argue, though, about how advertising adds value to products, affects prices, encourages or discourages competition, promotes consumer demand, narrows or widens consumer choice, and affects business cycles.

Although controversy surrounds some of these economic issues, few dispute the abundance principle: In an economy that produces more goods and services than can be consumed, advertising gives consumers more complete information about the choices available to them, encourages more sellers to compete more effectively, and thereby serves the self-interest of both consumers and marketers.

Critics say advertising is deceptive; it manipulates people into buying unneeded products, it makes our society too materialistic, and there's just too much of it. Further, they say, advertising perpetuates stereotypes, and all too frequently, it is offensive and in bad taste.

Proponents admit that advertising is sometimes misused. However, they point out that despite its problems, advertising offers many social benefits. It encourages the development of new products and speeds their acceptance. It fosters employment, gives consumers and businesses a wider variety of product choices, and helps keep prices down by encouraging mass production. It stimulates healthy competition among companies and raises the overall standard of living.

The federal and state courts are involved in several advertising issues, including First Amendment protection of commercial speech, and infringements on the right to privacy. Advertising is regulated by federal, state, and local government agencies, business-monitoring organizations, the media, consumer groups, and the advertising industry itself. All of these groups encourage advertisers to give more complete information to consumers and eliminate any negative externalities in the process.

Key Terms

abundance principle, 31
added value, 27
affirmative disclosure, 46
broadcast standards department, 52
cease-and-desist order, 46
comparative advertising, 46
consent decree, 46
consumer advocate, 53
consumerism, 53
copyright, 49

corrective advertising, 47
deceptive advertising, 44
endorsements, 46
ethical advertising, 39
externalities, 27
intellectual property, 49
limen, 33
patent, 49
primary demand, 30
privacy rights, 43

puffery, 32
selective demand, 30
social responsibility, 39
stereotypes, 36
subliminal advertising, 33
substantiation, 46
testimonials, 46
trademark, 49
unfair advertising, 44

Review Questions

1. Why is it good that advertising stimulates competition?
2. Describe the two types of social criticism of advertising.
3. What is puffery? Give some examples. Do you ever feel deceived by puffery in advertising?
4. Does advertising affect our value system? In what ways?
5. What is the difference between an advertiser's ethics and its social responsibility?
6. What are some examples of stereotypes used in advertising?
7. How does commercial speech differ from political speech? Do you think advertisers should have the same First Amendment rights as everyone else? Explain.
8. What arguments were used to selectively ban certain forms of tobacco advertising? What are the arguments against such a ban?
9. What is the role of the FTC in advertising? Do you think this role should be expanded or restricted?
10. What is the difference between *unfair* and *deceptive* advertising?

Exploring Advertising

1. Find advertising that satisfies the following criteria. Describe the advertising and answer the related questions.
   a. *Adds value to the brand.* Explain what value is added and how.
   b. *Stimulates primary or secondary demand (or both).* Explain what kind of demand is stimulated and how you determined this.
   c. *Provides an example of puffery.* Describe the puffery and explain why you do or don't consider it deceptive.
   d. *Tries to manipulate you into buying something you didn't previously want or need.* How is it doing that? Were you effectively manipulated?
   e. *Stereotypes a person or group.* Do you find the approach offensive or acceptable?
   f. *Makes a comparison to a competitive product.* Does the comparison seem fair and supportable? Does it influence your attitude?
   g. *Tries to deceive you.* Is the advertiser being dishonest? How is your opinion of the advertiser or product affected?
   h. *Shows social responsibility.* Did it make you feel differently about the company or its products?

2. Watch 30 minutes of television during at least one daypart or program format (e.g., morning, afternoon, evening, late night, news, sports, soaps). Note the time of day and type of programming you watched. Count the number of commercials during that 30-minute period and bring your results to class.

chapter three

The Advertising Industry

Objectives

To introduce the people and groups who sponsor, create, produce, and run advertising here and abroad. Advertising people may serve in a variety of roles. This chapter discusses the basic tasks of both the client and the advertising agency, the roles of suppliers and the media, the ways agencies acquire clients and are compensated, and the overall relationship between the agency and the client.

After studying this chapter, you will be able to:

* **Describe** the various groups in the advertising business and explain their relationship to one another.

* **Discuss** the differences between local and national advertisers.

* **Explain** how advertisers organize themselves to manage their advertising both here and abroad.

* **Define** the main types of advertising agencies.

* **Explain** the range of tasks people perform in an ad agency and an in-house advertising department.

* **Discuss** how agencies get new clients and how they make money.

* **Debate** the pros and cons of an in-house advertising agency.

* **Explain** how suppliers and the media help advertisers and agencies.

To get to the heartbeat of the market for her clients, Shelley Yamane spends much of her time talking directly with consumers. She works as a strategic planner at Muse Cordero Chen and Partners, an agency that focuses on multicultural communications—specifically the African American, Asian, and Latino markets in the United States. Now close to twenty years old, the Los Angeles–based shop has been one of the fastest growing ethnic agencies in the country and boasts a team of 45 employees who speak some 12 different languages and represent over 15 ethnicities. Muse Cordero Chen represents such plum accounts as Nike, Honda, and AT&T Wireless, and has garnered innumerable awards for its sometimes edgy, always creative work.

When the client approached the agency with the task of creating a new African American campaign for the Honda Civic, it was Shelley's job to research the market and develop some strategic alternatives. In the process, Shelley began to notice a trend and, after further study, it had a dramatic effect on the agency's approach. What she discerned was that in the urban market African American consumers were only one faction of a considerably larger group that was already buying the Civic. An entirely new target market was surfacing: one that was geographically concentrated and similar in age, lifestyle, and attitude. What characterized them was not their ethnicity, but that they were all young and urban, and they loved fixing up their cars.

When Honda first introduced the Civic over a quarter century ago, it was seen as something of a pioneer. Its low emissions and high gas mileage made it a frontrunner in its category. But over time, as competing manufacturers began to offer similarly priced alternatives, the Civic's market share suffered, and its image began to fade in the minds of the general car-buying public. They started looking at it as a family's second car. At the same time, though, something very quiet, but very exciting, was happening. Droves of young urban-ites, attracted to the car's quality, low price, and simple, customizable design, were starting to buy Civics, and they were spending a great deal of time and energy personalizing their vehicles. They took pride in their work and began to share that pride with other Civic drivers. Soon, all over the country, communities of young, urban Civic owners were gathering in ad hoc venues to trade ideas and show off their tricked-out cars, and in time this became an actual subculture. What Shelley had discovered was the birth of a new group of people. A Civic Nation.

The Advertising Industry

The range of work performed by advertising people goes far beyond what we see daily on TV. In fact, that's barely the tip of the iceberg. Moreover, many people and organizations besides those usually thought of as advertising folks are involved in the advertising business. That's because every successful company needs to advertise.

The Organizations in Advertising

The advertising business has evolved into four distinct groups. The two main ones are the *advertisers* and the *agencies.* The **advertisers** (or *clients*) are the companies—like Honda, Coca-Cola, or the local shoe store—that sponsor advertising for themselves and their products. Advertisers range in size from small independent businesses to huge multinational firms, and in type from service organizations to industrial manufacturers to local charities and political action committees. The second group, **advertising agencies,** assists the advertisers to plan, create, and prepare ad campaigns and other promotional materials.

A third group, the **suppliers,** includes the photographers, illustrators, printers, digital service bureaus, color film separators, video production houses, Internet Web developers, and others who assist both advertisers and agencies in preparing advertising materials. Suppliers also include consultants, research firms, and professional services that work with both advertisers and agencies. The fourth group, the **media,** sells time (on radio and TV) and space (in print, outdoor, and digital media) to carry the advertiser's message to the target audience.

The People in Advertising

When most people think of advertising, they imagine the copywriters and art directors who work for ad agencies. But the majority of people in advertising are actually employed by advertisers, rather than by their agencies. Most companies have an advertising department, even if it's just one person.

In addition, many other people work for the suppliers and the media. They're in advertising, too. The fact is, advertising is a very broad field that employs a wide variety of people in sales, research, management, accounting, computer science, and law, as well as specialists in the various communication arts—artists, writers, photographers, musicians, performers, and cinematographers.

In this chapter, we'll see what all these people do at the various places where they work. In the process, we'll get a good understanding of how the advertising industry operates both in the United States and abroad.

CONCEPT CHECK

What are the four major groups involved in the advertising industry and what are their primary functions?

The Advertisers (Clients)

While every company has some sort of advertising department, its importance depends on the size of the company, the type of industry it operates in, the size of the advertising program, the role advertising plays in the company's marketing mix, and most of all, the involvement of top management.

To get a sense of the diversity of companies that advertise, we'll look first at local advertisers to see how they operate. Then, we'll examine regional and national advertisers. Finally we'll look at the companies that market their products in foreign countries.

Local Advertising: Where the Action Is

Not long after graduating from San Diego State, Ralph Rubio opened his first Mexican restaurant. He offered an unusual specialty: fish tacos—lightly battered and fried whitefish served in soft corn tortillas with white sauce, salsa, cabbage, and a wedge of lime. At the time, very few other Mexican eateries offered fish tacos, and none specialized in them. So Rubio found fish tacos hard to sell, even with his secret batter recipe (which he'd gotten from a street vendor in San Felipe, Mexico). The first month's sales at the restaurant averaged only $163 a day.

Rubio started using small newspaper ads with coupons to lure courageous customers. It worked. As business picked up, he expanded his advertising to radio and TV, targeting his market with ads on Hispanic stations (whose listeners knew what fish tacos were). And he went after younger, venturesome customers ages 18 to 34 by advertising at local movie theaters. Business picked up some more. Rubio soon opened another restaurant, and then another.

With each new opening, Rubio distributed direct-mail flyers in the area and took free samples to nearby stores. Working with an artist, he created a cartoon character named Pesky Pescado based on the fish taco. He purchased a 15-foot inflatable Pesky to display at his restaurants. Employee T-shirts sported Pesky's picture, and Rubio sold Pesky T-shirts and sweatshirts to enthusiastic patrons. He also offered bumper stickers and antenna balls to add some fun to his promotions. To further integrate his activities, Rubio took an active part in community affairs, including tie-ins with a blood bank, a literacy program, and fundraising activities for both a Tijuana medical clinic and a local university's athletic program.

As the popularity of the fish taco grew, so did Rubio's revenues, doubling every year for the first five years. He trademarked the phrase "Rubio's, Home of the Fish Taco," and a local restaurant critic, commenting on things San Diegans couldn't do without, called fish tacos "the food San Diegans would miss the most." After 19 years, Rubio had 137 restaurants in five states. Together they produced more than $112 million in annual sales.[1]

Every year, advertisers spend billions of dollars in the United States. Almost half of that is spent on **local advertising** by local businesses targeting customers in their geographic area.

Local advertising is sometimes called *retail advertising* because so much is placed by retail stores. But retail advertising isn't always local; Sears and JCPenney advertise nationally. And many businesses besides retail stores use local advertising: banks, real estate developers, movie theaters, auto mechanics, plumbers, radio and TV stations, funeral homes, museums, and local politicians, to name a few.

Local advertising is critically important because most consumer sales are made (or lost) locally. Auto manufacturers may spend millions advertising new cars nationwide, but if their dealers don't make a strong effort locally, the dollars may be wasted. When it comes to making the sale and dealing with customers, local advertising is where the action is—where relationships often start and truly develop.

Types of Local Advertisers

There are four main types of local advertisers.

- Dealers or local franchisees of national companies that specialize in one main product line or service (Honda, Wendy's, Mail Boxes Etc., Kinko's, H&R Block).

Local advertising represents almost half of the advertising dollars spent in the United States. Much of this is placed by local retailers and service businesses looking to attract customers in their geographic area.

Many local advertisements are for retail stores that sell a variety of branded merchandise or for specialty businesses. This ad for Loehmann's Plaza promotes the shopping center, anchored by Loehmann's (www.loehmanns.com) and Albertsons (www.albertsons.com), as well as all of the individual stores and restaurants that serve the local community.

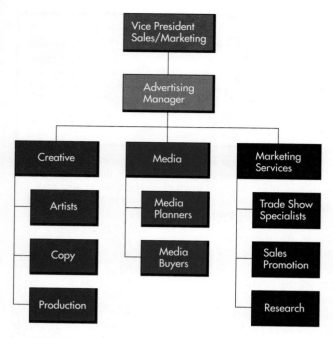

Exhibit 3–1

Typical department structure for small advertisers with high volumes of work, such as grocery store chains.

- Stores that sell a variety of branded merchandise, usually on a nonexclusive basis (convenience, grocery, and department stores).

- Specialty businesses and services (banks, insurance brokers, restaurants, music stores, shoe-repair shops, remodeling contractors, florists, hair salons, travel agencies, attorneys, accountants).

- Governmental, quasi-governmental, and nonprofit organizations (municipalities, utility companies, charities, arts organizations, political candidates).

A small, local business—say, a hardware, clothing, or electronics store—may have just one person in charge of advertising. That person, the advertising manager, performs all the administrative, planning, budgeting, and coordinating functions. He or she may lay out ads, write ad copy, and select the media. A manager with some artistic talent may even design the actual ads and produce them on a desktop computer.

Chain stores often maintain a completely staffed advertising department to handle production, media placement, and marketing support services. The department needs artists, copywriters, and production specialists. The department head usually reports to a vice president or marketing manager, as shown in Exhibit 3–1.

Types of Local Advertising

Most of the ads placed in local media are product, institutional, or classified advertising. Each type serves a different purpose.

Product advertising   **Product advertising** promotes a specific product or service and stimulates short-term action while building awareness of the business. To stimulate sales of particular merchandise or increase store traffic, local merchants frequently use **sale advertising,** placing items on sale and offering two-for-one specials or other deals.

Institutional advertising   **Institutional advertising** attempts to create a favorable long-term perception of the business as a whole, not just of a particular product or service. Many types of businesses (stores, restaurants, banks, professional firms, hospitals) use institutional advertising to promote an idea about the company and build long-term goodwill. It makes the public aware of what the business stands for and attempts to build reputation and image.

Classified advertising   Advertisers use **classified advertising** in the newspaper for a variety of reasons: to locate and recruit new employees, offer services (such as those of an employment agency or business opportunity broker), or sell or lease new and used merchandise (such as cars, real estate, and office equipment).

Local Advertisers: The Original Integrators

When Ralph Rubio built his restaurant business, his promotional activities involved a lot more than just running ads in the media. In fact, he did everything he could to

Local merchants like Michaels Stores (www.michaels.com) often use sale advertising to stimulate product sales or increase store traffic.

develop a relationship with his customers and to promote good word-of-mouth. That meant using publicity, sales promotion, and direct response as well as media advertising—all integrated with consistently good food, reasonable prices, and excellent service. This combination constitutes **integrated marketing communications (IMC)**—joining together in a consistent manner every element that communicates with customers. We will spend more time defining and discussing IMC in Chapter 7.

Creating Local Advertising

Cal Worthington first pitched his car dealership on Los Angeles TV stations in 1951 and 50 years later, he's still at it. He sponsors third-rate movies on late-night and Saturday afternoon TV. In his zany ads, he often appears in cowboy garb with a variety of domesticated wild animals, all introduced as "my dog Spot."

The principles for the development of good local advertising are really no different than the general principles we will discuss throughout this book. However, given limited budgets and the need to see immediate results, local advertisers have to make every word and every dollar count. To direct and control the creative aspects of their ads and commercials and ensure consistency, local advertisers should develop a checklist of creative do's and don'ts. (See the Checklist, "Creating Local Advertising" on page 64.)

Local advertisers can turn to a number of sources for creative help, including reps from the local media, local ad agencies, freelancers and consultants, creative boutiques, syndicated art services, and the cooperative advertising programs of wholesalers, manufacturers, and trade associations.

Manufacturers, such as Hoover (www.hoover.com), provide retailers with advertising materials and co-op dollars to encourage dealers like Sears (www.sears.com) to promote the manufacturer's products. If these products are not promoted at the local level, the manufacturer's national advertising efforts will be less effective.

Cooperative Advertising

As a service to their distributors and dealers, and to ensure proper reproduction of their products, wholesalers and manufacturers as well as some trade associations often provide local advertisers with ready-made advertising materials and cooperative advertising programs where the costs are shared.

There are two key purposes for **cooperative (co-op) advertising:** to build the manufacturer's brand image and to help its distributors, dealers, or retailers make more sales.[2] Every year, national manufacturers give their local retailers more than $20 billion for co-op projects. Newspapers, television, and radio are the favored media of co-op spending, with newspapers claiming 55 percent of co-op dollars.[3] Intel alone spends more than $800 million annually to help PC marketers who display the "Intel Inside" logo.[4] Exhibit 3–2 demonstrates how important co-op advertising dollars are for certain retail businesses. (Commercial Break 3–A provides questions to consider when contemplating co-op advertising.)

Regional and National Advertisers

Some companies operate in one part of the country—in one or several states—and market exclusively within that region. These are referred to as **regional advertisers.** Typical examples include regional grocery and department store chains, governmental bodies (such as state lotteries), franchise groups (such as

Exhibit 3–2

The importance of co-op advertising dollars.

Store	Co-op dollars as a percentage of total ad budget
Appliance dealers	80%
Food stores	75
Drugstores	70
Department stores	50
Shoe stores	50
Clothing stores	35
Furniture stores	30
Household goods	30
Jewelers	30
Discount stores	20

Checklist

Creating Local Advertising

- **Stand out from the competition.** Make your ads easily recognizable. Ads with unusual art, layout, and typefaces have higher readership. Make the ads distinctive but keep their appearance consistent.

- **Use a simple layout.** The layout should carry the reader's eye through the message easily and in proper sequence from headline to illustration to explanatory copy to price to store name. Avoid using too many typefaces.

- **Use a dominant element.** A large picture or headline ensures quick visibility. Photos of real people and action pictures win more readership, as do photos of local people or places. Color attracts more readers.

- **Stress the benefits.** Present the emotional reason to buy or the tangible performance element customers seek.

- **Make the headline count.** Use a compelling headline to feature the main benefit.

- **Watch your language.** Make your writing style active, lively, and involving. Make the readers feel they already own the product. Avoid negativism and profanity.

- **Let white space work for you.** White space focuses the reader's attention and makes the headline and illustration stand out.

- **Make the copy complete.** Emphasize the benefits most appealing to customers.

- **Make your visual powerful and eye-catching.** Make sure it demonstrates your message. The main visual is often more important than the headline. Photos work better than artwork.

- **State price or range of prices.** Dollar figures have good attention value, and readers often overestimate omitted prices. Spell out credit and layaway plans.

- **Specify branded merchandise.** If the item is a known brand, say so.

- **Include related items.** Make two sales instead of one by offering related items along with a featured one.

- **Urge readers to buy now.** Ask for the sale. Stimulate prompt action by using "limited supply" or "this week only."

- **Don't forget the store name and address.** Check every ad to be certain the store name, address, phone number, and hours are included.

- **Don't be too clever.** Many people distrust or misunderstand cleverness.

- **Don't use unusual or difficult words.** Everyone understands simple language. Use it.

- **Don't generalize. Be specific.** Shoppers want all the facts before they buy.

- **Don't make excessive claims.** Advertisers lose customers when they make claims they can't back up.

- **Plan ad size carefully.** Attention usually increases with size.

- **Consider your target customers.** People notice ads more if they are directed at their own gender or age group.

- **Use tie-ins with local or special news events.**

---

the Southern California Honda dealers), telephone companies (such as SBC), and statewide or multistate banks (Bank of America).

Other companies sell in several regions or throughout the country and are called **national advertisers.** These include consumer packaged-goods manufacturers (such as Procter & Gamble and Johnson & Johnson), national airlines (Delta, American), media and entertainment companies (Disney, Time Warner), electronics manufacturers (Apple, Hewlett-Packard), and all the auto companies. These firms also make up the membership of the *Association of National Advertisers (ANA)* and comprise the largest advertisers in the country (see Exhibit 3–3).

How National and Local Advertisers Differ

The basic principles of advertising are the same in both local and national advertising. However, local advertisers have special challenges stemming from the day-to-day realities of running a small business (see Exhibit 3–4).

Exhibit 3–3

Top 10 advertisers ranked by total U.S. advertising in 2005 (figures in millions of U.S. dollars).

Rank	Company	U.S. ad spending
1	General Motors Corp.	$3,997.4
2	Procter & Gamble Co.	3,919.7
3	Time Warner	3,283.1
4	Pfizer	2,957.3
5	SBC Communications	2,686.8
6	DaimlerChrysler	2,462.1
7	Ford Motor Co.	2,458.0
8	Walt Disney Co.	2,241.5
9	Verizon Communications	2,197.3
10	Johnson & Johnson Co.	2,175.7

Commercial Break 3–A

The Co-op Marriage

On the surface, cooperative advertising seems like a great arrangement for retailers. A manufacturer supplies advertising materials (saving the retailer production costs) and pays a percentage of the media cost. The retailer drops in the store's logo, arranges for the ad to run, and collects the co-op dollars from the manufacturer. The small retail business can stretch its ad budget and associate its business with a nationally advertised product. The retailer receives professionally prepared ads and acquires greater leverage with the local media that carry the co-op ads.

But as with any marriage, there is give and take.

A retailer may have to sell a lot of merchandise to qualify for significant co-op funds. More often, the retailer and manufacturer have different advertising objectives and different ideas about how the ads should be executed.

The manufacturer often wants total control. The manufacturer expects co-op ads to tie in with its national advertising promotions. It wants the right product advertised at the right time. Manufacturers prepare guideline pamphlets specifying when and where the ads should appear, what form they should take, and what uses of the name and logo are not allowed.

Retailers have their own ideas about which products to advertise when. They're more concerned with daily volume and with projecting an image of value and variety. An appliance store might prefer to advertise inexpensive TVs even though the manufacturer wants to emphasize its top-of-the-line models.

Manufacturers worry that retailers will place the product in a cluttered, ugly ad or next to inferior products; that the ad will run in inappropriate publications; and that it will not run at the best time. Retailers counter that they know the local market better. In short, manufacturers think they don't have enough control; retailers think they have too much.

A retailer contemplating co-op funds should consider the following questions:

- What requirements must be met in order for ads to qualify for co-op money?
- What percentage is paid by each party?
- When can ads be run?
- What media can be used?
- Are there special provisions for message content?
- What documentation is required for reimbursement?
- How does each party benefit?
- Do cooperative ads obscure the retailer's image?

Applying the Breaks

1. Look through today's edition of a daily paper in your city. Identify two ads that can qualify as co-op. Do the ads fit both the store's image and the manufacturer's image? Explain.

2. A store may develop its own ad and drop in the manufacturer's logo or it may take an ad created by the manufacturer and simply add the store's location. Which do your two ads do?

Focus National companies are concerned about building their *brands,* so their advertising tends to focus on the competitive features of one brand over another. Local merchants or dealers often carry hundreds of different brands, so they focus on attracting customers to a particular *location*—their place of business.

Big companies battle for market *share* against a few competitors, and every share point is worth millions of dollars. Local advertisers compete with many companies, so their focus is on gross sales or *volume:* 60 cars a month, five new insurance policies a week, 55 oil changes a day.

National advertisers plan *strategically* to launch, build, and sustain brands. Local advertisers think *tactically.* Will a new $15,000 sign bring more people into the store? Should we stay open Labor Day? Can we attract more lunchtime customers by reducing our prices or by offering free refills on soft drinks?

The relationship with the customer may be the greatest difference between national and local advertisers. National advertisers' marketing executives rarely see their customers; instead, they traditionally think of them in terms of large groups of people—segments, niches, target *markets*—with various geographic, demographic, or psychographic descriptions. They design their strategies and campaigns to appeal to these large groups.

Exhibit 3–4

Differences between local and national advertisers.

	National	Local
Focus	Brand	Location
	Market share	Volume
	Strategies	Tactics
	Markets	Customers
Time	Long-term campaigns	Short-term ads
Resources	$5–$10 million+	Less than $1 million
	Many specialists	A few generalists

But local advertisers deal with individual *customers* every day. The local advertiser gets regular feedback on the company's advertising, prices, product performance, customer service, store decor, and the new sign out front. The national marketer may get occasional feedback—from surveys and from customer complaint lines.

Time orientation   National companies think long term. They develop five-year strategic plans and budget for annual advertising campaigns. Local advertisers worry that this week's ad didn't *pull* (a term rarely used by national marketers) as well as last week's; a New York advertiser may have months to develop a network TV campaign; the little market on Main Street may have to churn out a new newspaper ad every week.

Resources   Finally, national advertisers have more resources available—both money and people. The national advertiser has millions of dollars and an army of *specialists* dedicated to the successful marketing of its brands. The local advertiser may have a small staff of *generalists* or just one person—the owner—to market the business. So the local entrepreneur has to know more about every facet of marketing communications.

CONCEPT CHECK

What are the elements that characterize local, regional, and national advertisers? In what key ways do they differ?

How Large Companies Manage Their Advertising

In large companies, many people are involved in the advertising function. Company owners and top corporate executives make key advertising decisions; sales and marketing personnel often assist in the creative process, help choose the ad agency, and evaluate proposed ad programs; artists and writers produce ads, brochures, and other materials; product engineers and designers give input to the creative process and provide information about competitive products; administrators evaluate the cost of ad campaigns and help plan budgets; and clerical staff coordinate various promotional activities, including advertising.

A large company's advertising department may employ many people and be headed by an advertising manager who reports to a marketing director or marketing services manager. The exact department structure depends on many variables. Most large advertisers tend to use some mix of two basic management structures: *centralized* and *decentralized*.

Centralized organization   Companies are concerned with cost efficiency and continuity in their communications programs. Thus, many embrace the **centralized advertising department** because it gives the greatest control and offers both efficiency and continuity across divisional boundaries. In centralized departments, an advertising manager typically reports to a marketing vice president. But beyond this one feature, companies may organize the department in any of five ways:

- By product or brand.

- By subfunction of advertising (copy, art, print production, media buying).

- By end user (consumer advertising, trade advertising).

- By media (radio, TV, newspapers, outdoor).

- By geography (western advertising, eastern advertising, international advertising).

Companies that sell their products or services throughout the country are called national advertisers. Unlike their local counterparts, national advertisers plan strategically to launch, build, and sustain brands. A company like Dunkin' Donuts (www.dunkindonuts.com) targets large demographic groups and is concerned with issues of market share and brand equity. This ad creatively demonstrates the quality of Dunkin' Donuts coffee—it's so good, "you just can't wait."

Coffee so good
you just can't wait.

DUNKIN' DONUTS

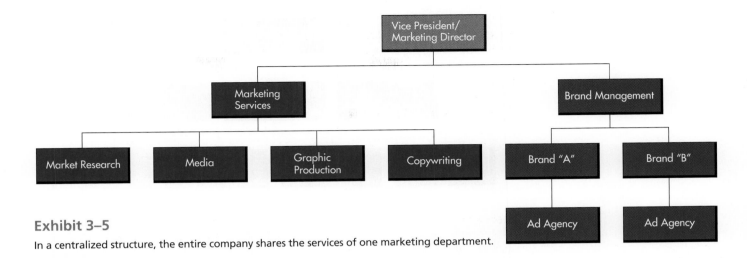

Exhibit 3–5

In a centralized structure, the entire company shares the services of one marketing department.

The cereal giant General Mills, for example, is one of the nation's largest advertisers. It operates a vast advertising and marketing services department with some 350 employees. It spends more than $555 million annually in media advertising and other promotional activities.[5]

General Mills' Marketing Services is really many departments within a department. Its centralized structure enables it to administer, plan, and coordinate the promotion of more than 60 brands. It also supervises five outside ad agencies and operates its own in-house agency for new or smaller brands.[6]

Organized around functional specialties (market research, media, graphics), Marketing Services helps General Mills' **brand managers** consolidate many of their expenditures for maximum efficiency. The media department, for example, prepares all media plans for the marketing divisions. The production and art department designs the packages for all brands and the graphics for the company's in-house agency. From one department, Marketing Services handles a wide variety of brands efficiently and effectively (see Exhibit 3–5).

Decentralized organization As some companies become larger, diversify their product line, acquire subsidiaries, and establish divisions in different regions or even different countries, a centralized advertising department often becomes impractical.

In a **decentralized system,** the company sets up separate ad departments for different divisions, subsidiaries, regions, brands, or other categories that suit the company's needs. The general manager of each division or brand is responsible for that group's advertising. A brand manager, who oversees each individual brand, typically works under a marketing manager, who reports to a category manager. While the brand manager's primary goal is to use advertising and promotion to build market share, the category manager focuses on sharpening overall strategy and building profits. This system gives significant authority to the individuals responsible for each brand.

For large companies with many divisions, decentralized advertising is more flexible. Campaigns and media schedules can be adjusted faster. New approaches and creative ideas can be introduced more easily, and sales results can be measured independently of other divisions. In effect, each division has its own marketing department, with the marketing manager reporting to the division head (see Exhibit 3–6).

A drawback, though, is that decentralized departments often concentrate on their own budgets, problems, and promotions rather than the good of the

> **CONCEPT CHECK**
>
> What are the advantages and disadvantages of the two ways to organize large company marketing departments?

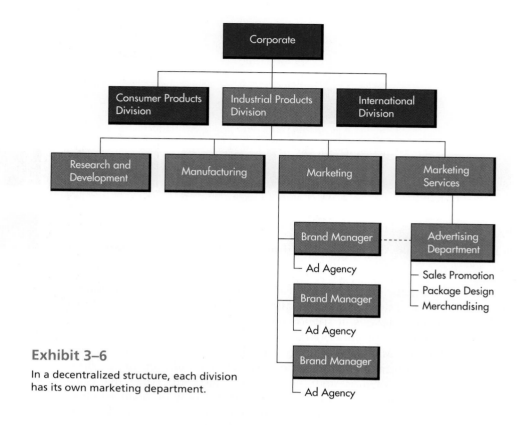

Exhibit 3–6

In a decentralized structure, each division has its own marketing department.

whole company. Across divisions, ads may lack uniformity, diminishing the power of repetitive corporate advertising. Rivalry among brand managers may even escalate into unhealthy competition or deteriorate into secrecy and jealousy.

Transnational Advertisers

Companies advertising abroad typically face markets with different value systems, environments, and languages. Their customers have different purchasing abilities, habits, and motivations. Media customary to U.S. and Canadian advertisers may be unavailable or ineffective. The companies will therefore likely need different advertising strategies. But they face a more basic problem: How should they manage and produce the advertising? Should their U.S. agency or in-house advertising department do it? Should they use a foreign agency or set up a local advertising department?

Procter & Gamble is a 165-year-old, $40 billion company. It sells more than 300 consumer brands to more than five billion consumers in 160 countries. These brands include such market leaders as Tide, Ivory soap, Pampers, Folgers, Pringles, and Crest toothpaste.[7]

P&G is one of the biggest and most influential consumer advertisers in the world; its expenditures in the United States alone exceed $3.3 billion annually. But more than half of its sales come from abroad.[8] Each overseas division is set up almost like a separate company with its own research and development department, manufacturing plant, sales force, and finance and accounting staff. Each division also has an advertising department to help coordinate sales promotion and merchandising programs across brands within that division.

As companies continue to grow and prosper around the world, they may invest directly in many countries. True **multinational corporations** strive for full, integrated participation in world markets.[9] Foreign sales often grow faster

With an international structure, advertisers' local divisions are responsible for their own product lines and create customized ads for each market. This Heinz ketchup (www.heinz.com) ad was created by Leo Burnett Group, Copenhagen, and only ran in Denmark. The translation: "The only American you can hit without being sued."

In Canada, all packages and labels must be printed in both English and French, and most major companies also run their ads in both languages. The layout of the French version of this HP (www.hp.com) ad is modified to accommodate the slightly longer text.

than domestic sales. Multinationals such as ExxonMobil and IBM earn about 50 percent of their sales abroad; Kodak and Xerox, about 25 percent. Typically, the top 25 U.S. multinational corporations earn more than 40 percent of their revenues and two-thirds of their profits overseas.[10]

Multinationals that use a *standardized approach* to marketing and advertising in all countries are considered **global marketers,** and they create global brands. Their assumption is that the way the product is used and the needs it satisfies are universal.[11] Max Factor, for example, markets its cosmetics globally. In the 1990s, it ran a campaign aimed at making the brand more relevant by using as spokespersons a variety of strong, contemporary, and self-confident women. The campaign drew favorable reactions from women worldwide.[12] Other global advertisers include Coca-Cola, British Airways, British Petroleum, TGI Friday's, FedEx, and Chiclets.[13]

Companies must research extensively before attempting a global advertising strategy. So much depends on the product and where they try to sell it. A "no" answer to any of the following questions means the attempt will probably fail.

1. *Has each country's market for the product developed in the same way?* A Ford is a Ford in most markets. On the other hand, many Europeans use clotheslines, so they don't need fabric softeners for dryers.

2. *Are the targets similar in different nations?* Japanese consumers like jeans, running shoes, and rock and roll. The same is true for consumers in Europe and the United States. But they might not like certain foods or other fashions.

3. *Do consumers share the same wants and needs?* Breakfast in Brazil is usually a cup of coffee. Kellogg's Corn Flakes won't be served the same way as in the United States, where people commonly eat cereal for breakfast.[14]

Advertisers who cannot answer "yes" to the above questions will often take a *localized approach* to international marketing and advertising. They will consider differences in product use, economic development, media options, local laws, technology, and customs. The outcome will often be the adaptation of products, packages, and advertising campaigns to suit each market.

According to the worldwide creative director of J. Walter Thompson, the secret to success in global advertising is knowing how to tap into basic human emotions and uncover universal appeals that don't depend solely on language.[15]

Media Around the World

In the United States, if you want to promote a soft drink as a youthful, fun refresher, you use television. In some parts of Europe, Asia, South America, and Africa you may not be able to. Around the world, most broadcast media are owned and controlled by the government, and many governments do not allow commercial advertising on radio or television. In Egypt, the current hot medium used by Coca-Cola and others is the fleet of boats plying the Nile with corporate logos emblazoned on their sails.[16]

Where TV ownership is high, it cuts across the spectrum of income groups. In less-developed countries, though, TV sets may be found only among upper-income groups. This means advertisers may need a different media mix in foreign markets.

Virtually every country has access to radio, television, newspapers, magazines, outdoor media, and direct mail. However, the legalities of different media forms vary from country to country. Generally, the media available to the international advertiser can be categorized as either *international* or *foreign media,* depending on the audience they serve.

International Media

In the past, **international media**—which serve several countries, usually without any change in content—have been limited to newspapers and magazines. Several large American publishers such as Time, McGraw-Hill, and Scientific American circulate international editions of their magazines abroad. Usually written in English, they tend to be read by well-educated, upper-income consumers and are therefore good vehicles for advertising high-end, brand-name products. *Reader's Digest,* on the other hand, is distributed to 126 foreign countries and printed in the local language of each. Today, television is also becoming a viable international medium. We are beginning to see the emergence of *global media vehicles,* such as CNN.

Foreign Media

Advertisers use **foreign media**—the local media of each country—for large campaigns targeted to consumers or businesses within a single country. Because foreign media cater to their own national audience, advertisers must produce their ads in the language of each country. In countries such as Belgium and Switzerland, with more than one official language, ads are produced in each language.

Unlike the United States, most countries have strong national newspapers that are a good medium for national campaigns. Advertisers also get broad penetration of lower-income markets through radio, which enjoys almost universal ownership. And cinema advertising is a viable alternative to TV in markets with low TV penetration or restricted use of commercial TV.

The Advertising Agency

Why does a company such as Honda hire an advertising agency in the first place? Couldn't it save money by hiring its own staff and creating its own ads? How does Muse Cordero Chen win such a large account? Must an agency's accounts be that big for it to make money? This section sheds some light on these issues and gives a clearer understanding of what agencies do and why so many advertisers use agencies.

The Role of the Advertising Agency

The American Association of Advertising Agencies (AAAA) defines an **advertising agency** as an independent organization of creative people and businesspeople who specialize in developing and preparing marketing and advertising plans, advertisements, and other promotional tools. The agency also purchases advertising space and time in various media on behalf of different advertisers, or sellers (its clients), to find customers for their goods and services.[17]

This definition offers clues to why so many advertisers hire ad agencies. First, an agency like Muse Cordero Chen (MCC) is *independent*. The agency isn't owned by the advertiser, the media, or the suppliers, so it can bring an outside, objective viewpoint to the advertiser's business—a position the advertiser can never attain.

Second, like all agencies, MCC employs a combination of *businesspeople* and *creative people,* including administrators, accountants, marketing executives, researchers, market and media analysts, writers, and artists. They have day-to-day contact with outside professional suppliers who create illustrations, take photos, retouch art, shoot commercials, record sound, and print brochures.

The agency provides yet another service by researching, negotiating, arranging, and contracting for commercial space and time with the various print, electronic, and digital media. Because of its *media expertise,* Muse Cordero Chen saves its clients time and money.

Agencies don't work for the media or the suppliers. Their moral, ethical, financial, and legal obligation is to their clients. Just as a well-run business seeks professional help from attorneys, accountants, bankers, or management specialists, advertisers use agencies out of *self-interest,* because the agencies can create more effective advertising and select more effective media than the advertisers can themselves. Today, almost all sizable advertisers rely on an ad agency for expert, objective counsel and unique creative skills—to be the "guardian of their brands."[18]

Finally, a good agency serves its clients' needs because of its daily exposure to a broad spectrum of marketing situations and problems both here and abroad. As technology has enabled companies to work across borders with relative ease, the advertising business has boomed worldwide. All the large U.S. agencies maintain offices in many foreign countries.

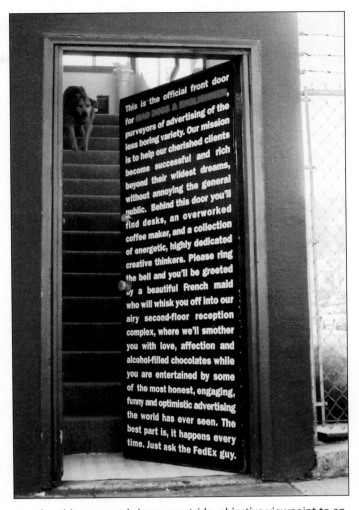

An advertising agency brings an outside, objective viewpoint to an advertiser's business. In order to do so, the agency must also promote itself so that advertisers may choose its services. Here, Mad Dogs & Englishmen, San Francisco, does so by creatively altering its front door.

Types of Agencies

Advertising agencies are typically classified by their geographic scope, the range of services they offer, and the type of business they handle.

Geographic Scope

Every community of any size has reputable **local agencies** that offer expert assistance to local advertisers. Unfortunately, local advertisers use ad agencies less extensively than do national advertisers. Many local advertisers simply don't spend enough money on advertising to warrant hiring an agency. And some large agencies don't accept local advertisers because their budgets are too low to support the agency's overhead.

Every major city has numerous ad agencies that can produce and place the quality of advertising suitable for national campaigns. **Regional** and **national agencies** typically participate in either the 4As (American Association of Advertising Agencies) or some similar trade group such as the Western States Advertising Agency Association (WSAAA). The *Standard Directory of Advertising Agencies* (the Red Book) lists these agencies geographically, so they're easy to find.

The largest national agencies are also **international agencies.** That is, they have offices or affiliates in major communications centers around the world and can help their clients market internationally or globally as the case may be. Likewise, many foreign-based agencies have offices and affiliates in the United States. For example, the largest advertising agency organization in the world today, WPP Group, is based in London. But it owns several of the top agencies in the United States, such as Ogilvy & Mather and J. Walter Thompson.

Range of Services

The modern **full-service advertising agency** supplies both advertising and nonadvertising services in all areas of communications and promotion. *Advertising services* include planning, creating, and producing ads; performing research; and selecting media. *Nonadvertising services* run the gamut from packaging to public relations to producing sales promotion materials, annual reports, and trade-show exhibits. With the trend toward IMC, many of the largest agencies today are in the forefront of the emerging *interactive media.*[19]

Full-service agencies may specialize in certain kinds of clients. Most, though, can be classified as either *general consumer agencies* or *business-to-business agencies.*

General consumer agencies   A **general consumer agency** represents the widest variety of accounts, but it concentrates on *consumer accounts*—companies that make goods purchased chiefly by consumers (soaps, cereals, cars, pet foods, toiletries). Most of the ads are placed in consumer media (TV, radio, magazines, and so on) that pay a *commission* to the agency. General agencies often derive much of their income from these commissions.

General agencies include the international superagency groups headquartered in communication capitals such as New York, London, Paris, and Tokyo, as well as many other large firms in New York, Chicago, Los Angeles, Minneapolis, Montreal, and Toronto. A few of the better-known names in North America are McCann-Erickson; Ogilvy & Mather; Foote, Cone & Belding; Grey Advertising; BBDO; DDB Needham; Young & Rubicam; and Cossette Communications-Marketing (Canada). But general agencies also include the thousands of smaller *entrepreneurial agencies* located in every major city across the country (Martin Agency, Richmond, Virginia; Rubin/Postaer, Los Angeles; Ruhr/Paragon, Minneapolis; Wieden & Kennedy, Portland, Oregon).

Profit margins in entrepreneurial agencies are often slimmer, but these shops are typically more responsive to the smaller clients they serve. They offer the hands-on involvement of the firm's principals, and their work is frequently startling in its creativity. For these very reasons, many large agencies are spinning off smaller subsidiaries. Gotham Advertising, for example, is a hot creative shop in New York that was spun off by the Interpublic Group of Companies to do work for a variety of clients its bigger sister agencies couldn't serve.[20] Some entrepreneurial agencies, such as Muse Cordero Chen, carve a niche for themselves by serving particular market segments.

Business-to-business agencies   A **business-to-business agency** represents clients that market products to other businesses. Examples are electronic components for computer manufacturers, equipment used in oil and gas refineries, and MRI equipment for radiology. High-tech advertising requires some technical knowledge and the ability to translate that knowledge into precise, as well as persuasive communications.

Most business-to-business advertising is placed in trade magazines or other business publications. These media are commissionable, but their circulation is smaller, so their rates are far lower than those of consumer media. Because commissions usually don't cover the cost of the agency's services, business agencies typically charge their clients service fees. They can be expensive, especially for small advertisers, but failure to obtain a business agency's expertise may carry an even higher price in lost marketing opportunities.

Business and industrial agencies may be large international firms such as MacLaren/Lintas in Toronto or HCM/New York, or smaller firms experienced in areas of recruitment, biomedical, or electronics advertising.

Some advertising agencies specialize in business-to-business advertising. In this ad, DHL (www.dhl.com) is promoting its shipping services to small businesses.

Specialized Service Agencies

Many agencies assist their clients with a variety of limited services. In the early 1990s the trend toward specialization blossomed, giving impetus to many of the small agency-type groups called *creative boutiques* and other specialty businesses such as *media-buying services* and *interactive agencies.*

Creative boutiques   Some talented artists—such as graphic designers and copywriters—set up their own creative services, or **creative boutiques.** They work for advertisers and occasionally subcontract to ad agencies. Their mission is to develop exciting creative concepts and produce fresh, distinctive advertising messages. In the 1990s, Creative Artists Agency (CAA), a Hollywood talent agency, caused a stir on Madison Avenue (the collective term for New York agencies) by taking on the role of a creative boutique, using its pool of actors, directors, and cinematographers to create a series of commercials for Coca-Cola. McCann-Erickson Worldwide remained Coke's *agency of record,* but the majority of the creative work came from CAA. Since that time, Coke has allowed numerous other smaller shops to work on its account. In fact, in 1999, it had 16 agencies and boutiques on its roster.[21]

Advertising effectiveness depends on originality in concept, design, and writing. However, while boutiques may be economical, they usually don't provide the research, marketing, sales expertise, or deep customer service that full-service agencies offer. Thus, boutiques tend to be limited to the role of creative suppliers.

Media-buying services   Some years ago, a few experienced agency media people started setting up organizations to purchase and package radio and TV time.

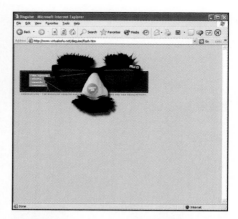

Because of the technical expertise needed for interactive media, some small agencies have made big names for themselves. Boutiques can demonstrate their creative power through ads for their services, such as this interactive Web ad from AgenciaClick (Brazil) (www.agenciaclick.com.br) for AgenciaClick International. To see the ad itself, visit www.virtualsofa.net/disguise/. The ad demonstrates the agency's flair for creating banner ads that are actually Web sites. AgenciaClick (Brazil) garnered a 2004 Cannes Silver Lion for this effort.

CONCEPT CHECK

What are the distinguishing characteristics of the different types of advertising agencies?

The largest **media-buying service** (or *media agency*) is Initiative Media. Based in Los Angeles, it is owned by the Interpublic Group, has offices around the world, and places more than $21 billion worth of advertising annually for a wide variety of clients from Coors and Nextel to Victoria's Secret.[22]

Media time and space is perishable. A 60-second radio spot at 8 p.m. can't be sold later. So radio and TV stations presell as much time as possible and discount their rates for large buys. Media-buying services negotiate a special discount with the media and then sell the time or space to agencies or advertisers.

Media-buying firms provide customers (both clients and agencies) with a detailed analysis of the media buy. Once the media package is sold, the buying service orders spots, verifies performance, sees that stations "make good" for any missed spots, and even pays the media bills. Compensation methods vary. Some services charge a set fee; others get a percentage of what they sell or how much they save the client.

Media agencies have experienced so much growth in the last decade that they have become major players on the advertising stage. We'll discuss them in greater detail in Chapter 15, "Media Planning and Buying."

Interactive agencies With the stunning growth of the Internet and the heightened interest in integrated marketing communications has come a new breed of specialist—the **interactive agency.** Think New Ideas (owned by AnswerThink) is one of the many firms that have sprung up within the last few years with specialized experience in designing Web pages and creating fun, involving, information-rich, online advertising.[23]

Other specialists, such as *direct-response* and *sales promotion agencies,* are also growing in response to client demands for greater expertise and accountability.

What People in an Agency Do

The American Association of Advertising Agencies (AAAA), the national trade association of the advertising agency business, explains that an agency's purpose is to interpret to the public, or to desired segments of the public, information about a legally marketed product or service. How does an agency do this? First, it studies the client's product to determine its strengths and weaknesses. Next, it analyzes the product's present and potential market. Then, using its knowledge of how the product is distributed and media alternatives, the agency formulates a plan to carry the advertiser's message to consumers, wholesalers, dealers, or contractors. Finally the agency writes, designs, and produces ads; contracts for media space and time; verifies media insertions; and bills for services and media used.

The agency also works with the client's marketing staff to enhance the advertising's effect through package design, sales research and training, and production of sales literature and displays. To understand these functions, consider the people who were involved, directly and indirectly, in the creation, production, and supervision of the Honda Civic campaign created by Muse Cordero Chen and Partners.

Account Management

The **account executives (AEs)** at Muse Cordero Chen are the liaison between the agency and the client. Large agencies typically have many account executives, who report to **management** (or **account**) **supervisors.** They in turn report to the agency's director of account (or client) services.

Account executives are often caught in the middle of the fray, as they are responsible for formulating and executing advertising plans (discussed in Chapter 7), mustering the agency's services, representing the client's point of view to the agency, and the agency's point of view to the client. As one observer commented, to succeed today, an AE needs to be more of a strategist than an advocate. She must be well versed in an extraordinary range of media and demonstrate how her agency's creative work satisfies both her client's marketing needs and the market's product needs. That means she must be enterprising and courageous, demanding yet tactful, artistic and articulate, meticulous, forgiving, perceptive, persuasive, ethical, and discreet—all at once. And she must always deliver the work on time and within budget.

Research and Account Planning

Clients and agencies must give their creatives (artists and copywriters) a wealth of product, market, and competitive information because, at its core, advertising is based on information. Therefore, before creating any advertising, agencies research the uses and advantages of the product, analyze current and potential customers, and try to determine what will influence them to buy. After the ads are placed, agencies use more research to investigate how the campaign fared. Chapter 6 discusses some of the many types of research ad agencies conduct.

Account planning is a hybrid discipline that uses research to bridge the gap between account management and creatives. The account planner also defends the consumer's point of view and the creative strategy in the debate between the agency's creative team and the client.

Account planners study consumer needs and desires through phone surveys and focus groups, but primarily through personal interviews. They help the creative team translate their findings into imaginative, successful campaigns. Not attached to either account management or creative, the account planner balances both elements to make sure the research is reflected in the ads.[24]

Working on the Honda Civic account, Shelley Yamane spent a lot of time in Los Angeles talking to young people in their own environments with the goal of better understanding their attitudes, feelings, language, and habits. She then represented the views of those young people in agency meetings with Honda. The result was the discovery of a new market segment for Honda: urban youth—shaped by inner-city life, hip-hop music, and the desire to display both one's success and individuality. This group is defined not by ethnicity but by a cultural attitude that crosses demographic lines to foster the market's core values: irreverence, fitness, athleticism, and discipline.

By putting the consumer, rather than the advertiser, at the center of the process, account planning changes the task from simply creating an advertisement to nurturing a relationship between the consumer and brand. To get the job done right, Shelley had to be receptive, approachable, and most importantly, a good listener—essential characteristics of a good account planner. When performed properly, planning provides the brilliant, simplifying insight that lights the way for the client and the creatives. Interestingly, the U.S. agencies that have adopted account planning in the last decade are the ones now considered to be the hottest shops—performing the best work and getting the biggest accounts.

Media Planning and Buying

Ad agencies perform a variety of media services for their clients: research, negotiating, scheduling, buying, and verifying. **Media planning** is critical, because the only way advertisers can communicate is through some medium. We discuss media planning extensively in Chapter 15, but for now it's important to understand that changes over the last decade have made the media function even more important.

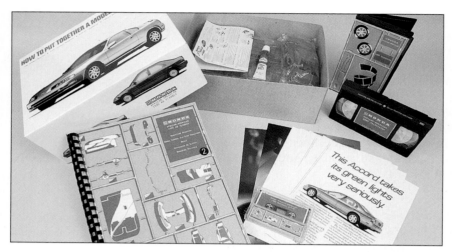

Items in the Honda (www.honda.com) dealer promotional kit included an 8 $\frac{1}{2}$ × 11 inch spiral-bound notebook with three color magazine ad slicks, five black-and-white newspaper ad slicks, and marketing and media information; a 25-second "I Am Me" video commercial; an audiocassette with three 55-second radio commercials; and an actual model kit of the Honda Prelude for the dealer to assemble.

With the unprecedented fragmentation of audiences from the explosion of new media options and the trend toward IMC and relationship marketing, the media task has taken on added significance. Tightening budgets demand ingenious thinking, tough negotiating, and careful attention to detail. Media planners must understand how advertising works in coordination with other marketing communication tools and come up with creative media solutions to tough marketing challenges. Today, many products owe their success more to creative media planning and buying than to clever ads.

Creative Concepts

Most ads rely heavily on **copy,** the words that make up the headline and message. The people who create these words, called **copywriters,** must condense all that can be said about a product into a few pertinent, succinct points.

Ads also use nonverbal communication. That is the purview of the **art directors,** graphic designers, and production artists, who determine how an ad's verbal and visual symbols will fit together. (The creative process is discussed in Part 4.) The agency's copywriters and artists work as a creative team under a **creative director.** Each team is usually assigned a particular client's business.

In the case of the Honda Civic, the creative director was Wilky Lau. He put together a creative team consisting of a copywriter, Mike Whitlow, and an art director, Alfonso ("Fons") Covarrubias. With the research that Shelley Yamane passed on to them, they began to brainstorm. Wilky, Mike, and Fons all agreed that it was important to generate a campaign that would show urban youth in their own world. The big idea was launched from that very notion: how better to accurately capture the essence of urban youth than to actually include them in the campaign? Maybe all they had to do was define this growing group of Civic-loving people and portray them realistically. And, in so doing, they would effectively position the car. The notion of a "Civic Nation" was born. They followed through with this initial concept in every aspect of the campaign—from the print ads and commercials, which featured authentic souped-up Civics, down to the radio spots, which they created by using a DJ to mix beats with sound bites from genuine interviews with Civic drivers. Not your average radio spot.

As with any good writing, ad copy should look like it was written with ease. Though simple and straightforward, the copy used in the Civic campaign was a long time in the making. But when Mike Whitlow came up with the line "Represent," used in both the print ads and commercials, it was met with glowing approval. "Represent" serves as both a command to be yourself and convey your individuality, as well as a caption to describe what the ad is doing, since it is in fact representing the personal, creative expression of many Civic drivers.

Advertising Production: Print and Broadcast

Once an ad is designed, written, and approved by the client, it is turned over to the agency's print production manager or broadcast producers.

For print ads, the **production department** buys type, photos, illustrations, and other components and works with printers, engravers, and other suppliers.

For a broadcast commercial, production people work from an approved script or storyboard. They use actors, camera operators, and production specialists (studios, directors, editors) to produce a commercial on audiotape (for radio) or on film or videotape (for TV).

But production work is not just limited to ads and commercials. Dealer kits and direct mailings are just two examples of other media types that may be created as part of a campaign. For instance, several years ago Muse Cordero Chen assembled a promotional kit for dealers that included, among the marketing and media literature, an actual model kit of the Honda Prelude (including glue) for the dealer to construct.

Traffic Management

One of the greatest sins in an ad agency is a missed deadline. If an agency misses a deadline for a monthly magazine for example, the agency will have to wait another month before they can run the ad, much to the client's displeasure.

The agency **traffic department** coordinates all phases of production and makes sure everything is completed before client and/or media deadlines. Traffic is often the first stop for entry-level college graduates and an excellent place to learn about agency operations. (See the *Essentials of Contemporary Advertising* Web site for more information about careers in advertising.)

Additional Services

The growth of IMC has caused many agencies to employ specialists who provide services besides advertising. While Muse Cordero Chen uses its regular creative department for both advertising and nonadvertising services, larger agencies may have a fully staffed **sales promotion department** to produce dealer ads, window posters, point-of-purchase displays, and dealer sales material. Or, depending on the nature and needs of their clients, they may employ public relations people and direct marketing specialists, Web page designers, home economics experts, or package designers.

Agency Administration

In small agencies, administrative functions may be handled by the firm's principals. Large agencies often have departments for accounting, human resources, data processing, purchasing, financial analysis, legal issues, and insurance.

> What are the key roles in a typical advertising agency and what functions do they perform?

CONCEPT CHECK

How Agencies Are Structured

An ad agency organizes its functions, operations, and personnel according to the types of accounts it serves, its size, and its geographic scope.

The owner or general manager usually supervises daily business operations, client services, and new-business development. Account executives generally handle day-to-day client contact. In smaller agencies, AEs may also do some creative work, such as writing copy. Artwork may be produced by an art director or purchased from an independent studio or freelance designer. Most agencies have production and traffic departments or an employee who fulfills these functions. They may have a media buyer, but in very small agencies account executives also purchase media time and space. Exhibit 3–7 shows how a typical advertising agency might be organized.

Medium and large agencies are usually structured in a *departmental* or *group system*. In the **departmental system,** the agency organizes its various

Thanks to modern telecommunications, clients and agencies can locate themselves almost anywhere. Today, virtual manufacturers work out of seaside resorts and their agencies can operate the same way—tied to their researchers, creatives, media departments, and suppliers by phones, fax machines, personal digital assistants, and high-speed Internet connections.

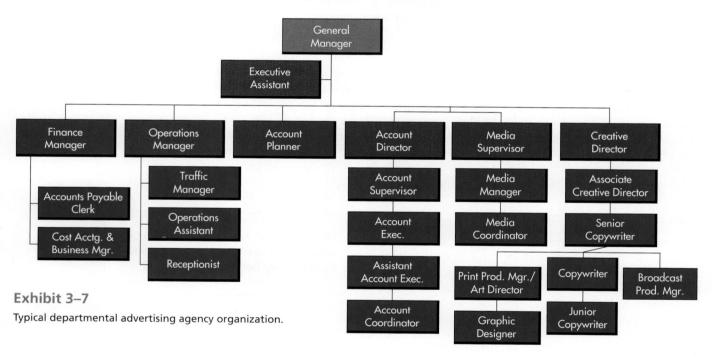

Exhibit 3–7

Typical departmental advertising agency organization.

functions—account services, creative services, marketing services, and administration—into separate departments.

In the **group system,** the agency is divided into a number of "little" agencies or groups. Each group may serve one large account or, in some cases, three or four smaller ones. An account manager heads each group's staff of account executives, copywriters, art directors, a media director, and any other necessary specialists. A very large agency may have dozens of groups with separate production and traffic units.

How Agencies Are Compensated

To survive, agencies must make a profit. But recent trends in the business—mergers of superagencies, shifts in emphasis from advertising to sales promotion and direct marketing, increased production costs, and the fragmentation of media vehicles—have all cut into agency profits.[25] Moreover, different clients demand different services, forcing agencies to develop various compensation methods. Still, there are really only three ways for agencies to make money: *media commissions, markups,* and *fees* or *retainers*.

Media Commissions

As we saw in Chapter 1, when ad agencies first came on the scene more than 100 years ago, they were really space brokers, or reps, for the newspapers. Because they saved the media much of the expense of sales and collections, the media allowed the agencies to retain a 15 percent **media commission** on the space or time they purchased on behalf of their clients. That started a tradition that endures to this day, although it is now changing rapidly. Let's see how it works.

Say a national rate-card price for a full-page color magazine ad is $100,000. The magazine bills the agency, and the agency in turn bills the client for the $100,000. The client pays that amount to the agency, and the agency sends $85,000 to the magazine, keeping its 15 percent commission ($15,000). For large accounts, the agency typically provides extensive services (creative, media, accounting, and account management) for this commission. With dwindling profits, though, and clients negotiating smaller commissions, many agencies now must charge a fee for services that used to be free.[26]

Markups

In the process of creating an ad, the agency normally buys a variety of services or materials from outside suppliers—for example, photos and illustrations. The agency pays the supplier's charge and then adds a **markup** to the client's bill, typically 17.65 percent of the invoice (which becomes 15 percent of the new total).

For example, a markup of 17.65 percent on an $8,500 photography bill yields a $1,500 profit. When billing the client, the agency adds the $1,500 to the $8,500 for a new total of $10,000. When the client pays the bill, the agency keeps the $1,500 (15 percent of the total)—which, not coincidentally, is the standard commission agencies normally receive.

$$\$8,500 \times 17.65\% = \$1,500$$

$$\$8,500 + \$1,500 = \$10,000$$

$$\$10,000 \times 15\% = \$1,500$$

Some media—local newspapers, for example—allow a commission on the higher rates they charge national advertisers but not on the lower rates they charge local advertisers. So, to get their commission, local agencies have to use the markup formula above.

Today many agencies find that the markup doesn't cover their costs of handling the work, so they're increasing their markups to 20 or 25 percent. While this helps, agency profits are still under pressure, forcing many agencies to a fee system in place of, or in addition to, commissions and markups.

Fees

Clients today expect agencies to solve problems rather than just place ads, so fees are becoming more common. In fact, one study shows that only about one-third of national advertisers still rely on the traditional 15 percent commission system. An equal number now use some fee-based system. The rest use some modified commission or incentive system.[27]

There are two pricing methods in the fee system. With the **fee-commission combination,** the agency charges a basic monthly fee for all its services to the client and retains any media commissions earned. In the **straight-fee** or **retainer method,** agencies charge for all their services, either by the hour or by the month, and return any media commissions earned to the client. This latter method addresses a common objection to the commission system, namely that commissions incent agencies to recommend more media spending, rather than looking for ways to spend the client's money more efficiently. The fee method also addresses the fact that many clients are now using media buying services to purchase space and time.

Accountability is a major issue in client/agency relationships. With a new type of agency compensation, the **incentive system,** the agency earns more if the campaign attains specific, agreed-upon goals. DDB Needham, for example, offers its clients a "guaranteed results" program. If a campaign is successful, the agency earns more; if it fails, the agency earns less. Kraft General Foods rewards its agencies based on their performance. An A grade gets an extra 3 percent commission; C grades are put on review.[28] To avoid compensating agencies altogether, some advertisers create their own in-house advertising agencies.

CONCEPT CHECK

What are the pros and cons of the various methods of agency compensation?

The In-House Agency

Some companies set up a wholly owned **in-house agency** (or *house agency*) to save money and tighten control over their advertising. The in-house agency may do all the work of an independent full-service agency, including creative tasks, production, media placement, publicity, and sales promotion.

Advertisers with in-house agencies hope to save money by cutting overhead, keeping the media commission, and avoiding markups on outside purchases. Small, local advertisers in particular seek this goal.

Advertisers also expect more attention from their house agencies, which know the company's products and markets better and can focus all their resources to meet its deadlines. Management is often more involved in the advertising when it's done by company people, especially in "single-business" companies. And some in-house advertising is outstanding, especially in the fashion field.

Some companies such as Benetton (www.benetton.com) prefer to create ads using their own in-house agency. Advertisers hope to save money and gain more attention to their needs by using their house agency, but they can lose the greater experience, objectivity, and talent of an outside agency.

But usually companies sacrifice more than they gain. In-house flexibility is often won at the expense of creativity. Outside agencies typically offer greater experience, versatility, and a larger talent pool. In-house agencies have difficulty attracting and keeping the best creative people, who tend to prefer the variety and challenges offered by independent agencies.

The biggest risk for in-house agencies may be a loss of objectivity. In the shadow of internal politics, linear-thinking policymakers, and criticism from management, ads may become bland and self-serving, rather than imaginative messages relevant to customers. In advertising, that's the kiss of death.

> **CONCEPT CHECK**
>
> What might a company gain or lose by using an in-house agency?

The Client/Agency Relationship

Many factors affect the success of a company's advertising program, but one of the most important is the relationship between the advertiser and its agency.

How Agencies Get Clients

To succeed, advertising agencies need clients. New clients come from personal contact with top management, referrals from satisfied clients or advertising consultants, publicity on recent successful campaigns, trade advertising, direct-mail solicitation, or an agency's general reputation.[29] The three most successful ways to develop new business are having clients who strongly champion the agency, having superior presentation skills, and cultivating a personal relationship with a network of top executives.

Referrals

Most good agencies get clients by referral—from existing clients, friends, review consultants, or even other agencies. The head of one company asks another who's doing her ads, and the next week the agency gets a call. If a prospective client presents a conflict of interest with an existing client, the agency may decline the business and refer the prospect to another agency.[30]

Independent *agency review consultants* often help arrange marriages between agencies and clients. In fact, independent advisers were involved in many important account shuffles on Madison Avenue: Domino's Pizza, DirecTV, Burger King, Compaq computers, and Monster.com, to name just a few.[31]

Sales reps for media and suppliers frequently refer local advertisers to an agency they know. So it's important for agencies to maintain good relations with the media, suppliers, other agencies, and, of course, their existing clients.

Presentations

An advertiser may ask an agency to make a presentation (a pitch)—anything from a simple discussion of the agency's philosophy, experience, personnel, and track record to a full-blown audiovisual presentation of a proposed campaign. Successful agencies, therefore, need excellent presentation skills.

Some advertisers ask for or imply that they want a **speculative presentation,** meaning they want to see what the agency intends to do for them before they sign on. But most agencies prefer to build their presentations around the work they've already done, to demonstrate their capabilities without giving away ideas for a new campaign. Invariably, the larger the prospective client, the

Ethical Issues

Accounting for Account Reviews

Periodically, advertisers review the effectiveness of their campaigns and invite presentations from a variety of agencies. This process is referred to as an agency or account review. If the client's current agency is invited to participate, and the review is handled responsibly and respectfully, it can serve as a mutually beneficial tool in keeping the relationship between the client and the agency honest and open for both sides. Conversely, when used in an unethical manner, account reviews can be very destructive to the relationship, tarnishing the reputation of the client and/or the agency and damaging the integrity of the brand.

Historically, advertisers have been expected to show some allegiance to their current agency, unless that agency has mishandled a campaign through incompetence, misconduct, or simple ineffectiveness. Recently, though, client loyalty seems to be on the wane and agency reviews are on the rise. A survey by the American Association of Advertising Agencies, covering 175 agencies and their 3,700 accounts, shows that, between 1984 and 1997, the average length of the client/agency relationship dropped from 7.2 years to 5.3 years. Several examples illustrate this trend: United Airlines dumped Leo Burnett Chicago after 31 years; Delta Air Lines reviewed its 50-year relationship with BBDO Worldwide; and Colgate-Palmolive Co. shifted $200 million in billing from Foote, Cone & Belding to Y&R Advertising.

The increase in account reviews is linked to two recent changes in the traditional client/agency relationship. The first change lies in the very nature of the client/agency bond. The historical, brand-building marriage is on the decline, and vendor-based services are on the rise. Today's advertisers, focused on the bottom line, increasingly settle for a quick fix that will temporarily increase sales volume, as opposed to the long-run investment of working with one agency to create an established brand. Used in this way, agencies are treated like specialized vendors, hired to spur the movement of the product or service, and called in for review the moment that movement slows. Once a review is called, the chances of an agency keeping the account are slim—an informal survey by *Adweek* revealed that only 1 incumbent agency out of 12 actually survives a review.

The second change in the traditional client/agency relationship is agency consolidation. As the industry transforms from a wide array of agencies into a handful of superpowers, the odds of rival advertisers falling under the services of the same shop have increased. Many clients believe same-house representation creates a conflict of interest, sparking more account reviews. The agency BBDO provided a good example by pitching for an assignment from Eastman Kodak while still handling a competing client, Polaroid. When one found out about the other, BBDO lost both the Kodak pitch and the Polaroid business.

In addition to the fundamental changes in the structure of the client/agency relationship, many agency people cite other, more questionable motives as causes for review increases. One such basis for review, tied closely to the bottom line–oriented approach, is what Roger Lewis, a partner at Hoffman/Lewis, San Francisco, dubs the "BOSS Theory of Marketing—Blame Others, Save Self." The BOSS theory states: In the event an advertiser's sales decline, marketing directors look for the quick fix by calling an agency into review to create the perception that action is being taken to reverse the decline. Although unfair to the agency, the advertiser has an incentive to do so as an

bigger the presentation. Some agencies now spend upwards of $500,000 to stage a new business presentation.

The presentation process also allows the agency and the advertiser to get to know each other before they agree to work together. Advertising is a people business, so human qualities—mutual regard, trust, and communication—play an important role.

Networking and Community Relations

Agencies frequently find that the best source of new business is the people their employees know socially in the community. Some agencies work *pro bono* (for free) for charities or nonprofit organizations. Jo Muse at Muse Cordero Chen contributes time to the Rebuild L.A. campaign, which started after the civil disorders of 1992. He also serves the profession by volunteering on the government relations committee of the AAAA.

immediate means of bolstering management and shareholder confidence.

The lure of free creative work is a second questionable motivation for clients to hold account reviews. In conducting a review, clients ask the participating agencies to create mock presentations as a means of assessing the capabilities and creativity of each, in relation to the prospective account's current campaign. After reviewing these presentations, they may later incorporate these ideas into their campaigns without compensating the participating agencies.

The involvement of agency review consultants has also been questioned. Many within the industry believe that since review consultants are in the business of account reviews, it is in their best interest to see that account reviews happen more often. To stimulate account reviews, some review consultants are believed to have encouraged the BOSS theory, or suggested account reviews as a way of obtaining free creative work. In an article on "Conducting an Effective Advertising Agency Review," one marketing strategist suggests that "four agencies should be asked to produce twelve campaigns in total . . . [as] an opportunity to look at a vast amount of work built specifically to your needs."

On the agency side, the costs of participating in a review are escalating; the average per-pitch cost to an agency runs in the range of $60,000 to $75,000. This enormous cost incurred by participating agencies keeps many smaller agencies from competing for accounts, greatly reducing the competition within the industry over time.

Reviews can also be extremely damaging to the reputation of the incumbent agency, as other clients can only be led to wonder what caused their agency to lose an account. For Peter Drakoulias, director of business development at Interpublic's Deutsch, New York, agencies are "perceived as damaged goods" after losing an account—a status from which an agency may never recover.

On the client side, reviews can be equally damaging in terms of the health of a brand. If a brand is changing its identity and public perception often, it loses its integrity as consumers become skeptical of the product. Loyalty to one agency can create the stable brand recognition that comforts consumers and propels the sales of a brand. Before the rise in account reviews, long-term marriages were believed to give an agency "deep knowledge of the client and product, a deep knowledge of the essence of the brand, a deep knowledge of retail relationships and a deep knowledge of the customer," all of which are important in creating a strong brand.

If these questionable motivations continue to drive the desire for account reviews, client/agency relationships will suffer. Advertisers and agency review consultants have the power to ensure this does not happen by changing the way that account reviews are used and, in doing so, defining a fair and stable role for ad agencies in the years to come.

Questions

1. What degree of loyalty should clients have to agencies and vice versa? Is it ethical for agencies to represent multiple clients within the same industry?

2. Do you view some of the reasons for agency review to be unethical? What do you think might be done to reduce the number of account reviews driven by these questionable motivations?

3. How can the account review process be structured to more fairly incorporate smaller agencies? What can be done to lower the cost of participating in an agency review?

Agencies may help local politicians (a controversial practice in some areas) or contribute to the arts, education, religion, or the community. Some agencies sponsor seminars; others assist ad clubs or other professional organizations. All these activities help an agency gain visibility and respect in its community.

Soliciting and Advertising for New Business

Lesser-known agencies must take a more aggressive approach. An agency may solicit new business by advertising, writing letters, making cold calls, or following up leads from sources in the business. An agency principal usually takes the responsibility for soliciting new business, but staffers help prepare presentations.

Today, more agencies are advertising themselves. Many agencies submit their best ads to competitions around the world to win awards and gain publicity and professional respect for their creative excellence.[32]

The use of creative collateral material is often an effective way to get the attention of prospective customers, as demonstrated by the Honda dealer kit shown earlier. Fallon Worldwide (www.fallon.com) solicits new business in a similar manner, by mailing prospects an empty box with their phone number inside, along with a quarter to place the call.

Factors Affecting the Client/Agency Relationship

Many forces influence the client/agency relationship. Generally they can be grouped into the four Cs: *chemistry, communication, conduct,* and *changes.*

The most critical factor is the personal *chemistry* between the client's and the agency's staffs.[33] Agencies are very conscious of this factor and wine and dine their clients in hopes of improving relations. Smart clients do the same.

Poor *communication,* a problem often cited by both agencies and advertisers, leads to misunderstandings about objectives, strategies, roles, and expectations—and to poor advertising. Constant, open communication and an explicit agreement on mutual contribution for mutual gain are key to a good relationship.[34]

Dissatisfaction with agency *conduct,* or performance, is the most commonly cited reason for agency switches in every country.[35] The service the agency gave two years ago may not be valued by the client in the same way today.[36] Or perhaps the agency doesn't understand the client's marketing problems. And clients change, too. Does the client give the agency timely, accurate information? Does it appreciate good work, or does it treat the agency like a vendor?[37]

Changes occur in every relationship. Unfortunately, some of them damage the agency/client partnership. The client's market position or policies may change, or new management may arrive. Agencies may lose key staff people. Client conflicts may arise if one agency buys another that handles competing accounts. Legally, an ad agency cannot represent a client's competition without the client's consent.[38] Saatchi & Saatchi was forced to resign Helene Curtis under pressure from Saatchi's biggest client, Procter & Gamble.[39]

Perhaps the best way to improve understanding between clients and agencies would be to have staff members change places for a while. A Foote, Cone & Belding account executive did just that with great success, filling in temporarily as marketing manager at Levi's Jeans for Women. It gave her a whole new perspective on her agency job and the daily challenges faced by her client.[40]

CONCEPT CHECK

What can ad agencies do to increase their opportunities to get new clients and to retain existing ones?

The Suppliers in Advertising

The people and organizations that provide specialized services to the advertising business are called **suppliers.** Without their services it would be impossible to produce the billions of dollars' worth of advertising placed every year.

Although we can't mention them all, important suppliers include *art studios and Web design houses, printers, film and video production houses,* and *research companies.*

Art Studios and Web Designers

Art studios design and produce artwork and illustrations for advertisements. They may supplement the work of an agency's art department or even take its place for small agencies. Art studios are usually small organizations with as few as three or four employees. Some, though, are large enough to employ several art directors, graphic designers, layout artists, production artists, and sales reps.

Most studios are owned and managed by a graphic designer or illustrator, who calls on agencies and advertising managers to sell the studio's services, takes projects back to the office to be produced, and then delivers them for the client's approval. The work is very time-consuming and requires a talent for organization and management as well as a core competency in art direction and computer graphics.

Similar to art studios, **Web design houses** employ specialists who understand the intricacies of HTML and Java programming languages and can design ads and Web pages that are both effective and cost efficient.

Printers and Related Specialists

The printers who produce brochures, stationery, business cards, sales promotion materials, and point-of-purchase displays are vital to the advertising business. Ranging from small instant-print shops to large offset operations, **printers** employ or contract with highly trained specialists who prepare artwork for reproduction, operate digital scanning machines to make color separations and plates, operate presses and collating machines, and run binderies.

As we discuss in Chapter 10, printers may specialize in offset lithography, rotogravure, letterpress, or other techniques. Their sales reps must be highly skilled, and they often earn very large commissions.

Film and Video Houses

Few agencies have in-house TV production capabilities. Small agencies often work with local TV stations to produce commercials. But the large agencies normally work with independent **production houses** that specialize in film or video production or both.

Research Companies

Advertisers are concerned about the attitudes of their customers, the size of potential markets, and the acceptability of their products. Agencies want to know what advertising approaches to use, which concepts communicate most efficiently, and how effective past campaigns have been.

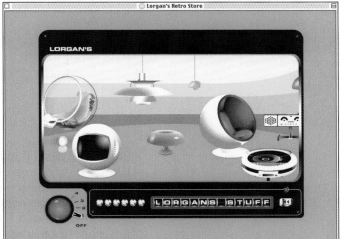

As the Internet continues to grow at an alarming speed, so does the demand for Web design houses that understand both the intricacies of programming languages and the various elements of good Web design. This Web site for Lorgan's, The Retro Store (www.lorgans.com), a specialist store dealing in retro furnishings, won a gold from the One Show Interactive in the category Corporate Image. A unique feature of the site was that it was created so that a person interested in '70s stuff would find himself or herself immersed in a '70s environment as he or she browsed the merchandise.

Exhibit 3–8

Top media companies in 2004, by category (revenue figures in millions of U.S. dollars).

Newspapers		Broadcast Television	
1. Gannett Co.	$4,951	1. Viacom	$8,505
2. Tribune Co.	4,109	2. NBC Universal	7,487
3. New York Times Co.	3,143	3. Walt Disney Co.	4,756
4. Knight Ridder	2,900	4. News Corp.	4,538
5. Advance Publications	2,285	5. Tribune Co.	1,354

Magazines		Cable Networks	
1. Time Warner	$4,851	1. Time Warner	$8,354
2. Advance Publications	2,420	2. Viacom	6,698
3. Hearst Corp.	1,837	3. Walt Disney Co.	6,410
4. Meredith Corp.	1,534	4. News Corp.	2,492
5. Primedia	1,206	5. NBC Universal	2,110

Radio		Internet	
1. Clear Channel Comm.	$3,754	1. Time Warner	$8,692
2. Viacom	2,096	2. Yahoo!	2,653
3. Walt Disney Co.	612	3. Google	2,083
4. Westwood One	562	4. MSN Network	1,197
5. Cox Enterprises	438	5. Dow Jones & Co.	381

The media are concerned with the reading and viewing habits of their audiences, the desired markets of their advertiser-customers, and public perceptions toward their own particular medium.

Research, therefore, is closely allied to advertising and an important tool for marketing professionals. But most firms do not maintain a fully staffed research department. Instead, they use independent **research suppliers** or consultants. Research firms come in all sizes and specialties, and they employ statisticians, field interviewers, and computer programmers, as well as analysts with degrees in psychology, sociology, and marketing. We discuss research in Chapter 6.

The Media of Advertising

The *medium* that carries the advertiser's message is the vital connection between the company that manufactures a product or offers a service and the customer who may wish to buy it. Although the plural term **media** commonly describes channels of mass communication such as television, radio, newspapers, and magazines, it also refers to other communications vehicles such as direct mail, out-of-home media (transit, billboards, etc.), specialized media (aerial/blimps, inflatables), specialty advertising items (imprinted coffee mugs, balloons), and new communication technologies such as digital media, interactive TV, and satellite networks. (Exhibit 3–8 shows the largest U.S. media companies.)

It is important to understand the various media, their role in the advertising business, and the significance of current media trends. For a person seeking a career in advertising, the media may offer the first door to employment, and for many they have provided great financial rewards.

We classify advertising media into six major categories: print, electronic, digital interactive, out-of-home, direct mail, and other media. Due to recent media trends, there is some overlap. These media categories are discussed in Chapters 11–14.

Chapter Summary

The advertising business comprises four main groups: advertisers (clients), agencies, suppliers, and media. It employs a wide range of artists and businesspeople, sales reps and engineers, top executives, and clerical personnel.

There are four main categories of advertisers based on their geographic activities: local, regional, national, and transnational. Local advertising is placed by businesses in a particular city or county and aimed at customers in the same geographic area. It is important because most sales are made or lost in the local arena.

Regional advertisers operate in one or several states and market exclusively within that region. National advertisers operate in several regions or throughout the country and comprise the largest advertisers.

A large company's advertising department may be centralized or decentralized. Each structure has advantages and disadvantages. The centralized organization is the most typical and may be structured by product, subfunction of advertising, end user, or geography. Decentralized departments are typical of large, far-flung organizations with numerous divisions, subsidiaries, products, countries, regions, and/or brands.

Transnational advertisers face unique challenges. Their markets have different value systems, environments, and languages with customers of different purchasing abilities, habits, and motivations. Media that are customary in the United States may be unavailable or ineffective. Companies therefore often need different advertising strategies. To manage their advertising, transnational advertisers use an international, multinational, or global marketing structure.

Ad agencies are independent organizations of creative people and businesspeople who specialize in developing and preparing advertising plans, ads, and other promotional tools on behalf of their clients.

Like their clients, ad agencies may be local, regional, national, or international in scope. Agencies can be classified by the range of services they offer and the types of business they handle. The two basic types are full-service agencies and specialized service agencies, such as creative boutiques, media-buying services, and interactive agencies. Agencies may specialize in either consumer or business-to-business accounts. The people who work in agencies may be involved in account management, research, account planning, creative services, production, traffic, media, new business, administration, or a host of other activities.

Agencies may be organized into departments of functional specialties or into groups that work as teams on various accounts. Agencies charge fees or retainers, receive commissions from the media, or mark up outside purchases made for their clients.

Some advertisers develop in-house agencies to save money by keeping agency commissions for themselves. However, they risk losing objectivity and creativity.

Most agencies get clients through referrals, publicity on successful campaigns, advertising, personal solicitation, or networking. Numerous factors can affect the client/agency relationship, including chemistry, communication, conduct, and changes.

The suppliers in advertising are all the people and organizations that assist in the business. Examples are art studios and Web designers, printers, film and video houses, talent agencies, research firms, and consultants.

The media of advertising include the traditional mass media of print, electronic, and out-of-home as well as more specialized channels such as direct mail, digital interactive media, and specialty advertising.

Key Terms

account executive (AE), 74
account planning, 75
account supervisor, 74
advertiser, 60
advertising agency, 60, 71
art directors, 76
art studios, 85
brand manager, 67
business-to-business agency, 73
centralized advertising department, 66
classified advertising, 62
cooperative (co-op) advertising, 63

copy, 76
copywriter, 76
creative boutique, 73
creative director, 76
decentralized system, 67
departmental system, 77
fee-commission combination, 79
foreign media, 70
full-service advertising agency, 72
general consumer agency, 72
global marketer, 69
group system, 78

incentive system, 80
in-house agency, 80
institutional advertising, 62
integrated marketing communications (IMC), 63
interactive agency, 74
international agency, 72
international media, 70
local advertising, 61
local agency, 72
management supervisor, 74
markup, 79

Review Questions

1. Almost half of advertising dollars are spent on local advertising. Why is local advertising so important?

2. What are the three types of local advertising and what purposes do they serve?

3. Why do wholesalers and manufacturers provide co-op advertising funds and materials to local advertisers?

4. What services might a modern full-service advertising agency offer a large business-to-business advertiser?

5. What additional challenges are faced by companies that advertise internationally?

6. How do the media in other countries tend to differ from that which we are accustomed to in the United States?

7. Why do so many advertisers hire ad agencies?

8. In what ways does the role of an Account Planner differ from that of an Account Executive?

9. What are the most important things an advertiser should consider when selecting an agency?

10. What is the best way to compensate an agency? Explain your answer.

Exploring Advertising

1. Select the advertising agency position that is most appealing to you. Describe what educational background, work experience, skills, and personality might be most appropriate for that position. Search the Internet for recruitment ads for that position to confirm your answers.

2. Your agency is paid on a traditional 15 percent media commission. You purchase $300,000 in network TV time to run an ad for your client. How much will your client pay for the TV time? How much will the network receive? How much will the agency be paid?

   The ad you ran cost $30,000 to produce. Your agency charges a 17.65 percent markup for production costs. How much will your client pay for the production? How much will your agency receive?

3. Select an advertising agency that interests you. You may admire its campaigns or you might be interested in it as a possible employer. Write a review of the agency organization and philosophy including as much of the following information possible. Consider using the *Standard Directory of Advertising Agencies,* Web sites, annual reports, *Advertising Age,* and *Adweek* as sources.

   - Agency size: billings and number of employees
   - Corporate affiliation (part of a holding company?)
   - Locations of major offices
   - Top officers of the company
   - Key clients
   - Most notable campaigns
   - Brief agency history
   - Agency philosophy
   - What makes this agency unique?

   If you were an advertiser seeking an agency, why might this agency appeal to you? What if you were a job seeker?

chapter four

Segmentation, Targeting, and the Marketing Mix

Objectives

To describe how marketers use behavioral characteristics to cluster prospective customers into market segments. Because no product or service pleases everybody, marketers need to select specific target markets that offer the greatest sales potential. Thus, they can fine-tune their mix of product-related elements (the four Ps), including advertising, to match the needs or wants of the target market.

After studying this chapter, you will be able to:

* **Describe** the role of marketing in creating satisfying exchanges.

* **Explain** the role of advertising in communicating a product's utility.

* **Identify** the various methods advertisers use to segment and aggregate consumer and business markets.

* **Discuss** how target marketing affects the firm's advertising strategy.

* **Describe** the elements of the marketing mix and the role of advertising in the mix.

* **Explain** the purpose and importance of branding.

"It's how the last place you'd go for a burger will become the first." Apologies for past mistakes rarely appear in advertising campaigns, but after years of declining sales, bloated menus, and failed comeback attempts, Hardee's had to innovate. The fast-food hamburger chain went with Mendelsohn/Zien's surprising approach as a way to level with consumers and give the brand a fresh start, said Brad Haley, Hardee's executive vice president of marketing.[1]

But what would the fast-food hamburger chain, owned by CKE Restaurants, Inc., do differently now? Something unorthodox: sell big, premium hamburgers in the midst of the 2001–2002 "burger wars," when the major burger chains were slashing prices on their sandwiches.[2] Building on the Six-Dollar Burger concept pioneered by Carl's Jr. (another CKE-owned chain), Hardee's introduced its Thickburger in January 2003. At the same time it began marketing its heftier sandwiches, Hardee's tightened the focus of its menu, eliminating dozens of lunch and dinner menu items.[3]

The Thickburger television ad campaign targeted the young male demographic by featuring brawny, "real" men enjoying the burgers. Further underscoring the campaign's focus, subsequent Thickburger spots proclaimed that the burgers "don't come with toys, because they're not for little boys."

As these examples illustrate, ads target their demographic on more than one level. The burgers must meet consumer taste expectations, of course, but the Thickburger commercials also trade directly on the notion of male identity ("real" men want "real," substantial burgers) and indirectly (eating Thickburgers shows that you're a "real" man). In a twist on the old saying "you are what you eat," the campaign implicitly tells young males that eating Thickburgers is more than just a fast-food choice; it says something about who you are.

Hardee's followed up their machismo campaign with recycled Carl's Jr. spots that showed women enjoying juicy, sloppy burgers in racy scenes. For a Western Thickburger spot, a model rides a mechanical bull, sensuously swaying and chewing, to the soundtrack of Foghat's "Slow Ride." A letter from the American Families Association demanded the ad be pulled because "it is degrading to women and not an appropriate message for our children. . . . Hardee's should not be in the business of marketing sex in order to sell hamburgers."[4]

Despite the criticism, Hardee's and Mendelsohn/Zien's decision to zero in on such a narrow group is paying off thus far. The advertising campaign's savvy combination of frankness, higher-quality ingredients, and testosterone helped the company's recovery. In early 2004, Hardee's began to look toward a different market segment. Thanks in part to broad interest in protein-heavy, low-carbohydrate diets—which the chain specifically catered to by introducing its lettuce-wrapped Low-Carb Thickburger[5]—same-store sales and profit margins improved markedly in 2004 over the previous year, sparking positive comments from the business community.

The Larger Marketing Context of Advertising

All advertisers face a perennial challenge: how to present their products, services, and ideas effectively through the media to buyers. To do this, they must comprehend the important relationship between the product and the marketplace. That relationship is the province of marketing.

Unfortunately, marketing's role is often misunderstood and occasionally overlooked. For example, everybody knows that a business can't survive with-

The Honda Element (www.honda.com) was designed to provide form utility—to meet the functional needs of its target market. This print ad clearly communicates the Element's utility.

Commercial Break 4–A

Understanding Needs and Utility

Superior quality will not close a sale by itself. Marketing people must make the product available and promote its advantages, whether it's a graphite tennis racket, a high-performance sports car, or even the prompt, friendly service of a bank.

A key fact in any product's success is that it must satisfy consumers' *needs*. The capability to satisfy those needs is called *utility*. Five types of functional utility are important to consumers: form, task, possession, time, and place. A product may provide psychic utility as well as functional utility.

Companies create *form utility* whenever they produce a tangible good, such as a bicycle. They provide *task utility* by performing a task for others. However, merely producing a bicycle—or repairing it—doesn't guarantee consumer satisfaction. Consumers must want the bicycle or require the repair, or no need is satisfied and no utility occurs. Thus, marketing decisions should guide the production side of business too.

Even when a company provides form or task utility, marketers must consider how consumers can take possession of the product. This includes distribution, pricing strategies, shelf availability, purchase agreements, and delivery. Money is typically exchanged for possession utility. An antique bicycle on display, but not for sale, lacks *possession utility* because the customer cannot purchase it.

Providing the consumer with the product when he or she wants it is known as *time utility*. Having an ample supply of jam, cars, or bank tellers on hand when the consumer has the need is thus another marketing requirement.

Place utility—having the product available where the customer can get it—is also vital to business success. Customers won't travel very far out of their way to get bicycles or cars. They're even less likely to travel long distances for everyday needs. That's why banks have branches. And that's why 24-hour convenience markets, which sell gasoline and basic food items, are so popular.

Finally, consumers gain *psychic utility* when a product offers symbolic or psychological need satisfaction, such as status or sex appeal. Psychic utility is usually achieved through product promotion (advertising) and may fulfill esteem and self-actualization needs.

Whether it be psychic utility or the functional utilities of form, task, possession, time, and place, product utility is an essential component of marketing success.

Applying the Breaks

Select an ad from a weekly newsmagazine and describe in detail what utilities it speaks to: psychic utility and/or the functional utilities of form, task, possession, time, and place.

out proper financing, and, without production, there are no products to sell. But how does a company know what products or services to produce? Or where to distribute them, or through what channels? That's where marketing comes in.

The key to a company's prosperity is the ability to attract and keep customers who are willing and able to pay for the firm's goods and services. This means a company must be able to locate prospective customers; create products and services to satisfy their desires; and finally communicate that information in a way that resonates with them.

Customer Needs and Product Utility

As we discussed in Chapter 1, marketing is the business process that management uses to plan and execute the conception, pricing, promotion, and distribution of its products, whether they be goods, services, brands, or even ideas. The ultimate purpose of marketing is to *create exchanges that satisfy the perceived needs and wants of individuals and organizations*.

One of the important elements of that definition is the special relationship between a customer's needs and a product's need-satisfying potential. This is known as the product's *utility*. **Utility** is the product's ability to satisfy both functional needs and symbolic (or psychological) wants.[6] One of the primary roles of advertising is to communicate this utility. Thus, some ads promote how well a product works (function); others tout glamour, sex appeal, or status (symbolism). Commercial Break 4–A discusses the important relationship between needs and utility.

Advertisers know that satisfying a consumer's self-interest is central to affecting purchasing behavior. This ad for Audi (www.audi.com) appeals to consumers' desire to feel eternally youthful.

Through the use of marketing research, companies try to discover what needs and wants exist in the marketplace. The goal is to use this information for product shaping—designing products, through manufacturing, packaging, or advertising, to satisfy more fully the customers' needs and wants.

To woo Gen Xers and Echo Boomers (the children of baby boomers), for example, Ford Motor Company developed Focus—a low-priced sporty compact car. Optional extras included a sports rack and an unconventional, removable pet holder with a foldable dish, designed to keep Rover from sliding around on the seat. The company also gave buyers the choice of flowers or swirls on the outside and fleece, jersey, or neoprene on the seats. Ford's marketers uncovered the customers' needs and wants and developed a product to satisfy them.

Businesspeople all too often give the marketing process short shrift. Some companies introduce a product without a clear idea of its utility to the customer, hoping advertising will move the product off the shelf.

Exchanges: The Purpose of Marketing and Advertising

Any transaction in which one person or organization trades something of value with someone else is an **exchange.** Exchange is the traditional, theoretical core of marketing. We all engage in exchanges. It's a natural part of our human self-interest. Buyers do it to acquire more things and better their situation. Sellers do it to grow their business and make a profit.

Marketing facilitates these exchanges, thus increasing our potential for satisfaction. How does it do this? In a variety of ways: by developing goods and services we might want; by pricing them affordably; by distributing them to convenient locations; and by informing us about them through advertising and other communication tools. By providing information, advertising makes people aware of the availability of products and of the selection alternatives among different brands. Advertising communicates product features and benefits, various price options, and locations where the product can be found. In the case of direct marketing, advertising may even close the sale.

This chapter defines and outlines marketing issues to clarify advertising's proper role in the marketing function. As we shall see, the relationship between advertising and marketing is critical.

CONCEPT CHECK

Describe the role advertising plays in facilitating exchanges and satisfying needs and wants.

The Market Segmentation Process

Recall from our discussion in Chapter 1 that marketing and advertising strategies evolved over time as more and more products entered the marketplace and competed for consumer dollars and approval. During the 1950s and 1960s, the *unique selling proposition (USP)* held sway as marketers built new and different properties into their products to tout in their advertising. Then in the 1960s and 1970s, as me-too products glutted mass markets, the strategy of *market segmentation* came to the fore. This meant developing products to meet the needs and wants of particular market segments. Then, as major market segments became saturated and product life cycles grew shorter, marketers developed new approaches, such as positioning, marketing warfare, niche marketing, micromarketing, and now even one-to-one marketing.

All of these are variations on basic market segmentation strategy, except that today segments are getting smaller. Thanks to modern technology, companies can satisfy the needs of smaller segments and still make a profit. It's important for advertising people to have a solid understanding of the principles of market segmentation. In the twenty-first century, the task of finding profitable market segments will be even more challenging.

In the voiceover for the ad that shows model Cameron Richardson riding a mechanical bull in slow motion, Hardee's (www.hardees.com) confirms that market segmentation is at work: "We could've shown you some cowboy, sitting around a campfire, eating a Western Bacon Thickburger . . . but who'd wanna see that?" The answer, of course, is not the young men at whom the campaign is targeted.

Marketing and advertising people constantly scan the marketplace to see what various consumer segments need and want and how they might be better satisfied. Today, the process of **market segmentation** is actually a two-step strategy of *identifying* groups of people (or organizations) with certain shared needs and characteristics within the broad markets for consumer or business products and *aggregating* (combining) these groups into larger market segments according to their mutual interest in the product's utility. This process gives a company a selection of market segments large enough to target and lays the foundation for developing the proper mix of marketing activities—including advertising.

Markets often consist of many segments. A company may differentiate products and marketing strategy for every segment, or concentrate its marketing activities on only one or a few segments. Either task is far from simple. Hardee's worked to rebuild its brand by targeting a broad segment: its disaffected former clientele. After the damage-control phase, Hardee's was ready to reconnect with a narrower market segment. The company began to differentiate its advertising campaigns; although it mostly attempted to lure young males with ever-bigger burgers, Hardee's also made some attempt to target other segments with different products. Catering to all these needs on a global level requires a sophisticated marketing and communications system. In this chapter, we look first at how marketers identify and categorize *consumer markets* and second at the techniques they use to segment *business markets*. Then we discuss various strategic options companies use, including advertising, to match their products with markets and create profitable exchanges.

Types of Markets

A firm's marketing activities are always aimed at a particular segment of the population—its *target market*. Likewise, advertising is aimed at a particular group called the *target audience*. When we see an ad that doesn't appeal to us, it may be because the ad is not aimed at any of the groups we belong to. For example, a TV commercial for denture cream isn't meant to appeal to youngsters. They're not part of either the target market or the target audience. There are two main types of target markets, consumers and businesses.

Consumer Markets

Most of the advertising we see daily in the mass media—TV, radio, newspapers, and magazines—falls under the broad category of consumer advertising. Usually sponsored by the producer (or manufacturer) of the product or service, these ads are typically directed at consumers, people who buy the product for their own or someone else's personal use. The consumer market is huge, spending close to $7.4 trillion every year on products and services in the United States alone.[7]

In the end, customers are people. So advertising professionals must understand how people act and think—and why they buy what they buy. This requires great skill. In fact, this area of study is the province of another specialty in marketing, consumer behavior, a topic we'll discuss in Chapter 5.

Business Markets

Companies use business advertising to reach people who buy goods and services that they resell, use to conduct their business, or use to manufacture another product. It tends to appear in specialized business publications or professional journals, in direct-mail pieces sent to businesses, or in trade shows. Since business advertising (also called business-to-business, or BTB, advertising) rarely uses consumer mass media, it is typically invisible to consumers.

However, nearly half of all marketing is business-to-business. In the United States, business buyers purchase nearly $4 trillion worth of manufactured goods every year, billions more of raw materials, and billions more for the services of law firms, accountants, airlines, and advertising agencies.[8]

Business customers are often very knowledgeable, sophisticated buyers, and they may require extensive technical information before making the purchase decision. So people who work in business-to-business advertising often need more specialized product knowledge and experience than their consumer advertising colleagues.

Segmenting the Consumer Market: Finding the Right Niche

The concept of *shared characteristics* is critical to market segmentation. Marketing and advertising people know that, based on their needs, wants, and mental files, consumers leave "footprints in the sand"—the telltale signs of where they live and work, what they buy, and how they spend their leisure time. By following these footprints, marketers can locate and define groups of consumers with similar needs and wants, create messages for them, and know how and where to send those messages. The goal is to find that particular niche (or space) in the market, where the advertiser's product or service will fit.

Marketers group these shared characteristics into categories *(behavioristic, geographic, demographic, and psychographic)* to identify and segment consumer markets (see Exhibit 4–1). The marketers' purpose is twofold: first, to identify people who are likely to be responsive; and second, to develop rich descriptions of them in order to better understand them, create marketing mixes for them, and reach them with meaningful advertising or other communications.

Behavioristic segmentation is one of the best ways to segment consumer markets. Purchase behavior variables, such as the benefits sought by the consumer, determine how the segmentations are made. In this ad, Hunan Garden targets Chinese food aficionados with a tongue-in-cheek promise that the Chinese food eaten is better than the English spoken.

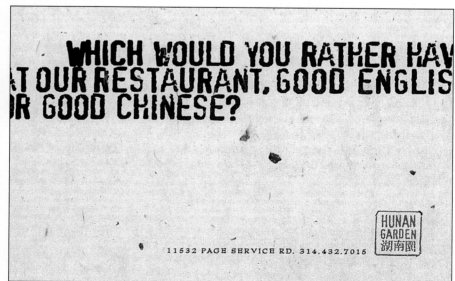

WHICH WOULD YOU RATHER HAV
T OUR RESTAURANT, GOOD ENGLIS
R GOOD CHINESE?

HUNAN
GARDEN
湖南園

11532 PAGE SERVICE RD. 314.432.7015

Exhibit 4–1

Methods for segmenting consumer markets.

Variables	Typical breakdowns	Variables	Typical breakdowns
Geographic		**Demographic**	
Region	Pacific; Mountain; West North Central; West South Central; East North Central; East South Central; South Atlantic; Middle Atlantic; New England	Age	Under 6, 6–11, 12–19, 20–34, 35–49, 50–64, 65+
County size	A, B, C, D	Sex	Male, female
Climate	Northern; southern	Family size	1–2, 3–4, 5+
City or SMSA size	Under 5,000; 5,000–19,999; 20,000–49,999; 50,000–99,999; 100,000–249,000; 250,000–499,999; 500,000–999,999; 1,000,000–3,999,999; 4,000,000 or over	Family life cycle	Young, single; young, married, no children; young, married, youngest child under 6; young, married, youngest child 6 or over; young, unmarried, with children; older, married, with children; older, unmarried, with children; older, married, no children under 18; older, single; other
Density	Urban, suburban, rural		
Behavioristic		Income	Under $10,000; $10,000–20,000; $20,000–30,000; $30,000–40,000; $40,000–60,000; $60,000–100,000; $100,000–150,000; $150,000 and over
Purchase occasion	Regular occasion, special occasion		
Benefits sought	Economy, convenience, prestige		
User status	Nonuser, ex-user, potential user, first-time user, regular user	Occupation	Professional and technical; managers, officials, and proprietors; clerical, sales; craftspeople, supervisors; operatives; farmers; retired; students; homemakers; unemployed
Usage rate	Light user, medium user, heavy user		
Loyalty status	None, medium, strong, absolute		
Readiness stage	Unaware, aware, informed, interested, desirous, intending to buy		
Marketing-factor sensitivity	Quality, price, service, advertising, sales promotion	Education	Grade school or less; some high school; high school graduates; some college; college graduates
Psychographic		Religion	Catholic, Protestant, Jewish, other
Societal divisions	Upper crust, movers and shakers, successful singles, social security, middle of the road, metro ethnic mix	Race	White, Black, Asian
		Nationality	American, British, French, German, Scandinavian, Italian, Latin American, Middle Eastern, Japanese
Lifestyle	Strivers, achievers, actualizers		
Personality	Compulsive, gregarious, authoritarian, ambitious		

Behavioristic Segmentation

One of the best ways to segment markets is to group consumers by purchase behavior. This is called **behavioristic segmentation.** Behavioral segments are determined by many variables, but the most important are *user status, usage rate, purchase occasion,* and *benefits sought.* These categories tell us who our customers are now, when and why they buy, and how much they consume.

User-status variables   Many markets can be segmented by the **user status** of prospective customers. Researchers Stephan and Tannenholz have identified six categories of consumers based on user status.

Sole users are the most brand loyal and require the least amount of advertising and promotion. *Semisole* users typically use Brand A but have an alternate selection if it is not available or if the alternate is promoted with a discount. *Discount users* are the semisole users of competing Brand B. They don't buy Brand A at full price but perceive it well enough to buy it at a discount. *Aware nontriers* use competitive products in the category but haven't taken a liking to Brand A. A different advertising message could help, but these people rarely offer much potential. *Trial/rejectors* bought Brand A's advertising message, but didn't like the product. More advertising won't help; only a reformulation of Brand A will bring them back. *Repertoire users* perceive two or more brands to have

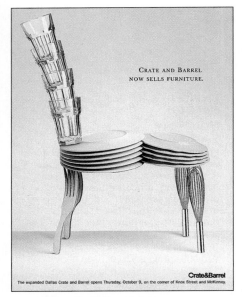

CRATE AND BARREL
NOW SELLS FURNITURE.

Crate&Barrel

The expanded Dallas Crate and Barrel opens Thursday, October 9, on the corner of Knox Street and McKinney.

While Crate and Barrel (www.
crateandbarrel.com) is better known for its
extensive kitchenware, it uses its strong
brand name to promote its furniture. For
sole users, this ad reinforces the brand and
for repertoire users—those most likely to
alternate between brands they believe to be
equally superior—it enhances brand
perception.

superior attributes and will buy at full price. They are the primary brand
switchers and respond to persuasive advertising based on their fluctuating
wants and desires. Therefore, they should be a primary target for brand
advertising.[9]

Usage-rate variables   It's usually easier to get a heavy user to increase
usage than a light user. In **volume segmentation,** marketers measure
people's **usage rates** to define consumers as light, medium, or heavy
users of products (see Exhibit 4–2). Often, 20 percent of the population
consumes 80 percent of the product. Marketers want to define that 20
percent and aim their advertising at them. Hardee's even has a pet name
for its prized 17- to 34-year-old male market segment: the HFFU (pronounced who-foo). According to Andrew Pudzer, CKE's CEO, "That's
the 'heavy fast-food user,' someone who eats there four or five times a
week. . . . It is the sweet spot of the industry and what appeals to him is
drippy, messy burgers. He is not interested in little 99-cent burgers or
low-carb anything."[10]

By finding common characteristics among heavy users of their products, marketers can define product differences and focus ad campaigns
more effectively. For example, heavy users of bowling alleys tend to be
working-class men between 25 and 50 who watch more than three and
one-half hours of television a day and prefer sports programs. So a bowling equipment company would probably want to advertise on TV sports
programs.

Marketers of one product sometimes find that their customers are also
heavy users of other products and can define target markets in terms of the
usage rates of the other products. Research indicates that heavy users of
home computers are also heavy users of foreign luxury cars, sports cars, back-
packing equipment, binoculars, expensive bicycles, and literary magazines.[11]

Purchase-occasion variables   Buyers can also be distinguished by when they buy
or use a product or service—the **purchase occasion.** Air travelers, for example, may fly for business or vacation so one airline might promote business
travel while another promotes tourism. The purchase occasion might be
affected by frequency of need (regular or occasional), a fad (candy, computer

Exhibit 4–2

Usage rates vary for different products.

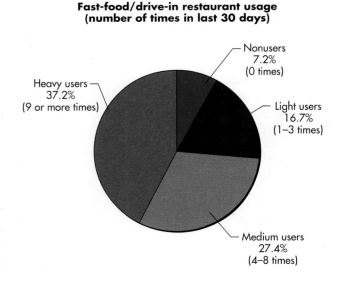

**Fast-food/drive-in restaurant usage
(number of times in last 30 days)**

Nonusers
7.2%
(0 times)

Heavy users
37.2%
(9 or more times)

Light users
16.7%
(1–3 times)

Medium users
27.4%
(4–8 times)

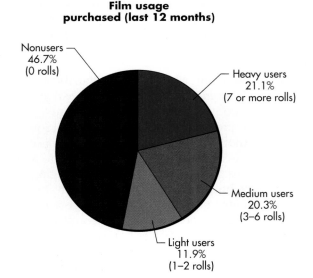

**Film usage
purchased (last 12 months)**

Nonusers
46.7%
(0 rolls)

Heavy users
21.1%
(7 or more rolls)

Medium users
20.3%
(3–6 rolls)

Light users
11.9%
(1–2 rolls)

games), or seasons (water skis, raincoats). The Japan Weather Association tracked buying patterns on 20,000 items and correlated them to the outside temperature. Not surprisingly, when the temperature goes up, people buy more sunshades, air conditioners, watermelons, and swimwear. When there's a chill in the air, sales of suits, sweaters, and heaters take off.[12] A marketer who discovers common purchase occasions for a group has a potential target segment and can better determine when to run specials and when to promote certain product categories.

Benefits-sought variables   Marketers may segment consumers on the benefits being sought. Consumers seek various **benefits** in the products they buy—high quality, low price, status, sex appeal, good taste, health-conscious. Hardee's customers may value the size and taste of Thickburgers, or they may prefer the low-carb, bunless chicken sandwich that has only half the fat. And often consumers are motivated by *symbolism*—what the brand name means to them, to associates, or to some social reference group. **Benefit segmentation** is the prime objective of many consumer attitude studies and the basis for many successful ad campaigns.

This Hardee's ad is clearly using behavioristic segmentation. Marketing of the Thickburger is directed at consumers who seek the benefit of large, meaty burgers.

Some product categories are characterized by substantial *brand switching* from one purchase occasion to the next. Researchers have determined that switching occurs in response to different *need states* that consumers may experience from one occasion to another.

Using behavioristic segmentation, we can accomplish the first step of identifying likely prospects for our marketing and advertising efforts. The next step in developing rich profiles of these customers involves the use of geographic, demographic, and psychographic characteristics.

Geographic Segmentation

One simple way to define markets is by using **geographic segmentation.** People in one region of the country (or the world) have needs, wants, and purchasing habits that differ from those in other regions. People in Sun Belt states, for example, buy more suntan lotion. Canadians buy special equipment for dealing with snow and ice—products many Floridians have never seen in stores.

Seasonal usage is a common way to segment users. In fact, the purchase occasion provides insight into the most opportune sales periods. For this reason, Columbia Sportswear (www.columbia.com) may run its ads in fall and winter—just before and during the peak season for snow sports.

When marketers analyze geographic data, they study sales by region, country size, city size, specific locations, and types of stores. Many products sell well in urban areas but poorly in suburban or rural ones, and vice versa. As we'll see in Chapter 15, this type of information is critical in developing advertising media schedules because with limited budgets, marketers want to advertise in areas where their sales potential is best.

Even in local markets, geographic segmentation is important. For example, a local progressive politician might send a mailer only to precincts where voters typically support liberal

Ethical Issues

Brand Niching May Cause Brand Switching

Advertisers recognize that offensive advertisements don't pay. They know that alienating or stereotyping minorities and other demographic groups causes serious controversy and bad PR for their clients. And, in addition to avoiding the negative effects, there are benefits to being politically correct in advertising: Hispanics, African Americans, Asian Americans, gays, and other minority groups are all sizable target markets with considerable buying power—so much buying power, in fact, that many marketing campaigns are designed specifically to appeal to these market sectors.

Unfortunately, even advertisements that are designed to be sensitive can sometimes backfire. During the 2000 Olympics, John Hancock Financial Services made a sudden revision to a commercial set to air during the events. In the spot, two women were shown together in an airport holding an Asian infant whom they presumably had just adopted. Although the ad never specifically identified the child's nationality, international adoption agencies pressured Hancock to amend the ad to avoid offending the Chinese government, which would be opposed to the evident homosexuality of the American parents. But Hancock was lucky—the ad was caught before it aired. This isn't always the case, and the results can be disastrous when a controversial ad is aired.

To counter recent accusations that they favored white clientele over their African American patrons, Denny's created some ads that attempted to resolve the issue—badly. The three-spot television campaign featured black customers being "welcomed back" to Denny's and having the time of their lives. However, 100 percent of the people Denny's "welcomed back" were black, affluent, well-dressed, and apparently aristocratic and successful. One would think that if they were going to solely feature African American customers in the ad, they would do so with a fair representation of the group. Instead of creating an ad that proved Denny's was racially unbiased, as intended, the company had displayed the same behavior it was trying to resolve. Although the company later worked to improve its image, the damage was done.

Not only businesses and retailers have these problems; not-for-profit and government organizations also have to watch their step. During the 2002 Super Bowl, the White House introduced a new series of antidrug public service announcements. The campaign tried to link the money spent on drugs to the funding of terrorist activities. Print and television ads in muted black-and-white traced teens' use of drugs for recreation through the supply chain back to tragic, violent episodes in drug-producing regions. To say that the guilt-trip method did not go over well with teenagers would be putting it mildly. Teens felt that the ads were deliberately manipulative and misrepresented the facts in an attempt to support President George W. Bush's war on terrorism. As a result, studies showed that, over time, teens exposed to the ads shifted to a significantly more "prodrug" attitude than those of kids who did not view the ads. In short, the ads fostered enough resentment among their target audience that teens deliberately defied the message being sent.

Advertising sensitivity is a difficult issue. What is politically correct enough? When is something too politically correct? And what should be done when a conflict cannot be avoided? Some groups simply cannot be targeted without excluding, and thereby offending, other groups. When this happens, a choice must be made, and it must be made carefully, with serious consideration of all potential consequences.

causes, and a local retail store rarely draws customers from outside a fairly limited *trading area*.

Demographic Segmentation

Demographic segmentation is a way to define population groups by their statistical characteristics: sex, age, ethnicity, education, occupation, income, and other quantifiable factors. For example, research shows that people who identify themselves as "strongly Hispanic" tend to be very loyal to certain brands. And, as Exhibit 4–3 reveals, Hispanic media have recently experienced a boom. Many blue-chip advertisers, such as Procter & Gamble, AT&T, McDonald's, and General Motors, now aim a significant portion of their advertising specifically at this $675 billion market.[12b]

Demographics are often combined with geographic segmentation to select target markets for advertising. This is called **geodemographic segmentation.** JCPenney, for example, discovered that its Sandra Salcedo line of clothing for Hispanic women sold well in Texas and Northern California stores but not in heavily Mexican-American Los Angeles, where urban influences hold greater sway. In other words, people's lives are influenced by their environment as well as by their ethnicity.[13]

As people grow older, their responsibilities and incomes change, and so do their interests in various product categories (see Exhibit 4–4). Buick, for instance, found a huge untapped market of mature single women who were financially secure and good prospects for its brand. The company now sponsors a newsletter specifically targeted to this group.[14]

At the same time, the auto industry didn't forget that over half of America's consumers are now young adults. In fact, Generation Y, the 71 million children of baby boomers now between the ages of 8 and 25, is the most multicultural, diverse generation ever. By 2010, this group will account for 4 million new car sales, according to Jim Lentz, vice president of Toyota's youth-targeted division Scion. Similarly, Mitsubishi is targeting the youth market with extensive use of hip music as its advertising theme. Recent studies have shown that 41.6 percent of Mitsubishi buyers are under 35 years old.[15]

Demographic segmentation has long been understood in the fast-food industry. Once stigmatized as unsanitary meat fit only for poor people, chains like White Castle and McDonald's used advertising to change the hamburger's image, fashioning it into the national cuisine by the 1950s.[16] Now, children are McDonald's primary target consumers. Decades of ads for Happy Meals have made an impression. Among fictional characters, Ronald McDonald's cultural penetration is surpassed only by Santa Claus: 96 percent of schoolchildren in the United States can identify the yellow-jump-suited clown.[17] Against this giant's brand value and advertising expenditures, competitors have returned to the hamburger's traditional consumer, the young male. In the segment where McDonald's is slightly weaker, Hardee's intends to be strong.

In international markets, the demographics of many populations are changing rapidly. From Kuala Lumpur to Brazil to Poland, middle-class life is becoming available to more people in former Third World countries. This emerging middle class has an apparently insatiable appetite for consumer goods—everything from color TVs and CD players to video cameras, cars, and refrigerators.[18] In China, for example, only 1 percent of the population has hot running water, but 84 percent

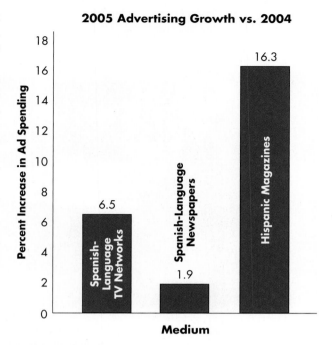

2005 Advertising Growth vs. 2004

Exhibit 4–3

Ad spending growth in U.S. hispanic media (from 2004 to 2005).

Exhibit 4–4

Heavy usage patterns of various age groups.

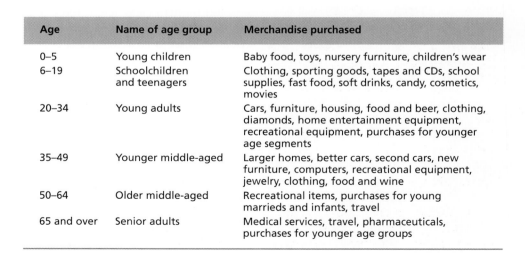

Age	Name of age group	Merchandise purchased
0–5	Young children	Baby food, toys, nursery furniture, children's wear
6–19	Schoolchildren and teenagers	Clothing, sporting goods, tapes and CDs, school supplies, fast food, soft drinks, candy, cosmetics, movies
20–34	Young adults	Cars, furniture, housing, food and beer, clothing, diamonds, home entertainment equipment, recreational equipment, purchases for younger age segments
35–49	Younger middle-aged	Larger homes, better cars, second cars, new furniture, computers, recreational equipment, jewelry, clothing, food and wine
50–64	Older middle-aged	Recreational items, purchases for young marrieds and infants, travel
65 and over	Senior adults	Medical services, travel, pharmaceuticals, purchases for younger age groups

GPS Navigator, as standard in all Mercedes-Benz models.

Mercedes Benz

Changing demographics in many international markets open up new opportunities for advertisers. In Spain, the growing upper middle class and the availability of good expressways enable Mercedes-Benz (www.mercedesbenz.com) to promote its navigation system in this very creative ad that won a Bronze Lion at Cannes.

Ads for Adidas (www.adidas.com) capture the attitude and lifestyle of its target market—young people around the world who like to make their own fashion statement. Segmentation along psychographic lines is difficult because it is not easily quantifiable. Nevertheless, lifestyle advertisements play a critical role in marketing products that involve feelings, personalities, values, and attitudes.

have television sets![19] In 2002, Russia emerged as the world's fastest growing advertising market as companies tried to reach that country's increasingly wealthy consumers.

Geographic and demographic data provide information about markets but little about the psychology of individuals. People in the same demographic or geographic segment may have widely differing product preferences and TV viewing habits. Rarely can demographic criteria alone predict purchase behavior.[20] That's why marketers developed the study of *psychographics.*

Psychographic Segmentation

For certain products, appeals to emotions and cultural values may be persuasive. So some advertisers use **psychographic segmentation** to define consumer markets. With **psychographics,** marketers group people by their values, attitudes, personality, and lifestyle. Psychographics enables marketers to view people as individuals with feelings and inclinations. Then, they can classify people according to what they feel, what they believe, the way they live, and the products, services, and media they use.[21]

For years, marketers have tried to categorize consumers by personality and lifestyle types to determine advertising appeals. One classification system, VALS™, originated by Stanford Research Institute (now SRI International and currently run by SRI Consulting Business Intelligence [SRIC-BI]), was quickly adopted by marketers across the country. In 1989, SRIC-BI released an updated version of VALS, for segmenting U.S. consumers and predicting their purchase behavior (see Exhibit 4–5). The new VALS was developed by a team of experts from Stanford University, University of California–Berkeley, and SRI International. The effort involved two nationally representative surveys and extensive theoretical work.

The VALS typology breaks consumers into eight groups based on the concept of *primary motivation* and *resources.* **Primary motivation** is based on psychological characteristics that underlie purchase decisions. There are three primary motivation categories: those who are primarily motivated by ideals, those by achievement, and those by self-expression. The **resources axis** in the VALS typology relates to the range of psychological, physical, demographic, and material capacities that consumers can draw upon. These include education, income, self-confidence, health, eagerness to buy, and energy level. People with the most resources are placed at the top of the typology; those with the least at the bottom. Each of the eight VALS groups exhibits distinctive behavior, decision-making patterns, and product/media usage traits.[22]

According to SRIC-BI, the purpose of VALS is to help marketers identify whom to target, uncover what the target group buys and does, locate where concentrations of the target group live, identify how best to communicate with them, and gain insight into why the target group behaves the way it does. The system has been applied to a variety of areas: new product development and design, target marketing, product positioning, advertising message development, media planning, and direct mail using GeoVALS™, which estimates the proportion of VALS types by zip code or block group.[23]

In one case, for example, a foreign car manufacturer used VALS to reposition its sports utility vehicle after its award-winning but ineffective television campaign failed to result in higher sales. Using VALS, the company targeted a new "rebellious" consumer group with a new campaign using a "breaking the rules" theme. Nothing changed but the advertising. But sales increased 60 percent in six months.[24]

VALS can also be used in the area of media planning. Different VALS groups have distinctive media preferences. For example, the VALS Believer and Maker segments, comprising about 29 percent of the U.S. population, often choose country music stations. VALS Innovators and Thinkers are more likely to listen to news and talk radio than country music.[25]

Limitations of Consumer Segmentation Methods

Advocates of all these psychographic systems claim they help address the emotional factors that motivate consumers. However, for some products psychographics may offer little real value—especially since it oversimplifies consumer personalities and purchase behavior. Some typologies, such as VALS, are also criticized for being complicated.[26]

Still, it's important for marketers to monitor and understand their customers. It helps them select target markets, create ads that match the attributes and image of their products with the types of consumers who use them, develop effective media plans, and budget their advertising dollars wisely.

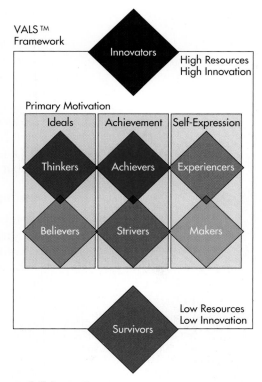

Exhibit 4–5

The VALS™ (www.sric-bi.com) classification system places consumers with abundant resources—psychological, physical, and material means and capacities—near the top of the chart and those with minimal resources near the bottom. The chart segments consumers by their basis for decision making: ideals, achievement, or self-expression. The boxes intersect to indicate that some categories may be considered together. For instance, a marketer may categorize Thinkers and Believers together.

Segmenting Business and Government Markets: Understanding Organizational Buying Behavior

Business markets (or industrial markets) include manufacturers, government agencies, wholesalers, retailers, banks, and institutions that buy goods and services to help them operate. These products may include raw materials, electronic components, mechanical parts, office equipment, vehicles, or services used in conducting the business. Many business marketers sell to **resellers,** such as retail businesses that resell to consumers. For example, much of Hardee's food is supplied by Siméus Foods International, a processing, production, and distribution conglomerate. Siméus's two plants produce and freeze menu items, such as hamburger and chicken patties, to the specifications of customers like Hardee's and Denny's. The end product is resold by Hardee's with no mention of Siméus. Hardee's reselling contract with Coca-Cola, however, is a much more visible *brand partnership*; Coke products are often featured in Hardee's advertising.

Identifying target markets of prospective business customers is just as complex as identifying consumer markets. Many of the variables used to identify consumer markets can also be used for business markets—for example, geography and behavior (purchase occasion, benefits sought, user status, and usage rate).

Business markets also have special characteristics. They employ professional buyers and use systematic purchasing procedures. They may be concentrated geographically. And in any single market there may be only a small number of buyers.

Business Purchasing Procedures

When businesspeople evaluate new products, they use a process far more complex and rigid than the consumer purchase process we will describe in Chapter 5. Business marketers must design their advertising programs with this in mind.

Large firms have purchasing departments that act as professional buyers. They evaluate the need for products, analyze proposed purchases, weigh competitive bids, seek approvals from users and managers, make requisitions, place orders, and supervise all product purchasing. This structured purchase decision process implies a rational approach. Recent research, however, showed that professional buyers often exhibit significant brand equity behaviors, such as willingness to pay a substantial premium for their favorite brand. This was especially true for buyers concerned about the negative consequences of a product failure. In other words, the buyers perceived well-known brands as a way to reduce risk. Moreover, their feelings about brands tended to transfer from one product category to another, even when the products were very different (e.g., from fax machines to floppy disks).[27] This suggests that advertising may play a larger role in business-to-business marketing than previously thought.

Making a sale in business markets may take weeks, months, or even years, especially to government agencies. Purchase decisions often depend on factors besides price or quality, among them product demonstrations, delivery time, terms of sale, and dependability of supply. Marketers often emphasize these issues in advertising and promotional appeals.

Before deciding on a target market, business marketers should consider how the purchase decision process works in various segments. New companies, for instance, may want to target smaller firms where the purchase decision can be made quickly. Or they may use commissioned reps to call on the larger prospects that require more time. These decisions will dictate where advertising should be placed.

Industrial Classification System

Industrial customers need different products, depending on their business. For example, apparel manufacturers such as Levi's are the main customers for buttons and zippers. Marketing managers need to focus their sales and advertising

Although business purchases are often made according to a company's well-defined needs and policies, the actual purchasers are people who might be persuaded by traditional forms of product branding. For this reason, business-to-business advertising for Sybase (www.sybase.com) places great significance on establishing and reinforcing the Sybase brand name.

efforts on those firms that are in the right business for their products.[28] The U.S. Census Bureau classifies all U.S. businesses—and collects and publishes industry statistics on them—using the **North American Industry Classification System (NAICS) codes.** The NAICS (pronounced "nakes") system replaces the old SIC (Standard Industrial Classification) system and includes many new industries that are relevant to today's changing economy. Because the system was developed in cooperation with Canada and Mexico, consistency throughout North America is guaranteed.

Level	Code	Sector
Sector	51	Information
Subsector	513	Broadcasting and telecommunications
Industry group	5133	Telecommunications
Industry	51332	Wireless telecommunications carriers (except satellite)
U.S. industry	513321	Paging

Exhibit 4–6

NAICS hierarchy and codes. A business marketer selling goods or services to firms in the paging industry can use the NAICS codes to locate prospective companies in directories or in subscription databases.

NAICS organizes all the industries in our economy into 20 broad sectors such as mining, manufacturing, wholesale trade, and information. These are then subdivided into four hierarchical levels of classification, including sectors, subsectors, industry groups, industries, and finally 1,170 distinct U.S. industries. (See Exhibit 4–6 for a breakdown of NAICS codes in the information and wireless telecommunications industry.) The U.S. Census Bureau uses NAICS to offer marketers an abundance of information, such as the number of firms, sales volumes, and number of employees by geographic area. Thus, the NAICS codes help companies segment markets and do research, and advertisers can even obtain lists of companies in particular NAICS divisions for direct mailings.[29]

Market Concentration

Many countries' markets for industrial goods are concentrated in one region or several metropolitan areas. In the United States, for example, the industrial market is heavily concentrated in the Midwest, the South, and California. Market concentration reduces the number of geographic targets for an advertiser.

Moreover, business marketers deal with fewer buyers than consumer marketers. Less than 15 percent of U.S. manufacturing establishments employ nearly 65 percent of all production workers and account for more than 80 percent of all manufacturing dollars.[30] Customer size is a critical issue for market segmentation. A firm may concentrate its marketing and advertising efforts on a few large customers, many smaller ones, or both.

Levi Strauss markets through three channels: independent department stores; specialty stores (such as Urban Outfitters); and chain stores (such as Wal-Mart and JCPenney). Its top 100 accounts provide 80 percent of the company's annual sales and are made through 13,000 retail outlets. Its remaining accounts (20 percent of sales) represent another 13,000 stores. Major accounts are served by sales reps from Levi's various divisions, smaller accounts by telemarketers and pandivisional sales reps. Bartle Bogle Hegarty creates and coordinates advertising for most Levi Strauss divisions in the United States.

Business marketers can also segment by end users. For example, a firm may develop software for one industry, such as banking, or for general use in a variety of industries. That decision, of course, affects advertising media decisions.

Aggregating Market Segments

Once marketers identify and locate broad product-based markets with shared characteristics (behavioristic, geographic, demographic, or psychographic), they can proceed to the second step in the market segmentation process. This involves (1) selecting groups that have a mutual interest in the product's utility and (2) reorganizing and aggregating (combining) them into larger market segments based on their potential for sales and profit. Let's take a look at how this process might work for Levi Strauss & Co. in the U.S. market.

PRIZM NE
Social Groups

Urban Uptown
Midtown Mix
Urban Cores

Elite Suburbs
The Affluentials
Middleburbs
Inner Suburbs

2nd City Society
City Centers
Micro-City Blues

Landed Gentry
Country Comfort
Middle America
Rustic Living

Unclassified

Exhibit 4–7

This exhibit shows how Claritas's PRIZM NE (for New Evolution) system classifies prospective customers in the Chicago area by census tract and labels each area by the residents' shared characteristics.

First, the company's management needs to know the market potential for jeans and casual pants in various market areas; that is, it needs to discover the *primary demand trend* of the total U.S. market for pants. To do this it uses a variety of marketing research techniques (discussed in Chapter 6).

Then management must identify the needs, wants, and shared characteristics of the various groups within the casual apparel marketplace who live near the company's retail outlets. It may use the services of a large marketing information company such as Claritas, which collects data on people's purchasing behavior and creates profiles of geographic markets across the country.

Claritas finds a huge market of prospective customers throughout the United States: students, blue-collar workers, young singles, professional people, homemakers, and so on. It then measures and analyzes household groups in each major retail area by demographic, lifestyle, and purchasing characteristics; sorts them into 66 geodemographic segments within 14 social groups; and refers to them with terms such as those in Exhibit 4–7: Urban Uptown, Affluentials, Micro-City Blues, Middle America, and the like. All these people have apparel needs, and many may be interested in the style, cachet, and durability of the Levi's brand.

Selecting Groups Interested in Product Utility

Levi Strauss next selects groups that would like and be able to afford the utilities or benefits of Levi's apparel—suitability for work or play, comfort, style, reasonable cost, durability, and so on. Groups interested in all these features make up the total possible market for Levi's clothes.

Part of the challenge of market segmentation is estimating the profits the company might realize if it (1) aimed at the whole market or (2) catered only to a specific market segment. Apparel is a highly competitive market, but 10 percent of 1,000 is always larger than 90 percent of 100. So for a company such as Levi Strauss, the target market must be a large mass market or it won't be profitable.[31]

Combining Groups to Build Target Market Segments

The company needs to find groups that are relatively homogeneous (similar) and offer good potential for profit. Market data turn up a large number of demographic and lifestyle groups, including ethnically diverse families, young singles, and seniors with lower education and income who often live in rented homes or apartments: On Their Own (3.4 percent), Back Country (6.0 percent), and Settled In (5.1 percent). Because of their minimal retail or credit activity, these groups are not prime targets for premium-branded department store products.

Other segments offer greater potential—young to middle-aged households with medium-to-high incomes and average-to-high retail activity: Movers & Shakers (2.5 percent), Prosperous Ethnic Mix (2.8 percent), and Home Sweet Home (5.7 percent). By combining these (and similar) groups with the young professionals in the Good Step Forward (2.1 percent) and Great Beginnings (3.6 percent) segments, Levi Strauss can target young to middle-aged people on their way up. Nationally, that amounts to 20 million U.S. households. That's not everybody, but it's a large and potentially very profitable mass-market segment. These people might like the style and comfort of Levi's 550s as well as the tradition of a brand they know and trust, and the company could develop a campaign to appeal to their particular needs, wants, and self-image.

> **CONCEPT CHECK**
>
> What is the advertiser's goal in segmenting the marketplace?

The Target Marketing Process

Once the market segmentation process is complete, a company can proceed to the **target marketing** process. This will determine the content, look, and feel of its advertising.

Target Market Selection

The first step in target marketing is to assess which of the newly created segments offer the greatest profit potential and which can be most successfully

No product appeals universally to every customer, so advertisers must carefully choose their target markets. Although Land Rover (www.landrover.com) typically targets consumers in the market for more rugged, off-roading automobiles, this ad is aimed at parents who want the safety and comfort of a family car and the function of a sport utility vehicle.

Understanding the Product Element: Starbucks Coffee

America's java giant began as the seed of an idea by a man with a dream whose tender care and commitment eventually built the familiar coffee empire of today. While on a trip to Italy in 1983, Howard Schultz discovered and fell in love with the coffee bars of Milan and Verona. They were a combination of coffee and community. He was sure Americans would love this concept.

At the time, Starbucks was a little 11-store chain of roasted coffee stores in Seattle. Schultz was in charge of marketing. He pitched the coffee bar concept to the company's management but received only a lukewarm response. They didn't want to be in the restaurant business. Howard held on to his vision, though. Leaving Starbucks in 1987, he launched a handful of coffee bars on his own and named them Il Giornale. Two years later, with some investor backing, his demonstrated success enabled him to acquire Starbucks. Today, he is chairman and chief global strategist of a publicly traded company that boasts more than 9,600 retail locations in North America, Latin America, Europe, the Middle East, and the Pacific Rim. Serving tens of millions of Americans each week, Starbucks has definitely become a household name.

To Schultz, the most important component for success is consistent product quality. "Our long-range goal is to be nothing less than the most recognized and respected brand of coffee in the world," Schultz says.

Thanks to management's demand for consistency, a double-tall latte tastes the same in New York as it does in Seattle; and your perfectly pulled espresso won't sit for more than 10 seconds before being poured into your cup. This attention to detail has earned Starbucks its place in the premium coffee category.

Of course a good product is best prepared and served by skilled, happy employees. And that also adds to an organization's profitability. Ranked as number 11 by the Fortune "100 Best Companies to Work for in 2005" poll, Starbucks's management believes that if it takes care of its workers, they in turn will take care of the public. Employees who work at least 20 hours a week receive full benefits, with dental and extended health care, including eyeglass and contact lens prescriptions—after only 90 days with the company. Starbucks even offers these benefits to the same-sex partners of employees. To further ensure consistent product quality, Starbucks has implemented procedures for monitoring the working conditions of the overseas producers who supply materials to the company.

Today, the coffee market is quite competitive, but Starbucks retains its leading position by continually introducing new products. With PepsiCo, Starbucks formed a partnership to produce its Frappuccino beverage in 1995. In 1996, Starbucks entered into a joint venture with Dreyers Grand Ice Cream to market "Starbucks Coffee Ice Cream." In 1998 and 1999, Starbucks strengthened its presence within the tea segment by introducing a mixture of tea, fruit juice, and ice called Tiazzi, and it aquired Tazo, a Portland, Oregon–based tea company. In 2002, a bottled espresso drink dubbed the DoubleShot joined the long line of creative products. And in 2005, Chantico drinking chocolate and Starbucks Coffee Liqueur joined the portfolio of products. If you're drinking a coffee or tea beverage these days, Starbucks may well have created it—even if it doesn't say so on the label.

Applying the Breaks

A basic rule of advertising is that the most ingenious campaign in the world cannot save a bad product. Think of a brand in the marketplace that you consider successful and analyze which product elements make it profitable and unique. Are there any similarities to the elements that made Starbucks successful? If so, what?

penetrated. The company designates one or more segments as a **target market**—that group of segments the company wishes to appeal to, design products for, and tailor its marketing activities toward.[32] It may designate another set of segments as a secondary target market and aim some of its resources at it.

Let's look at the most likely target market for loose-fitting jeans: young to middle-aged customers with moderate to high income and education who like the style, comfort, and fashion of Levi's apparel. This group represents a large percentage of the apparel market, and if won, will generate substantial profits. Levi's offers what these prospects need and want: the style and fashion of the jeans they grew up with, updated to be more comfortable for the adult body.

If the young, comfort-oriented segment wasn't large enough to be profitable, the company would select a different target market, and its other marketing and advertising activities would have to change as well. For an example, look at Commercial Break 4–B and consider how Starbucks selected its new target market.

The Marketing Mix: A Strategy for Matching Products to Markets

Once a company defines its target market, it knows exactly where to focus its attention and resources. Marketers and advertisers generally try to shape their basic product into a total **product concept:** the consumer's perception of a product or service as a bundle of utilitarian and symbolic values that satisfy functional, social, psychological, and other wants and needs. Companies have many strategic options they can employ to enhance this product/service concept and effect marketing exchanges (make sales). The company can design special features for its target market (such as certain colors or special sizes). It can establish proper pricing. And it can determine the criteria for locating stores or dealers and prepare the most convincing advertising messages.

Marketers categorize these options under four headings: (1) *product,* (2) *price,* (3) *distribution,* and (4) *communication.*[33] The way the marketer mixes and blends these different elements creates the company's marketing strategy—often called the **marketing mix.** For convenience, marketing educator E. Jerome McCarthy developed a mnemonic device to help recall these four functions: *product, price, place,* and *promotion*—or the **four Ps (4Ps).**[34]

The 4Ps are a simple way to remember the basic elements of the marketing mix. But within each element are numerous marketing activities a company can employ to fine-tune its product concept and improve sales. Advertising, for example, is one instrument of the communication (promotion) element. The remainder of this chapter focuses on the relationship between advertising and the other elements of the marketing mix.

> How do advertisers use the results of market segmentation to maximize the impact of their marketing efforts?

CONCEPT CHECK

Advertising and the Product Element

In developing a marketing mix, marketers generally start with the **product element.** Major activities typically include the way the product is designed and classified, positioned, branded, and packaged. Each of these affects the way the product is advertised.

Product Life Cycles

Marketers theorize that just as humans pass through stages in life from infancy to death, products (and especially product categories) also pass through a **product life cycle** (see Exhibit 4–8).[35] A product's position in the life cycle influences the target market selected and the marketing mix used. There are four major stages in the product life cycle: *introduction, growth, maturity,* and *decline.*

When a company introduces a new product category, nobody knows about it. By using market segmentation, though, the company may try to identify those prospects who are known to be **early adopters**—willing to try new things—and begin promoting the new category directly to them. The idea is to stimulate **primary demand**—consumer demand for the whole product category, not just the company's own brand.

During the **introductory phase** of any new product category, the company incurs considerable costs for educating customers, building widespread dealer distribution, and encouraging demand. It must spend significant advertising sums at this stage to establish a position as a market leader and to gain a large share of market before the growth stage begins.

Exhibit 4–8

A product's life cycle curve may vary, depending on the product category. Marketing objectives and strategies change as the product proceeds from one stage to the next.

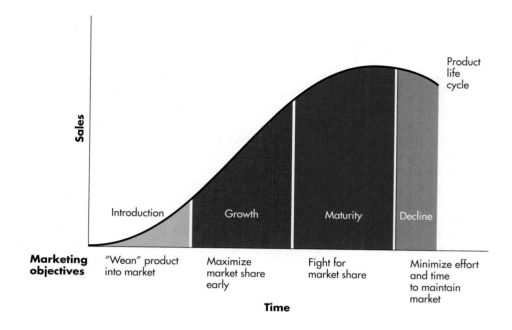

Sales

Product life cycle

Introduction | Growth | Maturity | Decline

Marketing objectives

"Wean" product into market | Maximize market share early | Fight for market share | Minimize effort and time to maintain market

Time

When cellular telephones were introduced in the late 1980s, advertisers had to first create enough consumer demand to pull the product through the channels of distribution (called **pull strategy**). Advertising communications educated consumers about the new product and its category, explained what cellular phones are, how they work, and the rewards of owning one. Promotional efforts aimed at the retail trade (called **push strategy**) encouraged distributors and dealers to stock, display, and advertise the new products.

When sales volume begins to rise rapidly, the product enters the **growth stage.** This period is characterized by rapid *market expansion* as more and more customers, stimulated by mass advertising and word-of-mouth, make their first, second, and third purchases. Competitors jump into the market, but the company that established the early leadership position usually reaps the biggest rewards. As a percentage of total sales, advertising expenditures should decrease, and individual firms will realize their first substantial profits.

Advertisers use a variety of strategies to extend the life cycle of a product in its maturity stage. Procter & Gamble (www.pg.com), testing two new flavors of Crest toothpaste in mass-merchant chains, used Telestar Interactive's MicroTalk shelf units to play audio messages about the products to approaching consumers.

During the early 1990s, the demand for cell phones exploded, and category sales quadrupled every year. Many competitors suddenly appeared. With increased production and competition, prices started to fall, which brought even more consumers into the market. By 2003, almost two-thirds of all U.S. families owned cell phones.

In the **maturity stage,** the marketplace becomes saturated with competing products and the number of new customers dwindles, so industry sales reach a plateau. Competition intensifies and profits diminish. Companies increase their promotional efforts but emphasize **selective demand** to impress customers with the subtle advantages of their particular brand. At this stage, companies can increase sales only at the expense of competitors.

The strategies of market segmentation, product positioning, and price promotion become more important during this shakeout period as weak companies fall by the wayside and those remaining fight for market share.

By the mid-1990s, for example, cellular phones that once sold for $1,500 were suddenly advertised regularly for $100 to $200. Ads emphasized features and low prices, and the product became a staple of discount merchandisers. Today, of course, one can get a cell phone for free, just by signing up for the service.[36]

Late in the maturity stage, companies may have to scramble to extend the product's life cycle. Without innovation or marketing support, name brands eventually see their sales erode. If the advertised brand has no perceived advantage, people will buy whatever's cheapest or most convenient. Professor Brian Wansink, who directs the Brand Lab at the University of Illinois Urbana–Champaign, suggests that the reason many old brands die is less for life cycle reasons and more for marketing neglect. He points out that aging brands often pack plenty of brand equity. The challenge for marketers is to determine which brands can be revitalized and then decide how to do it. With today's high price tag on introducing new products (often $100 million or more), revitalization should be the strategy of choice whenever possible. Marketers may try to find new users for the brand, develop new uses for the product, change the size of packages, design new labels, improve quality, or use promotions to increase frequency of use.[37]

If they're not revitalized, products will finally enter the **decline stage** because of obsolescence, new technology, or changing consumer tastes. At this point, companies may cease all promotion and phase the products out quickly, as in the case of record turntables and albums, or let them fade slowly with minimal advertising.

Product Classifications

The way a company classifies its product is important in defining both the product concept and the marketing mix. As Exhibit 4–9 shows, there are many ways

Exhibit 4–9

Product classifications.

By market	By rate of consumption and tangibility	By purchasing habits	By physical description
Consumer goods Products and services we use in our daily lives (food, clothing, furniture, cars). Industrial goods Products used by companies for the purpose of producing other products (raw materials, agricultural commodities, machinery, tools, equipment).	Durable goods Tangible products that are long-lasting and infrequently replaced (cars, trucks, refrigerators, furniture). Nondurable goods Tangible products that may be consumed in one or a few uses and usually need to be replaced at regular intervals (food, soap, gasoline, oil). Services Activities, benefits, or satisfaction offered for sale (travel, haircuts, legal and medical services, massages).	Convenience goods Purchases made frequently with a minimum of effort (cigarettes, food, newspapers). Shopping goods Infrequently purchased items for which greater time is spent comparing price, quality, style, warranty (furniture, cars, clothing, tires). Specialty goods Products with such unique characteristics that consumers will make special efforts to purchase them even if they're more expensive (fancy photographic equipment, special women's fashions, stereo components). Unsought goods Products that potential customers don't yet want (insurance, encyclopedias) or don't know they can buy (new products), so they don't search them out.	Packaged goods Cereals, hair tonics, and so forth. Hard goods Furniture, appliances. Soft goods Clothing, bedding. Services Intangible products.

Jeep

At a time when sport utility vehicles are so popular that competing companies all seem to be offering the same services, Jeep (www.jeep.com) positions itself as the "only one" to go anywhere on the planet. Positioning is important in tight markets to assist in differentiation between like products.

to classify tangible goods: by markets, by the purchasing habits of buyers, by the consumption rate or degree of tangibility, or by physical attributes.

Product Positioning

Once an advertising person understands the product's stage in the life cycle, how it's classified, and how it's currently perceived by the marketplace, the first strategic decision can be made: how to **position** the product. The basic goal of positioning strategy is to own a word that establishes the product in the prospect's mind. Levi's owns "jeans" (or at least they did for a long time). BMW owns "performance." Maytag owns "reliability." And Volvo owns "safety." By developing a unique position for the brand in the consumer's mind, the marketer helps the consumer remember the brand and what it stands for.

Product Differentiation

Product differentiation creates a product difference that appeals to the preferences of a distinct market segment. In advertising, nothing is more important than being able to tell prospects truthfully that your product is new and different. Unfortunately, in response to increased competitive pressures, burgeoning innovation and technology, and various constraints on distribution, new-product development cycles have shortened dramatically. As a result, many brand managers find themselves launching new products that are "only 85 percent there."[38] So it's not surprising that many "new" products fail to impress consumers. (See Exhibit 4–10.)

Differences between products that are readily apparent to the consumer are called **perceptible differences.** Snapple, for example, received its initial impetus because of its unique taste, and the company now spends $40 million annually to advertise this difference to consumers nationwide.[39] **Hidden differences** are not so readily apparent. Trident gum may look and taste the same as other brands, but it is differentiated by the use of artificial sweeteners. While hidden differences can enhance a product's desirability, advertising is usually needed to let consumers know about them.

For many product classes, such as aspirin, salt, gasoline, packaged foods, liquor, and financial services, advertising can create **induced differences.** Banks, brokerage houses, and insurance companies, for example, which offer virtually identical financial products and services, use advertising and promo-

Exhibit 4–10

What's new? Not much. Consumers didn't think these products were as new as they claimed to be, as indicated by the grades awarded.

Product	New and different	Purchase probability	Price/ value	Overall grade
Airwick Botanicals	F	A	A	B
Mr. Clean Glass & Surface Cleaner	F	A	A	B
Spic & Span with Bleach	F	A	B	B
Aspirin-Free Bayer Select	F	B	B	C
Sugar Twin Plus low-calorie sweetener	F	B	A	C
Lady Power Clear Roll-On antiperspirant	F	B	A	C

If there's one thing kids are good at, it's figuring out how to make it difficult to take their temperature. They squirm. They wiggle. They whine. They even cry. But don't give up hope. Just throw out your old thermometer. And replace it with a Thermoscan® Instant Thermometer.

In one short second, it takes a temperature at the ear. It's easy. It's accurate. It's safe. (No wonder over a half-billion temperatures are being taken this way every year in doctors' offices and hospitals.)

And now you can get it for a new lower price. Which means the perfect family thermometer just got better.

The first name in fast temperatures

THERMOSCAN.
INSTANT THERMOMETER

THE GREAT THING ABOUT THIS **THERMOMETER** IS THAT CHILDREN HAVE YET TO LEARN HOW TO CLENCH THEIR **EARS SHUT.**

Most of us might stick a thermometer in our mouths when we come down with a fever, but the Braun Thermoscan (www.braun.com) isn't just any thermometer. The company's product concept, using the ear rather than the mouth, differentiates its thermometer as one that is gentle yet effective for the temperament of children.

tion to differentiate themselves. However, few have yet discovered the image asset of **branding** as used by the national packaged-goods marketers. That is created through the accumulation of consistent advertising campaigns, favorable publicity, special-event sponsorship, and good word-of-mouth.[40]

Product Branding

The fundamental differentiating device for all products is the **brand**—that combination of name, words, symbols, or design that identifies the product and its source and distinguishes it from competing products. Without brands, consumers couldn't tell one product from another, and advertising them would be nearly impossible.

A manufacturer may establish an **individual brand** for each product it produces. Unilever, for example, markets its toothpastes under the individual brand names Aim, Pepsodent, and Close-Up. Such companies designate a distinct target market for each product and develop a separate personality and image for each brand. However, this strategy is very costly.

On the other hand, a company might use a **family brand** and market different products under the same umbrella name. When Heinz promotes its ketchup, it hopes to help its relishes too. This decision may be cost effective, but one bad product in a line can hurt the whole family.

Because it is so expensive for manufacturers to market **national brands** (also called *manufacturer's brands*), some companies use a *private-labeling* strategy. They manufacture the product and sell it to resellers (distributors or dealers), who put their own brand name on the product. **Private labels,** typically sold at lower prices in large retail chain stores, include such familiar names as Kenmore, Craftsman, Cragmont, Kroger, and Party Pride. They now account for almost 20 percent of grocery purchases.[41] The responsibility for creating brand image and familiarity with private label brands rests with the distributor or retailer, who is also the principal benefactor if the brand is successful. Recent trends have moved toward premium private labels, such as President's Choice, which has enjoyed immense success. These products feature better packaging, superior quality, and a higher price, often comparable to national brands.

Branding decisions are critical because the brands a company owns may be its most important capital asset. Imagine the value of owning a brand name such as Coca-Cola, Nike, Porsche, or Levi's. *Business Week's*

Creating a brand name is key to differentiation for a product. Without this, the consumer is left with a generic commodity. Large companies can actually oversee many different products and brand names, as in the case of the many popular and well-known items marketed by Procter & Gamble.

Rank	Brand	2004 brand value (in billions)
1	Coca-Cola	$67.39
2	Microsoft	61.37
3	IBM	53.79
4	GE	44.11
5	Intel	33.50
6	Disney	27.11
7	McDonald's	25.00
8	Nokia	24.04
9	Toyota	22.67
10	Marlboro	22.13

Exhibit 4–11

World's most valuable brands (2004).

Package design is an integral part of this Nestlé España (www.nestle.es) product. The high-quality package for Bombones Caja Roja (which simply means "red box chocolates") is always red, but the design changes every year. Customers eagerly await every new design. Caja Roja is a very successful assortment of chocolates produced mainly for the Spanish, Portuguese, and Chilean markets.

annual brand-value report ranks Coca-Cola as the most valuable brand in the world, followed by Microsoft, IBM, GE, Intel, and Nokia (see Exhibit 4–11).[42] Some companies pay a substantial fee for the right to use another company's brand name. Thus, we have **licensed brands** such as Sunkist vitamins, Coca-Cola clothing, Porsche sunglasses, and Mickey Mouse watches.

The Role of Branding

For consumers, brands offer instant recognition and identification. They also promise consistent, reliable standards of quality, taste, size, or even psychological satisfaction, which adds value to the product for both the consumer and the manufacturer. In a study by McKinsey & Co., a computer's brand name ranked second (behind performance) in what consumers considered important when choosing a personal computer. Price, by the way, ranked fifth.[43]

Brands must be built on differences in images, meanings, and associations. It's up to manufacturers to differentiate their products clearly and deliver value competitively. The product has to taste better, or get clothes cleaner, or be packaged in a more environmentally friendly container.[44] Advertising for an established brand, particularly a well-differentiated one, is much more effective if it exploits the brand's positioning.[45] Ideally, when consumers see a brand on the shelf, they instantly comprehend the brand's promise and have confidence in its quality. Of course, they must be familiar with and believe in the brand's promise (a function of advertising effectiveness). The goal is *brand loyalty*—because it serves both the consumer and the advertiser. For the consumer, it reduces shopping time. For the advertiser, it builds **brand equity,** the totality of what consumers, distributors, dealers—even competitors—feel and think about the brand over an extended period of time. In short, it's the value of the brand's assets.

High brand equity offers a host of blessings to the product marketer: customer loyalty, price inelasticity, long-term profits. A loyal customer can be nine times as profitable as a disloyal one.[46] But building brand equity requires time and money. Brand value and preference drive market share, but share points and brand loyalty are usually won by the advertisers who spend the most. Charlotte Beers, the former head of J. Walter Thompson, believes companies must maintain consistency in their message by integrating all their marketing communications—from packaging and advertising to sales promotion and publicity—to maintain and reinforce the brand's personality and avoid doing something stupid such as changing the distinctive color of a Ryder rental truck.[47]

Product Packaging

The product's package is a component of the product element that can determine the outcome of retail shelf competition. In fact, packaging may be a particular brand's one differential advantage—and it's the marketer's last chance to communicate at the point of sale. Package designers (who sometimes work in agencies) must make the package exciting, appealing, and at the same time functional. The four considerations in package design are *identification; containment, protection, and convenience; consumer appeal;* and *economy*. These functions may even become **copy points**—copywriting themes—in the product's advertising.

CONCEPT CHECK

Describe the various ways a marketer can use the product element of the marketing mix to enhance the product/service concept and improve sales.

Advertising and the Price Element

As we all know, the **price element** of the marketing mix influences consumer perceptions of a brand. Companies that don't compete on price typically use image advertising to create a particular perception of the company or personality for the brand. Companies that are more price-competitive may regularly use sale advertising, clearance advertising, or loss-leader advertising.

Consumers frequently associate higher prices with higher quality. Volvo (www.volvo.com) capitalizes on that concept by reinforcing that the safety value of its automobiles is worth a slightly higher cost.

Key Factors Influencing Price

Companies typically set their prices based on market demand for the product, costs of production and distribution, competition, and corporate objectives. Interestingly, though, a company often has relatively few options for determining its price strategy, depending on the desired product concept.

Marketers believe that, in many product categories, consumers are less concerned with a product's actual price than with its perceived price relative to competitors. Many premium-priced brands, such as L'Oréal, are touted for the very fact that they cost more. Setting a high price to make a product seem more valuable is an example of **psychological pricing.** Image advertising may be used to justify the higher price. The important thing is that the price be consistent with the brand image; you can't charge a Rolex price for a Timex watch. And similarly, the brand's advertising must be consistent with its pricing strategy.

> **CONCEPT CHECK**
>
> Describe the various ways a marketer can use the price element of the marketing mix to enhance the product/service concept and improve sales.

Advertising and the Distribution (Place) Element

Before the first ad can be created, the **place, or distribution, element** must be decided. It is important for marketers to understand that the method of distribution, like the price, must be consistent with the brand's image. People will not pay Nordstrom prices at Kmart. To understand Starbucks's distribution strategy, see Commercial Break 4–C.

Companies use two basic methods of distribution: *direct* or *indirect*.

Direct Distribution

When companies sell directly to end users or consumers, they use **direct distribution.** Avon, for example, employs sales reps who work for the manufacturer rather than for a retailer and sell directly to consumers. Encyclopedia publishers

Commercial Break 4–C

Starbucks and the Place Element

The *place* (or distribution) element of marketing strategy is always integral to successful business. You may have the most wonderful product in the world—but potential customers won't buy it if they can't find it.

Starbucks is a phenomenon that changed the way people view coffee. This can be explained, in large part, by the creative use of the place element. You'll notice that Starbucks cafés are found in high-traffic, high-visibility locations in each of their market areas. In some markets, Starbucks seems to appear on virtually every street corner. Although the average consumer may find this excessive, Starbucks actually picks and plans each retail location with great care.

To a company like Starbucks, street space is the same as shelf space. In this sense, buying out existing coffeehouses is the same as Coca-Cola buying shelf space in supermarkets. Starbucks's management believes that chain expansion is as much a part of the company's success as is its coffee bar and customer service concepts. Since its opening, stores have sprouted up in virtually every major city across the globe, and Starbucks has no intention of stopping. Opening stores at a rate of three to four per day, management expects, by the end of 2005, to have 10,000 Starbucks stores in 60 countries, with a long-term goal of 25,000 stores worldwide.

Aside from its store locations, Starbucks's unique coffee blends are now found in selected airlines, restaurants, hotels, and supermarkets. Additional venues include a mail-order business, a coast-to-coast alliance with Barnes & Noble bookstores, partnerships with major grocery chains, distribution to the Washington State Ferry system, Holland America Line–Westours cruises, Safeco Field in Seattle, Hyatt Hotels, and Chicago's Wrigley Field. Starbucks is also joining the Internet craze. Starting in 2001, Starbucks began a campaign to integrate high-speed wireless Internet access terminals at some stores. With more than 4,000 stores currently up and running with Internet access, customers are now able to browse the Net, send e-mails, and drink their coffee all at the same time.

Obviously, Starbucks intends to fully saturate every coffee market. When consumers go shopping for groceries, they aren't likely to make a separate trip to Starbucks for coffee. So Starbucks now competes directly with other specialty coffees sold in supermarkets. In 1998 Kraft Foods signed on with Starbucks and agreed to distribute and market Starbucks coffee beans in more than 25,000 grocery stores in the United States. Kraft is the largest packaged-food company in North America. This collaboration is a major stepping-stone in surpassing Folgers as the leading coffee brand in the United States. Other placement strategies include the incorporation of Starbucks's latest product, the DoubleShot, into supermarkets. By partnering with PepsiCo in developing and implementing the new drink, Starbucks can take advantage of PepsiCo's vast network of distribution channels, and place its product almost anywhere, bringing the company one step closer to its original dream—"Planet Starbucks."

Applying the Breaks
Take the product you used in Commercial Break 4–B and compare the distribution principles used by Starbucks with your product. In addition, think about the factors that should be considered when placing your product or service in other venues. How does it compare with Starbucks?

---

and insurance companies often sell and distribute their products and services directly to customers without the use of wholesalers or retailers. In these cases, the advertising burden is carried entirely by the manufacturer.

One of the fastest-growing methods of direct distribution today is **network marketing** (also called *multilevel marketing*), in which individuals act as independent distributors for a manufacturer or private-label marketer. These people sign up friends and relatives to consume the company's products and recruit others to join. Through a gradual, word-of-mouth process, they form a "buying club" of independent distributors who buy the products wholesale direct from the company, use them, and tout them to more and more friends and acquaintances.

Many people believe that the Internet is the ultimate direct distribution vehicle. As we will discuss in Chapter 13, Web sites allow marketers to make direct contact with their customers, develop interactive relationships, and consummate the sale of their products or services, all at a lower cost than any other method. The Internet is not appropriate for the distribution of all products, but its acceptance is rapidly spreading.

Indirect Distribution

Manufacturers usually don't sell directly to end users or consumers. Most companies market their products through a *distribution channel* that includes a network of *resellers*. A **reseller** (also called a *middleman*) is a business firm that operates between the producer and the consumer or industrial purchaser. It deals in trade rather than production.[48] Resellers include both wholesalers and retailers, as well as manufacturers' representatives, brokers, jobbers, and distributors. A **distribution channel** comprises all the firms and individuals that take responsibility for the product as it moves from the producer to the consumer.

The advertising a company uses depends on the product's method of distribution. Much of the advertising we see is not prepared or paid for by the manufacturer, but by the distributor or retailer.

An important part of the marketing strategy is determining the amount of coverage necessary for a product. Procter & Gamble, for example, distributes Crest toothpaste to virtually every supermarket and discount, drug, and variety store. Other products might need only one dealer for every 50,000 people. Consumer goods manufacturers traditionally use one of three distribution strategies: *intensive, selective,* or *exclusive.*

Intensive Distribution

Soft drinks, candy, Timex watches, and other convenience goods are available at every possible location because of **intensive distribution.** In fact, consumers can buy them with a minimum of effort. The profit on each unit is usually very low, but the volume of sales is high. The sales burden is usually carried by the manufacturer's national advertising. Ads in trade magazines push the product into the retail "pipeline," and in mass media they stimulate consumers to pull the products through the pipeline. As a manufacturer modifies its strategy to more push or more pull, special promotions may be directed at the trade or at consumers to build brand volume.

Some advertising addresses the distribution element of the marketing mix by targeting wholesalers and/or retailers of the product. Package delivery companies like FedEx (www.fedex.com) enable business owners, who may not have many retail outlets, a means of distributing their products to consumers. FedEx's advertising campaign, "Business Legends," compares business owners to historical pioneers, and describes how the company's latest features and services empower business owners to "ship confidently all over the planet."

Selective Distribution

By limiting the number of outlets through **selective distribution,** manufacturers can cut their distribution and promotion costs. Many hardware tools are sold selectively through discount chains, home-improvement centers, and hardware stores. Levi Strauss sells through better department and chain stores. Manufacturers may use national advertising, but the sales burden is normally carried by the retailer. The manufacturer may share part of the retailer's advertising costs through a **cooperative advertising** program, as we discussed in Chapter 3. For example, a Levi's retailer may receive substantial allowances from the manufacturer for advertising Levi's clothing in its local area. In return, the retailer agrees to advertise and display the clothing prominently.

Describe the various ways a marketer can use the distribution element of the marketing mix to enhance the product/service concept and improve sales.

CONCEPT CHECK

Exclusive Distribution

Some manufacturers grant **exclusive distribution** rights to a wholesaler or retailer in one geographic region. For example, a town of 50,000 to 100,000 people will have only one Buick dealer. This is also common in high fashion, major appliances, and furniture lines. What is lost in market coverage is often gained in the ability to maintain a prestige image and premium prices. Exclusive distribution agreements also force manufacturers and retailers to cooperate closely in advertising and promotion programs.

Advertising and the Promotion (Communication) Element

Once it determines product, price, and distribution, a company is ready to plan its marketing communications, of which advertising is just one component. The **promotion,** or **communication, element** includes all marketing-related communications between the seller and the buyer. (See Commercial Break 4–D.)

Marketing communications (often called *marcom*) typically refers to all the planned messages that companies and organizations create and disseminate to support their marketing objectives and strategies. In addition to advertising, major marketing communication tools include *personal selling, sales promotion, direct marketing,* and *public relations activities.* The extent to which an organization uses any or all of these tools again depends on its marketing needs.

Each marketing communication tool offers particular opportunities and benefits to the marketer. In Chapters 16 and 17 we will discuss how these tools can best be integrated into the *marketing mix.* Since advertising people are frequently called on to solve a variety of marketing problems, it is critical that they understand and know how to integrate the whole mix of communications techniques.

For creating brand awareness, familiarity, and image, as well as for reinforcing prior purchase decisions, advertising is usually the marcom tool of choice. Certain products lend themselves to advertising so much that it plays the dominant communications role. The following factors are particularly important for advertising success:

- Strong primary demand trend.
- Chance for significant product differentiation.
- Hidden qualities highly important to consumers.
- Opportunity to use strong emotional appeals.
- Substantial sums available to support advertising.

Where these conditions exist, companies spend large amounts on advertising, and the ratio of advertising to sales dollars is often quite high. For completely undifferentiated products, such as sugar, salt, and other raw materials or commodities, advertising is usually less important and the other marketing mix elements play a more significant role.

Checkout Coupon is an electronic in-store sales promotion that delivers incentives to shoppers at the checkout counter, based on what they buy. Catalina Marketing Network (www.catalinamarketing.com) helps the retailer coordinate the campaigns with tie-in of the coupons to in-store posters, shelf-talkers, savings on related store products, and newspaper ads.

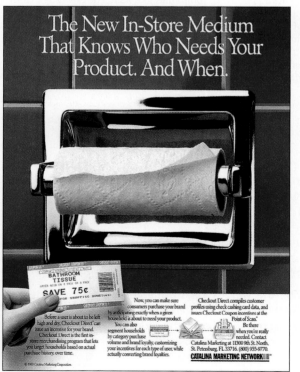

Commercial Break 4–D

Price and Promotion

Starbucks classifies its product as a "gourmet" coffee—in other words, it's positioned as a premium product. This suggests that it probably costs more than the typical coffee in the supermarket. However, since Starbucks targets a younger demographic of 20- to 49-year-olds, it must still be careful about how much it charges. Currently, regular brewed coffee at Starbucks costs $1.40, but the most expensive beverage runs approximately $5.00. Whole-bean coffee ranges from $9.95 to $43.90 per pound. Overall, Starbucks coffee may be a bit pricier, but it offers a higher-quality product and tries to add value through superior employee service.

To promote awareness, many new companies dedicate enormous budgets to advertising. However, this is not always necessary. Starbucks certainly never dreamed it could establish the degree of brand loyalty that it did in such a short time. But it managed to do so with only a minimal amount of advertising. It wasn't that the company didn't believe in advertising; it just didn't think it could afford to advertise. So Starbucks focused on creating product value and giving better service.

Initially, the only promotional elements the company used were public relations and some small sales promotions. These were designed to create initial awareness and interest in its gourmet coffees. As interest and awareness have grown, so have promotional activities. Among the new campaigns is the "Matches Made over Coffee" contest. To strengthen its brand and celebrate coffeehouse romances, Starbucks devised a competition in which the winner with the most "creative, romantic, and coffee-rich, true love story" would receive an all-expense-paid trip for two to Vienna, Austria.

To demonstrate its social concern, Starbucks also ventured into philanthropic activities. In fact, it is now the largest corporate sponsor of CARE, an international relief and development organization that aids the very communities from which the company buys its coffee.

With the coffee culture trend growing, increased competition was a given, forcing Starbucks to spend more on advertising to maintain its market share. Initially, Starbucks spent $17.8 million on a direct-response campaign. It also sold merchandise such as mugs, coffee grinders, espresso machines, and gourmet food bearing the Starbucks logo via catalog and the Internet. While Starbucks continues its public relations involvement with communities, it recognizes the growing need to invest in mass-media advertising. Its first major campaign began in 1997, under the creative design of Goodby, Silverstein & Partners, to promote its new Frappuccino beverage. Three television and three radio spots were created for the campaign, focusing on the jingle "Starbucks, purveyors of coffee, tea, and sanity." In the fall of 1997, though, Starbucks changed agencies and hired BBDO West, claiming that Goodby hadn't yet found the right "creative voice" for Starbucks. Since then, Starbucks has utilized the creative input of numerous top agencies, including Fallon McElligott as well as Saatchi & Saatchi.

The current focus of Starbucks's advertising is split between individual promotions for its wide array of products, including the "What Stirs You?" tagline for the "Toffee Nut Latte," as well as more cause-related marketing programs that focus on philanthropic endeavors abroad. In an ad that ran in *The New York Times,* Starbucks conveyed its charitable efforts in coffee-producing countries through an ad that began "Every sip is born out of respect" and concluded with the tagline "We're always serving more than coffee." As more corporations such as Starbucks spread to a global level, many experts believe we are likely to see more such cause-related advertisements in the future, as these companies attempt to maintain a positive image around the world.

Applying the Breaks

When constructing the marketing mix for your chosen product or service (refer to Commercial Breaks 4–B and 4–C), consider these last two elements: price and promotion. At what level should you price your product and why? What media should you use to advertise your product or service, and why? Do you think that Starbucks should advertise in more traditional mass media or continue to focus on public relations efforts?

The Marketing Mix in Perspective

With the target market designated and the elements of the marketing mix determined, the company has a complete product concept and a strategic basis for marketing to that target. Now it can formalize its strategies and tactics in a written marketing and advertising plan. As part of the planning process, companies use marketing and advertising research.

> Describe the various ways a marketer can use the communication element of the marketing mix to enhance the product/service concept and improve sales.

CONCEPT CHECK

We will discuss this in Chapter 6 before dealing with the formal planning process in Chapter 7. But first we'll examine the process of human communication and some theories of consumer behavior.

Chapter Summary

Market segmentation is the process of identifying groups of people with certain shared characteristics within a broad product market and aggregating these groups into larger market segments according to their mutual interest in the product's utility. From these segments, companies can then select a target market. Marketers use a number of methods to identify behavioral groups and segment markets. The most common are behavioristic, geographic, demographic, and psychographic.

Business markets are often segmented in the same way as consumer markets. They may also be grouped by business purchasing procedures, NAICS code, or market concentration.

In the target marketing process, companies designate specific segments to target and develop their mix of marketing activities. The product concept is the consumer's perception of the product as a bundle of utilitarian and symbolic need-satisfying values.

Every company can add, subtract, or modify four major elements in its marketing program to achieve a desired marketing mix. These elements are product, price, distribution (place), and communications (promotion)—the 4 Ps.

The product element includes the way the product is designed and classified, positioned, branded, and packaged. Just as humans pass through a life cycle, so do products—and

product categories. The stage of a product's life cycle may determine how it is advertised.

To satisfy the variety of consumer tastes and achieve competitive advantages, marketers build differences into their products. Even the product's package is part of the product concept. The concept may also be developed through unique positioning against competing products.

Price refers to what and how a customer pays for a product. Companies use many common pricing strategies. Some products compete on the basis of price, but many do not.

Distribution refers to how the product is placed at the disposal of the customer: where the product is distributed, how it is bought, and how it is sold. Companies may use direct or indirect methods of distribution. Consumer goods manufacturers use several types of distribution strategies.

Communications refers to all marketing-related communications between the seller and the buyer. Tools of the communications element include personal selling, advertising, direct marketing, public relations activities, collateral materials, and sales promotion. Marketers try to integrate all their marketing communications programs for greater effectiveness and consistency.

Key Terms

behavioristic segmentation, 97
benefits, 99
benefit segmentation, 99
brand, 113
brand equity, 114
branding, 113
business markets, 103
cooperative advertising, 117
copy points, 114
decline stage, 111
demographic segmentation, 100
direct distribution, 115
distribution channel, 117
early adopter, 109
exchange, 94

exclusive distribution, 118
family brand, 113
four Ps (4Ps), 109
geodemographic segmentation, 100
geographic segmentation, 99
growth stage, 110
hidden differences, 112
individual brand, 113
induced differences, 112
intensive distribution, 117
introductory phase, 109
licensed brand, 114
market segmentation, 95
marketing communications, 118
marketing mix, 109

maturity stage, 110
national brand, 113
network marketing, 116
North American Industry Classification System (NAICS) codes, 105
perceptible differences, 112
place (distribution) element, 115
position, 112
price element, 115
primary demand, 109
primary motivation, 102
private label, 113
product concept, 109
product element, 109
product life cycle, 109

Review Questions

1. How does the concept of shared characteristics relate to the market segmentation process?
2. How could you use VALS to develop the marketing strategy for a product of your choice?
3. How does the segmentation of business markets differ from that of consumer markets?
4. What is the most important factor to consider when determining the elements of the marketing mix?
5. What is the difference between a product and a product concept?

6. What are some examples of product positioning not discussed in this chapter?
7. What effect does the product life cycle have on the advertising a company uses?
8. What factors influence the price of a product?
9. How do the basic methods of distribution affect advertising?
10. What product characteristics encourage heavy advertising? Little advertising? Why?

Exploring Advertising

1. Find a print ad and identify the *utility* that is communicated in the ad. Does it address a functional need or a symbolic want? Describe that need or want.
2. Bring in or describe an advertisement that seems to be directed toward a specific target market. Describe what you perceive to be the targeted market segment. Define it using behavioristic, demographic, psychographic, and geographic variables.
3. Select a consumer product and describe what stage of the Product Life Cycle you believe it to be in. How would being in that stage affect the target market selected and the marketing mix used for this product or service?

4. Think of a product or service (not mentioned in this chapter) that is strongly positioned. Describe its positioning. Does its advertising differentiate it from other products with perceptible, hidden, or induced differences?
5. Go to the VALS Web site (www.sric-bi.com) and take the VALS Survey. Do you agree with the results? Do they correctly describe your segment? How would this information be useful to a marketer who was trying to target its product or service to you?

chapter five

Communication and Consumer Behavior

Objectives

To explain advertising communication and how it is used to persuade consumers to behave in a certain way. The successful advertising practitioner must understand the unique role advertising plays in the communication process and the way consumers behave in response to advertising communications. Ideally, this understanding results in the creation of effective advertising.

After studying this chapter, you will be able to:

* **Explain** how advertising differs from the basic communication process.

* **Outline** the consumer perception process and explain why advertising people say "perception is everything."

* **Describe** the fundamental motives behind consumer purchases.

* **Discuss** the various influences on consumer behavior.

* **Explain** how advertisers deal with cognitive dissonance.

* **Describe** how a consumer's level of involvement with a product influences the decision-making process and the advertising approach

HomeGrocer.com was born of the minds of three entrepreneurs with visions of staking a claim in this rapidly evolving world. Terry Dayton, Ken Deering, and Mike Donald sought to make grocery shopping an experience that would no longer require getting in the car, sitting in traffic, weaving through crowded aisles, and waiting in long lines. With the creation of HomeGrocer.com in 1997, the founders envisioned people shopping from home on a regular basis, their fresh groceries arriving the following day with a friendly smile. As they put it, they wanted to be the "milkmen of the 90s."

Within two years, the venture received more than $160 million in funding from big-time investors.[1] HomeGrocer developed an aggressive plan to maintain swift and steady growth. By year's end, top management vowed to expand into 20 new locations throughout the United States, lease 2 million square feet of warehouse space and more than 1,000 new Freightliner delivery trucks, hire 7,000 employees, and launch a multimillion-dollar ad campaign.[2] With a solid business plan aimed at taking advantage of a $500 billion market and strong financial backing, HomeGrocer.com had all the earmarks of a sure-fire winner.

Yet, despite this fantastic start, HomeGrocer.com was doomed from the beginning. Even with all of the money it had raised, all the capital it had invested, and all the new locations it had opened, HomeGrocer.com still lacked one important thing: a product that appealed to a broad enough customer base to turn a profit. The result? On June 26, 2000, just three months after going public, HomeGrocer.com was sold to its main rival, Webvan, for $1.1 billion in stock—one year later, after losing $697 million in three years, Webvan also closed its doors.[3]

How did this happen? How could the e-grocers, and HomeGrocer.com in particular, attract so much attention, raise so much money, and expand so quickly, only to close shop within two years? The answer is simple: poor marketing. More specifically, HomeGrocer failed to identify its potential customers and lacked a complete understanding of potential customers' wants. HomeGrocer was not just creating a new service; it was seeking to change peoples' grocery-shopping behavior as well.[4] For most shoppers, the only true way of choosing a ripe piece of fruit is to pick it up, squeeze it, and smell it. The online world was simply too foreign. Changing this behavioral trend would be a slow and time-consuming process. Yet time was the one thing that the market would not allow. With hungry investors, tight competition, and an ever-evolving marketplace, HomeGrocer.com needed to grow big, and it needed to do this quickly. Instead of taking the time needed to foster a change in customer behavior, HomeGrocer expanded as quickly as Wall Street dictated, spending millions marketing a service that few were ready to pay for.

At the time, the majority of customers were not willing to pay a premium for delivery when they could either get their groceries themselves or have an existing supermarket deliver their groceries at a lower cost.

To succeed in business, a company's top managers must understand the basic principles of marketing. Specifically, they must understand who their customers are, and they must listen and respond to their customers' desires. They cannot assume anything about the market. Companies that suffer from the assumption syndrome court failure and have swift endings. Even superior advertising won't save a mismarketed service. Unfortunately, advertising all too often becomes the scapegoat for management's marketing mistakes.

Communication: What Makes Advertising Unique

In the last chapter, we learned that communication is a key element of the marketing mix. However, for communication to be effective, the marketer must be able to construct a message that is meaningful to consumers and that will elicit the desired behavior.

In Chapter 1, we defined advertising as "the structured and composed non-personal communication of information." Advertising is a special kind of communication. McCann-Erickson, the ad agency for Coca-Cola and MasterCard, says that advertising is "Truth well told." This means that ethical advertisers, and the agencies they employ, work as a team to discover and use the best methods possible to tell their story truthfully and creatively to the marketplace. To succeed, they must understand the elements of the advertising communication process, which is derived from the basic human communication process.

The Human Communication Process

From our first cry at birth, our survival depends on our ability to inform others or persuade them to take some action. As we develop, we learn to listen and respond to others' messages. The traditional model in Exhibit 5–1 summarizes the series of events that take place when people share ideas in informal oral communication. The process begins when one party, called the source, formulates an idea, encodes it as a message, and sends it via some channel to another party, called the receiver. The receiver must decode the message in order to understand it. To respond, the receiver formulates a new idea, encodes it, and then sends the new message back through some channel. A message that acknowledges or responds to the original message constitutes feedback, which also affects the encoding of a new message.[5] And, of course, all this takes place

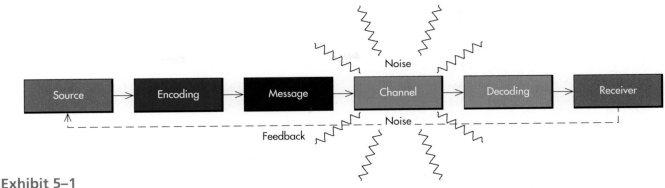

Exhibit 5–1

The human communication process.

in an environment characterized by noise—the distracting cacophony of many other messages being sent at the same time by other sources.

Applying the Communication Process to Advertising

Applying this model to advertising, we could say that the source is the sponsor, the message is the ad, the channel is the medium, the receiver is the consumer or prospect, and the noise is the din of competing ads and commercials. Most advertising today is a one-way process, with the message moving from the sponsor to the consumer. However, more interactive forms of marketing—personal selling, telemarketing, online advertising, interactive television—let consumers participate in the communication by extracting the information they need, manipulating what they see and hear, and responding in real time.

The Source

The ultimate **source** of a marketing message is the organization that has information it wishes to share with others. However, within the context of an advertisement, a real or imaginary spokesperson actually lends voice or tone to the communication. Because the receiver's perception of the source influences the effectiveness of the communication, the spokesperson must appear to be knowledgeable, trustworthy, and relevant to the audience.

The Message

The information contained in a **message** must be **encoded** in such a way that the receiver understands what is being communicated. This involves using words or symbols that are familiar to the intended audience. Depending on the medium used, the message may be verbal or nonverbal. **Semiotics** is the study of how humans use words, gestures, signs, and symbols to convey feelings, thoughts, ideas, and ideologies.[6] For example, the cowboy in the Marlboro advertisements symbolizes ruggedness and individualism. The Energizer bunny communicates reliability and persistence.

The Channel

The **channel** is the means by which the encoded message travels from the source to the receiver. Communications channels can be categorized as personal or nonpersonal. **Personal channels,** such as

Symbols are often used in advertising to encode messages. In this ad, Evian (www.evian.com) uses a flower to symbolize water's ability to restore, revitalize, replenish, and hydrate. Evian would like you to think of its spring water as a beauty product.

Interactive television will provide TV viewers with the ability to provide feedback to advertisers, request more information, or order products without leaving their chairs. This interactive television ad for the Honda CR-V, featured on *Interactive TV Today* (www.itvt.com), allows viewers to order T-shirts or learn more about the CR-V shower accessory by simply pressing a button on their TV remotes.

personal selling, involve direct contact between the parties. **Nonpersonal channels** of communication are those that rule out interpersonal contact between the sender and the receiver. Mass communications, such as television, newspapers, magazines, radio, and billboards, are sent to many individuals at one time.

The Receiver

The **receiver** is usually the consumer who reads, hears, or sees the advertiser's message. The advertiser must always be concerned about how the consumer will **decode,** or interpret, a message. The last thing an advertiser wants is to be misunderstood. Unfortunately, message interpretation is only partially determined by the words and symbols in the ad. The medium used may have an effect as well. As Marshall McLuhan said, "The medium is the message." Further, the unique characteristics of the receivers themselves are also very important, and the sponsor may know little or nothing about them. As we shall see later in this chapter, attitudes, perceptions, personality, self-concept, and culture are just some of the many important influences that affect the way people receive and respond to messages and how they behave as consumers in the marketplace.

As mentioned earlier, complicating this problem is the fact that the sponsor's advertising message must compete with hundreds of other commercial and noncommercial messages every day. This is referred to as **noise.** So the sender doesn't know how the message is received, or even if it is received, until a consumer acknowledges it.

Feedback and Interactivity

That's why **feedback** is so important. It completes the cycle, verifying that the message was received. Feedback employs the sender-message-receiver pattern, except that it is directed from the receiver back to the source.

In advertising, feedback can take many forms: redeemed coupons, phone inquiries, visits to a store, requests for more information, increased sales, responses to a survey, or e-mail inquiries. Dramatically low responses to an ad indicate a break in the communication process. Questions arise: Is the product wrong for the market? Is the message unclear? Are we using the right media? Without feedback, these questions cannot be answered.

In the past, the consumer's feedback used different channels than the original message. But now, thanks again to technology, the audiences of advertising are no longer just passive receivers of impersonal mass messages. They are now active decision makers who can control what communications they receive and choose the information they want about a particular product. With the growth of **interactive media** such as the Internet and interactive television, they can give instantaneous, real-time feedback on the same channel used by the original message sender.

CONCEPT CHECK

Equate the elements of advertising to the steps in the human communication process.

Consumer Behavior: The Key to Advertising Strategy

Now we know that effective communication is accomplished when the marketer selects a relevant source, develops an appropriate message, encodes it correctly, and then selects a suitable medium that will best reach the target audience. All of these steps rely upon the marketer knowing the receiver of the message and understanding how that individual might respond.

Take a look at your friends in class, or the people you work with. How well do you know them? Could you describe their lifestyles and the kinds of products they prefer? Do they typically eat out or cook for themselves? Do they ski? Play tennis? If so, what brands of equipment do they buy? Do you know which radio stations they listen to? What TV programs they watch? Do they read a daily newspaper? If you were Sanyo's advertising manager and wanted to advertise a new DVD player to these people, what type of appeal would you use? What media would you use to reach them?

Perception. | Reality.

For a new generation of Rolling Stone readers, drugs are out of their minds and into the frying pan. They know the truth; that if you tune in and turn on, you burn out. For twenty five years, Rolling Stone magazine has reflected the changing attitudes, ideas and lifestyles of the people who are changing the world. If you want to reach seven million of these people, we invite you to alter a few minds in the pages of Rolling Stone.

Rolling Stone

From the viewpoint of the customer, perception is reality. Companies must therefore carefully monitor the messages they send, since those messages may either enhance their image or damage it. Some advertisers, for example, perceive the readers of *Rolling Stone* to be hedonistic dopeheads—leftovers from the hippie era. So the magazine (www.rollingstone.com) attempts to change this perception by specifically addressing it and offering a counterargument of what the reality actually is. This highly successful campaign has garnered innumerable awards for creativity from the advertising industry.

The Importance of Knowing the Consumer

Advertisers spend a lot of money to keep individuals and groups of individuals (markets) interested in their products. To succeed, they need to understand what makes potential customers behave the way they do. The advertiser's goal is to get enough relevant market data to develop accurate profiles of buyers—to find the common ground (and symbols) for communication. This involves the study of **consumer behavior:** the mental and emotional processes and the physical activities of people who purchase and use goods and services to satisfy particular needs and wants.[7]

The Consumer Decision Process: An Overview

Social scientists develop many theories of consumer behavior to explain the process of making a purchase decision. Let's look at this information from the viewpoint of the advertiser.

Advertising's primary mission is to reach prospective customers and influence their awareness, attitudes, and buying behavior. As we just learned, to succeed, an advertiser must make the marketing communications process work very effectively.

The moment a medium delivers an advertising message to us, our mental computer runs a rapid evaluation called the **consumer decision process.** The conceptual model in Exhibit 5–2 presents the basic steps consumers go through in making a purchase decision. As you can see, the full process involves a rather lengthy sequence of activities: *problem recognition* (which may occur as a result of seeing an ad), *information search, evaluation and selection* of alternative brands, *store choice and purchase,* and finally *postpurchase behavior.* For simple, habitual, everyday purchases with low levels of involvement, the decision-making process is typically very abbreviated. But in those situations where the consumer is highly involved in the purchase, it's not at all unusual for the consumer to substantially extend the decision process.

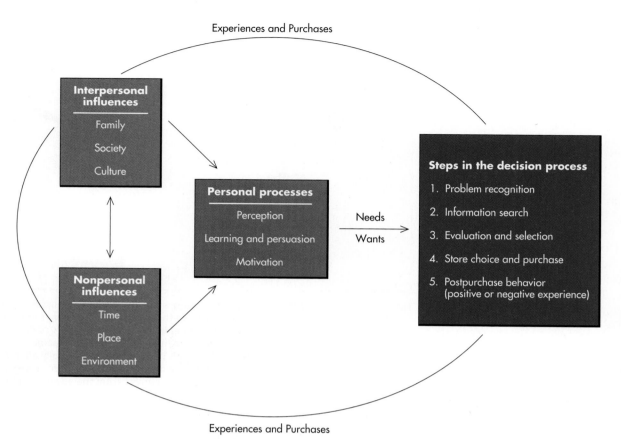

Experiences and Purchases

Interpersonal influences

Family

Society

Culture

Nonpersonal influences

Time

Place

Environment

Personal processes

Perception

Learning and persuasion

Motivation

Needs

Wants

Steps in the decision process

1. Problem recognition

2. Information search

3. Evaluation and selection

4. Store choice and purchase

5. Postpurchase behavior (positive or negative experience)

Experiences and Purchases

Exhibit 5–2

The basic consumer decision process comprises a set of fundamental steps that the consumer experiences during and after the purchase process. Advertising can affect the consumer's attitude at any point in this process. For the complete model of the process, see RL 5–1 in the Reference Library on the *Essentials of Contemporary Advertising* Web site.

Regardless of whether the process is limited or extended, though, numerous sociological and psychological factors invariably play a role in the way consumers behave. These include a series of personal subprocesses that are themselves shaped by various influences.

The three **personal processes** govern the way we discern raw data *(stimuli)* and translate them into feelings, thoughts, beliefs, and actions. The personal processes are the *perception,* the *learning and persuasion,* and the *motivation processes.*

Second, our mental processes and behavior are affected by two sets of influences. **Interpersonal influences** include our *family, society,* and *culture.* **Nonpersonal influences**—factors often outside the consumer's control—include *time, place,* and *environment.* These influences further affect the personal processes of perception, learning, and motivation.

After dealing with these processes and influences, we face the pivotal decision: to buy or not to buy. But taking that final step typically requires yet another process, the **evaluation of alternatives,** in which we choose brands, sizes, styles, and colors. If we do decide to buy, our **postpurchase evaluation** will dramatically affect all our subsequent purchases.

Like the communications process, the decision process is circular in nature. The advertiser who understands this process can develop messages more likely to reach and make sense to consumers.

CONCEPT CHECK

Why is it important for an advertiser to understand the basic steps consumers go through in making a purchase decision?

Personal Processes in Consumer Behavior

Assume you are the advertising manager preparing to launch a new high-tech, vitamin-laden beverage brand for athletes and sports participants. We'll call it MonsterMalt. What's your first objective?

The first task in promoting any new product is to create awareness *(perception)* that the product exists. The second is to provide enough compelling information *(learning and persuasion)* about the product for prospective customers to become interested and make an informed decision. Finally, you want your advertising to stimulate customers' desire *(motivation)* to satisfy their needs and wants by trying the product.

If they find MonsterMalt satisfying, they likely will continue to purchase it. These three personal processes of consumer behavior—perception, learning and persuasion, and motivation—are extremely important to advertisers. By studying these, advertisers can better evaluate how their messages are perceived.

The Consumer Perception Process

Perception is everything. It guides all our activities from the people we associate with to the products we buy. How a consumer perceives each of the different brands in a category determines which ones he or she uses.[8] The perception challenge, therefore, is the first and greatest hurdle advertisers must cross. Some marketers spend millions of dollars on national advertising, sales promotion, point-of-purchase displays, and other marketing communications only to discover that many consumers don't remember the product or the promotion. The average adult may be exposed to thousands of ads each day but notices only a handful and remembers even fewer.[9] How does this happen? The answer lies in the principle of perception.

We use the term **perception** to refer to the personalized way we sense, interpret, and comprehend various *stimuli.* This definition suggests there are several key elements to the consumer perception process, as shown in Exhibit 5–3.

Stimulus

A **stimulus** is physical information we receive through our senses. When we look at a new car, we receive a number of stimuli. We might note the color of the paint, the smell of the leather, the purr of the engine. When we look at a theater ad in the newspaper, we see a collection of type, art, and photography

Exhibit 5–3

The model of the consumer perception process portrays how consumers perceive, accept, and remember an ad or other stimulus to buy.

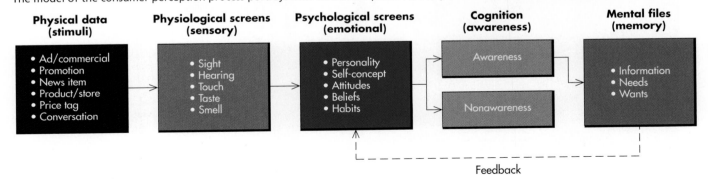

arranged in a way that we interpret as an ad. That's the stimulus. So, for our purposes, assume that a stimulus is any ad, commercial, or promotion that we see.

Advertising stimuli can appear in a variety of forms: a window display at a local department store, the brightly colored labels on cans of Campbell's tomato soup, or even the red price tag on a pair of skis at the Sport Chalet. These objects are all physical in nature; they stimulate our senses (with varying degrees of intensity) in ways that can be measured.

Perceptual Screens

The second key element in perception is the personalized way of sensing and interpreting the stimulus data. Before any data can be perceived, they must first penetrate a set of **perceptual screens,** the subconscious filters that shield us from unwanted messages. There are two types of screens, *physiological* and *psychological.*

The **physiological screens** comprise the five senses: sight, hearing, touch, taste, and smell. They detect the incoming data and measure the dimension and intensity of the physical stimuli. A sight-impaired person can't read an ad in *Sports Illustrated.* And if the type in a movie ad is too small for the average reader, it won't be read, and perception will suffer. Similarly, if the music in a TV commercial for a furniture store is not complementary to the message, the viewer may tune out, change channels, or even turn off the TV. The advertiser's

Screens are physical and psychological barriers that advertisers must penetrate in order to gain notice and convey their message. This ad for Tibor Nemeth Photography (www.tibornemeth.com) first grabs the viewers' attention with the sheer natural beauty of the ad. It then throws in what seems like a completely random headline. The attention is then directed to the copy below the photo, which puts the pieces together with the tagline, "Great photography can make you read anything."

How much wood could a woodchuck chuck if a woodchuck could chuck wood?

Great photography can make you read anything. Tibor Nemeth Photography · tibornemeth.com

message is effectively screened out when the viewer can't interpret it; perception does not occur, and the furniture goes unsold.[10]

We are limited not only by the physical capacity of our senses but also by our feelings and interests. Each consumer uses **psychological screens** to evaluate, filter, and personalize information according to subjective emotional standards. These screens evaluate data based on *innate factors,* such as the consumer's personality and instinctive human needs, and *learned factors,* such as self-concept, interests, attitudes, beliefs, past experiences, and lifestyle. They help consumers summarize unwieldy or complex data.

After extensive consumer research, Bally's Health & Tennis determined that the perfectly chiseled body, glorified by earlier health club advertising and exemplified by such icons as Cher, Victoria Principal, and Don Johnson, was no longer penetrating the psychological screens of its 4.5 million members. As the new millennium approached, that premise no longer fit their **self-concept** (the image we have of who we are and who we want to be). In a major strategy shift, Bally's refocused its advertising on customers such as Beth from Costa Mesa, California, who is seen rock climbing in a TV commercial while telling viewers, "I think I climb because I'm afraid of heights. . . . There is nothing better than being able to conquer that fear. That's why I work out at Bally's, so I can do more on the rocks." The tagline: "If you can get here [Bally's], you can get there [a mountaintop]."

As this example shows, advertisers face a major problem dealing with consumers' perceptual screens. As overcommunicated consumers, we unconsciously screen out or modify many of the sensations that bombard us, rejecting those that conflict with our experiences, needs, desires, attitudes, and beliefs.[11] We simply focus on some things and ignore others. This is called **selective perception.** Hence, Panasonic may run a series of outstanding ads for its new digital camcorder in the daily newspaper, but they won't penetrate the psychological screens of consumers who don't need or want a new camera. Later these people probably won't even remember seeing the ads.

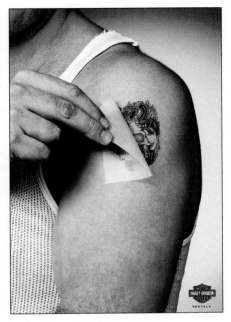

Advertisers frequently capitalize on consumers' concepts of themselves to generate attention and interest in a particular product. This ad—a 2004 Cannes Bronze Lion winner from Ogilvy & Mather RSTM—takes the next step: It shows consumers that they can temporarily identify with their wilder sides by renting a Harley-Davidson (www.harleydavidson.com).

Cognition

The third key element in perception is **cognition:** comprehending the stimulus. Once we detect the stimulus and allow it through our perceptual screens, we can understand and accept it. Now perception has occurred, and the stimulus reaches the consumer's reality zone. Awareness has been achieved.

But each of us has his or her own reality. For example, you may consider the tacos advertised by Taco Bell to be "Mexican" food. That perception is your reality. But someone from Mexico might tell you that a fast-food taco bears little resemblance to an authentic Mexican taco. That person's reality, based on another perception, is considerably different. Advertisers thus seek commonly shared perceptions of reality as a basis for their advertising messages.

Mental Files

The mind is like a memory bank, and the stored memories in our minds are called the **mental files** (or perceptual files). Just as stimuli bombard our senses, information crowds our mental files in today's overcommunicative society. To cope with the complexity of stimuli such as advertising, we rank products and other data in our files by importance, price, quality, features, or a host of other descriptors. Consumers can rarely hold more than seven brand names in any one file—more often only one or two. The remainder either get discarded to some other file category or rejected altogether.[12] How many brands of running shoes can you quickly name, for example?

Because of our limited memory, we resist opening new mental files, and we avoid accepting new information inconsistent with what is already filed. The experience consumers receive from using a brand solidifies their perceptions of it. These fixed perceptions can rarely be changed through advertising alone.[13]

What are the various factors that influence how a consumer might perceive an advertising message?

But once a new perception does enter our mental files, the information alters the database on which our psychological screens feed.

Because perceptual screens are such a major challenge to advertisers, it's important to understand what's in the consumer's mental files and, if possible, modify them in favor of the advertiser's product. That brings us to the second process in consumer behavior: *learning and persuasion*.

Learning and Persuasion: How Consumers Process Information

Each time we file a new perception in our minds it's a learning process. Many psychologists consider learning to be the most fundamental process in human behavior. From the advertiser's perspective, though, perception is the most important because it precedes learning. In truth, perception and learning are a continuum, overlapping each other.

By definition, **learning** is a relatively permanent change in thought process or behavior that occurs as a result of reinforced experience. Like perception, learning works off the mental files and at the same time contributes to them. Learning produces our habits and skills. It also contributes to the development of interests, attitudes, beliefs, preferences, prejudices, emotions, and standards of conduct—all of which affect our perceptual screens and our eventual purchase decisions.

Theories of Learning

There are numerous theories of learning, but advertisers classify most into two broad categories—*cognitive theory* and *conditioning theory*—depending on the level of consumer involvement (high or low) required to make a purchase. **Cognitive theory** views learning as a mental process of memory, thinking, and the rational application of knowledge to practical problems. This theory may be an accurate description of how we learn from the experience of others, such as our parents, and how we evaluate a complex purchase such as insurance, stocks and bonds, or business products. **Conditioning theory**—also called **stimulus-response theory**—treats learning as a trial-and-error process. Some stimulus (perhaps an ad) triggers the consumer's need or want, and this in turn creates the drive to respond. If the consumer's response reduces the drive, then satisfaction occurs, and the response is rewarded or reinforced. And that produces repeat behavior the next time the drive is aroused, demonstrating that learning has taken place. Exhibit 5–4 shows simple diagrams of these two theories.

Conditioning theory is more applicable to the simple, basic purchases consumers make every day, such as soap, cereal, toothpaste, paper towels. And it is here that reinforcement advertising plays its most important role—along with superior product performance and good service. If learning is reinforced enough and repeat behavior is produced, a purchasing habit may result.

Learning and persuasion are closely linked. **Persuasion** occurs when the change in belief, attitude, or behavioral intention is caused by promotion communication (such as advertising or personal selling).[14] Naturally, advertisers are very interested in persuasion and how it takes place.

The Elaboration Likelihood Model

Researchers have identified two ways promotion communication can persuade consumers: the *central* and *peripheral routes to persuasion*. Like learning theory, each depends on the consumer's level of involvement with the product and the message. When the consumer's level of involvement is higher, the central route to persuasion is more likely. On the other hand, the peripheral route to persuasion is more likely when consumer involvement is low.[15]

We can see how this works by looking at the **Elaboration Likelihood Model** in Exhibit 5–5. In the **central route to persuasion,** consumers have a higher level of involvement with the product or the message, so they are motivated to pay attention to the central, product-related information, such as product attributes and benefits or demonstrations of positive functional or psychological consequences. Because of their high involvement, they tend to learn cognitively and comprehend the ad-delivered information at deeper, more elaborate levels. This can lead to product beliefs, positive brand attitudes, and purchase intention.[16]

Suppose you are in the market for a significant purchase, say, a new camera or a computer. Because the purchase is relatively expensive, your level of involvement is higher. Perhaps you ask for advice from some friends or family members. You may shop different stores to compare models and prices. And you probably read ads for these products thoroughly to understand the variety of product features and benefits. That's central processing. And in that situation, a well-written, informative ad can be very persuasive.

The **peripheral route to persuasion** is very different. It's more like stimulus-response learning. People who are not in the market for a product typically have low involvement with the product message. They have little or no reason to pay attention to it or to comprehend the central information of the ad. As a result, direct persuasion is also low, and consumers form few if any brand beliefs, attitudes, or purchase intentions. However, these consumers might attend to some peripheral aspects—say, the pictures or the colors in an ad or the actors in a commercial—for their entertainment value. And whatever they feel or think about these peripheral, nonproduct aspects might integrate into a positive attitude toward the ad. At some later

Exhibit 5–4

Cognitive theory views learning as a mental process; conditioning theory treats learning as a trial-and-error process.

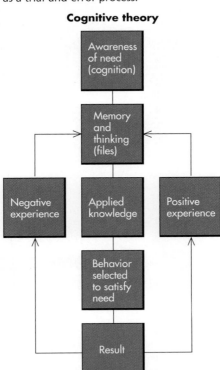

Exhibit 5–5

The Elaboration Likelihood Model.

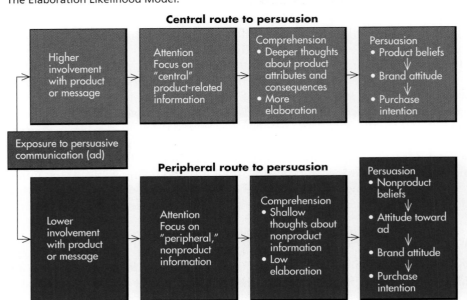

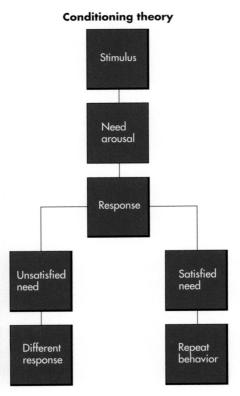

available at select macy's . keds.com

new tricks in keds stretch™

keds

every wear™

A consumer may have only low involvement with a product at the time an ad runs. A peripherally processed ad, like this fun ad for Keds (www.keds.com), hopes to create a positive attitude so that consumers will remember the brand once they are in the market to purchase.

date, if a purchase occasion does arise and the consumer needs to make some brand evaluation, these ad-related meanings could be activated to form some brand attitude or purchase intention.

Because very few people are actually in the market at any given time, most mass media advertising probably receives peripheral processing. We all know that most of the ads we see have little relevance to our immediate goals or needs, so we are not motivated to pay close attention to, much less think about, them. Our involvement is very low. That's why we also have very little recall of ads we saw yesterday. In cases where there is little product differentiation, advertisers may actually *want* us to engage in peripheral processing. Their ads focus more on image or entertainment than product features. This is typical of advertising for many everyday low-involvement purchases, such as soap, cereal, toothpaste, and chewing gum.

But when a product has a distinct advantage, the advertiser's goal should be to encourage central route processing by increasing consumers' involvement with the message. This is where we see a lot of comparative advertising.[17]

One key to learning and persuasion is repetition. Just as a student prepares for an exam by repeating key information to memorize it, an advertiser must repeat key information to prospective and current customers so they remember the product's name and its benefits. Repeat messages penetrate customers' perceptual screens by rekindling memories of information from prior ads. Quebec-based Cossette Communications-Marketing used pairs of billboards for the Provigo grocery store chain. They featured similar strong visual elements and were positioned to be seen in succession. The repetition proved highly successful, producing $100 million in sales in just six months.

Learning Produces Attitudes and Interest

An **attitude** is our acquired mental position regarding some idea or object. It is the positive or negative evaluations, feelings, or action tendencies that we learn and cling to. To advertisers, gaining positive consumer attitudes is critical to success. Attitudes must be either capitalized on or changed.

In Japan, for instance, dishwashers are not a common household appliance. Not only is there very little space for them, Japanese housewives feel guilty about using the labor-saving device. As a result, dishwasher manufacturers have designed smaller, space-saving machines and then promoted them using good hygiene themes rather than convenience appeals.[18]

For mature brands in categories with familiar, frequently purchased products, *brand interest* is even more critical for motivating action. **Brand interest** is an individual's openness or curiosity about a brand.[19] Enjoyable, entertaining advertising can enhance interest in the brand and reduce the variety-seeking tendencies of consumers who become bored with using the same old product.[20]

Learning Leads to Habits and Brand Loyalty

Attitude is the mental side and *habit* the behavioral side of the same coin. **Habit**—the acquired behavior pattern that becomes nearly or completely involuntary—is the natural extension of learning. We really are creatures of habit.

"Bird Seed" :30

(Open on an elderly man standing in a quiet park feeding pigeons)

SFX: Cooing pigeons.

(The peace is shattered when a high-revving sports car whips into a nearby parking spot. The driver skids to a stop. The birds scatter into the air.)

SFX: Screeching tires.

(Freeze frame.)

Super: That's low.

SFX: Ding!

(The businessman, talking on his cell phone, steps out of the car, hits the

car alarm and leaves. The birdless man watches the rude driver walk off. Cut to the convertible now filled with pigeons. The elderly man is tossing birdseed into the car. Freeze frame.)

Super: That's lower.

SFX: Ding!

Super: But not as low as Southwest Airline's click 'n' Save fares. (Fades.)

Super: They're our lowest fares and available only at southwest.com.

SFX: Ding!

Logo: southwest.com a symbol of e-freedom

Brett Stiles, art director

Christopher Staub, writer

David Crawford/Jeremmy Postaer, creative directors

Karen Jacobs, producer

Peter Darley Miller, director

Steifel & Co., production company

GSD&M Advertising (Austin, TX), ad agency

Southwest Airlines, client

Brand interest is an important component of marketing for products in the highly competitive field of travel and leisure. Creatives strive to gain additional awareness and interest in the brand, often through enjoyable and entertaining advertisements like this one for Southwest.com (www.southwest.com).

Most consumer behavior is habitual for three reasons: It's safe, simple, and essential. First, regardless of how we learned to make our purchase decision (through either central or peripheral route processing), if we discover a quality product, brand, or service, we feel *safe* repurchasing it through habit.

Second, habit is *simple*. To consider alternatives we must evaluate, compare, and then decide. This is difficult and time-consuming.

Finally, because habit is both safe and easy, we rely on it for daily living. Imagine rethinking every purchase decision you make. It would be virtually impossible, not to mention impractical. So it's really *essential* to use habit in our lives.

The major objective of all brand marketers is to produce *brand* loyalty, a direct result of the habit of repurchasing and the reinforcement of continuous advertising. **Brand loyalty** is the consumer's conscious or unconscious decision, expressed through intention or behavior, to repurchase a brand continually.[21] It occurs because the consumer *perceives* that the brand offers the right product features, image, quality, or relationship at the right price.

In the quest for brand loyalty, advertisers have three aims related to habits:

1. *Breaking habits*. Get consumers to unlearn an existing purchase habit and try something new. Advertisers frequently offer incentives

to lure customers away from old brands or stores. Or they may use comparative advertising to demonstrate their product's superiority.

2. *Acquiring habits.* Teach consumers to repurchase their brand or repatronize their establishment. To get you started, Columbia House advertises free CDs when you sign up, tied to a contract to purchase more later on.

3. *Reinforcing habits.* Remind current customers of the value of their original purchase and encourage them to continue purchasing. Many magazines, for example, offer special renewal rates to their regular subscribers.

Developing brand loyalty is much more difficult today due to consumers' increased sophistication and to the legions of habit-breaking activities of competitive advertisers.[22] Only recently have advertisers come to realize that their years of habit-breaking activities have undermined their own *habit-building* objectives. In the quest for instant results, they shifted much of their advertising budgets to sales promotions (deals, coupons, price cuts). But advertising, unlike sales promotion, is an integral part of what makes a brand salable. It's advertising that reinforces brand loyalty and maintains market share.[23] We revisit this topic in our discussion of sales promotion in Chapter 16.

CONCEPT CHECK

Describe the steps that lead consumers from perception to learning and persuasion.

Learning Defines Needs and Wants

The learning process is both immediate and long term. The moment we file a perception, some learning takes place. When we see a succulent food ad, we may suddenly feel hungry; we *need* food. As we collate the information in our mental files, comparing new perceptions with old ones, further learning takes place. The need may become a *want*. This leads to the next personal process, motivation.

Maslow's hierarchy of needs explains the levels of physical and psychological needs that humans must fulfill. Porsche (www.porsche.com) hints at several levels of needs in its ad touting the car's access to "instant freedom."

What a dog feels when the leash breaks.

The Consumer Motivation Process

Motivation refers to the underlying forces (or motives) that contribute to our actions. These motives stem from the conscious or unconscious goal of satisfying our needs and wants. **Needs** are the basic, often instinctive, human forces that motivate us to do something. **Wants** are "needs" that we learn during our lifetime.[24]

Motivation cannot be observed directly. When we see people eat, we assume they are hungry, but we may be wrong. People eat for a variety of reasons besides hunger: They want to be sociable, it's time to eat, or maybe they're nervous or bored.

People are usually motivated by the benefit of satisfying some combination of needs, which may be conscious

Need	Product	Promotional appeal
Self-actualization	Golf lessons	"Realize your full potential"
Esteem	Luxury car	"Be in control of the road"
Social	Pendant	"Show her you care"
Safety	Tires	"Bounces off hazards"
Physiological	Breakfast cereal	"The natural energy source"

Exhibit 5–6

The hierarchy of needs suggests that people meet their needs according to priorities. Physiological and safety needs carry the greatest priority.

In advertising, the message must match the need of the market or the ad will fail.

Advertisers use marketing research to understand the need levels of their markets and use this information in determining the marketing mix.

or unconscious, functional or psychological. *Motivation research* offers insights into the underlying reasons for certain observed consumer behavior. The reasons *(motives)* some people stop shopping at Ralph's Supermarket and switch to Vons may be that the Vons market is closer to home, it has a wider selection of fresh produce, and (most likely) they see other people like themselves shopping at Vons. Any or all of these factors might make a shopper switch even if prices are lower at Ralph's.

To better understand what motivates people, Abraham Maslow developed the classic model shown in Exhibit 5–6 called the **hierarchy of needs.** Maslow maintained that the lower, physiological and safety needs dominate human behavior and must be satisfied before the higher, socially acquired needs (or wants) become meaningful. The highest need, self-actualization, is the culmination of fulfilling all the lower needs and realizing one's true potential.

The promise of satisfying a certain level of need is the basic promotional appeal for many ads. In such affluent societies as the United States, Canada, Western Europe, and Japan, most individuals take for granted the satisfaction of their physiological needs. So advertising campaigns often portray the fulfillment of social, esteem, and self-actualization needs, and many offer the reward of satisfaction through personal achievement.

In focus groups for Nabisco SnackWells, for example, it became apparent that middle-aged women today have a high sense of self-worth. Wellness, to them, is no longer about looking good in a bathing suit, but rather celebrating what they do well. The advertiser wondered if it could use women's positive attitude about themselves to change their attitude toward the concept of snacking. Nabisco's agency, Foote, Cone & Belding, capitalized on the idea in a new campaign aimed at boosting women's self-esteem. The message: "Snacking is not about 'filling' yourself, but 'fulfilling' yourself."[25]

We all have needs and wants, but we are frequently unaware of them. Before the advent of the desktop computer, people were completely unaware of any need for it. But the moment a consumer consciously recognizes a product-related want or need, a dynamic process begins. The consumer first evaluates the need and either accepts it as worthy of action or rejects it. Acceptance converts satisfaction of the need into a goal, which creates the motivation to reach a particular result. In contrast, rejection removes the necessity for action and thereby eliminates the goal and the motivation to buy.

Modern researchers translated Maslow's theory about needs and motives into more strategic concepts for use by marketers and advertisers. Rossiter and Percy, for example, identify eight fundamental purchase and usage motives (see Exhibit 5–7). They refer to the first five as *negatively originated (informational) motives* and the last three as *positively originated (transformational) motives.*[26]

Exhibit 5–7

Rossiter and Percy's eight fundamental purchase and usage motives.

Negatively originated (informational) motives

1. Problem removal
2. Problem avoidance
3. Incomplete satisfaction
4. Mixed approach–avoidance
5. Normal depletion

Positively originated (transformational) motives

6. Sensory gratification
7. Intellectual stimulation or mastery
8. Social approval

Negatively Originated (Informational) Motives

The most common energizers of consumer behavior are the **negatively originated motives,** such as problem removal or problem avoidance. Whenever we

VISUAL: Inside St. Patrick's Church, we see a statue of the Virgin Mary. A tear seems to fall from the statue's eye. We follow this tear, and other droplets that seem to come from the statue's eye, down the length of its body until they drip from the statue's foot and into a bucket underneath.

As we cut to the head of the statue, we see drips of water falling onto the head and over the face. We follow the drips up and see that the water is coming from a hole in the ceiling above the statue.

Cut to exterior shot of the St. Patrick's Church sign. It's raining heavily.
SUPER: Donations needed for urgent repairs.

Negative motivation is a powerful tool to affect human behavior. This ad by St. Patrick's Church in England evokes a sense of religious or civil responsibility to help renovate the religious sanctuary and historical landmark. The implication in the ad is that one can eliminate negative feelings of responsibility or guilt by donating to the church's repair.

run out of something, for instance, we experience a negative mental state. To relieve those feelings, we actively seek a new or replacement product. Thus, we are temporarily motivated until the time we make the purchase. Then, if the purchase is satisfactory, the drive or motivation is reduced.

These are also called **informational motives** because the consumer actively seeks information to reduce the negative mental state. In fact, Rossiter and Percy point out, these could also be called "relief" motives because consumers work to find relief from a problem.

Positively Originated (Transformational) Motives

Ads that make use of positively originated motives promise to reward consumers in some way. This Minute Maid Light ad (www.minutemaid.com) addresses two positively originated motives—sensory gratification and social approval—by promising the consumer both great taste and an attractive figure.

From time to time, we all want to indulge ourselves by buying some brand or product that promises some benefit or reward. With the **positively originated motives,** a positive bonus is promised rather than the removal or reduction of some negative situation. The goal is to use positive reinforcement to increase the consumer's motivation and to energize the consumer's investigation or search for the new product.

The three positively originated motives—sensory gratification, intellectual stimulation, and social approval—are also called **transformational motives** because the consumer expects to be transformed in a sensory, intellectual, or social sense. They could also be called "reward" motives because the transformation is a rewarding state.[27]

For some consumers, the purchase of a particular product (say, a new suit) might represent a negatively originated motive (they don't really want to spend the money on it, but they have to have it for work). But for other consumers, it might be positively originated (they love to shop for new clothes). This suggests two distinct target markets that advertisers must understand and that may call for completely different advertising strategies.

Before creating messages, advertisers must carefully consider the goals that lead to consumer motivations. Denny's Restaurants would make a costly mistake if its ads portrayed the reward of a romantic interlude if the real motive of most Denny's customers is simply to satisfy their need to reduce hunger with a filling, low-priced meal.

The issues of high-involvement and low-involvement products and informational and transformational motives are so important that we will revisit them in Chapter 7 when we discuss the development of marketing and advertising plans.

Interpersonal Influences on Consumer Behavior

For advertisers, it's not enough just to know the personal processes of perception, learning and persuasion, and motivation. Important **interpersonal influences** affect—sometimes even dominate—these processes. They also serve as guidelines for consumer behavior. These influences can best be categorized as the *family,* the *society,* and the *cultural environment* of the consumer.

Family Influence

From an early age, family communication affects our socialization as consumers—our attitudes toward many products and our purchasing habits. This influence is usually strong and long-lasting. A child who learns that the "right" headache relief is Bayer aspirin and the "right" name for appliances is General Electric has a well-developed adult purchasing behavior.

From 1970 to 1990, married couple households with children declined sharply—from 40 to 26 percent of all households. Since 1990, that decline has been slower—to 23 percent in 2003. Still, this suggests that family influence has greatly diminished in the United States over the last 30 years as working parents take a less active role in raising their children and youngsters look outside the family for social values.[28] As this happens, the influence of the social and cultural environments intensifies.

Societal Influence

The community we live in exerts a strong influence on all of us. When we affiliate with a particular societal division or identify with some reference group or value the ideas of certain opinion leaders, it affects our views on life, our perceptual screens, and eventually the products we buy.

Societal Divisions: The Group We Belong To

Sociologists traditionally divided societies into **social classes:** upper, upper-middle, lower-middle, and so on. They believed that people in the same social class tended to have similar attitudes, status symbols, and spending patterns.

But today this doesn't apply to most developed countries. U.S. society, especially, is extremely fluid and mobile—physically, socially, and economically. Americans, regardless of their social class, believe strongly in getting ahead, being better than their peers, and winning greater admiration and self-esteem. As the famous Army campaign illustrates, advertisers capitalize on this desire to "Be All You Can Be."

Because of this mobility, dramatic increases in immigration, and the high divorce rate, social-class boundaries have become quite muddled. Single parents, stockbrokers, immigrant shopkeepers, retired blue-collar workers, and bankers all see themselves as

Sometimes social class can affect how we see ourselves and how we fit into the larger social fabric. Although class differences are not as distinct in the United States as in many parts of the world, marketers of high-end purchases often capitalize on class distinction for product positioning purposes. In this ad, Cross Pens (www.cross.com) targets the alternative segment of the high-end purchasing crowd.

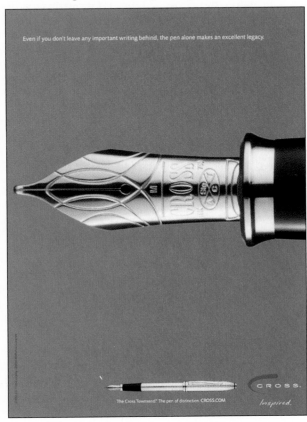

Even if you don't leave any important writing behind, the pen alone makes an excellent legacy.

The Cross Townsend™ The pen of distinction. CROSS.COM

CROSS.

Inspired.

Ethical Issues

Is It Marketing or Is It Exploitation?

Commercial sponsorship is one way to help fund primary and secondary schools. San Francisco–based School Properties, Inc., offers various sponsorship programs—including licensing school names and mascots, fund-raising catalogs, and affinity credit cards—to national and regional marketers. They test products and hold focus groups at schools, display banners at events, and use former student athletes for company appearances. School Properties, aware that budget cuts jeopardize extracurricular school activities, feel this program is a natural outgrowth of existing athletic and special-event sponsorships. Supporters feel it will help mobilize resources for schools, but opponents say that school funding is the government's problem and commercial product logos don't belong in education. Others wonder if this allows advertisers to take unfair advantage of captive kids.

The ethical dilemma concerns promoting products for advantage or profit at the unreasonable expense of the customer. Commercial products work only if they meet consumer needs, and advertising must appeal to those needs. But what happens if advertisers overstep a need, in a crisis situation, for example, and edge into exploitation?

Look at the public concern about the commercialization of children. In response to complaints about Saturday morning advertising to kids, broadcasters of children's TV are now banned from advertising toys during shows that feature those toys and they must clearly separate commercials from the program by announcing commercial breaks. In a different arena, most baby formula companies don't yet advertise directly to consumers because many doctors think breast-feeding is preferable to using formula. The companies don't want to be accused of exploitation; instead, they market their products through health care professionals, hospitals, and new-mother clubs.

Drastic changes in particular market segments may make new fields fertile for exploitation. For example, the emerging Third World middle class seems to have an insatiable appetite for buying things. While tradition and culture play a big role in what people buy and why, the evolving role of women, a burgeoning youth culture, and a middle class with higher expectations and more money than ever before make whole groups of consumers ripe for new products.

Some critics believe China is especially vulnerable to exploitation. A couple living in a cramped Beijing apartment may have a $270 refrigerator, a $700 foreign-made color TV, a telephone that came with a $600 installation charge, a $600 Panasonic VCR, a $1,200 Toshiba air conditioner, and a $1,200 piano—all purchased on a salary of $300 a month. In Mexico, companies pitch credit cards to people earning as little as $650 a month. The National Association of Credit Card Holders estimates five million Mexicans carry credit cards, but one million of them can't pay their bills. In the United States, the elderly and mentally incapacitated are targeted and exploited by sweepstakes promoters, misleading them into believing they've won contest monies and prizes. The elderly are bilked out of thousands of dollars in fees and merchandise they don't need and can't afford. State lotteries also prey on the hopes of the poor in their advertising, underplaying the long odds of winning significant prizes and exploiting gambling addictions.

Critics say that companies act irresponsibly when they target these groups for marketing and advertising activities because the average consumer can't afford the products being advertised.

However, researchers have investigated how advertising messages influence people to act. One finding, known as the third-person effect, holds that people generally believe others are more influenced by the media than they are. Perhaps the critics need to consider this. While they themselves can resist advertising appeals, they seem to believe the average consumer lacks their sophistication. So where do you draw the line between what is ethical (marketing) and what is not (exploitation)?

Questions

1. Do you think playing on people's desire for material possessions has a place in advertising? When does this become exploitation?

2. Is it the advertiser's responsibility to determine whether prospective customers can afford a product or service? Why or why not?

3. Are marketers enhancing the quality of life in developing countries or are they exploiting vulnerable consumers? Is this an example of the third-person effect?

part of the great middle class. So "middle class" doesn't mean anything anymore. From the advertiser's point of view, social class seldom represents a functional or operational set of values.

To deal with these often bewildering changes, marketers seek new ways to classify societal divisions and new strategies for advertising to them. We discussed some of these in Chapter 4. Exhibit 5–8 outlines some of the classifications marketers use to describe society today: for example, Upper Crust, Movers and Shakers, American Classics, and Big City Blues. People in the same group tend to have similar patterns of behavior and product usage.

Young Digerati

Young Digerati are the nation's tech-savvy singles and couples living in fashionable neighborhoods on the urban fringe. Affluent, highly educated and ethnically mixed, Young Digerati communities are typically filled with trendy apartments and condos, fitness clubs and clothing boutiques, casual restaurants and all types of bars—from juice to coffee to microbrew.

Urban Achievers

Concentrated in the nation's port cities, Urban Achievers is often the first stop for up-and-coming immigrants from Asia, South America and Europe. These young singles and couples are typically college-educated and ethnically diverse: about a third are foreign-born, and even more speak a language other than English.

Big City Blues

With a population that's 50 percent Latino, Big City Blues has the highest concentration of Hispanic Americans in the nation. But it's also the multi-ethnic address for downscale Asian and African-American households occupying older inner-city apartments. Concentrated in a handful of major metros, these young singles and single-parent families face enormous challenges: low incomes, uncertain jobs and modest educations. More than 40 percent haven't finished high school.

Upper Crust

The wealthiest lifestyle in America—a haven for empty-nesting couples over 55 years old. No segment has a higher concentration of residents earning over $200,000 a year or possessing a postgraduate degree. And none has a more opulent standard of living.

Movers & Shakers

Home to America's up-and-coming business class: a wealthy suburban world of dual-income couples who are highly educated, typically between the ages of 35 and 54, often with children. A high percentage of executives and white-collar professionals; Movers & Shakers rank number-one for owning a small business and having a home office.

Kids & Cul-de-Sacs

Upscale, suburban, married couples with children—an enviable lifestyle of large families in recently built subdivisions. With a high rate of Hispanic and Asian Americans, this segment is a refuge for college-educated, white-collar professionals with administrative jobs and upper-middle-class incomes. Their nexus of education, affluence and children translates into large outlays for child-centered products and services.

New Beginnings

Filled with young, single adults, a magnet for adults in transition. Many of its residents are twentysomething singles and couples just starting out on their career paths—or starting over after recent divorces or company transfers. Ethnically diverse, with nearly half its residents Hispanic, Asian or African-American. They tend to have the modest living standards typical of transient apartment dwellers.

American Classics

They may be older, lower-middle class and retired, but are still living the American Dream of home ownership. Few segments rank higher in their percentage of home owners, and that fact alone reflects a more comfortable lifestyle for these predominantly white singles and couples with deep ties to their neighborhoods.

Upward Bound

The home of those legendary Soccer Moms and Dads. In small satellite cities, these upper-class families boast dual incomes, college degrees and new split-levels and colonials. Residents of Upward Bound tend to be kid-obsessed, with heavy purchases of computers, action figures, dolls, board games, bicycles and camping equipment.

Shotguns & Pickups

Scores near the top of all lifestyles for owning hunting rifles and pickup trucks. These Americans tend to be young, working-class couples with large families—more than half have two or more kids—living in small homes and manufactured housing. Nearly a third of residents live in mobile homes, more than anywhere else in the nation.

Exhibit 5–8

The societal divisions described in this exhibit represent just 10 of the 66 PRIZM NE (New Evolution) segments defined by Claritas. Marketers believe that consumers in each segment have a great deal in common.

Reference Groups: The People We Relate To

Most of us care how we appear to people whose opinions we value. We may even pattern our behavior after members of some groups we affiliate with. This is the significance of **reference groups**—people we try to emulate or whose approval concerns us. Reference groups can be personal (family, friends, co-workers) or impersonal (political parties, religious denominations, professional associations). A special reference group, our peers, exerts tremendous influence on what we believe and how we behave. They determine which brands are cool and which are not.[29] To win acceptance by our peers (fellow students, co-workers, colleagues), we may purchase a certain style or brand of clothing, choose a particular place to live, and acquire behavioral habits that will earn their approval.

Often an individual is influenced in opposite directions by two reference groups and must choose between them. For example, a college student might feel pressure from some friends to join a Greek house and from others to live independently off campus. In ads targeted to students, a local apartment complex might tap the appeal of reference groups by showing students splashing in the complex's pool.

Opinion Leaders: The People We Trust

An **opinion leader** is some person or organization whose beliefs or attitudes are respected by people who share an interest in some specific activity. All fields (sports, religion, fashion, politics) have opinion leaders. An opinion leader may be some expert we find credible. We reason, "If Picabo Street thinks Marker makes the best ski bindings, then it must be so. She knows more about the sport than I do." Thus, the purchasing habits and testimonials of opinion leaders are important to advertisers.

When choosing an opinion leader as a spokesperson for a company or product, advertisers must understand the company's target market thoroughly. Even if executives in the company do not relate to the spokesperson, they must follow market tastes and interests. A spokesperson out of sync with the market undermines his or her credibility—and the company's. On the other hand, an internal person such as Dave Thomas, the founder of Wendy's, might turn out to be a highly credible spokesperson without the risks associated with outside celebrities and athletes.[30]

Of course, using a superstar spokesperson such as Michael Jordan is extremely expensive. It is estimated that Mr. Jordan's annual endorsement income exceeds $45 million. Analysts also estimate that, due to his stature and credibility, he produces some $500 million in sales for the companies he represents.[31]

Cultural and Subcultural Influence

Culture has a tenacious influence on consumers. **Culture** refers to the whole set of meanings, beliefs, attitudes, and ways of doing things that are shared by some homogeneous social group and typically handed down from generation to generation.[32] Americans love hot dogs, peanut butter, corn on the cob, and apple pie. Canada, Russia, Germany—every country has its own favorite specialties. And advertisers find it much easier to work with these tastes than try to change them.

Global marketers are especially concerned with the purchase environment. According to Professor Carolyn Lin, of all business functions, marketing activities are the most susceptible to cultural error.[33]

When creating ads for foreign consumption, marketers must consider many environmental factors: cultural trends, social norms, changing fads, market dynamics, product needs, and media channels.[34]

In countries where people earn little income, demand for expensive products

As the old saying goes, you must feed a cold and starve a fever, or at least that's what we say in the West. Every culture is characterized by unique idiosyncrasies that advertisers must be aware of when addressing a particular audience. This ad from the Ai Sin Foot Reflexology Centre capitalizes on the notion of Asian expertise in holistic therapies.

is low. So the creative strategy of an automobile advertiser might be to target the small group of wealthy, upper-class consumers. In a country with a large middle class, the same advertiser might be better off mass-marketing the car and positioning it as a middle-class product.

The United States and Canada embrace many subcultures, some of them quite large. They may be based on race, national origin, religion, language, or geographic proximity. The advertiser must understand these subcultures, for differences among them may affect responses to both products and advertising messages.

The United States, in particular, is a great melting pot of minority subcultures. A **subculture** is a segment within a culture that shares a set of meanings, values, or activities that differs in certain respects from those of the overall culture.[35] According to the U.S. Census, 37 million African Americans, 40 million Hispanics, and 12 million Asians live in the United States (plus an unknown number of undocumented foreign nationals). These three minority groups alone account for more than 30 percent of the American population.[36] Canada has two major subcultures, anglophones and francophones, based on language (English and French), plus a mosaic of many other cultures based on ethnic and national origins.

Subcultures tend to transfer their beliefs and values from generation to generation. Racial, religious, and ethnic backgrounds affect consumers' preferences for styles of dress, food, beverages, transportation, personal care products, and household furnishings, to name a few. As we saw in Chapter 3, many ad agencies now specialize in minority markets as more advertisers realize that tailoring their appeals to minorities makes good business sense. Recognizing the rapid growth of the Hispanic population, for example, Procter & Gamble spends more than $55 million per year to understand and tap this market. Other major Hispanic marketers include Ford Motor Co., AT&T, and Sears Roebuck.[37]

The social environments in countries from Italy to Indonesia, from Sweden to Surinam are also based on language, culture, literacy rate, religion, and lifestyle. Advertisers who market products globally can't ignore these distinctions.

In North America, advertising encourages us to keep our mouths clean, our breath fresh, and our teeth scrubbed. But people in some southern European countries consider it vain and improper to overindulge in toiletries. Consumers in the Netherlands and the United Kingdom use three times as much toothpaste as those in Spain and Greece. To communicate effectively with Spanish consumers, who view toothpaste as a cosmetic product, advertisers use chic, creative executions rather than dry, therapeutic pitches.[38]

Clearly, many interpersonal factors influence consumers. They have an important effect on our mental files, screens, and subsequent purchase decisions. Awareness of these interpersonal influences helps marketers, both domestic and international, create the strategies on which much advertising is based.

Increasingly, advertisers realize that English-speakers are not the only market in the United States. Other ethnic and linguistic cultures exist and pose enormous markets for the culturally savvy. Here, the U.S. Army (www.goarmy.com) encourages the Spanish-speaking audience to "Se Todo Lo Que Puedes Ser," or "Be All You Can Be." Recently, the U.S. Army updated its campaign slogan to "An Army of One."

Explain the forms of influences other people and cultures can have on consumers' perception, learning, and persuasion.

CONCEPT CHECK

The Purchase Decision and Postpurchase Evaluation

Now that we understand the elements in the consumer purchase decision process, let's examine how it might work in a typical situation. A hypothetical consumer named Chris is thinking about buying an MP3 player.

Chris is enrolled at a state university and financed in part by a small scholarship. He also has a part-time job but must act conservatively when it comes to spending money because tuition, books, and other expenses are costly.

One day, thumbing through a consumer electronics magazine, Chris sees an exciting ad for a new, top-of-the-line MP3 player. A beautiful photograph shows the product's modern, yet understated design. The ad copy highlights the player's special features. They exude high-tech class—it's just the right style. The ad's signature: "Exclusively at Tech 2000." (See Commercial Break 5–A.)

In a split second Chris leaps from perception to motivation. Got to have it! He is highly involved and he wants this personal reward for all his hard work.

The next day Chris visits Tech 2000. While looking for the advertised MP3 player, he encounters a variety of alternative styles and models by well-known manufacturers.

High-involvement purchases often result in more highly involved postpurchase evaluations, and people will go to great lengths to avoid cognitive dissonance. For example, if someone just spent a lot of money for a customized built-in refrigerator from Jenn-Air (www.jennair.com), they are more likely to be interested in ads like this one that reinforce the purchase decision they already made.

Some of the most beautiful things remain unseen.

So naturally beautiful, it's perfect in any environment. Introducing the Jenn-Air® Luxury™ Series built-in refrigerator. Featuring a customizably exterior that can blend seamlessly with your cabinetry or stand as the centerpiece of your kitchen. Just as beautiful is the spacious interior waiting to be personalized by you. When it comes to refrigerators, nothing has ever matched your needs so perfectly. Until now.

JENN-AIR

The ad has already done its work; the purchase decision process is well under way. At the point of making a purchase decision, though, consumers typically search, consider, and compare alternative brands.

Consumers evaluate selection alternatives (called the **evoked set**). To do this, they establish **evaluative criteria,** the standards they use to judge the features and benefits of alternative products. Not all brands make it to the evoked set. In fact, based on their mental files, most consumers usually consider only four or five brands—which presents a real challenge to advertisers. If none of the alternatives meets the evaluative criteria, the consumer may reject the purchase entirely or postpone the decision.

Chris finally finds the advertised MP3 player. But it looks less stylish on the shelf than it did in the ad. Two other good players are also displayed; both are attractive, both expensive. While trying out the devices, Chris considers other unique qualities of style and design. "This one may be a little too bulky." "This one would fit in my pocket." "This one would be okay for relaxing, but I'm not sure about using it when I'm jogging."

Using central route processing, Chris compares the MP3 players, considering their style, technology, possible advantages, and price (the models are all within $35 of each other). The advertised player really is the best buy and would be the most satisfying. None of Chris's friends has one like it. The purchase decision is complete when Chris writes out a check for the MP3 player.

On the way home, the postpurchase evaluation begins. Chris suddenly envisions some friends' possible negative reactions to the purchase. Maybe it wasn't wise to spend so much money on a top-of-the-line MP3 player. Perhaps his friends made better choices. Chris starts to worry—and to plan.

"It's really a great player. It's excellent quality and worth the money. I'll get a lot of use out of it."

Commercial Break 5–A

Applying Consumer Behavior Principles to Ad Making

When Polaroid needed to capture the attention of photo enthusiasts, it turned to the creatives at Leonard/Monahan to design a series of ads that would exhibit the advantages of the instant film over other photo products. The first challenge for the creative design team was to break through the consumers' resistance, the subtle barrier that begins with perceptual screens. Second, the team had to present a picture as being worth a thousand words while avoiding clichés.

The advertisement's headline—"The victim refuses to speak. The pictures refuse to keep quiet."—commands your attention and expresses the big idea with urgency. The ad's black-and-white visual of a battered victim suggests the subject's grave nature while allowing the color Polaroids to jump out, emoting a raw portrayal of reality. The ad becomes credible by demonstrating the benefits of Polaroid photos and how effectively they can be used (to investigate, prosecute, and win). The tag line, "Instant evidence," sums up the product's features and helps the prospective consumer recall the product's benefits.

Applying the Breaks

Choose an ad from a popular magazine and explain how the visuals, the words, and the overall design of the ad accomplish the following tasks. Provide specific details to support your answers.

1. Penetrate consumers' perceptual screens.
2. Address consumers' existing mental files.
3. Stimulate consumer learning.
4. Persuade via the central or peripheral route.
5. Stimulate consumer needs and wants to achieve motivation and action.

A key feature of the postpurchase evaluation is *cognitive dissonance*. The theory of **cognitive dissonance** holds that people strive to justify their behavior by reducing the dissonance, or inconsistency, between their cognitions (their perceptions or beliefs) and reality.[39] In fact, research shows that, to combat dissonance, consumers are more likely to read ads for brands they've already purchased than for new products or competing brands.[40]

> Back at the dorm, Chris puts the magazine on the desk with a Post-it note marking the ad (for his roommate to discover). Then he phones a friend and describes the purchase, emphasizing its technology, its great design, the enjoyment it will bring, and how expensive it was.

During the postpurchase period, the consumer may enjoy the satisfaction of the purchase and thereby receive reinforcement for the decision. Or the purchase may turn out to be unsatisfactory for some reason. In either case, feedback from the postpurchase evaluation updates the consumer's mental files, affecting perceptions of the brand and similar purchase decisions in the future.

This story is common for a high-involvement purchase decision. Of course, if Chris's decision had merely involved the purchase of a pack of gum, the process would have been significantly simpler.

> **CONCEPT CHECK**
>
> Why is it important for advertisers to understand how consumers ultimately make and then reevaluate their purchase decisions?

Chris may typify a particular group of consumers, and that is important to marketers. As we saw in Chapter 4, marketers are interested in defining target markets and developing effective marketing strategies for groups of consumers who share similar characteristics, needs, motives, and buying habits.

Different Responses from Different Products

In the 1980s, Richard Vaughn at Foote, Cone & Belding took the fact that different kinds of products typically evoke different *levels* of consumer involvement (either high or low) and different *types* of involvement, either *cognitive* (think) or *affective* (feel) and concluded therefore that different products called for different kinds of advertising. He created a two-dimensional model known as the **FCB grid,** which categorized consumer products into four quadrants based on "high involvement" or "low involvement," and "think" or "feel." By positioning brands in the grid based on the degree and type of involvement consumers brought to the purchase decision, the agency could determine which type of advertising would be most appropriate.

As shown in Exhibit 5–9, a product's location on the grid also indicates how the product is purchased and how advertising copy should be written (more emotional or more rational).[41] High involvement/thinking products lend themselves to logical explanations and consumers will probably follow the tradi-

Exhibit 5–9

The Foote, Cone & Belding (FCB) grid.

	Thinking	Feeling

High involvement	**1. Informative (thinker)**
	
	Car-house-furnishing-new products
	model: Learn-feel-do
	           (economic?)
	
	Possible implications
	
	Test: Recall
	             Diagnostics
	Media: Long copy format
	             Reflective vehicles
	Creative: Specific information
	             Demonstration
		2. Affective (feeler)
		
		Jewelry-cosmetics-fashion apparel-motorcycles
		model: Feel-learn-do
		           (psychological?)
		
		Possible implications
		
		Test: Attitude change
		             Emotional arousal
		Media: Large space
		             Image specials
		Creative: Executional
		             Impact

Low involvement	**3. Habit formation (doer)**
	
	Food-household items
	model: Do-learn-feel
	           (responsive?)
	
	Possible implications
	
	Test: Sales
	Media: Small space ads
	             10-second I.D.s
	             Radio; POS
	Creative: Reminder
		4. Self-satisfaction (reactor)
		
		Cigarettes-liquor-candy
		model: Do-feel-learn
		           (social?)
		
		Possible implications
		
		Test: Sales
		Media: Billboards
		             Newspapers
		             POS
		Creative: Attention

Affective involvement (Feel)

Exhibit 5–10

The Kim-Lord grid.

tional learn-feel-do model. At the other extreme, high involvement/feeling products are more likely to stress emotional motives and consumers may follow a feel-learn-do sequence. In the case of low involvement products, which are associated with routinized or impulse purchase behavior, *learning* and *feeling* may not occur until after *doing*. In such cases, simply gaining exposure or awareness may be the primary advertising objective.

More recently, Kim and Lord recognized that people can be both cognitively and affectively involved at the same time. So they developed a variation of the FCB grid, shown in Exhibit 5–10. The **Kim-Lord grid** also depicts the degree and the kind of involvement a consumer brings to the purchase decision for different products. Some purchases, like cars, require a high degree of personal involvement on both the cognitive and affective levels.[42] For others, like detergent, involvement is low on both axes. Sometimes a marketer uses an advertising strategy aimed at shifting the product to higher involvement on either axis.

Chapter Summary

Because advertising is first and foremost communication, advertisers cannot afford to take the communication process for granted. The basic human communication process begins when one party (the source) formulates an idea, encodes it as a message, and sends it via some channel or medium to another party (the receiver). The receiver must decode the message in order to understand it. To respond, the receiver formulates a new idea, encodes that concept, and then sends a new message back through some channel. A message that acknowledges or responds to the original message is feedback, and it affects the encoding of a new message. In advertising, the communication process is complex because of the multidimensional nature of the source, the message, and the recipient. Traditionally, advertising has been principally a one-way process, but with today's new interactive technology, consumers can give feedback to advertising messages in real time using the same channels as the sender.

To reach consumers, advertisers must effectively blend data from the behavioral sciences with the communicating arts. Advertisers study the behavioral characteristics of large groups of people to create advertising aimed at those groups.

Successful advertising people understand the complexity of consumer behavior, which is governed by three personal processes: perception, learning and persuasion, and motivation. These processes determine how consumers see the world around them, how they learn information and habits, and how they actualize their personal needs and motives. Interpersonal influences (the consumer's family, society, and culture) also affect consumer behavior. These factors combine to determine how the consumer behaves, and their influence differs considerably from one country to another. Advertisers evaluate the effect of these factors on groups of consumers to determine how best to create their messages.

Once customers or prospects are motivated to satisfy their needs and wants, the purchase process begins. Based on certain standards they have established in their own minds, they evaluate various alternative products (the evoked set). If none of the alternatives meets their evaluative criteria, they may reject or postpone the purchase. If they do buy, they may experience cognitive dissonance in the form of postpurchase doubt and concern. An important role of advertising is to help people cope with dissonance by reinforcing the wisdom of their purchase decision. The result of the postpurchase evaluation will greatly affect the customer's attitude toward future purchases.

Consumers' level of involvement in a purchase decision will vary with the type of product. This will impact the complexity of the decision process and the type of advertising most appropriate for that product.

Key Terms

attitude, 134
brand interest, 134
brand loyalty, 135
central route to persuasion, 133
channel, 125
cognition, 131
cognitive dissonance, 145
cognitive theory, 132
conditioning theory, 132
consumer behavior, 127
consumer decision process, 127
culture, 142
decode, 126
Elaboration Likelihood Model, 133
encoded, 125
evaluation of alternatives, 128
evaluative criteria, 144
evoked set, 144
FCB grid, 146
feedback, 126

habit, 134
hierarchy of needs, 137
informational motives, 138
interactive media, 126
interpersonal influences, 128, 139
Kim-Lord grid, 147
learning, 132
mental files,131
message, 125
motivation, 136
needs, 136
negatively originated motives, 137
noise, 126
nonpersonal channels, 126
nonpersonal influences, 128
opinion leader, 142
perception, 129
perceptual screens, 130
peripheral route to persuasion, 133

personal channels, 125
personal processes, 128
persuasion, 132
physiological screens, 130
positively originated motives, 138
postpurchase evaluation, 128
psychological screens, 131
receiver, 126
reference groups, 141
selective perception, 131
self-concept, 131
semiotics, 125
social classes, 139
source, 125
stimulus, 129
stimulus-response theory, 132
subculture, 143
transformational motives, 138
wants, 136

Review Questions

1. What is semiotics? What are some examples (other than those mentioned) of semiotics used in advertising?
2. What is meant by noise and how might it affect an advertiser's efforts?
3. What does the term consumer behavior refer to, and why is it important to advertisers?
4. Which consumer behavior process presents the greatest challenge to advertisers? Why?
5. Why, as consumers, do we use perceptual screens to filter the advertisements to which we are exposed?
6. What is the difference between the cognitive theory and the conditioning theory of learning? To what types of purchases is each theory most applicable?
7. What is the difference between the central route and the peripheral route to persuasion?
8. What are the various approaches that advertisers use to develop brand loyalty among consumers?
9. What is the significance of negatively originated motives and positively originated motives to advertisers?
10. How does the theory of cognitive dissonance relate to advertising?

Exploring Advertising

1. Find two print ads, one that addresses consumers' negatively originated motives and one that addresses positively originated motives. Then identify the benefit offered by the product or service that addresses the motive. Do you believe each ad could possibly have been more effective if it had taken the opposite approach?

2. Find a print ad that uses semiotics to communicate feelings, thoughts, ideas, or ideologies. Describe the symbolism that is used. Does it make the advertisement more effective or is it confusing?

3. Find print ads that illustrate some of the following categories: family influence, social class, reference groups, opinion leaders, subcultures. Then describe the component of the ad that stressed that specific influence.

4. Select a product category and map several of the products/brands on the FCB grid. Then describe the implications for the purchase decision process for each of the brands and the type of advertising that should be considered. Is there anything the advertiser could do to move the product to a higher involvement level?

5. Make a conscious effort to notice advertising that you otherwise would not pay attention to. Why do you think you didn't notice those ads before? Did you learn anything new or different that changed your perception of the product or service? What could advertisers do to make these ads more conspicuous?

chapter six

Account Planning and Research

Objectives

To examine how advertisers gain information about the marketplace and how they apply their findings to marketing and advertising decision making.

After studying this chapter, you will be able to:

* **Describe** the role of account planners.

* **Discuss** how research helps advertisers select target markets, advertising messages, and media vehicles.

* **Explain** the basic steps in the research process.

* **Discuss** the differences between formal and informal research and primary and secondary data.

* **Explain** the methods used in qualitative and quantitative research.

* **Define** and explain the concepts of validity and reliability.

* **Recognize** the important issues in creating survey questionnaires.

* **Explain** the challenges international advertisers face in collecting research data abroad.

* **Debate** the pros and cons of advertising testing.

In the mid-1980s, Healthtex was a $350 million concern. But by the early 1990s, the 75-year-old company was barely hanging on. Fortunately, VF Corp., the parent of Wrangler jeans, realized the value of the brand and bought the company. Healthtex had been a leading manufacturer of children's clothing for many decades, but with the emergence of sophisticated competition, the company had not kept up. VF moved the company to offices close to Wrangler in Greensboro, North Carolina; installed new management; and proceeded to turn Healthtex around. John Martin was appointed director of marketing services and he brought in a new ad agency, The Martin Agency (no relation), in Richmond, Virginia.[1]

"Frankly, we needed help," says Martin. "And we weren't shy about requesting it. We didn't just need brilliant creative work; we needed extraordinarily savvy marketing counsel, too."

They got it. The people at The Martin Agency knew they had to know the product quickly. Beth Rilee-Kelley, now the agency's director of creative services, remembers the first days working on the account. "We went right out into the field and talked to retailers that car-ried the line and consumers that bought it," she says. "And we learned a lot—fast."

They got good news and bad news.

The bad news was that the trade was disappointed in the company and had lost confidence in the brand. Healthtex had missed shipping dates; customer service had declined; retailers saw the brand as underfunded in advertising and marketing; and even the product quality had slipped. In short, the long relationships Healthtex had enjoyed with retailers were rapidly deteriorating.

The good news was that consumers were unaware of these problems and still had great confidence in the Healthtex name. Moms saw the brand as high-quality, everyday playwear that lasts. They loved it.[2]

The agency also discovered that moms, the busiest customers on the planet, didn't find anything compelling or inspiring in advertising for any brand of kidswear. Magazines were full of ads showing beautiful, cuddly children in spotless clothes. But that just didn't resonate with these moms. There was no recognition of the hectic, untidy lives that moms of small children actually lead.

This was the nugget of insight the agency—and Healthtex—needed. This provided the opportunity for a unique position in the marketplace, for Healthtex to establish itself as the brand that understands moms and their lives.

In a series of award-winning ads, The Martin Agency made this position clear, sometimes explicitly, always implicitly. In one of the first ads, the headline reads: "Your baby's naked. Your phone's ringing. And your mother-in-law's walking up the driveway. Let's talk snaps." This was followed by four columns of factual, informative copy to explain precisely the practical, functional differences built into Healthtex infant wear. In another ad, the headline warns: "You've got 23 seconds to get your 2-year-old from the sandbox to the potty. Go."

To say the least, these ads resonated with parents. They showed that Healthtex really understood just how chaotic it can be to raise (and dress) small children. In short order, Healthtex became the only brand with a position that had more substance than cuteness. Thanks to good research, the campaign enabled Healthtex to reverse its decline immediately, increase its market share, and regain its lost luster with the trade. It also made The Martin Agency a household name in the advertising business.[3]

The success of "Got Milk?" and many other notable campaigns is often attributed to the ability of account planners to get into the heads of their prospects. This approach enables brands to develop meaningful relationships with their customers.

Grow Moore.

About 15% of your height is added during your teen years, and milk can help. What more can you ask for?

got milk?

The Account Planner as Consumer Advocate

Jeff Goodby, cochairman and creative director at Goodby, Silverstein & Partners, is famous for award-winning television ads including the Budweiser Lizards and the Got Milk? Campaign. He believes that everything an agency does should be geared toward getting into people's heads to figure out what they currently think and understand how best to influence them.[4]

This task is shared by many individuals during the process of planning advertising, but has, in recent years, been focused on the **account planner,** described in Chapter 3. The account planner's primary role is to represent the consumer in this process. The late Stanley Pollitt of the London agency Boase Massimi Pollitt is considered by some to be the "father" of account planning. He described planners as "the architects and guardians of their clients' brands, the detectives who uncovered long-hidden clues in the data and gently coerced consumers into revealing their inner secrets. . ."[5]

By putting the consumer, instead of the advertiser, at the center of the process, account planning changes the task from simply creating an advertisement to nurturing a relationship between consumer and brand. That requires tremendous understanding, intuition, and insight. But when performed properly, planning provides that mystical leap into the future—the brilliant, simplifying insight that lights the client's and the creative's way. Interestingly, the U.S. agencies that have adopted account planning in the last decade are the very ones now considered to be the hottest shops. They're performing the best work, getting the biggest accounts, and winning all the awards.

In large agencies, account planners work side-by-side with account managers. They share a common goal but with different orientations. Where the account planner brings a research perspective and represents the consumer, the account manager brings more of a business perspective and represents the client. In smaller agencies without account planning departments, the consumer's advocate would typically be someone from account management.

Whoever plays this role is responsible for assuring that the advertising strategy and executions are relevant to the target audience. The account planner is responsible for injecting a wealth of information into the planning process, monitoring the creative development, and testing the finished product to determine if it has achieved its goal of communicating with the intended audience.

Jon Steel summarizes the account planner's mission as follows: "They need to be able to take information of all sorts, shuffle it around, and rearrange it in new patterns until something interesting emerges."[6] One does not necessarily need to conduct research to get that information. Some questions can be answered without research or the answers may have been uncovered in previous explorations. But in all cases, the advertiser must understand what is happening in consumers' heads.

In this chapter we will examine various types of research and the role that research plays in the development of advertising.

> Describe the role of the account planner in the development of advertising.
>
> CONCEPT CHECK

The Need for Research in Marketing and Advertising

Every year companies spend millions of dollars creating ads and promotions that they hope their customers and prospects will notice and relate to. Then they spend millions more placing their communications in print and electronic media, hoping their customers will see and hear them and eventually respond.

Advertising is expensive. In the United States the cost of airing a single 30-second commercial on prime-time network TV averages around $140,000, not including the cost of production. Likewise, a single, full-page color ad in a national business magazine averages $100 to reach every thousand prospects.[7] That's too much money to risk unless advertisers have very good information about who their customers are, what they want and like, where they spend their media time, and whether the ads are effective. And that's why advertisers need research. Research provides the information that drives marketing and advertising decision making. Without that information, advertisers are forced to use intuition or guesswork. In today's fast-changing, highly competitive, global economy, that invites failure.

What Is Marketing Research?

To help managers make marketing decisions, companies develop systematic procedures for gathering, recording, and analyzing new information. This is

Marketing research is the important process of gathering, recording, and analyzing information about customers and prospects. Companies such as A. C. Nielsen (www.acnielsen.com) collect data for their clients and provide critical insight into current and potential markets.

called **marketing research.** Marketing research does a number of things: It helps identify consumer needs and market segments; it provides the information necessary for developing new products and devising marketing strategies; and it enables managers to assess the effectiveness of marketing programs and promotional activities.

What Is Advertising Research?

Before developing any advertising campaign, a company needs to know how people perceive its products, how they view the competition, what brand or company image would be most credible, and what ads offer the greatest appeal. To get this information, companies use *advertising research.* While marketing research provides the information necessary to make marketing decisions, **advertising research** uncovers the information needed for making advertising decisions. By definition, it is the systematic gathering and analysis of information to help develop or evaluate advertising strategies, individual ads, and entire campaigns.

In this chapter, we consider the importance of information gathering to the development of advertising plans and strategies; we look at how companies use research to test the effectiveness of ads before and after they run; and we explore a number of specific research techniques.

Applying Research to Advertising Decision Making

Advertising research serves various purposes, most of which can be grouped into four categories: *strategy research, creative concept research, pretesting,* and *posttesting.*

1. *Advertising strategy research.* Used to help define the product concept or to assist in the selection of target markets, advertising messages, or media vehicles.

When companies falter in their efforts to satisfy market expectations, regaining lost customers can be a formidable problem. What is needed is innovative marketing and outstanding communications. Ads like this one from Healthtex (www.healthtex.com), which demonstrate an understanding of modern mothers' concerns, can help restore faith in the company's brand.

Paint and ketchup and glue and mud and juice and markers and chalk and ravioli. Now that's what little girls are made of.

Healthtex

	Advertising Strategy Research	Creative Concept Research	Pretesting	Posttesting
Timing	Before creative work begins	Before agency production begins	Before finished artwork and photography	After campaign has run
Research problem	Product concept definition Target audience selection Media selection Message-element selection	Concept testing Name testing Slogan testing	Print testing TV storyboard pretesting Radio commercial pretesting	Advertising effectiveness Consumer attitude change Sales increases
Techniques	Consumer attitude and usage studies Media studies Qualitative interviews	Free-association tests Qualitative interviews Statement-comparison tests	Consumer juries Matched samples Portfolio tests Storyboard test Mechanical devices Psychological rating scales	Aided recall Unaided recall Attitude tests Inquiry tests Sales tests

Exhibit 6–1

Categories of research in advertising development.

2. *Creative concept research.* Measures the target audience's acceptance of different creative ideas at the concept stage.

3. *Pretesting of ads.* Used to uncover and diagnose possible communication problems before a campaign begins.

4. *Posttesting of ads.* Enables marketers to evaluate a campaign after it runs.

As Exhibit 6–1 shows, marketers use the different categories of advertising research at different stages of ad or campaign development. The techniques they use at each stage also vary considerably. We'll examine each of these categories briefly before moving on to discuss the research process.

Advertising Strategy Research

As we will discuss in the next chapter, an advertising strategy is comprised of the *creative strategy* and the *media strategy*. Developing these strategies requires a clear understanding of the *product concept,* the *target audience,* the *media* alternatives, and possible *message elements.* To gain this understanding, companies use **advertising strategy research.**

Product Concept

As we saw at the beginning of this chapter, advertisers need to know how consumers perceive their brands. They also want to know what qualities lead to initial purchases and, eventually, to brand loyalty.

Using this information, they try to establish a unique *product concept* for their brand—that bundle of values we discussed in Chapter 4 that encompasses both utilitarian and symbolic benefits to the consumer.

The Martin Agency asked consumers what would entice them to put their kids in Healthtex. They discovered that, overall, moms look for cuteness, durability, ease of dressing, and washability. Cuteness is the price of entry into the category— but to succeed a brand must have more than that.

Through the applied use of marketing research, Healthtex discovered that customers wanted more than just cute clothing. They needed clothing that was designed to be practical and would allow them to spend more quality time with their children. This ad, created by The Martin Agency, highlighted those qualities in the Healthtex brand.

Healthtex did. But they also discovered that mothers with full-time jobs want to spend any spare time they have with their kids. They don't want to waste time shopping. They want to be able to go in, pick out a trusted brand, and get home to spend time with the family.[8]

It's this kind of information that can lead to an effective positioning strategy for the brand. Advertising can shape and magnify a brand's position and image over time. In fact, this is one of the most important strategic benefits of advertising. But to use media advertising effectively, strategy research is essential to develop a blueprint for creatives to follow.[9]

Advertising works differently for different product categories and, often, even for different brands within a category. This means that each brand must develop a template for the creative based on an understanding of its particular consumers' wants, needs, and motivations. Only if this is done correctly over time (say, one to two years), can brand equity be built.[10]

Target Audience Selection

We pointed out in Chapter 4 that no market includes everybody. Therefore, one of the major purposes of research is to develop a rich profile of the brand's target markets and audiences. The marketer will want to know which customers are the primary users of the product category and will study them carefully to understand their demographics, geographics, psychographics, and purchase behavior. If the target audience is accurately defined, the advertising will be delivered to the most prospects with the least waste.

With any new product, the biggest problem is invariably the budget. There is never enough money to attack all geographic or demographic markets effectively at the same time. So the advertiser will often decide to employ the *dominance concept*—researching which markets (geographic or otherwise) are most important to product sales and targeting those where it can focus its resources to achieve advertising dominance. That way, spending is directed toward the most responsive audience.

In the case of Healthtex, the agency discovered that there were two distinct markets for their client's clothes: new mothers and experienced mothers. New mothers were categorized as first-time moms with infants between the ages of 0 and 20 months. The children of experienced mothers were between two and four years old. These were the primary markets and audiences for Healthtex's advertising. Later they discovered that grandparents were also a viable target market, so they designed a program to appeal to them also.

Media Selection

To develop media strategies, select media vehicles, and evaluate their results, advertisers use a subset of advertising research called **media research.** Agencies subscribe to syndicated research services (such as A. C. Nielsen, Arbitron,

Simmons, or Standard Rate & Data Service) that monitor and publish information on the reach and effectiveness of media vehicles—radio, TV, newspapers, and so on—in every major geographic market in the United States and Canada. (We'll discuss these further in Chapter 8 and in Part Five.)

For Healthtex, The Martin Agency researched what media were regularly used by mothers. It discovered that new moms read publications like *American Baby* and *Baby Talk,* while more experienced mothers read *Parents* magazine and *Parenting.*

Message Element Selection

Companies hope to find promising advertising messages by studying consumers' likes and dislikes in relation to brands and products. Kraft Foods, for example, was looking for ways to dissuade moms from switching to less-expensive brands of processed cheese. While its Kraft Singles brand dominated the processed cheese slices category, it was concerned that the brand wasn't keeping up with overall growth in the market.

Working with several research companies and its ad agency, J. Walter Thompson, the company conducted a series of qualitative consumer attitude studies to figure out how women, particularly mothers, felt about Kraft Singles with the hope of discovering possible advertising themes. The mothers said they felt good giving their kids Kraft Singles because of the brand's nutritional value. But there was a catch—they also said they'd switch to a competitive product if it were cheaper. Fortunately, a phone survey provided some clues for solving the problem. Among these polled, 78 percent considered the brand an extra source of calcium for their kids. And 84 percent of women with kids under 12 said they'd be motivated to buy the brand because of that added benefit.[11]

From this information, the agency used concept testing to determine which message elements might prove most successful.

> **CONCEPT CHECK**
>
> What contribution do marketing and advertising research make to the development of an advertising strategy?

Developing Creative Concepts

Once it develops an advertising strategy, the company (or its agency) will begin developing creative concepts for the advertising. Here again, research is helpful in determining which concepts to use.

From all their studies, Kraft researchers came up with two message elements that might keep mothers from defecting to competitive brands. First, show how much kids like Kraft Singles, and second, emphasize the fact that the brand provides the calcium kids need. J. Walter Thompson prepared two rough TV spots and then conducted focus groups of mothers to get their reaction. With a discussion leader moderating the conversation, each group viewed the commercials. The groups' reactions were measured, taped, and observed by JWT and Kraft staff behind a one-way mirror. Immediately, problems surfaced. The idea that kids love the taste of Kraft Singles just didn't come across strongly enough. And the statement that Kraft provides calcium wasn't persuasive. Moms said, "Of course it has calcium, it's cheese." The agency had to find a newsier way to communicate the information.

Tweaking the commercials, JWT came up with a new spot showing youngsters gobbling gooey grilled-cheese sandwiches while a voice-over announcer stated that two out of five kids don't get enough calcium. More focus groups ensued. Now the mothers agreed that the shots of kids devouring sandwiches

Advertisers can avoid mistakes and save money on production by testing creative concepts in animatic form. Animatics are illustrated by hand and then computer animated. This Windex animatic and others can be viewed at www.animaticmedia.com.

communicated the great taste theme, but some moms thought the two-out-of-five statement played too much on their guilt.

To soften the message, the agency switched to a female announcer and then brought in the Dairy Fairy, a character from an earlier campaign, to lighten the whole tone of the spot. This seemed to work better, so the agency proceeded to copy test a finished ad.

Pretesting and Posttesting

Advertising is one of the largest costs in a company's marketing budget. No wonder its effectiveness is a major concern! Companies want to know what they are getting for their money—and whether their advertising is working. And they'd like some assurance before their ads run.

Kraft was no exception. Millward Brown Research performed a number of copy tests to see how the agency's latest spot would perform. The tests showed that the spot performed significantly better than the norm on key measures such as branding and persuasion. Following the copy tests, the company aired "The Calcium They Need" commercial in five test markets to see how it would affect sales. They quickly achieved a 10 percent increase in sales in those markets. Based on such a strong showing, Kraft rolled the campaign out nationally in 1999 and sales took off, growing 11.8 percent.[12]

The campaign was so successful that in 2000, the Advertising Research Foundation named Kraft and J. Walter Thompson finalists for its prestigious David Ogilvy Research Award, given to the most effective ad campaign guided by research.

The Purpose of Testing

Testing is the primary tool advertisers use to ensure their advertising dollars are spent wisely. Testing can prevent costly errors, especially in judging which advertising strategy or execution is most effective. And it can give the advertiser some measure (besides sales results) of a campaign's value.

To increase the likelihood of preparing the most effective advertising messages, companies use **pretesting.** Some agencies, like DDB Needham, pretest all ad copy for communication gaps or flaws in message content before recommending it to clients.[13] When companies don't pretest their ads, they may encounter a surprising reaction from the marketplace. Schering Canada received a torrent of complaint letters from customers who said they didn't like its commercial introducing the antihistamine Claritin to the over-the-counter market in Canada. Most negative responses, though, are more insidious: Consumers sim-

The success of the Bissell "Life Testimonial" campaign was attributed to research that provided insight into attitudes and behaviors regarding home cleaning. Bissell's upright vacuum sales doubled and the campaign won the prestigious Advertising Research Foundation (ARF) Grand Ogilvy award.

Exhibit 6–2

The marketing research process begins with evaluation of the company's situation and definition of the problem.

ply turn the page or change the channel, and sales mysteriously suffer. This is why it's also important to evaluate the effectiveness of an ad or campaign *after* it runs. **Posttesting** (also called *ad tracking*) provides the advertiser with useful guidelines for future advertising.

Steps in the Research Process

Now that we understand the various types of decision-related information that marketers seek, let's explore how they gather this information by looking at the overall research process and some of the specific techniques they use.

There are five basic steps in the research process (see Exhibit 6–2):

1. Situation analysis and problem definition.

2. Informal (exploratory) research.

3. Construction of research objectives.

4. Formal research.

5. Interpretation and reporting of findings.

Step 1: Analyzing the Situation and Defining the Problem

The first step in the marketing research process is to *analyze the situation* and *define the problem*. Many large firms have in-house research departments. Often the marketing department also maintains a **marketing information system (MIS)**—a sophisticated set of procedures designed to generate a continuous, orderly flow of information for use in making marketing decisions. These systems ensure that managers get the information they need when they need it.[14]

Most smaller firms don't have dedicated research departments, and their methods for obtaining marketing information are frequently inadequate. These firms often find the problem-definition step difficult and time-consuming. Yet good research on the wrong problem is a waste of effort.

Step 2: Conducting Informal (Exploratory) Research

The second step in the process is to use **informal research** (or exploratory research) to learn more about the market, the competition, and the business environment, and to better define the problem. As we saw with Healthtex, researchers may discuss the problem with wholesalers, distributors, or retailers outside the firm; with informed sources inside the firm; with customers; or even with competitors. They look for whoever has the most information to offer.

There are two types of research data: *primary* and *secondary*. Information collected from the marketplace about a specific problem is called **primary data;**

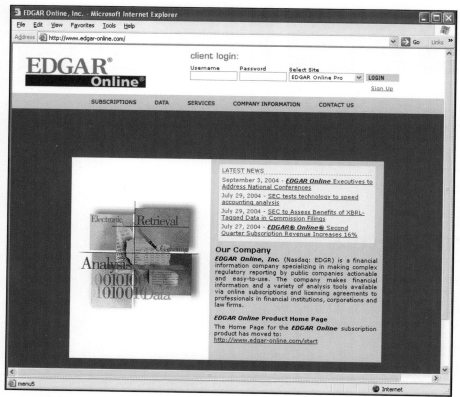

The Internet has evolved into a wellspring of secondary data that can be put to use for marketing purposes. Several well-known market research firms publish abbreviated market data on the World Wide Web, while other Internet services like Edgar Online (www.edgar-online.com) act as databases of news articles published in a wide range of trade and business journals. However, marketers must beware of the danger of potentially unreliable data sources on the Internet, as many sites may publish information that has not been verified by any independent organizations.

acquiring it is typically expensive and time-consuming. So during the exploratory stage, researchers frequently use **secondary data**—information previously collected or published, usually for some other purpose, by the firm or by some other organization. This information is readily available, either internally or externally, and can be gathered more quickly and inexpensively than primary data.

Assembling Internal Secondary Data

Company records are often a valuable source of secondary information. Useful internal data include product shipment figures, billings, warranty-card records, advertising expenditures, sales expenses, customer correspondence, and records of meetings with sales staffs.

A well-developed marketing information system can help researchers analyze sales data, review past tracking studies, and examine previous marketing research data. This information might point the way toward an interesting headline or positioning statement such as Jiffy Lube's: "America's favorite oil change."

Gathering External Secondary Data

Much information is available, sometimes at little or no cost, from the government, market research companies, trade associations, various trade publications, or computerized databases. Most large companies subscribe to any of a number of syndicated research reports about their particular industry. For example, as the advertising manager for a large nutritional company introducing a new line of vitamins, you might need to know the current demand for vitamins and food supplements, the number of competitors in the marketplace, the amount of advertising each is doing, and the challenges and opportunities the industry faces.

In the United States, frequently used sources of secondary data include:

- Library reference materials (*Business Periodicals Index* for business magazines, *Reader's Guide to Periodical Literature* for consumer magazines, *Public Information Service Bulletin,* the *New York Times Index,* and the *World Almanac and Book of Facts*).

- Government publications (*Statistical Abstract of the United States*).

- Trade association publications (annual fact books containing data gathered by various industry groups listed in the *Directory of National Trade Associations*).

- Research organizations and their publications or syndicated information (literature from university bureaus of business research, Nielsen retail store audits, MRCA consumer purchase diaries, Simmons' Study of Media and Markets, IRI's InfoScan market tracking service, and Standard Rate & Data Service).

- Consumer/business publications (*BusinessWeek, Forbes, Fortune, American Demographics, Advertising Age, Prevention,* and thousands more).

- Computer database services (DIALOG Information Service, ABI/Inform, Electric Library, Lexis-Nexis, and Dow Jones News Retrieval Service).

- Internet search engines (Google, Excite, About, AltaVista, Ask Jeeves, Dogpile, WebCrawler, Yahoo!, AOL, MSN, and others).

It's important to understand that secondary data carry some potential problems. Information may be out of date and therefore obsolete. Much of it is not relevant to the problem at hand. Some information from purported research is just wrong, so the findings are invalid. In other cases, the source may be unreliable. Finally, there is now so much information available (thanks to the Internet) that it's just overwhelming; it's extremely time-consuming to wade through it all.

Step 3: Establishing Research Objectives

Once the exploratory research phase is completed, the company may discover it needs additional information that it can get only from doing primary research. For example, it may want to identify exactly who its customers are and clarify their perceptions of the company and the competition. To do so, the company must first establish *specific research objectives.*

A concise written statement of the research problem and objectives should be formulated at the beginning of any research project. A company must be clear about what decisions it has to make that the research results will guide. Once it knows the application, it can set down clear, specific research objectives.[15] For example, a department store, noticing that it is losing market share, might write its problem statement and research objectives as follows:

Market Share

Our company's sales, while still increasing, seem to have lost momentum and are not producing the profit our shareholders expect. In the last year, our market share slipped 10 percentage points in the men's footwear department and 7 percentage points in the women's fine apparel department. Our studies indicate we are losing sales to other department stores in the same malls and that customers are confused about our position in the market. We need to make decisions about how we position ourselves for the future.

Research Objectives

We must answer the following questions: (1) Who are our customers? (2) Who are the customers of other department stores? (3) What do these customers like and dislike about us and about our competitors? (4) How are we currently perceived? and (5) What do we have to do to clarify and improve that perception?

This statement of the problem is specific and measurable, the decision point is clear, and the questions are related and relevant. The research results should provide the information that management needs to decide on a new positioning strategy for the company. The positioning strategy facilitates the development of marketing and advertising plans that will set the company's course for years to come.

	Qualitative	Quantitative
Main techniques for gathering data	Focus groups and in-depth interviews.	Surveys and scientific samples.
Kinds of questions asked	Why? Through what thought process? In what way? In connection with what other behavior or thoughts?	How many? How much?
Role of interviewer	Critical: interviewer must think on feet and frame questions and probes in response to whatever respondents say. A highly trained professional is advisable.	Important, but interviewers need only be able to read scripts. They should not improvise. Minimally trained, responsible employees are suitable.
Questions asked	Questions vary in order and phrasing from group to group and interview to interview. New questions are added, old ones dropped.	Should be exactly the same for each interview. Order and phrasing of questions carefully controlled.
Number of interviews	Fewer interviews tending to last a longer time.	Many interviews in order to give a projectable scientific sample.
Kinds of findings	Develop hypotheses, gain insights, explore language options, refine concepts, flesh out numerical data, provide diagnostics on advertising copy.	Test hypotheses, prioritize factors, provide data for mathematical modeling and projections.

Exhibit 6–3

Differences between qualitative and quantitative research.

Step 4: Conducting Formal Research

When a company wants to collect primary data directly from the marketplace about a specific problem or issue, it uses **formal research.** There are two types of formal research: qualitative and quantitative.

To get a general impression of the market, the consumer, or the product, advertisers typically start with **qualitative research.** This enables researchers to gain insight into both the population whose opinion will be sampled and the subject matter itself. Then, to get hard numbers about specific marketing situations, they may perform a survey or use some other form of **quantitative research.** Sophisticated agencies use a balance of both qualitative and quantitative methods, understanding the limits of each and how they work together.[16] (See Exhibit 6–3.)

In this section we'll discuss the basic methods advertisers use for conducting qualitative and quantitative research and then we'll look at how they apply these techniques to testing ads.

Basic Methods of Qualitative Research

To get people to share their thoughts and feelings, researchers use qualitative research that elicits in-depth, open-ended responses rather than yes or no answers. Some marketers refer to this as *motivation research.* Unfortunately, no matter how skillfully posed, some questions are uncomfortable for consumers to answer. When asked why they bought a particular status car, for instance, consumers might reply that it handles well or is economical or dependable, but they rarely admit that it makes them feel important. The methods used in qualitative research are usually either *projective* or *intensive techniques.*

Projective techniques Advertisers use **projective techniques** to understand people's underlying or subconscious feelings, attitudes, interests, opinions, needs, and motives. By asking indirect questions (such as "What kind of people do you think shop here?"), the researcher tries to involve consumers in a situation where they can express feelings about the problem or product.

Projective techniques were adapted for marketing research after their use by psychologists in clinical diagnosis. But such techniques require the skill of highly experienced researchers.

Intensive techniques **Intensive techniques,** such as in-depth interviews, also require great care to administer properly. In the **in-depth interview,** carefully planned but loosely structured questions help the interviewer probe respondents' deeper feelings. The big pharmaceutical company Schering, for example, uses in-depth interviews with physicians to find out what attributes doctors consider most important in the drugs they prescribe and to identify which brands the doctors associate with different attributes.[17] While in-depth interviews help reveal individual motivations, they are also expensive and time-consuming, and skilled interviewers are in short supply.

A focus group is an intensive research technique used to evaluate the effectiveness of the various elements of a sponsor's ad or advertising campaign. Focus groups are especially effective used in conjunction with market surveys.

One of the most common intensive research techniques is the **focus group,** in which the company invites six or more people typical of the target market to a group session to discuss the product, the service, or the marketing situation. The session may last an hour or more. A trained moderator guides the often freewheeling discussion, and the group interaction reveals the participants' true feelings or behavior toward the product. Focus-group meetings are usually recorded and often viewed or videotaped from behind a one-way mirror.

Focus groups don't represent a valid sample of the population, but the participants' responses are useful for several purposes. They can provide input about the viability of prospective spokespeople, determine the effectiveness of visuals, concepts, and strategies, and identify elements in ads that are unclear or claims that don't seem plausible. Focus groups are best used in conjunction with surveys. In fact, focus-group responses often help marketers design questions for a formal survey.[18] Following a survey, focus groups can put flesh on the skeleton of raw data.[19]

As in the cases of Healthtex and Kraft, focus groups can be particularly useful in gaining a deeper understanding of particular market segments. A show-and-tell focus group conducted by Grieco Research Group in Colorado provided a glimpse of the core values of baby boomers. Participants were asked to bring to the session three or four items that they felt represented their ideal environment. Items ranged from photographs to magazine pictures to mementos and souvenirs. One mother of two brought tickets to a retro rock concert; a conservative corporate executive brought in a pack of cigarettes to show he was still rebellious; a middle-aged father brought a lucky fishing lure given to his kids by his father.

The process uncovered five key themes regarding what matters most to urban boomers. Family love and support and a good home life are viewed as important achievements. Long-term friendships are also very important and provide continuity to boomers. City-dwelling boomers are driven to "get away from it all" and escape to the big outdoors. Spiritual fitness is as important as physical fitness, so they love to develop their intellectual potential. They also feel that they're never too old to improve themselves. Clearly, all these values can translate into interesting platforms for ads and commercials.[20]

Basic Methods of Quantitative Research

Advertisers use quantitative research to gain reliable, hard statistics about specific market conditions or situations. There are three basic research methods used to collect quantitative data: *observation, experiment,* and *survey.*

The Universal Product Code on packaging is scanned at checkout counters. It improves checkout time and inventory control, and provides a wealth of accessible data for use in measuring advertising response.

Observation In the **observation method,** researchers monitor people's actions. They may count the traffic that passes by a billboard, measure a TV audience through instruments hooked to television sets, or study consumer reactions to products displayed in the supermarket. Most observation method research is performed by large, independent marketing research companies, such as the A. C. Nielsen Co., Information Resources, Inc., and Audits and Surveys Worldwide, whose clients subscribe to their various services. Healthtex, for example, subscribes to the services of NPD (National Panel Diary), which tracks the clothing purchases of 16,000 homes as a nationwide sample. From this, Healthtex can find out its market share and better understand statistical trends in the marketplace.

Technology has greatly facilitated the observation method. One example is the **Universal Product Code (UPC)** label, an identifying series of vertical bars with a 12-digit number that adorns every consumer packaged good. By reading the codes with optical scanners, researchers can tell which products are selling and how well. The UPC label not only increases speed and accuracy at the checkout counter; it also enables timely inventory control and gives stores and manufacturers accurate point-of-purchase data sensitive to the impact of price, in-store promotion, couponing, and advertising.

For example, A. C. Nielsen's ScanTrack service provides weekly data on packaged-goods sales, market shares, and retail prices from 3,000 UPC scanner-equipped supermarkets. A companion service, ScanTrack Electronic Household Panel, provides packaged-goods purchase data via in-home UPC scanning based on 40,000 U.S. households. As a result, marketers suddenly have reliable data on the effectiveness of the tools they use to influence consumers. With that information, they can develop empirical models to evaluate alternative marketing plans, media vehicles, and promotional campaigns.[21] In one case, for instance, data might indicate that a 40-cent coupon for toothpaste would create $150,000 in profits, but a 50-cent coupon on the same item would create a $300,000 loss.

Video cameras have also affected observation techniques. Envirosell, a New York–based research company, uses security-type cameras to capture consumer in-store shopping habits. To determine the effectiveness of packaging and displays, the company analyzes how much time people spend with an item and how they read the label.[22]

This video frame from Envirosell shows how the company uses security-type cameras to observe in-store consumer shopping habits.

Experiment To measure actual cause-and-effect relationships, researchers use the **experimental method.** An experiment is a scientific investigation in which a researcher alters the stimulus received by a *test group* and compares the results with that of a *control group* that did not receive the altered stimulus. This type of research is used primarily for new product and new campaign introductions. As we saw in the Kraft story, marketers go to an isolated geographic area, called a **test market,** and introduce the product in that area alone or test a new ad campaign or promotion before a *national rollout.* For example, a new campaign might run in one geographic area but not another. Sales in the two areas

	Data Collection Method			
	Personal Interview	Telephone	Mail	Internet
Data collection costs	High	Medium	Low	Low
Data collection time required	Medium	Low	High	Medium
Sample size for a given budget	Small	Medium	Large	Large
Data quantity per respondent	High	Medium	Low	Low
Reaches widely dispersed sample	No	Maybe	Yes	Yes
Interaction with respondents	High	High	None	Medium
Degree of interviewer bias	High	Medium	None	None
Severity of nonresponse bias	Low	Low	High	Medium
Presentation of visual stimuli	Yes	No	Maybe	Yes
Field worker training required	Yes	Yes	No	No

Exhibit 6–4

Comparison of data collection methods.

are then compared to determine the campaign's effectiveness. However, researchers must use strict controls so the variable that causes the effect can be accurately determined. Because it's hard to control every marketing variable, this method is difficult to use and quite expensive.

Survey The most common method of gathering primary quantitative research data is the **survey,** in which the researcher gains information on attitudes, opinions, or motivations by questioning current or prospective customers (political polls are a common type of survey). Surveys can be conducted by personal interview, telephone, mail, or on the Internet. Each has distinct advantages and disadvantages (see Exhibit 6–4).

Basic Methods for Testing Ads

Although there is no infallible way to predict advertising success or failure, pretesting and posttesting can give an advertiser useful insights if properly applied.

Pretesting methods Advertisers often pretest ads for likability and comprehension by using a variety of qualitative and quantitative techniques.

For example, when pretesting print ads, advertisers often ask direct questions: What does the advertising say to you? Does the advertising tell you anything new or different about the company? If so, what? Does the advertising reflect activities you would like to participate in? Is the advertising believable? What effect does it have on your perception of the merchandise offered? Do you like the ads?

Through **direct questioning,** researchers can elicit a full range of responses from people and thereby infer how well advertising messages convey key copy points. Direct questioning is especially effective for testing alternative ads in the early stages of development, when respondents' reactions and input can best be acted on. There are numerous techniques for pretesting print ads, including: *focus groups, order-of-merit tests, paired comparisons, portfolio tests, mock magazines, perceptual meaning studies,* and *direct-mail tests.* (See the Checklist of Methods for Pretesting Ads.)

Several methods are used specifically to pretest radio and TV commercials. In **central location tests,** respondents are shown videotapes of test commercials, usually in shopping centers, and questions are asked before and after exposure. In **clutter tests,** test commercials are shown with noncompeting control commercials to determine their effectiveness, measure comprehension and attitude shifts, and detect weaknesses.

Researchers often collect information on attitudes, opinions, or motivations by conducting surveys of current or prospective customers. A common technique is the mall intercept, in which an interviewer at a shopping mall intercepts a sample of those passing by to ask if they would be willing to participate in a brief research study.

Checklist

Methods for Pretesting Ads

Print Advertising

- **Direct questioning.** Asks specific questions about ads. Often used to test alternative ads in early stages of development.
- **Focus group.** A moderated but freewheeling discussion conducted with six or more people.
- **Order-of-merit test.** Respondents see two or more ads and arrange them in rank order.
- **Paired-comparison method.** Respondents compare each ad in a group.
- **Portfolio test.** One group sees a portfolio of test ads interspersed among other ads and editorial matter. Another group sees the portfolio without the test ads.
- **Mock magazine.** Test ads are "stripped into" a magazine, which is left with respondents for a specified time (also used as a posttesting technique).
- **Perceptual meaning study.** Respondents see ads in timed exposures.
- **Direct-mail test.** Two or more alternative ads are mailed to different prospects on a mailing list to test which ad generates the largest volume of orders.

Broadcast Advertising

- **Central location test.** Respondents see test commercials in a central location such as a shopping center.
- **Clutter test.** Test commercials are shown with non-competing control commercials to measure effectiveness, comprehension, and attitude shifts.

- **Trailer test.** Respondents see TV commercials in trailers at shopping centers and receive coupons for the advertised products; a matched sample of consumers just get the coupons. Researchers measure the difference in coupon redemption.
- **Theater test.** Electronic equipment enables respondents to indicate what they like and dislike as they view TV commercials in a theater setting.
- **Live telecast test.** Test commercials are shown on closed-circuit or cable TV. Respondents are interviewed by phone and/or sales audits are conducted at stores in the viewing areas.
- **Sales experiment.** Alternative commercials run in two or more market areas.

Physiological Testing

- **Pupilometric device.** Dilation of the subject's pupils is measured, presumably to indicate the subject's level of interest.
- **Eye-movement camera.** The route the subject's eyes traveled is superimposed over an ad to show the areas that attracted and held attention.
- **Galvanometer.** Measures subject's sweat gland activity with a mild electrical current; presumably the more tension an ad creates, the more effective it is likely to be.
- **Voice-pitch analysis.** A consumer's response is taped and a computer used to measure changes in voice pitch caused by emotional responses.
- **Brain-pattern analysis.** A scanner monitors the reaction of the subject's brain.

The challenge of pretesting There is no best way to pretest advertising variables. Different methods test different aspects, and each has its own advantages and disadvantages—a formidable challenge for the advertiser.

Pretesting helps distinguish strong ads from weak ones. But since the test occurs in an artificial setting, respondents may assume the role of expert or critic and give answers that don't reflect their real buying behavior. They may invent opinions to satisfy the interviewer, or be reluctant to admit they are influenced, or vote for the ads they think they *should* like. This is why some creative people mistrust ad testing; they believe it stifles creativity.

Researchers encounter problems when asking people to rank ads. Respondents often rate the ones that make the best first impression as the highest in all categories (the **halo effect**). Also, questions about the respondent's intended buying behavior may be invalid; behavior *intent* may not become behavior *fact*.

Despite these challenges, the issue comes down to dollars. Small advertisers rarely pretest, but their risk isn't as great, either. When advertisers risk millions of dollars on a new campaign, they *must* pretest to be sure the ad or commercial is interesting, believable, likable, memorable, and persuasive—and reinforces the brand image.

Checklist

Methods for Posttesting Ads

- **Unaided recall.** Respondents are asked to recall advertisements they have seen recently but are not given any clues to help them remember.
- **Aided recall (recognition-readership).** Respondents are asked to recall advertisements they have seen recently; they are given names of products or brands to jog their memories.
- **Attitude tests.** Respondents are asked questions, before and after an advertising campaign, to measure changes in their attitudes.
- **Inquiry tests.** Additional product information, product samples, or premiums are offered to readers or viewers of an ad; ads generating the most responses are presumed to be the most effective.
- **Sales tests.** Measures of past sales compare advertising efforts with sales. Controlled experiments test different media in different markets. Consumer purchase tests measure retail sales from a given campaign. Store inventory audits measure retailers' stocks before and after a campaign.

Posttesting methods Posttesting can be more costly and time-consuming than pretesting, but it can test ads under actual market conditions with finished ads. As we saw with Kraft, some advertisers benefit from pretesting and posttesting by running ads in select test markets before launching a campaign nationwide.

As in pretesting, advertisers use both quantitative and qualitative methods in posttesting. Most posttesting techniques fall into five broad categories: *aided recall, unaided recall, attitude tests, inquiry tests,* and *sales tests.* (See the Checklist of Methods for Posttesting Ads.)

Some advertisers use **attitude tests** to measure a campaign's effectiveness in creating a favorable image for a company, its brand, or its products. Presumably, favorable changes in attitude predispose consumers to buy the company's product.

Impact Research in Montreal developed a proprietary posttest called TES (Tracking Efficiency Study) that it administers regularly for clients.[23] Using a random sample of 200 people in each market, Impact researchers phone or visit respondents and ask 8 to 10 questions to determine which ads or commercials they remember seeing, if they can identify the sponsor, which message elements they remember, and how well they liked the ads.

Similarly, Nissan interviews 1,000 consumers every month to track brand awareness, familiarity with vehicle models, recall of commercials, and shifts in attitude or image perception. If a commercial fails, it can be pulled quickly.[24]

Following its initial campaign, Healthtex conducted some posttesting and discovered that, while the new moms appreciated the information in the long copy format of their ads, more experienced mothers didn't. For them, the headline and one line of copy were sufficient to get the point across. They already understood the rest. As a result, The Martin Agency redesigned the ads aimed at experienced moms, using the shorter format.

The challenge of posttesting Each posttesting method has limitations. **Recall tests** reveal the effectiveness of ad components, such as size, color, or themes. But they measure what respondents noticed and remembered, *not* whether they actually intend to buy the product.

For measuring sales effectiveness, attitude tests are often better than recall tests. An attitude change relates more closely to product purchase, and a measured change in attitude gives management more confidence to make informed decisions about advertising plans.

Ethical Issues

Research Statistics Can Be Friends or Foes

Marketing research gives the advertiser and its agency the data they need to identify consumer needs, develop new products and communication strategies, and assess the effectiveness of marketing programs. It also often provides the basis for advertising claims.

However, the way some advertisers use research data can lead to serious ethical lapses. Clever researchers can hide, shape, and manipulate statistics. Unfortunately, some researchers and marketers deliberately withhold information, falsify figures, alter results, misuse or ignore pertinent data, compromise the research design, or misinterpret the results to support their points of view.

Trying to spin the nutritional numbers to its advantage with consumers on the Atkins, South Beach, and other high-protein, low-carbohydrate diets, KFC created two television ads "aimed at educating the public that fried chicken can actually be part of a healthy diet." One ad showed a wife plopping down a bucket of fried chicken in front of her TV-engrossed husband, proudly explaining that they are starting to eat better ("healthier" is implied). A second ad showed a man sitting on the tailgate of a truck, again with a bucket of fried chicken; his friend compliments him on his "fantastic" appearance. Compared to a Burger King Whopper, the company claimed, its fried chicken was veritable health food. Not really. According to the Federal Trade Commission (FTC), "although it is true that the two fried chicken breasts have slightly less total fat and saturated fat than a Whopper, they have more than three times the trans fat and cholesterol, more than twice the sodium, and more calories."

It didn't take a lawsuit or months of investigation for the public to discover that KFC's statistics were skewed. Consumer-protection groups were up in arms as soon as the ads aired, forcing the company to pull the ads within a month of their October 2003 launch. In response to the FTC's inquiry, KFC marketing executive Scott Bergen said, "We have always believed our ads to be truthful and factually accurate." In their settlement with the FTC, the company agreed to simply stop running the ads. Six months after the debacle, KFC tried the healthy tack again, this time promoting roasted chicken.

Sometimes misleading health information in advertisements can be hazardous to more than just the waist-line. Consider the fen-phen controversy in which Wyeth-Ayerst, a division of American Home Products, was accused of ignoring research findings. Wyeth manufactures the "fen" portion of fen-phen. In 1996, fen-phen was approved for distribution in the United States, and by the end of 1996 thousands of people had reported health complications. In 1997, it was found that fen was linked to heart valve damage and an often-fatal lung disease. Subsequently, the manufacturer was pressured to pull the drug off the shelf.

By the end of 1997, American Home Products was the subject of thousands of civil lawsuits over fen-phen by people who claimed that the drug had caused their health problems. In 1999, American Home Products went under fire for allegedly withholding important information from the FDA (Food and Drug Administration).

American Home Products had also hired "ghostwriters" to write articles that promoted fen-phen. According to lawsuit evidence cited in the Associated Press, the company used respected researchers to publish these articles under their own names. Dr. Jeffery Drazen, editor-in-chief of the *New England Journal of Medicine*, believes "that line between the author's independent conclusions and the company's conclusions has been blurred." Critics allege that oftentimes drug companies influence authors to bury unfavorable results and that this undue influence leads the public to believe that these drugs are safer and more effective than they actually are.

In November 1999, American Home Products agreed to settle the more than 11,000 fen-phen lawsuits for a whopping $4.83 billion. This was one of the biggest product-liability settlements ever. Of course, as part of the settlement, the company admitted no wrongdoing.

There is a lot of money to be made in the pharmaceutical industry; companies go to great lengths and great expense to get their products approved. But ignoring, manipulating, or omitting pertinent research findings is not only unethical, it's potentially lethal.

Questions

1. Are there any circumstances where you could justify distorting or concealing research findings to improve a product's sales performance?

2. Do you think KFC was attempting to deceive the public? Should they have been penalized more severely for airing that advertising?

By using **inquiry tests**—in which consumers respond to an ad for information or free samples—researchers can test an ad's attention-getting value, readability, and understandability. These tests also permit fairly good control of the variables that motivate reader action, particularly if a *split-run* test is used (split runs are covered in Chapter 11). The inquiry test is also effective for testing

Type of research	Features	Cost
Telephone	500 20-minute interviews, with report	$24,000–$28,000
Mail	500 returns, with report	$15,000–$18,000
Intercept	500 interviews, four or five questions, with report	$20,000–$22,000
Executive interviews (talking to business administrators)	20 interviews, with report	$7,500–$10,000
Focus group	One group, 8 to 10 people, with report and videotape	$5,000–$8,000

Exhibit 6–5

The cost of professional research.

small-space ads. Unfortunately, inquiries may not reflect a sincere interest in the product, and responses may take months to receive.

When advertising is the dominant element or the only variable in the company's marketing plan, **sales tests** are a useful measure of advertising effectiveness. However, many other variables can affect sales (competitors' activities, the season of the year, and even the weather). Sales response may not be immediate, and sales tests, particularly field studies, are often costly and time-consuming.

For consumer packaged goods, though, the cost of sales tests has been greatly reduced thanks to grocery store scanners. Finally, sales tests are typically more suited for gauging the effectiveness of campaigns than of individual ads or components of ads.

Step 5: Interpreting and Reporting the Findings

The final step in the research process involves interpreting and reporting the data. Research is very costly (see Exhibit 6–5), and its main purpose is to help solve problems. The final report must be comprehensible to the company's managers and relevant to their needs.

Tables and graphs are helpful, but they must be explained in words management can understand. Technical jargon (such as "multivariate analysis of variance model") should be avoided, and descriptions of the methodology, statistical analysis, and raw data should be confined to an appendix. The report should state the problem and research objective, summarize the findings, and draw conclusions. The researcher should make recommendations for management action, and the report should be discussed in a formal presentation to allow management feedback and to highlight important points.

> Describe the objectives that advertisers are striving to accomplish at each step in the research process.

CONCEPT CHECK

Important Issues in Advertising Research

When marketers conduct primary research, there is always one legitimate concern—the accuracy of the findings. This is especially true when conducting formal quantitative research and when doing research in international markets.

Considerations in Conducting Formal Quantitative Research

Quantitative research requires formal design and rigorous standards for collecting and tabulating data to ensure its accuracy and usability. When conducting

Validity

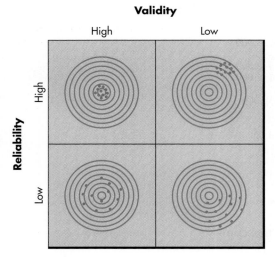

Exhibit 6–6

The reliability/validity diagram. Using the analogy of a dartboard, the bull's-eye is the actual value of some measure within a population. The top row shows high reliability (repeatability) because the darts are closely clustered. When reliability drops, the darts land more randomly and spread across a wider area, as in both examples in the bottom row. The left column demonstrates high validity because in both examples the darts center around the bull's-eye. The right column represents low validity because bias in the testing process drew all the darts to one side. The upper-left quadrant reflects the truest picture of the data.

formal research, advertisers must consider certain issues carefully, especially whether the research is *valid* and *reliable.*

Validity and Reliability

Assume you want to determine a market's attitude toward a proposed new toy. The market consists of 10 million individuals. You show a prototype of the toy to five people and four say they like it (an 80 percent favorable attitude). Is that test valid? Hardly. For a test to have **validity,** *results must be free of bias* and reflect the *true status of the market.*[25] Five people aren't enough to be representative of the market, and the fact that *you* showed a prototype of only *your* toy to these people would probably bias their response.

Moreover, if you repeated the test with five more people, you might get an entirely different response. So your test also lacks **reliability.** For a test to be reliable it must be *repeatable*—it must produce approximately the same result each time it is administered (see Exhibit 6–6).

Validity and reliability depend on several key elements: the specification and size of the sample, the sampling methods, the survey questionnaire design, and the data tabulation and analysis methods.

Sampling Methods

When a company wants to know what consumers think, it typically cannot ask everybody. But its research should as nearly as possible reflect the **universe** (the entire target population) of prospective customers. Researchers therefore select from that population a **sample** that they expect will represent the population's characteristics. To accomplish this, they must decide whom to survey, how many to survey, and how to choose the respondents.

A sample must be large enough to achieve precision and stability. The larger the sample, the more reliable the results. However, reliability can be obtained with even very small samples, a fraction of one percent of the population, if the sample is drawn correctly. There are two types of samples: probability samples and nonprobability samples.

The greatest accuracy is gained from **probability samples** (sometimes referred to as *random samples*) because everyone in the universe has a quantifiable chance of being selected.[26] For example, a researcher who wants to know a community's opinion on an issue could select members of the community at random. But this method has difficulties. Every unit (person) must be known, listed, and numbered so each can be given an equal chance of being selected, an often prohibitively expensive and sometimes impossible task, especially with customers of nationally distributed products.

Instead, researchers often use **nonprobability samples** because they're easier, less expensive, and less time-consuming than probability samples. Sometimes referred to as *convenience samples,* respondents are selected on the basis of their availability (e.g., because they volunteered) or because of the researcher's personal judgment that they are representative. The consequence is that an unknown portion of the population is excluded (e.g., those who did not volunteer). Nonprobability samples don't give every unit in the universe a chance of being included, so there's no guarantee the sample is representative. As a result, researchers can't be as confident in the validity of the responses.[27] However, most marketing and advertising research only needs approximate measures of the data. For example, the nonprobability method of interviewing shoppers in malls may be sufficient to determine the shopping preferences, image perceptions, and attitudes of target customers.

1. Do you intend to shop at _(Store name)_ between now and Sunday?
Yes   1   No   2   (If no, skip to question 5)

2. Do you intend to buy something in particular or just to browse?
Buy   1   Browse   2

3. Have you seen any of the items you intend to buy advertised by _(Store name)_ ?
Yes   1   (continue)   No   2   (skip to question 5)

4. Where did you see these items advertised? Was it in a _(Store name)_ advertising insert included with your newspaper, a _(Store name)_ flyer you received in the mail, the pages of the newspaper itself, on TV, or somewhere else?
☐ Insert in newspaper   ☐ On TV
☐ Flyer in mail   ☐ Somewhere else (specify) _____
☐ Pages of newspaper   ☐ Don't recall

5. Please rate the _(Store name)_ advertising insert on the attributes listed below. Place an X in the box at the position that best reflects your opinion of how the insert rates on each attribute. Placing an X in the middle box usually means you are neutral. The closer you place the X to the left or right phrase or word, the more you believe it describes the _(Store name)_ insert.

Looks cheap							Looks expensive
Unskillful							Cleverly done
Unappealing							Appealing
Does not show clothing in an attractive manner	1	2	3	4	5	6	7	Shows clothing in an attractive manner

6. Please indicate all of the different types of people listed below you feel this _(Store name)_ advertising insert is appealing to.

☐ Young people   ☐ Quality-conscious people
☐ Bargain hunters   ☐ Low-income people
☐ Conservative dressers   ☐ Budget watchers
☐ Fashion-conscious people ☐ Older people
☐ Rich people   ☐ Middle-income people
☐ Professionals   ☐ Blue-collar people
☐ High-income people   ☐ Women
☐ Men   ☐ Office workers
☐ Someone like me   ☐ Smart dressers
☐ Career-oriented women   ☐ Other (specify) _____

Exhibit 6–7

A personal questionnaire like this helps determine shoppers' feelings toward a chain of stores, its merchandise, and its advertising.

How Questionnaires Are Designed

Constructing a good questionnaire requires considerable expertise. Much bias in research is blamed on poorly designed questionnaires. Typical problems include asking the wrong types of questions, asking too many questions, using the wrong form for a question (which makes it too difficult to answer or tabulate), and using the wrong choice of words. Exhibit 6–7 shows some typical questions that might be used in a survey for a retail store.

Consider the simple question: "What kind of soap do you use?" The respondent doesn't know what *soap* means. Hand soap, shampoo, laundry detergent, or dishwashing soap? Does *kind* mean brand, size, or type? Finally, what constitutes *use?* What a person buys (perhaps for someone else) or uses personally—and for what purpose? In fact, one person probably uses several different kinds of soap, depending on the occasion. It's impossible to answer this question accurately. Worse, if the consumer does answer it, the researcher doesn't know what the answer means and will likely draw an incorrect conclusion. For these reasons, questionnaires *must* be pretested. (See the Checklist for Developing an Effective Questionnaire.)

Checklist

Developing an Effective Questionnaire

- **List specific research objectives.** Don't spend money collecting irrelevant data.
- **Write short questionnaires.** Don't tax the respondent's patience; you may get careless or flip answers.
- **State questions clearly** so there is no chance for misunderstanding. Avoid generalities and ambiguities.
- **Write a rough draft first,** then polish it.
- **Use a short opening statement.** Include the interviewer's name, the name of the organization, and the purpose of the questionnaire.

- **Put the respondent at ease** by opening with one or two inoffensive, easily answered questions.
- **Structure questions so they flow logically.** Ask general questions before more detailed ones.
- **Avoid questions that suggest an answer or could be considered leading.** They bias the results.
- **Include a few questions that cross-check earlier answers.** This helps ensure validity.
- **Put the demographic questions (age, income, education) and any other personal questions at the end of the questionnaire.**
- **Pretest the questionnaire** with 20 to 30 people to be sure they interpret the questions correctly and that all the information sought is covered.

Effective survey questions have three important attributes: *focus, brevity,* and *clarity.* They focus on the topic of the survey. They are as brief as possible. And they are expressed simply and clearly.[28]

The four most common types of questions are *open-ended, dichotomous, multiple choice,* and *scale.* But there are many ways to ask questions within these four types. In Exhibit 6–8, for example, more choices can be added to the multiple-choice format. Neutral responses (the middle choice) can be removed from the scale question so the respondent must answer either positively or negatively. And there is obvious bias in the dichotomous question.

Questions should elicit a response that is both accurate and useful. By testing questionnaires on a small subsample, researchers can detect any confusion, bias, or ambiguities and make revisions.

Data Tabulation and Analysis

Collected data must be validated, edited, coded, and tabulated. Answers must be checked to eliminate errors or inconsistencies. For example, one person might answer two years, while another says 24 months; such responses must be changed to the same units for correct tabulation. Some questionnaires may be

Exhibit 6–8

Different ways to phrase research questions.

Type	Questions
Open-ended	How would you describe (*Store name*) advertising?
Dichotomous	Do you think (*Store name*) advertising is too attractive? ____ Yes ____ No
Multiple choice	What description best fits your opinion of (*Store name*) advertising? ____ Modern ____ Unconvincing ____ Well done ____ Old-fashioned ____ Believable
Scale	Please indicate on the scale how you rate the quality of (*Store name*) advertising.

1   2   3   4   5
Poor   Excellent

rejected because respondents' answers indicate they misunderstood the questions. Finally, the data must be tabulated and summarized, usually by computer.

Many researchers want *cross-tabulations* (for example, product use by age group or education). Software programs such as SPSS® and MINITAB® Statistical Software make it possible for small advertisers as well as large corporations to tabulate data on a personal computer and apply advanced statistical techniques.[29] Many cross-tabulations are possible, but researchers must use skill and imagination to select only those that show meaningful and significant relationships. On small samples, using additional cross-tabs dramatically reduces the level of confidence.

Collecting Primary Data in International Markets

International marketers face a number of challenges when they collect primary data. For one thing, research overseas is often more expensive than domestic research. Many marketers are surprised to learn that research in five countries costs five times as much as research in one country; there are no economies of scale.[30]

But advertisers must determine whether their messages will work in foreign markets. (Maxwell House, for example, had to change its "great American coffee" campaign when it discovered that Germans have little respect for U.S. coffee.)

Advertisers need more than just facts about a country's culture. They need to understand and appreciate the nuances of its cultural traits and habits, a difficult task for people who don't live there or speak the language. Knowledgeable international advertisers such as Colgate-Palmolive work in partnership with their local offices and use local bilingual marketing people when conducting primary research abroad.[31]

For years, Mattel tried unsuccessfully to market the Barbie doll in Japan. It finally sold the manufacturing license to a Japanese company, Takara, which did its own research. Takara found that most Japanese girls and their parents thought Barbie's breasts were too big and her legs too long. It modified the doll accordingly, changed the blue eyes to brown, and sold two million dolls in two years.

Conducting original research abroad can be fraught with problems. First, the researcher must use the local language, and translating questionnaires can be tricky. Second, many cultures view strangers suspiciously and don't wish to talk about their personal lives. U.S. companies found that mail surveys and phone interviews don't work in Japan; they have to use expensive, time-consuming personal interviews.[32]

Despite these problems—or perhaps because of them—it's important for global advertisers to perform research. Competent researchers are available in all developed countries, and major international research firms have local offices in most developing countries.

Marketers are often surprised by some of the differences they encounter when trying to conduct international research. Lead times to begin projects are typically longer, with the Far East being particularly troublesome. The structures differ

This example from Procter & Gamble's Bonux detergent campaign in Lebanon illustrates some of the difficulties inherent in international advertising. Lebanese housewives take great pride in clean washing, so much so that they even brag about laundry secrets and hang their laundry on balconies to be seen by neighbors. Bonux created the "housewives moment of fame" campaign and bought advertising space on the roofs of buses so the ads could be seen from balconies. Radio spots featured interviews with housewives riding the buses. The campaign raised awareness 85 percent, increased market share by 20 percent, and won a Media Lion at the Cannes Advertising Festival.

too. Focus groups, for instance, rarely use more than 4 to 6 people rather than the 8 to 10 typical of the United States. Screening requirements for participants abroad are typically less rigid, and foreign moderators tend to be much less structured than their U.S. counterparts. Finally, the facilities don't usually have all the amenities of U.S. offices, but the costs are frequently twice as high in Europe and three times as high in Asia.[33]

Thanks to a combination of computer-based interviewing, the Internet, e-mail, telephones, faxes, and courier services, the time required to conduct worldwide business-to-business research has been drastically reduced. Today, nearly three-quarters of market research firms use the Internet to conduct some form of market research.[34] With the global adoption of the Internet, experts anticipate further cuts in costs and time for getting valuable customer input for marketing and advertising decision making.

CONCEPT CHECK

Define the issues that advertisers must consider when conducting primary research.

Chapter Summary

The account planner's role in an advertising agency is to nurture a relationship between consumer and brand. The account planner brings a research perspective and represents the consumer, assuring that the advertising strategy and executions are relevant to the target audience.

Marketing research is the systematic procedure used to gather, record, and analyze information to help managers make decisions about the marketing of goods and services. Marketing research helps management identify consumer needs, develop new products and communication strategies, and assess the effectiveness of marketing programs and promotional activities. The many types of information gathered can help marketers recruit, retain, and regain customers.

Advertising research, a subset of marketing research, is used to gather and analyze information for developing or evaluating advertising. It helps advertisers develop strategies and test concepts. The results of research help define the product concept, select the target market, and develop the primary advertising message elements.

Advertisers use testing to make sure their advertising dollars are spent wisely. Pretesting helps detect and eliminate weaknesses before a campaign runs. Posttesting helps evaluate the effectiveness of an ad or campaign after it runs.

The research process involves several steps: analyzing the situation and defining the problem, conducting informal (exploratory) research by analyzing internal data and collecting external secondary data, setting research objectives, conducting formal research using qualitative or quantitative methods, and, finally, interpreting and reporting the findings.

Marketers use qualitative research to get a general impression of the market. The methods used may be projective or intensive. Quantitative techniques include observation, experiment, and survey.

Techniques used in pretesting include central location tests, clutter tests, and direct questioning. Pretesting has numerous problems, including artificiality, consumer inaccuracy, and the halo effect of consumer responses. The most commonly used posttesting techniques are aided recall, unaided recall, attitude tests, inquiry tests, and sales tests.

The validity and reliability of quantitative surveys depend on the sampling methods used and the design of the survey questionnaire. The two sampling procedures are random probability and nonprobability. Survey questions require focus, brevity, and simplicity.

In international markets, research is often more expensive and less reliable than in the United States. But advertisers must use research to understand cultural traits and habits in overseas markets.

Key Terms

account planner, 152

advertising research, 154

advertising strategy research, 155

attitude test, 167

central location test, 165

clutter tests, 165

direct questioning, 165

experimental method, 164

focus group, 163

Review Questions

1. Why do you think that the agencies that have adopted account planning are the ones performing the best work, getting the biggest accounts, and winning all the awards?

2. Describe the difference between marketing research and advertising research.

3. Which kind of research data is more expensive to collect, primary or secondary? Why?

4. How have you personally used observational research?

5. As a marketer, how might you combine the information you can obtain from UPC scanning and retailer loyalty cards?

6. Which of the major surveying methods is most costly? Why?

7. How could the halo effect bias a pretest for a soft-drink ad?

8. When might research offer validity but not reliability?

9. Why is a probability sample more expensive and more reliable than a nonprobability sample?

10. How would you design a controlled experiment to test new advertising for a chain of men's clothing stores?

Exploring Advertising

1. Find five print ads that are directed to a specific target audience (e.g., women, men, teens, pet owners). Then show these ads to five members of that target audience, giving them approximately two minutes to review all of the ads and then take them away. Then ask questions that will demonstrate recall, comprehension, and persuasion. For example: "For what products do you remember seeing ads?" "What did those ads say about the products?" "Did the ads increase your interest in the products?" What did you learn from this exercise?

2. Spend some time in a retail store (e.g., a grocery store, bookstore, hardware store, or bank) and observe the customers. What do the customers do first when they arrive? What patterns do they follow when they shop? How do they decide which product(s) to purchase? What could you, as a marketer for this business or its products, learn from simply observing the customers?

3. Think of an advertised product or service that is targeted specifically to your demographic or lifestyle. How effective is the advertiser at getting into your head and figuring out what you think and how best to influence you? If you were an account planner for that product or service, could you have done a better job? What would you have done differently?

4. Your college is planning to remodel the cafeteria and introduce a new menu. The administration has approached you to help determine what students would like. Design a research project to answer their questions. Outline the steps you would take and specify what kind of research you would conduct. Explain your choices.

5. Select one of your favorite brands in a specific category. Then write a questionnaire with about 10 questions with the goal of determining how people make brand decisions in that category. Interview 10 people you have never met before and tabulate the results. Then write a brief memo explaining how people select the brand they are going to buy.

chapter seven

Developing Marketing and Advertising Plans

Objectives

To describe the process of marketing and advertising planning. Marketers and advertisers need to understand the various ways plans are created. They must also know how to analyze situations; set realistic, attainable objectives; develop strategies to achieve them; and establish budgets for marketing communications.

After studying this chapter, you will be able to:

* **Explain** the role and importance of a marketing plan.

* **Give** examples of need-satisfying and sales-target objectives.

* **Explain** the difference between objectives, strategies, and tactics in marketing and advertising plans.

* **Discuss** the suitability of top-down, bottom-up, and integrated marketing communications (IMC) planning.

* **Describe** how marketing and advertising plans are related.

* **Explain** how to establish specific, realistic, and measurable advertising objectives.

* **Explain** how advertising budgets are determined.

Sixty years ago, Ally and Barney Hartman of Knoxville, Tennessee, decided to make their own mixer for hard liquor. The two brothers cooked up a 7Up-type brew and tested it on their families and friends. They seemed to like it, so they started bottling the concoction and distributing it to the locals. In 1946, they designed a label for their beverage featuring a hillbilly toting a gun and a signature that read "By Barney and Ollie." In honor of the mountain moonshine famous in Tennessee, they named their drink "Mountain Dew." They debuted the bottle that year at a soft-drink convention in Gatlinburg, Tennessee, and quickly became convinced they had a good thing going. They had no idea how good.

Over the course of time, the brand grew. The gun-toting Willy the Hillbilly and their apt slogan, "Ya-hoo Mountain Dew," helped build it into a regional player. In 1964, PepsiCo bought the brand and, for some years, continued using the old advertising approach. But as sales failed to increase substantially, the marketing brains at Pepsi decided a new direction was called for.

In 1973, after a great deal of research, debate, and months of marketing and advertising planning, they completely repositioned and relaunched Mountain Dew. No longer would it be a hillbilly mixer. Rather, the Dew would be cast as a high-energy, youth-oriented, flavored soft drink. New ads created by BBDO New York featured active young people enjoying outdoor activities to the theme "Hello Sunshine, Hello Mountain Dew." By 1978, the action-oriented approach sent Dew sales over the 100-million-case mark. In the 1980s they added high-octane sports and adventure to the advertising.[1] Then, in 1985, Mountain Dew went nationwide.

Since that time, Mountain Dew has set a standard of how to remain true to its own definition of exuberance across a variety of marketing platforms. "We have a great unity of message and purpose that has been consistent over time about what we are and what we aren't," says Scott Moffitt, director of marketing for Mountain Dew.[2] "The brand is all about exhilaration and energy, and you see that in all that we do, from advertising and community to grass-roots programs and our sports-minded focus. We have a very crystal clear, vivid positioning."

The positioning concept has allowed Mountain Dew great latitude: The brand's marketing extends from skateboarding parks and alternative events to mainstream extravaganzas such as the Super Bowl. Marketing across such a broad spectrum from grass roots to grandiose advertising events is known within PepsiCo as "mass intimacy."[3]

This positioning took it to the top of the "heavy citrus" soda category in the early 1990s. Then, in 1999, it reached a new benchmark. It briefly passed Diet Coke to become the number three soft drink in the United States after Classic Coke and Pepsi. In the $62 billion carbonated soft drink industry, that is a huge success.

To say the least, Barney and Ally would be proud. Mountain Dew has come a long way since its hillbilly days. Yahoo!

The Marketing Plan

In spite of the brilliant creativity employed by BBDO in its ads for Mountain Dew, the Dew story actually demonstrates that business success often depends more on careful marketing and advertising planning than on advertising creativity. Yet, every year, companies waste millions and millions of dollars on ineffective advertising due to a woeful lack of prior planning.

The Importance of Marketing Planning

Since marketing typically drives a company's income, the marketing plan may well be its most important document.

The **marketing plan** assembles all the pertinent facts about the organization, the markets it serves, and its products, services, customers, competition, and so on. It forces all departments—product development, production, sales, advertising, finance, transportation—to focus on the customer. Finally, it sets goals and objectives for specified periods of time and lays out the precise strategies and tactics to achieve them.

The written marketing plan must reflect the goals of top management and be consistent with the company's mission and capabilities. Depending on its scope, the plan may be long and complex or, in the case of a small firm or a single product line, very brief. Formal marketing plans are typically reviewed and revised yearly, but planning is not a one-time event; it's a continuous process that includes research, formulation, implementation, evaluation, review, and reformulation.

The Effect of the Marketing Plan on Advertising

The marketing plan has a profound effect on an organization's advertising. It helps managers analyze and improve all company operations, including marketing and advertis-

Careful marketing and advertising planning can be the principal reason for a successful ad campaign. Mountain Dew's edgy and exhilarating ads are a great example of how these aspects can work effectively together (www.mountaindew.com).

ing programs. It dictates the role of advertising in the marketing mix. It enables better implementation, control, and continuity of advertising programs, and it ensures the most efficient allocation of advertising dollars.

Successful organizations do not separate advertising plans from marketing. They view each as a vital building block for success. Companies have a choice in how they plan. Most still use the traditional top-down planning model; some use a bottom-up model; and now, increasingly, companies are starting to use an integrated marketing communications (IMC) model. We'll look at the first two briefly before delving into the newer discipline of IMC.

Top-Down Marketing

The traditional **top-down marketing** plan is still the most common format. It has been used for over 30 years and fits the hierarchical organization of most companies. It is often appropriate for companies planning to launch completely new products. As Exhibit 7–1 shows, the top-down plan has four main elements: *situation analysis, marketing objectives, marketing strategy,* and *marketing tactics* (or *action programs*). Large companies with extensive marketing plans sometimes include additional sections. (Appendix A on the *Essentials of Contemporary Advertising* Web site outlines a complete top-down marketing plan.)

Situation Analysis

The **situation analysis** section is a *factual* statement of the organization's current situation and how it got there. It presents all the relevant facts about the company's history, growth, products and services, sales volume, share of market, competitive status, markets served, distribution system, past advertising programs, marketing research studies, company capabilities, strengths and weaknesses, and other pertinent information. To plan successfully for the future, company executives must agree on the accuracy of the data and its interpretation. The Checklist for Situation Analysis (in the Reference Library on the *Essentials of Contemporary Advertising* Web site) shows the most important elements to consider.

Once the historical information is gathered, the focus changes to potential threats and opportunities based on key factors outside the company's control—for example, the economic, political, social, technological, or commercial environments in which the company operates.[4]

Look at the situation Mountain Dew faced in the mid-1990s. While the 1980s had been the decade of the diet colas, the 1990s were turning into the decade of the big flavored brands. The soft-drink category was still dominated by the two mainstream colas with the most marketing muscle, Coca-Cola and Pepsi-Cola, and they were followed fairly closely by Diet Coke. But noncola drinks such as Sprite, Dr Pepper, and Mountain Dew were producing consistent gains. In fact, the noncolas were growing faster than the colas; and the folks at Mountain Dew were celebrating because, with scant resources and extraordinary competitive pressure, their little niche brand had reached the number six position overall and the number two noncola brand behind Dr Pepper. They were still some distance away from Diet Coke, but the brand was emerging as a growth leader even while being outspent in advertising by Dr Pepper. In a nutshell, that was the situation. And it spelled opportunity.

Marketing Objectives

The organization's next step is to determine specific marketing objectives. These must consider the amount of money the company has to invest in marketing and production, its knowledge of the marketplace, and the competitive environment.

Exhibit 7–1

Traditional top-down marketing plan.

The best service anticipates your needs. To help you arrive feeling ready for business, our Arrivals Lounge at Heathrow has the services of a spa. You can step off the plane and straight into a shower, a robe, even a Molton Brown facial – all while your suit is being pressed. Our goal is simple: to deliver the best service you could ask for, without you having to ask. So whether you're enjoying a gourmet meal, or our infinitely more comfortable flat bed, we think you'll find our business class like no other.

Visit ba.com/clubworld   Business class is different on BRITISH AIRWAYS

Need-satisfying objectives address the real value that a product or service delivers to its customers. British Airways (www.ba.com) knows that its business-class customers want more than just transportation from one city to another; they want to be refreshed and ready to conduct business when they arrive at their destination.

For example, in 1998, Mountain Dew budgeted about $40 million for media advertising, far less than the $83 million spent by Pepsi or the $116 million spent by Coke.[5] As a result, Dew had to set less ambitious marketing objectives in terms of total volume, but not in terms of growth.

Marketing objectives follow logically from a review of the company's current situation, management's prediction of future trends, and the hierarchy of company objectives. For example, **corporate objectives** are stated in terms of profit or return on investment, or net worth, earnings ratios, growth, or corporate reputation. **Marketing objectives,** which derive from corporate objectives, should relate to the needs of target markets as well as to specific sales goals. These may be referred to as general *need-satisfying objectives* and specific *sales-target objectives.*

To shift management's view of the organization from a producer of products to a satisfier of target market needs, companies set **need-satisfying objectives.** These have a couple of important purposes. First, they enable the firm to view its business broadly. For example, Revlon founder Charles Revson once said a cosmetic company's product is hope, not lipstick. An insurance company sells financial security, not policies. Since customer needs change, maintaining a narrow view may strand a company in a market where its products are no longer relevant. For example, if a button manufacturer thought his need-satisfying objective was to satisfy people's need for buttons, he might have completely missed the opportunity presented by new products such as Velcro and zippers, which satisfy a similar but broader need—fastening clothes.

Second, by setting need-satisfying objectives, managers force the company to look through the customer's eyes. They have to ask "What are we planning to do for the customer?" and "What is the value of that to our customer?" One of the best ways to define a market is to think about customer needs first and then identify the products that meet those needs.[6]

The second kind of marketing objective is the **sales-target objective.** This is a specific, quantitative, realistic marketing goal to be achieved within a specified period of time. A sales-target objective could be phrased as "What are we planning to do for ourselves?" They may be expressed in several ways: total sales volume; sales volume by product, market segment, customer type; market share in total or by product line; growth rate of sales volume in total or by product line; and gross profit in total or by product line.

Mountain Dew, for example, uses a number of measures for its sales-target objectives: case volume, share of market, growth, and/or share of growth. In 1998 and 1999, it defined its goal as outpacing its competitors and growing at twice the soft-drink category rate. These objectives were specific as to product and market, quantified as to time and amount, and—judging by the results—fairly realistic. In 1998, the category growth rate was 3 percent, and in 1999 it was 0.5 percent because of an industrywide price increase. Mountain Dew sold 665 million cases in 1998, at a growth rate of 9.9 percent; and in 1999, it sold 705 million cases, a solid 6 percent gain, and a dramatic 12 times the category rate.[7] Only by setting specific objectives can management measure its marketing success.

Commercial Break 7–A

The Strategies of Marketing Warfare

Jack Trout and Al Ries's *Marketing Warfare* is based on the classic book of military strategy, *On War*, written by Prussian general Carl von Clausewitz and published in 1832. The book outlines the principles behind all successful wars, and two simple ideas dominate: *force* and *the superiority of the defense*.

The Strategic Square

How do the principles of warfare apply to marketing? It comes down to the "strategic square":

Out of every 100 companies:
One should play defense.
Two should play offense.
Three should flank.
And 94 should be guerrillas.

Defensive Warfare

Datril opened its war on Tylenol with a price attack. Johnson & Johnson immediately cut Tylenol's price, even before Datril started its price advertising. Result: It repelled the Datril attacks and inflicted heavy losses on the Bristol-Myers entry.

Here are the rules for defensive marketing warfare:

1. Participate only if you are a market leader.
2. Introduce new products and services before the competition does.
3. Block strong competitive moves by copying them rapidly.

Offensive Warfare

Colgate had a strong number one position in toothpaste. But rival Procter & Gamble knew a thing or two about Carl von Clausewitz.

P&G launched Crest toothpaste with not only a massive $20 million advertising budget, but also the American Dental Association "seal of approval." Crest went over the top to become the best-selling toothpaste in the country.

But overtaking the leader is not that common. Most companies are happy if they can establish a profitable number two position.

The rules for waging offensive marketing warfare are:

1. Consider the strength of the leader's position.
2. Launch the attack on as narrow a front as possible, preferably with single products.
3. Launch the attack at the leader's weakest position.

Flanking Warfare

The third type of marketing warfare is where the action is for many companies. In practice, it means launching products where there is no competition. Unilever introduced Mentadent, the first baking soda/peroxide toothpaste, which became a very successful brand.

Here are the principles of flanking marketing warfare:

1. Make good flanking moves into uncontested areas.
2. Use surprise. Too much research often wastes precious time.
3. Keep up the pursuit; too many companies quit after they're ahead.

Guerrilla Warfare

Most of America's companies should be waging guerrilla warfare. The key to success in guerrilla wars is flexibility. A guerrilla should abandon any product or market if the tide of battle changes.

Here are the principles of guerrilla marketing warfare:

1. Find a market segment small enough to defend.
2. No matter how successful you become, never act like the leader.
3. Be prepared to "bug out" at a moment's notice.

Bottom Up

Trout and Ries's later book, *Bottom-Up Marketing* (discussed later in this chapter), continues the military analogy.

"Deep penetration on a narrow front is the key to winning a marketing war," they say. By this they mean that smaller companies should keep their product narrowly focused on a single concept. Many companies spread their forces over too wide a front. In fact, most large corporations today expend significant resources fending off focused attacks by smaller companies.

Applying the Breaks

Think of a successful product and explain its success in terms of marketing warfare. Then select a new or less successful product and explain how it might use marketing warfare strategy to achieve greatness.

Marketing Strategy

The **marketing strategy** describes how the company plans to meet its marketing objectives (see Commercial Break 7–A, "The Strategies of Marketing Warfare"). "Developing and following a strategy is what keeps you and everybody else on the same course so that you can maximize the effectiveness of your marketing."[8]

Marketing strategy typically involves three steps: (1) defining the particular target markets; (2) determining the strategic positioning; and (3) developing an

THE ION RED LINE. With a 205-horsepower supercharged and intercooled engine, oil-jet-cooled pistons, and sport seats from RECARO. Check the static zero-to-sixty in 6.2 seconds, 200-ft. lbs. of torque, and the cornering power to generate 0.85 lateral Gs. Starting at $21,450. As shown: $21,650. To build your own ION Red Line, visit saturn.com.

People first.

The photography and the copy in this print ad communicate that General Motors has a clear definition of the target market for its Saturn Ion Red Line. The 18- to 34-year-old male pictured in the ad grew up "eating, drinking, breathing cars."

Positioning helps differentiate products from the competition. In the crowded detergent category, Procter & Gamble has clearly positioned this Tide product as an alternative to using bleach. When a consumer wants to get clothes white without bleach, this is the product that should come to mind.

NO RUNNING
NO JUMPING
NO BALLPLAYING
NO PLAYING IN DIRT
NO GOING ANYWHERE NEAR DIRT
NO EVEN THINKING ABOUT DIRT

IF YOU WANT TO AVOID USING BLEACH, CONSIDER YOUR ALTERNATIVES
You could avoid getting dirty. That's one alternative. Or you could use the detergent that gives you brilliant whites without a drop of chlorine bleach. And is safe on colors too. TIDE WITH BLEACH ALTERNATIVE.

appropriate marketing mix for each target market. A company's marketing strategy has a dramatic impact on its advertising. It determines the role and amount of advertising in the marketing mix, its creative thrust, and the media to be employed.

Selecting the target market In top-down marketing, the first step in strategy development is to define and select the target market, using the processes of market segmentation and research discussed in Chapters 4 and 6.

When General Motors introduced its new Saturn SC1 model, for instance, it defined its target market as "college-educated import owners and intenders"—highly educated young adults (18 to 34) considering their first or second car purchase. They were further defined as 60 percent female, living in one- or two-person households, and seeking a vehicle with sporty styling, fun performance, fuel economy, a good warranty, and sound quality/reliability/dependability.[9] They typically drive a Honda Civic, Toyota Corolla, or Nissan 240SX.

Similarly, Mountain Dew defines its target market as active, young people in their teens as well as young adults 20 to 39 years old. In addition, the brand aims a significant portion of its marketing activities at urban youth, especially African Americans and Latinos.[10] To Mountain Dew, their prototypical consumer is an 18-year-old, street-smart, male teen.[11]

Positioning the product The famous researcher and copywriter David Ogilvy said one of the first decisions in marketing and advertising is also the most important: how to position the product. **Positioning** refers to the place a brand occupies competitively in the minds of consumers. Every product has some position—whether intended or not—even if the position is "nowhere." Positions are based on consumer perceptions, which may or may not reflect reality. Strong brands have a clear, often unique position in the target market. Ogilvy's agency (Ogilvy & Mather), for example, differentiated Dove soap in 1957 by positioning it as a complexion bar for women with dry skin. Now, a half-century later, every commercial still uses the same cleansing cream demonstration, and Dove is consistently the number one brand, spending some $93.2 million in advertising annually to maintain its 24 percent share of the multibillion-dollar bar soap market.

Many positions are available in a market. The big mistake many companies make is not staking out any position. They can't be everything; but they don't want to be nothing.[12] A company might pick a position similar to a competitor's and fight for the same customers. Or it might find a position not held by a competitor—a niche in the market—and fill it quickly, perhaps through product differentiation or market segmentation.

Professor Ernest Martin at Virginia Commonwealth University proposes seven distinct approaches to developing a positioning strategy:

1. *Product attribute*—setting the brand apart by stressing a particular product feature important to consumers.

2. *Price/quality*—positioning on the basis of price or quality.

3. *Use/application*—positioning on the basis of how a product is used (e.g., Arm & Hammer).

4. *Product class*—positioning the brand against other products that, while not the same, offer the same class of benefits.

5. *Product user*—positioning against the particular group who uses the product.

6. *Product competitor*—positioning against competitors (e.g., Avis/Hertz), using the strength of the competitor's position to help define the subject brand.

7. *Cultural symbol*—positioning apart from competitors through the creation or use of some recognized symbol or icon.[13]

5 - Love

We would add an eighth approach: *By category*—positioning by defining or redefining a business category. A simple way for a company to get the number one position is to invent a new product category.

Xerox, for example, was originally known as *the* copier company, but with increased competition, the copier market became glutted, so Xerox tried to reposition itself as a problem solver. Now calling itself "The Document Company," it offers to use technology to find ways for everyone in an organization to manage and share useful information. But what it has really done is create a new business category occupied by one company: Xerox.[14]

With all its high energy and exhilaration, "youth" is not only the positioning of Mountain Dew, it's the heartbeat of the brand.[15] PepsiCo defines the Dew positioning this way:

Strong brands have a clear and consistent positioning, often evident in their advertising taglines. BMW (www.bmw.com) has been advertised as "The Ultimate Driving Machine" since 1973.

> To 18-year-old males who embrace excitement, adventure, and fun, Mountain Dew is the great-tasting soft drink that exhilarates like no other because it is energizing, thirst quenching, and has a unique citrus flavor.

Often, a product's positioning can be discerned from its advertising tagline—*BMW, the ultimate driving machine; Nobody doesn't like Sara Lee; Bounty, the quicker picker-upper; You're in good hands with Allstate.*

Determining the marketing mix The next step in developing the marketing strategy is to determine a cost-effective marketing mix for *each* target market the company pursues. As we discussed in Chapter 4, the mix blends the various marketing elements the company controls: *product, price, distribution,* and *communications.*

Mountain Dew was blessed with a broad marketing toolbox to draw upon. First, it offered consumers an energizing, thirst-quenching soft-drink *product* with a unique citrus flavor and an image of youthful exuberance, exhilaration, and adventure. Then, to build *distribution,* it used a variety of promotions to the trade that would enable grocers and other resellers to increase both volume and profits. While its *price* was competitive with other soft drinks, Mountain Dew promoted itself aggressively with free samples, premiums, and prizes at various street and sporting events—which effectively lowered the price to consumers.

Finally, Mountain Dew initiated an integrated *communications* program that included extensive advertising on TV, radio, outdoor, print, and the Internet; sports and event sponsorships; appearances at grass-roots geographical events; plus a host of public relations activities—all designed to develop and promote the distinct Mountain Dew personality.

Companies have a wide variety of marketing strategy options. They might increase distribution, initiate new uses for a product, change a product line, develop entirely new markets, or start discount pricing. Each option emphasizes one or more marketing mix elements. The choice depends on the product's target market, its position in the market, and its stage in the **product life cycle,** the progression of growth and decline through which a successful product typically moves.

Exhibit 7–2

Bottom-up marketing plan.

Marketing Tactics (Action Programs)

A company's objectives indicate where it wants to go; the strategy indicates the intended route; and the **tactics** (or **action programs**) determine the specific short-term actions to be taken, internally and externally, by whom, and when. Advertising campaigns live in the world of marketing tactics. These tactics are the key to *bottom-up marketing.*

Bottom-Up Marketing: How Small Companies Plan

In a small company, everybody is both player and coach, and the day-to-day details seem to come first, leaving little or no time for formal planning. However, there is a solution to this dilemma: **bottom-up marketing** (see Exhibit 7–2).

Jack Trout and Al Ries think one of the best ways for a company to develop a competitive advantage is to focus on an ingenious tactic first and then develop that tactic into a strategy. By reversing the normal process, advertisers sometimes make important discoveries.[16] Researchers at Vicks developed an effective liquid cold remedy but discovered that it put people to sleep. Rather than throw out the research, Vicks positioned the formula as a nighttime cold remedy. NyQuil went on to become the number one cold remedy and the most successful new product in Vicks's history.

The *tactic* is a singular, competitive technique. By planning from the bottom up, entrepreneurs can find unique tactics to exploit. But caution is required. Advertisers should find just *one* tactic, not two or three. The advertiser can then focus all elements of the marketing mix on this single-minded tactic. The tactic becomes the nail, and the strategy is the hammer that drives it home.

The artful combination of tactic and strategy creates a position in the consumer's mind. When Tom Monaghan thought of the tactic of delivering pizza to customers' homes, he focused his whole strategy on that singular idea. He ended up making a fortune and marketing history with Domino's Pizza.

Managers of small companies have an advantage here. Surrounded by the details of the business, they are more likely to discover a good tactic that can be developed into a powerful strategy. However, that's not to say that a large company cannot profit from bottom-up marketing. Many have, like 3M with its Post-it notes.

CONCEPT CHECK

What is accomplished during each of the four main elements of top-down marketing plan development?

The New Marketing Mantra: Relationship Marketing

Today, many advertisers are discovering that the key to building brand equity in the twenty-first century will be to develop interdependent, mutually satisfying relationships with customers.

A market-driven firm's overriding purpose is to create happy, loyal customers. Customers, not products, are the lifeblood of the business.[17] This realization has created a new trend away from simple *transactional marketing* to **relationship marketing**—creating, maintaining, and enhancing long-term relationships with customers and other stakeholders that will result in exchanges of information and other things of mutual value.[18]

Today's affluent, sophisticated consumers can choose from a wide variety of products and services offered by producers located around the world. As a result, the customer relationship—in which the sale is only the beginning—is the key strategic resource of the successful twenty-first-century business.[19] As

Ethical Issues

A War of Comparisons

Across the advertising battlefield, marketers wage a war called comparative advertising. Ads wield charges and countercharges, and the main players are no longer just second-rate brands looking to make their mark.

Comparative advertising, a technique where one company explicitly compares its brand to another in an effort to gain a competitive edge, was actually endorsed by the Federal Trade Commission in the 1970s "as a means of improving competition." Since its inception into the advertising world, comparative advertising has turned out to be a bit of a double-edged sword.

Ideally, comparative advertising should provide consumers with more information about competing products, thereby allowing them to make better-informed purchase decisions. However, research indicates that direct product comparisons often create greater awareness for the lesser-known brand, and that has been directly linked to a decline in sales for the more established brand, since at the point of purchase the consumer often confuses the two.

When taken too far, comparative advertising can be illegal. If an ad's comparisons are shown to be false, deceptive, or deliberately misleading, the campaign may result in litigation. Even ads that are literally correct can be found liable. According to one court, "innuendo, indirect intimations, and ambiguous suggestions" can unjustly injure a competitor. McNeil Consumer Products' Extra-Strength Tylenol, for example, successfully sued American Home Products' Maximum Strength Anacin even though Anacin's ad was literally true. Anacin had implied superiority over Tylenol when in fact both products contain the same amount of pain reliever.

A further complication arises when advertisers manipulate comparisons to cast a more favorable light on their products. In Australia, Duracell ran an ad showing a bunny powered by a Duracell battery outracing one powered by an Energizer battery. What Duracell neglected to mention in the ad was that they were comparing their top-of-the-line alkaline battery to one of Energizer's midrange carbon zinc batteries—apples and oranges in the world of batteries. Energizer took the unfair comparison to court, and Duracell had to add clarifying text to their ad before they could put it back on the air.

MCI goes after AT&T. Visa attacks American Express, and Jack in the Box and Burger King taunt McDonald's.

Name-calling, finger pointing, and insulting the competition are all contemporary weapons used in the marketing wars waged between virtually identical brands, who are desperate to stand apart from the competition.

Some researchers estimate that 40 percent of all advertising in the United States is now comparative, whereas in most of the world it is either illegal or strictly regulated. In France, a recent telecom ad was able to bypass the national ban on comparative advertising. The campaign claimed that Tele2's rates were up to 50 percent cheaper than those of rival phone companies. Tele2 was recently awarded a winning judgment by French courts, which ruled that its campaign targeting competitors Cegetel and France Telecom "met French standards on comparative advertising . . . the ads were clearly focused on identical products."

In the United States, to keep comparison battles from getting out of hand, numerous groups, including the American Association of Advertising Agencies, the National Association of Broadcasters, and the FTC, issued guidelines for comparative advertising that are often stricter than current laws. TV network NBC, for example, insists that "advertisers shall refrain from discrediting, disparaging, or unfairly attacking competitors, competing products, or other industries."

This is a good step, but the legal language governing comparisons is vague, allowing for a blurry line between healthy one-upmanship and illegal behavior. As competition continues to increase, and ethical and legal guidelines remain ambiguous, the public will no doubt continue to be bombarded by comparative ads. The responsibility, therefore, will continue to fall on consumers to sift through the ads and differentiate fact from fiction.

Questions

1. How do you feel about ads that compare the features and benefits of competitive products and services? Do you believe they are unethical even if the comparisons are honest? Should they be allowed? Why or why not?

2. Select a comparative ad and study the copy. What points of comparison does the ad make? Are the points made honestly and directly, or are they masked by innuendo and implication? Is the ad literally true but still potentially misleading? Do you feel the ad is ethical or not?

Dartmouth professor Frederick Webster points out: "The new *market-driven conception* of marketing will focus on *managing strategic partnerships* and positioning the firm between vendors and customers in the value chain with the aim of delivering *superior value* to the customer."[20]

We define **value** as the ratio of *perceived benefits* to the price of the product.[21]

Microsoft (www.microsoft.com) understands the lifetime value of a customer. This ad suggests that Microsoft wants to help its software users develop their potential. By nurturing relationships early in individuals' careers, Microsoft is likely to retain their business for years to come.

The Importance of Relationships

To succeed, companies must focus on managing loyalty among carefully chosen customers and **stakeholders** (employees, centers of influence, stockholders, the financial community, and the press).[22] This is important for a number of reasons:

1. *The cost of lost customers.* No amount of advertising is likely to win back a customer lost from shoddy products or poor service. The real profit lost is the **lifetime customer value (LTV)** of a customer to a firm. For example, the average customer of one major transportation firm represented a lifetime value of $40,000. The company had 64,000 accounts and lost 5 percent of them due to poor service. That amounted to an unnecessary loss of $128 million in revenue and $12 million in profits![23] Moreover, negative word of mouth can have a terrible snowballing effect. Imagine if one lost customer influences only one other customer to not patronize the business. That immediately doubles the LTV loss. Negative word of mouth is why bad movies disappear so quickly from theaters.

2. *The cost of acquiring new customers.* Defensive marketing typically costs less than offensive marketing because it requires a great deal of effort to lure satisfied customers away from competitors.[24] The fragmentation of media audiences and the resistance of sophisticated consumers to advertising messages make it increasingly difficult for a brand to break out of the ghetto of advertising clutter by stepping up the advertising volume.[25] In fact, it costs five to eight times as much in marketing, advertising, and promotion to acquire a new customer as it does to keep an existing one.[26]

3. *The value of loyal customers.* Lester Wunderman, the founder of Wunderman Worldwide (the second largest direct-response agency in the world), says that 90 percent of a manufacturer's profit comes from repeat purchasers; only 10 percent comes from trial or sporadic purchasers.[27] Reducing customer defections by even 5 percent can improve profit potential by 25 to 85 percent.[28] And the longer customers stay with a company, the more willing they are to pay premium prices, make referrals, increase their annual buying, and demand less hand-holding.[29]

Thus, a company's first market should always be its current customers. In the past, most marketing and advertising effort focused on *presale* activities aimed at acquiring new customers. But today sophisticated marketers are shifting more of their resources to *postsale* activities, making customer retention their first line of defense. They have discovered the primary benefit of focusing on relationships: increasing retention and optimizing lifetime customer value.[30]

Levels of Relationships

Kotler and Armstrong distinguish five levels of relationships that can be formed between a company and its various stakeholders, depending on their mutual needs:

- *Basic transactional relationship.* The company sells the product but does not follow up in any way (Target).

- *Reactive relationship.* The company (or salesperson) sells the product and encourages customers to call if they encounter any problems (Men's Wearhouse).

- *Accountable relationship.* The salesperson phones customers shortly after the sale to check whether the product meets expectations and asks for product improvement suggestions and any specific disappointments. This information helps the company to continuously improve its offering (Acura dealers).

- *Proactive relationship.* The salesperson or company contacts customers from time to time with suggestions about improved product use or helpful new products (Nextel).

- *Partnership.* The company works continuously with customers (and other stakeholders) to discover ways to deliver better value (Nordstrom's Personal Shopper).[31]

Most of a company's profit comes from repeat purchasers. So Marriott (www.marriott.com) tries to generate repeat business by rewarding its loyal customers with free vacations. It must work; nearly 75 percent of shoppers in the United States now belong to at least one loyalty program.

Different stakeholders require different types of relationships. The relationship a company seeks with a customer will rarely be the same as it seeks with the press. However, there is often significant overlap in stakeholder roles. An employee may also be a customer and own stock in the company. Knowing intimately the customers and stakeholders is critical to the success of relationship marketing.

The number of stakeholders is also important. The more there are, the more difficult it is to develop an extensive personal relationship with each. Moreover, some customers may not want anything more than a transactional relationship.[32] Most people wouldn't want a phone call from Oscar Mayer asking if the hot dogs tasted good or from Gillette asking about the smoothness of their last shave. However, when Coca-Cola changed its formula in the early 1980s, legions of Coke loyalists besieged the company with angry letters and phone calls. They believed their relationship with the brand had been violated. The company quickly brought back Classic Coke. Clearly, therefore, brand relationships can be psychological or symbolic as well as personal, and they can be created by brand promotion, publicity, and advertising as well as by people.

Realizing this, Mountain Dew places a great deal of emphasis on creating a "Dew-x-perience" for its customers. Using guerilla-marketing tactics to reach out to urban youth, it employs a variety of hip-hop and Latin recording artists in various "street marketing" efforts to distribute bottles of Dew. It also sponsors extreme athletes and appears at sporting events such as the Gravity Games and ESPN's X Games with vans full of merchandise and giveaways.[33]

The final consideration is the profit margin. High-profit product or service categories make deeper, personal relationships more desirable (see Exhibit 7–3). Low profit margins per customer suggest that the marketer should pursue basic transactional relationships augmented by brand image advertising.[34]

> Why is it so important for companies to carefully manage relationships with their customers?

CONCEPT CHECK

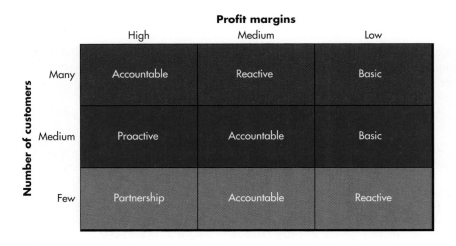

Exhibit 7–3

Relationship levels as a function of profit margin and number of customers.

	Profit margins		
	High	Medium	Low
Many	Accountable	Reactive	Basic
Medium	Proactive	Accountable	Basic
Few	Partnership	Accountable	Reactive

Number of customers (axis label)

Using IMC to Make Relationships Work

This interest in relationship marketing coincided with the interest in *integrated marketing communications* (IMC). In fact, according to Northwestern professor Don Schultz, IMC is what makes relationship marketing possible.[35]

IMC: The Concept and the Process

Technology has enabled marketers to adopt flexible manufacturing, customizing products for customized markets. Being "market driven" today means bundling services together with products to create a "unique product experience." It means companies and customers working together to find solutions.[36]

The counterpart to flexible manufacturing is flexible marketing—and integrated marketing communications—to reach customers at different levels in new and better ways.

IMC is both a concept and a process. The *concept* of integration is *wholeness*. Achieving this wholeness in communications creates **synergy**—the principal benefit of IMC—because each element of the communications mix reinforces the others for greater effect.[37]

For example, when a Mountain Dew grocer runs an **endcap promotion** (a special display at the end of an aisle) alone, it might generate a 10 percent increase in volume. If he runs an ad for Dew with a coupon, that might deliver a 15 percent increase. But running both together might grow volume by 35 percent. That's synergy—because the whole is greater than the sum of its parts.

Tom Duncan, director of the IMC program at the University of Denver, points out that IMC is also a *process* in which communication becomes the driving, integrating force in the marketing mix and throughout the organization.

The Evolution of the IMC Concept

As we discussed in Chapter 1, with the phenomenal technological changes in the last decade came a host of specialized media and the fragmentation of the mass market. At the same time we witnessed a flood of mergers and acquisitions, the ascension of the global marketplace, the escalation of competition between various internal departments and external suppliers, and

The company eBay (www.ebay.com) was in search of an integrated promotion to stimulate activity during the summer season when people traditionally spend more time outdoors and away from their computers. The promotion featured a Camp eBay bus touring at concerts and venues all across the country. Camp eBay was also featured at Loews theaters and Baskin-Robbins. Camp eBay campers could win prizes by unscrambling online messages with their very own Camp eBay decoder card. Nearly 300,000 people registered for Camp eBay and made over 80,000 purchases.

Mobile Tour Exhibit | Collateral

the arrival of more sophisticated, critical, and demanding customers. Suddenly, companies faced costly redundancies and inefficiencies as company departments with different missions and agendas all sought to achieve their particular goals, often at odds with either corporate or customer needs. For efficiency, companies needed to coordinate the multiplicity of inconsistent company and product messages being issued.[38]

Many companies initially took a narrow, *inside-out* view of IMC. They saw it as a way to coordinate and manage their marketing communications (advertising, sales promotion, public relations, personal selling, and direct marketing) to give the audience a consistent message about the company.[39] The coordination of these communications elements is certainly important and we will examine them more closely in Chapters 16 and 17.

But a broader, more sophisticated, *outside-in* perspective of IMC sees customers as partners in an ongoing relationship, recognizes the references they use, acknowledges the importance of the whole communications system, and accepts the many ways they come into contact with the company or the brand. Companies committed to IMC realize their biggest asset is not their products or their factories or even their employees, but their customers.[40] Defined broadly:

> **Integrated marketing communications** is the process of building and reinforcing mutually profitable relationships with employees, customers, other stakeholders, and the general public by developing and coordinating a strategic communications program that enables them to have a constructive encounter with the company/brand through a variety of media or other contacts.

Whether a company employs the narrow view or the broad view depends to a great extent on its corporate culture. Some companies enjoyed rapid growth and strong customer relationships because they intuitively integrated and focused all corporate and marketing activities. Saturn, Apple, Honda, Nike, and Banana Republic are just a few.

How the Customer Sees Marketing Communications

To truly understand IMC, we have to look through the customer's eyes. In one study, consumers identified 102 different media as "advertising"—everything from TV to shopping bags to sponsored community events.[41] Customers also develop perceptions of the company or brand through a variety of other sources: news reports, word of mouth, gossip, experts' opinions, financial reports, and even the CEO's personality.

All these communications or brand contacts, sponsored or not, create an *integrated product* in the consumer's mind.[42] In other words, customers automatically integrate all the brand-related messages that emanate from the company or some other source. The way they integrate those messages determines their perception of the company. IMC gives companies a better opportunity to manage or influence those perceptions and create a superior relationship with those stakeholders.

The Four Sources of Brand Messages

To influence customers' perceptions, marketers must understand one of the basic premises of IMC: that *everything we do (and don't do) sends a message*. That is to say, every corporate activity has a message component. Duncan categorized four types of company/brand-related messages stakeholders receive: *planned, product, service,* and *unplanned*. Each of these influences a stakeholder's relationship decision, so marketers must know where these messages originate, what effect they have, and the costs to influence or control them.

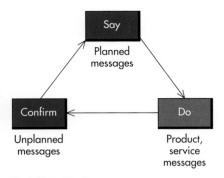

Exhibit 7–4

The integration triangle.

1. **Planned messages.** These are the traditional marketing communication messages—advertising, sales promotion, personal selling, merchandising materials, publicity releases, event sponsorships. These often have the *least* impact because they are seen as self-serving. Planned messages should be coordinated to work toward a predetermined set of communications objectives. This is the most fundamental aspect of (inside-out) IMC.

2. **Product messages.** In IMC theory, every element of the marketing mix (not just promotion) sends a message. Messages from the product, price, or distribution elements are typically referred to as product (or inferred) messages. For example, customers and other stakeholders receive one product message from a $2,500 Rolex watch and a totally different one from a $30 Timex. Product messages also include packaging, which communicates a lot about the product through the use of color, type fonts, imagery, design, and layout.

   Product messages have great impact. When a product (or service) performs well, the customer infers a positive message that reinforces the purchase decision. However, a gap between the product's performance and advertised promises is likely to convey a negative message. Managers must realize that all marketing mix decisions are also communication decisions.

3. **Service messages.** Many messages result from employee interactions with customers. In many organizations, customer service people are supervised by operations, not marketing. Yet the service messages they send have greater marketing impact than the planned messages. With IMC, marketing people work with operations to minimize negative messages and maximize positive ones.

4. **Unplanned messages.** Companies have little or no control over the unplanned messages that emanate from employee gossip, unsought news stories, comments by the trade or competitors, word-of-mouth rumors, or major disasters. Unplanned messages may affect customers' attitudes dramatically, but they can sometimes be anticipated and influenced, especially by managers experienced in public relations.[43]

Companies have control over their advertising, but they must be careful about any unplanned messages they may inadvertently engender. Over the years, the fashion designer Benetton (www.Benetton.com) has developed a number of highly controversial ads addressing social issues. However, much like Calvin Klein, Benetton has suffered criticism for its advertising. In this case, critics blasted the company for trying to gain publicity by exploiting human suffering. Benetton's ad was actually a statement against the war in the Balkans. Criticism, of course, is just one kind of unplanned message. Good word of mouth is another. In both cases, the company has little control over these kinds of messages.

The Integration Triangle

The integration triangle developed by Duncan and Moriarty is a simple illustration of how perceptions are created from the various brand message sources (see Exhibit 7–4). Planned messages are *say* messages, what companies say about themselves. Product and service messages are *do* messages because they represent what a company does. Unplanned messages are *confirm* messages because that's what others say and confirm (or not) about what the company says and does. Constructive integration occurs when a brand does what its maker says it will do and then others confirm that it delivers on its promises.[44]

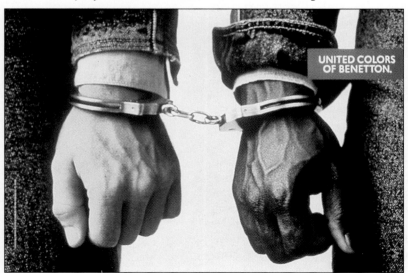

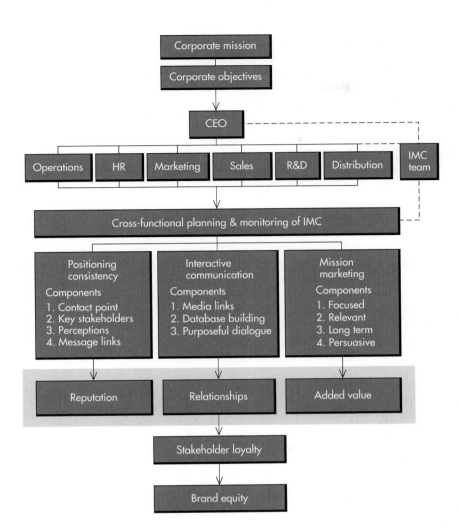

Exhibit 7–5
IMC macro model.

The Dimensions of IMC

To maximize the synergy benefits of IMC, Duncan suggests three dimensions to an organization's integration process. It should first ensure consistent positioning, then facilitate purposeful interactivity between the company and its customers or other stakeholders, and finally actively incorporate a socially responsible mission into the organization's relationships with its stakeholders.

As Duncan's IMC macro model shows in Exhibit 7–5, the cross-functional planning and monitoring of IMC activities results in an enhanced relationship with customers and other stakeholders, which leads to stakeholder loyalty and ultimately to greater brand equity.[45] (See RL 7–2 in the Reference Library on the *Essentials of Contemporary Advertising* Web site for more details on this model.)

The interest in IMC is already global, moving from North America to Europe, Asia, and Latin America.[46] The $38 billion Swiss company Nestlé, for example, used a variety of IMC strategies, such as building highway rest stops for feeding and changing babies, designed to establish deep, caring relationships between families and the Nestlé Baby Foods division in France.[47]

In short, IMC offers accountability by maximizing resources and linking communications activities directly to organizational goals and the resulting bottom line.[48]

The IMC Approach to Marketing and Advertising Planning

For many companies, integrated marketing communications represents a new approach to planning marketing and communications activities. It differs substantially from the traditional process by mixing marketing and communications planning together rather than separating them. Using the outside-in process, the IMC approach starts with the customer. Marketers study what media customers use, the relevance of their message to the customers, and when customers and prospects are most *receptive* to the message. They begin with the customer and work back to the brand.[49]

Thanks to computer technology, marketers now have a wealth of information at their fingertips. With supermarket scanner data, for instance, packaged-goods marketers can (1) identify specific users of products and services; (2) measure their actual purchase behavior and relate it to specific brand and product categories; (3) measure the impact of various advertising and marketing communications activities and determine their value in influencing the actual purchase; and (4) capture and evaluate this information over time.[50]

This ever-expanding database of customer behavior can be the basis for planning all future marketing and communications activities, especially if the database contains information on customer demographics, psychographics, purchase data, and brand or product category attitudes.

Starting the whole planning process with the database forces the company to focus on the consumer, or prospect, not on the company's sales or profit goals. Communications objectives and strategies are established for making contact with the consumer and influencing his or her attitudes, beliefs, and purchase behavior. The marketer then decides what other elements of the marketing mix (product, price, distribution) can be used to further encourage the desired behavior. Finally, the planner determines what communications tactics to use—media advertising, direct marketing, publicity, sales promotion, special events. All forms of marketing are thus turned into communication, and all forms of communication into marketing.[51]

The Importance of IMC to the Study of Advertising

Because customers see all sponsored communications as advertising, advertising people (account managers, creatives, media planners) must grow beyond their traditional specialty to become enlightened generalists, familiar with and able to integrate all types of marketing communications.

In a survey of 122 *Fortune* 500 marketing, advertising, and communications executives, most respondents indicated a general understanding of IMC and agreed that synergy is the key benefit of integrated marketing.[52] However, the study also showed that confusion remains among professionals concerning IMC use. This suggests that most practitioners today still lack the broad knowledge required to develop, supervise, and execute full IMC programs.[53]

CONCEPT CHECK

In what ways does the more sophisticated, outside-in view of IMC differ from the narrower, inside-out view and why is this important?

The Advertising Plan

The **advertising plan** is a natural outgrowth of the marketing plan and is prepared in much the same way. It picks up where the marketing plan leaves off, building on the goals that have been established for the advertising program.

Those goals are translated into specific advertising objectives, from which creative and media strategies are developed. The advertising plan typically also incorporates the rationale for a proposed budget and a plan for conducting research. (A top-down advertising plan and an IMC plan outline can be found on the *Essentials of Contemporary Advertising* Web site.)

Reviewing the Marketing Plan

The advertising manager first reviews the marketing plan to understand where the company wants to go, how it intends to get there, and what role advertising plays in the marketing mix. The first section of the advertising plan should organize information from the marketing plan's situation analysis into four categories: internal *strengths* and *weaknesses* and external *opportunities* and *threats* (**SWOT analysis**). Internal factors are those that are under the company's control, and external factors are those over which a company has little or no control.

For example, McDonald's restaurants' *strengths* include its strong name identity and thousands of retail locations. However, the company's *weaknesses* included a menu loaded with unhealthy food choices and an image to match. McDonald's is now taking advantage of an *opportunity* to capitalize on nutritious food trends by promoting healthier menu items and a fresh, new image. In doing so, it is combating *threats* from competitive restaurants and posting its biggest sales gains in nearly 20 years.

Setting Advertising Objectives

Based on the marketing plan, the advertising manager determines what tasks advertising must take on. What strengths and opportunities can be leveraged? What weaknesses and threats need to be addressed? Unfortunately, some corporate executives (and advertising managers) state vague goals for advertising, like "increase sales and maximize profits by creating a favorable

impression of the product in the marketplace." When this happens, no one understands what the advertising is intended to do, how much it will cost, or how to measure the results. Advertising objectives should be specific, realistic, and measurable.

Advertising cannot be assigned full responsibility for a product's success or failure. In 2003, Heinz (www.heinz.com) launched a major ad campaign to introduce new varieties, like its hot ketchup. This campaign, from Leo Burnett's Lisbon office, attracted critical acclaim and earned a Cannes Bronze Lion, but could not sustain interest in specialty condiments.

Understanding What Advertising Can Do

Most advertising programs encourage prospects to take some action. However, it is unrealistic to assign advertising the whole responsibility for achieving sales. Sales goals are marketing objectives, not advertising objectives. Before an advertiser can persuade customers to buy, it must inform, persuade, or remind its intended audience about the company, product, service, or issue. A simple adage to remember when setting objectives is "Marketing sells,

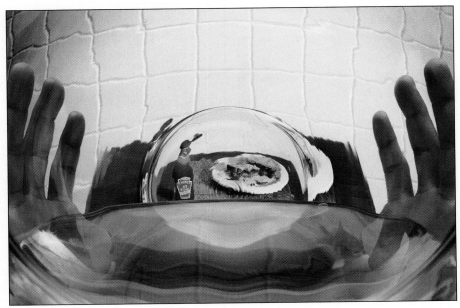

Exhibit 7–6

The advertising pyramid depicts the progression of advertising effects on mass audiences—especially for new products. The initial message promotes *awareness* of the product to a large audience (the base of the pyramid). But only a percentage of this large group will *comprehend* the product's benefits. Of that group, even fewer will go on to feel *conviction* about, then *desire* for the product. In the end, compared with the number of people aware of the product, the number of people who take *action* is usually quite small.

The advertising pyramid represents the learn-feel-do model of advertising effects. Oneida (www.oneida.com), for instance, is renowned for its quality glassware and china. It uses the learn-feel-do approach in this ad, where consumers learn about the resiliency of the porcelain, feel positively about the durability, and fulfill the do element by visiting the store and/or purchasing the product.

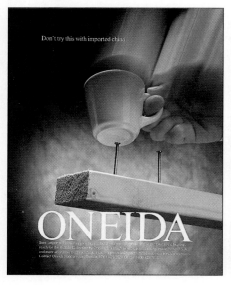

advertising tells." In other words, advertising objectives should be related to communication effects.

The Advertising Pyramid: A Guide to Setting Objectives

Suppose you're advertising a new brand in a new product category, but you're not sure what kind of results to expect. The pyramid in Exhibit 7–6 shows some of the tasks advertising can perform. Obviously, before your product is introduced, prospective customers are completely unaware of it. Your first communication objective therefore is to create *awareness*—to acquaint people with the company, product, service, and/or brand.

The next task might be to develop *comprehension*—to communicate enough information about the product that some percentage of the aware group will recognize the product's purpose, image, or position, and perhaps some of its features.

Next, you need to communicate enough information to develop *conviction*—to persuade a certain number of people to actually believe in the product's value. Once convinced, some people may be moved to *desire* the product. Finally, some percentage of those who desire the product will take *action*. They may request additional information, send in a coupon, visit a store, or actually buy the product.

The pyramid works in three dimensions: time, dollars, and people. Advertising results may take time, especially if the product is expensive or not purchased regularly. Over time, as a company continues advertising, the number of people who become aware of the product increases. As more people comprehend the product, believe in it, and desire it, more will take the final action of buying it.

Let's apply these principles to a hypothetical case. Suppose you are in charge of advertising for the new "Lightning Bug," a hybrid car built by Volkswagen that runs on both gasoline and electricity. Your initial advertising objectives for this fictional car might read as follows:

1. Within two years, communicate the existence of the Lightning Bug to half of the more than 500,000 people who annually buy foreign economy cars.

2. Get two-thirds of this "aware" group to comprehend that the Lightning Bug is a superior economy car with many design, safety, and environmentally friendly features; that it is a brand-new nameplate backed with unmatched service, quality, and value; and that it is sold only through dedicated Volkswagen dealers.

3. Convince two-thirds of the "comprehending" group that the Lightning Bug is a high-quality car, reliable, economical, and fun to drive.

4. Stimulate desire within two-thirds of the "convinced" group for a test drive.

5. Motivate two-thirds of the "desire" group to visit a retailer for a test drive.

These advertising objectives are specific as to time and degree and are quantified like marketing objectives. Theoretically, at the end of the first year, a consumer attitude study could determine how many people are aware of the Lightning Bug, how many people understand the car's primary features, and so on, thus measuring the program's effectiveness.

Volkswagen's advertising may accomplish the objectives of creating awareness, comprehension, conviction, desire, and action. But once the customer is in the store, it's the retailer's responsibility to close the sale with effective selling and service.

With the advent of integrated marketing communications, we can look at the pyramid in another way. By using a variety of marketing communication tools and a wide menu of traditional and nontraditional media, we can accomplish the communication objectives suggested by the pyramid in a more efficient manner. For instance, for creating sheer awareness for the new Lightning Bug as well as brand image for the car and the company, an intensive program of public relations activities supported by mass media advertising would be the communication tools of choice. Comprehension, interest, and credibility can be augmented by media advertising, press publicity, direct mail brochures, and special events such as a sports car show. Desire can be enhanced by a combination of the buzz created by good reviews in car enthusiast magazines, plus media advertising, beautiful brochure photography, and the excitement generated by a sales pro-

There are many ways to deliver a message besides using traditional media. In keeping with its theme of fun and adventure, Mountain Dew traveled around the country in a colorful subway car that was packed with all kinds of treats and memorabilia given away at key events.

motion (such as a sweepstakes). Finally, action can be stimulated by direct mail solicitation, sales promotion, and the attentive service of a retail salesperson in an attractive new car showroom. Following the sale, media advertising should continue to reinforce the purchase decision. But at the same time, outbound telemarketing calls from the retailer can be used to thank the customer, solicit feedback on that customer's experience, and offer any needed assistance. This acknowledges that the sale was just the beginning of a valuable relationship.

The Old Model versus the New

The advertising pyramid represents the *learn-feel-do* model of advertising effects. That is, it assumes that people rationally consider a prospective purchase, and once they feel good about it, they act. The theory is that advertising affects attitude, and attitude leads to behavior. That may be true for certain expensive, high-involvement products that require a lot of consideration. But other purchases may follow a different pattern. For example, impulse purchases at the checkout counter may involve a *do-feel-learn* model, in which behavior leads to attitude which leads to knowledge. Other purchases may follow some other pattern. Thus, there are many marketing considerations when advertising objectives are being set, and they must be thought out carefully (see RL 7-3, Checklist for Developing Advertising Objectives, in the Reference Library on the *Essentials of Contemporary Advertising* Web site).

The advertising pyramid also reflects the traditional mass-marketing monolog. The advertiser talks and the customer listens.[54] That was appropriate before the advent of computers and databases, and it may still be appropriate in those categories where the marketer has no choice.

But today, as the IMC model shows, many marketers have databases of information on their customers—about where they live, what they buy, and what they like and dislike. When marketers can have a dialogue and establish a relationship, the model is no longer a pyramid but a circle (see Exhibit 7-7).

Exhibit 7–7

Messages go to the customer through advertising and other communication channels. Messages come back via direct response, surveys, and a purchase behavior database. The marketer's message can evolve based on this feedback.

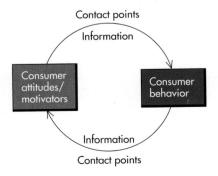

Nutrition Facts
Serving Size: depends. So how was your day?
Serving Per Container: see above

Amount Per Serving	
Calories huh?	
	% Daily Value
Total Euphoria	**94%**
Rapture	82%
Ecstasy	89%
Bliss	90%
Indulgence	**100%**
Decadence	**75%**
Fulfillment	**97%**
Thiamin	0%
Niacin	0%

SEATTLE CHOCOLATES

Seattle Chocolates are available in seven flavours: espresso, passion fruit, mint, toffee, hazelnut, raspberry and white chocolate orange. For more information, call 1-800-335-3662.

The creative strategy represents what a company wants to communicate about its product. The benefit communicated by the Seattle Chocolate Company (**www.seattlechocolate. com**) is that its candies provide sweet tooth decadence and gratification to consumers willing to indulge themselves for a moment. It accomplishes this through tongue-in-cheek humor by parodying the nutritional facts label on other food products.

CONCEPT CHECK

What sort of objectives should realistically be established for advertising in an advertising plan?

Consumers and business customers can send messages back to the marketer in the form of coupons, phone calls, surveys, and database information on purchases. With interactive media, the responses are in real time. This feedback can help the marketer's product, service, and messages evolve.[55] And reinforcement advertising, designed to build brand loyalty, will remind people of their successful experience with the product and suggest reuse.

By starting with the customer and then integrating all aspects of their marketing communications—package and store design, personal selling, advertising, public relations activities, special events, and sales promotions—companies hope to accelerate the communications process, make it more efficient, and achieve lasting loyalty from *good* prospects, not just prospects.[56]

Determining the Advertising Strategy

The advertising *objective* declares what the advertiser wants to achieve with respect to consumer awareness, attitude, and preference; the advertising *strategy* describes how to get there. **Advertising strategy** consists of two substrategies: the creative strategy and the media strategy.

The **creative strategy** is a guide for those developing the advertising. At a minimum, the creative strategy defines the *target audience,* restates the *objective* of the advertising, specifies the key *benefits* to be communicated, and offers *support* for those benefits. We will discuss the development of the creative strategy in Chapter 8.

The **media strategy** provides direction to the media planners. It defines the communication objectives that must be achieved and then describes how these will be accomplished through the use of media vehicles. The media planning process will be covered in Chapter 15.

Allocating Funds for Advertising

In the early 1990s, after eight years of unprecedented growth, the United States and Canada experienced the first throes of a recession. Interest rates rose, real estate sales dropped, construction of new homes slowed, defense spending was cut, and unemployment began to rise. To make matters worse, threats of war in the Persian Gulf caused fear of higher fuel prices. Consumer confidence declined, and with it sank retail sales.

As sales dropped, many executives cut back their marketing communication budgets, some to zero. Two years later, when the government announced the recession was over, these executives wondered why sales were still down and how their companies had lost so much market share.

Money is the motor that drives every marketing and advertising plan. If you suddenly shut the motor off, the car may coast for a while, but before long it will stop running. The marketing department has the tough job of convincing top management that communication spending makes good business sense, even during adverse economic conditions.

Advertising: An Investment in Future Sales

Accountants and the Internal Revenue Service consider advertising a current business expense. Consequently, many executives treat advertising as a budget item to be trimmed or eliminated like other expense items when sales are either very high or very low. This is understandable but extremely shortsighted.

The cost of a new factory or warehouse is an investment in the company's future ability to produce and distribute products. Similarly, advertising—as one element of the communication mix—is an investment in future sales. While advertising is often used to stimulate immediate sales, its greatest power is in its cumulative, long-range, reinforcement effect.[57]

Advertising builds consumer preference and promotes goodwill. This, in turn, enhances the reputation and value of the company name and brand. And it encourages customers to make repeat purchases.

So while advertising is a current expense for accounting purposes, it is also a long-term investment. For management to see advertising as an investment, however, it must understand how advertising relates to sales and profits.

The Relationship of Advertising to Sales and Profits

Many variables, both internal and external, influence the effectiveness of a company's marketing and advertising efforts. Methods to measure the relationships between advertising and sales and between sales and profits are far from perfect. However, substantial research does support the following principles:

- In consumer goods marketing, increases in market share are closely related to increases in the marketing budget. And market share is a prime indicator of profitability.[58]

- Sales normally increase with additional advertising. At some point, however, the rate of return plateaus and then declines. (See Commercial Break 7–B, "The Economic Effect of Advertising on Sales.")

- Sales response to advertising may build over time, but the durability of advertising is brief, so a consistent investment is important.

- There are minimum levels below which advertising expenditures have no effect on sales.

- There will be some sales even if there is no advertising.

- There are saturation limits above which no amount of advertising can increase sales.

To management, these facts might mean: Spend more until it stops working. In reality, the issue isn't that simple. Advertising isn't the only marketing activity that affects sales. A change in market share may

Although the relationship between advertising and sales can at times be difficult to ascertain, certain profit trends can be linked directly to the intensity and frequency of advertising. A locally based business like Classic Bi-Plane Rides (www.classicbiplanerides.com) can expect to have some sales even if it does not advertise—mostly through word of mouth. But advertising in a high-exposure medium like outdoor is likely to provide significant sales improvement. Local businesses are hit particularly hard during times of recession; but, if at all possible, they should maintain advertising levels to prevent losing market share over the long run.

Commercial Break 7–B

The Economic Effect of Advertising on Sales

As a rule, the level of sales of a product is proportional to the level of advertising expenditure—that is, within reasonable limits, the more you spend the more you sell (assuming the advertising program is effective). Yet, even the most enthusiastic ad agency will admit, reluctantly, that it is possible to spend too much.

Ideally, managers would like to know how much more they will be able to sell per additional dollar of advertising and when additional advertising dollars cease being effective. They would like to have a graph or a sta-

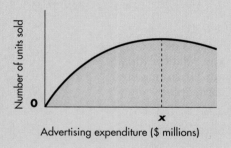

Advertising expenditure ($ millions)

tistical equation describing the relationship between advertising and sales.

In our illustration, most of the curve goes uphill as we move to the right (it has a positive slope). This means that additional advertising will continue to bring in business until (at a budget of *x* million dollars) people become so saturated by the message that it begins to repel them and turn them away from the product.

Even if the saturation level cannot be reached within the range of expenditures the firm can afford, the curve is likely to level off, becoming flatter and flatter as the amount spent on advertising becomes greater and greater and saturation is approached. The point at which the curve begins to flatten is the point at which returns from advertising begin to diminish. When the total advertising budget is small, even a $1 addition to the campaign may bring in as much as $10 in new sales. But when the market approaches saturation, each additional dollar may contribute less than a dollar in new sales, if any at all.

Applying the Breaks
What other factors might influence the level of sales of a product? Why might it be difficult to clearly establish a relationship between advertising levels and sales results?

---

occur because of quality perceptions, word of mouth, the introduction of new products, competitive trade promotion, the opening of more attractive outlets, better personal selling, or seasonal changes in the business cycle.

Furthermore, most companies don't have a clear-cut way to determine the relationship between advertising and sales and profit. What if the company sells a variety of products? Which advertising contributes to which sales?

One thing remains clear. Because the response to advertising is spread out over an extended time, advertising should be viewed as a long-term investment in future profits. Like all expenditures, advertising should be evaluated for wastefulness. But historically, companies that make advertising the scapegoat during tough times end up losing substantial market share before the economy starts growing again.[59]

The corollary is also true. Sustained ad spending during difficult times protects, and in some cases even increases, market share and builds brands. During the last global recession, the leading European marketers recognized this fact, and fewer than 40 percent of the top spenders in Italy, Austria, Germany, France, and Spain cut their budgets.[60]

Methods of Allocating Funds

Most business executives will spend more money on advertising as long as they are assured it will mean more profit. However, the point of equilibrium is hard to predict when advertising budgets are being developed.

Companies use a number of methods to determine how much to spend on advertising, including *the percentage-of-sales, percentage-of-profit, unit-of-sale,*

Checklist

Ways to Set Advertising Budgets

- **Percentage of sales.** Advertising budget is determined by allocating a percentage of last year's sales, anticipated sales for next year, or some combination of the two. The percentage is usually based on an industry average, company experience, or an arbitrary figure.
- **Percentage of profit.** Like the above, but the percentage is applied to profit, rather than sales.
- **Unit of sale.** Also called the case-rate method. A specific dollar amount is set for each box, case, barrel, or carton produced. Used primarily in assessing members of co-ops or trade associations for advertising costs.
- **Competitive parity.** Also called the self-defense method. Allocates dollars according to the amounts spent by major competitors.

- **Share of market/share of voice.** Allocates dollars by maintaining a percentage share of total industry advertising comparable to or slightly ahead of desired share of market. Often used for new-product introductions.
- **Objective/task.** Also referred to as the budget buildup method, this method has three steps: defining objectives, determining strategy, and estimating the cost to execute that strategy.
- **Empirical research.** By running experimental tests in different markets with different budgets, companies determine which is the most efficient level.
- **Quantitative mathematical models.** Computer-based programs developed by major advertisers and agencies rely on sophisticated data, history, and assumptions.
- **All available funds.** Go-for-broke technique generally used by small firms with limited capital, trying to introduce new products or services.

competitive-parity, share-of-market, and *objective/task methods* (see the Checklist of Ways to Set Advertising Budgets).

No technique is appropriate for all situations. The three methods discussed here are commonly used for setting national advertising budgets. However, local retailers can use them too.

Percentage-of-Sales Method

The **percentage-of-sales method** is one of the most popular techniques for setting advertising budgets. It may be based on a percentage of last year's sales, anticipated sales for next year, or a combination of the two. Businesspeople like this method because it is the simplest, it doesn't cost them anything, it is related to revenue, and it is considered safe. The problem is knowing what percentage to use. As Exhibit 7–8 shows, even leaders in the same industry use different percentages. Across industries, they range from just 1.5 percent to more than 22 percent.

Usually the percentage is based on an industry average or on company experience. Unfortunately, it is too often determined arbitrarily. An industry average assumes that every company in the industry has similar objectives and faces the same marketing challenges. Using company experience assumes that the market is static, which is rarely the case.

However, when applied against a forecast of future sales, this method often works well. It assumes that a certain number of dollars is needed to sell a certain number of units. If the advertiser knows what that relationship is, the correlation between advertising and sales should remain reasonably constant, assuming the market is stable and competitors' advertising remains unchanged. And because this method is common in the industry, it diminishes the likelihood of competitive warfare.

The greatest shortcoming of the percentage-of-sales method is that it violates a basic marketing principle. Marketing activities are supposed to *stimulate* demand and thus sales, not occur as a *result* of sales. If advertising only

Exhibit 7–8

Advertising expenditures by the top 15 advertisers in 2005 ($ millions).

Rank	Company	U.S. advertising expenditures (in millions)	U.S. sales (in millions)	Advertising as a percentage of U.S. sales
1	General Motors Corp.	$3,997.4	134,380	2.97%
2	Procter & Gamble Co.	3,919.7	23,688	16.55
3	Time Warner	3,283.1	33,572	9.78
4	Pfizer	2,957.3	29,539	10.01
5	SBC Communications	2,686.8	40,787	6.59
6	DaimlerChrysler	2,462.1	80,224	3.07
7	Ford Motor Co.	2,458.0	100,208	2.45
8	Walt Disney Co.	2,241.5	24,012	9.33
9	Verizon Communications	2,197.3	69,269	3.17
10	Johnson & Johnson Co.	2,175.7	27,770	7.83
11	GlaxoSmithKline	1,828.3	17,513	10.44
12	Sears Holdings Corp.	1,823.0	31,230	5.84
13	Toyota Motor Corp.	1,821.0	55,007	3.31
14	General Electric Co.	1,819.0	90,954	2.00
15	Sony Corp.	1,665.3	19,741	8.44

increases when sales increase and declines when sales decline, an opportunity is lost that might encourage an opposite move.

Share-of-Market/Share-of-Voice Method

In markets with similar products, a high correlation usually exists between a company's share of the market and its share of industry advertising.

The **share-of-market/share-of-voice method** is a bold attempt to link advertising dollars with sales objectives.[61] It holds that a company's best chance of maintaining its share of market is to keep its share of advertising (voice) comparable to its market share. For example, a company with a 30 percent share of the market should spend roughly 30 percent of the industry's advertising dollars.

The share-of-market/share-of-voice method is commonly used for new product introductions.[62] According to this formula, when a new brand is introduced, the advertising budget for the first two years should be about one and one-half times the brand's targeted share of the market in two years. This means that if the company's two-year sales goal is 10 percent of the market, it should spend about 15 percent of total industry advertising during the first two years.

One hazard of this method is the tendency to oversimplify. Maintaining the targeted percentage of media exposure usually isn't enough to accomplish the desired results. The top national packaged-goods marketers still spend 25 to 30 percent of their marketing budgets on consumer and trade promotion rather than consumer advertising.[63] Companies must be aware of *all* their competitors' marketing activities, not just advertising.

Objective/Task Method

The **objective/task method,** also known as the *budget buildup method,* is used by the majority of major national advertisers in the United States. It considers advertising to be a marketing tool to help generate sales.

The task method has three steps: defining objectives, determining strategy, and estimating cost. After setting specific, quantitative marketing objectives, the advertiser develops programs to attain them. If the objective is to increase the sales of cases of coffee by 10 percent, the advertiser determines which advertising approach will work best, how often ads must run, and which media to use. The estimated cost of the program becomes the basis for the advertising budget. Of course, the company's financial position is always a consideration. If the cost is too high, objectives may have to be scaled back. If results are better or worse than anticipated after the campaign runs, the next budget may need revision.

The task method forces companies to think in terms of accomplishing goals. Its effectiveness is most apparent when the results of particular ads or campaigns can be readily measured. The task method is adaptable to changing market conditions and can be easily revised.

However, it is often difficult to determine in advance the amount of money needed to reach a specific goal. Techniques for measuring advertising effectiveness still have many weaknesses.

The Bottom Line

The principal job of advertising is to influence perception by informing, persuading, and reminding. Advertising *affects* sales, but it is just one of many influences on consumer perception. Advertising managers must keep this in mind when preparing their plans and budgets.

> **CONCEPT CHECK**
>
> What are the pros and cons of the most common methods for determining advertising budgets?

Chapter Summary

The marketing plan may be the most important document a company possesses. It assembles all the pertinent and current facts about a company, the markets it serves, its products, and its competition. It sets specific goals and objectives and describes the precise strategies to use to achieve them. It musters the company's forces for the marketing battlefield and, in so doing, dictates the role of advertising in the marketing mix and provides focus for advertising creativity.

There are three types of marketing planning models: top-down, bottom-up, and integrated marketing communications planning.

The top-down marketing plan contains four principal sections: situation analysis, marketing objectives, marketing strategy, and tactics. A company's marketing objectives should be logical deductions from an analysis of its current situation, its prediction of future trends, and its understanding of corporate objectives. They should relate to the needs of specific target markets and specify sales objectives. Sales-target objectives should be specific, quantitative, and realistic.

The first step in developing a top-down marketing strategy is to select the target market. The second step is to determine the product's positioning. The third step is to construct a cost-effective marketing mix for each target market the company pursues. The marketing mix is determined by how the company blends the elements it controls: product, price, distribution, and communications. Advertising is a communications tool.

One way for small companies to construct the marketing and advertising plan is to work from the bottom up, taking an ingenious tactic and building a strategy around it.

Integrated marketing communications can help build long-term relationships with customers. IMC planning is driven by technology. Thanks to computers and databases, marketers can learn more about their customers' wants and needs, likes and dislikes. IMC is both a concept and a process that offers the synergy of various communications media, strategically managed to enhance the relationship between the customer and the brand or company. In the IMC model, all marketing becomes communications and all communications become marketing.

Advertising is a natural outgrowth of the marketing plan, and the advertising plan is prepared in much the same way as the top-down marketing plan. It includes a SWOT (strengths, weaknesses, opportunities, and threats) analysis, advertising objectives, and strategy.

Advertising objectives may be expressed in terms of moving prospective customers up through the advertising pyramid (awareness, comprehension, conviction, desire, action). Or they may be expressed in terms of generating inquiries, coupon response, or attitude change. Whereas the advertising *objective* declares what the advertiser wants to achieve, the advertising *strategy* describes how to get there. Advertising strategy consists of two substrategies: the creative strategy and the media strategy. The creative strategy is a guide for those developing the advertising. The media strategy provides direction to the media planners.

Several methods are used to allocate advertising funds. The most popular are the percentage-of-sales approach and the objective/task method. The share-of-market/share-of-voice method is often used for new product introductions.

Key Terms

action programs, 184
advertising plan, 192
advertising strategy, 196
bottom-up marketing, 184
corporate objectives, 180
creative strategy, 196
endcap promotion, 188
integrated marketing communications, 189
lifetime customer value (LTV), 186
marketing objectives, 180
marketing plan, 178

marketing strategy, 181
media strategy, 196
need-satisfying objectives, 180
objective/task method, 200
percentage-of-sales method, 199
planned messages, 190
positioning, 182
product life cycle, 183
product messages, 190
relationship marketing, 184
sales-target objective, 180

service messages, 190
share-of-market/share-of-voice method, 200
situation analysis, 179
stakeholders, 186
SWOT analysis, 193
synergy, 188
tactics, 184
top-down marketing, 179
unplanned messages, 190
value, 185

Review Questions

1. What is a marketing plan and why is it a company's most important document?

2. What are some examples that illustrate the difference between need-satisfying objectives and sales-target objectives?

3. What are the various approaches to developing a positioning strategy?

4. What basic elements should be included in a top-down marketing plan?

5. How can small companies use bottom-up marketing to become big companies?

6. What are the differences between a company's objectives, strategies, and tactics?

7. What are the elements of an advertising plan and an advertising strategy?

8. What is synergy and how is it created by IMC?

9. What types of companies tend to use the percentage-of-sales method? Why?

10. How might a packaged-foods manufacturer use the share-of-market/share-of-voice method to introduce a new product?

Exploring Advertising

1. Conduct a SWOT analysis on a product or service brand with which you are familiar. If you were responsible for that brand's planning process, how would they use their SWOT analysis to develop objectives and strategies for the next one to three years?

2. Locate advertising for a brand with which you are familiar. Then, working from the bottom up, determine what the strategy might be that resulted in that tactic. And then deduce what marketing objective may have resulted in that strategy. Describe what you believe to be the brand's target market and positioning. What other elements of the brand's marketing mix can you determine?

3. Select a local service business (e.g., a retailer, restaurant, bank, hospital, movie theater) and recommend several relationship marketing tactics. Refer to Kotler and Armstrong's five levels of relationships. Describe how that business could use IMC to enhance its customer relationships.

4. You have been asked to determine an advertising budget for Dave's Donuts. Your only competitor is Patty's Pastries. You have been provided with the following sales estimates. Use the following methods to develop budget alternatives. Which approach would you recommend? Why?

	Last Year	Forecast for Next Year
Dave's Unit Sales	50,000	60,000
Dave's $ Sales	$40,000	$50,000
Patty's $ Sales	$80,000	$100,000

   a. Unit-of-sale method. Last year Dave spent 4 cents per unit (donut) on advertising, but he needs to adjust for 6 percent media inflation next year.

   b. Percentage-of-sales method. The industry typically spends 5 percent of donut sales on advertising.

   c. Share-of-market/share-of-voice method. Patty is expected to spend $6,500 next year on advertising.

   d. Competitive parity.

chapter eight

Creative Strategy and the Creative Process

Objectives

To show how advertising strategies are translated into creative strategies and message strategies that guide the creative process. The chapter examines the characteristics of great advertising, styles of thinking, the nature of creativity, its importance in advertising, and the role of the agency creative team. We discuss how research serves as the foundation for creative development and planning, and we review common problems and pitfalls faced by members of the creative team.

After studying this chapter, you will be able to:

* **Discuss** the meaning and the importance of creativity.
* **Identify** the members of the creative team and their primary responsibilities.
* **Tell** how to differentiate great advertising from the ordinary.
* **Explain** the role of the creative strategy and its principal elements.
* **Explain** the purpose of the message strategy and how it differs from the creative strategy.
* **Describe** the two basic styles of thinking.
* **Define** the four roles people play at different stages of the creative process.
* **List** several techniques creatives can use to enhance their creativity.

Bob Taylor has designed and assembled guitars for more than 25 years. He's an artisan, and his instruments show it. The average Taylor guitar sells for around $2,000, some for as much as $7,000. The company makes some of the best guitars in the world. But its sales volume didn't reflect that fact.

So Taylor and Kurt Lustig, the company's CEO, put in a call to John Vitro who had been an outstanding art director for some time, and John Robertson who was a great copywriter. But when they got together, they were even better. Call it creative synergy—where one plus one is greater than two. The two Johns had been the principal creative team at Taylor Guitar's previous ad agency but had gone out on their own. Now, not only Taylor Guitar but also AirTouch Cellular (formerly PacTel) and Thermoscan wanted them back. And Chiat/Day, the L.A. agency they had worked for prior to moving to San Diego, wanted them to do some freelance work.

What did these guys have that everybody wanted?

For starters, they were winning more awards than any other creative team around. And not just local medals, but major national honors from the New York Art Director's Club, the One Show, and the leading trade press. Vitro and Robertson never had great notions about owning an agency of their own, but with clients knocking their doors down, there seemed little choice. They formed VitroRobertson, and the clients started coming.

The first meetings with Taylor Guitar were successful. The agency and the client saw eye to eye and seemed to share similar values. Lustig and Taylor both understood marketing and advertising. They wanted advertising that would make a statement about the company and its ideals—not just words and pictures, but something genuine and visceral, yet subtle.

Their marketing problem was clear. In limited circles, people recognized the Taylor guitar as a quality instrument. But to the vast majority of amateur guitar enthusiasts, Taylor was completely unknown. Dealers told Rick Fagan,

Taylor's national sales rep, "We know Taylor makes a great guitar, but our customers have never heard of it. Nobody knows the name." Vitro and Robertson had to develop a creative strategy that would put the Taylor name on the tip of the tongue of every serious guitarist. If the campaign was successful, these people would ask to strum a Taylor when considering their next instrument.

"We had plenty of research data to give them," said Fagan. The Johns looked at the research, listened to the founders, and reviewed guitar publications. Competitors used two general approaches: feature comparisons or celebrity artist endorsements.

Vitro and Robertson understood the parameters. To increase name recognition, Taylor's ads had to be completely different. They had to stand out, and they had to reflect the quality that goes into every Taylor guitar. Moreover, they had to appeal to the sensibilities of today's musicians. The ads should talk to them, not at them.

The creative process began. VitroRobertson started playing with ideas, putting them down on paper. "A lot of times, it's based on their gut instinct," says AirTouch/San Diego's marketing manager Mary Bianchetti, "and their gut instinct is usually very good."

The challenge was to integrate all the concepts into a single big idea. If they could accomplish that, they could develop individual messages for a series of ads. Unfortunately, finding the big idea is rarely a simple task. It's usually a frustrating, laborious process of developing an initial stream of concepts—5, 10, 20, whatever it takes. Sifting, sorting, evaluating, throwing them out, and starting over again. It's 90 percent perspiration and 10 percent inspiration.

Vitro and Robertson plugged away, discarding one concept after another. And then suddenly it came. The big idea was trees. Because wood comes from trees.

They would use magnificent photos of trees: trees alone, trees in a forest, trees in the fog. Big photos. Not just a full-page ad but a spread, two full pages. And they would use very short, slightly humorous copy lines to speak about wood's subtle relationship with people's lives. In contrast to Taylor's competitors, they would appeal to the sensitive, emotional side of the marketplace and make their prospects think.

They prepared two-page, horizontal layouts of their ideas for Taylor and Lustig to evaluate. One ad featured a lone tree in a barren landscape. The headline read: "In its simplest form, a guitar is just a hollow box made of wood. It's up to you to decide how to fill it." Taylor and Lustig loved it. The proposed campaign passed the review, and the rest is history.

"The recognition has been fantastic," reports Rick Fagan. "No one mentions the name problem since these ads have appeared. And sales are up."

The recognition has also been good for VitroRobertson. The Taylor Guitar campaign has won national awards and been applauded in *Advertising Age* and *Adweek.* And when the Magazine Publishers of America invited Ken Mandelbaum, CEO of the New York agency Mandelbaum Mooney Ashley, to choose a favorite for its "I wish I'd done that ad" series, he chose a VitroRobertson ad for Taylor Guitars.[1]

The Creative Team: The Authors and Encoders of Advertising

In Chapter 5 we discussed the marketing communications process, in which a source encodes a message that is sent through a channel to be decoded by a receiver. In advertising, the *encoding* of messages—the conversion of mental concepts into symbols—is the responsibility of the creative team.

Each member of the creative team plays an essential role. The team's **copywriter** develops the *verbal* message, the copy (words) within the ad. The copywriter typically works with an **art director** who is responsible for the *nonverbal* aspect of the message, the design, which determines the look and feel of the ad. Together, they work under the supervision of a **creative director** (typically, a former copywriter or art director), who is ultimately responsible for the creative product—the form the final ad takes. As a group, the people who work in the creative department are generally referred to as **creatives,** regardless of their specialty.

In the Taylor Guitar ads, we see how the creative team's taste, talent, and conceptual skill determine an ad's overall character and its ability to communicate. George Gier, the creative partner and cofounder of the Leap Partnership, says, "The only thing agencies have left to sell to clients that they can't get anywhere else is creative ideas."[2]

This chapter focuses on the creative process: where it comes from, how it's developed, and how it relates to a company's marketing and advertising strategy. But to get a proper perspective on creativity, we need to understand the characteristics of great advertising. What is it? Where does it come from?

What Makes Great Advertising?

We've all seen ads we love, and we've all seen ads we hate (probably a lot more of the latter). The ads we love we refer to as "great." But what do we really mean when we say an ad is great?

If we look at some of the classic ads in history, we may get a clue: Volkswagen's famous "Think small" ad; DeBeers' "A diamond is forever" line; Clairol's "Does she or doesn't she?"; Arpege's "Promise her anything, but give her Arpege"; the Army's "Be all you can be"; and Coca-Cola's "The real thing." What do all these ads and campaigns have in common that have made them universally considered great?

This is a very important question, since most recent research indicates that "ad liking" has a tremendous impact on "ad success." But is liking all that is required for an ad to be great?

Whether the "ad" is a billboard, a page in a magazine, a TV or radio

A great ad is one so remarkable or stunning that it leaves a long-lasting impression on the audience of the product or service. Advertisers typically begin with a headline or visual that quickly grabs attention and resonates with the reader. This ad for Lego (www.lego.com) immediately catches audience's eyes by featuring the awesome beauty of the Great Wall of China. The succinct message is delivered with one simple line of copy, "The Power of the Brick."

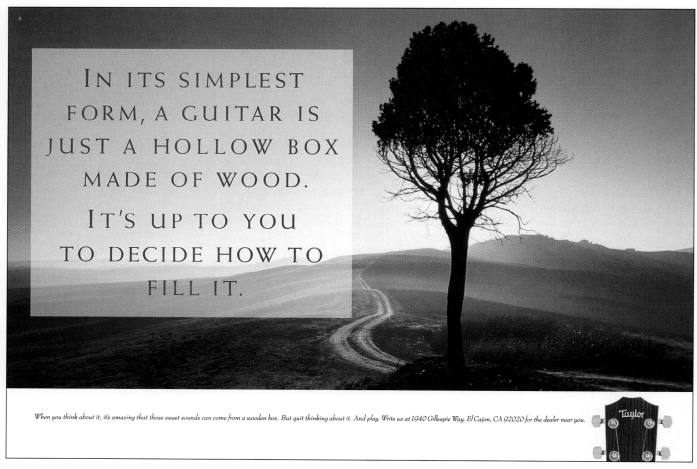

In its simplest form, a guitar is just a hollow box made of wood. It's up to you to decide how to fill it.

When you think about it, it's amazing that those sweet sounds can come from a wooden box. But quit thinking about it. And play. Write us at 1940 Gillespie Way, El Cajon, CA 92020 for the dealer near you.

Taylor

Every ad should seek to achieve the elusive "boom factor"—that essential quality that makes an immediate and lasting impression on the mind of the reader or viewers. VitroRobertson earned respect and envy from colleagues and competitors for its Taylor Guitar series.

spot, or a hot new Web site, great ads do have certain commonalities. We can probably lump most of these characteristics into two dimensions of greatness: *audience resonance* and *strategic relevance*.[3]

The Resonance Dimension

To resonate means to echo, reverberate, or vibrate. It also means to boom, ring, or chime. And that's what a great ad does with the audience. It rings their chimes. It echoes in their ears. It reverberates and gives them good vibes. It *resonates*.

Why? Because of the boom factor.

When a cannon goes "boom," it gets your attention—right now! The same is true with an ad. It's the surprise element—the "aha," the "gee," or the "wow." But in advertising, it not only gets your attention, it catches your imagination. In this sense it's like great art. It invites you to stop and think about the message.

Look at the Taylor Guitar ad, juxtaposing the image of a box with a musical instrument. They're both made of wood. So they are the same, but oh so different! We recognize this reality at an instinctive level, and we are left to think about it. More important, we associate the profundity of the question with the company that thinks to pose it. We like it, and we respect Taylor for it. The ad resonates.

Other ads may resonate for different reasons. In some of the classic cases we just mentioned, it's simply the headline that resonates—so much so that it becomes a part of our daily lexicon. Other memorable classics include California Milk Processors' "Got Milk," and Budweiser's "Whassup?!"

Recall from Chapter 5 our discussion of consumer motives. *Negatively originated motives,* such as problem avoidance or problem removal, provide the foundation for many great ads. These resonate with the audience by being highly **informational,** by offering relief from some real or perceived problem (FedEx's "When it absolutely, positively has to be there overnight."). Other motives are *positively originated* as consumers seek sensory gratification, intellectual stimulation, or social approval. Here, ads may

WARNING: SMOKING CAUSES IMPOTENCE

Ads that appeal to the avoidance or removal of a problem are based on negatively originated motives. This ad for the California Department of Health discourages smoking by depicting the stereotypical Marlboro man with a limp cigarette, suggesting that smoking causes impotence. The copy, imitating the standard warning labels found on cigarettes, reinforces the ad's visual.

achieve greatness by being **transformational,** using positive reinforcement to offer a reward ("Be all you can be.").

Unfortunately, most ads, whether they're informational or transformational, fail to resonate with the audience. Why? Because they lack a "big idea" or they fall down in the *execution.* The copy may be uninspiring, the visual may be less than attractive, or the production techniques used may be low quality. From the consumer's point of view, these ads are just a waste of time.

From the advertiser's point of view, ads that don't resonate are a terrible waste of money. In fact, for them the greatness of the advertising is in the "bang per buck." Great ads give their sponsors much more advertising effectiveness per dollar spent. Given this reality, isn't it amazing how much money is invested in ads that are simply not great?

The Relevance Dimension

The second dimension of great advertising is strategic relevance. An ad may get you to think, but what does it get you to think about? A classic example is the old Alka-Seltzer ad "I can't believe I ate the whole thing." It captured everyone's imagination, but it reinforced the wrong feeling—the feeling of the problem (overeating) rather than the solution (Alka-Seltzer). The agency lost the account.

While the text and the visual carry the ad message, behind the creative team's choice of tone, words, and ideas lies an advertising strategy. When the ad is completed, it must be relevant to the sponsor's strategy, or it will fail—even if it resonates with the audience. In other words, it may be great *entertainment,* but not great *advertising.* Great advertising always has a strategic mission to fulfill. In fact, strategy is at the root of all great creative work.

> What are some of the factors that make great advertising great?

CONCEPT CHECK

Formulating Creative Strategy: The Key to Great Advertising

Recall from Chapter 7 that the purpose of the advertising *objective* is to state what the advertiser wants to achieve with respect to consumer awareness, attitude, and preference. The advertising *strategy* then describes a means to achieve that objective through the development of advertising executions and media plans. The *creative strategy* is the component of the advertising strategy that guides those responsible for developing creative advertising.

To be sure that everyone has the same understanding of the task at hand, account managers (or, in larger agencies, account planners) develop a brief statement summarizing the agreed upon objectives and strategies. Many individuals from both the client and agency—including representatives from creative, media, and research—should have input into this document. The agency and client team should agree to the finished document before the creative process commences. This **creative strategy** serves as the creative team's guide for writing and producing the advertising. In some agencies it may be referred to as a **creative brief**, a **work plan**, a **copy strategy**, or a **copy platform.**

Writing the Creative Strategy

Regardless of the name, the creative strategy is a simple written statement of the most important issues to consider in the development of an ad or campaign. It typically includes many of the following elements:

- The basic problem the advertising must address.
- The objective of the advertising.
- A definition of the target audience.
- The key benefits to communicate.
- Support for those benefits.
- The brand's personality.
- Any special requirements.

Let's look at the creative strategy Vitro and Robertson developed for Taylor Guitar. Then we'll see how they translated that into a message strategy and a big idea and, finally, into effective ads.

- What is the **problem the advertising must solve?** Although Taylor was well known in the trade for its quality guitars, the word was not filtering down to the larger guitar-buying public. *This information often comes straight from the marketing plan's situation analysis.*

- What is the *objective of the advertising?* Taylor Guitar wants to make its brand a household name for serious guitarists. It wants prospective customers to ask for the Taylor name when they shop for a guitar. The **advertising objective** is initially spelled out in the marketing plan.

- What is Taylor Guitar's **target audience?** Resellers (or retailers) are Taylor's *primary market*—that's who the company sells to. So Taylor definitely wants them to see its advertising. The primary target audience also includes a segment of the retailers' customers—serious musical enthusiasts who play acoustic guitars and are willing to spend $2,000 to $5,000 for a superior instrument. Professional guitarists typically circumvent the normal distribution channels; however, they might act as *centers of influence* (or *key influentials*). In that case they would be considered a *secondary target audience* for the advertising. The target audience is usually a refinement of the marketing plan's target market, focusing on those to whom the advertising should be directed.

- What is Taylor Guitar's *key benefit?* Taylor guitars display a unique, distinguishable sound quality—a certain ring in the tone—that customers like. In other words, there is something special about a Taylor guitar that makes it worth more. The **benefit statement** is the heart of the creative strategy. It is very important to make it as succinct and single-minded as possible. Complex benefit statements can lead to creative executions that promise everything and focus on nothing.

- How is that benefit *supported?* Taylor's acoustic guitars are top-quality, handcrafted musical instruments made from the finest woods available. They are designed and constructed differently from other guitars. The **support statement** should provide information about the product or service that will convince the target audience that the key benefit is true.

- What is the **brand personality?** Taylor wants its guitars known for their quality, sophistication, beauty, and value. The creatives will consider this statement when they develop the message strategy.

- Are there any **special requirements?** The company has a small budget and uses limited media. It advertises in special-interest consumer magazines targeted to well-defined segments of the guitar enthusiast market. Magazines offer high-quality reproduction and color and are read by members of the trade as well as professional musicians. The company supplements its advertising with high-quality brochures that detail the instruments' features and construction. It is important for the creatives to understand budget and media constraints before they begin creative development.

The creative strategy identifies the benefits to be presented to consumers, but it doesn't cover execution. How the benefits will be presented is the creative team's job.

Procter & Gamble and Leo Burnett use a simple creative strategy with only three parts:[4]

1. *An objective statement.* A specific, concise description of what the advertising is supposed to accomplish or what problem it is supposed to solve. The objective statement also includes the name of the brand and a brief, specific description of the target consumer. For example:

   Advertising will convince serious guitar players that the Taylor guitar is a distinctive, high-value instrument and persuade them to consider it the next time they are in the market for an acoustic guitar.

2. *A support statement.* A brief description of the evidence that backs up the product promise; the reason for the benefit. For example:

   Support is that Taylor guitars are handcrafted from the finest woods available, which gives the instrument a distinctive sweet sound.

3. *A tone or brand character statement.* A brief statement of either the advertising's tone or the long-term character of the brand. Tone statements are emotional descriptions of the advertising strategy. Brand character statements are descriptions of the enduring values of the brand. A tone statement might be phrased:

   The tone of Taylor Guitar advertising should convey beauty, quality, and sophistication, with just a touch of good-natured humor.

   On the other hand, a brand character statement might be phrased:

   The Taylor brand is known for its quality, heritage, and value.

Diet Coke (www.dietcoke.com) exemplifies the art of nonverbal communication in advertising. In ads such as this, well-known brands benefit from consumer awareness of their name or logo, and that can eliminate the need for extraneous copy.

The delivery of the creative strategy to the creative department concludes the process of developing an advertising strategy. It also marks the beginning of the next step: the **creative process,** in which the creative team develops a *message strategy* and begins the search for the *big idea.* After writing the first ad, the copywriter should review the creative strategy to see if the ad is "on strategy." If it isn't, the team must start again.

Elements of Message Strategy

From the information given by the account team (in the creative strategy) and any additional research it may perform, the creative team develops the message strategy. This may actually occur before, during, or after the creative process of searching for the big idea.

The **message strategy** is a simple description and explanation of an ad campaign's overall creative approach—the main idea, details about how the idea will be executed, and a rationale. The message strategy has three components:

- *Verbal.* Guidelines for what the advertising should say; considerations that affect the choice of words; and the relationship of the copy approach to the medium (or media) that will carry the message.

- *Nonverbal.* Overall nature of the ad's graphics; any visuals that must be used; and the relationship of the graphics to the media in which the ad will appear.

- *Technical.* Preferred execution approach and mechanical outcome, including budget and scheduling limitations (often governed by the media involved); also any **mandatories**—specific requirements for every ad, such as addresses, logos, and slogans.

The verbal elements are the starting point for many advertising campaigns. However, because all these elements of the message strategy intertwine, they typically evolve simultaneously. Language affects imagery, and vice versa.

The message strategy helps the creative team sell the ad or the campaign concept to the account managers and helps the managers explain and defend the creative work to the client. Of course, the message strategy must conform to the creative strategy or it will probably be rejected.

In the development of message strategy, certain basic questions need to be answered: How is the market segmented? How will the product be positioned? Who are the best prospects for the product? Is the target audience different from the target market? What is the key consumer benefit? What is the product's (or company's) current image? What is the product's unique advantage?[5] At this point, research data are important. Research helps the creative team answer these questions and support their proposed approach.

CONCEPT CHECK

What important information should be communicated in the creative strategy and the message strategy?

How Creativity Enhances Advertising

The powerful use of imagery, copy, and even humor in the Taylor Guitar campaign demonstrates how creativity enhances advertising. But what exactly is creativity? What is the role of creativity in advertising? And where does creativity come from?

What Is Creativity?

To create means to originate, to conceive a thing or idea that did not exist before. Typically, though, **creativity** involves combining two or more previously unconnected objects or ideas into something new. As Voltaire said, "Originality is nothing but judicious imitation."

Many people think creativity springs directly from human intuition. But as we'll see in this chapter, the creative process is actually a step-by-step procedure that can be learned and used to generate original ideas.

The Role of Creativity in Advertising

Advertisers often select an agency specifically for its creative style and its reputation for coming up with original concepts. While creativity is important to advertising's basic mission of informing, persuading, and reminding, it is vital to achieving the boom factor.

Creativity Helps Advertising Inform

Advertising's responsibility to inform is greatly enhanced by creativity. Good creative work makes advertising more vivid, and many researchers believe vividness attracts attention, maintains interest, and stimulates consumers' thinking.[6] A common technique is to use plays on words and verbal or visual metaphors, such as "Put a tiger in your tank," "Fly the friendly skies," or "Own a piece of the rock." The metaphor describes one concept in terms of another, helping the reader or viewer learn about the product.[7]

Other creative techniques can also improve an ad's ability to inform. For example, visual cues such as lighting, pose of the model, setting, and clothing style can instantly signal viewers nonverbally whether a fashion ad reflects a romantic adventure or a sporting event.[8]

Creativity Helps Advertising Persuade

The ancients created legends and myths about gods and heroes—symbols for humankind's instinctive, primordial longings and fears—to affect human behavior and thought. To motivate people to some action or attitude, advertising copywriters have created new myths and heroes, like the Jolly Green Giant and the Energizer Bunny. A creative story or persona can establish a unique identity for the product in the collective mindset, a key factor in helping a product beat the competition.[9]

To be persuasive, an ad's verbal message must be reinforced by the creative use of nonverbal message elements. Artists use these elements (color, layout, and illustration, for example) to increase vividness. Research suggests that, in print media, *information graphics* (colorful explanatory charts, tables, and the like) can raise the perception of quality for some readers.[10] Artwork can also stimulate emotions. Color, for example, can often motivate consumers, depending on their cultural background and personal experiences (see Commercial Break 8–A, "The Psychological Impact of Color").

Metaphors help readers understand the intended message. In this ad, Capital One (**www.capitalone.com**) uses both visual and verbal metaphors to inform you that your credit card rate will never change.

The Psychological Impact of Color

National origin or culture can play a role in color preferences. For example, people from warmer climates, apparently, are most responsive to warm colors—red, yellow, and orange. These colors tend to stimulate, excite, and create an active response. Certain color combinations have ethnic connotations. Metallic golds with reds, for example, are associated with China. Turquoise and beige are associated with the Indian tribes of the American Southwest.

Colors can also convey lifestyle preferences. Vivid primary colors (red, blue, yellow) juxtaposed with white stripes exude decisiveness and are often used in sporting events as team colors. Thus, they are associated with a sporting lifestyle.

The colors we experience during the four seasons often serve as guides for combining colors and for guessing the temperaments of individuals who dress themselves or decorate their houses in specific seasonal colors. Spring colors such as yellows, greens, and light blues, for example, suggest a fresh, exuberant character. Winter colors such as dark blues, deep violets, and black are associated with cool, chilly attitudes.

Because we usually feel refreshed from sleeping, we associate the colors of the morning—emerald green, raspberry, and pale yellow—with energy. And because the mellow colors of sunset predominate when we're usually home relaxing after work, we may associate sunset colors—peach, turquoise, and red-orange—with relaxation and reflective moods.

Some colors are ambiguous. Violet and leaf-green fall on the line between warm and cool. They can be either, depending on the shade.

Here are some more observations:

Red
Symbol of blood and fire. Second to blue as people's favorite color but more versatile, the hottest color with highest "action quotient." Appropriate for soups, frozen foods, and meats (Campbell's, Ore-Ida). Conveys strong masculine appeal, so is often used for shaving cream containers.

Brown
Another masculine color, associated with earth, woods, mellowness, age, warmth, comfort. Used to sell anything, even cosmetics (Revlon's Braggi).

Yellow
High impact to catch consumer's eye, particularly when used with black. Good for corn, lemon, or suntan products.

Green
Symbol of health and freshness; popular for mint products and soft drinks (7Up).

Blue
Coldest color with most appeal; effective for frozen foods (ice impression); if used with lighter tints becomes "sweet" (Yoplait yogurt, Lowenbrau beer, Wondra flour).

Black
Conveys sophistication and high-end merchandise, and is used to stimulate the purchase of expensive products. Good as background and contrast for other colors.

Orange
Most "edible" color, especially in brown-tinged shades; evokes autumn and good things to eat.

Applying the Breaks
Explain the moods or feelings that are stimulated by two color ads or packages illustrated in this text.

Creativity Helps Advertising Remind

Imagine using the same invitation to ask people to try your product again and again, year after year. Your invitation would become stale and tiresome. Only creativity can transform your boring reminders into interesting, entertaining advertisements. Nike is proof. Several commercials in a Nike campaign never mentioned the company name or even spelled it on the screen. The ads told stories. And the only on-screen cue identifying the sponsor was the single, elongated "swoosh" logo inscribed on the final scene. A Nike spokesperson said the ads weren't risky "given the context that the Nike logo is so well known."[11] We are entertained daily by creative ads—for soft drinks, snacks, and cereals—whose primary mission is simply to remind us to indulge again.

Creativity Puts the "Boom" in Advertising

Successful comedy also has a boom factor—the punchline. It's that precise moment when the joke culminates in a clever play on words or turn of meaning, when the audience suddenly gets it and guffaws its approval.

Good punchlines are the result of taking an everyday situation, looking at it creatively, adding a bit of exaggeration, and then delivering it as a surprise. Great advertising often does the same thing.

When a group of friends greet each other with wagging tongues and an exaggerated "Whassup?" while "watching the game and having a Bud," the audience is completely caught off guard and roars with laughter. Boom!

In advertising, though, the boom doesn't always have to be funny. It may come from the sudden understanding of a subtle profundity, as in the case of Taylor Guitars. Or from the gentle emotional tug of a Hallmark Cards commercial. Or the breathtaking beauty of a magnificent nature photograph for Timberland shoes. In a business-to-business situation, it may come from the sudden recognition of how a new high-tech product can improve workplace productivity. In short, the boom factor may come from many sources. But it always requires the application of creativity.

International ads must appeal to the target audience within a given country. Here, mobile phone service provider Embratel (www.embratel.com) uses some rather dark humor in its campaign to promote its rates. Other ads in the campaign featured a derailed train and a wrecked airplane, all with the same tagline: "If you have a lot to explain, we have the best phone rates." Such dry wit is probably appreciated by the ads' British audience. The judges at Cannes were amused, at least; they awarded the campaign a Silver Lion.

Understanding Creative Thinking

Some people may exhibit more of it than others, but creativity lives within all of us. Human creativity, developed over millions of years, enabled our ancestors to survive. Without creativity we wouldn't have discovered how to harness fire, domesticate animals, irrigate fields, or manufacture tools. As individuals, we use our natural creativity every time we select an outfit to wear, style our hair, contrive an excuse, decorate our home, or cook a meal.

Fact-Based versus Value-Based Thinking

Most theories of thinking fit into two general categories: value-based or fact-based. Let's examine these styles of thinking more closely.

People whose preferred style of thinking is **fact-based** tend to fragment concepts into components and to analyze situations to discover the one best solution. Although fact-based people can be creative, they tend to be linear thinkers and prefer to have facts and figures—hard data—they can analyze and control. They are not comfortable with ambiguous situations. They like logic, structure, and efficiency.[12]

In contrast, **value-based** thinkers make decisions based on intuition, values, and ethical judgments. They are better able to embrace change, conflict, and paradox. This style fundamentally relies on melding concepts together. Value-based thinkers, for example, attempt to integrate the divergent ideas of a

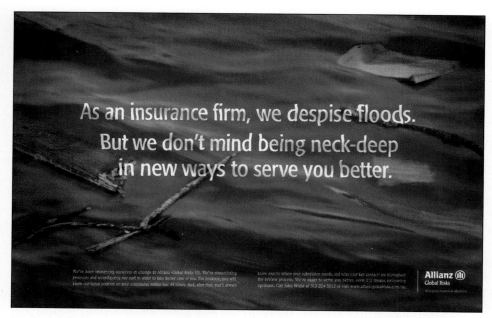

As an insurance firm, we despise floods.
But we don't mind being neck-deep
in new ways to serve you better.

We've been immersing ourselves in change at Allianz Global Risks US. We're streamlining processes and reconfiguring our staff in order to take better care of you. For instance, you will know our initial position on your submission within just 48 hours. And, after that, you'll always know exactly where your submission stands, and who your key contacts are throughout the review process. We're eager to serve you better, even if it means swimming upstream. Call John White at 312-224-3312 or visit www.allianzglobalrisks.com/us.

Allianz (ⅲ)
Global Risks

Fact-based thinking can also be creative. In this fact-based ad, Allianz (www.allianz.com) creatively explains the ways that they provide superior service to their global insurance customers.

group into an arrangement that lets everyone win. They are good at using their imagination to produce a flow of new ideas and synthesizing existing concepts to create something new.[13]

How Styles of Thinking Affect Creativity

If the creative team prefers a value-based thinking style, it tends to produce ads such as those in the Taylor Guitar and Nike campaigns—soft, subtle, intuitive, metaphorical. That's fine if the client also prefers that style of thinking.

On the other hand, clients who prefer a fact-based style often seek agencies that produce practical, hard-edged work characterized by simple, straightforward layouts, rational appeals, and lots of data. A fact-based client may even find a value-based campaign to be unsettling.

The creative team needs to understand the campaign's target audience. In some market segments (high-tech, for example) customers may tend toward one style of thinking over another. And that could dictate which approach to use.

This slightly absurd commercial doesn't concentrate on Pepsi's calorie count or great taste—the ad's strictly value-based thinking is designed to entertain and build brand personality and value.

SYNOPSIS: In an empty recreation room, there is a foosball table whose inanimate players, one team representing Manchester United and the other, Juventus, suddenly come alive and play an intense game of football. There is a Pepsi bottle sitting on the edge of the table.

DAVID BECKHAM (Manchester United): You thinkin' what I'm thinkin'?

EDGAR DAVIDS (Juventus): Winner take the Pepsi?

DAVID BECKHAM: Sure.

VISUAL: The game begins. Yorke (Manchester United) ricochets the ball off the Pepsi bottle and into the Pepsi net.

YORKE: Sco-o-o-re!

JUVENTUS PLAYERS: You cheated.

VISUAL: Two boys enter a now quiet rec room.

BOY 1: There it is.

VISUAL: The boy grabs the Pepsi and takes a drink. They start to leave the room.

ROY KEANE (Manchester United): Hey! Get back here! We won that!

BOY 2: Did you hear something?

FOOTBALLER VO: Hey mate! That's our Pepsi!

BOY 1: No.

VISUAL: The two boys leave the room.

FOOTBALLERS (grumbling): Big idiots.

SUPER: Pepsi logo.

Ask for More.

As we shall see in the next section, the best art directors and copywriters use both styles to accomplish their task. In the creative process, they need to use their imagination (value-based thinking) to develop a variety of concepts. But to select the best alternative and get the job done, they probably have to use the fact-based style.

The Creative Process

The creative process is the step-by-step procedure used to discover original ideas and reorganize existing concepts in new ways. By following it, people can improve their ability to unearth possibilities, cross-associate concepts, and select winning ideas.

Over the years, many notions of the creative process have been proposed. Although most are similar, each format has unique merits. In 1986, Roger von Oech published a four-step creative model used today by many *Fortune* 100 companies. It offers flexibility for fact-based and value-based thinkers alike. Von Oech describes four distinct, albeit imaginary, roles (Explorer, Artist, Judge, and Warrior) that every art director and copywriter has to personally take on at some point in the creative process:[14]

1. *The Explorer* searches for new information, paying attention to unusual patterns.

2. *The Artist* experiments and plays with a variety of approaches, looking for an original idea.

3. *The Judge* evaluates the results of experimentation and decides which approach is most practical.

4. *The Warrior* overcomes excuses, idea killers, setbacks, and obstacles to bring a creative concept to realization.

The Explorer Role: Gathering Information

Copywriters and art directors thrive on the challenge of creating **advertising messages**—the encoding process. But first they need the raw materials for ideas: facts, experiences, history, knowledge, feelings.

Taking on the role of the **Explorer,** the creatives examine the information they have. They review the creative strategy and the marketing and advertising plan; they study the market, the product, and the competition (see RL 8–1, Checklist of Product Marketing Facts for Creatives, in the Reference Library on the *Essentials of Contemporary Advertising* Web site). They may seek additional input from the agency's account managers and from people on the client side (sales, marketing, product, or research managers).

When John Vitro and John Robertson began work for Taylor Guitar, they first assumed the Explorer role. They spoke with people about the nature of the company, its products, its marketing history, its competitors, and the competitors' styles of advertising. They reviewed all appropriate sources of advertising for acoustic guitars and studied the company's marketing environment.

Develop an Insight Outlook

In advertising, it's important that when creatives play the Explorer role, they get off the beaten path to look in new and uncommon places for information—to discover new ideas and to identify unusual patterns. Vitro and Robertson might have hiked in the wilderness to spark a new idea for Taylor Guitar. Or they could have opened a book on national parks and experienced the same flash of insight.

Von Oech suggests adopting an "insight outlook" (a positive belief that good information is available and that you have the skills to find and use it). If you're curious and poke around in new areas, you'll improve your chances of discovering new ideas. Ideas are everywhere: visit a museum, an art gallery, a hardware store, an airport. The more diverse the sources, the greater your chance of uncovering an original concept.

Know the Objective

Philosopher John Dewey said, "A problem well-stated is a problem half-solved." This is why the creative strategy is so important. It helps define what the creatives are looking for. The creatives typically start working on the message strategy during the Explorer stage because it, too, helps them define what they're looking for.

Brainstorming is a useful process for generating a wealth of ideas. Creativity is encouraged by not allowing ideas to be evaluated or discussed until everyone has run dry. The more ideas the better, and every idea is recorded exactly as stated. Any and all ideas are considered legitimate and often the most far-fetched prove to be the most valuable.

Brainstorm

As Explorers, the art director and copywriter look first for lots of ideas. One technique is **brainstorming,** a process (conceived in 1939 by Alex Osborn, the former head of BBDO) in which two or more people get together to generate new ideas. A brainstorming session is often a source of sudden inspirations. To succeed, it must follow a couple of rules: all ideas are above criticism (no idea is "wrong"), and all ideas are written down for later review. The goal is to record any inspiration that comes to mind, a process that psychologists call free association, allowing each new idea an opportunity to stimulate another.

Von Oech suggests other techniques for Explorers: leave your own turf (look in outside fields and industries for ideas that could be transferred); shift your focus (pay attention to a variety of information); look at the big picture (stand back and see what it all means); don't overlook the obvious (the best ideas are right in front of your nose); don't be afraid to stray (you might find something you weren't looking for); and stake your claim to new territory (write down any new ideas or they will be lost).

To get their creative juices flowing, most copywriters and art directors maintain an extensive library of advertising award books and trade magazines. Many also keep a *tickler* (or *swipe*) *file* of ads they like that might give them direction.

The Artist Role: Developing and Implementing the Big Idea

The next step in the creative process, playing the Artist's role, is both tough and long, but it's also rewarding. The **Artist** must actually accomplish two major tasks: searching for the big idea and then implementing it.

Task 1: Develop the Big Idea

The first task for Artists is the long, tedious process of reviewing all the pertinent information they gathered when they played the Explorer role, analyzing the problem, and searching for a key verbal or visual concept to communicate what needs to be said. It means creating a mental picture of the ad or commercial before any copy is written or artwork begun.

This step (also called **visualization** or **conceptualization**) is the most important in creating the advertisement. It's where the search for the **big idea**—that flash of insight—takes place. The big idea is a bold, creative initiative that builds on the strategy, joins the product benefit with consumer desire in a fresh, involving way, brings the subject to life, and makes the audience stop, look, and listen.[15]

Some images make the point so well they require no words. This ad for Globetrotter outdoor gear connects the idea of giant seals snug in their skins with campers snug in their sleeping bags. It's amazing how much they look alike. The clever ad garnered a Bronze Lion at Cannes.

What's the difference between a strategy and a big idea? A strategy describes the direction the message should take. A big idea gives it life. For example, the creative strategy proposed earlier for the Taylor Guitar campaign contained a strategic brand character statement:

> Taylor Guitars—handcrafted from the finest materials to give the sweetest sound.

Vitro and Robertson could have used that brand character statement as a headline. But it would have been dreadfully dull for an ad aimed at musicians. It lacks what a big idea headline delivers: a set of multiple meanings that create interest, memorability, and, in some cases, drama.

John O'Toole said, "While strategy requires deduction, a big idea requires inspiration."[16] The big idea in advertising is almost invariably expressed through a combination of art and copy. Most ads use a specific word or phrase to connect the text to the visual, like "wood" in the Taylor Guitar ad. Think what this ad would look like without the beautiful photograph of the trees in the background, with just the headline and body copy on an otherwise bare page. It would have saved a lot of money. But it would have greatly reduced the boom factor and lost a lot more money due to low readership.

Transforming a Concept: Do Something to It

Creative ideas come from manipulating and transforming resources. Von Oech points out that when we take on the Artist role, we have to do something to the materials we collected as Explorers to give them value. That means asking lots of questions: What if I added this? Or took that away? Or looked at it backward? Or compared it with something else? The Artist has to change patterns and experiment with various approaches.

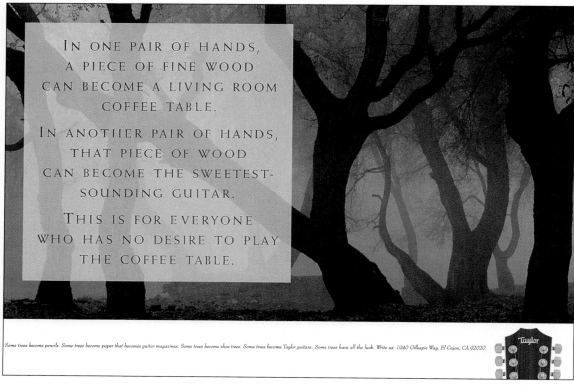

IN ONE PAIR OF HANDS,
A PIECE OF FINE WOOD
CAN BECOME A LIVING ROOM
COFFEE TABLE.

IN ANOTHER PAIR OF HANDS,
THAT PIECE OF WOOD
CAN BECOME THE SWEETEST-
SOUNDING GUITAR.

THIS IS FOR EVERYONE
WHO HAS NO DESIRE TO PLAY
THE COFFEE TABLE.

Some trees become pencils. Some trees become paper that becomes guitar magazines. Some trees become shoe trees. Some trees become Taylor guitars. Some trees have all the luck. Write us: 1940 Gillespie Way, El Cajon, CA 92020.

Adapting an idea means looking at it in a way that is different than the obvious. This example from Taylor Guitar transforms the idea of trees. While the wood is used for a wide variety of rather inanimate objects, the lucky ones are reinvented into an almost lifelike creature, a Taylor Guitar. The small print continues the witty approach of the headline: Some trees become pencils. Some trees become paper that becomes guitar magazines. Some trees become shoe trees. Some trees become Taylor guitars. Some trees have all the luck.

Vitro and Robertson had two concepts to begin with: "guitar" and "music." Looking at the guitar, they noted it was made of wood—special wood. So "wood" became a third concept. Thinking about wood led them to "trees." Interesting notion. But now they had to figure out how to turn these four concepts into a "big idea."

At this point in the creative process, a good Artist may employ a variety of strategies for transforming things. Von Oech suggests several techniques for manipulating ideas:[17]

1. *Adapt.* Change contexts. Think what else the product might be besides the obvious. A Campbell's Soup ad showed a steaming bowl of tomato soup with a bold headline underneath: "HEALTH INSURANCE."

2. *Imagine.* Ask what if. Let your imagination fly. Be zany. What if people could do their chores in their sleep? What if animals drank in saloons? Clyde's Bar in Georgetown actually used that idea. The ad showed a beautifully illustrated elephant and donkey dressed in business suits and seated at a table toasting one another. The headline: "Clyde's. The People's Choice."

3. *Reverse.* Look at it backward. Sometimes the opposite of what is expected has great impact and memorability. A cosmetics company ran an ad for its moisturizing cream under the line: "Introduce your husband to a younger woman." A vintage Volkswagen ad used "Ugly is only skin deep."

4. *Connect.* Join two unrelated ideas together. Ask yourself: What ideas can I connect to my concept? A Target ad showed the rear view of a high-fashion-type model clad only with a backpack and a lampshade—the latter wrapped around her middle like a miniskirt. Next to the Target logo the ad said simply "fashion and housewares." To get people to send for its catalog, Royal Caribbean Cruises ran an ad that showed the catalog cover under the simple headline "Sail by Mail."

5. *Compare.* Take one idea and use it to describe another. Ever notice how bankers talk like plumbers? "Flood the market, laundered money, liquid assets, cash flow, take a bath, float a loan." The English language is awash in metaphors because they help people understand. Jack in the Box advertised its onion rings by picturing them on a billboard and inviting motorists to "Drive thru for a ring job." An elegant magazine ad for the Parker Premier fountain pen used this sterling metaphor: "It's wrought from pure silver and writes like pure silk."

6. *Eliminate.* Subtract something. Or break the rules. In advertising, there's little virtue in doing things the way they've always been done. Seven-Up became famous by advertising what it wasn't ("the Uncola") and thereby positioned itself as a refreshing alternative. To introduce its new models one year, Volkswagen used a series of humorous teaser ads that didn't show any cars. In one, a shaggy dog sat patiently in front of a fan. He was presumably replicating what dogs do in cars, sticking their heads out the window to catch the breeze. The only difference was he was doing it indoors.

7. *Parody.* Fool around. Have some fun. Tell some jokes—especially when you're under pressure. There is a close relationship between the ha-ha experience of humor and the aha! experience of creative discovery. Humor stretches our thinking and, used in good taste, makes for some great advertising. A classical radio station ran a newspaper ad: "Handel with care." And speaking of classics, Fila USA got a rave review from *Advertising Age* for its "bizarre, absolutely hilarious, and totally cool" spot of a praying mantis racing up a leaf stem in Fila sneakers to escape his murderous mate.[18]

Blocks to Creativity

Everybody experiences times when the creative juices just won't flow. There are many causes: information overload, mental or physical fatigue, stress, fear, insecurity. Often, though, the problem is simply the style of thinking being used.

In the Explorer stage, when creatives study reams of marketing data, the facts and figures on sales and market share may put them in a fact-based frame of mind. But to create effectively, they need to shift gears to a value-based style of thinking.

Creative blocking may occur when people in the agency start "thinking like the client," especially if the client is a fact-based thinker. This can also be hazardous to the agency's creative reputation and is one reason agencies sometimes resign accounts over "creative differences."

Creative fatigue sometimes happens when an agency has served an account for a long time and all the fresh ideas have been worked and reworked. It can also happen when a client has rejected a series of concepts; the inspiration is lost and the creatives start trying to force ideas. If this becomes chronic, the only solutions may be to appoint an entirely new creative team or resign the account.

Incubating a Concept: Do Nothing to It

When the brain is overloaded with information about a problem, creatives sometimes find it's best to just walk away from it for a while, do something else, and let the unconscious mind mull it over. This approach yields several benefits. First, it puts the problem back into perspective. It also rests the brain, lets the problem incubate in the subconscious, and enables better ideas to percolate to the top. When they return to the task, the creatives frequently discover a whole new set of assumptions.

Task 2: Implement the Big Idea

Once the creatives latch onto the big idea, they have to focus on how to implement it. When Vitro and Robertson suddenly thought "trees" and connected that idea to "guitars" and "music," they then had to translate that concept into a tangible ad. This is where the real art of advertising comes in—writing the exact words, designing the precise layout. To have a sense of how advertising creatives do that, we need to understand what art is in advertising, how artistic elements and tools are selected and used, and the difference between good art and bad art.

In advertising, art shapes the message into a complete communication that appeals to the senses as well as the mind. So while **art direction** refers to the act or process of managing the visual presentation of the commercial or ad, the term **art** actually refers to the whole presentation—visual and verbal. For example, the artful selection of words not only communicates information but also stimulates positive feelings for the product. An artfully designed typeface not only makes reading easier, it also evokes a mood. By creatively arranging format elements—surrounding the text with lines, boxes, and colors, and relating them to one another in proportion—the art director can further enhance the ad's message. Art also shapes the style of photography and illustration. An intimate style uses soft focus and close views, a documentary style portrays the scene without pictorial enhancements, and a dramatic style features unusual angles or blurred action images.

In short, if *copy* is the verbal language of an ad, *art* is the body language. TV uses both sight and sound to involve viewers. Radio commercials use sound to create word *pictures* in the minds of listeners. The particular blend of writing, visuals, and sounds makes up an ad's expressive character. So while the quality may vary, every ad uses art.

In advertising, balance, proportion, and movement are guides for uniting words, images, type, sounds, and colors into a single communication so they relate to and enhance each other. We'll discuss more of these concepts in Chapter 9, "Creative Execution: Art and Copy."

The Creative Pyramid: A Guide to Formulating Copy and Art

The **creative pyramid** is a model that can help the creative team convert the advertising strategy and the big idea into the actual physical ad or commercial. The cognitive theory of how people learn new information uses a simple five-step structure (the first pyramid in Exhibit 8–1).

The purpose of much advertising copy and design is to either persuade prospective customers to take some action to satisfy a need or want or to remind them to take the action again. In a new-product situation, people may first need to be made aware of the problem or, if the problem is obvious, that a solution exists. For a frequently purchased product, the advertiser simply has to remind people of the solution close to the purchase occasion. In either case, the advertiser's first job is to get the prospect's *attention*. The second step is to stimulate the prospect's *interest*—in either the message or the product itself. Next, it's important, especially for new products, to build *credibility* for the product claims. Then the ad can focus on generating *desire* and finally on stimulating *action*. These five elements (the second pyramid in Exhibit 8–1) should be addressed in just about every ad or commercial. We'll deal with each step briefly.

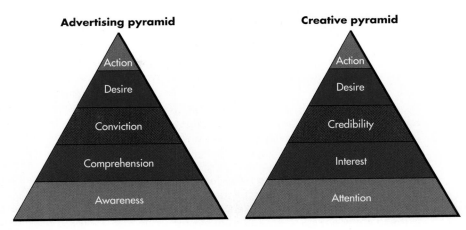

Exhibit 8-1

The advertising pyramid, discussed in Chapter 7, reflects how people learn new information. Each level of that pyramid can be related to a role that creativity must play. The creative pyramid thus translates advertising objectives into copywriting objectives.

This ad for K2 skis (www.k2skis.com) exemplifies the five steps of the creative pyramid. The ad gains attention with its stark imagery and resemblance to the American flag. Then, it retains interest with the reference to Betsy Ross. Credibility is established with Betsy Ross's opinion of Jonny Moseley. The tagline, "This little red light makes you a better, faster American. God bless," is consistent with the patriotic theme and creates a desire to be a better, faster American. The final words, "You are an American and these are your skis," is an indirect call to action.

Does Sex Appeal?

It's one of the more blatant uses of sex in advertising in recent memory: a billboard features a young woman, holding a grease gun cartridge in each hand, and leaning over to exhibit an ample amount of cleavage. The headline reads "This is Debbie. She wants you to have this pair in your car." The ad is for auto parts, but the implication seems to be that if you buy this manufacturer's auto parts, you'll get Debbie or someone like Debbie in the bargain. Nothing in the ad says so explicitly, but the innuendo is all that's required to capture the viewer's attention.

Advertisers frequently use the power of suggestion to imply sex, encouraging viewers to come to their own conclusions. However, advertisers who run such risqué ads must contend with the critics and with the often tricky legal distinction between obscenity and indecency. Obscenity is illegal and carries criminal charges, whereas indecency does not. To be considered obscene, an ad must meet three conditions: it appeals to prurient interests, it is patently offensive, and it lacks any redeeming social value.

In general, most ads with sexual appeals don't meet the criteria for obscenity, but they may still be considered indecent, since indecency is in the eyes of the beholder. If enough people believe sexually oriented material is indecent, then "community standards" reflect this belief. In such cases, citizen pressure groups, along with media organizations and local courts, can enforce community standards by disallowing advertising that offends those standards.

Consider Abercrombie & Fitch. The clothing retailer sparked controversy at a mall in Omaha when its window posters featured a topless model covering her breasts with her hands. A Christian group, Family First, quickly objected, claiming that Abercrombie's posters created a "sexualized walkway." Family First began pressuring shoppers and other retailers in the mall to object to the photographs, and within nine days the window displays were changed.

Were the posters obscene or indecent? Advertisers like A&F, who continue to strive for the "sexy" appeal, are beginning to find it increasingly difficulty to draw the line between simple sex appeal and unethical exploitation.

There is no easy solution to this dilemma, especially since research shows that sexual appeals can be very effective when sexuality relates to the product. However, when it doesn't, it can distract audiences from the main message and severely demean the advertiser in the consumer's eyes. Many argue that sexually oriented advertising is not only a distraction, but also a source of negative *externalities*—the social costs to consumers outside the target market, such as children who might be indirectly affected.

Advertisers must examine, on a case-by-case basis, at what point sexual appeals become unethical and therefore counterproductive. In one case, an executive on the Valvoline advertising account justified using "girlie calendars" for mechanics by noting that "the calendar may offend some groups—but they aren't our customers."

Attention

An ad or commercial is a *stimulus*. It must break through consumers' physiological screens to create the kind of attention that leads to perception. *Attention,* therefore, is the first objective of any ad and the foundation of the creative pyramid. The Artist may spend as much time and energy figuring out how to express the big idea in an interesting, attention-getting way as searching for the big idea itself.

The attention step is critically important to triggering the ad's boom factor. Print ads often use the headline as the major attention-getting device. Usually designed to appear in the largest and boldest type in the ad, the headline is often the strongest focal point. Many other devices also help gain attention. In print media, they may include dynamic visuals, unusual layouts, vibrant color, or dominant ad size. In electronic media, they may include special sound effects, music, animation, or unusual visual techniques.

The attention-getting device should create drama, power, impact, and intensity. It must also be appropriate, relating to the product, the tone of the ad, and the needs or interests of the intended audience. This is especially true in business-to-business advertising, where rational appeals and fact-based thinking dominate.

Miller Lite's "Catfight" campaign recently raised a few eyebrows. The campaign appeared to signal the company's return to "beer and babes" ads, depicting women as sexual objects. In the commercial, two women in a restaurant begin the classic "tastes great/less filling" debate over Miller Lite. The debate quickly turns into a full-fledged catfight, with the two women stripped down to their bras and panties, splashing around in an adjacent fountain. Moments later, we see the two buxom brawlers going at it in a soggy cement pit. The ad cuts to a bar. It turns out the fight was only the fantasy of two guys in a bar who were dreaming of the perfect beer commercial, much to the shock and disgust of their girlfriends, who were with them at the time.

So what does any of this have to do with selling beer? Hillary Chura, who covers the beer industry for *Advertising Age,* explains that ads such as the "Catfight" commercial are "aspirational." After watching these two beautiful women wrestle around for 30 seconds, Miller wants guys to say, "Hey, if I drink Miller Genuine Draft, I'll get those hot women." And Miller wants women to think "If I drink this beer, I'll look like those women."

But what is the social cost of these unrealistic "aspirations"? In a society rife with confidence-related disorders, should advertisers exploit consumer insecurities in an effort to sell more of their product? At what point do advertisers need to accept some ethical responsibility for the interests of the society to which they owe their existence?

Unfortunately, this debate over sex in advertising may actually be fueling advertisers' desire to continue using blatant sex appeals. The "Catfight" campaign sparked nationwide attention on talk radio, CNN's *Cross-fire,* in *USA Today,* and in other media outlets. Similarly, Abercrombie & Fitch's quarterly catalog of scantily clad models makes national headlines with every issue. Controversy equals publicity. Publicity stimulates interest. And interest spawns sales.

In short, sex and the controversy surrounding it, sells. Until this changes, industry or government policymakers will certainly continue to encounter difficulties in treating advertising sex in a way satisfactory to everyone.

Questions

1. Explain why you believe that sexual appeals in advertising do or do not have "redeeming value."

2. Even if sexual appeals are considered okay by the audiences that are directly targeted, what responsibility does the advertiser have for any effect on indirect targets, such as adults who are offended or children? How can advertisers protect themselves from this problem?

3. Is it acceptable for advertisers to exploit consumer insecurities in an effort to sell more of their product? Should advertisers accept some ethical responsibility for creating unrealistic "aspirations" and intensifying confidence-related disorders?

Interest

The second step in the creative pyramid, *interest,* is also extremely important. It carries the prospective customer—now paying attention—to the body of the ad. The ad must keep the prospect excited or involved as the information becomes more detailed. To do this, the copywriter may answer a question asked in the attention step or add facts that relate to the headline. To maintain audience interest, the tone and language should be compatible with the target market's attitude. As we discussed earlier, the successful ad resonates.

The writer and designer must lead prospects from one step to the next. Research shows that people read what interests them and ignore what doesn't, so the writer must maintain prospects' interest at all times.[19] One way to do so is to sneak through prospects' psychological screens by talking about their problems, their needs, and how the product or service will answer them. Copywriters use the word *you* a lot.

There are many effective ways to stimulate interest: a dramatic situation, a story, cartoons, charts. In radio, copywriters use sound effects or catchy dialogue. Television frequently uses quick cuts to maintain interest. We discuss some of these techniques in Chapter 10, "Producing Ads for Print, Electronic, and Digital Media."

Credibility

The third step in the creative pyramid is to establish *credibility* for the product or service. Customers today are sophisticated and skeptical. They want claims to be backed up by facts. Comparison ads can build credibility, but they must be relevant to customers' needs—and fair.

Well-known presenters may lend credibility to commercials. For example, actress Catherine Zeta Jones effectively represents T-Mobile with her personable, believable, and elegant style.

Advertisers often show independent test results to substantiate product claims. To work, such "proofs" must be valid, not just statistical manipulation. Advertisers and agencies must remember that many consumers have extensive product knowledge, even in specialized areas.

Desire

In the *desire* step, the writer encourages prospects to picture themselves enjoying the benefits of the product or service.

In print ads, copywriters use phrases like "Picture yourself" or "Imagine." In TV, the main character pulls a sparkling clean T-shirt from the washer, smiles, and says "Yeah!" In radio, the announcer says, "You'll look your best."

In print advertising, the desire step is one of the most difficult to write (which may be why some copywriters omit it). In TV, the desire step can simply show the implied consumer experiencing the benefit of the product. Ever notice how advertisers almost invariably show the happy life that awaits their product's user?

Action

The final step up the creative pyramid is *action*. The purpose is to motivate people to do something—send in a coupon, call the number on the screen, visit the store—or at least to agree with the advertiser.

The call to action may be explicit—"Call for more information"—or implicit—"Fly the friendly skies." Designers cue customers to take action by placing dotted lines around coupons to suggest cutting and by highlighting the company's telephone number with large type or a bright color.

This block of the pyramid reaches the smallest audience but those with the most to gain from the product's utility. So the last step is often the easiest. If the copy is clear about what readers need to do and asks or even nudges them to act, chances are they will (see Commercial Break 8–B, "Applying the Creative Pyramid to Advertising").

With today's technology, it's important to not only ask people to act but facilitate their action, through either a toll-free phone number or an attractive Web site. In relationship marketing, the ad basically enables people to select themselves as being interested in a relationship. Then the marketer can use more efficient one-on-one media to develop the relationship.

The Judge Role: Decision Time

The next role in the creative process is the **Judge.** This is when the creatives evaluate the practicality of their big ideas and decide whether to implement, modify, or discard them.[20]

The Judge's role is delicate. On the one hand, the creatives must be self-critical enough to ensure that when it's time to play the Warrior they will have

Commercial Break 8–B

Applying the Creative Pyramid to Advertising

Notice how the five objectives of advertising copy apply to the ad shown here.

Attention. The photograph of an oversized egg sitting in a chair with a remote control and a bag of potato chips grabs the reader's attention quickly. The reader jumps to the headline, despite its small size, in an attempt to understand the visual.

Interest. If the reader has any money invested for the future, this headline will pique his or her interest. All investors are concerned that their nest eggs may not be earning as much as they could be.

Credibility. The fact that six A.G. Edwards' analysts were singled out by the *Wall Street Journal* and that 3 million clients use their services adds tremendous credibility to this ad's claims.

Desire. The ad has created doubt in the reader's mind about the effectiveness of his or her current investment strategy. As we learned in Chapter 5, the reader will actively seek information to reduce that negative mental state.

Action. A.G. Edwards suggests that the reader visit a Web site or dial a phone number to satisfy the need for more information about their services. This is where the relationship building can begin.

Applying the Breaks

Find an ad that exhibits the five elements of the creative pyramid. (A print ad will be the easiest to find and talk about, but radio and TV commercials also feature the five elements. Beware: The desire step may be hard to find.)

---

an idea worth fighting for. On the other hand, they need to avoid stifling the imagination of their internal Artist. It's easier to be critical than to explore, conceptualize, or defend. But the Judge's purpose is to help produce good ideas, not to revel in criticism. Von Oech suggests focusing first on the positive, interesting aspects of a new idea. The negatives will come soon enough.

When playing the Judge, the creatives need to ask certain questions: Is this idea an aha! or an uh-oh? (What was my initial reaction?) What's wrong with this idea? (And what's right with it?) What if it fails? (Is it worth the risk?) What is my cultural bias? (Does the audience have the same bias?) What's clouding my thinking? (Am I wearing blinders?)

Risk is an important consideration. When the advertising scores a hit, everybody's happy, sales go up, people get raises, and occasionally there's even positive publicity. But when a campaign flops, all hell breaks loose, especially on high-profile accounts. Sales may flatten or even decline, competitors gain a couple of points in market share, distributors and dealers complain, and the phone rings incessantly with calls from disgruntled client executives. Perhaps worst of all is the ridicule in the trade press. This is not good for either the agency's stock or the client's. And it's how agencies get replaced. So the Judge's role is vital.

If the Artist-as-Judge does a good job, the next role in the creative process, the Warrior, is easier to perform.

The Warrior Role: Overcoming Setbacks and Obstacles

In the final step of the creative process, the **Warrior** wins territory for big new ideas in a world resistant to change. The Warrior carries the concept into action. This means getting the big idea approved, produced, and placed in the media.

To get the big idea approved, the Warrior has to battle people within the agency and often the client, too. So part of the Warrior's role is turning the agency account team into cowarriors for the presentation to the client. At this point, it's imperative that the creatives finish their message strategy document to give their rationale for the copy, art, and production elements in the concept they're trying to sell. And the message strategy had better mesh with the creative strategy, or the valiant Warrior will likely face a wide moat with no drawbridge.

Part of the Warrior's task may be to help the account managers present the campaign to the client. Bruce Bendinger says, "How well you *sell* ideas is as important as how good those ideas are." To give a presentation maximum selling power, he suggests five key components:[21]

1. *Strategic precision.* The selling idea must be *on strategy.* The presenting team must be able to prove it, and the strategy should be discussed first, before the big selling idea is presented.

2. *Savvy psychology.* The presentation, like the advertising, should be receiver-driven. The idea has to meet the client's needs.

3. *Slick presentation.* The presentation must be prepared and rehearsed; it should use great visuals and emotional appeals.

4. *Structural persuasion.* The presentation should be well structured, since most clients relate well to organized thinking. The opening is all-important because it sets the tone for the entire presentation.

5. *Solve the problem.* Clients have needs, and they frequently report to big shots who ask tough questions about the advertising. Solve the client's problem and you'll sell the big idea—and do it with style.

For clients, recognizing a big idea and evaluating it are almost as difficult as coming up with one. (For some examples of big ideas, see the Portfolio Review, "The Creative Director's Greatest Ads" on the *Essentials of Contemporary Advertising* Web site.) When the agency (or the in-house advertising department) presents the concepts, the client is suddenly in the role of the Judge, without having gone through the other roles first. David Ogilvy recommended that clients ask themselves five questions: Did it make me gasp when I first saw it? Do I wish I had thought of it myself? Is it unique? Does it fit the strategy to perfection? Could it be used for 30 years?[22]

As Ogilvy pointed out, campaigns that run five years or more are the superstars: Dove soap (one-quarter cleansing cream), Ivory soap (99 and 44/100 percent pure), Perdue chickens ("It takes a tough man to make a tender chicken"), the U.S. Army ("Be all you can be"). Some of these campaigns are still running today, and some have run for as long as 30 years. Those are big ideas!

Big ideas tend to be around for a long time. The Sara Lee (www.saralee.com) slogan "Nobody Doesn't Like Sara Lee" has been used as a campaign tagline since 1968. Fortunately, the client recognized it as a big idea and stuck with it.

When the client approves the campaign, the creative's role as a Warrior is only half over. Now the campaign has to be executed. That means the Warriors shepherd it through the intricate details of design and production to see that it is completed, faithful to the concept, on time, under budget, and with the highest quality possible. At the same time, the creatives revert to their Artist roles to finalize the design and copy and produce the ads.

The next step in the process, therefore, is to implement the big idea, to produce the ads for print and electronic media—the subject of our next two chapters.

> **CONCEPT CHECK**
>
> Describe the tasks that face copywriters and art directors in each role they must assume during the creative process.

Chapter Summary

In the marketing communications process, the creative team is responsible for encoding advertising messages. It is the author of the communications. The creative team typically comprises an art director and a copywriter who report to a creative director.

Their job is to create great advertising for their clients. Great advertising is characterized by two dimensions: audience resonance and strategic relevance. To truly resonate, ads need the boom factor—that element of surprise that instantly attracts the audience's attention, gets them involved, and stirs their imagination. Some ads are informational and resonate with the audience by offering relief from some real or perceived problem. Other ads are transformational and achieve resonance through positive reinforcement by offering some reward.

The second dimension of great advertising, strategic relevance, is behind the visuals and the text of every ad. In fact, advertising strategy is the key to great creative work.

Typically written by the account management team, with the client's concurrence, the creative strategy outlines the key strategic decisions. Provided by the account team to the creatives, it contains at least three elements: an objective statement, a support statement, and either a tone or brand character statement. This document gives strategic guidance to the art director and copywriter, but it is their responsibility to develop a message strategy that lays out the specifics of how the advertising will be executed. The three elements of message strategy are copy, art, and production.

Copy is the verbal and art is the nonverbal (visual) presentation of the message strategy. Production refers to the mechanical details of how the ads and commercials will be produced.

To create means to originate. Creativity involves combining two or more previously unconnected elements, objects, or ideas to make something new. Creativity helps advertising inform, persuade, and remind customers and prospects by making the advertising more vivid.

Scholars believe certain styles of thinking are more conducive to creativity than others. The two basic thinking styles are fact-based and value-based. People who prefer the fact-based style tend to be linear thinkers, analytical, and rational. Value-based thinkers tend to be less structured, more intuitive, and more willing to use their imagination. They are good at synthesizing diverse viewpoints to arrive at a new one. And, with their ability to think metaphorically, they tend to be more creative.

In one model of the creative process, the creative person must play four roles along the way to acceptance of a new idea: the Explorer, Artist, Judge, and Warrior. The Explorer searches for new information, paying attention to unusual patterns. The Artist experiments with a variety of approaches looking for the big idea. The Artist also determines how to implement it. For this, the creative pyramid may help. The pyramid models the formation of an ad after the way people learn new information, using five steps: attention, interest, credibility, desire, and action.

The Judge evaluates the results of experimentation and decides which approach is most practical. The Warrior overcomes excuses, idea killers, setbacks, and obstacles to bring a creative concept to realization. Each role has unique characteristics, and there are many techniques for improving performance in each role. During the creative process, it's better to use a value-based style of thinking. During the Judge and Warrior phases, a fact-based style may be more effective.

Key Terms

advertising objective, 210
advertising message, 217
art, 222
art direction, 222
art director, 207
Artist role, 218
benefit statement, 211
big idea, 219
brainstorming, 218
brand personality, 211
conceptualization, 219
copy platform, 210

copy strategy, 210
copywriter, 207
creative brief, 210
creative director, 207
creative process, 212
creative pyramid, 222
creatives, 207
creative strategy, 210
creativity, 213
Explorer role, 217
fact-based thinking, 215
informational, 209

Judge role, 226
mandatories, 212
message strategy, 212
problem the advertising must solve, 210
special requirements, 211
support statement, 211
target audience, 210
transformational, 209
value-based thinking, 215
visualization, 219
Warrior role, 228
work plan, 210

Review Questions

1. What does it mean for advertising to resonate? What causes an ad to resonate?

2. What is creativity? Find some additional definitions on the Internet.

3. What qualities characterize the two main styles of thinking? Which style do you usually prefer? Why?

4. What are some techniques you personally might use to adopt an "insight outlook" and to discover new ideas?

5. Why is the creative strategy so important?

6. In your own words, describe the difference between the creative strategy and a big idea.

7. Creative ideas come from manipulating or transforming things. Describe Von Oech's suggested techniques for manipulating ideas.

8. What does it mean to "start thinking like the client"? Why might this be a problem for an agency?

9. Describe the five steps through which advertising must take customers according to the creative pyramid.

10. What five questions does David Ogilvy recommend that clients ask themselves when evaluating creative concepts? Do you think his standards are too high?

Exploring Advertising

1. Find an ad that you believe has a big idea and describe the idea. Is there a boom factor? Compose what you believe the creative strategy might have been.

2. Select five creative ads from a magazine. What techniques of the Artist can you recognize in those ads? In those same ads, can you identify each step of the creative pyramid?

3. Select an ad that you particularly like or admire. Imagine you are one of the creatives, presenting this ad concept to the client. Outline how you would make the presentation and the points you would be sure to make. Pay attention to Bruce Bendinger's five key components of a campaign presentation.

4. Incorporating the seven typical elements, write a creative strategy to promote an issue of importance to you. Examples could be why college tuition shouldn't be increased, why there should be a national health plan, or why your parents should help you purchase a new car. Remember to keep the strategy focused and succinct.

5. In a brainstorming session with two or more people, generate ideas for ways you could communicate the creative strategy developed in #4 above. List as many ideas as possible, resisting the temptation to evaluate any of them.

part 4
The Creative Process

chapter nine

Creative Execution: Art and Copy

Objectives

To present the role of art and copy—the nonverbal and verbal elements of message strategy—in print, radio, and television advertising. Artists and copywriters include a variety of specialists who conceptualize, design, write, and produce advertising materials. To be successful, advertising people must know the copywriting and commercial art terms and formats used in the business. They must also develop an aesthetic sensitivity so they can recognize, create, evaluate, or recommend quality work.

After studying this chapter, you will be able to:

* **Describe** the roles of the various types of artists in the advertising business.
* **Explain** the use of advertising layouts and the steps in creating them.
* **Outline** the creative approval process.
* **Explain** the purpose and selection of visuals in print advertising.
* **Describe** the format elements of an ad and discuss how they relate to the objectives of advertising copywriting.
* **Identify** the art director's role in radio and television commercials.
* **Debate** the advantages and disadvantages of the different television commercial formats.
* **Discuss** the unique requirements in writing for the Web.

Sandra T.
Identity Theft Victim

Ruth F.
Identity Theft Victim

The flush years of the 1990s were awash with sentimental, softly lit, quiet ads about the benefits of credit card use. Feeling good about spending money was the message. But new realism pervades turn-of-the-century advertising for banking services. We're told how to insulate ourselves against every nightmare from stock market crashes to escalating interest rates to identity theft and credit card fraud.

In 2004, about one out of every twenty people discovered (usually months after the fact) that their credit report had been tarnished by identity theft.[1] Reports of identity theft had increased tenfold since 1998, when the FTC began tracking the trend. The crime wave is costly for victims, averaging $4,800 per reported incident, and creditors often hold victims liable for some part of the unauthorized charges.[2] Among others, Citibank has been working hard to restore confidence in its services by touting its Identity Theft Solutions service and its cards that feature "$0 liability" for unauthorized charges.

Brad Jakeman, Citigroup's consumer division advertising director, described the difficulty of squeezing the complex message into a 30-second television spot: "Identity theft was a broad-scale problem for millions of people. . . . It was, 'How can we create a piece of advertising that could communicate it could happen to you, but not just scare people?'"[3]

The creative team at Fallon/Minneapolis responded to the challenge by radically juxtaposing the visual and the verbal, and their efforts earned them a spot on the Cannes Lions Shortlist in 2004. Each TV spot contrasts two archetypal characters, one flamboyant and the other mild. A boasting thief provides the voice and a stunned victim is shown lip-synching. Art director Steve Driggs explained of the first few ads that "even though there are three characters, there are really six, and I think you can identify with all of them."[4]

The thieves detail a disturbing variety of lavish purchases, whereas the victims sit or stand and speak into a fixed camera. The voices and accents are jarringly different than the lip-synching victims would be expected to use. But the purchases are the most unlikely and hilarious aspect of the ads. Vocal actors were given the freedom to embellish copywriter Ryan Peck's memorable scripts. Each list of fraudulent purchases has a racy highlight: a leather bustier to "lift and separate"; "those mud flaps with the naked ladies on 'em"; a "girl robot" prom date; and a full-body "wax job on the old chassis."

Creativity in advertising must be connected to the business of product promotion. After the thief/victim duos rattle off their shopping sprees, Citibank's "identity theft solutions" logo, "live richly" tagline, and toll-free hotline number appear briefly. However, it was the audacious criminals who lived richly, not their relatively humble targets. Artistic concepts can backfire if not sufficiently relevant to the campaign's message. The flipside of a humorous advertising treatment of a crime wave is that once customers realize how vulnerable they are, they may remain unconvinced that the advertiser can protect them. Joyce King Thomas, deputy creative director at McCann Erickson in New York, praised the identity-theft campaign for its resonance, but noted, "For me, it's just creepy. And when it's over, I'm not sure if I should apply for a card from Citibank or cut up all the cards I own."[5]

Delivering on the Big Idea: The Visual and the Verbal

The Citibank "Identity Theft" campaign was applauded worldwide in a variety of advertising competitions, and it has set the tone for a new series of Citibank ads. What characterizes this campaign more than anything else is its layered message strategy. Every element, from the production values to the slight tension evident in the actors' performances, reinforces the creative concept.

In advertising, what is shown is just as important as what is said—sometimes more. The nonverbal aspect of an ad or commercial carries at least half the burden of communication. It helps position the product and create personality for the brand. It creates the mood of the ad, determining the way it *feels* to the audience. That mood flavors the verbal message, embodied in the *copy*.

In this chapter, we discuss how advertising concepts are executed from the standpoint of both art and copy. We examine the visual and the verbal details, first of print advertising and then of electronic media.

The Art of Creating Print Advertising

The next challenge for Citibank and Fallon was to integrate print ads into the media mix for the identity theft campaign: How could the concept be illustrated without the striking dissonance of the voiceovers? Again, creative director Steve Driggs found the answer in pairing the unlikely. The magazine ads depict people in places they probably wouldn't be caught dead. And, although the TV spots resonated with viewers, print media allowed Fallon to *execute* the company's objectives and strategy even more successfully. The ad copy elaborates on the benefits of the Identity Theft Solutions service, an area where the TV spots came up short.

Fallon/Minneapolis creative director Steve Driggs used a combination of nightmarishly realistic photography and an engaging headline to translate Citibank's award-winning "Identity Theft" campaign from TV to print. Executives and big wheelers alike are protected from unauthorized purchases, large or small, by Citigroup's antifraud programs.

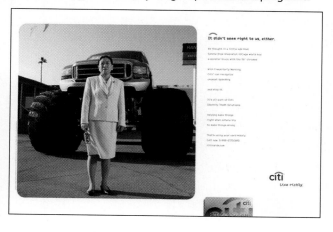

Designing the Print Ad

The term **design** refers to how the art director, graphic artist, or graphic designer chooses and structures the artistic elements of an ad. A designer sets a style—the manner in which a thought or image is expressed—by choosing particular artistic elements and blending them in a unique way.

The Citibank photographs enhance the message by capturing an atmosphere of anxiety and tension. "Something's wrong with this picture," thinks the viewer. This reaction is confirmed by the tagline, "It didn't seem right to us, either." The rounded edges of the photo and bankcard contribute to the design, mirroring the Citi logo.

In general, clean lines, formally composed photographs, and sparse copy give an ad the breathing room it needs to draw the reader's eye from one element to the next. Notice the empty space along the right edge of the ad. The uncomfortable situation in the photograph has been resolved by the copy; Citibank's Early Fraud Warning problem has fixed the problem. Sufficient *white space* gives an ad unity and balance in spite of the diversity of its elements.

A number of designers, working under the art director, may produce initial layouts of the ad concept. In collaboration with copywriters, these artists draw on their expertise in graphic design (including photography, typography, and illustration) to create the most effective ad or brochure.

The Use of Layouts

A **layout** is an overall orderly arrangement of all the format elements of an ad: visual(s), headline, subheads, body copy, slogan, seal, logo, and signature. The layout serves several purposes. First, it helps both the agency and the client develop and evaluate, in advance, how the ad will look and feel. It gives the client (usually not an artist) a tangible item to correct, change, comment on, and approve.

Second, the layout helps the creative team develop the ad's psychological elements: the nonverbal and symbolic components. Sophisticated advertisers want their advertising to do more than just bring in store traffic. They want their ads to create personality for the product and to build the brand's equity with the consumer. To do this, the "look" of the ad needs to elicit an image or mood that reflects and enhances both the advertiser and the product.

Third, once the best design is chosen, the layout serves as a blueprint. It shows the size and placement of each element in the ad. Once the production manager knows the dimensions of the ad, the number of photos, the amount of typesetting, and the use of art elements such as color and illustrations, he or she can determine the cost of producing the ad (see Commercial Break 9–A, "The Role of the Advertising Artist").

Advertising Design and Production: The Creative and Approval Process

The design process is both a creative and an approval process. In the creative phase, the designer uses thumbnails, roughs, dummies, and comprehensives (comps) to establish

When designing an ad, the layout is the preliminary version of the ad that shows where all the key formatting elements are placed. Both the agency and the client use it to evaluate and develop the ad's look and feel. To announce the arrival of its VW Bugs, the creatives for Volkswagen South Africa cleverly featured the VW in a way that looks much like the tummy of an expectant mother.

Due date February 28th.

Commercial Break 9–A

The Role of the Advertising Artist

All the people employed in commercial art are called artists, but they may perform very different tasks. Some can't even draw well; instead, they're trained for different artistic specialties.

Art Directors

Art directors are responsible for the visual presentation of the ad. Along with a copywriter, they develop the initial concept. They may do initial sketches or layouts, but after that they may not touch the ad again. Their primary responsibility is to supervise the ad's progress to completion.

The best art directors are good at presenting ideas in both words and pictures. They are usually experienced graphic designers with a good understanding of consumers. They may have a large or small staff, depending on the organization. Or they may be *freelancers* (independent contractors) and do most of the work themselves.

Graphic Designers

Graphic designers (or artists) are precision specialists preoccupied with shape and form. In advertising they arrange the various graphic elements (type, illustrations, photos, white space) in the most attractive and effective way possible. While they may work on ads, they often design and produce collateral materials, such as posters, brochures, and annual reports.

In an agency, the art director often acts as the designer. Sometimes, however, a separate designer is used to offer a unique talent to a particular ad.

Illustrators

Illustrators paint or draw the visuals in an ad. They frequently specialize in one type of illustrating, such as automotive, fashion, or furniture. Very few agencies or advertisers retain full-time illustrators; most advertising illustrators freelance. Typically, agencies hire different illustrators for different jobs, depending on an ad's particular needs, look, and feel.

Photographers

Like the illustrator, the advertising photographer creates a nonverbal expression that reinforces the verbal message. Photographers use the tools of photography—cameras, lenses, and lights—to create images. They select interesting angles, arrange subjects in new ways, carefully control the lighting, and use many other techniques to enhance the subject's image quality. Many photographers specialize—in cars, celebrities, fashion, food, equipment, or architecture. Agencies and advertisers rarely employ staff photographers. They generally hire freelancers by the hour or pay a fee for the assignment. Photographers also sell stock photography, which are photos on file from prior shootings.

Production Artists

Production (or pasteup) artists assemble the various elements of an ad and mechanically put them together the way the art director or designer indicates. Good production artists are fast, precise, and knowledgeable about the whole production process. Production artists today must be highly computer literate; they use a variety of software programs for pagemaking, drawing, painting, and photo scanning. Most designers and art directors start their careers as production artists and work their way up. It's very difficult work, but it is also very important, for this is where an ad actually comes together in its finished form.

Applying the Breaks

Select a print ad from any chapter. Explain which types of advertising artists were probably involved in its creation and what the responsibility of each artist was.

---

the ad's look and feel. Then in the *prepress* (or *production art*) phase, the artist prepares a mechanical: the final artwork with the actual type in place along with all the visuals the printer or the media will need to reproduce the ad. In Chapter 10, "Producing Ads for Print, Electronic, and Digital Media," we'll see how this design process works to produce a finished ad.

The approval process takes place at each step along the way. At any point in the design and production process, the ad—or the ad concept—may be altered or even canceled.

Thumbnail Sketches

The thumbnail sketch, or **thumbnail,** is a very small (about three-by-four inch), rough, rapidly produced drawing that the artist uses to visualize layout approaches without wasting time on details. Thumbnails are very basic. Blocks of straight or squiggly lines indicate text placement, and boxes show placement of visuals. The best sketches are then developed further.

Rough Layout

In a **rough,** the artist draws to the actual size of the ad. Headlines and subheads suggest the final type style, illustrations and photos are sketched in, and body copy may be simulated with lines or random gibberish *(greek).* The agency may present roughs to clients, particularly cost-conscious ones, for approval. Several examples of rough layouts are presented in Commercial Break 9–B, "The Art Director's Guide to Layout Styles."

Dummy

A **dummy** presents the handheld look and feel of brochures, multipage materials, or point-of-purchase displays. The artist assembles the dummy by hand, using color markers and computer proofs, mounting them on sturdy paper, and then cutting and folding them to size. A dummy for a brochure, for example, is put together, page by page, to look exactly like the finished product.

Thumbnail sketches are usually the first step in the advertising design process. They allow designers to quickly evaluate several layout options for further development. Rough lines and boxes are used to represent copy and graphics.

Comprehensive

The **comprehensive layout,** or **comp,** is a highly refined facsimile of the finished ad. A comp is generally quite elaborate, with colored photos, the final type styles and sizes, subvisuals, and a glossy spray coat. Today, copy for the comp is typeset on a computer and positioned with the visuals, and the ad is printed as a full-color proof. At this stage, all visuals should be final.

Mechanical (Pasteup)

The type and visuals must be placed in their exact position for reproduction by a printer. Today, most designers do this work on the computer, completely bypassing the need for a mechanical. A very few advertisers, however, still make traditional **mechanicals,** where type and line art are pasted in place on a piece of white art board (called a **pasteup**). Printers refer to the mechanical or pasteup as **camera-ready art** because they photograph it using a large production camera.

At any time during the design process—until the printing press lays ink on paper—changes can be made on the art. However, the expense may grow tenfold with each step from roughs to mechanicals to printing.

Approval

The work of the copywriter and art director is always subject to approval. The larger the agency and the larger the client, the more formidable this process becomes. A new ad concept is first approved by the agency's creative director. Then the account management team reviews it. Next, the client's product managers and marketing staff review it, often changing a word or two or sometimes rejecting the whole approach. Both the agency's and client's legal departments

Ads that employ a standard poster-style format tend to gain higher readership and recall scores than other types of layouts. As this poignant ad for 3M shows, the visual is the dominant element in a poster-style ad. The compassionate image of Mother Teresa stops the reader and gains interest. The message on the Post-it note reminds audiences "Don't forget."

scrutinize the copy and art for potential problems. Finally, the company's top executives review the final concept and text.

The biggest challenge in approval is keeping approvers from corrupting the style of the ad. The creative team works hard to achieve a cohesive style. Then a group of nonwriters and nonartists has the opportunity to change it all. Maintaining artistic purity is extremely difficult and requires patience, flexibility, maturity, and the ability to articulate an important point of view and explain why artistic choices were made.

Effect of Computers on Graphic Design

By using graphics or imaging programs on computers, today's graphic artist or designer can do much of the work previously performed by hand. On the screen, the artist can see an entire page layout, complete with illustrations and photos, and easily alter any of them in a few minutes. Before computers, designing a variety of layouts could take days, and final art was not as detailed or complete as designs created today on the computer.

Small PC- and Macintosh-based systems are ideal for computer design, and sophisticated PC graphics software is now available for pagemaking (*QuarkXPress, Ventura,* and *InDesign*), painting and drawing (*CorelDRAW, Macromedia Free-Hand, Adobe Illustrator),* and image manipulation (*ColorStudio, PhotoStyler, Adobe Photoshop).* For word processing the most popular programs include *Microsoft Word, WordPerfect,* and *Claris MacWrite.*[6] Their moderate cost makes such software accessible to freelancers, small businesses, and agency creative departments. Today's graphic artist, illustrator, and retoucher must be computer literate in addition to having a thorough knowledge of aesthetics, rendering, and design.

Principles of Design: Which Design Formats Work Best

Ads must be designed to attract the customer, and they have to do it fast. Typically, the advertiser has only a second or two to grab the reader's attention. Indeed, studies of ad readership show that 74 percent of readers claim that they completely ignore ads.[7] They also show virtually no relationship between how much the advertiser spends and how well the ad is recalled. But the quality of the advertising is important.[8] Good design not only commands attention but holds it. Good design also communicates as much information as possible in the shortest amount of time and makes the message easier to understand.[9]

Advertisers use many different types of layouts (see Commercial Break 9–B, "The Art Director's Guide to Layout Styles"). Traditionally, the ads that score the highest recall employ a standard, **poster-style format** (also called a **picture-window layout** and **Ayer No. 1** in the trade) with a single, dominant visual

(continued on p. 242)

Commercial Break 9–B

The Art Director's Guide to Layout Styles

Art directors use many different types of layouts. Creating an ad for the fictitious Imperial Cruise Lines, Tom Michael, the president and creative director of Market Design (Encinitas, California), first prepared several rough layouts using a variety of different styles and headlines to see which ideas would work best.

Note how the copy in each ad is indicated by lines of recurring gibberish. Art directors frequently represent layout text with such incoherent ramblings, referred to in the business as "greek." This saves time, but provides a graphic representation of the actual copy.

Applying the Breaks

Study the different layouts and discuss the advantages and disadvantages of each. Which approach would you recommend for Imperial Cruise Lines? Why? What additional layout or copy ideas can you come up with?

Poster-style layout—"Warm up to the beauty of Alaska."
Also called a picture window layout, note how the single, large visual occupies about two-thirds of the ad. The headline and copy may appear above or below the "window."

Mondrian grid layout—"Alaska: The last frontier for family fun."
Named after Dutch painter Piet Mondrian, the Mondrian layout uses a series of vertical and horizontal lines, rectangles, and squares within a predetermined grid to give geometric proportion to the ad.

Circus layout—"Picture Yourself Here."
Filled with multiple illustrations, oversize type, reverse blocks, tilts, or other gimmicks to bring the ad alive and make it fun and interesting.

Picture frame layout—"Guaranteed to disrupt your biological clock."
The copy is surrounded by the visual. Or, in some cases, the visual may be surrounded by the copy.

Copy-heavy layout—"Get rocked to sleep on our water bed."
When you have a lot to say and visuals won't say it, use text. But be sure the headlines and subheads make it interesting. In this case, the heavy copy actually frames the headline and visual to add visual interest. However, the headline could just as well have run above or below the copy.

Montage layout—"Open all night. Loitering encouraged."
Similar to the circus layout, the montage brings multiple illustrations together and arranges them by superimposing or overlapping to make a single composition.

Combo layout—"Warm up to Alaska."
Creativity often involves combining two or more unrelated elements to make a new element. The same is true in design. To make an ad more interesting or contemporary, the art director may combine two or more layout types to make a combo layout. This ad, for instance, starts out with a grid layout, but in the center of the grid note how the copy surrounds the headline and logo as in a frame layout.

(continued from p. 238)

that typically occupies 60 to 70 percent of the ad's total area.[10] In fact, some research shows that ads scoring in the top third for stopping power devote an average of 82 percent of their space to the visual.[11] Next in ranking are ads that have one large picture and two smaller ones. The visuals are intended to stop the reader and arouse interest, so their content must be interesting.

As we discuss in the next section, headlines also stop the reader and may actually contribute more to long-term memory than the visual.[12] As a design element, the total headline area should normally fill only 10 to 15 percent of the ad, so the type need not be particularly large. Headlines may appear above or below the visual, depending on the situation. However, when the headline appears below the illustration, the ad typically gains about 10 percent more readership.[13] This is probably because the eye tends to follow a Z pattern as it scans down the page. It sees the picture first, then the headline, then the body copy and the signature. Ads that don't interrupt this natural flow seem to score higher.

Research also shows that readership drops considerably if ads have more than 50 words. So to attract a large number of readers, copy blocks should be kept to less than 20 percent of the ad. However, with many high-involvement products, the more you tell, the more you sell. If communicating detailed information is the objective, then informative body copy becomes important. And long copy works when it's appropriate—when the advertiser is more interested in quality of readership than quantity.[14]

Finally, most people who read ads want to know who placed the ad. Company signatures or logos need not be large or occupy more than 5 to 10 percent of the area. For best results, they should be placed in the lower right-hand corner or across the bottom of the ad.

Advertising author Roy Paul Nelson points out that the principles of design are to the layout artist what the rules of grammar are to the writer. The basic rules include the following:

- The design must be in balance.

- The space within the ad should be broken up into pleasing proportions.

- A directional pattern should be evident so the reader knows in what sequence to read.

- Some force should hold the ad together and give it unity.

- One element, or one part of the ad, should have enough emphasis to dominate all others.[15]

For more on the basic principles of advertising design (balance, proportion, sequence, unity, and emphasis), see RL 9–1, Checklist of Design Principles, in the Reference Library on the *Essentials of Contemporary Advertising* Web site.

The Use of Visuals in Print Advertising

The artists who paint, sketch, and draw in advertising are called **illustrators.** The artists who produce pictures with a camera are **photographers.** Together they are responsible for all the **visuals,** or pictures, we see in advertising.

Purpose of the Visual

When confronted with a print ad, most prospects spot the picture first, then read the headline, and then peruse the body copy, in that order. Since the visual carries so much responsibility for an ad's success, it should be designed with several goals in mind. Some of the most obvious follow:

- Capture the reader's attention.
- Clarify claims made by the copy.
- Identify the subject of the ad.
- Show the product actually being used.
- Qualify readers by stopping those who are legitimate prospects.
- Help convince the reader of the truth of copy claims.
- Arouse the reader's interest in the headline.
- Emphasize the product's unique features.
- Create a favorable impression of the product or advertiser.
- Provide continuity for the campaign by using a unified visual technique in each ad.[16]

Determining the Chief Focus for Visuals

The Citibank "identity theft solutions" ads are dominated by a large, single visual that demonstrates the situation in which the service is useful rather than focusing on the card itself. The visuals capture a mood and create a feeling, a context for the consumer's perception of the product.

Selecting the focus for advertising visuals is a major step in the creative process. It often determines how well the big idea is executed. Print advertising uses many standard subjects for ad visuals, including

1. *The package containing the product.* Especially important for packaged goods, it helps the consumer identify the product on the grocery shelf.

2. *The product alone.* This usually does not work well for nonpackaged goods.

3. *The product in use.* Automobile ads typically show a car in use while talking about its ride, luxury, handling, or economy. Cosmetic ads usually show the product in use with a close-up photo of a beautiful woman or a virile man.

4. *How to use the product.* Recipe ads featuring a new way to use food products have historically pulled very high readership scores.

5. *Product features.* Computer software ads frequently show the monitor screen so the prospect can see how the software features are displayed.

6. *Comparison of products.* The advertiser shows its product next to a competitor's and compares important features.

7. *User benefit.* It's often difficult to illustrate intangible user benefits. However, marketers

This Cannes Silver Lion–winning ad for Axe deodorant body spray appeals to man's dual nature, both visually and with the headline. It doesn't take itself too seriously—ads that use humor are more likely to be remembered.

know that the best way to get customers' attention is to show how the product will benefit them, so it's worth the extra creative effort.

8. *Humor.* If used well, a humorous visual can make an entertaining and lasting impression. But it can also destroy credibility if used inappropriately.

9. *Testimonial.* Before-and-after endorsements are very effective for weight-loss products, skin care lotions, and bodybuilding courses.

10. *Negative appeal.* Sometimes visuals point out what happens if you don't use the product. If done well, that can spark interest.

Selecting the Visual

The kind of picture used is often determined during the conceptualization process (see RL 9–2, Techniques for Creating Advertising Visuals, on the *Essentials of Contemporary Advertising* Web site). But frequently the visual is not determined until the art director or designer actually lays out the ad.

Selecting an appropriate photo or visual is a difficult creative task. Art directors deal with several basic issues. For example, not every ad needs a visual to communicate effectively. Some all-type ads are quite compelling. If the art director determines that a visual is required, how many should there be: one, two, or more? Should the visual be black-and-white or color? These may be budgetary decisions.

The art director must then decide the subject of the picture. Should it be one of the standard subjects listed earlier? Or something else altogether? And how relevant is that subject to the advertiser's creative strategy? The art director also has to decide how the visual should be created. Should it be a hand-rendered illustration? A photograph? What about a computer-generated illustration?

Finally, the art director has to know what technical and/or budgetary issues must be considered. With so many options, selecting visuals is obviously no simple task. In Chapter 10, we'll see how all these decisions come together in the process of producing the final ad.

CONCEPT CHECK

Which elements of print ad design have the greatest impact on the effectiveness of the advertising?

Copywriting and Formats for Print Advertising

Now that we understand the objectives and format elements of good design, let's examine some basic copywriting formats to see how art and copy are linked.

In print advertising, the key format elements are the *visual(s), headlines, subheads, body copy, slogans, logos,* and *signatures.* As Exhibit 9–1 shows, copywriters can correlate the visual and headline to the *attention* step of the creative pyramid (discussed in Chapter 8). The *interest* step typically corresponds to the subhead and the first paragraph of body copy. Body copy handles *credibility* and *desire,* and the *action* step takes place with the logo, slogan, and signature block. We'll discuss these elements first and then look at the formats for radio and television commercials.

Headlines

The **headline** contains the words in the leading position in the advertisement—the words that will be read first and are situated to draw the most attention. That's why headlines usually appear in larger type than other parts of the ad.

Ethical Issues

Imitation, Plagiarism, or Flattery?

When two companies run strikingly similar ads, is it imitation, plagiarism, or coincidence? In December 1999, two beverage companies began running television commercials that closely resembled each other. The commercials, for Michelob Light beer and Colombian coffee, were set in supermarkets and shared the same plot: grocery baggers manhandle products until the item being advertised comes down the conveyer belt. For both Michelob Light and Colombian, the bagger wraps the advertiser's package in bubble wrap and carefully gives it to the buyers.

Advertisers and the media commonly point to "coincidence." Bob Garfield, ad critic for *Advertising Age*, said, "It's seldom plagiarism, especially if the ads are appearing simultaneously." Both of the agencies representing Michelob Light beer and Colombian coffee agree. Peter le Comte, president of DDB Worldwide Marketing, said, "We have written it off as an incident of coincidence. Besides, I don't think we share the same consumers. They will run their commercial and we will run ours."

Stephen Bergerson, an attorney specializing in advertising and promotion law at Fredrikson & Byron, Minneapolis, is skeptical. "When you get four or five words that are so specific, simultaneously used by people in the same category, the nose starts to quiver." But Ron Redfern, senior vice president of sales and marketing for the Orange County Register, calls it "coincidental invention. It's like the automobile being invented in France and in the U.S. within weeks of each other."

Some advertisers try to ignore the problem by convincing themselves that being copied is actually good. Hugh Thrasher, executive VP of marketing for Motel 6 ("We'll leave the light on for you."), says of his often-imitated Tom Bodett commercials: "We think these copycat ads just remind people of the originality of our concept." Nancy Shalek, president of L.A.'s Shalek Agency, maintains that only the best ads are imitated: "If you haven't been ripped off, you're really in trouble."

But Ellen Kozak, a Milwaukee copyright and publishing lawyer, warns against this form of flattery. "There's a fine line between the kind of borrowing that constitutes an admiring bow to a classic work and the kind that's really the theft of another writer's efforts."

Unfortunately, plagiarism is almost impossible to prove, as long as you make a few changes. There is no set number of words that make up a plagiarized effort. And plagiarism covers not only words but ideas, plots, and characters. In 1996, Kendall-Jackson Winery filed a suit against E&J Gallo Winery, charging that Gallo's Turning Leaf Vineyards brand and labeling infringed on Kendall-Jackson's Colored Leaf trademark. A jury determined there was no infringement and that judgment was affirmed on appeal. It seems that grape-leaf designs have become generic emblems for wine.

The crux of the problem may be that imitation is an accepted part of the business, at least unofficially. Clients tend to avoid the debate, perhaps because they're more comfortable with well-worn ideas than with bold, original concepts. Many art directors and writers collect competitive ads for inspiration. And advertising is such a highly collaborative process that it's often difficult to determine each individual's creative contribution. With personal responsibility so unclear, ignoring professional ethics is relatively easy.

But every so often, someone creates an ad that moves beyond the gray zone of imitation into outright plagiarism. In July 2000, Anheuser-Busch asked Heiser Automotive Group to drop its TV spots with animated frogs croaking, "Buy . . . Hei . . . ser." Heiser had manipulated its "Be Wiser . . . Buy Heiser" slogan to imitate the Budweiser frogs without permission from Anheuser-Busch.

"There are very few original ideas," according to Philip Circus, an advertising law consultant to the Newspaper Society in London. "Plagiarism is the name of the game in advertising. It's about recycling ideas in a useful way."

That's why some industry leaders are passionate about the need for personal ethics. Jim Golden, executive producer of DMH MacGuffin, says, "All we have in this business are creativity and ideas. The moment someone infringes on that, they're reaching into the very core of the business and ripping it out." Ultimately, advertisers must stop "borrowing" ideas from each other and demand greater creativity from themselves.

Questions

1. Some art directors claim that "coincidental invention" explains why many ads look the same. Do you think that's really possible?

2. Who wins and who loses when advertising is imitated? Do you believe that it's actually a benefit to be copied?

3. What would you do if a client asked you to copy an ad that was already running? Is it acceptable to plagiarize advertising ideas, as long as they are recycled "in a useful way"?

4. Is plagiarism justified by the contention that "there are very few original ideas"?

Creative pyramid

Format elements

5. Action
4. Desire
3. Credibility
2. Interest
1. Attention

← Headline and visual

← Subhead

← Body copy

← Slogan

← Logo

← Contact information

Exhibit 9–1

An ad's success depends on the viewer's ability to absorb and learn its message. The creative pyramid helps the copywriter present the conceptual elements of the message. The format elements (headlines, subheads, body copy, slogan) segment the copy to help audiences decode the message.

Role of Headlines

Headlines should offer a benefit and be easy to understand. They should also engage readers and pull them into the ad.

Effective headlines attract attention, engage the audience, explain the visual, lead the audience into the body of the ad, and present the key benefit.

Another goal of a headline is to engage the reader—fast—and give a reason to read the rest of the ad. If the headline lacks immediacy, prospects turn their attention to another subject and pass the ad's message by.[17]

Ideally, headlines communicate the complete selling idea. Research shows that, on average, three to five times as many people read the headline as read the body copy. So if the ad doesn't sell in the headline, the advertiser is wasting money.[18] Nike uses beautiful magazine and outdoor ads featuring just an athlete, the logo, and the memorable headline: "Just do it." Working off the visual, the headline creates the mood and tells the reader, through implication, to take action—buy Nikes.

The traditional notion is that short headlines with one line are best but a second line is acceptable. Many experts believe that headlines with 10 words or more gain greater readership.[19] In one study of more than 2,000 ads, most headlines averaged eight words in length.[20] David Ogilvy said the best headline he ever wrote contained 18 words—and became a classic: "At 60 miles an hour, the loudest noise in the new Rolls-Royce comes from the electric clock."[21]

Headlines should offer a benefit that is apparent to the reader and easy to grasp. For example: "When it absolutely, positively has to be there overnight" (FedEx) or "Folds flat for easy storage" (Honda Civic Wagon).[22]

Finally, headlines should present *product news*. Consumers look for new products, new uses for old products, or improvements on old products. If they haven't been overused in a category, "power" words that suggest newness can increase readership and improve the boom factor of an ad. They should be employed whenever honestly applicable.[23] Examples include *free, now, amazing, suddenly, announcing, introducing, it's here, improved, at last, revolutionary, just arrived, new,* and *important development.*

Types of Headlines

Copywriters use many variations of headlines depending on the advertising strategy. Typically, they use the headline that presents the big idea most successfully. Headlines may be classified by the type of information they carry: *benefit, news/information, provocative, question,* and *command.*

Advertisers use **benefit headlines** to promise the audience that experiencing the utility of the product or service will be rewarding. Benefit headlines shouldn't be too cute or clever, just simple statements of the product's most important benefit.[24] Two good examples are

Gore-Tex® Fabrics
Keep you warm and dry.   and
Regardless of what falls
Out of the sky.

Speak a foreign language in 30 days or your money back.

Note that both of these headlines focus on the benefit of using the product, not the features of the product itself.[25]

The **news/information headline** announces news or promises information. Sea World began its TV announcement of a new baby whale with the headline "It's a girl." The information must be believable, though. A claim that a razor "shaves 200% smoother" probably isn't.[26]

Copywriters use **provocative headlines** to provoke the reader's curiosity—to stimulate questions and thoughts. For example: "Betcha can't eat just one" (Lay's Potato Chips). To learn more, the reader must read the body copy. The danger, of course, is that the reader won't read on. To avoid this, the creative team designs visuals to clarify the message or provide some story appeal.

A **question headline** asks a question, encouraging readers to search for the answer in the body of the ad. An ad for 4 Day Tire Stores asked: "What makes our tire customers smarter & richer than others?" A good question headline piques the reader's curiosity and imagination.

A **command headline** orders the reader to do something, so it might seem negative. But readers pay attention to such headlines. Sprite soft-drink ads target youth with the hip headline: "Obey your thirst." Some command headlines make a request: "Please don't squeeze the Charmin" (bathroom tissue).

Subheads

The **subhead** is an additional smaller headline that may appear above the headline or below it. A subhead above

Florida Orange Juice.
The best start under the sun.

Benefit headlines offer a reward to the reader. They should be straightforward and preferably include the name of the product that's providing the benefit.

Combining visual humor and a provocative headline is a difficult task, but if done correctly, it can ensure an ad's resonance. This simple but effective ad, promoting the freshness of the seafood in Thailand's Tesco Lotus supermarkets, won a Bronze Lion at Cannes. With such brevity of text, we can see an example of a picture being worth exactly 998 words.

the headline is called a **kicker** (or *overline*) and may be underlined. Subheads may also appear in body copy.

Subheads are usually set smaller than the headline but larger than the body copy or text. Subheads generally appear in **boldface** (heavier) or **italic** (slanted) type or a different color. Like a headline, the subhead transmits key sales points fast. But it usually carries less important information than the head-line. Subheads are important for two reasons: Most people read only the head-line and subheads, and subheads usually best support the interest step.

Subheads are longer and more like sentences than headlines. They serve as stepping-stones from the headline to the body copy, telegraphing what's to come.[27]

Body Copy

The advertiser tells the complete sales story in the **body copy, or text.** The body copy comprises the interest, credibility, desire, and often even the action steps. It is a logical continuation of the headline and subheads, set in smaller type. Body copy covers the features, benefits, and utility of the product or service.

The body copy is typically read by only 1 out of 10 readers, so the writer must speak to the reader's self-interest, explaining how the product or service satisfies the customer's need.[28] The best ads focus on one big idea or one clear benefit. Copywriters often read their copy aloud to hear how it sounds, even if it's intended for print media. The ear is a powerful copywriting tool.[29]

Some of the best copywriting techniques of leading experts are highlighted in the Checklist, "Writing Effective Copy."

Body Copy Styles

Experienced copywriters look for the technique and style with the greatest sales appeal for the idea being presented. Common copy styles include *straight sell, institutional, narrative, dialogue/monologue, picture caption,* and *device.*

In **straight-sell copy,** writers immediately explain or develop the headline and visual in a straightforward, factual presentation. The straight-sell approach appeals to the prospect's intelligence. The Citibank print ads at the beginning of this chapter use a straight sell to describe its service. Although the topic of fraud can be emotional, the copy is reassuring because it presents hard facts and clear solutions. Because it ticks off the product's sales points in order of importance, straight-sell copy is particularly good for high think-involvement products or products that are difficult to use. It's very effective for direct-mail advertising and for industrial or high-tech products. Advertisers use the straight-sell approach more than all other techniques combined.[30]

Advertisers use **institutional copy** to promote a philosophy or extol the merits of an organization rather than product features. Institutional copy is intended to lend warmth and credibility to the organization's image. Banks, insurance companies, public corporations, and large manufacturing firms use institutional copy in both print and electronic media. However, David Ogilvy warned against the "self-serving, flatulent pomposity" that characterizes the copy in many corporate ads.[31]

Copywriters use **narrative copy** to tell a story. Ideal for the creative writer, narrative copy sets up a situation and then resolves it at the last minute by having the product or service come to the rescue. The Citibank headline ("It didn't seem right to us, either.") engages readers in dialogue and tells them that the company thinks the same way they do. Narrative copy offers good opportunities for emotional appeals. An insurance company, for example, might tell the poignant story of the man who died unexpectedly but, fortunately, had just renewed his policy.[32]

Checklist

Writing Effective Copy

- **Get to the main point—fast.**
- **Emphasize one major idea simply and clearly.** And be sure the idea is on strategy.
- **Be single-minded.** Don't try to do too much. If you chase more than one rabbit at a time, you'll catch none.
- **Position the product clearly.**
- **Keep the brand name up front and reinforce it.**
- **Write with the consumer's ultimate benefit in mind.**
- **Write short sentences.** Use easy, familiar words and themes people understand.
- **Don't waste words.** Say what you have to say—nothing more, nothing less. Don't pad, but don't skimp.
- **Avoid bragging and boasting.** Write from the reader's point of view, not your own. Avoid "we," "us," and "our."
- **Avoid clichés.** They're crutches; learn to get along without them. Bright, surprising words and phrases perk up readers and keep them reading.

- **Write with flair. Drum up excitement.** Make sure your own enthusiasm comes through in the copy.
- **Use vivid language.** Use lots of verbs and adverbs.
- **Stick to the present tense, active voice.** It's crisper. Avoid the past tense and passive voice. Exceptions should be deliberate, for special effect.
- **Use personal pronouns.** Remember, you're talking to just one person, so talk as you would to a friend. Use "you" and "your" whenever appropriate.
- **Use contractions.** They're fast, personal, natural. People talk in contractions (listen to yourself).
- **Don't overpunctuate.** It kills copy flow. Excessive commas are the chief culprits. Don't give readers any excuse to jump ship.
- **Read the copy aloud.** Hear how it sounds; catch errors. The written word is considerably different from the spoken word so listen to it.
- **Rewrite and write tight.** Edit mercilessly. Tell the whole story and no more. When you're finished telling the story, stop!

By using **dialogue/monologue copy,** the advertiser can add the believability that narrative copy sometimes lacks. The characters portrayed in a print ad do the selling in their own words. A caution: Poorly written dialogue copy can come off as dull or, even worse, hokey and unreal.

Sometimes it's easier to tell a story with illustrations and captions. A photo with **picture-caption copy** is especially useful for products that have a number of different uses or come in a variety of styles or designs.

With any copy style, the copywriter may use some device copy to enhance attention, interest, and memorability. **Device copy** uses figures of speech (such as puns, alliteration, and rhymes) as well as humor and exaggeration. Verbal devices help people remember the brand and tend to affect attitude favorably.[33]

Humor can be effective when the advertiser needs high memorability in a short time, wants to dispel preconceived negative images, or needs to create a distinct personality for an undifferentiated product. However, humor should always be used carefully and never be in questionable taste. Humor also grows old very quickly; the same joke is not funny for long. Therefore, a variety of executions should be created to keep the idea fresh. Some researchers believe humor distracts from the selling message and can even be detrimental when used for serious services like finance, insurance, and crematoriums.[34]

Formatting Body Copy

The keys to good body copy are simplicity, order, credibility, and clarity. Or, as John O'Toole says, prose should be "written clearly, informatively, interestingly, powerfully, persuasively, dramatically, memorably, and with effortless grace. That's all."[35]

Four basic format elements are used to construct long copy ads: the *lead-in paragraph, interior paragraphs, trial close,* and *close.*

Lead-in paragraph The **lead-in paragraph** is a bridge between the headline and the sales ideas presented in the text. Like a subhead, the lead-in paragraph is part of the *interest* step. It must be engaging and able to convert a prospect's reading interest to product interest.

Interior paragraphs The **interior paragraphs** of the body copy should develop *credibility* by providing proof for claims and promises and they should build *desire* by using language that stirs the imagination. Advertisers should support their product promises with research data, testimonials, and warranties. Such proofs convince customers of the validity of the product, improve goodwill toward the advertiser, and stimulate sales.

Trial close Interspersed in the interior paragraphs should be suggestions to *act* now. Good copy asks for the order more than once; mail-order ads ask several times. Consumers often make the buying decision without reading all the body copy. The **trial close** gives them the opportunity to make the buying decision early.

Close The **close** is the real *action* step. A good close asks consumers to do something and tells them how. The close can be indirect or direct (a subtle suggestion or a direct command). A direct close seeks immediate response in the form of a purchase, a store or Web site visit, or a request for further information.

The close should simplify the audience's response, making it easy for them to order the merchandise, send for information, or visit a showroom or a Web site. A business reply card or a toll-free phone number may be included.

Of course, not all ads sell products or services. Advertisers may want to change attitudes, explain their viewpoints, or ask for someone's vote. By giving a Web site address, the advertiser can offer additional information to those readers who are interested in learning more at their leisure.

Slogans

Many **slogans** (also called **themelines** or **taglines**) begin as successful headlines, like AT&T's "Reach out and touch someone." Through continuous use, they become standard statements, not just in advertising but for salespeople and company employees.

Slogans have two basic purposes: to provide continuity to a series of ads in a campaign and to reduce an advertising message strategy to a brief, repeatable, and memorable positioning statement. Wheaties cereal, for example, positions itself as the "Breakfast of Champions." And ads for DeBeers still use the famous "Diamonds are forever" slogan.

Seals, Logos, and Signatures

A **seal** is awarded only when a product meets standards established by a particular organization, such as the Good Housekeeping Institute or Underwriters Laboratories. Because these organizations are recognized authorities, their seals provide an independent, valued endorsement for the advertiser's product.

Logotypes (logos) and **signatures** are special designs of the advertiser's company or product name. They appear in all company ads and, like trademarks, give the product individuality and provide quick recognition at the point of purchase.

CONCEPT CHECK

Describe the functions that the various copy elements perform in print advertising.

Checklist

Creating Effective Radio Commercials

- **Make the big idea crystal clear.** Concentrate on one main selling point (which must be on strategy). Radio is a good medium for building brand awareness, but not for making long lists of copy points or complex arguments.

- **Mention the advertiser's name early and often.** If the product or company name is tricky, consider spelling it out.

- **Take time to set the scene and establish the premise.** A 30-second commercial that nobody remembers is a waste of money. Fight for 60-second spots.

- **Use familiar sound effects.** Ice tinkling in a glass, birds chirping, or a door shutting can create a visual image. Music also works if its meaning is clear.

- **Paint pictures with your words.** Use descriptive language to make the ad more memorable.

- **Make every word count.** Use active voice and more verbs than adjectives. Be conversational. Use pronounceable words and short sentences.

- **Be outrageous.** The best comic commercials begin with a totally absurd premise from which all developments follow logically. But remember, if you can't write humor really well, go for drama.

- **Ask for the order.** Try to get listeners to take action.

- **Remember that radio is a local medium.** Adjust your commercials to the language of your listeners and the time of day the spots will run.

- **Presentation counts a lot.** Even the best scripts look boring on paper. Acting, timing, vocal quirks, and sound effects bring them to life.

Copywriting for Electronic Media

For electronic media, the fundamental elements—the five steps of the creative pyramid—remain the primary guides, but the copywriting formats differ. Radio and television writers prepare *scripts* and *storyboards*.

Writing Radio Copy

A **script** resembles a two-column list. On the left side, speakers' names are arranged vertically, along with descriptions of any **sound effects** (abbreviated **SFX**) and music. The right column contains the dialogue, called the **audio.**

Copywriters first need to understand radio as a medium. Radio provides entertainment or news to listeners who are busy doing something else—driving, washing dishes, reading the paper, or even studying. To be heard, an advertising message must be catchy, interesting, and unforgettable. Radio listeners usually decide within five to eight seconds if they're going to pay attention. To attract and hold the attention of listeners, particularly those not attracted to a product category, radio copy must be intrusive.

Intrusive, yes; offensive, no. An insensitive choice of words, an overzealous effort to attract listeners with irritating everyday sounds (car horn, alarm clock, screeching tires), or characters that sound too exotic, odd, or dumb can cause listener resentment and ultimately lose sales. Tom Bodett's often-imitated ads for Motel 6 demonstrate the effectiveness of a personal, relaxed, and natural style. Other guidelines are given in the Checklist, "Creating Effective Radio Commercials."

One of the most challenging aspects is making the script fit the time slot. The delivery changes for different types of commercials, so writers must read

Healthier America
Lost Campaign
Radio: 60
"Neighbor"
Expiration date: 2/23/05

SFX: Phone ringing	
Bill:	Hello...?
George:	Hi, Bill? This is George Dewey from up the street.
Bill:	Hey, George. How ya doin?
George:	Good, good. Say, I noticed you've been walking to work these days instead of driving...and I, uh, don't quite know how to say this, but...but...
Bill:	But what?
George: *(stammering)*	But...But...Your butt, your buttocks, your butt—I think I found your butt on my front lawn. Have you recently lost it?
Bill:	As a matter of fact, I have, George *(pleased)* It's about time someone noticed.
George: *(playful)*	Well, it was kinda hard to miss if you know what I mean... ...Anyways, would you like it back?
Bill:	Would I like it back? No, not really.
George:	So, it's okay if I throw it out?
Bill:	Sure, that's fine. Take it easy, George.
SFX: Phone ringing	
Announcer:	Small step #8—Walk instead of driving whenever you can. It's just one of the many small steps you can take to help you become a healthier, well, you. Get started at www.smallstep.gov and take a small step to get healthy.
Legal:	A public service announcement brought to you by the U.S. Department of Health and Human Services and the Ad Council.

A radio script format resembles a two-column list, with speakers' names and sound effects on the left and the dialogue in a wider column on the right. This national public service announcement (PSA) was created by McCann-Erickson and is one of many in a campaign designed to inspire Americans to take small steps toward a healthier lifestyle.

the script out loud for timing. With electronic compression, recorded radio ads can now include 10 to 30 percent more copy than text read live. Still, the following is a good rule of thumb:

10 seconds: 20–25 words
20 seconds: 40–45 words
30 seconds: 60–70 words
60 seconds: 130–150 words[36]

Radio writing has to be clearer than any other kind of copywriting. For example, the listener can't refer back, as in print, to find an antecedent for a pronoun. Likewise, the English language is so full of homonyms (words that sound like other words) that one can easily confuse the meaning of a sentence ("who's who is whose").[37]

Writing Television Copy

Radio's basic two-column script format also works for television. But in a TV script, the left side is titled "Video" and the right side "Audio." The video column describes the visuals and production: camera angles, action, scenery, and stage directions. The audio column lists the spoken copy, sound effects, and music.

Broadcast commercials must be believable and relevant. Even zany commercials must exude quality in their creation and production to imply the product's quality. While the art director's work is very important, the copywriter typically sets the tone of the commercial, establishes the language that determines which visuals to use, and pinpoints when the visuals should appear. Research shows the techniques given in the Checklist, "Creating Effective TV Commercials" work best.

To illustrate these principles, let's look at a particular commercial. Many people want smooth, soft skin and consider a patch of rough, flaky skin anywhere on their body a disappointment. If you were the copywriter for Lubriderm skin lotion, how would you approach this somewhat touchy, negative subject?

The creative staff of J. Walter Thompson crafted an artistic solution for Lubriderm. An alligator was the big idea. The gator's scaly sheath was a metaphor for rough, flaky skin. Its appearance ignited people's survival instincts; they paid attention, fast. A beautiful, sophisticated woman with smooth, feminine skin was seated in a lounge chair, completely unruffled by the passing gator. The swing of the animal's back and tail echoed the graceful curves of the two simple pieces of furniture on the set, and its slow stride kept the beat of a light jazz tune.

Checklist

Creating Effective TV Commercials

- **Begin at the finish.** Concentrate on the final impression the commercial will make. And be sure that final impression is on strategy.

- **Create an attention-getting opening.** An opening that is visually surprising or full of action, drama, humor, or human interest sets the context and allows a smooth transition to the rest of the commercial.

- **Use a situation that grows naturally out of the sales story.** Avoid distracting gimmicks. Make it easy for viewers to identify with the characters.

- **Characters are the living symbol of the product.** They should be appealing, believable, nondistracting, and most of all, relevant.

- **Keep it simple.** The sequence of ideas should be easy to follow. Keep the number of elements in the commercial to a bare minimum.

- **Write concise audio copy.** The video should carry most of the weight. Fewer than two words per second is effective for demonstrations. For a 60-second commercial, 101 to 110 words is most effective; more than 170 words is too talky.

- **Make demonstrations dramatic but believable.** They should always be true to life and avoid the appearance of camera tricks.

- **Let the words interpret the picture and prepare viewers for the next scene.** Some of the best TV ads communicate just as well with the sound turned off. Use conversational language; avoid "ad talk," hype, and puffery.

- **Run scenes for five or six seconds on average.** Rarely should a scene run less than three seconds. Offer a variety of movement-filled scenes without "jumping."

This commercial opened with an attention-getting big idea that was visually surprising, compelling, dramatic, and interesting. It was also a quasi-demonstration: we saw the alligator's scaly, prickly skin and the woman's confidence and willingness to touch the alligator as it passed by, which symbolized the confidence Lubriderm can bring.

This ad follows the creative pyramid. The alligator captures attention visually while the announcer's first words serve as an attention-getting headline: "A quick reminder." The ad commands us to listen and sets up the interest step that offers this claim: "Lubriderm restores lost moisture to heal your dry skin and protect it." Now for the credibility step: "Remember, the one created for dermatologists is the one that heals and protects." And then the desire step recaps the primary product benefit and adds a touch of humor: "See you later, alligator."

CONCEPT CHECK

In what ways does the challenge of writing copy for radio and television differ from that of writing for print?

The Role of Art in Radio and TV Advertising

According to *Advertising Age* columnist Bob Garfield, the best commercial in the world in 1997 was from Delvico Bates, Barcelona, for Esencial hand cream. The spot opens with a woman riding her bicycle to the persistent squeak of its unlubricated chain. She dismounts, opens a jar of Esencial, and rubs some of the cream onto the chain. Then she rides away—but the squeak is still there. Why? Because, as the voice-over points out, "Esencial moisturizes, but it has no grease."

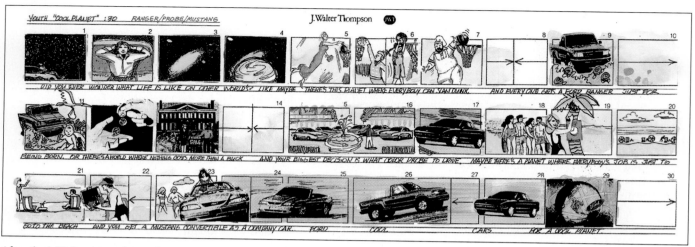

YOUTH "COOL PLANET" :30   RANGER/PROBE/MUSTANG   J.Walter Thompson

After the initial concepts for a television ad are finalized, creatives develop a storyboard rough composed of small sketches that depict the various scenes of the ad. The storyboard rough is used to present the creative concept to the account team and the client.

No big production. No digital effects. No jingle. No celebrity. No big comedy payoff. Just a pure advertising idea: a problem/resolution spot where the brand pointedly cannot solve the problem. It's a vivid demonstration of brand nonattributes. Inspired. Cunning. Brilliant.

Developing the Artistic Concept for Commercials

Creating the concept for a radio or TV commercial is similar to creating the concept for print ads. The first step is to determine the big idea. Then the art director and copywriter must decide what commercial format to use. Should a celebrity present the message? Or should the ad dramatize the product's benefits with a semifictional story? The next step is to write a script containing the necessary copy or dialogue plus a basic description of any music, sound effects, and/or camera views.

In both radio and TV, the art director assists the copywriter in script development. But in television, artistic development is much more extensive. Using the TV script, the art director creates a series of **storyboard roughs** to present the artistic approach, the action sequences, and the style of the commercial.

Good casting is critical. The most important consideration is relevance to the product; agencies don't use a comic to sell financial products—or cremation services. And in spite of Michael Jordan's success for Nike, Gatorade, and McDonald's, some experts don't believe in using celebrities. David Ogilvy, for example, thought viewers remember the celebrity more than the product.[38]

Formats for Radio and TV Commercials

Similar to print advertising, the format for a broadcast ad serves as a template for arranging message elements into a pattern. Once the art director and copywriter establish the big idea, they must determine the commercial's format.

Many radio and TV commercial styles have been successful. Here we consider eight common commercial formats that can be used in either radio or television: *straight announcement, presenter, testimonial, demonstration, musical, slice of life, lifestyle,* and *animation.*

Presenter commercials often use celebrities, experts, or actors playing a role. Jack has been well established as the spokesperson for Jack in the Box. Here, Jack shares the stage with his son, in an execution that does an excellent job reinforcing the name of Jack's new Ciabatta sandwich.

"Spelling Bee": 30

(Open on boy standing on stage at a grade school spelling bee)

Boy #1: Ciabatta. C-B-A . . .

(Buzzer sounds. Cut to the next contestant)

Girl: Ciabatta. C-A . . .

(Buzzer sounds. Cut to the next contestant)

Boy #2: Can you use it in a sentence?

(Cut to Jack, buzzer in hand, officiating the spelling bee off stage)

Jack: My original Ciabatta burger is made with a juicy jumbo patty topped with greenleaf lettuce, onions, tomatoes, pickles and a zesty sauce all served on delicious, lightly toasted ciabatta bread.

(Cut to shot of Ciabatta burger and accompaniments)

Boy #2: J . . .

(Buzzer sounds)

(Bag drops)

Bag 1: Original Ciabatta Burger

Bag 2: Experience Ciabatta

(Cut to next contestant with Jack-in-the-Box head on stage)

Boy (with Jack head): C-I-A-B-A-double T-A. Ciabatta. Peace out.

Straight Announcement

The oldest and simplest type of radio or TV commercial and probably the easiest to write is the **straight announcement.** One person, usually a radio or TV announcer, delivers the sales message. Music may play in the background. Straight announcements are popular because they are adaptable to almost any product or situation. In radio, a straight announcement can also be designed as an **integrated commercial**—that is, it can be woven into a show or tailored to the style of a given program.

For TV, an announcer may deliver the sales message **on camera** or off screen, as a **voice-over,** while a demonstration, slide, or film shows on screen. If the script is well written and the announcer convincing, straight announcements can be very effective. Since they don't require elaborate production facilities, they save money, too.

Presenter

The **presenter commercial** uses one person or character to present the product and carry the sales message. Some presenters are celebrities, such as Catherine Zeta-Jones for T-Mobile. Others may be experts, such as corporate officers (Lee

Iacocca) or professionals (doctors), or they may be actors playing a role (the lonely Maytag repairman). A *man-on-the-street* may interview real people and get them to share their thoughts about a client's products or services. And, of course, a presenter doesn't have to be a real person. Remember Tony the Tiger?

A **radio personality,** such as Rush Limbaugh or Larry King, may *ad lib* an ad message live in his or her own style. Done well, such commercials can be very successful, as evidenced by the initial success of Snapple. However, the advertiser surrenders control to the personality.

Testimonial

The true **testimonial**—where a satisfied user tells how effective the product is—can be highly credible in both TV and radio advertising. Celebrities may gain attention, but they must be believable and not distract from the product. Actually, people from all walks of life endorse products, from known personalities to unknowns and nonprofessionals. Which type of person to use depends on the product and the strategy. Satisfied customers are the best sources for testimonials because their sincerity is usually persuasive. Ogilvy suggested shooting candid testimonials when the subjects don't know they're being filmed.[39] Of course, advertisers must be sure to get their permission before using the piece.

Demonstration

Television is uniquely suited to visual demonstrations. And a **demonstration** convinces an audience better and faster than a spoken message. So don't say it, show it.[40] Naturally, it's easier to demonstrate the product on TV than on radio, but some advertisers have used the imaginative nature of radio to create humorous, tongue-in-cheek demonstrations.

Products may be demonstrated in use, in competition, or before and after. These techniques help viewers visualize how the product will perform for them.

Musical

The **musical commercials,** or **jingles,** we hear on radio and TV are among the best—and worst—ad messages produced. Done well, they can bring enormous success, well beyond the average nonmusical commercial. Done poorly, they can waste the advertising budget and annoy audiences beyond belief.

Advertisers have three sources of music. They can buy the right to use a tune from the copyright owner, which is usually expensive. They can use a melody in the public domain, which is free. Or they can hire a composer to write an original song. Some original tunes, including Coke's famous "I'd like to teach the world to sing," have become hits.

Slice of Life (Problem Solution)

A commercial that dramatizes a real-life situation is called **slice of life.** It usually starts with just plain folks, played by professional actors, discussing some problem or issue. Often the situation deals with a problem of a personal nature: bad breath, loose dentures, dandruff, body odor, or yellow laundry. A relative or a co-worker drops the hint, the product is tried, and the next scene shows the result—a happier, cleaner, more fragrant person off with a new date. The drama always concludes with a positive outcome. Such commercials can get attention and create interest, even though they are often irritating to viewers and hated by copywriters.

The key to effective slice-of-life commercials is simplicity. The ad should concentrate on one product benefit and make it memorable. Often a **mnemonic device** (a technique that helps you remember something) can dramatize the product benefit and trigger instant recall. Users of Imperial margarine, for example, suddenly discover crowns on their heads.

Believability in slice-of-life commercials is difficult to achieve. People don't really talk about "the sophisticated taste of Taster's Choice," so the actors must be highly credible to pull it off. That's why most *local* advertisers don't use the slice-of-life technique. Creating that believability takes very professional talent and money. In all cases, the story should be relevant to the product and simply told.

Lifestyle

To present the user rather than the product, advertisers may use the **lifestyle technique.** For example, Diesel pitches its denim to urbanites by showing characters working and playing while wearing its latest line. Likewise, beer and soft-drink advertisers frequently target their messages to active, outdoorsy young people, focusing on who drinks the brand rather than on specific product advantages.

Animation

Cartoons, puppet characters, and demonstrations with computer-generated graphics are very effective **animation** techniques for communicating difficult messages and reaching specialized markets, such as children. The way aspirin or other medications affect the human system is difficult to explain. Animated pictures of headaches and stomachs can simplify the subject and make a demonstration clear and understandable.

Computer animation requires a great deal of faith on the part of advertisers. Since most of this very expensive work is done on the computer, there's nothing to see until the animation is well developed and a good bit of money has been spent (this is more fully discussed in Chapter 10).

Basic Mechanics of Storyboard Development

After the creative team selects the big idea and the format for a TV commercial, the art director and the writer develop the script. Television is so visually powerful and expressive that the art director's role is particularly important. Art directors must be able to work with a variety of professionals—producers,

Ads that appeal to lifestyle present the type of user associated with the product, rather than the product itself. This ad for MasterCard is aimed at sports fans, and specifically Boston Red Sox fans, who are willing to do just about anything for their team.

VO: Red Sox World Series tickets

Baseball Enthusiast #1: Five hundred bucks.

Man Waiting in Line: I'd pay four grand.

Weightlifter: My car. My truck. My computer.

Girl #1: Two months' salary.

Weightlifter: . . . my entire savings account.

Man with Painted Face: Anything, anything.

Little Boy: My fish.

Young Woman: My dog.

Weightlifter: My girlfriend.

Fan at Ballpark: My first-born kid.

Girl #3: Really.

VO/Super: Seeing the Red Sox in the World Series: Priceless.

VO/Super: There are some things money can't buy.

VO/Super: For everything else there's MasterCard.

VO/Super: Devoted fan of the devoted fans.

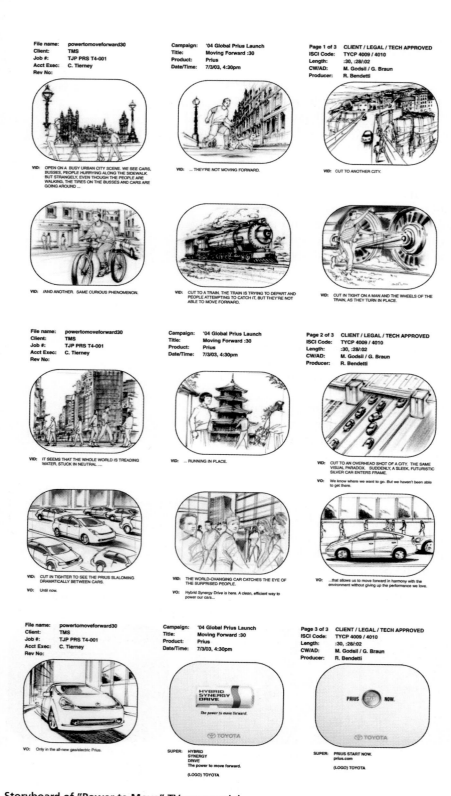

Storyboard of "Power to Move" TV commercial
The storyboard is a visual representation of the ad, made up of sketches that indicate the art director's concept of the various scenes, camera angles, sound effects, and special effects to be used in the final production.

directors, lighting technicians, and set designers—to develop and produce a commercial successfully. Producing ads will be discussed in the next chapter.

Storyboard Design

Once the basic script is completed, the art director must turn the video portion of the script into real images. This is done with a **storyboard,** a sheet preprinted with a series of 8 to 20 blank windows (frames) in the shape of TV screens. Below each frame is room to place the text of the commercial, including the sound effects and camera views. The storyboard works much like a cartoon strip.

Through a process similar to laying out a print ad (thumbnail, rough, comp) the artist carefully designs how each scene should appear, arranging actors, scenery, props, lighting, and camera angles to maximize impact, beauty, and mood. The storyboard helps the creatives visualize the commercial's tone and sequence of action, discover any conceptual weaknesses, and make presentations for final management approval. It also serves as a guide for filming.

Even when designed to the level of a comp, though, the storyboard is only an approximation of the final commercial. Actual production often results in many changes in lighting, camera angle, focal point, and emphasis. The camera sees many things that the artist couldn't visualize, and vice versa.

Animatic: The Video Comp

To supplement the storyboard or pretest a concept, a commercial may be taped in rough form using amateur talent as actors. Or an **animatic** may be shot—a film strip of the sketches in the storyboard accompanied by the audio portion of the commercial synchronized on tape. A standard animatic costs more than $10,000 to produce, but computers are cutting costs dramatically. Avid Technologies, for example, developed a Macintosh-based editing system that lets the agency create moving pictures on the screen, lay sound behind them, and transfer the entire package onto videotape to send to the client. This system cuts the cost to produce testable material from about $10,000 to $1,000. This kind of technology is being adopted by many agencies as they look for ways to better serve clients' creative needs for less money.

Upon approval of the storyboard and/or the animatic, the commercial is ready for production, a subject we cover in detail in Chapter 10.

CONCEPT CHECK

What are the potential advantages and disadvantages of the formats commonly used for radio and television commercials?

Writing for the Web

The Internet is a whole new medium for communication, and many advertising people are still learning how to use it. This is an important issue since Web users are both savvy and skeptical as well as influential.

According to research by Burson-Marsteller, a large New York public relations firm, there are 11 million heavy online users in the United States, and their opinions affect the buying decisions of 155 million consumers both online and off. Burson-Marsteller refers to these opinion leaders as e-fluentials.

"An e-fluential is the rock that starts the ripple," said Chet Burchett, president and chief executive officer, Burson-Marsteller USA. "Each one communicates with an average of 14 people." E-fluentials can be reputation builders or busters.[41] You can find out if you are an e-fluential at **www.efluentials.com**.

So writing effectively for the Web is critical. Company Web sites that provide e-fluentials with straightforward, easy-to-use information are crucial to building and enhancing brand value.

People don't really read a Web site. They scan it, so the information presented must be at once concise and comprehensive. Numbered lists and bulleted items thus can be used more than in print media. Rather than scanning down the page like newspaper readers, Web users often just read the first text screen of any site and then move on. But if they like what they see, then they will want more, and they will stay on the site to search for more information. Having fewer space limitations than any other medium, the Web is ideal for in-depth elaboration.

A study measuring the usefulness of Web sites found that a sample Web site scored 58 percent higher when it was written concisely, 47 percent higher when the text was scannable, and 27 percent higher when it was written in an objective rather than promotional style. When these three characteristics were combined in a single site, the result was 124 percent higher usefulness.[42]

Finally, Web sites should always offer interactivity—a way for the reader to respond, either through e-mail or Web response forms. The Web is about interactivity. Companies that overlook that feature are wasting their money.

CONCEPT CHECK

What are guidelines for writing effectively for the Web?

The most effective Web sites can be quickly scanned for useful information. This GEICO page (**www.geico.com**) has clear navigation buttons, helpful links, and bulleted benefits. Multiple opportunities are presented for users to interact with this site.

Creating Ads for International Markets

International advertisers have debated the transferability of campaigns for years. One side believes it's too expensive to create a unique campaign for each national group. They simply translate one overall campaign into each language. Another method is to think globally but act locally, creating ads in various languages and reflecting the needs of different groups, but maintaining a consistent theme worldwide. Other advertisers believe the only way to ensure success is to create a special campaign for each market. Citigroup uses a variation of this approach. With branches in 100 countries, the financial service giant adapts its ads and products to the needs of each market. For example, the large Indian population working abroad can open checking accounts in rupees instead of the local currency; family members back home can access the accounts via 250 Citibank ATMs in 28 cities in India, avoiding the steep fees usually associated with transferring money. Some advertisers find such solutions expensive and unnecessary. They run their ads in English worldwide, promoting their products generically rather than specifically.

Advertisers must address their unique situations. Moreover, they have to weigh the economics of various promotional strategies.

Translating Copy

In international markets, the most important consideration for copywriters and creative directors is language. In Western Europe, people speak at least 15 different

Global advertisers often use a single basic ad, translating it into the languages of the various countries where it will run.

languages and more than twice as many dialects. A similar problem exists in Asia, Africa, and, to a lesser extent, South America.

Classic examples of mistranslations and faulty word choices abound in international advertising. A faulty Spanish translation for Perdue chickens reads "It takes a sexually excited man to make a chick affectionate" instead of "It takes a tough man to make a tender chicken."[43]

A poorly chosen or badly translated product name can undercut advertising credibility in foreign markets. A classic case was when Coke's product name was widely translated into Chinese characters that sounded like "Coca-Cola" but meant "bite the wax tadpole."[44]

People in the United States, Canada, England, Australia, and South Africa all speak English, but with wide variations in vocabulary, word usage, and syntax. Similarly, the French spoken in France, Canada, Vietnam, and Belgium may differ as much as the English spoken by a British aristocrat and a Tennessee mountaineer. Language variations exist even within countries. The Japanese use five lingual "gears," ranging from haughty to servile, depending on the speaker's and the listener's respective stations in life. Japanese translators must know when to change gears.

Advertisers should follow some basic rules in using translators:

- **The translator must be an effective copywriter.** In the United States and Canada, most people speak English, yet relatively few are good writers and even fewer are good copywriters. Too often advertisers simply let a translation service rewrite their ads in a foreign language. That's not good enough.

- **The translator must understand the product.** The translator must also know the product's features and its market. It is always better to use a translator who is a product or market specialist rather than a generalist.

- **Translators should translate into their native tongue.** Ideally, they should live in the country where the ad will appear. This way the advertiser can be sure the translator has a current understanding of the country's social attitudes, culture, and idioms.

- **The advertiser should give the translator easily translatable English copy.** The double meanings and idiomatic expressions that make English such a rich language for advertising rarely translate well. They only make the translator's job more difficult.

There is no greater insult to a national market than to misuse its language. The translation must be accurate and punctuated properly, and it must also be good copy.

English is rapidly becoming the universal language for corporate ad campaigns directed to international businesspeople, and some firms print their instructional literature and brochures in English as well. But this approach can incite nationalistic feelings against the company. Worse yet, it automatically limits a product's use to people who understand technical English.[45]

Art Direction for International Markets

Philosophers often refer to the arts as a kind of international language whose nonverbal elements translate freely regardless of culture. A nice idea but, in advertising, a very costly one. People ascribe different meanings to color depending on their culture. When designing ads for use in other countries, the art director must be familiar with each country's artistic preferences and peculiarities.

Some consider color to indicate emotion: Someone "has the blues" or is "green with envy" (refer back to Commercial Break 8–A, "The Psychological Impact of Color").

An **icon,** a visual image representing some idea or thing, can have a meaning that cuts across national boundaries and reflects the tastes and attitudes of a group of cultures. An ad with a snake (an icon for the devil and eroticism in many Western cultures) could easily lose sales in North American markets. But in the Far East, where the snake represents renewal (by shedding its skin), the same visual might work as a dynamic expression of a product's staying power.

Similarly, a model considered attractive in one culture is not necessarily seen that way in another, however. Just as with copy translation, advertisers working in global markets must pretest art and design concepts with natives of each country.

CONCEPT CHECK

Define the issues that advertisers should be concerned about when developing advertising that will be used in international markets.

Legal Restraints on International Advertisers

Finally, all advertising creativity, including what the ads say, show, or do, is at the mercy of foreign governments and cultures. As we discussed in Chapter 2, many countries strongly regulate advertising claims and the use of particular media.

Chapter Summary

The nonverbal aspect of an ad or commercial carries half the burden of communicating the big idea. In fact, the nonverbal message is inseparable from the verbal. Either can enhance the other or destroy it.

Design refers to how the art director and graphic artist choose and structure the artistic elements that make up an ad's appearance or set its tone. For print advertising, the first work from the art department is a simple, undeveloped design of the ad's layout. The layout has several purposes: It shows where the parts of the ad are to be placed; it is an inexpensive way to explore creative ideas; it helps the creative team check the ad's psychological or symbolic function; and it serves as a blueprint for the production process.

As advertising copy goes through the editing process, copywriters must be prepared for edits and reedits from agency and client managers and legal departments. Copywriters must be more than creative; they must be patient, flexible, mature, and able to exercise great self-control.

Several steps are used to develop an ad's design: thumbnail sketch, rough layout, and comprehensive layout. The mechanical is the final art ready for reproduction. Brochures and other multipage materials use a three-dimensional rough called a dummy.

The computer has dramatically affected graphic design. Various software programs allow artists to paint and draw, compose pages, and manipulate images in ways that would not be possible manually. Every graphic designer must now be computer literate.

In print advertising, the visual has a great deal of responsibility for an ad's success. The picture may be used to capture the reader's attention, identify the subject of the ad, create a favorable impression, or serve a host of other functions.

The two basic devices for illustrating an ad are photos and drawings. Photography can contribute realism; a sense of immediacy; a feeling of live action; the enhancement of mood, beauty, and sensitivity; and speed, flexibility, and economy. Drawn illustrations do many of these things, too, and may be used if the artist feels they can achieve greater impact than photos. The chief focus for visuals may be the product in a variety of settings, a user benefit, a humorous situation, a testimonial, or even some negative appeal.

The key format elements for writing print ads are headlines, subheads, body copy, slogans, seals, logos, and signatures. Many headline types and copy styles are used in print advertising. There are five basic types of advertising headlines: benefit, provocative, news/information, question, and command. Copy styles also fall into several categories: straight sell, institutional, narrative, dialogue/monologue, picture caption, and device.

The creative pyramid and the format elements come together in creating effective print ads. The headline carries the attention step; the subhead and lead-in paragraph hold the interest; and the interior paragraphs, the trial close, and close of body copy contain the credibility and desire steps. The action step takes place with the last line of copy or with the logo, slogan, and signature block.

In electronic media, copy is normally spoken dialogue that is prepared using a script; it is referred to as the audio portion of the commercial. The copy may be delivered as a voice-over by an unseen announcer or on camera by an announcer, spokesperson, or actor.

Radio commercials must be intrusive to catch and hold the attention of people who are usually doing something else. Radio copy must be more conversational than print copy and should paint word pictures for listeners to see in their mind's eye.

Television copywriters use scripts and storyboards to communicate the verbal and nonverbal ideas of a commercial. When writing TV ads, the creative team must strive for credibility, relevance, and consistency in tone. While TV commercials should be entertaining, the entertainment should not interfere with the selling message.

In radio and TV advertising, art plays an important role. Art includes concept development, character definition, set and scene design, costuming, lighting, scripting, camera angles—everything having to do with the visual value of the commercial.

Common formats for radio and TV commercials include straight announcement, presenter, testimonial, demonstration, musical, slice of life, lifestyle, and animation. The art director works with a writer to develop the artistic qualities of the big idea, the format, and the storyboard. The storyboard, the basic rough design of a TV commercial, contains sketches of the scenes along with the script. To supplement the storyboard and pretest a commercial, an animatic may be used.

The Internet presents a new challenge for artists and copywriters. People do not read a Web site in the same way as they read a print ad; they scan it. Web sites must be concise yet comprehensive, objective in style, and interactive.

When creating ads for international markets, advertisers must consider the variations in language and the legal restrictions imposed by foreign governments or cultures. Art direction for international markets requires an in-depth knowledge of the foreign culture. Even if the verbal message translates well, the icons and images may not.

Key Terms

animatic, 258
animation, 257
audio, 251
Ayer No. 1, 238
benefit headline, 247
body copy, 248
boldface, 248
camera-ready art, 237
close, 250
command headline, 247
comprehensive layout (comp), 237
demonstration, 256
design, 235
device copy, 249
dialogue/monologue copy, 249
dummy, 237
headline, 244
icon, 262
illustrators, 242
institutional copy, 248
integrated commercial, 255
interior paragraphs, 250

italic, 248
jingle, 256
kicker, 248
layout, 235
lead-in paragraph, 250
lifestyle technique, 257
logotype (logo), 250
mechanical, 237
mnemonic device, 256
musical commercial, 256
narrative copy, 248
news/information headline, 247
on camera, 255
pasteup, 237
photographers, 242
picture-caption copy, 249
picture-window layout, 238
poster-style format, 238
presenter commercial, 255
provocative headline, 247
question headline, 247

radio personality, 256
rough, 237
script, 251
seal, 250
signature, 250
slice of life, 256
slogan, 250
sound effects (SFX), 251
storyboard, 258
storyboard roughs, 254
straight announcement, 255
straight-sell copy, 248
subhead, 247
tagline, 250
testimonial, 256
text, 248
themeline, 250
thumbnail, 236
trial close, 250
visuals, 242
voice-over, 255

Review Questions

1. What is a layout? What purposes does it serve in the process of print ad development, approval, and production?
2. What are the benefits of preparing a rough layout prior to generating a comp?
3. Describe the various types of headlines.
4. Which print ad design formats tend to achieve the highest recall scores? Why do you think that is the case?
5. In what order do prospects typically view the elements of a print ad?
6. Correlate the key format elements of a print ad with the steps on the creative pyramid.
7. What is a storyboard, and what is its role?
8. How is an animatic created? Why would an ad agency recommend testing an animatic rather than a finished commercial?
9. Why are there different guidelines for writing for the Web than for traditional print advertising?
10. What guidelines should advertisers use in selecting translators for international advertising?

Exploring Advertising

1. Find a newspaper or magazine ad with a headline that you don't think is very effective. Rewrite the headline. What classification of headline did you choose? Explain the reasons for the changes that you made.
2. Find examples of print ads that use three of the standard subjects for the visual focus of the ads. Explain why you believe the art director chose that visual focus.
3. On a print ad, identify all of the key format elements and describe what classification or style of each element was used. Indicate which element you believe is the focal point and what path your eye takes when it first views the ad.
4. Critique a print ad based on the Checklist: "Writing Effective Copy." Give the ad a grade for each of the points and explain why you assigned that grade. Repeat this exercise for radio and television, using the appropriate checklists.
5. Go to www.freetranslations.com and translate a common slang term or advertising tagline from English to one of the languages offered. Then take the result and translate it back to English. Could you have used the translation in your client's advertising?
6. Print the home page for a Web site of your choosing. Explain which elements you believe work particularly well and which ones do not.

chapter ten

Producing Ads for Print, Electronic, and Digital Media

Objectives

To present an overview of how ads and commercials are produced for print, electronic, and digital media. With their dynamic effect on the production process, computers now give advertisers many more options for saving money and time and enhancing production quality. But to control cost and quality, advertisers still need a basic knowledge of the processes and methods used in printing and broadcasting as well as in the new digital media.

After studying this chapter, you will be able to:

* **Explain** the development process for print ads and brochures from initial concept through final production.

* **Discuss** how materials for printing are prepared for the press.

* **Explain** the development process for radio and TV commercials from initial concept through final production.

* **Describe** the major production techniques for TV commercials.

* **Understand** ways to save money in print, radio, and television production.

* **Explain** the major types of digital media and their evolving role in advertising.

For a client as big and powerful as Toyota, choosing an agency to collaborate with on a global campaign for Prius, its brand-new, technologically superior hybrid car, was a monumental project unto itself. Hundreds of agencies would have loved to handle the account, but the competition was limited to the client's roster agencies, meaning that bidding was open only to firms that already worked for Toyota.

That meant that the offices of Saatchi & Saatchi, which has more than 100 branches in 85 countries, and a handful of other agencies around the world would be competing for the account. Saatchi & Saatchi looked like the favorite, but the question was which Saatchi office would be assigned the responsibility of creating and overseeing the project.

In offices around the world, teams of copywriters and creative directors produced and discarded countless concepts. Finally, each agency selected one or several of their best ideas. They presented their work to the client and then crossed their fingers. The winning agency would produce local and international print ads and create and develop a global TV spot—one that would be translated into dozens of different languages and aired all over the world.

Saatchi & Saatchi Los Angeles already handled U.S. advertising for Toyota, a major American account. In fact, it was the largest advertising account west of the Mississippi River. Naturally, the agency wanted the assignment, but it wasn't a slam-dunk. It was up against some of the biggest agencies in the world and was even forced to compete with many of their own offices, some of which—London, Paris, New York—were famous for their outstanding creativity.

It didn't hurt that the Prius was the kind of car the agency could really get behind. With little to no advertising, the previous limited-production model had already become the leader in its field. Equipped with Bluetooth technology, low emission rates, and fantastic fuel economy, this sleek hybrid was already a favorite among environmentally conscious consumers and the Hollywood set. Now that Toyota was rolling the car out globally, Saatchi knew that to win the campaign it would have to speak to a new segment of the market.

There were ample challenges. Saatchi wanted to create a campaign for the Prius that would be broad enough to appeal to a wide audience, regardless of national and cultural differences, but that would still be specific enough to truly speak to the buyer. Two creative directors, Max Godsil and Doug Van Andel, were assigned the project in Los Angeles. They spent hours, days, and weeks reviewing the research and analyzing the markets. They started developing ideas, and more ideas, and then even more. After about 30 tries, they hit upon a concept that was complex but friendly, futuristic but warm, and clean without being clinical.

They brought their concept to Saatchi's senior creative director, Steve Rabosky, and he concurred. They were confident that this was the idea that would win the account, and they were right. Toyota Japan awarded the global introduction of the Prius to Saatchi & Saatchi Los Angeles.[1]

A few months later, when Toyota asked them to cut back on the advertising, they knew for certain that they had done something right. There simply weren't enough cars to meet the growing demand. In this chapter, we'll see what they did and study how they did it.

Managing the Advertising Production Process

The average reader has little idea of the intricate technical stages that ads go through from start to finish. But experienced advertising people do, especially art directors, designers, print production managers, and producers. They know it's the details that give an ad added impact and completeness. Since careful management is the key to success in producing advertising, we'll discuss some of the management issues before examining the details of the production processes.

The Role of the Production Manager or Producer

Every ad or commercial represents the completion of a highly complex process that includes many steps, such as the reproduction of visuals in full color, the shooting and editing of scenes, the precise specification and placement of type, and the checking, approving, duplicating, and shipping of final art, negatives, tape, or film to various communications media (newspapers, magazines, radio and TV stations, and even Web publishers).

These tasks are usually the responsibility of a **print production manager** or, for electronic media, a **producer.** The overall responsibility of this manager is to keep the project moving smoothly and under budget, while maintaining the required level of quality through every step of the production process.

While a national ad like this one for Toyota's Prius may require only 15 seconds to read, what most people don't realize is that, from initial concept to completion, an ad of this caliber may require three weeks to a month, or even longer, to create. As ideas are born and discarded and then meticulously crafted into a finished work, an advertisement passes through many hands before it is finally ready to make its first public appearance.

Essentially, production managers and producers perform the four classic functions of management: *planning, organizing, directing,* and *controlling.* At Saatchi, for example, Johanna Leovey was the print producer. Her job was to review the conceptual art and then plan which production process to use to fulfill each requirement. Next she organized the tasks and established priorities in order to meet the client's media schedule. She then directed the production staff in completing each section of the art. Finally, to perform the *control* function—essential for optimizing quality, economy, and speed—she carefully reviewed the work of each staffer and subcontractor and solicited feedback from her supervisor and the art director, just to be sure they were all on the same track.

Planning and Organizing

An important facet of management is the *allocation of time.* Each phase of a project comprises many tasks, so the production manager must anticipate where irregularities may occur within each phase.

Directing and Controlling

Supervising the production staff and suppliers is another challenge. If artists fail to follow the art director's design correctly, they can kill an ad's power, beauty, and effectiveness. Improper printing processes, papers, or inks can also weaken the impact of the image, increase costs, and even lead to time-consuming reprinting. Print production managers can lose tens of thousands of their client's or agency's dollars (and sometimes their jobs) by forgetting to double-check the details of print production and the work of the production staff.

The producer also has to keep up with all the technological changes occurring in print and electronic production, including the emerging forms of *digital media* (multimedia, interactive media, and online networks). And because virtually all ad agency employees now use computers, the manager must also understand how computers serve the production process and which software programs offer the best results.[2]

Managing Production Costs

When Saatchi began working on the Prius campaign, it submitted an estimate for anticipated production costs, including computer artwork and subcontracted work such as photography, reproduction services, and delivery. When Johanna Leovey received the approved ad concepts a couple of weeks later, it was understood that she would make every effort to keep the actual costs below the estimate.

A good production manager continually monitors the time spent on a job and the charges submitted by outside suppliers so as to not exceed the budget.

Common Budget Busters

There are five problems that commonly break budgets. The most frequent cause of cost overruns is inadequate planning and lack of preparation. Another culprit is production luxuries. When the creative director wants to reward the staff by taking everyone to lunch at the company's expense, the first question should be: Was money budgeted for this? The third budget buster is overtime: night and weekend work. Whenever possible, managers should develop alternative plans to avoid overtime hours. Special equipment for unusual production effects can also wreak havoc on budgets. It's often far more expensive to use an exotic computer gizmo than standard equipment. Finally, a complex hierarchy of decision makers, approvers, and lawyers can stall decision making, cause negative debate, and stop progress.

Some other budget issues are unique to each medium.

Managing the Cost of Print Production

The term **print production** refers to the systematic process an approved design goes through from concept to final publication in a printed medium such as magazines, newspapers, or collateral materials like brochures and direct-mail packages.

For print media, production managers must translate the rough or comprehensive design into a final assembly of black-and-white artwork called a *mechanical* or *pasteup*. Then, working with an engraver or printer, they make sure the mechanical is converted into a correct set of negatives for the printer to use to make printing plates.

A big cost factor in the production of many print ads is the *engraver* that provides all the color separations, retouching, press proofs, and digital files. Paper costs affect budgets, too. When agencies place ads in print media, the cost of paper is included in the charge for the ad. They don't notice this pass-along cost. But when an agency prints collateral materials such as data sheets, brochures, or packaging for a client, the cost of paper is noticeable.

For the Prius campaign, Saatchi assembled a teaser promo to send to car shows and dealers, designed to create interest in the Prius before the rest of the promotional material came out. It was encased in an elegant, origami-style pocket made of vellum paper. Among other things, Saatchi included a small flyer made of coarse, toothed paper embedded with seeds. The copy read: "Hybrid Synergy Drive: Sometimes the seeds of change are brilliantly designed as a car. Or in this case, a card." The recipient simply planted the piece of paper and could expect the seeds to come into bud.

Managing the Cost of Electronic Production

The term **electronic production** refers to the process of converting a script or storyboard to a finished commercial for use on radio, TV, or digital media. While the overall process is similar to print production, the technical details and the costs of electronic production are quite different. And the end result, rather than print film or negatives, may be audio or videotape, motion picture film, or some digital format such as CD-ROM or DVD.

Radio Radio is the least expensive electronic medium to produce because it deals only with the dimension of sound. There's no need for hairstylists, makeup artists, or cue-card holders. And commercials are duplicated on inexpensive audiotape.

The primary control factors in producing radio spots, therefore, are the costs of talent and music. Celebrity talent can be very expensive. But even the cost of standard union talent, paid at **scale** (the regular charge agreed to in the union contract), can mount rapidly if there are multiple voices or if the commercial is aired in many markets or for an extended period of time. The advertiser, for example, may initially contract for a four-week or a thirteen-week run. If the commercial is extended beyond that time, the advertiser will have to pay a **residual fee** to the talent.

Likewise, the cost of original music (composing, scoring, and orchestration) can range from very inexpensive to frightful, depending on the talent and scope of use. For this reason, many clients—especially small local and regional advertisers—prefer to use prerecorded **stock music** available for commercial use from a studio or radio station.

Television In 2003, the average cost of producing a 30-second national television spot was $372,000.[3] Numerous factors can increase TV production budgets. They include the use of children and animals, superstar talent and directors, large casts, animation, special effects, stop-motion photography, use of both location and studio shooting for one commercial, expensive set decoration or construction, additional shooting days, and major script changes during a shoot.[4] Commercial producers have to be aware of all these factors and plan for them very carefully.

There is a belief in the industry that high-priced celebrity talent and extravagant effects get attention and increase memorability. It turns out that's not always true. A recent study showed that advertising that features a brand differentiation message along with a demonstration of the product is actually more effective and costs on average 28 percent less to produce. The study further indicated that advertisers sometimes use lavish production values to compensate for having nothing to say.[5]

Digital media The computer has engendered a whole new class of digital media. This has dramatically increased the importance of the tasks performed by the agency producer and creative staff and made it critical for them to stay current with new recording and duplicating processes as well as special-effects technology.

From airport check-in to grocery check-out, consumers have become accustomed to the self-service touch screens and credit card readers on digital **kiosks.** Agencies are busy preparing digital presentations for kiosks, which often automatically present the customer with options to upgrade or add on to their orders: the self-service grocery checkstand asks if you need ice, and the kiosk at the airport may feature tickets to attractions in your destination city.[6]

Some ads are totally created by computers for use on computers—electronic images and text designed for transmission around the world via the Internet. For this service, most production managers subcontract the work. Saatchi & Saatchi, for instance, has a special design and interactive media group that creates advertising for Toyota and other clients.[7] The Prius campaign included many interactive components, including an in-depth look at the vehicle via the Toyota Web site (**www.toyota.com/prius**).

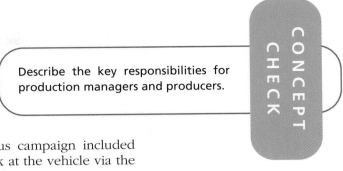

Describe the key responsibilities for production managers and producers.

CONCEPT CHECK

The overall production process for creating images, graphic design, texts, and interactive digital programs for various electronic media is similar to working in print. Final output, though, is to a medium suitable for electronic storage and transmission.

The Print Production Process

Once Toyota's advertising managers gave the go-ahead on the Prius ad concept, Johanna Leovey could turn her full attention to it. The process she used was the same as for any other print job, whether a brochure, a poster, or a direct-mail piece. Her goal is always the same—to produce the job as closely as possible to the concept intended by the creative team.

The **print production process** consists of four major phases: *preproduction, production, prepress,* and *printing and distribution.* For a simple model of this process, see Exhibit 10–1 (a more detailed version appears in RL 10–1 in the Reference Library on the *Essentials of Contemporary Advertising* Web site).

The Preproduction Phase: Planning the Project

The first step, **preproduction,** begins when the creative department submits the approved creative concepts—rough or comprehensive layout and copy—to the production department. The production manager's first task is to communicate with the agency's traffic manager and log the project into the department's *traffic system.* Together they will open a **job jacket** for storing the various pieces of artwork and ideas that will be generated throughout the process, and then they will examine the general nature of the job and consider several questions pertinent to managing it efficiently. For example,

- What equipment will be needed?
- How will we get it? (Will we have to lease another machine?)
- What materials are necessary? (If this is a packaging job, what material will we be printing on: tin, paper, cardboard?)
- What human resources are needed? (Do we need to hire any freelancers like photographers or illustrators?)
- Will there be any special expenses associated with the job? (Do we need to do location photography, for example, or use the specialized services of a food designer?)

Exhibit 10–1

The print production process.

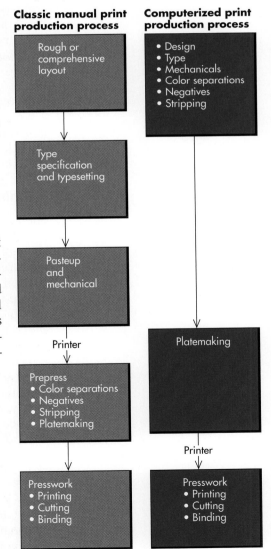

Classic manual print production process

Rough or comprehensive layout

↓

Type specification and typesetting

↓

Pasteup and mechanical

↓ Printer

Prepress
• Color separations
• Negatives
• Stripping
• Platemaking

↓

Presswork
• Printing
• Cutting
• Binding

Computerized print production process

• Design
• Type
• Mechanicals
• Color separations
• Negatives
• Stripping

↓

Platemaking

↓ Printer

Presswork
• Printing
• Cutting
• Binding

- How many production artists will be needed? (Is the deadline so near that we'll have to call up the reserves?)

Once these general questions are answered, the production manager can look more closely at the specific needs of the project.

Working backward from publication **closing dates** (deadlines), the traffic and production managers decide when each step of the work must be completed. Deadlines can vary from hours to months. The manager tries to build extra time into each step because every word, art element, and aesthetic choice may need some last-minute change. The traffic manager's job is to make sure deadlines are not missed and that all the proper approvals are obtained in a timely fashion. The team at Saatchi & Saatchi was given a prototype of the Prius for a total of only five days. In this time they were required to photograph the vehicle for use in all of the print ads, collateral work, as well as several 15-second spots used in their prelaunch campaign.

Typography

Art directors select type styles to enhance the desired personality of the product and complement the tone of the ad. Typefaces affect an ad's appearance, design, and readability. Good type selection can't compensate for a weak headline, poor body copy, or an inappropriate illustration, but it can create interest and attract readers.

It is imperative that production managers as well as graphic artists understand **typography,** the art of selecting and setting type. They should consider four important concepts when selecting type: *readability, appropriateness, harmony or appearance,* and *emphasis.* Commercial Break 10–A, "The Characteristics of Type," describes these and other type-related topics.

To make their ads unique and exclusive, some advertisers even commission a new type design. Other companies tailor their typography to blend with the magazines or newspapers their advertising appears in. This gives the ad an editorial look and, the advertiser hopes, enhanced credibility (or at least interest). For consistency, Saatchi & Saatchi uses a particular type style in all Toyota ads.

Planning the Job

The overall purpose of the preproduction phase is to plan the job thoroughly, which usually entails making a number of strategic choices before launching into full production. For example, since the art director's conceptual rough layouts are often made with marker colors that do not match printing inks, the production manager should consult with the art director to formally select a color palette in advance, using a color guide such as the PANTONE® system.

For brochures, there is also the question of which printing process and which type of printing press to use for the job (see RL 10–3, Choosing the Best Method of Printing, in the Reference Library on the *Essentials of Contemporary Advertising* Web site). This will affect the budget and dictate how art is to be prepared in the production and prepress phases.

Finally, the production manager must decide early which is most important for a particular project: *speed, quality,* or *economy.* Typically, the manager must sacrifice one in favor of the other two. The answer determines the production methods used and the personnel employed. Once all these decisions are made, the manager can begin the production phase.

The Production Phase: Creating the Artwork

Essentially, the **production phase** involves completing ancillary functions such as illustration or photography, setting up the artwork and typesetting, and then melding all these components into a final tangible form for the printer or publisher.

Creating the Visual

Almost every ad has some kind of a visual besides typography. And many ads have several pictures. The visual may be an illustration or a photograph or even a combination of the two. But where do these pictures come from?

When reviewing the layout with the art director, the decision will be made whether to use illustration or photography and how to get the pictures the creatives envisioned. In many cases, to save the client money, the art director or producer will choose to purchase one or more pictures from a stock photography house for a reasonable licensing fee. The fee will typically be based on the intended use and the length of time the use will continue.

Most expensive is commissioning an illustrator to draw an original picture or hiring a photographer to go on location to shoot a specific visual, especially if it's out of town. For photography, there are several important considerations, the first being who to use. That depends on the style of photograph desired. Some photographers are well-versed in photojournalistic techniques. Others are especially good at shooting interiors. And some specialize in food or fashion photography.

Other considerations include any special equipment, props, or sets that will be needed. In the case of the print work for the Prius ad, the creative team worked in a studio, photographing the car against a white backdrop. Later, they completed the image by adding visuals and text.

Artists prepare mechanicals electronically on computers or by pasting artwork and type onto artboards.

Preparing Mechanicals

The **mechanical** is the camera-ready pasteup of the artwork. It includes type, photos, and line art, all attached to an art board. To create the mechanical for an ad, brochure, or package, the production artist normally begins by marking out a grid on which to lay the type and art. Artists used to do this by hand on a piece of artboard in light-blue pencil. Today, pagemaking computer software does this with commands for setting up columns and guides. The grid provides an underlying consistency to the spacing and design of the piece.

The production artist then specifies the style and size of the typefaces for the text and inputs this information, along with the copy, into the computer. The type may be positioned electronically, or it may be output onto paper and glued onto an artboard within the image area.

When an additional color is to be printed, a second artboard marked to the same dimensions is used for the second image. The second image may be glued onto a clear plastic **overlay** that lies on top of the first image (called the **base art**). The production artist places crossmarks in the corners of the base art and then superimposes crossmarks on the transparent overlay precisely over those on the base art. This registers the exact position of the two layers of art in relation to one another.

The art elements must be properly positioned in the artwork (whether mechanical or computer generated) because the printer needs to have layers of art that can be reproduced individually. The total image is then constructed as each layer is printed over the previous one. Because the printer must photograph each layer to make separate plates, this kind of artwork is called **camera-ready art.**

Camera-Ready Art and Halftones

Production art for the printing process is like an on/off switch: Where the art is black, ink will stick; where the art is white, ink won't stick. The production artist adheres to this printing principle by using *line art* and *halftones*.

The Characteristics of Type

Readability

The most important consideration in selecting a typeface is readability. As David Ogilvy said, good typography helps people read; bad typography prevents them from doing so. General factors that contribute to readability include the type's style, boldness, and size; the length of the line; and the spacing between words, lines, and paragraphs. An ad is meant to be read, and reduced readability kills interest. Difficult-to-read typefaces should be used infrequently and only to create special effects.

Large, bold, simply designed typefaces are the easiest to read. However, the amount of space in the ad and the amount of copy that must be written limit the use of these type forms. The length of the line of copy can also affect the readability. Newspaper columns are usually less than two inches wide; magazine columns slightly wider. For readability, columns of copy should be less than three inches wide.

Spacing between lines also influences an ad's readability. Space between lines of type allows for descenders (the part of the letter that extends downward, as in the letters j, g, p) and ascenders (the part of the letter that extends upward, as in the letters b, d, k). When this is the only space between lines, type is said to be "set solid." Sometimes an art director adds extra space between lines (called **leading,** pronounced "ledding") to give a more "airy" feeling to the copy. The name comes from the thin lead strips that used to be inserted between lines of metal type.

Kerning (the space between letters) also affects an ad's appearance and readability. The narrower the kerning, the more type can fit into the available space. Narrow kerning is effective in headlines because people read large type faster when the letters are close together. But narrow kerning is hard to read if overdone, especially in smaller type sizes.

Appropriateness

A typeface must be appropriate to the product being advertised. Each typeface and size conveys a mood and feeling quite apart from the meanings of the words themselves. One typeface whispers "luxury," another screams "bargain!" A typeface that looks old-fashioned is probably inappropriate for a digital watch.

Harmony/Appearance

Advertising novices often mix too many typefaces, creating disharmony and clutter. Type should harmonize with the other elements of an ad, including the illustration and layout. Skilled artists often choose typefaces in the same family or faces that are closely related in appearance.

Emphasis

Contrast creates emphasis. Artists often use more than one type style or mix italic and roman, small and large type, lowercase and uppercase. But they must be careful not to emphasize every element or they won't emphasize any.

Classes of Type

Two classes of type are used in advertising.

Display type is larger and heavier than text type; useful in headlines, subheads, logos, and addresses, and for emphasis.

Text type is smaller and finer, used in body copy.

Type Groups

Serif (roman) type is the most popular type group due to its readability and warm personality. It is distinguished by small lines or tails called serifs that finish the ends of the main strokes and by variations in the thickness of the strokes. It comes in a wide variety of designs and sizes.
Sans serif (gothic) type is the second most popular type

Roman type	Square serif type
Typography	Typography
Typography	
Typography	Script type
Typography	*Typography*
	Typography
Sans serif type	
Typography	Ornamental type
Typography	Typography
TYPOGRAPHY	Typography

a.

Line art Any artwork or type that is comprised of a solid color, such as black, is called **line art.** There are no shades of gray or shades of any other color. Line art can be printed with line plates.

Halftones Most photographs and some drawings contain images with **continuous tones,** such as shades of gray. However, printing presses cannot print

group; it is also referred to as block or contemporary. Characterized by lack of serifs (*sans* is French for *without*) and relatively uniform thickness of the strokes, it is not as readable as roman but is widely used because the simple, clean lines give a slick, modern appearance (see **a**).

Square serif type combines sans serif and serif typefaces. It has serifs, but letter strokes have uniform thickness.

Cursive or script type resembles handwriting; letters often connect and may convey a feeling of femininity, formality, classicism, or beauty. It is difficult to read and is used primarily in headlines, formal announcements, and cosmetic and fashion ads.

Ornamental type uses novel designs with a high level of embellishment and decorativeness. It adds a "special effects" quality but is often difficult to read.

Type Families

A **type family** is made up of related typefaces. The serif typeface used for the text of this book is called Garamond. Within a family, the basic design remains the same but varies in the proportion, weight, and slant of the characters. The type may be light, medium, bold, extra bold, condensed, extended, or italic. Variations enable the typographer to provide contrast and emphasis without changing the family (see **b**).

A **font** is a complete assortment of capitals, small capitals, lowercase letters, numerals, and punctuation marks for a particular typeface and size.

Measuring Type

Type characters have height, width, weight, and, for some ornamental typefaces, depth. They also come in shapes called a case.

Size is the height of a character (or letter) measured in **points** (72 points to the inch) from the bottom of the descenders to the top of the ascenders (see **c**).

The width of a letter, known as an em space, is usually based on the maximum width and proportions of the capital letter M for that particular typeface. The width of the letter N is called an en space.

Capital letters are uppercase, small letters lowercase (in the days of manual typesetting, the case containing the capital letters was stored above the one with the small letters). It's easiest to read a combination of uppercase and lowercase. Type may be set in all caps (for emphasis) or in commoncase (caps and small caps).

Applying the Breaks

Use the various figures and terms in this Commercial Break to answer the following:

1. Describe the class, group, family, and size of the type used in the title "Producing Ads for Print, Electronic, and Digital Media," which appears on the first page of this chapter.

2. Do the same for the captions that appear in the exhibits in this book.

Garamond Book	Garamond Condensed Book
Garamond Book Italic	*Garamond Condensed Book Italic*
Garamond Bold	**Garamond Condensed Bold**
Garamond Bold Italic	***Garamond Condensed Bold Italic***
Garamond Light	Garamond Condensed Light
Garamond Light Italic	*Garamond Condensed Light Italic*
Garamond Ultra	**Garamond Condensed Ultra**
Garamond Ultra Italic	***Garamond Condensed Ultra Italic***

b.

Text type	Display type
6 pt. Type size	16 pt. Type size
8 pt. Type size	18 pt. Type size
9 pt. Type size	20 pt. Type size
10 pt. Type size	24 pt. Type size
12 pt. Type size	30 pt. Type size
14 pt. Type size	36 pt. Type size

c.

gray—just black or white. Continuous-tone artwork must therefore be broken up into dots, by shooting it through a *halftone screen*. The combination of dots, when printed, produces a **halftone,** an optical illusion of shading, as in a photo. In the dark areas of the image, large dots bump into each other and make the paper appear nearly black. In the gray areas, smaller black dots allow more of the white paper to show through; in the white areas, tiny black dots are

A halftone screen breaks up continuous-tone artwork into tiny dots. The combination of printed dots produces an optical illusion of shading, as in a photograph. The color dots show the separation for the color photo above. The other set of dots shows the range that would appear in a black-and-white photo.

surrounded by a lot of white or are completely missing. The human eye perceives the dots as gradations of tone.

The fineness of the halftone screen determines the quality of the illusion. Glossy magazine ads are printed with halftone screens as fine as 200 lines per inch (lpi), while newspaper photos appear very coarse at 80 to 100 lpi. Coarser screens are used to print on coarse, ink-absorbent paper (like newsprint) because the ink spreads when it hits the paper and fills in the white areas. Fine-quality, glossy magazine paper can take fine-screen halftones because the surface doesn't let the ink spread into the white areas. The dots in a coarse screen can be seen quite easily with the naked eye.

The artist's final step is to mark any halftones and line art for size and indicate where they should be placed. The artist simply sticks a photocopy of the visual to the artboard in its exact location with the letters FPO (for position only) written across the image. That way the printer doesn't think this is the actual final art.

The Prepress Phase: Stripping, Negs, and Plates

When Saatchi & Saatchi completed all the production for the Prius ad on its computers, the next step was to get the finished artwork ready for the press.

In the **prepress phase,** the printer makes plates from the mechanical. The various elements of the ad are converted into film negatives, which are carefully mounted together in perfect registration—through a process known as **stripping**—onto opaque plastic sheets called **flats.** A completed flat is a mask that allows light to pass through only where lines and dots are to appear on the plate. The flat is pressed against the printing plate, and ultraviolet light exposes the plate's photosensitive emulsion. Once exposed, the emulsion is developed, etching the plate in the process. This leaves some areas of the plate capable of holding ink and others unable to do so. Once dry, the plates are "hung" on the press, ready for printing.

New digital solutions allow printers to go directly from "computer to plate," eliminating labor-intensive, complex, and costly steps required in the conventional prepress process.

Special screens lend an artistic look to photos. Whether the screens use lines, scratches, or some other technique, they work on the same principle as the halftone dot screen.

Two-color texture   Random line

Mezzo tint   Wavy line (dry brush)

Printing in Color

A printing plate can print only one color at a time. An advertiser who wants to print an ad or a brochure in blue, green, and black needs three different plates (one for each color), and the job is referred to as a three-color job. To print in full color, though, the **four-color process** is used. This process can simulate nearly all colors by combining the four primary colors: *process blue* (cyan), *process yellow, process magenta,* and *black* (which provides greater detail and density as well as shades of gray). In the parlance of the trade, this is also called **CYMK printing,** the K standing for black. To print in full color, therefore, the printer prepares four different printing plates—one for each process color plus black.

Designs that don't need full color are printed in blended inks rather than process colors. For example, it would take two process colors (magenta and yellow) to make red or three process colors (magenta, yellow, and cyan) to make burgundy. To print a brochure in black and burgundy, it's cheaper to use only those two ink colors rather than black plus three process colors.

A PANTONE® color, one of a spectrum of colors that makes up the **PANTONE Matching System® (PMS),** is a single ink premixed according to a formula and given a specific color number. The PANTONE swatch book features more than 1,000 colors in solid and screened blocks printed on different paper finishes.[8]

Four-Color Separations

Four separate halftone negatives are needed to make a set of four-color plates: one each for cyan, yellow, magenta, and black. Each of the resulting negatives appears in black and white, and the set is called the **color separation.** In printing, the process color inks are translucent, so two or three colors can overlap to create another color. For example, red is reproduced by overlapping yellow and magenta dots (see Exhibit 10–2(e)).

Until recently, most color separations were done using a photographic process. Today, sophisticated electronic scanning systems can produce four-color separations and screens in one process. And all this can be accomplished in minutes instead of the hours or days previously needed for camera work and hand etching.

Regardless of the separation method used, when properly printed, tiny clusters of halftone dots in various colors, sizes, and shapes give the eye the illusion of seeing the colors of the original photograph or painting.

The Duplication and Distribution Phase: Printing, Binding, and Shipping

The last phase of the print production process involves the actual printing, proofing, and finishing steps of drying, cutting, binding, and shipping.

Several printing processes are available—letterpress, offset, rotogravure, flexography—the choice largely dependent on the type of surface being printed, the quality required, and the size of the job. However, all of the processes involve applying ink to a plate and then transferring the inked impression to the paper (or some other surface).

The Press Run

Once the paper, plates, and ink are readied, the press is started and stopped a few times to adjust the image's alignment on the paper. In multicolored printing, proper alignment of all the colors is critical. When the initial proofs show good alignment, the presses are started again and gradually sped up to maximum output.

Finishing

Once all the pieces are printed, the ink must dry. Then the excess paper is cut away using huge cutting machines. Depending on the nature of the job, the pieces may be delivered to special subcontractors who emboss or die-cut or perform other special techniques to enhance the final printed piece. The final stop may be the bindery for two- and three-hole drilling, wire stapling, and folding.

> **CONCEPT CHECK**
>
> What tasks are accomplished and what decisions are made during each phase of the print production process?

(a)

(b)

(c)

(d)

(e)

(f)

Exhibit 10–2

Four-color ads are created by combining translucent inks from four printing plates. Here we show the separation of four-color artwork into its (a) yellow, (b) magenta, and (c) cyan components. When these three process colors are combined with (d) the fourth color (black) on the printing press, the resulting ad will closely resemble (f) the original artwork.

Quality Control in Print Production

At various stages of the print production process, the production manager needs to verify the quality. Artwork for a newspaper or magazine ad, for example, must be camera-ready. Many agencies now just send a disk, and the publisher converts the computer image to negatives. Magazines provide specific instructions and measurements for each ad size they offer.

Finally, the production manager must check all proofs for errors and obtain approvals from agency and client executives before releasing ads to publications or artwork to printers. Proofing is a time-consuming task made more so by the fact that not everyone is available when the work is ready for approval.

For the production process to run smoothly, everyone concerned must understand the procedure. The later in the process errors are discovered, the more expensive they are to fix. Changing a single comma may cost as much as $50 after copy is typeset, or $500 once negatives are made, or $5,000 if the job is already printed.[9]

Production Phase Quality Issues

The task of quality control really begins in the production phase. Proofs of the production art, with all its type and images, must be carefully inspected for misspellings, mismeasured lines, improperly sized images, misplaced cropmarks, or a myriad of other minutiae that could lead to a problem later.

Prepress Quality Issues

The slightest flaw in the final printed piece can have serious repercussions. The production manager must check and double-check, even triple-check, the film negatives before they're sent off to a magazine. An analog or digital proof (described below) of the negatives should be carefully checked and sent with the negatives.

Ways to Proof Print Production

When printing collateral materials or projects like brochures, the production manager will typically see a blueline, color key, analog or digital proof, and press proof from the printer.

Blueline proof A **blueline** is a proof that is created by shining light through the negatives and exposing a light-sensitive paper that turns from white to blue. The blueline helps reveal scratches and flaws in the negatives as well as any assembly errors, such as a reversed illustration. The blueline is usually trimmed, folded, and stapled like the final product to check if the crop and fold marks have been properly registered.

Color keys and analog or digital proofs The **analog proof** (also called a **Chromalin**) uses a series of four very thin sheets of plastic pressed together. Each layer's light-sensitive emulsion turns one of the process colors when exposed to certain wavelengths of light. Together they form a full, four-color image proof. The **color key** is a less expensive form of the Chromalin with relatively thick plastic sheets that can be lifted up. The most recent innovation is the **digital proof** (also called an *Iris*). It uses ink-jet technology and offers accuracy as well as lower cost and faster turnaround time.[10]

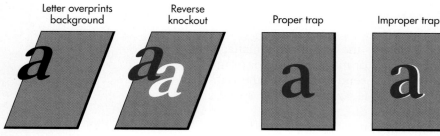

| Letter overprints background | Reverse knockout | Proper trap | Improper trap |

Exhibit 10–3

Black ink can overprint a background color (far left). However, art or text printed in a color other than black should have no background color underneath. For example, if a green letter "a" appears on an orange field, a white reverse knockout will keep the green from being affected by the orange (second from left). If the green letter and the reverse knockout aren't properly aligned or the green letter is smaller than the white knockout, the letters will not trap, and white paper will show between the two colors (far right).

Press proof When the presses begin printing, the press operator "pulls" a few proofs to align the press and check ink densities. At this time the production manager should sign one of these actual **press proofs** as a guide for the operator to follow and for the agency's protection if something goes wrong later during the printing process.

What to Look for in a Proof

When checking proofs, production managers and art directors look for any scratches, minute holes or dots, blemishes, or unevenness of ink coverage. Using a *loupe* (magnifying glass), they inspect the dot pattern in halftones to make sure the registration of color is perfectly tight. Then they check *traps* and *bleeds*.

Traps A **trap** occurs where the edge of one color or shade overlaps its neighbor by a fraction of an inch to make sure the white paper underneath doesn't show through (see Exhibit 10–3).

To save money and avoid trapping problems, designers often plan for the typesetting to *overprint* (print on top of) the background color with black ink. But when colored type is printed over a different background color, the background color must let white show to avoid distorting the true color of the colored type. This **reverse knockout** requires careful trapping.

For full-color ads, it's often wise to print text in black ink. When ads or brochures are reprinted, advertisers often make type changes. If all the text is black, the advertiser needs only to change the black negative and plate. If the text is any other color, all the negatives, stripping, and plating will have to be changed.

Bleeds Finally, designers also need to consider **bleeds**—colors, type, or visuals that run all the way to the edge of the page. Production artists must set up their artwork for at least a quarter inch of extra color *outside* the image area to accommodate variations in the printing and cutting processes.

> **CONCEPT CHECK**
>
> Discuss some of the problems that can be detected in the production phase of the print production process.

The Radio Commercial Production Process

Radio commercials, called **spots,** are among the quickest, simplest, and least expensive ads to produce. In fact, many radio stations provide production services free to local advertisers.

Some spots are delivered live by the announcer, in which case the station gets a script or highlight sheet and any recorded music to be used. The material must be accurately timed. A live commercial script should run about 130 to 150 words per minute so the announcer can speak at a normal, conversational pace. The best way to do this is to use a popular DJ and let him or her improvise. It's a lot more entertaining and links the DJ's credibility to the product.[11]

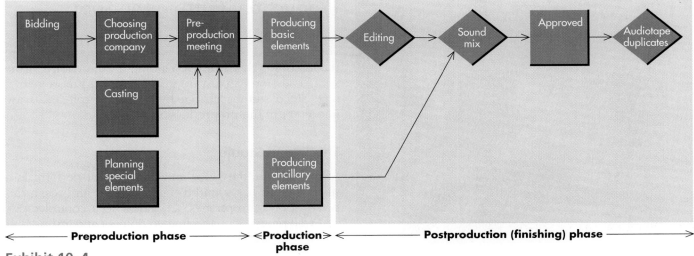

Exhibit 10–4

Radio commercials have three production phases. The preproduction and finishing phases are usually the most complex. Preproduction and postproduction editing and mixing typically require far more time than the actual recording session.

The disadvantages of live commercials are that announcers may be inconsistent in their delivery, and sound effects are quite limited. Uniform delivery requires a recorded commercial. The process of producing a recorded commercial includes *preproduction, production,* and *postproduction* (or finishing) phases (see Exhibit 10–4).

Preproduction

In the preproduction phase, the advertiser and agency perform a variety of tasks that allow production to run smoothly, on time, and within budget. The agency assigns a radio producer from its staff or hires a freelance producer. Based on the script, the producer selects a studio and a director, determines what talent will be needed, estimates costs, and prepares a budget for the advertiser's approval.

To control the production process and get the finest sound reproduction, most ad agencies use independent recording studios. The best audio studios have experienced sound directors and technicians, close ties to well-known talent, and the latest recording equipment.

During the preproduction phase, the producer (or a casting director) searches for the right talent. The advertiser and the agency consider several factors before arriving at a decision: the person's tone of voice, vocal acting skills and creativity, intelligence, style of thinking, and reputation. The unusual effect of Tom Bodett's vocal style for Motel 6, for instance, shows how valuable good talent can be. In just three years, Motel 6 went from near-bankruptcy to incredible profitability and became the largest chain of budget motels in the United States—using only radio and Bodett's folksy commercials ("We'll only charge you about 20 bucks and we'll leave the light on for you").

If the script calls for music, the producer decides whether to use prerecorded music or hire a composer and/or arranger. Any needed sound effects can be created or, most often, collected from prerecorded sources. All these decisions, of course, affect the budget, but they also have a dramatic impact on the effectiveness of the spots.

Once the talent is hired and music prepared, the **director** supervises rehearsals until everything is ready for recording.

A sophisticated audio console manipulates sound electronically, making sounds sharper or fuzzier, with more echo, or more treble or bass. Its multitrack mixing and sound enhancement capabilities are most useful during postproduction.

Production: Cutting the Spot

All of the elements to be used in the commercial—voices, music, sound effects—come together and are recorded at a **session.** Depending on the nature of the spot, a session can last from a half-hour to more than a day. Since studios charge by the hour, rehearsals are important in the preproduction phase.

The Sound Studio

At the session, the voice and music talent perform in a studio, which has sound-dampening wall surfaces, a carpeted floor, microphones, a window to a control room, and wall plugs for connecting equipment and instruments to the control room.

Standard items in the sound studio are microphones, headphones, and speakers. Announcers and singers wear headphones to hear instructions from the director in the control room or to monitor prerecorded instrumental tracks as they sing (keeping the music track from being recorded onto the voice track).

Studio technicians and engineers carefully select, disperse, and aim the appropriate microphones to capture the full spectrum of sounds. The studio may have a separate sound booth (a small windowed room or partitioned area) to isolate drums or louder backup talent so the sound technicians can better balance the collection of sounds.

The Control Room

The agency producer, director, and sound engineer (and often the client and account executive) sit in the **control room,** where they can monitor all the sounds generated in the sound studio. The control room is separated from the studio by a thick glass window and soundproofed walls, so the people monitoring the session can hear the sounds on quality speakers and discuss the various takes.

The director and sound engineer work at an **audio console** (also called a **board**), the central "switchboard" for controlling the sounds and channeling them to the appropriate recording devices. As they monitor the sounds coming from the studio, they keep the pitch and loudness within acceptable levels for broadcast.

The board also serves as a sound mixer, blending both live and prerecorded sounds for immediate or delayed broadcast.

Postproduction: Finishing the Spot

After the commercial is recorded a number of times, a selection is made from the best takes. The sound engineer usually records music, sound effects, and vocals separately and then mixes and sweetens them during the **postproduction phase** (or finishing phase). The final recording is referred to as the **master tape.**

From the master tape, the engineer makes duplicates called **dubs,** records them onto quarter-inch magnetic tape, and sends them to radio stations for broadcast.

CONCEPT CHECK

Describe the important tasks that take place during each stage of the radio commercial production process.

The Television Commercial Production Process

While Johanna Leovey was working on the Prius print ads, another team across the office was working on the television commercials. The creatives had come up with a great concept for the Prius, and it was right on the money strategically, but it would have to be produced exceedingly well to communicate the idea credibly and resonate with the company's diverse audiences. That meant bringing in one of the agency's top TV producers, and Richard Bendetti was selected to do the job.

The commercial to be produced is portrayed by the storyboard in Chapter 9 (page 258). The spot features cars, buses, and people hurrying along the sidewalk. However, instead of moving forward, the tires on the vehicles would simply go round and round, and the people on the street would appear to be walking in place. This would happen in various locations, urban and rural, all over the world. Suddenly, the Prius emerges—the only forward-moving motion in the shot.

The Role of the Commercial Producer

Students of advertising need to know basic TV production concepts to understand how commercials are made, why production is so expensive, and what methods they can use to cut costs without sacrificing quality or effectiveness.

As with radio, the process of producing a TV commercial always involves three stages, as shown in Exhibit 10–5:

1. *Preproduction:* all the work prior to the actual day of filming.

2. *Production:* the actual day (or days) the commercial is filmed or videotaped.

3. *Postproduction (or finishing):* all the work done after shooting to edit and finish the commercial.

The Preproduction Phase

Good planning before production can save advertisers a lot of money. That's the purpose of the preproduction phase. The first thing the producer must do, therefore, is study the script and storyboard and analyze the production techniques that will be called for in the commercial. Three major categories of production techniques are used today: *live action, animation,* and *special effects.*

Live Action

To portray people and things in lifelike, everyday situations, like typical slice-of-life TV commercials, advertisers use the **live action** technique.

If a commercial calls for live action, the producer must consider whether the action will be staged indoors in a studio, outside on a studio lot, or on location away from the studio. Will it be taped or filmed? All these factors have a bearing on what equipment and personnel are required, where costumes can be obtained, what permissions may be required, what talent can be used, and, of course, what the commercial costs.

Working with the creative team, Richard Bendetti concurred that shooting on location was crucial to the Prius spot, which meant finding several locations around the world. This would mean coordinating with foreign ministries for visas and local city officials to get the necessary permits, police security, and environmental clearances. This created a bit of a problem in Japan, where the government doesn't allow traffic flow to be impeded at major intersections.

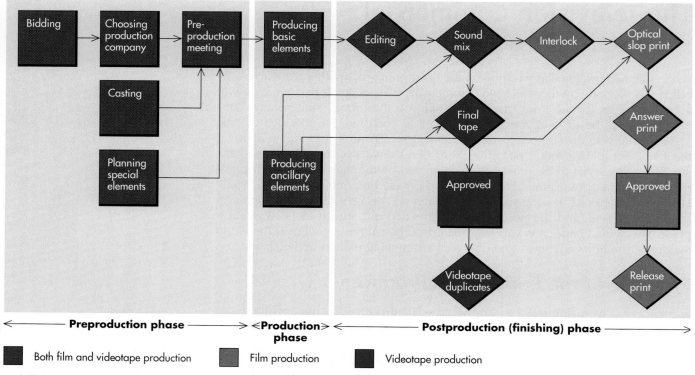

Exhibit 10–5

The production processes for film and videotape are very similar to that for radio until the sound-mixing stage. Computerized editing speeds up the finishing phase for videotape.

Animation

Animation—cartoons, dancing puppets, and demonstrations in which inanimate objects come to life—can effectively communicate difficult messages or reach special markets such as children.

Traditional animation techniques include *cartoons, photo animation, stop-motion photography,* and *video animation.* Cartoons often score the highest viewer interest and the longest life, so over time they cost the least per showing. However, initial production is very expensive. A fully animated commercial can easily cost more than $200,000.[12]

Special Effects

Today, much video animation and most **special effects,** such as moving titles and whirling logos, are done with a joystick. All major video production companies use dedicated **digital video effects (DVE)** units that can manipulate graphics on the screen in many ways: fades, wipes, zooms, rotations, and so on.

No technique should so enthrall viewers that they pay more attention to it than to the product—or the strategic message. Further, more than one fantasy or **mnemonic device** (Energizer Bunny or Jolly Green Giant) might confuse audiences. David Ogilvy suggested that, to make the strongest impression on the viewer, fantasies should relate to the product's claims and be repeated heavily.[13]

Planning Production

The commercial is a group effort; the team includes a writer, art director, producer, director, and sometimes a musical composer and choreographer. The agency pro-

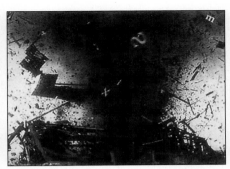

SFX: Music throughout
(Aerial shot of barn roof as surrounding countryside blows in the wind.)
VO (MAYA ANGELOU): The truth does not stand still for a moment.

(A tornado approaches. High winds blow against a wheelbarrow and pick up telephone and utility poles.)
It twists and turns, picks up your opinions,

(The twister hits and the barn breaks up into splinters of debris that mix with typed letters.) and sets them down a thousand miles away.

(The letters fall from the grip of the tornado, neatly into place as part of *The New York Times* newspaper text.)
When was the last time something you read moved you?

(SUPER: *The New York Times* logo.)
The New York Times.

Special effects play a major role here in grabbing the viewer's attention and adding drama to the message. The metaphor of a tornado combined with simple, yet sophisticated copy distinguish this thoughtful spot for *The New York Times.*

ducer, who is responsible for completing the job on schedule and within budget, usually sends copies of the storyboard to three studios for competitive bids.

When the studio is chosen, the producer and casting director select the cast and hire the announcer. Next the set is built, and the crew and cast rehearse under the director's supervision.

For many commercials, the most important decision is the hiring of the director. Such was certainly the case for the Prius. When Saatchi was looking for a director, it was told several times that its concept for the Prius would necessarily involve a lot of special effects. Saatchi was hesitant; it wanted to film the commercial with as little special effects as possible. Tarsem Singh was an obvious choice as the director. Not only did Tarsem seem excited by the Prius concept, but he agreed that the ad should be shot in the most natural way possible.

During the preproduction period, meetings are necessary among the director, the agency producer, the account representative, the writer, the art director, the commercial director, possibly the advertiser, and anyone else important to the production. This is where they iron out any last-minute problems and make final decisions about the scenes, the actors, and the announcer. They should review everything—music, sets, action, lighting, camera angles. A finished 60-second film commercial takes only 90 feet of film, but the shooting often requires several days and 3,000 to 5,000 feet of film. And unlike videotape, film can't be used again.

The soundtrack may be recorded before, during, or after actual production. Recording sound in advance ensures that the commercial will be neither too long nor too short; it also helps when the subject has to move or dance to a specific music theme or rhythm.

Production: The Shoot

The actual shooting day (or days) can be very long and tedious. It may take several hours just to light the set to the director's liking. The Prius spot, for instance, took six full days to shoot—in five different locales in four countries—over the course of a two-week period.

Quiet on the Set: Sound

Procedures for recording and controlling music and sound effects are similar to those used in radio. Microphones capture sound; recorders transfer the sound and store it on a medium like magnetic tape. Then, with the use of a multichannel control board, a sound engineer manipulates sounds for effect and records them onto film, video, or a playback system synchronized with film.

Lights

The arrangement of lights—whether in the studio, on the studio lot, or on location—establishes a visual mood. Intense light from a single source gives a harsh appearance and may be used to create anxiety in the viewer. By using filters, warmer lights, diffusion screens, and reflectors, the cinematographer can create a more consistent, softer illumination—and a more romantic mood. The director works with the art director, the cinematographer, and the lighting engineer to choose the most appropriate placement, types, and intensities.

Camera

Professional film cameras used for making TV commercials shoot 16 millimeter (mm), 35 mm, and 75 mm film, the diagonal measurement of a single film frame.

Producers of local TV commercials used to shoot with the grainier but less expensive 16 mm film; national spots were shot on 35 mm for extra quality and precision; and 75 mm film provides the highest quality image. While film is still widely used for national spots because of the atmosphere it brings to an image, most local spots are now shot on video.

Unlike film cameras, studio video cameras are tied to a control room by electronic cables. In the control room, multiple video screens and sound channels are wired to a control panel. Working at the control panel, the director can switch from one camera to another and simultaneously set the input and output levels of sound and visuals. Control panels also have DVE units for creating text or visual effects on screen.

Different types of lighting can enhance a scene and create special moods. Here, strong keylights light up the actors. A fainter light casts a window-shaped pattern onto the background. The effect light above enhances the reflected glow of the candle on the table top. To bystanders the scene appears very bright, but when the camera's aperture is set properly, the film sees a darker, more shadowy play of lights and darks.

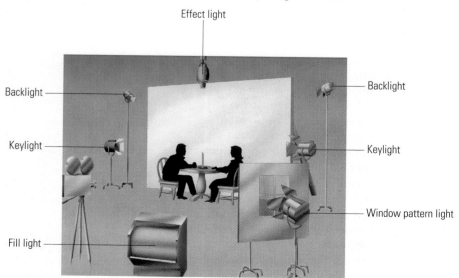

Effect light

Backlight

Backlight

Keylight

Keylight

Fill light

Window pattern light

Action: Staging and Talent

Staging for a commercial may be done in the isolation of a studio, outside on a studio lot, or on location. The studio offers the most control.

Most film and video studios have heavy sound-proofing to eliminate outside noises such as sirens and low-flying aircraft. The studios are lightproof, which allows for complete lighting control. Special equipment is easier to use in the controlled environment of a studio. But studio lighting can make a scene appear artificial.

For scenes requiring large amounts of space, historic or unique architecture, scenery, and the full effect of outdoor lighting, the **studio lot** offers the best control. The lot is outside acreage shielded from stray, off-site sounds. The lot is convenient to the studio's carpentry shop, and sets can be left standing until all shootings and retakes are completed.

Although it adds realism, **location** shooting is often a technical and logistical nightmare. Every location has natural and manufactured features that create obstacles. Natural lighting creates bright highlights that contrast with harsh shadows. Large reflective screens and high-intensity lights are required to brighten up shadows for a more even-toned exposure. Energy sources for lighting and equipment may be insufficient, requiring long cables and mobile generators. But because sets don't have to be built, location shooting can be good for some low-budget or short lead-time commercials. However, natural events such as rain and fog can cause costly interruptions and serious delays.

Whether at the studio or on location, most scenes require several takes for the **talent** (actors) to get them right. Lighting may need readjusting as unexpected shadows pop up. Each scene may be shot from two or three different angles: one to establish the characters, one to show only the speaker, and one to show the listener's reaction.

Scenes aren't necessarily shot in order. Those with no synchronized sound are usually shot last since they don't require the full crew.

A long time may be needed between scenes to move the camera, reset the lights, reposition the talent, and pick up the action, sound, and look to match the other scenes. Each action must match what comes before and after. Commercials with disconcerting jumps destroy credibility.

Once all the scenes are "in the can," the commercial enters the postproduction, or finishing, phase.

Postproduction

In the **postproduction phase,** the film editor, sound mixer, and director actually put the commercial together.

In any commercial production, it's typical to have many more people behind the camera than in front of it. In addition to the director and assistant director, other important players behind the scenes may include a sound editor, lighting technicians, electricians, and grips (skilled workers who set up and adjust the equipment).

In the postproduction phase, the director and editor can save a lot of time and money by using computerized video and sound editing equipment for the assembly of the final product. At this stage, the director and editor will select and splice scenes into their respective order, removing all the unneeded footage. Next, they add off-camera special effects, like supers, and incorporate any necessary music or voice-overs.

"Power to Move Forward" TV commercial
Following the shoot, the footage goes to the editing studios where music, voice-overs, special effects, and supers are all incorporated into the finished commercial. For the "Power to Move Forward" spot, treadmills, which had been placed under the talent and the vehicles to create a natural pacing, were removed during the postproduction stage.

With computer and videotape technology, editors can convert the film to tape and add effects such as wipes and dissolves electronically. Although a director will spend many hours editing a commercial shot on video, it will still be considerably less than what would be needed for film editing.

Many professionals still prefer film. The visual portion of the commercial appears on one piece of celluloid (film) without the effects of dissolves, titles, or **supers** (words superimposed on the picture). The sound portion is assembled on another piece of celluloid. This is the **work print** stage (also called the *rough cut* or *interlock*).

External sound is recorded next. The sound engineer records the musicians and singers, as well as the announcer's voice-over narrative. Prerecorded stock music may be bought and integrated into the commercial. The mixing also includes any sound effects, such as doorbells ringing or doors slamming.

CONCEPT CHECK

Describe the important tasks that take place during each stage of the television commercial production process?

Once sound editing is complete, the celluloid with the finished sound is combined with the almost-completed visual celluloid, yielding the **mixed interlock.** The addition of optical effects and titles results in the **answer print.** This is the final commercial. If it is approved, **dupes** (duplicate copies) are made for delivery to the networks or TV stations.

Producing Advertising for Digital Media

Have you seen the Academy Awards shows recently? The lavish Kodak Theatre, home to the presentation since 2002, has a "media cockpit" located in the middle of orchestra (main floor) seating. From there, technicians coordinate the multimedia extravaganza for each year's festivities. Home viewers are also participants in the huge digital media event. The live telecast of the Oscars often wins an Emmy for its smooth mixture of film clips, live performances, coverage of the action at the podium, and audience reaction shots.

The Emergence of Digital Media

The roots of this new phenomenon really go back to the 35 mm camera and the lowly slide show. Remember when the neighbors got back from Paris and came over to show you their slides?

Boring as it was, the home slide show was rapidly adopted by the business world and became a staple of sales presentations, corporate shareholder meetings, and luncheon speeches.

Some enterprising person thought the slide show could be perked up with a little music or a professional announcer. The professional slide presentation was born—and so was a new medium for advertising. The slide presentation was quickly adopted by sales forces, and companies sprang up all over the country to write, photograph, and produce high-quality, professional slide shows for businesses.

Sound + Music + Motion = Multimedia

Then came the idea of using multiple screens and multiple projectors. Quick cuts from one slide to another, in sync with the music and sound effects, created the feeling of motion. This was the birth of the **multimedia presentation,** which simply refers to presenting information or entertainment using several communications media simultaneously.

It wasn't long before video and animation were added to the mix. In one multimedia presentation, a prospect might be treated to both slides and video playing on two to twelve screens simultaneously, plus professional narration, music, and sound effects. It was very compelling.

Multimedia + Computer Technology = Digital Media

Then along came the personal computer, the breakup of AT&T, the deregulation of the broadcast and cable TV industry, the development of CD-ROM technology and fiber optics, and the stage was set for the media revolution now taking place—the emergence of digital media. Basically, **digital media** are channels of communication that join multimedia formats with the electronic system capabilities of modern telecommunications, television, and computer technologies. Digital media are a subset of electronic media. We already see them in many venues (settings).

Venues for Digital Media

The three categories of places where we experience digital media today are based on audience size: *mass audience, private audience,* and *personal audience venues.*

The Academy Awards show is a good example of a **mass audience venue.** With hundreds of people in the live audience and millions more watching at home, the multimedia presentation has a huge reach. Multimedia is also used in major sporting events, the Olympics opening ceremonies, political conventions, and other mass audience events.

Many digital media events are in **private audience venues,** though some of these may be quite large. A major marketer's national sales meeting, large corporate conferences, educational conferences, and training seminars all use computer-driven multimedia presentations, utilizing software programs such as PowerPoint to inform, persuade, remind, and entertain people.

The **personal audience venue** is experiencing the most growth today. One person sitting in front of a personal computer can receive multimedia information

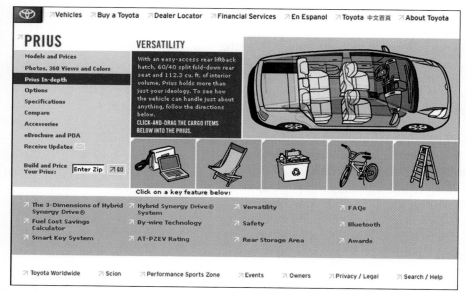

The emergence of digital media requires the development of an entirely new set of skills to produce ads. Art directors and designers must understand how to integrate print and video into a single medium, and they must also comprehend the features and limitations of the computer software used to produce such work.

off the Internet from an online service, or from software bought in a computer store. People can even create their own mini-multimedia programs with slides and animation by buying a turnkey authoring program (Hypercard®, Supercard®, Macromedia Director®) at any software store.

Finally, interactive TV is becoming available as another personal audience venue. While watching TV, people can use a remote control system to gain immediate access to the Internet or, in some limited cases, even tailor the programming to their personal tastes. Ironically, the most massive form of media—television—is now becoming one of the most personal.

The Role of Digital Media in Advertising

With the trend toward integrated marketing communications, the various digital media give marketers new ways to reach prospects and begin a relationship—or improve their relationship with current customers.

In some cases, the medium itself is the ad, as in the case of a multimedia sales presentation or a dedicated kiosk offering information about a company's wares. In other cases, though, the digital media are a form of narrowcasting in which advertisers can buy space or time for their commercial announcements. Often the spot is just an electronic billboard with the company or brand name. In Internet advertising, the advertiser sets up a virtual storefront, called a **Web page,** or places a billboard ad on another company's Web page. When viewers click certain "buttons" on the home page, a new page comes up with more detailed information about the company and its products, policies, or prices. We've gone back to the basics; it's a fancy slide show. But, in fact, it's multimedia. And the technology is getting better, faster, cheaper, and more impressive every day.

For the agency producer, this presents exciting challenges and opportunities. Not all the opportunities are available yet, but everybody knows what's around the corner: Touch a button on the screen and a full video commercial or technical film will run; click on another button and a personal representative will come online with you. The possibilities are endless. The challenge will be to keep current with the available technology.

The People Who Produce Digital Media Advertising

Some experts predict a virtual revolution in creative style and effectiveness as creative people learn to deal with the new media, offering more information and less glitz.[14] The ranks of production managers and producers are already swelling as media vehicles multiply beyond anybody's recent imagination. New titles are suddenly appearing on agency rosters: multimedia producers, directors, and technicians; interactive planners and writers; computer programmers and system designers; kiosk media buyers; and so on. At Saatchi & Saatchi, Nathan Hackstock holds the title of creative director for integrated marketing. Working with him is a staff of art directors, copywriters, and producers who specialize in creating interactive ads for Saatchi's clients. Outside the agencies are a host of new suppliers: kiosk manufacturers, interactive software developers, digital media-buying services, and so on.

The Production Process

For digital media, the production process is a hybrid of all the other processes we've discussed. That's because some of the digital media are akin to print and outdoor media (computer billboards and Web pages), while others are more closely associated with TV and radio.

As we've seen in this chapter, regardless of the medium, the production manager or producer goes through a planned sequence of activities: preproduction, production, and postproduction. Preproduction includes the planning, costing, and hiring activities. The production stage is when the artwork is created, the video and audio recorded, or the computer program developed. Postproduction includes the editing, duplicating, and distribution activities. The difference for digital media is in the details of activities in the production and postproduction stages (see RL 10–2, Production Process for Digital Media, in the Reference Library on the *Essentials of Contemporary Advertising* Web site).

An exciting new world awaits us. And it's not just around the corner. It's already here.

> What are some of the ways that digital media are being used today to communicate with various audiences and what directions might this take in the future?

CONCEPT CHECK

Chapter Summary

Careful management is the key to success in producing advertising. If the production process is not handled correctly, an otherwise well-conceived ad or commercial can be destroyed. The task of managing this process is the responsibility of a production manager. The manager's job is to keep the project moving smoothly and under budget, while maintaining the required level of quality through every step of the production process.

Production managers perform the classic functions of management: planning, organizing, directing, and controlling. They also have to keep up with changing technology, monitor costs, and meet budgets.

The print production process consists of four phases: preproduction, production, prepress, and printing and distribution. In the preproduction phase, the manager plans the overall job carefully and then starts to deal with the specific needs of the job, such as typography. Typography affects an ad's appearance, design, and legibility.

In the production phase, artists prepare mechanicals (or pasteups) of the art to be printed. Most agencies today use sophisticated desktop publishing. In the prepress stage, the printer makes a plate from the mechanical. For full color, four halftone plates are used (one for each color process color plus black). This work is now mostly done on large computerized scanner systems. The final phase of the production process includes the actual printing of the job, as well as cutting, embossing, binding, and shipping. Quality control is critical throughout the process.

Radio spots are among the quickest, simplest, and least expensive ads to produce. A producer manages the production process through the preproduction, production, and postproduction stages. The producer contracts with a recording studio, selects talent, and collects music and sound effects for the recording session. At the session, the talent works in a studio, while the director and sound engineer work in the control room at an audio console, monitoring and modulating the sound as it's recorded.

In the postproduction phase, the director and sound engineer select the best takes, splice them together, mix in sound effects and music, and then edit the sound until the master tape is completed. Dubs are made from this and sent to radio stations for airing.

Television production involves the same three stages. In preproduction, the producer determines which production technique is most suitable for the script: live action, animation, special effects, or a combination. The studio is chosen, the cast selected, and rehearsals held. As much work as possible is done during preproduction to reduce the shooting time required.

The production phase is when the commercial is actually shot, in a studio, on a lot, or on location. Specialized technicians are responsible for the sound, lights, and cameras, all of which can diminish the quality of the commercial if not handled correctly. Scenes are shot and reshot until the director and producer feel they have a good take.

In the postproduction stage, the commercial is actually put together on either film or videotape. External sound and music and special effects are added to the video and the sound track until the master (or answer print for film) is completed. Then dupes are made and shipped to TV stations.

A multimedia presentation provides information or entertainment using several communications media simultaneously, typically slides, video, and audio. The electronic capabilities of computer technology were added to the multimedia presentation to create digital media.

Digital media are used in mass audience venues, private audience venues, and personal audience venues. The personal audience venue includes PC applications such as advertising on the Internet or via interactive TV and kiosks. Digital media are a whole new industry. The overall production process is similar to those of print and electronic media, but the details involve new technologies and terminologies that advertisers and agencies are not yet familiar with. This means opportunities for new people coming into the field.

Key Terms

analog proof (Chromalin), 279

animation, 284

answer print, 288

audio console (board), 282

base art, 273

bleeds, 280

blueline, 279

camera-ready art, 273

closing date, 272

color key, 279

color separation, 277

continuous tone, 274

control room, 282

CYMK printing, 276

digital media, 289

digital proof, 279

digital video effects (DVE), 284

director, 281

display type, 274

dubs, 282

dupes, 288

electronic production, 270

flats, 276

font, 275

four-color process, 276

halftone, 275

job jacket, 271

kerning, 274

kiosks, 270

leading, 274

line art, 274

live action, 283

location, 287

mass audience venue, 289

master tape, 282

mechanical, 273

mixed interlock, 288

mnemonic device, 284

multimedia presentation, 289

overlay, 273

PANTONE Matching System® (PMS), 277

personal audience venue, 289

points, 275

postproduction phase, 282, 287

prepress phase, 276

preproduction, 271

press proof, 280

print production, 269

print production manager, 268

print production process, 271

private audience venue, 289

producer, 268

production phase, 272

residual fee, 270

reverse knockout, 280

sans serif, 274

scale, 270

serif, 274

session, 282

special effects, 284

spots, 280

stock music, 270

stripping, 276

studio lot, 287

supers, 288

talent, 287

text type, 274

trap, 280

type family, 275

typography, 272

Web page, 290

work print, 288

Review Questions

1. What are the five common budget busters every production manager should be aware of?
2. What is the primary role of the print production manager?
3. What does the traffic manager do and why is it such an important position?
4. What are the important concepts to consider when selecting type?
5. What is a halftone? Why is it important, and how is it produced?
6. How are color photographs printed? What are the potential problems with printing in color?
7. What are the advantages and disadvantages of animation?
8. What leads to the greatest waste of money in TV commercial production? Explain.
9. Who are the key individuals involved in the television commercial production process?
10. What are some ways an advertiser such as McDonald's could use digital media to enhance its IMC program? Explain.

Exploring Advertising

1. Typeface makes a strong contribution to the overall effect of an advertisement. Create ads with appropriate typefaces for three of the following media products. (Typefaces are not restricted to those discussed in Commercial Break 10–A.) You may design your own typefaces or select them from the choices in a word processing program.
    a. The Gettysburg Address
    b. *The King James Bible*
    c. Stephen King's (or Stanley Kubrick's) *The Shining*
    d. A DVD collection of *Friends* episodes
    e. A boxed set of "Barney's Greatest Hits" CDs
    f. An astronomy textbook
    g. A collection of *Lord of the Rings*

2. Prepare a mechanical pasteup of a print advertisement of your own design. You may cut and paste copy, graphics, and logos from magazines or other sources. The finished product should be "camera ready."

3. Looking through magazines and newspapers, find examples of line art, black and white halftones, and four-color process images.

chapter eleven

Print Advertising

Objectives

To examine how print advertising enhances the advertiser's media mix. Newspapers and magazines, with their unique qualities, can complement broadcast, direct mail, and other media. By using print wisely, advertisers can significantly increase the reach and impact of their campaigns and still stay within their budget.

After studying this chapter, you will be able to:

* **Explain** the advantages and disadvantages of magazine advertising.

* **Discuss** the various ways to analyze a magazine's circulation.

* **Describe** how newspapers are categorized.

* **Define** the major types of newspaper advertising.

* **Explain** the advantages and disadvantages of newspaper advertising.

* **Discuss** how rates are determined for print media.

* **Describe** the alternatives for print advertising in foreign markets.

Crowd-pleaser.

Milk has a lot of fans. And I'm one of them. Its nine essential nutrients help me give strong performances day after day. What can it do for you?

got milk?

KELLY CLARKSON ©2005 AMERICA'S MILK PROCESSORS

For today's increasingly health-conscious public, the steak and egg meals of yesteryear have lost their appeal. Now, Americans count their calories meticulously, right down to a simple can of soda.

Given this changing attitude, the National Fluid Milk Processor Promotion Board faced a considerable dilemma. How could it reestablish milk as sufficiently savvy for the country's modern beverage consumer? Milk from the dairies of the heartland didn't have the panache sought by the majority of people. Fortunately, unlike many food marketers, the milk board held a trump card of superior nutritional value that it felt could complete a winning hand. What it needed was to educate the public about its special secret and overcome fears of what had become that most taboo "F word": fat.

Science (and nature) worked in the organization's favor. Nutritionists began publishing study after study that confirmed that most Americans did not receive enough calcium from their diet. And calcium is easily obtained through the consumption of milk. The National Institutes of Health (NIH) warned that without enough calcium, middle-age people (especially women) could suffer from the bone-degenerating disease osteoporosis. It reported that after the age of 11, no age group of females achieves even 75 percent of the recommended levels of calcium, and that only one out of three males receives the levels recommended for adults.[1] Armed with this information, the milk board set out to create a campaign that would spark public interest in its solution to this health problem.

The board hired Bozell Worldwide, an advertising agency well known for its print ads. The puzzle was to create a campaign that would resonate with the times, one that would create appeal for a new era of milk, and one that could be supported by the data from the NIH.

From a marketing perspective, the beauty of print media is the ability to target audiences selectively and achieve maximum exposure for a product. Magazines open avenues to very specific niches of the public and facilitate high-quality presentations in the brilliance of full-color spreads. The efforts culminated in the "Milk, where's your mustache?" campaign, featuring celebrities from all walks of life with not-so-debonair milk mustaches smeared across their upper lip. Accompanying the quirky photos, Bozell incorporated testimonials from the models praising the positive effects of the vitamins, minerals, and protein from milk that helped them to achieve their success.

The campaign's initial phase focused on women to eliminate the stigma of milk's supposed high fat content. Ads featuring the likes of supermodel Kate Moss and actress Daisy Fuentes played up their glamour and health consciousness. The accompanying testimonials touted milk's bone-fortifying effects while assuring the audience of its minimal fat content. Another ad featured America's most famous homemaker, Martha Stewart, with a caption that advised the audience to substitute milk for water in their cooking recipes.

The ads ran in such consumer magazines as *Vogue, Cosmopolitan, People,* and *Good Housekeeping.* Following the campaign, research revealed a 17 percent increase in the belief by women that milk's health benefits outweigh its fat and calories. This success emboldened the National Fluid Milk Processor Promotion Board to double the campaign's advertising budget and led to more ambitious plans to target teenage boys and girls, college students, and men.[2]

By carefully selecting the vehicles, the milk board changed the public's attitude toward an entire industry. Use of consumer magazines emphasized the rich colors of the photos and displayed the desired tone of athleticism, sensuality, and humor to the fullest degree with each of the well-known celebrities.

In the end, the milk processors' $110 million "Where's your mustache?" integrated campaign endowed milk with its current and much-needed image of fun, glamour, and health.

Selecting Media

Selecting the most appropriate media mix for a campaign requires two distinct skills: understanding the unique characteristics of the various media alternatives and determining which medium will most efficiently and effectively reach the target audience.

These chapters in Part 5 will discuss the unique elements of the most common media classes. Then, in Chapter 15, we will examine how media planners and buyers decide which media to use, when to use them, and how to purchase them. In that chapter, we will also discuss audience measurements. For now, it will help if you have a basic understanding of two key terms: *reach*—the number of different people exposed, at least once, to a medium during a given period of time; and *frequency*—the average number of times those people are exposed to that medium during that period of time.

Understanding the characteristics of media options is important not only to media planners and buyers; account managers, planners, and creatives must also have an appreciation for the strengths and weaknesses of each medium so they can develop strategies and executions that will take full advantage of their alternatives.

Using Magazines in the Creative Mix

Advertisers use magazines in their **creative mix** for many reasons. First and foremost, magazines allow an advertiser to reach a particular target audience with a high-quality presentation. The National Fluid Milk Processor Promotion Board is just one of many leading advertisers that use magazines as an important element of their creative mix (Exhibit 11–1 lists the top U.S. magazine advertisers).

The Pros and Cons of Magazine Advertising

Magazines offer a wide variety of benefits to advertisers. The milk mustache campaign benefited greatly from the outstanding color reproduction available only from magazines. Further, by running in consumer magazines read by women of particular ages and lifestyles, the milk board could target its audience more precisely. Magazines offer a host of other features too: flexible design options, prestige, authority, believability, and long shelf life. Magazines may sit on a coffee table for months and be reread many times. People can read a magazine ad at their leisure; they can pore over the details of a photograph; and they can study carefully the information presented in the copy. This makes it an ideal medium for high-involvement think and feel products.

However, like every medium, magazines also have a number of drawbacks (see the Checklist, "The Pros and Cons of Magazine Advertising"). They are expensive (on a cost-per-reader basis), especially for color ads. And since they typically come out only monthly, or weekly at best, it's difficult to reach a large audience quickly or frequently. For these reasons, many advertisers use magazines in combination with other media—such as newspapers, which we'll discuss later in this chapter (see Commercial Break 11–A, "Magazines and the Creative Mix").

Special Possibilities with Magazines

Media planners and buyers need to be aware of the many creative possibilities magazines offer advertisers through various technical or mechanical features. These include bleed pages, cover positions, inserts and gatefolds, and special sizes, such as junior pages and island halves.

When the dark or colored background of the ad extends to the edge of the page (like the milk ad at the beginning of this chapter), it is said to **bleed** off the page. Most magazines offer bleed pages, but they charge 10 to 15 percent more for them. The advantages of bleeds include greater flexibility in expressing the advertising idea, a slightly larger printing area, and more dramatic impact.

If a company plans to advertise in a particular magazine consistently, it may seek a highly desirable **cover position.** Few publishers sell ads on the front cover, commonly called the *first cover.* They do however sell the inside front, inside back, and outside back covers (the *second, third,* and *fourth covers,* respectively), usually through multiple-insertion contracts at a substantial premium.

A less expensive way to use magazine space is to place the ad in unusual places on the page or dramatically across spreads. A **junior unit** is a large ad

Exhibit 11–1

Top 10 magazine advertisers in the United States (2004).

Rank	Company	Magazine ad spending ($ millions)
1	Procter & Gamble Co.	$619.8
2	General Motors Corp.	478.2
3	Altria Group (Philip Morris)	419.8
4	Ford Motor Co.	370.6
5	DaimlerChrysler	350.8
6	L'Oréal	329.1
7	Johnson & Johnson	314.6
8	Time Warner	309.2
9	Pfizer	243.3
10	Toyota Motor Corp.	241.7

Checklist

The Pros and Cons of Magazine Advertising

The Pros

- **Flexibility** in readership and advertising. Magazines cover the full range of prospects; they have a wide choice of regional and national coverage and a variety of formats, topics, and editorial tones.

- **Color** gives readers visual pleasure, and color reproduction is best in slick magazines. Color enhances image and identifies the package. In short, it sells.

- **Authority and believability** enhance the commercial message. TV, radio, and newspapers offer lots of information but lack the depth needed for readers to gain knowledge or meaning; magazines often offer all three.

- **Permanence,** or long shelf life, gives the reader time to appraise ads in detail, allowing a more complete education/sales message and the opportunity to communicate the total corporate personality.

- **Prestige** for products advertised in upscale or specialty magazines such as *Architectural Digest, Connoisseur,* and *Town and Country.*

- **Audience selectivity** is more efficient in magazines than any other medium except direct mail. The predictable, specialized editorial environment selects the audience and enables advertisers to pinpoint their sales campaigns. Examples: golfers *(Golf Digest)*, businesspeople *(BusinessWeek)*, 20-something males *(Details)*, or teenage girls *(Seventeen)*.

- **Cost efficiency,** because wasted circulation is minimized. Print networks also give advertisers reduced prices for advertising in two or more network publications.

- **Selling power** of magazines is proven, and results are usually measurable.

- **Reader loyalty** that sometimes borders on fanaticism.

- **Extensive pass-along readership.** Many people may read the magazine after the initial purchaser.

- **Merchandising assistance.** Advertisers can obtain reprints and merchandising materials that help them get more mileage out of their ad campaigns.

The Cons

- **Lack of immediacy** that advertisers can get with newspapers or radio.

- **Shallow geographic coverage.** Many different magazines must be used to approach the national reach of broadcast media.

- **Inability to deliver mass audiences at a low price.** Magazines are very costly for reaching broad masses of people.

- **Inability to deliver high frequency.** Since most magazines come out only monthly or weekly, it is difficult for advertisers to achieve high frequency levels in a short amount of time.

- **Long lead time** for ad insertion, sometimes two to three months.

- **Heavy advertising competition.** The largest-circulation magazines have 52 percent advertising to 48 percent editorial content.

- **High cost per reader.** Black-and-white ads in national consumer magazines can cost from $5 to $12 per thousand readers; color over $40 per thousand; and some trade publications with highly selective audiences charge over $50 per thousand readers for a black-and-white page.

- **Declining circulations,** especially in single-copy sales, is an industrywide trend that limits an advertiser's reach.

(60 percent of the page) placed in the middle of a page and surrounded with editorial matter. Similar to junior units are **island halves,** surrounded by even more editorial matter. The island sometimes costs more than a regular half-page, but because it dominates the page, many advertisers consider it worth the extra charge. Exhibit 11–2 shows other space combinations that create impact.

Sometimes, rather than buying a standard page, an advertiser uses an **insert.** The advertiser prints the ad on high-quality paper stock to add weight and drama to the message, and then ships the finished ads to the publisher for insertion into the magazine at a special price. Another option is multiple-page inserts. Calvin Klein once promoted its jeans in a 116-page insert in *Vanity Fair.* The insert reportedly cost more than $1 million, but the news reports about it in major daily newspapers gave the campaign enormous publicity value.

Commercial Break 11–A

Magazines and the Creative Mix

Read the Checklist, "The Pros and Cons of Magazine Advertising," and see if you can apply that information to the following situation:

You manage an elegant French restaurant in Los Angeles that is known for its intimate setting, excellent service, and a lovely outdoor garden patio. You decide to build the business by promoting the special ambience your restaurant offers. To enhance the sense of romance, you plan to give away a long-stem rose and a glass of cham-

pagne with each entrée. Your clientele consists primarily of wealthy, educated business leaders and celebrities. However, a growing segment of your customers are tourists and middle-class couples out for a special evening.

Applying the Breaks

1. Are magazines the best way to advertise this special? If not, explain why. If so, explain why and include which specific magazines would be best.

2. How can magazine advertising help you build the restaurant's image?

A **gatefold** is an insert whose paper is so wide that the extreme left and right sides have to be folded into the center to match the size of the other pages. When the reader opens the magazine, the folded page swings out like a gate to present the ad. Not all magazines provide gatefolds, and they are always sold at a substantial premium. Commercial Break 11–B discusses other innovations in magazine advertising.

How Magazines Are Categorized

In the jargon of the trade, magazines are called books, and media planners and buyers commonly categorize them by content, geography, and size.

Exhibit 11–2

An ad's position on the page influences its effectiveness. The size and shape of the ad often determine where it will fall on the page. These eight two-page spreads show most of the positions a fractional ad can take.

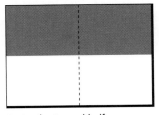

Facing horizontal half-pages to dominate a spread

Vertical halves across the gutter with the same objective

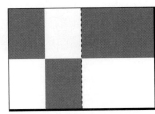

Checkerboard facing a half-page ad

Staggered horizontal half-pages

Outside halves of a spread

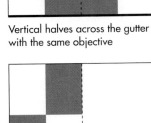

Checkerboard (multiple small space units on a single page)

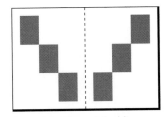

Staircase units and double staircases on facing pages

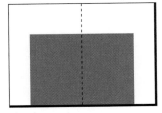

Island spread

Innovations in Magazine Advertising

Magazines work closely with advertisers to develop new technologies for presenting ideas and products. From these efforts have come such innovations as fragrance strips, color strips, and pop-up ads.

Fragrance strips are a great favorite with perfume advertisers. Similar to the familiar Scratch & Sniff, with the Scentstrip, readers sample a scent by opening a sealed flap tucked into a magazine. Despite some consumer complaints, Scentstrips have been incredibly popular. Fragrances are useful for other products as well. For example, a Rolls-Royce ad in *Architectural Digest* carried a Scentstrip bearing the essence of leather.

Cosmetics manufacturers insert **color strip** samples of eye shadow, blush, lipstick, and other makeup that readers can try immediately. Color strips are expensive to produce, but many advertisers think they're worth it.

Another costly innovation is the **pop-up ad**. Corporate advertisers such as Honeywell and TransAmerica were among the first to try this eye-catching approach. Product ads, such as a pop-up for the Dodge Dakota, followed.

Other intriguing approaches include **3-D ads** (complete with 3-D glasses), **product samples** (facial tissues and paper towels), and unusual shapes and sizes for **preprinted inserts.** An ad for Sara Lee cheesecake used a single heavy-stock page with what appeared to be a bite taken out of a life-size cheesecake slice. A half-page insert for Gleem toothpaste featured a metallic graphic of a mirror with the slogan "Check your mirror."

Researchers are probing the possibilities of holograms and ads that talk. Already ads can sing—liquor companies included microchips that played Christmas carols in their December magazine ads, and ads for a cigarette brand played "Happy Birthday" on the brand's 75th anniversary.

Recently, Global Commerce Group invented the Web Decoder™, a transparent device made of clear polyester Mylar. The recipient is invited to interact with an image on a Web site. When the piece is positioned over the designated image, a hidden word, icon, or phrase is revealed. Advertisers can tailor the Web Decoder to their specific promotional needs, from cents-off coupons to instant-winner prizes.

Such innovative approaches not only attract readers' attention but also involve them in the experience by appealing to more than just the visual sense.

Applying the Breaks

What are some other products that could benefit from the use of these technological innovations?

Go on, smell it.

Scratch & Sniff

It's Orchard Blossom. One of a new line of anti-perspirants that smells the way you want to smell. Fun. Exciting. And does it for 24 hours, with no white residue. Exciting armpits. Wow! It's a whole new concept.

Wear something new and exciting under your clothes.

Content

One of the most dramatic developments in publishing is the emergence of magazines with special content, which has given many books good prospects for long-term growth. The broadest classifications of content are *consumer magazines, farm magazines,* and *business magazines.* Each may be broken down into hundreds of categories.

- **Consumer magazines,** purchased for entertainment, information, or both, are edited for consumers who buy products for their own personal consumption: *Time, Sports Illustrated, Glamour, Good Housekeeping.* The Portfolio Review, "Outstanding Magazine Ads," on the *Essentials of Contemporary Advertising* Web site shows the range of creativity in consumer magazine advertising.

- **Farm publications** are directed to farmers and their families or to companies that manufacture or sell agricultural equipment, supplies, and services: *Farm Journal, Progressive Farmer, Prairie Farmer, Successful Farming.*

- **Business magazines,** by far the largest category, target business readers. They include *trade publications* for retailers, wholesalers, and other distributors *(Progressive Grocer, Bakery News); business* and *industrial magazines* for businesspeople involved in manufacturing and services *(Electronic Design, American Banker);* and *professional journals* for lawyers, physicians, architects, and other professionals *(Archives of Ophthalmology).*

Magazines that cater to specific geographic areas are considered local or regional publications. Most metropolitan areas publish magazines specific to their particular city, such as this example from *Chicago* magazine (www.chicagomag.com), providing news and information on issues and events of interest to the local population.

Geography

A magazine may also be classified as *local, regional,* or *national.* Today, most major U.S. cities have a **local city magazine:** *San Diego Magazine, New York, Los Angeles, Chicago, Palm Springs Life.* Their readership is usually upscale business and professional people interested in local arts, fashion, and business.

 Regional publications are targeted to a specific area of the country, such as the West or the South: *Sunset, Southern Living.* National magazines sometimes provide special market runs for specific geographic regions. *Time, Newsweek, Woman's Day,* and *Sports Illustrated* allow advertisers to buy a single major market. Exhibit 11–3 shows the 10 major geographic editions of *Reader's Digest.*

 National magazines range from those with enormous circulations, such as *TV Guide,* to small, lesser-known national magazines, such as *Nature* and *Volleyball Monthly.* The largest circulation magazine in the United States today is *AARP The Magazine,* distributed to the 21 million members of the American Association of Retired Persons.[3]

Size

It doesn't take a genius to figure out that magazines come in different shapes and sizes, but it might take one to figure out how to get one ad to run in different size magazines and still look the same. Magazine sizes run the gamut, which can make production standardization a nightmare. The most common magazine sizes follow:

CONCEPT CHECK

Describe how the unique elements of magazines enhance the creative mix. What are the downsides?

Size classification	Magazine	Approximate size of full-page ad
Large	*Life*	4 col. × 170 lines (9³/₈ × 12¹/₈ inches)
Flat	*Time, Newsweek*	3 col. × 140 lines (7 × 10 inches)
Standard	*National Geographic*	2 col. × 119 lines (6 × 8¹/₂ inches)
Small, pocket or digest	*Reader's Digest*	2 col. × 91 lines (4¹/₂ × 6¹/₂ inches)

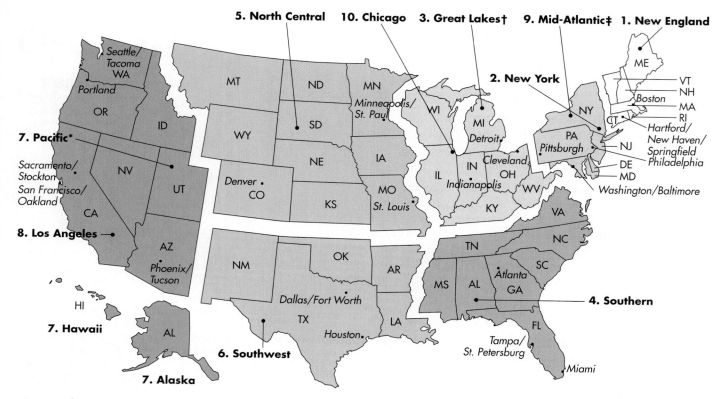

5. North Central   10. Chicago   3. Great Lakes†   9. Mid-Atlantic‡   1. New England

2. New York

7. Pacific*

8. Los Angeles

7. Hawaii

7. Alaska

6. Southwest

4. Southern

• Major market
* Pacific Ed. excludes counties covered by Metro L.A. Edition
† Great Lakes Ed. excludes counties covered by Metro Chicago
‡ Mid-Atlantic Ed. excludes counties covered by Metro N.Y.

Exhibit 11–3

Advertisers benefit from selecting regional editions similar to the 10 geographic editions of *Reader's Digest* shown on the map. With regional binding and mailing, advertisers can buy ad space for only the areas of distribution they need.

Buying Magazine Space

When analyzing a media vehicle, media planners and buyers consider readership, cost, mechanical requirements, and ad closing dates (deadlines). To buy effectively, they must thoroughly understand the magazine's circulation and rate-card information.

Understanding Magazine Circulation

The first step in analyzing a publication's potential effectiveness is to assess its audience. The buyer studies circulation statistics, primary and secondary readership, subscription and vendor sales, and any special merchandising services the magazine offers.

Guaranteed versus Delivered Circulation

A magazine's rates are based on its circulation. The **rate base** is the circulation figure on which the publisher bases its rates. It is generally equivalent to the **guaranteed circulation,** the minimum number of copies the publisher expects to circulate. This assures advertisers they will reach a certain number of people. If the publisher does not deliver its guaranteed figure, it must provide a refund. For that reason, guaranteed circulation figures are often stated safely below the average actual circulation.

Media buyers expect publications to verify their circulation figures. Publishers pay thousands of dollars each year for a **circulation audit**—a thorough analysis of the circulation procedures, outlets of distribution, readers, and other factors—by companies such as the **Audit Bureau of Circulations (ABC).**

Primary and Secondary Readership

Data from the ABC or other verified reports tell the media buyer the magazine's total circulation. This **primary circulation** represents the number of people who buy the publication, either by subscription or at the newsstand. **Secondary** (or **pass-along**) **readership**, which is an estimate determined by market research of how many people read a single issue of a publication, is very important to magazines. Some have more than six readers per copy. Multiplying the average pass-along readership by, say, a million subscribers can give a magazine a substantial audience beyond its primary readers.

Vertical and Horizontal Publications

There are two readership classifications of business publications: *vertical* and *horizontal*. A **vertical publication** covers a specific industry in all its aspects. For example, Cahners Publishing produces *Restaurants & Institutions* strictly for restaurateurs and food-service operators. The magazine's editorial content includes everything from news of the restaurant industry to institutional-size recipes.

Horizontal publications, in contrast, deal with a particular job function across a variety of industries. Readers of *Purchasing* work in purchasing management in many different industries. Horizontal trade publications are very effective advertising vehicles because they usually offer excellent reach and they tend to be well read.[4]

Subscription and Vendor Sales

Media buyers also want to know a magazine's ratio of subscriptions to newsstand sales. Today, subscriptions account for the majority of magazine sales. Newsstands (which include bookstore chains) are still a major outlet for single-copy sales, but no outlet can handle more than a fraction of the many magazines available.

From the advertiser's point of view, newsstand sales are impressive because they indicate that the purchaser really wants the magazine and is not merely subscribing out of habit. According to the Magazine Publishers Association, single-copy sales account for 34 percent of total revenues for a representative sampling of leading magazines.

Advertising Age is a good example of a vertical publication. The magazine is geared toward a variety of issues specific to the advertising industry. Unlike horizontal publications, which focus on a single job function across various industries, *Ad Age* is read by people in a wide range of functions throughout the advertising industry.

Paid and Controlled Circulation

Business publications may be distributed on either a *paid-circulation* or *controlled-circulation* basis. A paid basis means the recipient must pay the subscription price to receive the magazine. *BusinessWeek* is a **paid-circulation** business magazine.

In **controlled circulation,** the publisher mails the magazine free to individuals who the publisher thinks can influence the purchase of advertised products. Managers of corporate video departments receive *Corporate Video Decisions.* To qualify for the subscription list, people must indicate in writing a desire to receive it and must give their professional designation or occupation. Dues-paying members of organizations often get free subscriptions. For example, members of the National Association for Female Executives receive free copies of *Executive Female.*

Publishers of paid-circulation magazines say subscribers who pay are more likely to read a publication than those who receive it free. But controlled-circulation magazines can reach good prospects for the goods and services they advertise.

Merchandising Services: Added Value

Magazines, and newspapers too, often provide liberal added-value services to their regular advertisers, such as:

- Special, free promotions to retail stores.
- Marketing services to help readers find local outlets.
- Response cards that allow readers to request brochures and catalogs.
- Help handling sales force, broker, wholesaler, and retailer meetings.
- Advance copies for the trade.
- Marketing research into brand preferences, consumer attitudes, and market conditions.

If a publication's basic characteristics—editorial, circulation, and readership—are strong, these additional services can increase the effectiveness of its ads.[5] Magazines offer great potential for relationship marketing since they already have a relationship with their subscribers.

Reading Rate Cards

Magazine rate cards follow a standard format (see RL 11–1 in the Reference Library on the *Essentials of Contemporary Advertising* Web site). This helps advertisers determine costs, discounts, mechanical requirements, closing dates, special editions, and additional costs for features like color, inserts, bleed pages, split runs, or preferred positions.

Three dates affect magazine purchases. The **cover date** is the date printed on the cover. The **on-sale date** is the date the magazine is actually issued. And the **closing date** is the date all ad material must be in the publisher's hands for a specific issue. Lead time may be as much as three months.

Rates

As we will discuss in Chapter 15, one way to compare magazines is to look at how much it costs to reach a thousand people based on the magazine's rates for a one-time, full-page ad. You compute the **cost per thousand (CPM)** by dividing the full-page rate by the number of thousands of subscribers:

$$\frac{\text{Page rate}}{(\text{Circulation} \div 1,000)} = \text{CPM}$$

If the magazine's black-and-white page rate is $10,000, and the publication has a circulation of 500,000, then:

$$\frac{\$10,000}{(500,000 \div 1,000)} = \frac{\$10,000}{500} = \$20 \text{ CPM}$$

Consider this comparison. In 2003, the page rate for a full-color, one-page ad in *Car & Driver* was $142,235 on total paid circulation of 1,369,848; *Road & Track* offered the same ad space for $85,745 on total paid circulation of 762,688. Which was the better buy on a CPM basis?[6]

Exhibit 11–4 lists the circulations, color page rates, and CPMs for 12 leading consumer magazines.

Discounts

Magazines and newspapers often give discounts. **Frequency discounts** are based on the number of ad insertions, usually within a year; **volume discounts** are based on the total amount of space bought during a specific period. Most magazines also offer *cash discounts* (usually 2 percent) to advertisers who pay right away, and some offer discounts on the purchase of four or more consecutive pages in a single issue. In fact, more than half of all magazine publishers now negotiate their rates.

Premium Rates

Magazines charge extra for special features. Color printing normally costs 25 to 60 percent more than black and white. Some publications, such as *Money,* even offer metallic inks and special colors. Bleed pages can add as much as 20 percent to regular rates, although the typical increase is about 15 percent.

Second and third cover rates (the inside covers) typically cost less than the fourth (back) cover. According to SRDS, a service which compiles advertising rates for consumer and business magazines, in 2004 *Newsweek* charged $172,000 for a normal color page and the same for second and third covers, but it charged $245,460 for the fourth cover.[7]

Magazines charge different rates for ads in geographic or demographic issues. **Geographic editions** target geographic markets; **demographic editions** reach readers who share a demographic trait, such as age, income level, or professional status. *Time* offers one-page, four-color ads in its Boston edition for $21,495 and in its New York edition for $34,708. For full-page, four-color ads, advertisers in the top management edition pay $90,000 (circulation 805,489). To run the same ad in *Time Gold,* which is targeted to baby boomers and has a circulation of more than 1 million, advertisers pay $69,000.

Exhibit 11–4

Advertising costs in 2004 for U.S. consumer magazines with the largest circulations.

Magazine	Total paid circulation	Page cost per ad	CPM (cost per thousand)
Better Homes & Gardens	7,606,820	$313,207	$41.17
People	3,603,115	202,682	56.25
Parents	2,072,867	114,507	55.24
The New York Times Magazine	1,676,885	78,794	46.99
InStyle	1,652,906	96,223	58.21
Rolling Stone	1,288,324	108,375	84.12
Vogue	1,260,026	96,007	76.19
Travel & Leisure	965,977	76,418	79.11
Forbes	920,752	86,089	93.50
GQ	788,851	81,222	102.96
Road & Track	758,615	82,402	108.62
Bridal Guide	215,976	31,329	145.06

It's so nice that homosexuals, Jews and terrorists have a newspaper to read.

VOICE
NOT AMERICA'S FAVORITE PAPER

Newspapers are an important medium in the creative mix, second only to television in advertising volume, but costing much less. This ad for the *Village Voice* (www.villagevoice.com) shows how a niche business can use newspaper advertising to expand sales. Mimicking the freewheeling tone of the newspaper, the advertiser targeted those who already read the *Village Voice* but were not subscribers.

Using Newspapers in the Creative Mix

When a small, alternative newspaper in Manhattan asked one of the newest and hottest creative shops in the city for help in promoting subscriptions, it had no idea what the little agency with the funny name, Mad Dogs & Englishmen, would do for it.

The *Village Voice* newspaper had always knocked the Establishment with its radical coverage of social issues, politics, media, and culture. So perhaps it shouldn't have come as a surprise when the Mad Dogs took the newspaper's own prose style and turned it around in a series of impertinent, self-mocking ads.

"Hell, I wouldn't have my home contaminated with a subscription to your elitist rag if you were giving away five-speed blenders," rants one ad in the series. "You people think New York is the friggin' center of the world." But then a second paragraph offers a dramatic alternative: "YES, I want to buy a year's subscription to the *Village Voice*," along with a coupon.

Selecting the medium was easy. Because most people who would be interested in a subscription are *Village Voice* readers, the campaign ran in the paper itself. It proved to be a wise choice. In the first year of the campaign, the *Voice* saw a 30 percent increase in its subscriber base, surpassing all expectations.[8]

Who Uses Newspapers?

Newspapers are now the second-largest medium (after television) in terms of advertising volume, receiving 18.3 percent of the dollars spent by advertisers in the United States.[9]

Consider these important facts:

- More than half of all adults (55 percent) read a daily newspaper. Nearly two-thirds (63.1 percent) read the Sunday edition.

- Each section is read by about two-thirds of all adult readers, whereas almost all (88 percent) read the main news sections.

- More than 55 million newspapers are sold daily, and every copy has an average of 2.3 readers.

- In 2003, there were 1,456 daily newspapers in the United States, with a total circulation of 55.2 million. The same year, the nation's more than 6,700 weekly newspapers and shoppers had a combined circulation of more than 50.2 million.[10]

- Newspaper advertising expenditures in 2003 totaled $44.1 billion.[11]

- More than 1,500 newspapers in the United States have sites on the Internet. More and more online readers are completely abandoning the print product.

Although the newspaper is the major community-serving medium for both news and advertising, more and more national advertisers are shifting to radio and television. As a result, radio and TV carry most of the national advertising in the United States, while 83 percent of newspaper advertising revenue comes from local advertising. As Exhibit 11–5 shows, retailers and cellular phone companies are the primary advertisers in newspapers.

The Pros and Cons of Newspaper Advertising

The *Village Voice* promotion shows how small businesses with even smaller budgets can benefit from creative newspaper advertising. Print ads in general and newspapers in particular provide a unique, flexible medium for advertisers to express their creativity—especially with businesses that rely on local customers.

Newspapers offer advertisers many advantages. One of the most important is timeliness; an ad can appear very quickly, sometimes in just one day. Newspapers also offer geographic targeting, a broad range of markets, reasonable cost, and more. But newspapers suffer from lack of selectivity, poor production quality, and clutter. And readers criticize them for lack of depth and follow-up on important issues.[12]

Use the Checklist, "Pros and Cons of Newspaper Advertising," to answer the questions in Commercial Break 11–C, "Newspapers and the Creative Mix."

Exhibit 11–5

Top 10 newspaper advertisers in the United States (2004).

Rank	Company	Newspaper ad spending ($ millions)
1	SBC Communications	$804.8
2	Verizon Communications	644.3
3	Federated Department Stores	474.6
4	General Motors Corp.	459.3
5	Sprint Corp.	443.6
6	May Department Stores Co.	429.5
7	Time Warner	374.6
8	Walt Disney Co.	255.8
9	Dillard's	210.4
10	Sears Holding Corp.	202.0

How Newspapers Are Categorized

Newspapers can be classified by frequency of *delivery, physical size,* or *type of audience*.

Frequency of Delivery

A **daily newspaper** is published as either a morning or evening edition at least five times a week, Monday through Friday. Of the 1,457 dailies in the United States, 692 are evening papers and 777 are morning papers. (The total exceeds 1,457 because 12 "all day" newspapers print both morning and evening editions.)[13] Morning editions tend to have broader geographic circulation and a larger male readership; evening editions are read more by women.

With their emphasis on local news and advertising, **weekly newspapers** characteristically serve small urban or suburban residential areas and farm communities. They are now the fastest-growing class of newspapers. A weekly newspaper's cost per thousand is usually higher than a daily paper's, but a weekly has a longer life and often has more readers per copy.

Physical Size

There are two basic newspaper formats, standard size and tabloid. The **standard-size newspaper** is about 22 inches deep and 13 inches wide and is divided into six columns. The **tabloid newspaper** is generally about 14 inches deep and 11 inches wide. National tabloid newspapers such as the *National Enquirer* and the *Star* use sensational stories to fight for single-copy sales. Other tabloids, such as the *New York Daily News,* emphasize straight news and features.

Newspapers used to offer about 400 different ad sizes. But in 1984, the industry introduced the **standard advertising unit (SAU)** system, which standardized the newspaper column width, page sizes, and ad sizes. An SAU **column inch** is $2\frac{1}{16}$ inches wide by 1 inch deep. There are now 56 standard ad sizes for standard papers and 32 for tabloids. Virtually all dailies converted to the SAU system and so did most weeklies.

Checklist

The Pros and Cons of Newspaper Advertising

The Pros

- **Mass medium** penetrating every segment of society. Most consumers read a newspaper.
- **Local medium** with broad reach. Covers a specific geographic area that comprises both a market and a community of people sharing common concerns and interest.
- **Comprehensive in scope.** Covers an extraordinary variety of topics and interests.
- **Geographic selectivity** is possible with zoned editions for specific neighborhoods or communities.
- **Timeliness.** Papers primarily cover today's news and are read in one day.
- **Credibility.** Studies show that newspaper ads rank highest in believability. TV commercials are a distant second.
- **Selective attention** from the relatively small number of active prospects who, on any given day, are interested in what the advertiser is trying to tell them or sell them.
- **Creative flexibility.** An ad's physical size and shape can be varied to give the degree of dominance or repetition that suits the advertiser's purpose. The advertiser can use black and white, color, Sunday magazines, or custom inserts.
- **An active medium** rather than a passive one. Readers turn the pages, clip and save, write in the margins, and sort through the contents.
- **A permanent record,** in contrast to the ephemeral nature of radio and TV.
- **Reasonable cost.**

The Cons

- **Lack of selectivity** of specific socioeconomic groups. Most newspapers reach broad, diverse groups of readers, which may not match the advertiser's objectives.
- **Short life span.** Unless readers clip and save an ad or coupon, it's disposed of that day.
- **Low production quality.** Coarse newsprint generally produces a less impressive image than the slick, smooth paper stock of magazines, and some newspapers can't print color.
- **Clutter.** Each ad competes with editorial content and with all the other ads on the same page or spread.
- **Lack of control** over where the ad will appear unless the advertiser pays extra for a preferred position.
- **Overlapping circulation.** Some people read more than one newspaper. Advertisers may be paying for readers who were already reached in a different paper.

Type of Audience

Some dailies and weeklies serve special-interest audiences, a fact not lost on advertisers. They generally contain advertising oriented to their special audiences, and they may have unique advertising regulations.

Some serve specific ethnic markets. Today, more than 200 dailies and weeklies are oriented to the African-American community. Others serve foreign-language groups. In the United States there are newspapers printed in 43 languages other than English.

Specialized newspapers also serve business and financial audiences. *The Wall Street Journal,* the leading national business and financial daily, enjoys a circulation of 1.8 million. Other papers cater to fraternal, labor union, or professional organizations, religious groups, or hobbyists.

Other Types of Newspapers

The United States has 917 Sunday newspapers, mostly Sunday editions of daily papers, with a combined circulation of more than 58.4 million.[14] Sunday newspapers generally combine standard news coverage with special functions like these:

- Increased volume of classified ads.

- Greater advertising and news volume.

Newspapers and the Creative Mix

Study the Checklist, "The Pros and Cons of Newspaper Advertising," and see if you can apply that information to the following situation:

You're the product manager for a major brand of bar soap and you wish to go nationwide with an ad featuring a coupon.

Applying the Breaks

1. Which newspaper would be best?
   a. A weekly.   b. A daily.

2. If you use a daily, in what section of the paper do you want your ad to appear?

3. If you decided to run a coupon in the Sunday paper, which of the following would you choose and why?
   a. *Parade* magazine.   b. Color coupon insert.
   c. Display ad.

- In-depth coverage of business, sports, real estate, literature and the arts, entertainment, and travel.

- Review and analysis of the past week's events.

- Expanded editorial and opinion sections.

Most Sunday newspapers also feature a **Sunday supplement** magazine. Some publish their own supplements, such as the *Los Angeles Magazine* of the *Los Angeles Times*. Other papers subscribe to syndicated supplements; *Parade* magazine is now received by more than 35.7 million homes every week.[15]

Printed on heavier, coated paper stock, Sunday supplements are more conducive to color printing than newsprint, making them attractive to national advertisers who want better reproduction quality.

Another type of newspaper, the independent shopping guide or free community newspaper, offers advertisers local saturation. Sometimes called *pennysavers,* these **shoppers** offer free distribution and extensive advertising pages targeted at essentially the same audience as weekly newspapers—urban and suburban community readers. Readership is often high, and the publishers use hand delivery or direct mail to achieve maximum saturation.

North Americans also read national newspapers, including the *Globe and Mail* in Canada, *USA Today,* and the *Christian Science Monitor.* With a circulation of 2.1 million, *USA Today* surpasses *The Wall Street Journal* (1.8 million) and *The New York Times* (1.1 million) in national distribution.[16]

Types of Newspaper Advertising

The major classifications of newspaper advertising are display, classified, public notices, and preprinted inserts.

Display Advertising

Display advertising includes copy, illustrations or photos, headlines, coupons, and other visual components—such as the ads for the *Village Voice*

The picture of Alfred Hitchcock (director of the movie thriller *The Birds*) juxtaposed with the bird stamps, seemingly in flight, is a brilliant creative concept for a large newspaper ad.

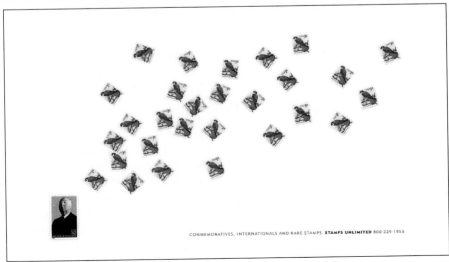

COMMEMORATIVES, INTERNATIONALS AND RARE STAMPS. **STAMPS UNLIMITED** 800-229-1955

discussed earlier. Display ads vary in size and appear in all sections of the newspaper except the first page of major sections, the editorial page, the obituary page, and the classified advertising section.

One common variation of the display ad, the **reading notice,** looks like editorial matter and sometimes costs more than normal display advertising. To prevent readers from mistaking it for editorial matter, the word *advertisement* appears at the top.

As we discussed in Chapter 3, retailers often run newspaper ads through **cooperative** (or **co-op**) **advertising** programs sponsored by the manufacturers whose products they sell. The manufacturer pays fully or partially to create and run the ad, which features the manufacturer's product and logo along with the local retailer's name and address.

Classified Advertising

Classified ads provide a community marketplace for goods, services, and opportunities of every type, from real estate and new-car sales to employment and business opportunities. A newspaper's profitability often relies heavily on a large and healthy classified section.

Classified rates are typically based on how many lines the ad occupies and how many times the ad runs. Some newspapers accept **classified display ads,** which run in the classified section of the newspaper but feature larger type and/or photos, art borders, and sometimes even color.

Public Notices

For a nominal fee, newspapers carry legal **public notices** of changes in business and personal relationships, public governmental reports, notices by private citizens and organizations, and financial reports. These ads follow a preset format.

Preprinted Inserts

Like magazines, newspapers carry **preprinted inserts.** The advertiser prints the inserts and delivers them to the newspaper plant for insertion into a specific edition. Insert sizes range from a typical newspaper page to a double postcard; formats include catalogs, brochures, mail-back devices, and perforated coupons.

Some large metropolitan dailies allow advertisers to limit their inserts to specific circulation zones. A retail advertiser that wants to reach only those shoppers in its immediate trading area can place an insert in the local-zone editions. Retail stores, car dealers, and large national advertisers are among those who find it less costly to distribute their circulars this way compared to mailing them or delivering them door to door.

CONCEPT CHECK

Describe how the unique elements of newspapers enhance the creative mix. What are the downsides?

Online Advertising

Most major local and national newspapers have developed online editions, which carry several types of advertising—display ads, classified ads, and banner ads. **Online advertising** is proving to be successful because online newspaper editions are often the dominant news and information Web sites in their trading areas. As a result, online advertising, though still in its infancy, has become the fastest growing source of revenue for newspapers. Online revenues of U.S. newspapers were expected to grow by 36 percent to $1.4 billion in 2005.

Newspapers are still trying to determine how best to charge for online advertising, but rates are generally based on the size and placement of the ads and the estimated volume of traffic coming to the Web site.

How Advertisers Buy Newspaper Space

To get the most from the advertising budget, the media planner and buyer must know the characteristics of a newspaper's readership: the median age, sex, occupation, income, educational level, as well as buying habits of the typical reader.

Understanding Readership and Circulation

Readership information is available from various sources, such as Simmons Market Research Bureau (SMRB) and Scarborough Research Corp. Most large papers also provide extensive data on their readers.

In single-newspaper cities, reader demographics typically reflect a cross section of the general population. In cities with two or more newspapers, however, these characteristics may vary widely. The *Los Angeles Times* is directed to a broad cross section of the community while *La Opinion* targets Los Angeles's large Hispanic population.

Advertisers must understand the full extent of the newspaper's circulation. The paper's total circulation includes subscribers and single-copy newsstand buyers, as well as secondary readers.

Rate Cards

Like the magazine rate card, the newspaper **rate card** lists advertising rates, mechanical and copy requirements, deadlines, and other information. Because rates vary greatly, advertisers should calculate which papers deliver the most readers and the best demographics for their money.

Local versus National Rates

Most newspapers charge local and national advertisers at different rates. The **national rate** averages 75 percent higher, but some papers charge as much as 254 percent more.[17] Newspapers attribute higher rates to the added costs of serving national advertisers. For instance, an ad agency usually places national advertising and receives a 15 percent commission from the paper. If the advertising comes from another city or state, then additional costs, such as long-distance telephone calls, are also involved.

But many national advertisers reject the high rates and take their business elsewhere. Only 3 percent of national ad money now goes to newspapers, and that proportion may shrink even further.[18] In response to declining national advertising revenue, newspapers are experimenting with simplified billing systems and discount rates for their national clients.

Flat Rates and Discount Rates

Many national papers charge **flat rates,** which means they allow no discounts; a few newspapers offer a single flat rate to both national and local advertisers.

Newspapers that offer volume discounts have an **open rate** (their highest rate for a one-time insertion) and **contract rates,** whereby local advertisers can obtain discounts of up to 70 percent by signing a contract for frequent or bulk space purchases. **Bulk discounts** offer advertisers decreasing rates as they use more inches. Advertisers earn **frequency discounts** by running a given ad repeatedly in a specific time period. Similarly, advertisers can sometimes get **earned rates,** a discount applied retroactively as the volume of advertising increases through the year.

OHIO

Cincinnati

Hamilton County—Map Location B-7

THE CINCINNATI ENQUIRER*THE CINCINNATI POST

312 Elm St., Cincinnati, OH 45202. Phone 513-768-8220. Fax 513-768-8250. Classified Phone 513-421-6300. Classified Fax 513-768-8320.
E-mail abaston@enquirer.com
URL http://www.cincinnati.com

ⒶABC   readerprofile

Location ID: 1 NSNL OH   **Mid 017122-000**
Member: ABC Coupon Distribution Verification Service; ACB, Inc.; NAA.
The Cincinnati Enquirer—Morning (Mon-Fri), Sat and Sun.
SHIPPING INSTRUCTIONS: Insertion orders to: The Cincinnati Enquirer, 312 Elm St. 17th Floor, Cincinnati, OH 45202.

1. PERSONNEL
EXEC, PUB—Harry Whipple, Pres/Pub
NSM—Karen Cruise, Nat'l Sales Mgr, P:513-768-8176

2. REPRESENTATIVES and/or BRANCH OFFICES
Newspapers First.
American Publishers' Representatives Ltd.

3. COMMISSION AND CASH DISCOUNT
15% to agencies. No cash discount.

4. POLICY-ALL CLASSIFICATIONS
30-day notice given of any rate revision.
Alcoholic beverage advertising accepted.

ADVERTISING RATES
Effective 12-27-04   Confirmed 10-05

5. BLACK/WHITE RATES

	M&E	Sun
SAU open, per inch	337.08	344.68
Full page rates	43,483.32	44,463.72

BULK SPACE CONTRACT RATES

	Per inch			Per inch	
	Combo	Sun.		Combo	Sun.
129*	309.05	319.60	2,580*	272.77	291.39
258*	286.87	303.48	3,354*	265.51	287.76
516*	284.49	300.45	4,902*	247.65	284.04
774*	283.49	299.83	6,708*	243.21	282.25
1,032*	281.04	298.60	9,804*	241.75	281.07
1,290*	278.18	293.22	13,416*	232.03	269.55
1,677*	275.20	292.55			

REPEAT RATE
30% discount off full rated ational ads. All ads must run within a seven-day priod and the entire order must be submitted at one time to earn discounts. No minimum ad size. Discounts do not apply to color or other charges. Sunday/Holiday ads is at full rate.

5a. ZONE EDITIONS
METRO ZONED EDITIONS
Per Inch, Per insertion

Zone	Enquirer and Post
West	107.45
East	112.32
North	56.41
Kentucky	73.31

6. GROUP COMBINATION RATES-B/W & COLOR
Target, Ohio Network—see listing at beginning of State.

7. COLOR RATES AND DATA
Use b/w rate plus the following applicable costs:

	Per inch		
	b/w 1 c	b/w 2 c	b/w 3 c
M & E Combo, Extra	34.00	50.00	55.00
Sunday, Extra	27.00	38.00	42.00

Closing dates: Advance deadline 24 hours earlier than normal deadlines.
A charge will be made for cancellations made after these times if it is mechanically impossible to cancel.

8a. INSERTS
PREPRINT INSERTS—FULL DISTRIBUTION

	CPM		CPM
FSS	54.50	25-28 tab pgs	87.25
4-8 tab pgs	57.00	29-32 tab pgs	90.50
9-12 tab pgs	61.25	33-36 tab pgs	93.75
13-16 tab pgs	72.50	37-40 tab pgs	96.50
17-20 tab pgs	74.00	41-44 tab pgs	103.00
21-24 tab pgs	80.25	45-48 tab pgs	106.00

Over 48 pages: Add 1.00 per page CPM. For all Monday and Tuesday inserts, add 10.00 CPM. For all Sunday inserts add 5.00 CPM.

PARTIAL DISTRIBUTION

	25,000+	100,000+	200,000
FSS	75.00	68.50	64.25
4-12 tab	80.00	74.00	72.00
13-24 tab	94.25	86.75	84.75
25-36 tab	107.00	99.75	97.50
37-48 tab	119.75	114.75	112.50

Over 48 pages—extra 1.00 per page/CPM.
Sunday inserts—5.00 extra CPM.
Delivery deadline:
Daily—Not more than 3 weeks of less than 8 days prior to insertion dates.
Sunday—Not more than 3 weeks or less than 12 days prior to insertion dates.
SHIPPING INSTRUCTIONS: The Cincinnati Enquirer Production Facility, 1531 Western Ave., Cincinnati, OH 45214.
Attn: Frank Woesman. Phone 513-369-3585.

9. SPLIT RUN
100.00 to agencies (commissionable). When necessary to set second ad, extra charge of 20.00 per col. inch. (noncommissionable.) Minimum 14 inches.
True split runs available Monday, Tuesday and Saturday only. Option dates required. A 2/3-1/3 split run can be run on Wednesday, Thursday and Friday.

11. SPECIAL DAYS/PAGES/FEATURES
Daily—Business, Employment, Women.
Sunday—Best Food Day, Arts, Real Estate, Travel, Women.
Tuesday—Books.
Wednesday—Technology, Health.
Friday—Family, Religion, Entertainment.
Saturday—Auto, Home.

12. R.O.P. DEPTH REQUIREMENTS
Ads over 18 inches deep charged full col.

13. CONTRACT AND COPY REGULATIONS

Per inch	186.47	Comb. per inch	267.54

FREQUENCY DISCOUNTS

7 weeks or 14 insert.	12%
13 weeks or 26 insert.	15%
26 weeks or 52 insert.	20%
39 weeks or 78 insert.	25%
52 weeks or 104 insert.	30%

COLOR RATES AND DATA
Use b/w rate plus the following applicable costs:
Available in full page, 1/2, 3/4 units:

b/w 1 c	678.00
b/w 2 c	1,308.00
b/w 3 c	1,726.00

POST
TV Magazine
SATURDAY
BLACK/WHITE RATES

Per inch	120.91	Comb. per inch	267.54

FREQUENCY DISCOUNTS

7 weeks or 14 insert.	12%
13 weeks or 26 insert.	15%
26 weeks or 52 insert.	20%
39 weeks or 78 insert.	25%
52 weeks or 104 insert.	30%

COLOR RATES AND DATA
Use b/w rate plus the following applicable costs:
Available in full page, 1/2, 3/4 units:

b/w 1 c	678.00	b/w 3 c	1,726.00
b/w 2 c	1,308.00		

ROP DEPTH REQUIREMENTS
1/16 page minimum.
CLOSING TIMES
Reservations for color 24 days; monotone 18 days.
Copy for color 22 days; monotone 16 days.
MECHANICAL MEASUREMENTS
PRINTING PROCESS: Offset.
4 cols. to page.
Page size 6-1/2" wide x 9-3/4" deep.

20. CIRCULATION
Enquirer established 1841, per copy daily .50; Sunday 1.50.
Post established 1881. per copy .50.
ENQUIRER
Net Paid—A. B. C. 3-31-05*
NEWSPAPER DESIGNATED MARKET

	Total	NDM	Outside
Morn (Mon-Thu)	192,562	186,125	6,437
Fri Morn	213,038	206,176	6,862
Sat Morn	189,409	182,674	6,735
Sun	296,989	282,724	14,265

Unpaid dist. (not included above):
Morn Total 124; Fri Total 124; Sat Total 124; Sun Total 1.
POST
Net Paid—A. B. C. 3-31-05*
NEWSPAPER DESIGNATED MARKET

	Total	NDM	Outside
Eve (Mon-Fri) except Sun.	35,544	34,384	1,160
Sat	47,631	46,060	1,571

Unpaid dist. (not included above):
Eve Total 11; Sat Morn 11.
Net Paid—A. B. C. Combined
NEWSPAPER DESIGNATED MARKET

	Total	NDM	Outside
Morn & Eve Comb.	228,106	220,509	7,597
Fri Morn	213,038	206,176	6,862
Sat Comb.	237,040	228,734	8,306
Sun	296,989	282,724	14,265

(*) 26 weeks.
For county, MSA & DMA data, see CIRCULATION 2006.

This partial rate card for the *Cincinnati Enquirer* and the *Cincinnati Post* (www.cincinnati.com) is similar to that for magazines. It shows the variety of ad units available and presents the costs, circulation figures, requirements, and deadlines.

Short Rate

An advertiser who contracts to buy a specific amount of space during a one-year period at a discount and then fails to fulfill the promise is charged a **short rate,** which is the difference between the contracted rate and the earned rate for the actual inches run. Conversely, an advertiser who buys more inches than contracted may be entitled to a rebate or credit because of the discounted earned rate for the additional advertising space.

Combination Rates

Combination rates are often available for placing a given ad in (1) morning and evening editions of the same newspaper; (2) two or more newspapers owned by the same publisher; and (3) in some cases, two or more newspapers affiliated in a syndicate or newspaper group.

Run of Paper versus Preferred Position

Run-of-paper (ROP) advertising rates entitle a newspaper to place a given ad on any newspaper page or in any position it desires. Although the advertiser has no control over where the ad appears in the paper, most newspapers try to place an ad in the position the advertiser requests.

Ethical Issues

What's at Stake with Sweepstakes?

Many of us have probably received an envelope in the mail with the phrase "You Are a Winner!" or something similar, plastered in large, bold type. And perhaps, for a split second you believed that you had won the $100,000 prize. Then you discovered otherwise. Perhaps you were misled into believing that purchasing magazine subscriptions would increase your chances of winning.

Until recently, this is how many sweepstakes were pitched to consumers. According to the Direct Marketing Association, sweepstakes are by definition, "an advertising or promotional device by which items of value (prizes) are awarded to participating consumers by chance, with no purchase or 'entry fee' required in order to win." However, by entering a sweepstakes you are volunteering your name and address to be put on lists for acquisition by other direct marketers. In turn you are offered a chance to win what seems like easy money. For years it was difficult for recipients to tell whether or not they had a winning entry. With statements claiming "You are a winner" and simulated checks, the line separating promotion and deception became very thin.

All of this changed in 2000. Following investigations of sweepstakes firms in more than 40 states, three of the biggest sweeps marketers—Publisher's Clearing House (PCH), Time Inc., and U.S. Sales Corp.—were each brought to court by numerous state regulators, alleging that the marketing giants conducted deceptive sweepstakes promotions. In California alone, state officials claimed that 5,000 consumers spent more than $2,500 each a year in unnecessary magazine subscriptions through PCH because they believed that it improved their odds of winning. Accusations were similar for all three companies, and each defended their marketing practices claiming they always believed their mailings were clear. One PCH spokesman stated that 98 percent of the consumers who purchased magazines through their promotions were spending less than $300 a year. How-

ever, because litigation in so many states—47 in Time Inc.'s case—would have been too costly, each company decided to settle and agreed to reform its practices. Combined, the three marketers refunded more than $50 million in fines and restitution to state regulators and consumers who excessively purchased unnecessary magazines.

The reforms agreed to by these companies were in accord with the Deceptive Mail Prevention and Enforcement Act that became effective in April 2000. The act changed how direct mail sweepstakes are presented and packaged. Some of the most significant changes included abandoning any "winner" proclamations unless the recipient had truly won a prize, and displaying a "fact box" that "clearly and conspicuously" explained all the terms and rules of the sweepstakes, including the odds of winning. Each mailing is also required to include the statements "No purchase is necessary to enter" and "A purchase does not improve your chances of winning" in boldfaced capital letters in the mailing, in the rules, and on the order/entry form itself. In addition, each company is required to include a statement providing an address or toll-free number where recipients can either write or call to have their name and address removed from the mailing list.

Does this mean an end to sweepstakes? Probably not, since many people seem to jump at the chance to strike it rich for the cost of a stamp.

How much harm, if any, are sweepstakes really causing? Isn't part of promotion getting consumers to believe that they want what is being advertised? Without question, the ethical issues involved are complicated, but at least now you won't have to read the fine print to get the whole story.

Questions

1. Are sweepstakes companies really at fault for misleading their consumers? Why or why not?

2. Do you believe it is ethical for sweepstakes to "disguise" their promotions for the purpose of advertising?

An advertiser can ensure a choice position for an ad by paying a higher **preferred-position rate.** A tire manufacturer, for example, may pay the preferred rate to ensure a position in the sports section.

There are also preferred positions on a given page. The preferred position near the top of a page or at the top of a column next to reading matter is called **full position.** It's usually surrounded by reading matter and may cost the advertiser 25 to 50 percent more than ROP rates.

Color Advertising

Color advertising is available in many newspapers on an ROP basis. Because of their high-speed presses and porous paper stock, newspapers are not noted for

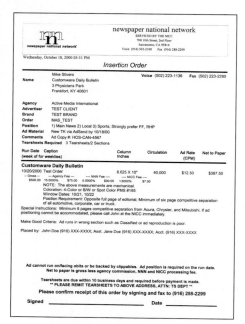

Co-ops and networks help simplify the ad buying process for advertisers by consolidating the purchasing paperwork and requirements for all local papers in a single location. This example of an insertion order for the Newspaper National Network is typical of what these contracts look like. Important information such as run date, size, and desired position is included.

high-quality color printing. So advertisers frequently preprint ads using processes known as HiFi color and Spectracolor. The cost of a color ad is usually based on the black-and-white rate plus an extra charge for each additional color.

Split Runs

Many newspapers (and magazines) offer **split runs** so that advertisers can test the *pulling power* of different ads. The advertiser runs two ads of identical size, but different content, for the same product on the same day in different press runs. The idea is to eliminate as many variables as possible. By measuring responses to the two ads, the advertiser is able to compare and contrast the effectiveness of each. For this service, newspapers typically charge extra and set a minimum space requirement.

Co-ops and Networks

As an aid to national advertisers, the National Advertising Bureau (NAB) created the Newspaper Advertising Co-op Network (NACON). Salespeople from participating newspapers helped national advertisers line up retailers for dealer-listing ads. The advertiser would produce the ad and include a blank space for each paper to insert local retailers' names. The system also helped manufacturers manage local advertising tie-ins to national campaigns and themes. Before the development of NACON, national advertisers had to place ads and recruit local dealers individually.

In 1992 the NAB merged with the American Newspaper Publishers Association and five other marketing associations to form the **Newspaper Association of America (NAA),** which continued to simplify national newspaper ad buys. In 1994 the NAA launched a one-order, one-bill system for national advertising, called the Newspaper National Network. Advertisers can make multimarket newspaper buys by placing one order and paying one bill, instead of having to contact—and pay—each paper individually.[19]

Chrysler was the first marketer to use the new network, placing ads for its national minivan sale in 75 newspapers in March 1994.[20] The Newspaper National Network offers advertisers competitive CPM pricing and guaranteed positioning in addition to its one-order, one-bill appeal.[21] It also allows smaller papers to participate in national advertising.[22]

Insertion Orders and Tearsheets

When advertisers place an ad, they submit an **insertion order** to the newspaper stating the date(s) on which the ad is to run, its size, the desired position, the rate, and the type of artwork accompanying the order.

When a newspaper creates ad copy and art, it gives the advertiser a **proof copy** to check. In contrast, most national advertising arrives at the newspaper *camera ready,* either in the form of a photo print or an electronic file via e-mail.

To verify that the ad ran, the newspaper tears out the page on which the ad appeared and sends it to the agency or advertiser. Today, most **tearsheets** for national advertisers are handled through a private central office, the Advertising Checking Bureau.

When a tearsheet arrives, the advertiser examines it to make sure the ad ran according to instructions: in the right section and page position, and with the cor-

CONCEPT CHECK

What are some of the options that advertisers must consider when purchasing space in newspapers?

rect reproduction. If the ad did not run per instructions, the agency or advertiser is usually due an adjustment, a discount, or even a free rerun.

Print: A Worldwide Medium

Every country has newspapers and magazines to serve its population. U.S. advertisers in foreign markets generally use either international or local media, depending on their campaign objectives and intended audience. Whether at home or abroad, advertisers must study the audience and remember the basics of print advertising, some of which are enumerated in the Checklist, "What Works Best in Print."

Several large U.S. publishers, including Time Warner and *Scientific American*, circulate international editions of their magazines abroad. The *International Herald Tribune, The Wall Street Journal,* and London's *Financial Times* are widely read in Asia, Europe, and the Middle East. In China, numerous publications such as *Elle* and *Avenue China* are now distributed to the country's wealthiest and most influential residents.[23]

Well-educated, upper-income consumers read these newspapers and magazines, even though they are typically printed in English. So these publications are the closest thing to global print media for reaching this audience. *Reader's Digest*—the oldest international mass-audience medium—reaches 170 foreign countries. However, the publisher prints the magazine in local languages and tailors it to each country, so advertisers often view it as a local medium.

The number of international business, trade, or specialty publications is growing. Switzerland's *European Business* and Belgium's *Electronic Product News,* both English-language magazines, are distributed throughout Europe.

Political changes in the former Soviet Union and Eastern bloc countries spurred many new trade publications. Most are published locally in association with foreign publishers. In 1990, for example, McGraw-Hill launched Russian-language editions of *Aviation Week & Space Technology* and *Business Week.* And International Data Group launched several trade publications, including *Mir PK Russia* (formerly *PC World USSR*) and *ComputerWorld Poland.*

Print Media and New Technologies

With computers came revolutionary media options, such as the Internet and CD-ROM, challenging both traditional print media and advertisers to adapt. Newspapers and magazines are rushing to make alliances with cable, regional telephone, and online companies to get a toehold in the interactive information market.

Over the last five years, for example, virtually all metropolitan news organizations and national magazines have incorporated electronic services. News organizations are information-rich, and much of the specialized information they don't run in the paper or the magazine fits perfectly with the online world's narrower interests. They are still, however, trying to figure out how to incorporate advertising into their new ventures. Most ads are still simply banners, but customers who are interested can click on the banners for more in-depth information. This becomes a value-added service for the print medium's advertising customers. George Gilder, media expert and author, believes that the newspaper industry is in a particularly advantageous position, because "the convergence of text and video will cause a revolution in advertising, with targeted messages leading consumers step-by-step to a transaction."[24]

We'll deal with these issues in greater depth in Chapter 13.

Chapter Summary

The printed page—in magazines and newspapers—provides a unique, flexible medium for advertising creativity.

In selecting magazines for advertising, the media buyer must consider a publication's circulation, its readership, its cost, and its mechanical requirements. A magazine's rates may be determined by several factors: its primary and secondary readership, the number of subscription and newsstand sales, and the number of copies guaranteed versus those actually delivered.

Magazine rate cards follow a standard format so advertisers can readily compare advertising costs. They list black-and-white and color rates, discounts, issue and closing dates, and mechanical requirements.

Magazines offer distinct advantages. They are the most selective of all mass media and are flexible in both readership and advertising. They offer unsurpassed color, excellent reproduction quality, authority and believability, long shelf life, and prestige at an efficient cost. However, they often require long lead times, have problems offering broad reach and high frequency, and are subject to heavy advertising competition. The cost of advertising in some magazines is also very high.

The newspaper is a mass medium read by almost everybody. It offers great flexibility, which assists creativity, and its printed message lasts longer than ads in electronic media. However, newspapers also have disadvantages: lack of audience selectivity, short life span, poor production quality, heavy advertising competition, potentially poor ad placement, and overlapping circulation. Still, the newspaper is the major community-serving medium today for both news and advertising.

The newspaper's rate card lists prices, deadlines, mechanical requirements, and other pertinent information. Rates vary for local and national advertisers. Also listed are the newspaper's short-rate policy, combination rates, frequency discounts, run-of-paper rates, and other data.

Print is a worldwide medium; every country has newspapers and magazines. The international advertiser may have to choose between local and international media. The most educated consumers in many countries often read English-language publications. Political changes in eastern Europe have spurred the introduction of many trade and business publications in local languages. Advertisers must study the audience they wish to reach before buying any media, whether at home or abroad.

Newspapers and magazines are making alliances with cable, regional telephone, and online computer companies to enter the interactive information market. They are still experimenting with ways to sell advertising on their electronic publications. Some experts believe that the convergence of text, video, and graphics will cause a creative revolution in advertising, with targeted, information-rich messages able to lead consumers step by step to a transaction without ever leaving home.

Key Terms

Audit Bureau of Circulations (ABC), 303
bleed, 297
bulk discounts, 311
business magazines, 301
circulation audit, 303
classified ads, 310
classified display ads, 310
closing date, 304
color strip, 300
column inch, 307
combination rates, 312
consumer magazines, 301
contract rate, 311
controlled circulation, 304
cooperative (co-op) advertising, 310
cost per thousand (CPM), 305
cover date, 304
cover position, 297
creative mix, 297
daily newspaper, 307
demographic editions, 305
display advertising, 309
earned rate, 311
farm publications, 301

flat rate, 311
fragrance strips, 300
frequency discounts, 305, 311
full position, 313
gatefold, 299
geographic editions, 305
guaranteed circulation, 302
horizontal publications, 303
insert, 298
insertion order, 314
island half, 298
junior unit, 297
local city magazine, 301
national magazine, 301
national rate, 311
Newspaper Association of America (NAA), 314
online advertising, 310
on-sale date, 304
open rate, 311
paid circulation, 304
pop-up ad, 300
preferred-position rate, 313

preprinted inserts, 300, 310
primary circulation, 303
product samples, 300
proof copy, 314
public notices, 310
rate base, 302
rate card, 311
reading notice, 310
regional publications, 301
run-of-paper (ROP) advertising rates, 312
secondary (pass-along) readership, 303
shoppers, 309
short rate, 312
split runs, 314
standard advertising unit (SAU), 307
standard-size newspaper, 307
Sunday supplement, 309
tabloid newspaper, 307
tearsheets, 314
3-D ads, 300
vertical publication, 303
volume discount, 305
weekly newspapers, 307

Review Questions

1. If you worked in the advertising department of a premium-priced furniture manufacturer, would you recommend magazine advertising? Why or why not?

2. If you were the advertising manager for a magazine aimed at senior citizens, what advantages would you cite to potential advertisers?

3. What is the advantage of magazine advertising to businesses that sell to other businesses?

4. What is the importance of the Audit Bureau of Circulations?

5. Why do magazines typically base their advertising rates on circulation figures that are below their average circulation?

6. Why do retailers advertise so heavily in local newspapers?

7. How can advertisers improve the selectivity of their newspaper ads?

8. What factors should advertisers consider in deciding among various local papers (including dailies and weeklies)?

9. Should national advertisers be charged a higher rate than local advertisers? Support your position.

10. What role do you see the Internet playing in the future for publishers of newspapers and magazines?

Exploring Advertising

1. Find examples of creative print media formats, such as bleed pages, cover positions, inserts and gatefolds, and special sizes, such as junior pages and island halves. Explain why you think those formats were chosen for those specific brands. Were they a good choice?

2. Cut several ads out of a magazine. Based on the Pros and Cons checklist, determine the primary reasons those advertisers chose to use this medium. Was it a good choice?

3. Cut several ads out of the local newspaper. Based on the Pros and Cons checklist, determine the primary reasons those advertisers chose to use this medium. Was it a good choice?

4. Critique a newspaper or magazine advertisement based on the Checklist, "What Works Best in Print." Give the ad a grade for each of the points and explain why you assigned that grade. What is your overall evaluation of the print ad?

5. Using the *Cincinnati Enquirer* rate card on page 312, answer the following questions:

    a. What is the cost of a full-page, black-and-white ad in the Sunday edition?

    b. Based on total circulation, calculate the CPM for the black-and-white ad.

    c. How much, on a CPM basis, would the *Enquirer* charge to insert an 8-page, preprinted advertisement into a Tuesday edition? What would that translate to in actual dollars for the total market?

    d. If you wanted to run an ad for an herbal remedy product, on what day and in which feature section might the ad be most effective?

chapter twelve

Electronic Media: Television and Radio

Objectives

To present the important factors advertisers need to evaluate when considering the use of radio and television in the media mix. Each medium has its own characteristics, advantages, and drawbacks. Advertisers must be able to compare their merits and understand the most cost-effective ways to buy advertising time.

After studying this chapter, you will be able to:

* **Describe** the advantages and drawbacks of broadcast television as an advertising medium.

* **Discuss** the advantages and drawbacks of cable television as an advertising medium and explain how it differs from broadcast television.

* **Explain** the process of buying cable and broadcast TV time.

* **Evaluate** the different types of television advertising available.

* **Describe** the process of TV audience measurement.

* **Discuss** the main factors to consider when buying television time.

* **Analyze** the pros and cons of using radio in the media mix.

* **Explain** the major factors to consider when buying radio time.

Milk! Milk! Milk!

Milk coming!

Milk may "do a body good," but for the dairy industry, the bottom line remains the same: How can we sell more of it? Unlike the national "Milk, where's your mustache?" magazine campaign, the California milk producers were concerned less with changing consumer attitudes toward milk than with increasing its consumption. The late 1980s and early 1990s were characterized by slumping sales that needed to be bolstered, not with an image enhancer but with an action campaign—one that would move more milk out of the supermarkets and into the homes of consumers.

The problem of declining milk consumption was not unique to California, of course. It plagued the industry nationwide. People simply weren't drinking the beverage on the scale they once did; milk was losing out to sexy colas and snappy fruit drinks. And while the campaigns of "Milk does a body good" and "America's favorite health kick" had managed to create a fun and healthy image for milk, they had done little to improve sales.

Enter Jeff Manning, executive director for the California Milk Processor Board. Founded by the state's milk producers in 1993, the board set out to solve the problem of poor sales. Manning started with a hunch—that people don't drink milk by itself. Previous ads featured milk alone, but he believed that food was a key component, and it was missing from the picture. "If you ask people when milk is crucial, they'll tell you it's when they have cereal in the bowl or cookies in their mouth," Manning explained. "The driver is not the milk. It's the food."[1]

With this idea, Manning hired San Francisco–based Goodby, Silverstein & Partners to develop an advertising campaign that would target people who already consume milk and encourage them to drink more. Research revealed that 88 percent of milk is consumed at home and, as Manning suspected, it is usually accompanied by food. People most often drink milk with cereal, but cookies, pastries, peanut butter and jelly sandwiches, and brownies are also popular milk partners.

The agency asked a group of research participants to go without milk for one week and then to share their experiences. The group quickly discovered the anguish of not having milk when they really needed it. One person woke up early in the morning and poured himself a bowl of cereal but then discovered there was no milk in the fridge. "It's so bad, you'd even steal milk from your kid," said one man, to which another replied, "Never mind your kid. You're so desperate you'd even steal it from your cat!"[2]

These stories found their way into the creative TV commercials that we all know: the businessman who dies and finds himself in what appears to be heaven with a plateful of cookies, only to discover that there is no milk; the angry Santa who takes back his gifts when he finds that no milk was left with the cookies. The question "Got milk?" became a punch line to jokes, not just a tagline for commercials.

Television proved to be the perfect vehicle for the "Got milk?" campaign because of its ability to tell the story in a unique manner and to dramatize the dilemma faced by milk-starved consumers. People began buying milk again. So successful was the regional advertising campaign, in fact, that Dairy Management, Inc., the national dairy industry board, quickly licensed it to run on the national circuit.

The growth in cable and satellite TV systems has dramatically increased the number of channels available to viewers. This has given consumers almost unlimited program alternatives, making it easier for advertisers to reach a more selective audience.

Electronic Media

The electronic media of radio and television used to be called the broadcast media. But with the advent of cable TV, many programs are now transmitted electronically through wires rather than broadcast through the air.

The United States alone has more than 1,000 local commercial TV stations and nearly 10,000 local radio stations as well as major TV and radio networks, including ABC, CBS, NBC, and Fox. More than 10,000 local cable systems blanket the country, serving more than 68 million subscribers. Major cable networks such as USA, A&E, and CNN serve these systems. Cable also provides channels with specialized offerings, such as QVC, which offers products that can be purchased by phone; Cinemax, which features recently released films; and American Movie Classics (AMC), which features vintage films.

The Medium of Television

Back in 1950, U.S. advertisers spent $171 million, or about 3 percent of total U.S. advertising volume, on the new medium of television. It didn't take long, though, for the nation's advertisers to discover the power of this new vehicle to reach mass audiences quickly and frequently. TV also offered unique creative opportunities to imbue their brands with personality and image like never before. By 2004, TV advertising had grown to more than $67 *billion* and accounted for more than 25 percent of all U.S. ad spending, surpassing newspapers as the leading U.S. advertising medium.[3] Exhibit 12–1 lists the top network television advertisers in the United States and their annual expenditures.

Today, the medium of television is available to advertisers in two principal forms: broadcast and cable. **Broadcast TV** reaches its audience by transmitting electromagnetic waves through the air across some geographic territory. **Cable TV** reaches its audience through wires, which may be strung from telephone poles or laid underground, or via satellite signals.

Exhibit 12–1

Top 10 network TV advertisers in the United States (2004).

Rank	Company	Network TV ad spending in 2004 ($ millions)
1	Procter & Gamble Co.	$858.2
2	General Motors Corp.	753.5
3	Johnson & Johnson	521.6
4	Ford Motor Co.	497.6
5	Time Warner	451.9
6	Pfizer	417.8
7	Walt Disney Co.	417.6
8	SBC Communications	396.2
9	PepsiCo	379.5
10	DaimlerChrysler	359.4

Broadcast TV

Until the advent of the Internet, broadcast television grew faster than any other advertising medium in history. As both a news and entertainment medium, it caught people's fancy very quickly. From its beginnings after World War II, broadcast TV rapidly emerged as the only medium that offered sight, sound, and motion. People could stay home and still go to the movies. As TV's legions of viewers grew, the big national brand advertisers quickly discovered they could use the medium very efficiently to expand distribution across the country and sell products like never before. Not only that, the medium was ideal for building an image for their brands—even better than magazines, which had previously been the image-building medium of choice. It didn't take long for marketers to switch their budgets from radio, newspapers, and magazines. Broadcast TV attracts the largest volume of *national* advertising, almost $42 billion in 2003.[4]

The United States now has 1,685 commercial TV stations.[5] Stations in the United States operate as independents unless they are affiliated with one of the national networks (ABC, NBC, CBS, Fox). Both network affiliates and independent stations may subscribe to nationally syndicated programs as well as originate their own programming. However, increasing competition from cable TV is taking viewers from the national network programs. To compensate, some networks are investing in cable TV systems or starting their own. NBC, for example, started CNBC and MSNBC, and ABC (which is now owned by Disney) has an 80 percent interest in ESPN.

Cable TV

For more than 30 years, broadcast TV, especially network TV, was the dominant entertainment medium for most Americans. Today, other electronic media have dramatically changed that dominance. Chief among the challengers is cable television.

Cable TV has been around since the late 1940s. Initially, it carried television signals by wire to areas with poor reception such as mountainous regions. But in the 1970s, the advent of satellite TV signals, the proliferation of channels, and the introduction of uncut first-run movies via premium cable channels such as Home Box Office (HBO) and Showtime made cable TV more attractive to all viewers, even people in urban areas.

At first, many subscribers valued cable simply for the full array of regional channels and access to premium services such as HBO. But once this novelty

Exhibit 12–2

Top 15 cable TV networks (as of April, 2005)

Network	Number of subscribers (millions)	Program type
Discovery Channel	89.9	Education/family/health/news/science
ESPN	89.9	Sports
Cable News Network (CNN)	89.4	News/information
Turner Network Television (TNT)	89.4	Family/general/sports
USA Network	89.2	Entertainment/movies/sports
Nickelodeon	89.1	Youth interest
TBS Superstation	89.1	Family/general/music/sports
Spike TV	89.1	Men's interest/movies
Arts & Entertainment (A&E)	89.0	Family/variety
Lifetime	88.9	Women's interest/family/general/health
ESPN2	88.8	Sports
The Weather Channel	88.8	Weather news/information
The Learning Channel (TLC)	88.7	Family/general/documentaries
Music Television (MTV)	88.5	Youth interest/music
C-SPAN	88.4	Public affairs/government proceedings

wore off, subscribers wanted more. A variety of advertiser-supported cable networks soon appeared with specialized programming in arts, history, sports, news, and comedy, along with diversified pay services and many more local shows. All of this attracted more and more subscribers—and consequently drew viewers away from the big broadcast networks.

In the last three decades, cable's growth has been extraordinary. In 1975, only 13 percent of TV households in the United States had cable. By 2005, cable (wired and satellite) reached 85 percent of all TV households.[6] Although cable subscribers may receive more than 100 channels, most households only watch 15 to 19 channels.[7]

Most channels are privately owned and operated. These include local network affiliates and independents, cable networks, superstations, local cable system channels, and community access channels. The cable fees represent about one-third of cable TV revenues; advertising makes up the remainder. Networks such as CNN, USA, the Discovery Channel, Arts & Entertainment, Lifetime, Comedy Central, and Spike TV now compete for advertisers' dollars, each selling its own niche audience.[8] For an additional price, subscribers can receive premium services such as HBO, Showtime, and Cinemax and see special events such as first-run films, championship boxing matches, and baseball and football games.

There are now some 65 ad-supported national cable networks in the United States and a growing number of regional networks.[9] Exhibit 12–2 lists the most widely carried ones. Included are a handful of *superstations* (such as WGN Chicago and TBS Atlanta), local over-the-air TV stations whose signals are delivered via satellite to cable systems across the country and that carry some national advertising.

TV Audience Trends

As a way to reach a mass audience, no other medium today has the unique creative abilities of television: the combination of sight, sound, and motion; the opportunity to demonstrate the product; the potential to use special effects; the empathy of the viewer; and the believability for viewers of seeing it happen right before their eyes (see the Checklist, "The Pros and Cons of Broadcast TV Advertising"). As Exhibit 12–3 shows, almost half of viewers believe TV is the most authoritative advertising source, compared to only 26 percent for newspapers, 11 percent for magazines, 9 percent for radio, and 5 percent for the Internet. Television was also rated as the most influential, persuasive, and exciting medium.[10]

Checklist

The Pros and Cons of Broadcast TV Advertising

The Pros

- **Mass coverage.** A full 98 percent of all U.S. homes have a TV (most have more than one), and viewing time for the average household increased from about five hours a day in 1960 to about eight hours in 2005.
- **Relatively low cost per viewer.** Despite the often huge outlays for commercial production and advertising time, TV's equally huge audiences bring the cost per exposure down to $2 to $10 per thousand viewers.
- **Some selectivity.** Television audiences vary a great deal depending on the time of day, day of the week, and nature of the programming. Advertising messages can be presented when desirable prospects are watching, and advertisers can reach select geographic audiences by buying local and regional markets.
- **Impact.** Television offers a kind of impact that other forms of advertising cannot achieve, displaying and demonstrating the product with sound, motion, and full color.
- **Creativity.** The various facets of the TV commercial—sight, sound, motion, and color—permit infinite original and imaginative appeals.
- **Prestige.** Because the public considers TV the most authoritative and influential medium, it offers advertisers a prestigious image.
- **Social dominance.** In North America, most people under age 35 grew up with TV as a window to their social environment. They continue to be stirred by TV screenings of the Olympics, space travel, assassinations, wars, and political scandals around the world.

The Cons

- **High production cost.** One of broadcast TV's greatest handicaps is the high cost of producing quality com-

mercials. Depending on the creative approach, the cost of filming a national commercial today may run from $200,000 to more than $1 million. However, some local stations are willing to produce low-cost commercials for local advertisers.
- **High airtime cost.** The average cost of a prime-time network commercial ranges from $200,000 to over $400,000. A single 30-second commercial in a top-rated prime time show may cost over $500,000. Special attractions like the Super Bowl cost over $2 million. The cost of mass coverage prices small- and medium-size advertisers out of the market.
- **Long lead times.** Producing commercials and purchasing airtime generally require a lot of advance planning.
- **Limited selectivity.** Broadcast TV is not cost effective for advertisers seeking a very specific, small audience. And it is losing some of its selectivity because of changing audience trends. For example, more women are working outside the home or watching specialized cable shows, hurting advertisers on network soap operas.
- **Brevity.** Studies show that most TV viewers can't remember the product or company in the most recent TV ad they watched—even if it was within the last five minutes. Recall improves with the length of the commercial; people remember 60-second spots better than 30-second spots.
- **Clutter.** TV advertising is usually surrounded by station breaks, credits, and public service announcements, as well as six or seven other ads. All these messages compete for attention, so viewers become annoyed and confused and often misidentify the product.
- **Zipping and zapping.** VCR and TiVo users who skip through commercials when replaying taped programs are zipping; remote-control users who change channels or mute the sound at the beginning of a commercial break are zapping.

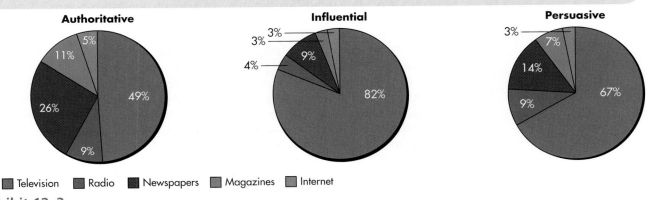

Authoritative
- 49%
- 5%
- 11%
- 26%
- 9%

Influential
- 82%
- 3%
- 3%
- 9%
- 4%

Persuasive
- 67%
- 3%
- 7%
- 14%
- 9%

■ Television ■ Radio ■ Newspapers ■ Magazines ■ Internet

Exhibit 12–3

In 2003, adult viewers rated television as the most authoritative, influential, and persuasive advertising medium.

The heaviest viewers of broadcast TV are middle-income, high school–educated individuals and their families, so most programming is directed at this group. People with considerably higher incomes and more education typically have a more diverse range of media and entertainment options.

The number of TV viewing hours continues to increase. In the average U.S. home, total viewers watch TV/cable/VCR for more than 8 hours every day. Children and teenagers view an average of 21 hours per week, 1 to 2 hours less than their parents.[11] Around the world, older women watch TV the most (36 hours per week in both the United States and Canada).

Cable in North American homes has significantly altered TV viewing patterns and the use of other media. Households with cable spend less time watching broadcast TV. They also spend less time listening to the radio, reading, or going to the movies. Cable seems to reach an audience that is difficult to get to in any other way. As a result of this audience fragmentation, advertising on broadcast networks has become less cost effective. Video and DVD rentals have also increased dramatically, drawing more viewers away from advertiser-supported TV, both broadcast and cable (which is why ads have now started appearing on videos).

Cable households watch more television than noncable households: 56.2 hours per week versus 32.6 hours. Cable households watch about 22.8 hours of cable programming a week.[12]

National advertisers have been using cable since the late 1970s and cable advertising revenues have grown steadily, reaching over $18.8 billion in 2004.[13] One reason is that cable's upscale audience buys proportionately more goods and services than noncable subscribers. However, local retailers also find local cable a good place to advertise. Fisher Big Wheel, a discount department store in Midvale, Ohio, became an enthusiastic cable devotee after its first cable promotion brought an extra 15,000 customers into the store.

For many years television was strictly a mass medium, used to great advantage by the manufacturers of mass consumption goods: toiletries and cosmetics, food, appliances, and cars. But today, thanks to the narrowcasting ability of cable TV, television can also be a highly selective niche medium. It's not unusual, for instance, to see ads for special feed for thoroughbreds and show horses on ESPN's Grand Prix of Jumping. And thanks to local cable, TV is now affordable for even small local advertisers.

In 2004, local cable advertising made up about 8 percent of the more than $60 billion U.S. TV advertising market. But it's growing at a faster clip than other advertising categories. PricewaterhouseCoopers estimates that the local cable ad market rose 11.9 percent in 2004 to $5.4 billion and should grow by nearly 21 percent to $7.3 billion by 2008.[14]

It appears that audiences are being offered a nearly infinite number of choices today. But there lies the crux of one of the major issues of modern media. While there is no doubt that the media play an ever-expanding role in our daily lives, there is a finite limit to the number of media exposures people can absorb. When that limit is reached (and we're certainly getting close to it now), any new media will simply be fighting for market share. This is the reason for the increasing fragmentation of the audience and the precipitous decline in the huge share of audience once held by the broadcast networks. This is also why media buyers and planners are growing in importance as advertisers search for the elusive audience and fight for their share of that audience in an overcrowded media environment.

The Impact of Technology

What if you could effortlessly record the entire season of your favorite show, pause a live broadcast while you answer the phone, and automatically skip

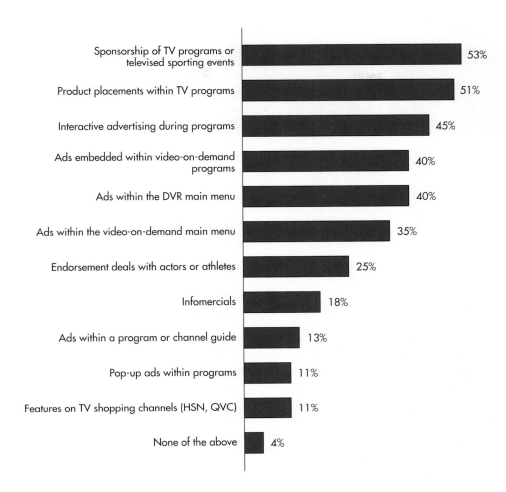

Exhibit 12–4

Responses of 55 national advertisers when asked "If large numbers of consumers could skip commercials while watching television, which of the following forms of advertising would you spend more on?"

every commercial? That's all possible today with the use of the **digital video recorder (DVR).** Introduced in 1999 under the TiVo and ReplayTV brands, DVRs could have a profound effect on the way we watch television and the way sponsors advertise. In response, several TV networks are beginning to offer some of their hit shows, commercial free, in a fee-based, video-on-demand format.

However, nobody expects the demise of the television commercial. Without commercials, there would be far less money to produce TV shows. Instead, it is expected that advertisers will find new ways to deliver their messages. As of 2003, only about 2 percent of TV households owned a DVR, but experts predict this could rise to 50 percent before the end of the decade, to the level of cable TV penetration within 10 years. Accordingly, advertisers like Coca-Cola, Pfizer, and Chrysler are scrambling to innovate and adapt to the new medium, which compels them to reach consumers with advertising vehicles other than the traditional 30-second commercial. In particular, television advertisers are working to increase program sponsorship and product placement and to make commercials more engaging and relevant. Forrester Research asked television advertising executives how they might cope in a DVR-saturated environment. Exhibit 12–4 shows how television advertising might differ.

The Use of Television in IMC

While single programs don't deliver the mass audience they once did, television is still the most cost-effective way to deliver certain kinds of messages to large, well-defined audiences. When it comes to awareness and image advertising, for

Television plays an important role in imparting brand personality. Television can deliver a "big idea" to a mass audience in a uniquely creative manner. In this television spot, an erupting volcano propels a Jeep Liberty from its cone and sends it crashing to the ground. In keeping with the Jeep's personality, the Liberty drives away unscathed.

instance, television has no rival. The same is true for brand reinforcement messages.[15] Through its unique ability to deliver a creative big idea, television can impart brand meaning (the symbolism or personality of the brand) to either attract people to the brand or reinforce their current relationship with it.

Television is also a good leverage tool. That is, an advertiser might take advantage of the efficiency of television to reach out to many prospects. Prospects can identify themselves by responding to the commercial, and then the advertiser can follow up with less expensive, one-to-one or addressable media.[16]

What's important to remember is that the high visibility of TV forces the sponsor to create ads that people find interesting and that consistently reinforce the brand's strategic position (remember our definition of great advertising). The brands that succeed are the ones that are the most popular. And "ad liking" has a lot to do with brand popularity.

CONCEPT CHECK

Explain how the unique elements of television enhance the media mix. What are the downsides?

Types of TV Advertising

Advertisers use different strategies to buy time on broadcast and cable television. The major broadcast networks offer a variety of *programs* that appeal to different audiences. So the advertiser buys ads based on the viewing audience of each program. A national advertiser that wants to reach a broad cross section of women ages 25 to 45, for example, might find *Desperate Housewives* an efficient buy.

When buying cable TV, an advertiser can buy ads over the full schedule of a channel because cable networks typically aim all of their programming to relatively specific *audiences*. The Lifetime and Family channels heavily weigh programs toward women; MTV targets viewers ages 16 to 25. Cable companies sell their network channels in bundles at a discount and offer discounts for *run-of-schedule* positioning—multiple ad purchases they can place throughout a channel's daily schedule (see the Checklist, "The Pros and Cons of Cable TV Advertising").

There are various ways advertisers can buy time on TV. They include sponsoring an entire program, participating in a program, purchasing spot announcements between programs, and purchasing spots from syndicators. Exhibit 12–5 shows how much money is spent nationally on the various types of television advertising.

Exhibit 12–5

Where does all of the money go? Measured TV spending in billions of dollars (2004).

Medium	2004 ad spending in billions of dollars	2003 ad spending in billions of dollars	Percent change
Network TV	$22.5	$20.3	10.7%
Syndicated TV	3.9	3.4	15.8
Spot TV	17.3	15.5	11.7
Cable TV networks	14.2	12.5	13.8
Total	58.0	51.8	11.9

Checklist

The Pros and Cons of Cable TV Advertising

The Pros

- **Selectivity.** Cable offers specialized programming aimed at particular types of viewers. Narrowcasting allows advertisers to choose programming with the viewer demographics that best match their target customers.
- **Audience demographics.** Cable subscribers are younger, better educated, and more affluent, have higher-level jobs, live in larger households, and are more likely to try new products and buy more high-ticket items, such as cars, appliances, and high-tech equipment.
- **Low cost.** Small companies can get TV's immediacy and impact without the enormous expenditures of broadcast TV. Cable advertising can sometimes cost as little as radio. Some national advertisers find sponsorship attractive, since an entire cable series can cost less to produce than a single broadcast TV commercial.
- **Flexibility.** Broadcast TV commercials need to be short because of the high costs of production and air time, but cable ads can run up to two minutes and, in the case of infomercials, much longer. They can also be tailored to fit the programming environment. And they do not have to adhere to strict network standards.
- **Testability.** Cable is a good place to experiment, testing both new products and various advertising approaches: ad frequency, copy impact, and different media mixes.

The Cons

- **Limited reach.** About 15 percent of TV households don't have cable. This was cable's main weakness in the past, but it is less so today.
- **Fragmentation.** With more than 100 channels at their disposal, cable viewers do not watch any one show in enormous numbers. To reach the majority of the cable audience in a particular market, ads must run on many stations.
- **Quality.** Cable, particularly local cable, sometimes has poorer production quality and less desirable programming than broadcast TV.
- **Zipping and zapping.** Cable TV has some of the same drawbacks as broadcast TV, such as zipping and zapping.

Network Advertising

Historically, major U.S. advertisers purchased airtime from one of the national broadcast **networks.** Cable has slowly eroded the networks' audiences. At one time the big three (ABC, CBS, and NBC) had more than 90 percent of the prime-time audience. Today their total share is about 29 percent, with ad-supported cable networks comprising 42 percent and other channels (pay cable, smaller networks, and public television) comprising another 29 percent.[17]

Networks offer large advertisers convenience and efficiency because they broadcast messages simultaneously across many affiliate stations throughout the country. Broadcast networks tend to reach masses of American consumers representing a cross section of the population, while cable networks tend to reach more selective niches. Further, because networks are centralized, the advertiser gets only one bill.

An advertiser who underwrites the cost of a program is engaging in **sponsorship.** In a sole sponsorship, the advertiser is responsible for both the program content and the total cost of production. Sponsorship is so costly that single sponsorships are usually limited to specials. Companies that sponsor programs (AT&T, Xerox, and Hallmark, for example) gain two important advantages. First, the public more readily identifies with the product(s) due to the prestige of sponsoring first-rate entertainment. Second, the sponsor controls the placement and content of its commercials. The commercials can be fit to the program and run any length the sponsor desires so long as they remain within network or station regulations.

Exhibit 12–6

Advertising cost per 30-second spot on the 10 most expensive shows (2005–2006 prime-time season).

Rank	Show and Network	Price
1	*American Idol* (Fox)	$705,000
2	*Desperate Housewives* (ABC)	560,000
3	*CSI: Crime Scene Investigation* (CBS)	465,000
4	*Grey's Anatomy* (ABC)	440,000
5	*ER* (NBC)	400,000
6	*Extreme Makeover, Home Edition* (ABC)	355,000
7	*Survivor: The Australian Outback* (CBS)	350,000
8	*The Apprentice* (NBC)	350,000
9	*The Apprentice, Martha Stewart* (NBC)	310,000
10	*Two and a Half Men* (CBS)	293,000

Sponsorship offers many opportunities. When the popular drama series *24* started its second season, the first episode was presented commercial-free, thanks to a full sponsorship by Ford Motor Company. The episode also featured numerous Ford vehicles in the show. To save money and reduce risks, many advertisers cosponsor programs, sponsoring on alternate weeks or dividing the program into segments. NFL games, for instance, are always sold as multiple sponsorships.

Most network TV advertising is sold on a **participation** basis, with several advertisers buying 30- or 60-second segments within a program. This enables them to spread their budgets and avoid long-term commitments to any one program. It also lets smaller advertisers buy a limited amount of time and still get the nationwide coverage they need.

Network advertising also has several disadvantages: lack of flexibility, long lead times, inconvenient restrictions, and forced adherence to network standards and practices, not to mention high prices. Costs can run as high as $705,000 for a spot on *American Idol* (see Exhibit 12–6). For this reason, most advertisers decide to buy *spot announcements*.

Spot Announcements

Spot announcements run in clusters between programs. They are less expensive and more flexible than network advertising because they can be concentrated in specific regions of the country. Therefore, local businesses are frequently seen on spot schedules. An advertiser with a small budget or limited distribution may use spots to introduce a new product into one area at a time. Or an advertiser can vary its message for different markets to suit promotional needs.[18]

Spots may run 10, 15, 30, or 60 seconds and be sold nationally or locally. Spot advertising is more difficult to buy than network advertising because it involves contacting each station directly. The national rep system, in which individuals act as sales and service representatives for a number of stations, alleviates this problem.

Meanwhile, a number of large cable rep firms are also working to make the purchase of spot cable more convenient for national advertisers through technology that interconnects various cable companies in a region.[19]

Spot advertising is available only at network station breaks and when network advertisers have not purchased all of the available time, so spot ads may get lost in the clutter—which is why they tend to have less viewers and a smaller piece of the ad spending pie.

Syndication

As audiences fragment, syndicated programs become an increasingly popular adjunct or alternative to network advertising. In a little over 10 years, the syndication industry has grown from almost nothing into a $3.3 billion advertising medium.[20]

Syndication is the sale of programs on a station-by-station, market-by-market basis. In other words, a producer (for example, Warner Bros. or Disney) deals directly with stations, often through a distribution company, rather than going through the networks (see Exhibit 12–7). This efficient "direct-from-the-factory" approach gives local TV stations more programming control and greater profits. It also gives advertisers access to **inventory** (commercial time) that they might not get on network programs—often at better prices.[21] Syndication has become the largest source of programming in the United States.

Television syndication comes in three forms: off-network, first-run, and barter. In **off-network syndication,** former popular network programs (reruns) are sold to individual stations for rebroadcast. Examples include *Frasier* and *The X-Files*. **First-run syndication** involves original shows, like *Inside Edition, The Jerry Springer Show,* and *Extra,* which are produced specifically for the syndication market. One of the fastest-growing trends in television is **barter syndication** (also called *advertiser-supported syndication*). These are off-network or first-run programs offered by producers to local stations free or for a reduced rate, but with some of the ad space (usually more than half) presold to national advertisers. *Wheel of Fortune, Jeopardy,* and *Oprah* are some of the most popular examples.[22]

Syndication is a popular tool for many national advertisers. It enables them to associate with popular programs and reach some otherwise difficult to reach audiences at a lower cost per viewer than network shows. However, syndicated shows tend to be more cluttered with advertising and may not air in all markets or at consistent times.

Program-Length Ads (PLAs)

In the fall of 1992, independent presidential candidate Ross Perot sat in front of a TV camera for 30 minutes with homemade flip charts and a down-home pitch for the White House and drew 20 million viewers. A month later, he pulled a respectable 19 percent of the vote.

Perot made advertising history by catapulting the **program-length advertisement (PLA),** or **infomercial,** into the limelight. He also proved what companies that produce and sell infomercials have been saying for years: Long-form advertising can communicate a message in a way other forms can't.[23] As a result, *Advertising Age* named Perot its adman of the year.

Infomercials aren't new, but their respectability is. Before Perot, most PLA users were off–Madison Avenue marketers of hand mixers, juicers, and car waxes. Today, major marketers such as Toshiba, Lexus, and Magnavox have ventured into the infomercial arena.[24] And now even networks air some of these ads, which were once relegated to independents and cable channels.[25] The reasons for this sudden growth are simple:

1. Consumers pay attention and can respond immediately.

2. Brand managers may be able to gain a competitive advantage by going where the competition is not.

3. PLAs can fulfill some message objectives, like product demonstration and brand differentiation, far better than 30-second commercials.

4. Results are both measurable and accountable.

5. The ad campaign can pay for itself while supporting the retail trade.

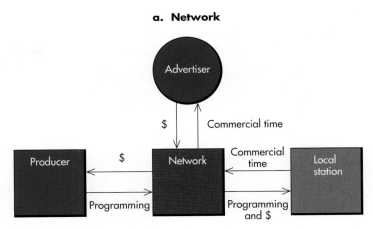

a. Network

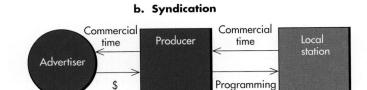

b. Syndication

Exhibit 12–7

TV network and syndication distribution.
a. The networks are essentially middlemen.
b. Syndication is often a more efficient way of financing and distributing programs.

Infomercials provide a unique opportunity for advertisers to demonstrate their products and generate immediate results.

6. PLAs combine the power of advertising, direct response, and sales promotion.[26]

Add to these factors the benefits of lower (though rising) production costs and attractive, upscale audience demographics, and it's easy to see why several national marketers have jumped on the PLA bandwagon. Advertisers spent over $900 million on infomercials in 2002.[27]

TV Audience Measurement

Efficient advertisers study the audiences of various programs and analyze their impact and cost effectiveness against other media vehicles. To do this, they must understand the techniques and terminology used in television audience measurement.

Rating Services

The companies that measure the program audiences of TV and radio stations for advertisers and broadcasters are called **rating services.** These firms attempt to pick a representative sample of the market and furnish data on the number and characteristics of the viewers or listeners. Several research organizations gather the data at their own expense and publish it. Companies subscribe to a service and use it as a basis for planning, buying, or selling media advertising.

In the United States, Nielsen Media Research is the major rating service for television. Its flagship service, the Nielsen Television Index (NTI), uses a national sample of households equipped with people meters to develop audience estimates for all national TV programming. The people meters are hooked up to TV sets in 55 markets across the country and continuously measure the channels to which each set is tuned. Household members are supposed to punch in and punch out as they come and go from the room. This provides Nielsen with demographic information about who specifically is watching and when.

At the local level, Nielsen surveys households in 210 TV markets. Household members record their viewing habits in diaries. Four times each year, during the **sweeps** month-long rating periods, Nielsen compiles the ratings from all 210 markets. This information is used by networks and local stations to determine how much they can charge for advertising on their shows. (See Commercial Break 12–A.)

Many advertisers and broadcasters maintain that Nielsen's reports are unstable and inaccurate.[28] Nielsen's biggest problem may be the low cooperation rate among viewers who are supposed to fill out diaries. In addition, some networks and local affiliates use elaborate schemes to improve their ratings during sweeps periods, making the results not necessarily representative of the balance of the year. These issues are critical to the networks and advertisers alike, since Nielsen's numbers determine the fate of billions of dollars' worth of programming and advertising every year.

For demographic studies of TV audiences, advertisers also use the Simmons Market Research Bureau and Mediamark Research. These companies perform extensive surveys of the U.S. marketplace and publish their findings on consumer lifestyles, product usage, and media habits. Advertisers use the results for strategic planning purposes.

Ethical Issues

Advertising to Children: Child's Play?

Kids make up a considerable consumer group whose number and purchasing power are growing. In 1999, children ages four to twelve took in $31.3 billion in income from allowances, jobs, and gifts, and spent 92 percent of it, says James MacNeal, a market researcher who specializes in the children's market. Today, children are influencing the family's buying behavior for everything from cars to orange juice—up to $500 billion a year. Whether they're spending their own money or asking their parents to spend theirs, marketing to kids is big business and it's only getting bigger.

The benefits of reaching children are great. If won over now, they tend to be loyal customers into adulthood. Besides selling to children, advertisers also sell through children. Some companies believe they can sell more by appealing to children's preferences than to those of adults. The minivan was created because children demanded more room, says Mr. MacNeal. When kids decided the vehicle was "uncool," their opinions helped to develop the SUV. Saturday morning cartoons are the traditional vehicle for ads promoting cereals, candy, and toys. But parents are asked to buy particular brands of vacuum cleaners and other household goods because their kids saw them advertised on TV. Marketers rely on kids' "pester power" to get their products sold.

The dangers of marketing to kids from an ethical perspective are fairly clear: Children are the "vulnerable" market. They are less experienced. Their concepts of self, time, and money are immature. As a result, they know very little about their own desires, needs, and preferences—or how to use economic resources rationally to satisfy them. It is likely that child-oriented advertising can lead to false beliefs or highly improbable product expectations. Telling children about a product and accurately describing that product is probably ethical. Convincing them that they must have a toy to be popular with their friends is probably not. Nothing is likely to enrage parents and society-at-large more than the prospect of marketers manipulating and taking advantage of children.

Cereal is better if a fun character is selling it; so are beer and cigarettes as the Budweiser frogs and lizards and Joe Camel proved. In the UK, there is criticism over the use of TV characters such as the Simpsons and Teletubbies, as well as the Spice Girls, to sell snack foods high in fat, sugar, and salt. The junk food firms face a crackdown on the hard sell of products that can make children overweight and unhealthy.

Both critics and defenders agree that advertisers should not intentionally deceive children. Federal legislation has been introduced that would reimpose the 1974 guidelines limiting advertising on children's programs. These guidelines deal with truth and accuracy.

The mood in several European countries is to tighten up children-and-advertising guidelines. Sweden has some of the strictest controls in Europe on children and advertising, banning all television advertisements aimed at children under 12. This ban includes advertisements on toys, foods, sweets, drinks, and any products that might appeal to preteens.

In the United States, the Children's Advertising Review Unit (CARU) of the Council of Better Business Bureaus (BBB) promotes responsible children's advertising and responds to public concerns. The basic activity of CARU is the review and evaluation of child-directed advertising to help avoid deceptive messages. When children's advertising is found to be misleading, inaccurate or inconsistent with its guidelines, CARU seeks changes through the voluntary cooperation of advertisers. The BBB Web site at www.bbbsilicon.org/guidelinechild.html discusses CARU's guidelines.

Questions

1. Do bans on marketing to children compromise a basic freedom of choice and speech? Whose responsibility is it to make sure children are not inappropriately influenced by advertising? Their parents? The government? Advertisers? How far should advertisers have to go to ensure that children are not misled by their ads?

2. Study the CARU guidelines and then watch the advertising on a children's network or Saturday morning television. How well do you feel the advertiser's are adhering to those guidelines?

Cable Ratings

Reliable information on the audiences for cable programs is even harder to gather. Traditional techniques often rely on too small a sample to be statistically significant, so major cable programming services provide their own reports of audience viewership by show. Interpreting cable ratings is a confusing process, since the media planner has to integrate so much information from so many different sources. Some companies are trying to remedy the situation. ADcom Information Services, for example, is a ratings service that installs in-home recording devices to provide more reliable information. One test with Continental Cablevision in Jacksonville, Florida, confirmed that Nielsen had

been underreporting cable TV audiences—in some cases dramatically.[29] Nielsen, meanwhile, has introduced its own cable TV ratings service but has been criticized for using older broadcast reporting technology.[30] This controversy is destined to rage for some time.

Defining Television Markets

Television rating services define unique geographic television markets to minimize the confusion of overlapping TV signals. The Nielsen station index uses the term **designated market areas (DMAs)** for geographic areas (cities, counties) in which the local TV stations attract the most viewing. For example, the DMA for Columbus, Georgia (see Exhibit 12–8), is the 17 counties in which the local area TV stations are the most watched.

Dayparts

Advertisers must decide when to air commercials and on which programs. Unlike radio listeners, TV viewers are loyal to programs, not stations. Programs continue to run or are canceled depending on their ratings (percentage of the population watching). Ratings also vary with the time of day a program runs. Television time is divided into dayparts as follows:

Daytime: 9 a.m.–4 p.m. (Eastern and Pacific)
Early fringe: 4–5:30 p.m.

November. Now the people meter—dubbed the Local People Meter—is being rolled into the top 10 markets across the country to provide more accurate, detailed, and timely measurements. This may some day make "sweeps" obsolete. Critics, however, are still convinced that people meter numbers are flawed and do not accurately measure viewing habits, especially of certain demographic groups.

Nielsen's competitor Arbitron is developing a passive people meter whose portable technology can register media exposure anywhere respondents are tuned in, even in the car or at the movie theater. The new Portable People Meter (PPM) is pager-sized and would be worn by each panelist. The meter works by detecting identification codes which can be implanted in any form of audio transmission. Respondents are not required to do anything except wear the device, which will eliminate problems with panelist participation inherent in the current people meter system. The Portable People Meter has already been tested successfully in Philadelphia and the next test is underway in Houston. You can read about the PPM at www.arbitron.com/portable_people_meters/home.htm.

Nielsen is also trying to meet the challenge of measuring viewership of the new digital technologies, including digital tuners, digital video recorders, and video on demand. They are testing a new system, called active/passive meters, which uses a technology similar to the PPM. The meters read a code embedded in the audio signal of each program (inaudible to viewers), that the meters tabulate and send back to Nielsen's data processing center.

An interesting development in audience measurement is the single-source data made available by supermarket scanners. A family's viewing habits can be related to its packaged-goods purchases. If a household purchases a specific product one day after they viewed a TV advertisement for that product, the manufacturer will know it. The implications are monumental for marketing and media planners. The leaders in single-source measurement today are Information Resources, Inc. (IRI), with its BehaviorScan service, and Nielsen, with its Home Scan service.

Applying the Breaks
1. Would you be willing to be in a Nielsen household? How would you feel about having your media and shopping habits tracked and analyzed? Is it an invasion of your privacy?
2. Does it sound to you like the rating data is reliable? If you were a network executive would you be willing to pay for it?

Combine as early fringe	Early news:	5 or 5:30–7:30 p.m.
	Prime access:	7:30–8 p.m.
	Prime:	8–11 p.m.
Combine as late fringe	Late news:	11–11:30 p.m.
	Late night:	11:30 p.m.–1 a.m.

Viewing is highest during **prime time** (8 to 11 p.m. Eastern and Pacific Time; 7 to 10 p.m. Central and Mountain Time). Late fringe ranks fairly high in most markets among adults, and daytime and early fringe tend to be viewed most heavily by women. To reach the greatest percentage of the advertiser's target audience with optimal frequency, the media planner determines a **daypart mix** based on TV usage levels reported by the rating services.

Audience Measurements

Rating services and media planners use many terms to define a station's audience, penetration, and efficiency. **TV households (TVHH)** refers to the number of households that own television sets. The number of TVHH in a particular market gives an advertiser a sense of the market's size. Likewise, the number of TVHH tuned in to a particular program helps the advertiser estimate the program's popularity and how many people a commercial is likely to reach.

The percentage of homes in a given area that have one or more TV sets turned on at any particular time is expressed as **households using TV (HUT).** If there are 1,000 TV sets in the survey area and 500 are turned on, HUT is 50 percent.

Exhibit 12–8

This map of the area surrounding Columbus, Georgia, shows media planners which counties are included in the designated market area (DMA) and will be reached by advertising placed on the local television stations. Columbus, Georgia, is the 125th largest DMA in the United States and contains over 200,000 TV households.

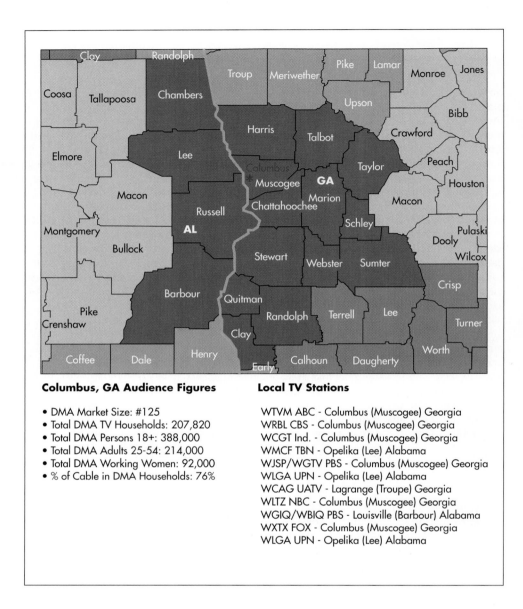

Columbus, GA Audience Figures

- DMA Market Size: #125
- Total DMA TV Households: 207,820
- Total DMA Persons 18+: 388,000
- Total DMA Adults 25-54: 214,000
- Total DMA Working Women: 92,000
- % of Cable in DMA Households: 76%

Local TV Stations

WTVM ABC - Columbus (Muscogee) Georgia
WRBL CBS - Columbus (Muscogee) Georgia
WCGT Ind. - Columbus (Muscogee) Georgia
WMCF TBN - Opelika (Lee) Alabama
WJSP/WGTV PBS - Columbus (Muscogee) Georgia
WLGA UPN - Opelika (Lee) Alabama
WCAG UATV - Lagrange (Troupe) Georgia
WLTZ NBC - Columbus (Muscogee) Georgia
WGIQ/WBIQ PBS - Louisville (Barbour) Alabama
WXTX FOX - Columbus (Muscogee) Georgia
WLGA UPN - Opelika (Lee) Alabama

The **program rating** refers to the percentage of TV households in an area that are tuned in to a specific program. The rating is computed as follows:

$$\text{Rating} = \frac{\text{TVHH tuned to specific program}}{\text{Total TVHH in area}}$$

Networks want high ratings because they measure a show's popularity. More popular shows can command higher advertising rates.

The percentage of homes with sets in use (HUT) tuned to a specific program is called the **audience share.** A program with only 500 viewers can have a 50 share if only 1,000 sets are turned on. *Ratings,* in contrast, measure the audience as a percentage of all TVHH in the area, whether the TV sets are on or off.

The total number of homes reached by some portion of a program is called **total audience.** This figure is normally broken down into demographic categories to determine **audience composition.**

Gross Rating Points

In television, **gross rating points (GRPs)** are the total rating points achieved by a particular media schedule over a specific period. For example, a weekly schedule of five commercials on programs with an average household rating of 20 would yield 100 GRPs.

GRPs allow advertisers to draw conclusions about the different markets available for a client's ads by providing a comparable measure of advertising weight. However, GRPs do not reflect a market's size. For example, while campaigns in Knoxville and Charlotte might have the same GRPs, they would differ significantly in the number of homes reached.

	TV homes (000s)	Average cost per spot	Average rating	Avg. homes reached (000)	Number of spots	GRPs
Knoxville	1,002	$1,500	15	150	5	75
Charlotte	638	$1,250	15	96	5	75

To better determine the relative value of television advertising markets, other measures are used, such as cost per rating point (CPP) and cost per thousand (CPM). These and other media terms will be described here and in Chapter 15.

Buying Television Time

The process of buying TV time can be lengthy and, depending on the number of stations in the buy, quite involved. Advertisers or media buyers must

- Determine which programs are available at what cost.
- Analyze the various programs for efficiency.
- Negotiate prices with station reps.
- Determine how many viewers they are reaching how often.
- Sign broadcast contracts.
- Review affidavits of performance to be sure the commercials ran as agreed.

These procedures are so complex that most large advertisers use ad agencies or media-buying services. Buying services have gained in popularity because they charge less and can save advertisers money by negotiating for desirable time slots at reduced rates. Local advertisers typically rely on station reps to determine the best buys for their money.

Requesting Avails

To find out which programs are available, media buyers contact stations' sales reps—local station salespeople, national media rep organizations that sell for one station in each market, or network reps. The media buyer gives the rep information about the advertiser's media objectives and target audiences and asks the rep to supply a list of **avails** (available time slots) along with prices and estimated ratings. Many media buyers ask for the information based on the last few Nielsen books to see whether a show's ratings are consistent, rising, or falling.

Selecting Programs for Buys

The media buyer selects the most efficient programs in relation to the target audience using the **cost per rating point (CPP)** and the **cost per thousand (CPM)** for each program:

$$\text{CPP} = \frac{\text{Cost}}{\text{Rating}} \qquad \text{CPM} = \frac{\text{Cost}}{\text{Thousands of people}}$$

For example, assume *CSI* has a rating of 25, reaches 200,000 people in the primary target audience, and costs $2,000 for a 30-second spot on station WALB-TV in Albany, Georgia. Then,

$$\text{CPP} = \frac{\$2,000}{25} = \$80 \qquad \text{CPM} = \frac{\$2,000}{(200,000 \div 1,000)} = \$10$$

By calculating CPP, the media buyer can compare the cost of a rating point (reaching 1 percent of TVHH) from one program or network to another. That's good information for beginning negotiations. But rating points relate to the whole market. The real important figure is the cost of reaching 1,000 prospects in the target market. That's why the CPM should be calculated against the size of the target audience, not the whole market. The lower the cost per 1,000/target audience (CPM-TA), the more efficient the show is at reaching real prospects.

To get the best buys within the available budget, then, the media buyer substitutes stronger programs for less efficient ones.

Negotiating Prices and Contracts

TV stations and cable companies publish rate cards to sell their air time. However, since TV audiences are estimated at best, television reps will always negotiate prices.

The media buyer contacts the rep and explains what efficiency the advertiser needs in terms of CPM to make the buy. The buyer has numerous ways to negotiate lower rates: work out a package deal, accept *run-of-schedule positioning* (the station chooses when to run the commercials), or take advantage of preemption rates. A **preemption rate** is lower because the advertiser agrees to be "bumped" (preempted) if another advertiser pays the higher, nonpreemption rate.

The media buyer must examine the advertising contract carefully before signing it. The contract indicates the dates, times, and programs on which the advertiser's commercials will run, the length of each spot, the rate per spot, and the total cost. The balance of the contract defines payment terms and responsibilities of the advertiser, agency, and station. After the spots run, the station returns a signed and notarized **affidavit of performance** to the advertiser or agency, specifying when the spots aired and what makegoods are available. **Makegoods** refer to free advertising time an advertiser receives to compensate for spots the station missed or ran incorrectly or because the program's ratings were substantially lower than guaranteed.[31]

Advertising on Video Rentals

Ever since Pepsi sponsored the successful home-video release *Top Gun* in 1987, industry analysts have been expecting advertising on video rentals to become a major new medium.

Research shows that home-video renters are younger and more upscale than the general population. And the majority of video renters do watch the commercials that precede the movie—sometimes more than once. A Schweppes ad starring comedian John Cleese was viewed by an astounding 95 percent of households renting Cleese's movie *A Fish Called Wanda*.[32] However, more recent research has shown that video renters find ads intrusive and somewhat offensive. Many just zip through them to get to the movie.[33]

Presently, the primary users of the medium are the movie studios themselves, advertising coming attractions.

Why are audience measurements and rating point costs so important to media planners?

CONCEPT CHECK

The Medium of Radio

Radio is a personal, one-on-one medium; people tend to listen alone. And radio is mobile. It can entertain people who are driving, walking, at home, or away from home. This makes it a particularly strong way to reach people who commute by car.

Radio is also adaptable to moods. In the morning, people may want to hear the news, upbeat music, or interesting chatter; in the afternoon, they may want to unwind with classical or easy-listening music.

Who Uses Radio?

In an average week, 95.4 percent of the U.S. population listens to radio; in an average day, over 75 percent. The average American listens to the radio more than three hours every weekday and over five hours on the weekend. In fact, during the prime shopping hours of 6 a.m. to 6 p.m., the average U.S. adult spends more time with radio than any other medium.[34] Radio is also cost-effective. In the last decade, the CPM for radio advertising has risen less than for any other major medium and substantially less than the consumer price index.[35] As a result, radio's advertising revenues have grown steadily.

More national advertisers are discovering radio's audience potential. Certainly it has worked well for the Got Milk campaign. Similarly, Snapple profited greatly from radio. Back when it was still a little company in Queens, New York, and strapped for money, Snapple Natural Beverages decided to use radio. It put its entire ad budget into a year-long schedule with a young, relatively unknown radio show host named Howard Stern. Snapple liked the way he delivered its spots as a live reader.

A few years later, Snapple began receiving letters and phone calls from people in the Midwest and West, where it didn't even have distribution. It seems that nationally syndicated talk show host Rush Limbaugh, on a restricted-calorie diet, had been giving enthusiastic on-air endorsements for Snapple Diet Iced Tea. The firm moved quickly to sign him as a paid endorser. What it learned was the power of radio, especially when combined with a popular radio personality. This combination doubled Snapple's sales every year for five years, propelled it into national distribution, and turned it into a major national advertiser, spending more than $30 million every year advertising in more than 100 U.S. radio markets.[36]

The Use of Radio in IMC

While television tends to be a passive medium that people simply watch, radio actively involves people. They listen intently to their favorite personalities; they call in to make requests, participate in a contest, or contribute to a discussion; they use their ears and imaginations to fill in what they cannot see. Most people listen faithfully to two or three different radio stations with different types of programming. This means that smart advertisers can use the medium to establish an immediate, intimate relationship with consumers and other stakeholders. This makes radio an ideal medium for integrated marketing communications.

With radio, national companies can tie in to a local market and target the specific demographic group they want to reach. Most important, radio enables advertisers to maintain strategic consistency and stretch their media dollars through **imagery transfer.** Research shows that when advertisers run a schedule on TV and then convert the audio portion to radio commercials, fully 75 percent of consumers replay the video in their minds when they hear the radio spot.[37] That extends the life and builds the impact of a TV campaign at greatly reduced cost.[38] In an IMC campaign, where message consistency is a primary objective, this is a very important feature of radio.

Local retailers like the medium for the same reasons. Also, they can tailor it to their needs. It offers defined audiences; its recall characteristics are similar to those of TV; and retailers can create an identity by doing their own ads. Finally, since radio is so mobile, retailers can reach prospects just before they purchase. Hence, recent years have seen major spending increases by local grocery stores, car dealers, banks, and home-improvement, furniture, and apparel stores.[39]

Radio Programming and Audiences

Radio stations plan their programming carefully to reach specific audiences and to capture as many listeners as possible. The larger the audience, the more a station can charge for commercial time. Therefore, extensive planning and research go into radio programming and program changes. Stations can use tried-and-true formats, subscribe to network or syndicated programming, or devise unique approaches. Programming choices are greatly influenced by whether a station is on the AM or FM band. FM has much better sound fidelity, fewer commercial interruptions, and more varied programming.

To counteract FM's inroads, many AM stations switched to programs that don't rely on sound quality, such as news, talk, and sports. Some stations are experimenting with all comedy, midday game shows with audience participation, or formats geared to specific regions. AM stations are also trying to win back music listeners by improving their sound quality and offering stereo broadcasting.

When buying radio time, advertisers usually buy the station's *format,* not its programs. Most stations adopt one of the dozen or so standard **programming formats:** contemporary hit radio, adult contemporary, country, rock, easy listening, news/talk, and so on, as shown in Exhibit 12–9. Each format tends to appeal to specific demographic groups. The most popular format is country music, which appeals to a broad cross section of Americans from 25 to 54 years old.

Contemporary hit radio (CHR) appeals to teenagers and women under 30. It provides a constant flow of top 40 hits, usually with minimal intrusion by disk jockeys. Another popular format, adult contemporary (or "easy oldies"), is often advertised as "light rock, less talk." This format aims at the desirable target group of working women between 25 and 54. The news/talk, easy-listening, and nostalgia formats tend to have high listenership among men and women over 35.[40]

A major trend in radio today is the resurgence of radio networks, which offer services and programs that complement a station's local programming. A station might subscribe to ABC Radio's daily Paul Harvey news and commentary, CBS's weekly *House of Blues Radio Hour,* EIB's Rush Limbaugh, and Westwood One's *Larry King Show.*

Radio is an important component of the media mix. It offers tremendous reach, attention, imagery, and selectivity, at a relatively low cost. In this ad, the Radio Advertising Bureau (www.rab.com) is publicizing the results of a research study that suggests advertisers can improve brand recall by replacing some of their TV and newspaper ads with radio spots (www.radioadlab.org).

Ironically, adding radio gives your customers a clearer picture.

Radio

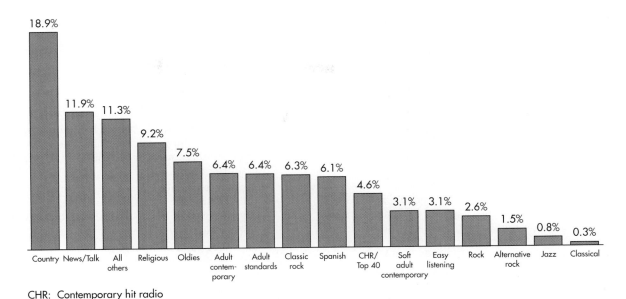

Exhibit 12–9

Percentage of radio stations in the most common programming formats. The country format appeals to the largest share of listeners.

There are now over 20 national radio networks, including numerous syndicators, offering programs from live rock concerts to public-affairs discussions. To stand out, 80 percent of licensed radio stations are opting for syndicated and network offerings.[41] As more stations carry these programs and more listeners tune in, national advertisers find them increasingly attractive.

A relatively new alternative on the national radio scene is satellite broadcast. XM and Sirius are the two major satellite players, each offering more than 100 channels of radio. They are just beginning to take listeners away from traditional radio stations. Subscribers are charged a monthly fee and must own a satellite radio, but they gain access to high-quality, exclusive programming from coast to coast. Presently, the music stations will not carry ads, just the news, sports and entertainment stations. There is no reliable data on how many people are listening to which satellite radio shows or the demographics of those listeners, so advertisers are holding back. But Mel Karmazin, the CEO of Sirius Satellite Radio, predicts that ad revenue on Sirius will reach $100 million by 2007.[42]

Although spending on radio advertising only accounts for about 8 percent of all ad spending, consumers spend about 40 percent of their total time with media listening to the radio.[43] Clearly, although it is much cheaper to produce than television advertising, radio ad spending has room to grow. In 2003, however, revenue for radio grew the least of all major media, to $10.08 billion for the top 20 companies, only 1.5 percent above the previous year.[44] The largest national radio advertisers are major retailers, entertainment conglomerates, and telecommunications companies (see Exhibit 12–10).

> CONCEPT CHECK
>
> Explain how the unique elements of radio enhance the media mix. What are the downsides?

Exhibit 12–10

Top 10 national spot radio advertisers (2004).

Rank	Company	National spot radio ad spending ($ millions)
1	SBC Communications	$102.7
2	Verizon Communications	101.7
3	Home Depot	86.0
4	Time Warner	78.6
5	News Corp.	50.6
6	Safeway	49.6
7	Viacom	39.7
8	Berkshire Hathaway	37.0
9	General Electric Co.	35.9
10	Walt Disney Co.	34.6

Checklist

The Pros and Cons of Radio Advertising

The Pros

- **Audience.** The average adult listens more than three hours a day, radio builds a large audience quickly, and a normal advertising schedule provides repeated impact on the listener.
- **Selectivity.** Specialized radio formats, with prescribed audiences and coverage areas, enable advertisers to select the market they want to reach: a specific sex, age group, ethnic or religious background, income group, employment category, educational level, or special interest.
- **Cost efficiency.** Radio offers one of the lowest costs per thousand, and radio production is inexpensive. National spots can be produced for about one-tenth the cost of a TV commercial. And local stations often produce local spots for free.
- **Visualization.** Creative radio spots can create imagery every bit as graphic as the visual media.
- **Other advantages.** Radio also offers timeliness, immediacy, local relevance, and creative flexibility.

The Cons

- **Limitations of sound.** Radio is heard but not seen, a drawback if the product must be seen to be understood. Some agencies think radio restricts their creative options.
- **Segmented audiences.** If a large number of radio stations compete for the same audience, advertisers who want to blanket the market have to buy multiple stations, which may not be cost-effective.
- **Short-lived and half-heard commercials.** Radio commercials are fleeting. They can't be kept like a newspaper or a magazine ad. Radio must compete with other activities for attention, and it doesn't always succeed.
- **Clutter.** Stations with the greatest appeal for advertisers have more commercials. Advertisers must produce a commercial that stands out from the rest.

Buying Radio Time

Advertisers need a basic knowledge of the medium to buy radio time effectively: the types of radio advertising available for commercial use, a basic understanding of radio terminology, and the steps involved in preparing a radio schedule.

Types of Radio Advertising

An advertiser may purchase network, spot, or local radio time. Although local purchases still account for fully 80 percent of all radio time sold, national spot radio advertising is surging.[45] Advertisers like the size of the audience, selectivity, and cost efficiency of radio (see the Checklist, "The Pros and Cons of Radio Advertising").

Networks

Advertisers may use one of the national radio networks to carry their messages to the entire national market simultaneously via stations that subscribe to the network's programs. In addition, more than 100 regional radio networks in the United States operate with information oriented toward specific geographic markets.

Networks provide national and regional advertisers with simple administration and low effective net cost per station. Disadvantages include lack of flexibility in choosing affiliated stations, the limited number of stations on a network's roster, and the long lead times required to book time.

Spot Radio

Spot radio affords national advertisers great flexibility in their choice of markets, stations, air time, and copy. They can put commercials on the air quickly—some stations require as little as 20 minutes' lead time—and advertisers can build local acceptance by using local personalities. Radio rep firms, like Katz Radio, represent a list of stations and sell spot time to national advertisers and agencies.

Local Radio

Local time denotes radio spots purchased by a local advertiser or agency. It involves the same procedure as national spots.

Radio advertising can be either live or taped. Most radio stations use recorded shows with live news in between. Likewise, nearly all radio commercials are prerecorded to reduce costs and maintain broadcast quality.

Radio Terminology

For the most part, the terminology used for radio is the same as for other media, but some terms are unique to radio. The most common of these are the concepts of dayparts, average quarter-hour audiences, and cumes (cumulative audiences).

Dayparts

The radio day is divided into five dayparts:

6 a.m.–10 a.m.	Morning drive
10 a.m.–3 p.m.	Daytime
3 p.m.–7 p.m.	Afternoon (or evening) drive
7 p.m.–midnight	Nighttime
Midnight–6 a.m.	All night

Rating services measure audiences for only the first four dayparts because all-night listening is very limited and not highly competitive. Heaviest radio use occurs during **drive times** (6–10 a.m. and 3–7 p.m.) during the week (Monday through Friday), when many listeners are commuting to or from work or school.

Radio stations base their rates on the time of day the advertiser wants commercials aired, but the rates are negotiable according to supply and demand at any given time. RL 12–1 in the Reference Library on the *Essentials of Contemporary Advertising* Web site shows standard rates for air time on KWOD-FM in Sacramento, California. To obtain the lowest rate, an advertiser orders spots on a **run-of-station (ROS)** basis, similar to ROP in newspaper advertising. However, this leaves total control of spot placement up to the station. So most stations offer a **total audience plan (TAP)** package rate, which guarantees a certain percentage of spots in the better dayparts if the advertiser buys a package of time.

Average Quarter-Hour Audience

Average quarter-hour audience (AQH persons) identifies the average number of people listening to a specific station for at least 5 minutes during an average 15-minute period of any given daypart. For example, station KKDA in Dallas/Fort Worth, Texas, has an average quarter-hour afternoon drive listenership of 33,800, meaning that any day, during an average 15-minute period between 3 and 7 p.m., about 33,800 people ages 12 and older are tuned in for at least 5 minutes (see RL 12–2 in the Reference Library on the *Essentials of Contemporary Advertising* Web site).

The **average quarter-hour rating** expresses the AQH persons as a percentage of the population. Since KKDA is located in an area of 3,072,727 people, its average quarter-hour persons could be expressed as an average quarter-hour *rating* of 1.1:

$$\frac{\text{AQH persons}}{\text{Population}} \times 100 = \text{AQH rating}$$

$$\frac{33,800}{3,072,727} \times 100 = 1.1\%$$

The same idea can be expressed in terms of **average quarter-hour share:** the station's audience (AQH persons) expressed as a percentage of the total radio listening audience in the area. For example, if the total average quarter-hour persons for all stations during afternoon drive is 676,000, then radio station KKDA's average quarter-hour afternoon drive share is 5:

$$\frac{\text{AQH persons of a station}}{\text{AQH persons of all stations}} \times 100 = \text{AQH share}$$

$$\frac{33,800}{676,000} \times 100 = 5\%$$

The **gross impressions** are arrived at by multiplying the station's audience (AQH persons) by the number of times a message is delivered to that audience. For example, if an advertiser runs 24 spots on KKDA during the afternoon drive, then 811,200 gross impressions will be delivered:

$$\text{AQH persons} \times \text{Number of spots} = \text{Gross impressions}$$

$$33,800 \times 24 = 811,200$$

The **gross rating points** of a radio schedule are the sum of all ratings points delivered by that schedule, or the gross impressions expressed as a percentage of the population being measured:

$$\text{AQH rating} \times \text{Number of spots} = \text{GRPs}$$

$$1.1 \times 24 = 26.4$$

or

$$\frac{\text{Gross impressions}}{\text{Population}} \times 100 = \text{GRPs}$$

$$\frac{811,200}{3,072,727} \times 100 = 26.4$$

Cume Estimates

The **cume persons** is the total number of *different* people who listen to a radio station for at least five minutes in a quarter-hour within a reported daypart (also called *unduplicated audience* or *reach*).

In the example, our schedule on station KKDA generated 811,200 gross impressions, but that does not mean that 811,200 different people heard our commercials. Many people heard the commercials three, four, or five times. By measuring the number of different people who listened to KKDA, rating services provide the *reach potential* of our radio schedule, which in this case was estimated to be 167,800.

The **cume rating** is the cume persons expressed as a percentage of the population being measured. For example,

$$\frac{167,800 \times 100}{3,072,727} = 5.5\%$$

This means that 5.5 percent of the Dallas/Fort Worth population listened to KKDA at least once during afternoon drive.

The Seven Steps in Preparing a Radio Schedule

The procedure advertisers use to prepare radio schedules is similar to that used for TV schedules.

1. Identify stations with the greatest concentration (cume) of the advertiser's target audience by demographics (say, men and women ages 35 to 49).

2. Identify stations whose formats typically offer the highest concentration of potential buyers.

3. Determine which time periods (dayparts) on those stations offer the most (average quarter-hour) potential buyers.

4. Using the stations' rate cards for guidance, construct a schedule with a strong mix of the best time periods. At this point, it is often wise to give the advertiser's media objectives to the station reps, suggest a possible budget for their station, and ask what they can provide for that budget. This gives the media buyer a starting point for analyzing costs and negotiating the buy.

5. Assess the proposed buy in terms of audience delivery.

6. Determine the cost for each 1,000 target people each station delivers. The key word is target; the media buyer isn't interested in the station's total audience.

7. Negotiate and place the buy (see RL 12–3 in the Reference Library on the *Essentials of Contemporary Advertising* Web site).

> **CONCEPT CHECK**
>
> In what ways is buying radio time different from buying television time?

Chapter Summary

As a means of reaching the masses, no other medium today has the unique creative ability of television. Broadcast TV grew faster than any previous advertising medium because of the unique advantages it offered advertisers: mass coverage at efficient cost, impact, prestige, and social dominance.

Television is a powerful creative tool, but the medium still has many drawbacks, including high actual cost, limited selectivity, brevity, clutter, and susceptibility to zipping and zapping.

Broadcast TV dominance is being challenged by new electronic media, particularly cable television. Cable offers advertisers the visual and aural appeal of broadcast TV at much lower cost and with greater flexibility. Cable audiences are highly fragmented, which helps advertisers target specific markets but is a drawback for those wanting to reach a mass audience.

TV advertising can be done at the national, regional, or local level and can take the form of sponsorships, participations, and spots of varying lengths, including program-length infomercials.

To determine which shows to buy, media buyers select the most efficient ones for their target audience. They compare the packages of each station, substitute stronger programs for less efficient ones, and negotiate prices to get the best buy. Media buyers must have a firm grasp of certain important terms: designated market areas (DMAs), TV households (TVHH), households using TV (HUT), program rating, share of audience, gross rating points, and cost per thousand.

Like television, radio is a highly creative medium. Its greatest attribute is its ability to offer excellent reach and frequency to selective audiences at a very efficient price. Its drawbacks are the limitations of sound, segmented audiences, and its short-lived and half-heard commercials.

Radio stations are normally classified by the programming they offer and the audiences they serve. Radio stations may be AM or FM. They may use network or syndicated programs and follow any of a dozen or more popular formats. Advertisers purchase radio time in one of three forms: local, spot, or network. Buying radio time requires a basic understanding of radio terminology. The most common terms are dayparts, average quarter-hour, and cumulative audiences.

Key Terms

affidavit of performance, 338
audience composition, 336
audience share, 336
avails, 337
average quarter-hour audience (AQH persons), 343
average quarter-hour rating, 344
average quarter-hour share, 344
barter syndication, 331
broadcast TV, 323
cable TV, 323
cost per rating point (CPP), 338
cost per thousand (CPM), 338
cume persons, 344
cume rating, 344
daypart mix, 335

designated market areas (DMA), 334
digital video recorder (DVR), 327
drive times, 343
first-run syndication, 331
gross impressions, 344
gross rating points (GRPs), 337, 344
households using TV (HUT), 335
imagery transfer, 340
infomercial, 331
inventory, 330
local time, 343
makegoods, 338
networks, 329
off-network syndication, 331
participation, 330

preemption rate, 338
prime time, 335
program-length advertisement (PLA), 331
program rating, 336
programming format, 340
rating services, 332
run-of-station (ROS), 343
sponsorship, 329
spot announcements, 330
spot radio, 343
sweeps, 332
total audience, 336
total audience plan (TAP), 343
TV households (TVHH), 335

Review Questions

1. What are the advantages of broadcast TV advertising for a product like milk?
2. What steps can advertisers take to overcome zipping and zapping?
3. Why has advertising on network TV become less desirable in recent years?
4. In what ways is cable TV's selectivity a strength? A drawback?
5. How can TV and radio be used best in an integrated marketing communications program?
6. How does syndication differ from network television?
7. What are the various ways to measure a TV program's audience and cost efficiency?
8. What is the format of the radio station you listen to most? How would you describe the demographics of its target audience?
9. What is the difference between average quarter-hour and cume persons? Which is better?
10. What is the significance of dayparts in radio and TV advertising? What are the best dayparts for each?

Exploring Advertising

1. Look through the TV listings for cable shows on several specialty cable channels. What audience do you think watches those channels? What products would you expect to see advertised?

2. While you are watching television, note which commercials are aired at what times. Do you see a pattern of advertisers during the shows versus between shows? What about at different times of day? What conclusions can you draw?

3. Pretend you are in a Nielsen TV Diary household for one week. Write down what shows you watched on which channels at what time of day. Was it difficult? How accurate do you think these surveys are?

4. Listen to some radio stations that you wouldn't normally consider listening to. Pay attention to the ads that you hear. Are the products different than those you normally hear advertised? If not you, whom are they trying to reach?

5. Valentine's Day is approaching and, as the owner of Dream Flower Florists, you want to increase your share of local business by advertising on the radio. After researching local stations, choose one whose format suits your target audience. Decide what kind of buys you will make and when they will be aired.

chapter thirteen

Digital Interactive Media and Direct Mail

Objectives

To explore the important factors advertisers weigh when considering digital interactive media and direct mail. Each medium has its own distinct characteristics and each has unique advantages and drawbacks. Advertisers must be able to compare the merits of these media and understand the most cost-effective ways to use them in their media mix.

After studying this chapter, you will be able to:

* **Discuss** the various opportunities and challenges presented by digital interactive media.

* **Explain** the evolution of interactive media.

* **Debate** the pros and cons of the Internet as an advertising medium.

* **Define** the various kinds of Internet advertising.

* **Discuss** the Net's audience and the challenges involved in measuring it.

* **Explain** how Internet advertising is sold and how much it costs.

* **Enumerate** the various types of direct-mail advertising.

* **Detail** the various costs associated with direct-mail advertising.

* **Assess** which kinds of mailing lists are best.

Anna is a college student who loves animals. At home, she has two dogs, a cat, two parakeets, and a goldfish. But that's not all. She also has an Aisha, a Shoryu, a Kau, and a Zafara. And on top of that, she has a couple of pets for her pets—called *petpets*. She gave her Aisha a Ghostkerfish, her Shoryu a Warf, her Kau a Huggy, and her Zafara a Triffin. The names aren't the only thing that's a little unusual. The dogs, cat, birds, and fish are real, but the others are *virtual*—they're the products of Anna's imagination and the creative folk at NeoPets.

NeoPets is an interactive community of virtual pet owners on the Internet. Members start by adopting one or several pets out of 48 different species. Then they name them, feed them, and play games with them. The warriors at heart can even train their pets and take them to the Battledome to fight other members' pets or other characters on the site. That's just the beginning. As we shall see, there are so many activities on this site it's mind-boggling, and nearly impossible for any one person to see and do everything that the site offers.

NeoPets went live in early 2000 with about 500 new registrations a day. To grow the site, the team at NeoPets did not use any conventional means of advertising. Instead, they used only one—the most powerful communication medium—word of mouth. And word spread like wildfire. With more than 25 million registrations worldwide, NeoPets is the largest global youth community on the Internet. Users range in age from 8 to 80. The bulk of its users—more than 40 percent—are between 13 and 17 years old, a very desirable and elusive market for many advertisers. In addition to the heavy traffic on NeoPets, the site is also the "stickiest" on the entire Internet, with its millions of users spending an average of four hours per month there.

Why is it that NeoPets appeals to so many? More important, how does NeoPets maintain members' interest and attention? Two words: content and quality. Early on, the team at NeoPets knew that content—lots of it—would be key to keeping members interested, so this was one of the first things they worked on. And equally important was the quality of the content. In fact, the site is updated daily and is monitored around the clock.

"It's all about quality of writing, quality of creative and quality of experience," says Stephanie Yost Cameron, senior vice president of business and legal affairs at NeoPets. "We're also completely CARU (Children's Advertising Review Unit) and COPPA (Children's Online Privacy Protection Act) compliant." As a result, most parents feel safe when their children are on the site. Many teachers also regard the site highly and even integrate it into their classroom lectures and activities.

For advertisers, NeoPets offers the opportunity to participate in *Immersive Advertising,* NeoPets's proprietary practice of integrating advertisers' products or services into the Neopian experience. Before the creative team starts on a project, Rik Kinney, executive vice president of NeoPets, explains that NeoPets gets to know a client to truly understand the company, its product or service, and its objectives. "Then we try to figure out how to communicate the advertiser's message in an imaginative, fun, Neopian way," Kinney says.

For example, in the virtual downtown Neopia Central, pet owners can spend their accumulated Neopoints—most stores are Neopian inventions, but the site is sprinkled with virtual stores for real businesses. NeoPets can "eat" at McDonald's or "watch" the latest Disney movies. Some of the site's 166 arcade-style games are sponsored by brands like General Mills' Honey Nut Cheerios. Games feature a familiar NeoPet using the product in a Neopian environment and are often huge hits with members.[1]

Instead of inundating the site with the virtual product, as many marketers would intuitively want to do, Kinney and his team, familiar with the psychology of NeoPets's members, recommended limiting the number of products available. This results in an immediate rush of participants seeking the products on the site because they are so "rare." In fact, less than 1 percent of the thousands of NeoPets pages contain any marketing or branding, and all advertising is marked as such. Word of mouth propagates an interest for the products more than any other conventional means of advertising can.

It's not surprising that MTV Networks acquired NeoPets in 2005.

Digital Interactive Media

Today, we are all participating in a new media revolution, brought on by incredible achievements in communications technology. We're talking, of course, about **digital interactive media** and the *information superhighway.* The highway is the Internet, and it is already the fastest-growing medium in history.

To understand the dramatic effect this is having on marketing and advertising, imagine for a moment what life was like before radio and TV. Back then, if you had a product to sell, you made your appeal to the consumer directly, often on her front door step. If she didn't like what you were peddling, she slammed the door in your face. She was in complete control of the selling environment.[2] Then along came radio and, 30 years later, TV. Now mass marketers had a captive audience, people who would willingly pay for an evening's entertainment at home by simply sitting through the commercials. Advertisers prospered—and so did consumers, as they participated in a rapidly growing standard of living.

But now the sands are shifting across the advertising landscape. The remote control was the first step toward convenient interactivity, and it had a major impact on commercial viewership. Instead of watching commercials, people could now use the station breaks to channel surf, effectively slamming the door in the salesperson's face.

Right on its heels came the widespread distribution of cable TV. In less than a decade, the network TV audience plunged from 90 percent to 60 percent. SLAM!

Then, of course, came the VCR. People could now record shows and watch them later at their convenience, zipping through the commercials. Or they could just rent a movie or use video on demand and skip the commercials altogether. TiVo brought ad-avoidance into the digital age, allowing viewers to customize their entertainment schedules. SLAM!

Meanwhile, technology keeps on going and going and going. It's already given us the personal computer, the cellular phone, the Internet and the World Wide Web, fiber optics, satellite communications, CD-ROM, DVD, and the software to make it all simple enough for virtually anybody to use. And on the launching pad, about to blast off, is interactive TV. With growing consumer acceptance of all this wizardry, prices have plummeted, making most of it affordable to the masses.

These are not just advertising media. In many cases, they represent completely new ways of living and doing business. The fastest growing advertising medium in history has also opened the door to electronic commerce.

From the convenience of your own personal computer, you can bank online, buy a car or a beautiful piece of art, trade on the stock exchange, book your airline reservations, purchase concert tickets, buy a complete new wardrobe from your favorite department store, or even order your week's groceries and have them delivered to your door.

The Internet has also changed the way we send mail, eliminating the need for an overseas airmail stamp if you want to communicate with your brother in Berlin. You can do library research in the comfort of your den, or you can start your own home-based business and market your products worldwide.

The new media are truly revolutionary in their effect on our daily lives, and it's a revolution for marketers too.

Back in 1996, the entire Internet services industry amounted to only $1.3 billion, and total ad spending was a mere $300 million. But the potential was already obvious. By the year 2000, online retail sales had soared to $42.2 billion, and online advertising reached $8.2 billion.[3] Then came the dot-com crash, the recession, and the September 11, 2001, terrorist attacks. Internet advertising took a major hit—along with the rest of the advertising industry—declining steeply for two straight years. But by 2003, the industry was back on a growth track. As the nation's biggest traditional advertisers suddenly realized that the Net offered wonderful opportunities for achieving real, bottom-line results, they started increasing their online spending dramatically.

In light of this, eMarketer projected that online advertising spending in the United States would reach $18.5 billion in 2008, more than double the spending in 2004.[4] And the Internet research company Gartner, Inc., predicted that worldwide business-to-business (B2B) e-commerce revenues would surpass $7.29 trillion in 2004, a 5,000% increase over 1999, with the United States accounting for only 39 percent of the total, a steep decline from its 63 percent share in 1999.[5]

In addition to this phenomenal growth, by offering true interactivity the new media enable businesses and other organizations to develop and nurture relationships with their customers and other stakeholders, in a way never before available, on a global scale at a very efficient cost. It's an environment where customers may spend 20 minutes or more, not just 30 seconds, and where advertising is a dialogue, not a monologue.

The new interactive media today include the Internet and all its associated online services, CD-ROM catalogs

Digital interactive media brings us full circle—back to before the advent of mass media when the consumer controlled the selling environment. Sites like BarnesandNoble.com (www.bn.com) offer interactivity with the consumer, to a degree unmatched by any other advertising medium. The site not only serves as an Internet-based mail-order retailer but also offers customers extensive search capabilities, book reviews, book suggestions tailored to each specific user, e-books, magazine subscriptions, DVDs, and software.

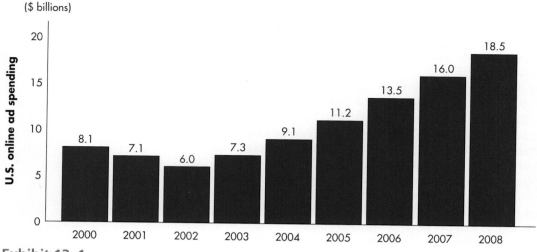

Exhibit 13–1

U.S. online advertising spending, 2000–2008 ($ billions). After three years of contraction, due to the recession and dot-com bust, eMarketer tracked a rebound in 2003 and predicts continued expansion.

CONCEPT CHECK

What aspects of the Internet make it such a unique medium?

and magazines, stand-alone kiosks, cellular telephone systems, and interactive television. Most prominent of all is the Internet, so that is what we will focus on in this chapter. In only 10 years as a commercial medium, the Internet has become a mass forum for advertising as well as other communications (see Exhibit 13–1). In recognition of this explosive growth, we need to understand what the medium is, how it is organized, how people get to it, and how advertisers buy it and use it in their marketing plans. Following that discussion, we'll examine some of the other new media briefly and then look at the most prominent form of *addressable media*—direct mail.

The Internet as a Medium

The Internet has come a long way from its simple roots. While some people assume it was just recently created by today's commercial online providers, such as America Online (AOL) and EarthLink, in fact the technological infrastructure of the Internet has been around for close to 40 years.

The Evolution of the Internet

The **Internet** actually began in the early 1960s as a twinkle in the eye of the U.S. Department of Defense, which saw it as a means of supercomputer communication for researchers and military facilities across the country. Until its commercial explosion in the 1990s, the Internet remained a relatively obscure network of linked computers used mostly by academics, military researchers, and scientists around the world to send and receive electronic mail, transfer files, and find or retrieve information from databases.

Commercial Online Services

During the 1980s, a number of commercial online services like Prodigy and AOL began their operations by capitalizing on the phenomenon of local *elec-*

tronic bulletin board services (BBSs). These new online providers managed to create, in effect, nationwide BBSs that delivered e-mail between subscribers, supplied catalogs for online shopping, provided chat rooms for discussion, organized interactive game playing, and offered software downloading capabilities, along with a host of other features. People could even advertise in the AOL classifieds just like in the newspaper.

At that time, anyone with a modem-equipped PC could join the several million members of EarthLink, Prodigy, and America Online for a basic fee of around $10 a month plus a charge for any time spent online beyond the basic monthly allowance. One drawback, though, was that subscribers were limited to sharing e-mail and information with users of the same service provider.

Still, it didn't take long for the country's most aggressive advertisers to understand the potential of being able to communicate with this lucrative market of computer users via a new medium. General Motors, Chrysler, MCI, 1-800-FLOWERS, *BusinessWeek* magazine, and Lands' End jumped on the bandwagon. Soon thousands of product marketers and business services were using the online services as a medium of both advertising and commerce.[6]

Commercial applications of the Internet itself were not as well received as online services until the development of graphical browsers. The Internet offered a tremendous wealth of information, but it wasn't as easy to use as the online services. First of all, to get access to the Internet, people had to find an **Internet service provider (ISP).** Then, once they were online, there was no simple way to navigate around the Internet unless they possessed a lot of technical know-how. The first form of the World Wide Web, for instance, was entirely text-based; it had no graphics, and the initial ads resembled simple print classifieds.

When the first commercially available **Web browser** software that accommodated graphics, Netscape Navigator, was released in 1994, the Internet drew even more public attention. People could now simply point and click on icons and pictures to find their way around in cyberspace. This made the Internet almost as user-friendly as the online services.

The World Wide Web

The **World Wide Web (WWW)** provides access to an enormous amount of information found mostly in the form of **Web pages.** These can best be likened to book covers, **portals,** or gateways, since they act as starting points to additional information. These pages are created by millions of online users and businesses, with content varying from culinary tips to sports commentary to corporate and business information. Early sites on the Web typically consisted of a home page that resembled a poorly designed brochure cover, with perhaps some limited information on subsequent Web pages about the company and its products. These were, in effect, corporate storefronts.

Once businesses (and the media) sensed the lucrative potential of the Internet, they bombarded the public with messages about how the technology would revolutionize global communication. This became a self-fulfilling prophecy, and the gold rush of the Information Age began. AOL and Prodigy, with their multimillion-customer databases, rushed to marry their services to the Internet to provide communication to users worldwide. The Web exploded from about 50 sites in 1993 to more than 70,000 sites in 1995 to 9 million sites worldwide in 2002.[7] It is estimated that the Web exceeded 70 million sites in 2005 and is growing at about one million sites per month.

Internet Search Engines

Imagine trying to find a book in the Library of Congress without the aid of a card catalog. It would be next to impossible. That's the problem people faced in their initial efforts to find information on the World Wide Web. And that's what

The development of the search engine greatly facilitated the explosion of the Internet because it provided a centralized source of information that made the medium accessible to the mainstream user. Without search engines like Google (www.google.com) the World Wide Web would not have captured such a significant consumer audience and the Internet may have developed for use only by technology-based businesses.

created the demand for another software program: the search engine. In rapid succession, a number of programs with catchy names like Yahoo!, Excite, and InfoSeek emerged to act as **search engines** for the cyberspace traveler. The user could simply type in a name, a word, or a phrase, and the search engine would scour the Net for relevant information and *Web site* addresses.

Because of their usefulness, many millions of people pass through the major search engines each month, and marketers quickly realized the advertising potential of these and other high-traffic Internet sites. Actual Internet advertising began in earnest in October 1994, when the first *banner ads*—little billboards of various sizes that pop up when a visitor lands on a particular Web page— were sold by *Hotwired* (the online edition of *Wired* magazine). Soon, other companies followed suit, buying banner advertising on other popular Web sites.

Today, Web surfers can browse everything from university libraries to the Louvre museum in Paris. Along the way, they can click on an ad banner and visit the commercial sites set up by IBM, AT&T, the city of Berlin, Ford, Merrill Lynch, Krispy Kreme Doughnuts, and Visa, to mention just a few.

Since the online services and the search engines are the gateways to all these sites, they also attract the greatest number of visitors, as well as the greatest amount of advertising. In October 1997, for instance, the top two Web sites by number of hits were Yahoo! and AOL.[8] By August 2005, both were still on top— only AOL had been folded into the Time Warner Network (see Exhibit 13–2).[9]

Exhibit 13–2

Top 25 most visited Web sites in August 2005.

Rank	Property	Number of unique visitors (000)
	Total Internet Users	*168,482*
1	Yahoo! sites	121,962
2	Time Warner Network	118,911
3	MSN–Microsoft sites	114,622
4	Google sites	85,658
5	eBay	66,693
6	Amazon sites	42,906
7	Ask Jeeves	40,084
8	Viacom Online	39,809
9	United Online, Inc.	33,448
10	Verizon Communications Corp.	32,968
11	Expedia, Inc.	32,479
12	New York Times Digital	31,977
13	CNET Networks	30,813
14	Walt Disney Internet Group (WDIG)	30,760
15	Vendare Media	30,224
16	Monster Worldwide	29,736
17	Weather Channel, The	27,136
18	Lycos, Inc.	26,297
19	AT&T Properties	25,331
20	Wal-Mart	22,767
21	Target Corporation	22,000
22	MySpace.com	21,819
23	Shopping.com sites	21,645
24	Real.com Network	21,464
25	Trip Network, Inc.	20,798

Number of people online (millions)			
Region	Population	Internet users	Penetration (%)
Africa	893.2	12.8	1.4%
Asia	3,607.5	256.5	7.1
Europe	730.9	224.5	30.7
Middle East	259.0	168.4	6.5
North America	325.2	223.0	68.6
Latin America/Caribbean	541.8	50.8	9.4
Oceania	32.5	15.8	48.5
World total	6,390.1	800.0	12.5

Exhibit 13–3

Data compiled from the July 2004 United Nations sources.

The percentage of the U.S. population able to access the Internet on a regular basis continues to climb. In 1997, only 50 million people were wired. This number had doubled by 2000 and has since doubled again. In 2004, more than 200 million people in the United States accessed the Internet each month.[10] Worldwide, the active Internet audience is estimated at 455 million, with many more occasional users (see Exhibit 13–3). According to Internet World Stats (www.internetworldstats.com), Internet penetration is currently growing fastest in the Middle East and Africa, where the percentage of users has tripled since 2000. Sweden (77 percent), Hong Kong (72 percent), and the United States (69 percent) top the list of the most-wired populations.[11]

Businesses ranging from your local florist to global manufacturers are using the Internet to present multimedia content that includes bulletin boards, interesting or entertaining information, product data, and even games. Many of them, like E*Trade and Amazon.com, conduct all their commerce right on the Web. Users move from page to page and site to site depending on what they are looking for. In other words, the user is in control. The consumer chooses what screens to watch, which banners to click, and which to ignore.[12]

That means marketers have to provide information that is useful and relevant. They have to keep updating it to get repeat visits. And a little entertainment with a few freebies tossed in doesn't hurt. Even Ragú (www.ragu.com) spaghetti sauce has a colorful site that offers Italian phrases, recipes, and occasionally a sweepstakes. Learning how to use this new medium challenges the creativity of the whole advertising community. And with the amount of daily updating that is required to keep Web sites current, the opportunity for career growth and specialization is great.

The Internet Audience

In the past several years we have seen a steady migration of people who used to spend time in front of the TV moving over to the computer. In a 2000 Jupiter Research study, researchers asked PC users which media activities they were giving up most to spend more time on the Internet. Almost 50 percent said they were watching less TV; a small but significant minority of users said they decreased their print media consumption, with 22 percent reading magazines less frequently and 21 percent reading newspapers less. Recent surveys confirm this trend. The number of Internet users, as well as the amount of time spent by each user, grows steadily while the TV audience dwindles. Although there has been some controversy about measurement methods (which have resulted in major discrepancies in the results reported by even well-respected researchers like Nielsen and comScore Media Metrix), the consensus remains that time spent on the Internet eats into time spent watching television.[13]

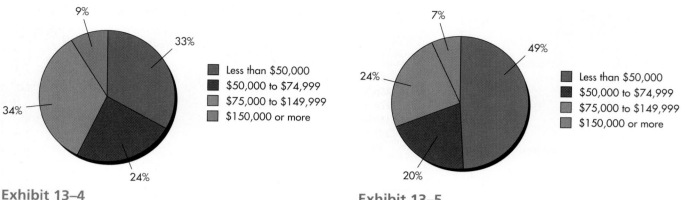

Exhibit 13–4

Household income composition of the World Wide Web in the United States (2004).

Exhibit 13–5

Household income composition of the United States (2004).

Who Uses the Net

Media budgets tend to be very pragmatic. As audiences migrate, so do the media dollars. As a result, media spending on Internet advertising has grown substantially. One of the great draws of the Internet from the marketer's point of view is its demographics. Historically, the majority of people who surfed the Internet were well-educated, upscale, white males who used the Net for business or scientific purposes. However, recent surveys of Internet demographics have found that women now represent more than half of the online population. Similarly, the growth of ethnic minorities on the Web shows that the Internet is starting to match America's diversity. The average age of Web users has also been increasing over the past several years. Twenty-two percent of U.S. adults over age 65 are regular Internet users; seniors are even more enthusiastic e-mailers than their younger counterparts and have begun to expand their Internet use into other areas, like product research and health information.[14]

Internet users also tend to be relatively affluent (see Exhibits 13–4 and 13–5).[15] Those in the lower annual income brackets (under $50,000) represent 49 percent of the U.S. population but only 33 percent of Internet users, whereas the upper income brackets (over $75,000 annually) comprise only 31 percent of the population but 43 percent of Internet users.[16] Internet users are also better educated than the general U.S. population. According to the U.S. Census Bureau, half of the population has attended at least some college, but this half comprises 69 percent of the online population.[17] To marketers this is a very attractive audience, especially for business-to-business advertisers.

As lower computer prices and easier access further democratizes the Net, the user group will continue to broaden, and this will enhance the medium's advertising opportunities to an even wider range of marketers. At first, the primary targets of advertising were businesspeople. But now, the growing number of women on the Net has pushed many of the traditional consumer advertisers (such as packaged goods companies) to consider the medium seriously. A recent study of a mixed-media campaign for Unilever's Dove Nutrium bar soap concluded that spending 15 percent of the campaign's TV/print/online budget on Web advertising resulted in a 24 percent boost in branding impact.[18] There are now numerous Web sites catering exclusively to women's interests, including iVillage (www.ivillage.com) and Ladies Home Journal Online (www.lhj.com).

How People Access the Net

To get on the Internet, people must first choose from two types of communication systems—*narrowband* and *broadband*. **Narrowband** is a type of digital data transmission in which each wire carries one signal at a time.[19] In contrast, **broadband** transmission enables a single wire to carry several signals simultaneously.[20] This high-**bandwidth** technology makes it possible to download large graphics files, watch video clips, play video games online, and surf the Net comfortably without having to endure what has been dubbed the "World Wide Wait."

Currently, there are several ways people can get online. The least expensive method is still narrowband via a dial-up modem, over a conventional telephone line, through an Internet service provider. While the dial-up method is universally available, the connections are unfortunately slow, so people can spend a lot of time drumming their fingers as they wait for pages to download.

That's why all the growth today is in broadband systems. By mid-2004, more than half of U.S. Internet users accessed it via broadband, a 47 percent increase in broadband use over 2003.[21] For home or small business use, there are essentially two choices: cable modem and DSL. Both options download files approximately ten times faster than dial-up. The **cable-modem** system is rapidly growing in popularity. It is obtainable from those cable TV companies that offer one of the cable-modem services such as Roadrunner. Cable modem may be subject to slowdowns during peak usage hours when everyone in the same neighborhood is online.[22]

The second method, **DSL**, which stands for **digital subscriber line**, is now competing with cable modem in popularity and price. This technology transforms a traditional telephone line into a high-speed digital link to provide homes and businesses with always-on, broadband Internet access.[23] DSL delivers speed comparable to cable[24]—but also has its drawbacks. One's distance from a telephone company's special switching facility, called a central office (CO), directly affects the speed of the DSL connection.

Two other methods, DirecPC and WebTV, are also available today, but they have yet to catch on like cable modem and DSL. Developed by Hughes Electronics, the same company that pioneered the DirecTV satellite system, DirecPC is also satellite based and offers very fast downloading—faster even than cable. However, it is very expensive and still requires a dial-up modem and separate phone line for sending material.

Microsoft's MSN TV (formerly WebTV) is much like cable modem except the receiving and viewing device used is the family TV instead of a computer. It includes a set-top box and offers constant connection to the Internet, even while the TV is playing. This is another gambit in the search for interactive TV technology and is really aimed at those people who don't want to invest in the cost and complexity of having a computer at home but would still like to have Internet access.

Critics contend that the Internet will never be as pervasive as television because many people either don't need to purchase an expensive computer or have no desire to use one. However, developers of MSN TV 2 (www.webtv.com) have incorporated the easy-to-use and interactive aspects of the World Wide Web directly into a typical television.

Types of Internet Advertising

Ads on the Internet can take a variety of forms, and as the Net matures, the number of forms continues to expand. Most advertising opportunities today can

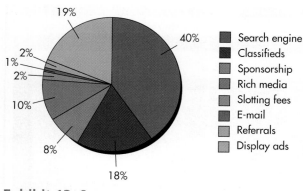

Exhibit 13–6

Percent of Internet ad revenues by type of advertising, 2004.

be classified as Web sites, banners, buttons, sponsorships, interstitials, search engine marketing, classified ads, and e-mail ads (see Exhibit 13–6). We'll discuss each briefly.

Web Sites

Some companies view their whole Web site as an ad. And in some ways it is. But in truth, the **Web site** is more than an ad—it's an alternative "storefront," a location where customers, prospects, and other stakeholders can come to find out more about the company, its products and services, and what it stands for.

Some companies use their Web site like an extended brochure to promote their goods and services; others act as information and entertainment publishers and try to create a cool place that people will visit often; still others treat their Web site as an online catalog store, perhaps their only store, conducting business right on the Net. Thus, except when used like a brochure, the Web site is really more than an ad; it's an "ad-dress." The NeoPets Web site, for example, is so full of activities that the average user spends between four and five hours per month at the site. As a result, Nielsen//NetRatings consistently ranks NeoPets as one of the top 10 "stickiest" sites on the Web. Advertisers like that a lot.

Web sites typically consist of a *home page* and an indefinite number of subsequent pages that users can visit for further information. A **Web page** does not refer to an $8\frac{1}{2}$- by 11-inch page. It refers to a single HTML *(hypertext markup language)* file, which, when viewed with a browser, may actually be several screens long. A large Web site may have hundreds of these pages of information. This means the site contains hundreds of different documents of various lengths, each probably covering a different subject.[25]

Banners and Buttons

The most basic form of Web advertising is the banner ad. A **banner** is a little billboard that spreads across the top or bottom of the Web page. When users click their mouse pointer on the banner, it sends them to the advertiser's site. The standard size for a banner ad is 468 pixels (picture elements) wide by 60 pixels high. That means that on a standard 8 1/2- by 11-inch page, the banner would measure just over 4 1/2 inches wide by 1/2 inch high.

While banners are the most common unit of Web advertising, the cost of a banner can range wildly—anywhere from free to thousands of dollars per month. Some standardization is taking place in the business, with most sites now charging, on a cost-per-thousand basis, anywhere from $3.00 to $100.00 per thousand impressions, depending on the number and type of visitors the site regularly receives. The industry average for the more popular sites is $30.00 per thousand.

In 2003, in response to many agency requests to simplify the ad buying process, the Interactive Advertising Bureau (IAB), the association of Web publishers, introduced the Universal Ad Package, a suite of sixteen standard ad sizes (including skyscrapers, rectangles, pop-ups, banners, and buttons) designed to improve the efficiency and ease of planning, buying, and creating online media.[26]

Similar to banners are **buttons,** small versions of the banner that often look like an icon and usually provide a link to an advertiser's **landing page,** a special Web page that leads people into the purchasing or relationship-building process. Because buttons take up less space than banners, they also cost less.

Today, a host of new software technologies, such as DHTML (dynamic hypertext markup language), Java, and Flash, have greatly enhanced the once-static banner and button ads. Full motion and animation, for example, are now commonplace. In fact, one of the greatest areas of recent growth has been **rich-media advertising,** which includes graphical animations and ads with audio and video elements that overlay or even float over the page.

Some of the more common types of rich-media ads include animated banners, interstitials, and rich mail. The **interstitial** is a catchall term for a variety of ads that play between pages on a Web site, popping up on the screen while the computer downloads a Web site that the user has clicked on. All of their various formats tend to perform well in terms of click-through rates and brand recall—which is what the advertisers care about.

Rich mail allows graphics, video, and audio to be included in e-mail messages. When you open up a rich e-mail, your e-mail client automatically calls up your Internet connection and launches an HTML page in your e-mail window. E-mail clients that are offline will invite you to click on the link when you have your Internet connection open again. We can anticipate seeing more audio and animation integrated into these ads as improving technology (and higher bandwidth) accommodates them.[27]

Interstitials are a form of interruption marketing, similar to a traditional television commercial. Visitors are forced to see these ads before they can continue on their intended path. As a result, they tend to get a lot of attention. Interstitials often contain large graphics, multimedia shows, or software applications.

Sponsorships and Added-Value Packages

A form of advertising on the Internet that is growing in popularity is the **sponsorship** of Web pages. Corporations sponsor entire sections of a publisher's Web page or sponsor single events for a limited period of time, usually calculated in months. In exchange for sponsorship support, companies are given extensive recognition on the site. Sometimes an added-value package is created by integrating the sponsor's brand with the publisher's content, as a sort of advertorial, or with banners and buttons on the page.

IBM has exclusively sponsored the Super Bowl Web page, at an estimated cost of $1 million for each event. Other forms of sponsorships have included Web serials (online soap operas), sites devoted to women's issues, contests, and giveaways.

Search Engine Marketing

When a user types a keyword or phrase into a search engine, two kinds of results are returned—those that have been *paid for* by advertisers, and those that are *natural*. **Pay per click (PPC) advertising** is a search engine marketing technique that requires the advertiser to pay a fee every time someone clicks onto its Web site from a search engine's paid results. The more an advertiser agrees to pay (or bid) per click for a specific search term (**keyword**), the higher a site will rank in the paid search results. Natural **search engine optimization** is a technique that involves enhancing a Web site's programming code and content so that a Web site is returned prominently in the natural search results of spider-based search engines (such as Google). A search engine **spider** (or **Web crawler**) is an automated browser that essentially builds an index of the Web by following every link it sees.

The most prominent results returned by the Yahoo! search engine are those that participate in Sponsored Search. The more an advertiser bids for a keyword, the higher it will appear in the results.

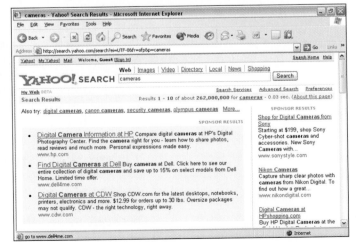

Classified Ads

Another growing area for Internet advertisers, and an excellent opportunity for local advertisers, is the plethora of **classified ad Web sites,** like CraigsList.org. Some of these offer *free* classified advertising opportunities because they are typically supported by banner ads for other advertisers. Others charge much in the same way as newspapers charge for printed classified ads. You can search for homes, cars, jobs, computer equipment, business opportunities, and so on. Moreover, the search can be narrowed to your city or expanded nationwide. Many of these sites are sponsored by the search engines themselves or by local newspapers around the country.

E-mail Advertising

According to Forrester Research, 77 percent of marketers send **e-mail advertising** to customers who have asked for it. Forrester predicted that U.S. marketers sent almost 210 billion e-mails in 2004.[28] Marketers have always known that direct-mail advertising (discussed in the second half of this chapter) is the most effective medium for generating inquiries and leads and for closing a sale. It's also been the most expensive medium on a cost-per-exposure basis. Now, thanks to the Internet, the cost of direct mail has been reduced dramatically.

A word of caution, though: It's important to differentiate responsible e-mail advertising from **spam,** which is really just electronic junk mail. Spam generally refers to unsolicited, mass e-mail advertising for a product or service that is sent by an unknown entity to a purchased mailing list or newsgroup. Spammers face the wrath of frustrated customers tired of having their inboxes filled with unwanted e-mails. Since January 2004, spammers also face litigation under the CAN-SPAM Act (Controlling the Assault of Non-Solicited Pornography and Marketing). Legitimate e-mail advertisers are required to (1) clearly mark the e-mail as advertising, (2) provide a valid reply-to e-mail address, and (3) allow recipients to opt out of future mailings. The first lawsuits under the act were filed in April 2004, against two companies that had sent nearly a million e-mails advertising bogus diet patches and growth hormones.[29] With this in mind, wary marketers are focusing their e-mail efforts on **customer relationship management (CRM)** rather than on cold prospecting.

One of the hottest trends on the Internet today is actually an application of e-mail. Thanks to *viral marketing,* Amazon.com, Napster, eBay, Blue Mountain Arts, and Hotmail all made it big on the Web, reaching unexpected heights in short time spans, most with surprisingly low marketing budgets.[30] **Viral marketing** is the Internet version of word-of-mouth advertising via e-mail. The term was coined in 1997 by Steven Jurvetson and his partners at the venture capital firm Draper Fisher Jurvetson. They were describing free e-mail provider Hotmail's incredible growth to 12 million users in just 18 months through the use of a little message at the bottom of every e-mail.[31] The message invited recipients to sign up for their own free Hotmail account.

Since that time, many other marketers have come up with ways to induce their satisfied customers to recommend their product or service to friends and family members. One of the keys to viral marketing success is to present an offer with real perceived value—one that people will want to share with one another. NeoPets, for example, uses a referral program whereby members are rewarded NeoPoints or rare items each time someone they refer to the site signs up and becomes a member.

Using the Internet in IMC

As we discussed in Chapter 7, one of the keys to successfully developing a meaningful relationship with customers is to promote purposeful dialogue between the company and its stakeholders. That is what interactivity really

The Pros and Cons of Internet Advertising

The Pros

- **Truly interactive medium.** More than any other medium, the Internet allows consumers to directly interact with an advertiser, thereby establishing stronger relationships.

- **Enormous audience.** With an audience of some 800 million people worldwide, the Internet is also the only true global medium, providing information and commerce opportunities that are immediately accessible around the world.

- **Immediate response** from consumers that cannot be rivaled, except through personal selling. Products and information are available on demand by the consumer, providing instantaneous feedback for the advertiser.

- **Highly selective targeting,** unmatched by any other medium. By effectively targeting their messages, advertisers can reach the best prospects.

- **Proximity to purchase** may be the greatest advantage of Internet advertising. Purchasers can be targeted right where and when they're considering making a purchase.

- **Affluent market.** Sixty-seven percent of Internet users have household incomes of $50,000 or more, compared with 51 percent of the U.S. population. Sixty-nine percent of Internet users attended college, compared with only 51 percent of the U.S. population.

- **In-depth information** provided about a company and its products. Commercial Web sites provide detailed information about products or services to information-hungry consumers. This feature can be used to enhance other forms of advertising.

- **A rapidly growing industry.** The Internet is expected to continue its stunning growth for some time, particularly as the children of today grow up with the technology and become the consumers of tomorrow.

- **Reaches business-to-business users** when television and radio often cannot—while they are at work. Even consumer advertising can reach these Internet users while they are working.

- **Advertorials** are effective tools for advertisers and are often incorporated into Web sites. An advertiser can place its name into an article to build credibility, increase exposure, and encourage adoption. With clever use, these advertorials can provide anything from tips and tricks on product use to new recipes requiring a certain product.

- **Virtual storefront.** Catalog companies have demonstrated the profitability of direct-mail campaigns, which can be replicated by Web pages on the Internet. Today's most commonly purchased online products are computers and supplies, travel arrangements, and entertainment-related products.

The Cons

- **Medium not standardized.** The Internet is still very young, with many unanswered questions about advertising effectiveness, accuracy of market research, and standardization of measurements for both ad exposure and pricing. The many unknowns still keep some advertisers from spending millions of dollars on online campaigns.

- **Targeting costs** used to be among the most expensive relative to other media; these have since come down to high, but not outrageous, levels.

- **Slow downloads,** due mostly to bandwidth, still hamper many users from the full online experience. Penetration of the high bandwidth DSL lines and cable modems has been accelerating, however. Before advertising on the Internet can realize its fullest potential, data transfer times will have to come down tremendously.

- **Security and privacy concerns** still prevent many users from engaging in online purchases, although with time these fears will likely be dispelled. Until most people believe the Internet is a safe place for financial transactions, it is unlikely to be accepted by everyone as a viable medium for commerce.

- **Global marketing limitations.** The Internet is rapidly growing in other countries as it is in the United States. However, many countries are still hampered by the high cost of local telephone services, and developing countries simply lack the technology infrastructure to provide Internet services to the general public.

means. And that is where the Internet offers its greatest potential. (See the Checklist, "The Pros and Cons of Internet Advertising.")

For the first time, customers and other stakeholders can truly respond to a company's media communications in real time, using the same channel for feedback that the company used for promotion. This means that even if a customer finds herself accidentally at the company's Web site and, if something there strikes her fancy, she can commence a dialogue (relationship) with the company immediately. Of course, this also means that, if the Web site triggers her memory of a less-than-satisfactory experience with the company, she can use the same mechanism for complaining. But that's actually good, because a customer that complains usually cares. And a complaint gives the company the opportunity to correct the situation and set things right. It also gives the company information on how to improve. Sophisticated marketers cherish complaints.

While all of this is well and good, it also brings up a new problem for marketers today. In the good old days of simple mass-media advertising, manufacturers placed their ads on network TV and went on about their business. The retailers took care of customers, so the manufacturers didn't really have to be concerned about them. In the new age of integrated marketing communications, that is no longer the case. Yes, the retailer is still there. But Mrs. Consumer doesn't want to talk to the retailer. She's a pretty sophisticated person. She knows who makes the product and if she's got a complaint that's who she wants to talk to. So it's not good enough for companies to put a pretty Web site up on the Internet and then walk away from it. It has to be adequately staffed and it must be kept up to date. Realizing this, companies are now finally staffing up. But this is very expensive—often requiring companies to double or triple their Internet budget with no increase in advertising exposure. So the decision to use the Internet for integration is a big one and cannot be taken lightly.

The Internet offers an enormous opportunity and challenge for advertisers to integrate this relatively new medium with traditional advertising vehicles. As the lines between television, movies, the Internet, and even cell phones begins to blur, companies are looking for ways to take advantage of them all. *Initiative,* a media-buying firm owned by Interpublic, compiled a database of more than 600 TV programs on the air. It then listed all the different ways that consumers could interact with these shows, through such things as promotional e-mails from the network, Web sites, cell phone text alerts, games or trivia contests. It concluded that there were 27 different avenues for advertisers to reach viewers interested in particular TV shows.[32] "There are a lot of advertisers looking for creative answers. It reminds me of the early days of the Web," says Larry Kramer, president of the digital-media arm of Viacom's CBS. "Everyone wants to do it, and they are not exactly sure how to do it yet."[33]

> **CONCEPT CHECK**
>
> Describe the different ways that advertisers can use the Internet to promote their goods or services.

Measuring the Internet Audience

When marketers and the media first began trumpeting the marvels of the Internet, they quickly noted the potentially vast size of its population. Today it's already up to 200 million people in the United States alone. Around the world, hundreds of millions of people use the Internet, and only citizens of developing countries are left without access.

Seeking Standardization

As much as Madison Avenue may want Web measurements to resemble traditional media measurements, the Internet cannot yet accommodate it. As we'll describe shortly, simply counting advertising impressions from a Web page is challenging. However, the basic questions remain the same: Do people see our ads? Are they effective? Until fairly recently, when a task force of the Interactive Advertising Bureau (IAB) provided some practical definitions, WWW audience measurement information lacked the standardization needed to be able to compare its advertising effectiveness to other media.

The most simple measurement, yet historically an area of great controversy, is the **ad impression.** The IAB defines an ad impression as "a measurement of responses from an ad delivery system to an ad request from the user's browser, which is . . . recorded at a point . . . closest to an actual opportunity to be seen by the user"[34] In other words, it is an ad that actually shows up on the computer screen. When a user loads a Web page with ads on it, the browser's intent is to pull the advertisement from its host ad server and bring it up as a banner, button, or interstitial. The number of successful ad requests can then be translated into the familiar CPM form. The goal of this definition, from the point of view of advertisers and agencies, is to guarantee to the extent possible, that a user will have an *opportunity to see* an ad. People often click away to some other site before a requested ad ever comes up. Or a pop-up blocker may intercept the ad. Under the IAB definition, an advertiser would not be charged for an ad that never had the opportunity to be seen. It is too soon to know whether marketers will now be able to obtain the foolproof numbers they want. But as technology improves the speed and methods of online advertising, we can anticipate increased accuracy in measurement. For more on Internet ratings, see Commercial Break 13–A.

A second measurement, unique to the Internet, is the **click rate** or *click-through rate.* A click occurs when a visitor moves the mouse's pointer to a Web link and clicks on the mouse button to get to another page. The click rate is the number of clicks on an ad divided by the number of times the ad is displayed. In essence, marketers are measuring the frequency with which users try to obtain additional information about a product by clicking on an advertisement. The click rate can then also be tabulated in CPM form to measure cost efficiency.

While most large companies have been caught by the allure of the Internet, advertisers are still nervous about spending millions of dollars in this largely unregulated and uncharted medium. Research firms like Media Metrix (www.mediametrix.com) specialize in gathering and testing Internet market data, from user demographics to ad effectiveness.

The Promise of Enhanced Tracking

Despite the controversy, today's software now provides some of the most precise targeting tools ever. In fact, every time you step into the Internet, some computer may be watching to see just where you go. The computers that send you Web pages interact with what are known as **cookies,** small pieces of information that get stored on your computer when you download certain Web sites. These cookies can keep track of whether you have ever before visited a specific site. This allows the Web site to identify you as a returning user and to customize the information based on your past browsing or purchase behavior.

From data gathered by sophisticated software, marketers' computers can determine your ISP, telephone area code, and industry code, what Web site you came from and where you went when you left. Marketers can then match this information with demographic and purchase data to create a clearer picture of consumer behavior than has ever before been available.

However, this new ability to track people's behavior on the Internet has stirred considerable debate. Although software developers claim that users are tracked anonymously with encrypted identification numbers, privacy advocates believe the marketing method is too invasive into consumers' lives (see Ethical Issues on page 366).

Commercial Break 13–A

Internet Ratings: The Next Frontier

While marketers are exploring the best ways to use the Internet in their campaigns, media research companies are trying to determine how to accurately measure the audiences using this new medium. These numbers are of interest not only to advertisers, but also to investment companies and venture capitalists who evaluate Web companies' stock prices and potential investment values, often without the benefit of traditional measures like earnings and profits.[35]

Nielsen, well known for its TV ratings, joined with NetRatings in 1999 to create Nielsen//NetRatings. Their flagship product, NetView, claims to be the industry's leading Internet audience measurement service. This leadership position might be refuted by Nielsen//NetRatings' primary competitor, Media Metrix, a service offered by comScore Networks.

Unlike Nielsen television ratings, which rely partly on weekly diaries and are often subject to a viewer's memory, Internet ratings data are collected by tracking software. Tracking software is installed on users' computers by the Internet ratings services. It tracks panelists' computer activity and automatically sends the collected information. These panel members have agreed to have their Internet use monitored and receive small cash incentives or gifts. Media Metrix and Nielsen//NetRatings each have about 50,000 panelists in the United States, far more than the Nielsen television panel. This is because of the enormous number of Web sites that must be monitored.

Some ratings services also use direct mailings and random calls to obtain data. The data are collected and compiled to produce monthly or weekly Internet ratings. The monthly Nielsen//NetRatings table below shows that Microsoft leads the list based on unique visitors to their Web sites, with several familiar names close behind. However, visitors stay much longer at the TimeWarner/AOL sites.

Unique Web site visitors for the month of October, 2005— Top 10 U.S. Parent Companies (Home Panel)

Parent name	Unique audience (000)	Reach %	Time per person
Microsoft	93,967	66.09	01:27:29
Time Warner (AOL)	85,272	59.98	03:51:55
Yahoo!	84,231	59.25	02:22:32
Google	69,333	48.77	00:25:58
eBay	44,778	31.50	01:36:36
InterActiveCorp	39,296	27.64	00:18:46
United States Government	35,706	25.11	00:17:35
Amazon	29,402	20.68	00:19:42
Walt Disney Internet Group	25,844	18.18	00:31:47
RealNetworks	24,620	17.32	00:48:09

Buying Time and Space on the Internet

There are many ways for companies to get involved in the new digital media. Most are proceeding cautiously; the particular vehicles selected must fit with the firm's overall marketing and media strategy. However, media planners must not think of these new vehicles in mass media terms. Interactive media are *personal audience venues*. That means one on one. So cost per thousand, rating points, and share of audience don't really mean the same things in the interactive world. With interactive media, we're not necessarily building sales volume. We're building relationships, one customer at a time. And the care companies exercise in buying and developing their interactive programs and integrating them with their mass media programs will determine their overall success.

Currently, the leading national advertisers spend the smallest piece of their marketing communications pie on interactive media—less than 2 percent of their budgets. But it's the fastest growing segment, having almost tripled in one year alone (see Exhibit 13–7).[38] The best marketers are testing extensively. Many direct marketers have launched online catalogs. Dell Computers (www.dell.com) generates several million dollars from online sales each day. Egghead Software (www.egghead.com) closed its retail stores in 1998 to operate 100 percent online.

But some advertisers and Internet companies do not believe these numbers are reliable. Critics point to a lack of standardization in how the numbers are produced. Each ratings service collects and computes data slightly differently. For example, Media Metrix combines home and at-work usage in its numbers while Nielsen//NetRatings breaks them out in separate charts. And if a consumer views the same Web page four times in one day, Media Metrix considers it one unique visitor. Most Web sites, conversely, interpret the data as four separate visits.[36]

As might be expected, the competitors' ratings, while similar, do not always match. In one month, for example, both companies reported Yahoo.com as the top-visited Web site. However, Nielsen//NetRatings said about 39.2 million home computer users came to the site, while Media Metrix put the number at 40.5 million. The next most popular site, according to Media Metrix, was MSN.com, with 32 million visitors, while Nielsen//NetRatings said it was AOL.com, with 35.3 million visitors. And there are sometimes large discrepancies between the rating companies' numbers and the logs kept by the Web sites themselves. "It's like wearing three watches at once—all with different times," says Ralph DiMuccio, head of industry relations at AltaVista, an Internet search firm. "You don't know what the right time is."

Once criticized for measuring only U.S. audiences[37] Internet rating services have gone global. For example,

Nielsen//NetRatings now measures audiences in 10 countries, representing an estimated 70 percent of the world's Internet usage. Media Metrix claims to capture data from 2 million global Internet users in 32 countries. The next big challenge for these ratings companies may be determining how to accurately measure Web surfing on the ever-more-popular, Internet-connected handheld devices (PDAs) and cellular phones.

Despite these improvements, some skeptical dot-com owners have turned to auditing companies for what they believe is a more accurate measurement of their audience. Companies like ABC Interactive and BPA International audit the Web traffic logs recorded by each individual site.

In 2004, the Interactive Advertising Bureau (IAB) issued a detailed definition and standard for global online ad impression measurement, which incorporates independent auditing. The standards are voluntary and have yet to be fully implemented, but they represent a good first step toward standardizing Internet audience measurements.

Applying the Breaks

Do you think we will ever be able to reliably measure Internet use? What approach do you think will ultimately generate the most accurate statistics?

One of the biggest question marks when advertising on the Internet is cost. Recent years have seen increased rate-card standardization, but advertisers still haven't found a completely satisfactory method of buying space on the Internet. This is no surprise really, since fully commercial advertising didn't really get going on the Internet until about 1996.

Pricing Methods

As we discussed earlier, advertising space on the World Wide Web can be purchased in several different ways. The most common means is the banner ad, typically billed on a cost-per-thousand basis determined by the number of impressions. On most Web pages, the base banner rate buys exposure on a rotating display that randomly selects which ads to show.

The real marketing power of the WWW, however, is the ability to specifically target an audience in a way that is virtually impossible in traditional media. In addition to general banners, media buyers may opt to purchase more selective space. For example, ads may be purchased in a portal's information

Exhibit 13–7

Top 10 Internet advertisers (2004).

Rank	Advertiser	Internet ad spending in 2004 ($ millions)
1	Netflix.com	170.4
2	Microsoft Corp.	153.7
3	Time Warner	145.3
4	Hewlett-Packard Co.	137.5
5	InterActiveCorp	131.9
6	Verizon Communications	124.6
7	Dell	119.5
8	Apollo Group	96.2
9	Lowermybills.com	78.4
10	Classmates Online	77.0

Ethical Issues

Profiling: Would You Take Cookies from a Stranger?

With the advance of Internet marketing technologies, privacy has become a primary concern among consumers. The ability of unknown persons to access personal online information has triggered widespread paranoia surrounding Internet security, some of it well deserved. Much of the paranoia has revolved around Internet profiling.

Internet profiling is the gathering of personal information on customers for the purpose of better targeting advertising and marketing. These profiles, stored in cookies or gathered by spyware, allow companies to remember who you are and what you did while you were on the Internet.

Cookies are small text files that contain information regarding the Web sites that you have visited. They were originally developed to assist Web surfers who were revisiting a favorite Web site by storing basic information about their past purchases and interests. Not all cookies are bad; most provide useful functions. Unfortunately, the original intent of the cookie has been subverted by some unscrupulous entities that have found ways to use this process to secretly plant their cookies and then retrieve them in such a way that allows them to build detailed profiles of a person's interests, spending habits, and lifestyle. This information is in many cases sold to third parties.

Adware was developed as a means to provide free software to consumers. Such **freeware** programs, games, or utilities often contain adware that tracks your surfing habits in order to serve ads that might be interesting to you. The companies providing the freeware receive revenue for the ads they serve. This allows them to stay in business.

Spyware works like adware but is usually a separate program that is installed unbeknownst to you when you install a freeware program, visit a Web site, or view a pop-up. Once installed, the spyware monitors your activity on the Internet and transmits that information in the background to someone else. Spyware can also gather e-mail addresses and even passwords and credit card numbers. Spyware has the ability to monitor your keystrokes, scan files on your hard drive, snoop other applications, install other spyware programs, and read cookies, while constantly relaying this information back to the spyware author who will either use it for advertising and marketing purposes or sell the information to another party. For example, if you are researching new cars, they know about it and provide you with car ads. Many say this is a good thing and would prefer ads targeted only to their needs. However, the information that adware marketers collect may be sold to less scrupulous third parties. One such company came under scrutiny because they literally replaced authorized paid advertising on Web sites with their clients' ads and did not pay the Web site owners a dime.

Perhaps the most redeeming feature of Internet profiling is that it keeps the Web free, much like broadcast television or radio. "In order to keep the Internet free, Web sites need to be profitable. And in order to be profitable, they need targeted ads that work," says Josh Isay, DoubleClick's director of public policy. DoubleClick, the Internet's largest advertising and profiling company, acquired database marketer Abacus Direct in 1999. It was no surprise that privacy rights activists responded with a class action lawsuit, and the Federal Trade Commission (FTC) launched an investigation. For the first time, the Internet profiles from DoubleClick's DART database could be matched with Abacus's marketing database of over two billion consumer retail and catalog purchases—complete with names and addresses.

For those who feel eerie about being "watched," Internet users have a number of options to protect their privacy. They can start by disabling or selectively rejecting cookies by changing their browser settings. And there are many spyware and adware programs that will detect and delete uninvited guests. A personal **firewall** will alert surfers to any outsider's attempts to access their computer as well as let them know if any program on their computer is attempting to transmit data without their knowledge. In addition, DoubleClick and many other companies provide users an **opt-out** function on their Web site that prevents their cookies from gleaning or storing any information on your system. And, of course, a good **antivirus** program should be installed and updated regularly.

There is no question that Internet profiling raises ethical issues about information security. But who should be responsible to remedy the situation? Although profiling has already been proven unpopular by consumers, DoubleClick still hopes to move forward in merging its online user profiles with the offline consumer database of Abacus when "industrywide privacy standards exist." Until then, marketers and advertisers are taking it upon themselves to establish trust with their online patrons. For example, the majority of the Fortune 500 companies have established and follow privacy policy standards.

Yet, Internet profiling is just one aspect of the never-ending dispute over Internet privacy. As new technologies are put to use, more policies and regulations will need to be addressed.

Questions

1. Do you think Internet profiling is a violation of personal privacy? Discuss the ethical issues involved.

2. If you were responsible for marketing products on the Internet, wouldn't you want available to you the kind of information provided by Internet profiling? Why or why not?

3. Is it better for companies to self-regulate issues of Internet privacy and security, or is federal intervention required?

MetaCrawler Keyword Packages:
Advertisers may select an industry-specific package of keywords such as travel, sports, business, or software.

Exclusive keywords Gross CPM	Net CPM	Impressions	Net price
$47.06	$40	200,000	$8,000

MetaCrawler front page promotions* Gross CPM	Net CPM	Impressions	Net price
$23.53	$20	200,000	$4,000
$17.65	$15	1 million	$15,000

*Exclusivity pricing is available on a case-by-case basis.

MetaCrawler search results pages (run-of-site) Gross CPM	Net CPM	Impressions	Net price
$17.65	$15	500,000	$7,500
$16.41	$13.95	1 million	$13,950

MetaCrawler targeting filters*	Gross CPM	Net CPM
One filter	$35.29	$30 CPM
Two filters	$43.52	$37 CPM

*Available on run-of-site purchases only.

Continuity discount Program duration	2–3 months	4–6 months	7–11 months	12+ months
Discount from base rate	5%	7%	10%	15%

Exhibit 13–8

An example of a rate card for WWW banner ads from the search engine MetaCrawler.

The "exclusive keywords" category provides advertisers with the opportunity to have their ad appear whenever someone conducts a search using a particular word. "Front page promotions" is for banners on the home page of the MetaCrawler site. "Search results pages" provides rates for banners that appear after a search has been conducted. And "targeting filters" provides advertisers with selectivity criteria for their ads. These rates for MetaCrawler are based on a minimum of 200,000 impressions per month, and calculated according to CPM. In this example, gross CPM reflects the cost to the advertiser, which includes the agency commission, and net CPM is the price the agency pays MetaCrawler.

categories and subcategories, such as finance, news, travel, or games. Prices vary according to category and the CPM increases as the advertiser targets a more selective audience (see Exhibit 13–8).

Another option discussed earlier is the **keyword** purchase, available on major search engines. Advertisers may buy specific keywords that bring up their ads when a user's search request contains these words. Keywords may be purchased individually or in packages that factor in the information categories and subcategories of a search engine site.

Some site publishers will charge their clients according to **click-throughs**—that is, when a user actually clicks on an ad to visit the advertiser's landing page. Although the cost for click-throughs is considerably higher than for simple impressions, this method is still unpopular with Web site publishers. When an advertiser pays only on a per-click basis, many users may be exposed to an advertiser's banner message without being charged for the value received. Some publishers have developed hybrid pricing that combines low-cost impression rates with higher-cost click-through rates.

For advertisers involved in e-commerce, some site publishers offer an **affiliate marketing program** whereby they charge a percentage of the transaction cost. For example, a site devoted to music reviews may have a banner link to an online music retailer. When consumers buy music from the retailer, the site publisher receives a percentage of the sale for attracting the customer.

The Cost of Targeting

The very selective nature of the Internet can, for additional cost, be combined with the tracking technology described earlier. This makes for a very focused campaign. Companies such as DoubleClick work behind the scenes using software that directs specific ads to a highly selective audience. Because DoubleClick technology "tags" users, it can build a consumer profile and show those ads that are likely to be of the greatest interest to specific Web users.

But contrary to popular belief, consumer targeting on the Internet is very cost intensive. While it is true that millions of people do indeed scour the Net each day, it is still difficult to find and reach the specific consumers that you want. Thus, prices for precise Internet business-to-business targeting can eclipse even those of direct mail.

Stretching Out the Dollars

One of the problems facing most Net marketers is how to reach enough prospects with their Internet advertising. The enormous numbers of users who utilize the major search engines make these sites very attractive to advertisers. Web browsers surf millions of Web pages each day, many of which are potential sites for effective ads. However, contacting all these sites and negotiating advertising contracts on each is a nearly impossible task.

For this reason, most advertisers work through **ad networks,** which act as brokers for advertisers and Web sites. Ad networks pool hundreds or even thousands of Web pages together and facilitate advertising across those pages. The advantage is that this allows advertisers to gain maximum exposure by covering even the smaller sites. The drawback is that such advertising is more difficult to monitor. Each site must be watched for traffic and content, which creates problems when trying to calculate costs. A few webmasters have been known to try to cheat the system by artificially increasing the number of page requests. So, as with any new medium, caution is always the watchword.

> **CONCEPT CHECK**
>
> Explain the different ways to track and charge advertisers for exposure to Internet advertising.

The Internet's largest potential is perhaps its ability to instantaneously create global commerce. Although currency exchanges can still be problematic, global commerce is becoming a common occurrence. A great example of how this enormous potential can be realized is eBay, the online marketplace, which has grown to be a huge presence on the Internet in more than 30 countries.

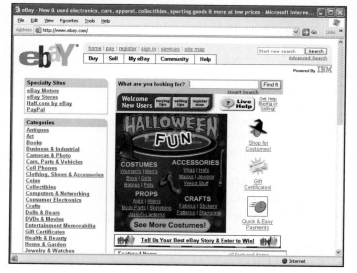

The Global Impact of the Internet

U.S. spending on Internet advertising has steadily increased in recent years. U.S. Web ad expenditures topped $10 billion in 2005 compared to $370 billion spent worldwide. Researchers predict U.S. spending could reach $26 billion by 2010.[39]

But as the Internet increasingly becomes a household word, the number of Web sites supporting local businesses overseas will also grow. Already Yahoo! has staked an early claim by servicing Japan, Germany, France, Norway, Sweden, Denmark, and Korea in their native languages. And while today most international Web surfers are proficient in English, this can be expected to change. As local online markets grow, so will the number of non-English-speaking users. American companies will need to cater to these new markets.

Other Interactive Media

In addition to the Internet, advertisers now also use other new media vehicles, such as CD-ROMs, kiosks, and interactive TV. While they are not major media forms, they do warrant some brief discussion.

CD-ROM Catalogs and Magazines

Virtually every new personal computer today comes equipped with **CD-ROM** (compact disk–read only memory) capabilities, and the CD is the fastest-growing segment of the software industry. The benefit of this technology is storage space; a tremendous volume of data, combined with full-motion video and high-quality audio, can be stored on one disk.

Marketers like the CD-ROM format because of its high quality and versatility. In fact, CompuServe, which already publishes a monthly magazine for its customers, is enhancing its online electronic mall with sound and video and mailing it as a bimonthly CD magazine. A number of its advertisers are participating. One of them, Chef's Catalog, included video clips about the creation of cookware and the proper way to carve a turkey.[40] The CD-ROM is also being linked to its online source and used to make transactions.[41]

Kiosks

An Internet **kiosk** is essentially a computer housed in a cabinet for public use. Internet kiosks are typically placed in settings such as hotel lobbies, retail stores, or airports for fast access to e-mail or Web pages. Kiosks sometimes have a bill acceptor or a credit card swipe, and nearly always have a keyboard, a mouse, and a monitor.

Kiosks are used around the globe for many purposes. The Singapore Postal Service has an award-winning, computerized vending kiosk that allows customers to pay utility bills; buy postcards, stamps, and envelopes; and get government information. The architectural firm Szabo International in Irvine, California, uses an elegant custom-built kiosk in its offices for impressive presentations of the firm's capabilities. BVR Group, the firm that developed Szabo's kiosk, won a gold medal for its creativity.[42]

Interactive TV

Imagine you're watching *Will & Grace* and a spot for State Farm Insurance appears. You remember you're not happy with your current insurance carrier. You pick up your TV remote and click the *information* button. A multimedia presentation begins. At various prompts, you click your remote to get more details. At the end you request the location of a State Farm agent. You accept an offer to have more information mailed to you. Then it's back to *Will & Grace*.[43]

As we discussed in Chapter 5, **Interactive TV (ITV)** allows viewers to interact with television content as they view it. An ITV is any television with what is called a **return path;** information flows not only from broadcaster to viewer, but also back from viewer to broadcaster. This return path can be through the cable, phone line, DSL, or the Internet. ITV is sometimes integrated with the digital video recorders (DVRs) discussed in Chapter 12, and is expected to benefit from the growth of those devices.

Interactive television promises to provide richer entertainment and more information pertaining to the shows and people involved in their creation. In

The stand-alone digital kiosk provides businesses and organizations with a new technology for communication and advertising. Kiosks today are used for a variety of purposes, ranging from the sale of train tickets to distribution of coupons to information about tourist attractions or new products.

a sense, it combines traditional TV viewing with the interactivity enjoyed by Internet users. Programming can include links to Web sites as well as electronic communication and commerce, such as home banking, home shopping, responding to surveys, participating in game shows, distance learning, or ordering a pizza. Research shows that people want additional facts pertaining to programming, alternative commentaries, and Web support. ITV can deliver all that and more.

Targeted Television

When Bermuda Tourism develops a television advertisement, they must decide if they should target middle-aged families with children or young single adults. Or do they? With new video production and distribution technology, advertisers could match the creative execution to the audience and send hundreds of different versions of ads to appropriate groups of viewers. And the ads can be updated or modified automatically, based on the weather or special promotions. Taglines at the end of the commercials could direct viewers to specific retailers near their homes. Seth Haberman's five-year-old company, Visible World, has developed the technology to make this all possible. It promises to give advertisers the "staggering reach of television but add the precise targeting ability of direct mail and the instant-updating capacity of the Internet."[44]

Cable providers such as Comcast can currently direct ads to zones of 1,000–20,000 homes in a growing number of cities. But Haberman hopes, within two years, to be able to target ads down to the level of individual households, based on criteria such as age, marital status, favorite leisure activities, and more. Of course, there are still major hurdles, such as delicate privacy issues, but technology such as this could allow television to compete with other narrowly targeted media like magazines, the Internet, and direct mail.

CONCEPT CHECK

What advertising opportunities are offered by other forms of interactive media?

Direct-Mail Advertising: The Addressable Medium

All forms of advertising sent directly to prospects through a government, private, or electronic mail delivery service are called **direct-mail advertising.** In dollars spent, direct mail is the third-ranked advertising medium today, surpassed only by newspapers and TV.

Both large and small companies use direct mail. New firms often use direct mail as their first advertising medium. The reason is clear: Of all media, direct-mail advertising offers the straightest line to the desired customer. Decades of mailboxes stuffed with catalogs, credit card offers, and music club packets have made today's advertising-weary consumers harder to reach, though. How does direct mail continue to generate a return on investment (ROI) in such a market?

Growth of Direct Mail

Direct methods of advertising and selling grew astronomically in the last decade. Robert Coen of McCann Erickson Worldwide estimates that national advertisers spent more than $48 billion on direct mail in 2003, more than 20 percent of all the ad dollars spent in the United States.[45]

Direct mail is successful for two reasons. First, it meets the needs of today's fast lifestyles. Families have less time, so shopping by mail is convenient. Second, it's the most effective medium for generating immediate results.

Marketers are expanding their profits by stuffing monthly credit card statements with tempting mail-order offers. Today's leading mail-order products include insurance and financial services, department-store merchandise, and the other products and services listed in Exhibit 13–9.

Types of Direct-Mail Advertising

Direct-mail advertising comes in a variety of formats, from handwritten postcards to **dimensional direct mail,** utilizing three-dimensional shapes and unusual materials. The message can be one sentence or dozens of pages. And within each format—from tiny coupon to thick catalog or box—the creative options are infinite. In addition to the dimensional direct-mail category are the following:

E-mail, as mentioned earlier, is one of the newest tools in direct marketing and is best used for customer retention and relationship management. It is most effective when the marketer first seeks *permission* to mail. In other words, advertisers should always give people the opportunity to opt in and to opt out of their e-mail programs. For new business acquisition, the best use is in a viral marketing campaign—otherwise it will probably be perceived as spam.

Sales letters, the most common direct-mail format, are often mailed with brochures, price lists, or reply cards and envelopes. **Postcards** are used to announce sales, offer discounts, or generate customer traffic. National postal services regulate formats and dimensions. Some advertisers use a double postcard, enabling them to send both an advertising message and a perforated reply card. To encourage response, some advertisers use **business reply mail** so the recipient can respond without paying postage. On receiving a response, the advertiser pays postage plus a handling fee of a few cents.

Folders and **brochures** are usually printed in multiple colors with photos or other illustrations on good paper stock. **Broadsides** are larger than folders and are sometimes used as window displays or wall posters in stores. They fold to a compact size to fit in a mailbag.

Self-mailers are any form of direct mail that can travel without an envelope. Usually folded and secured by a staple or seal, they have special blank spaces for the prospect's name and address.

Statement stuffers are ads enclosed in monthly customer statements from department stores, banks, oil companies, and the like. To order, customers write in their credit card number and sign the reply card.

Rank	Company	2003 sales ($ millions)	Market segment
1	Dell	$35,227.0	Computers, consumer electronics
2	International Business Machines Corp.	7,489.2	Computers
3	Corporate Express North America	4,456.7	Office and facility supplies
4	Boise Cascade Corp.	4,025.1	Office products
5	Office Depot	3,965.3	Office products
6	Staples	3,700.0	Office products
7	Fisher Scientific International	3,564.4	Scientific, medical, and lab supplies
8	Henry Schein	3,353.8	Dental, medical, and veterinary supplies
9	United Stationers	2,890.0	Wholesale office, janitorial, and computer supplies
10	CDW	2,741.0	Computers

Exhibit 13–9

Top 10 catalog companies (2003).

Direct-mail advertising can be uniquely creative and very targeted. Thomas & Betts wanted to announce its Safe-Ty product to a selective group of manufacturers. The new cable tie design is slimmer and less prone to snag. Conversant Relationship Marketing in Memphis, Tennessee, developed a box with a graphic of a guillotine on the outside. A hole was cut to emphasize the bulging head of the competitor's tie around a bundle of cables. When opened, the box revealed a Thomas & Betts tie wrapped around the cables to highlight the smoothness of their tie. Also included in the box were sample ties, along with a business reply card (BRC), for the prospect to return. Upon returning the BRC, the prospect received a bag of 100 ties, plus a cigar cutter. This promotion generated a 15 percent response rate (2,250 leads).

House organs are publications produced by associations or business organizations—for example, shareholder reports, newsletters, and dealer publications.

Catalogs are reference books that list, describe, and often picture the products sold by a manufacturer, wholesaler, jobber, or retailer. With more high-income families shopping at home, specialized catalogs are becoming very popular. Some mail-order companies prosper with specialized approaches, like outdoor clothing and equipment (L.L. Bean), electronic gadgets (Sharper Image), or gourmet foods (Sutton Place Gourmet).

Catalogs are big business. The industry was hit hard by the recent recession, but all indicators point to a recovery that began in 2003. Direct Media Catalog Tracker keeps tabs on circulation by counting how many catalogs hit its mailbox each month. In March 2005, it received 418 consumer catalogs, roughly the same number it had tallied in the same month in 2004.[46] But the percentage of catalogs offering free shipping and handling rose from 9 percent in March 2004 to 12 percent—one in every 8.5 catalogs.[47]

Using Direct Mail in the Media Mix

Direct mail is an efficient, effective, and economical medium for sales and business promotion (see the Checklist, "The Pros and Cons of Direct-Mail Advertising"). That's why it's used by a wide variety of companies, charity and service organizations, and individuals. Direct mail can increase the effectiveness of ads in other media. For example, Publishers Clearinghouse typically uses TV spots to alert viewers to the impending arrival of its direct-mail sweepstakes promotions.

Direct mail has two main drawbacks: cost and the "junk mail" image, both of which are almost inescapable. No other medium (except personal selling and consumer targeting on the Internet) has such a high cost per thousand. For this reason, many small advertisers participate in cooperative (rather than solo) mailings with companies such as ADVO, which serves most major U.S. cities. ADVO mails an envelope containing a coupon for each participating company to targeted zip codes.

Some large advertisers don't send unsolicited mail. To locate prospects, they use other direct-response media such as advertising with toll-free "800" numbers. Then they use direct mail to respond to inquiries. They save money by mailing only to qualified prospects, and by sending higher-quality materials, they build their image and improve their chances of establishing a worthwhile relationship.

CONCEPT CHECK

How do the unique elements of direct mail enhance the media mix? What are the downsides?

Buying Direct-Mail Advertising

Direct-mail advertising has three basic costs: list acquisition, creative production, and distribution.

Acquiring Direct-Mail Lists

The heart of any direct-mail program is the mailing list. Each list actually defines a market segment. Direct-mail advertisers use three types of lists: *house, mail-response,* and *compiled.*

House lists The company's database of current, recent, and long-past customers as well as identified prospects comprises the **house list** for direct-mail programs. Because customers are its most important asset, every company should focus suf-

Checklist

The Pros and Cons of Direct-Mail Advertising

The Pros

- **Selectivity.** Direct mail helps advertisers communicate directly with the people most likely to buy. Computerized mailing lists group people by occupation, region or state, income, and other characteristics.

- **Intensive coverage and extensive reach.** Everyone has a mailbox. With direct mail, an advertiser can reach 100 percent of the homes in a given area.

- **Flexibility.** Direct-mail advertising can be uniquely creative, limited only by the advertiser's ingenuity and budget and postal regulations. Advertisers can produce direct-mail pieces fast and distribute them quickly.

- **Control.** Preprinted direct-mail pieces enable an advertiser to precisely control circulation and reproduction quality.

- **Personal impact.** Advertisers can personalize direct mail to the needs, wants, and whims of specific audiences without offending other prospects or customers.

- **Exclusivity.** There are no distractions from competitive ads (in solo mailings).

- **Response.** Direct mail achieves the highest response of any advertising medium. About 15 percent of the responses arrive within the first week, so the advertiser can quickly judge a campaign's success.

- **Testability.** Direct mail is good for testing prospect reactions to products, pricing, promotions, copy approaches, sales literature, and so on.

The Cons

- **High cost per exposure.** Direct mail has the highest cost per exposure of any major medium, about 14 times as much as most magazine and newspaper advertising.

- **Delivery problems.** The mass media offer precise delivery times, but the postal service makes no delivery commitments on third-class mail. And up to 10 percent of mailings may be undeliverable because people move.

- **Lack of content support.** Direct mail must capture and hold the reader's attention without the support of editorial or entertainment content.

- **Selectivity problems.** Effective direct mail depends on correctly identifying the target audience and obtaining a good list. Some groups of prospects, such as physicians, are so saturated with direct mail they ignore it.

- **Negative attitudes.** Many consumers think of direct mail as junk mail and automatically throw it away. This may also negatively impact the product's image.

- **Environmental concerns.** Some consumers see direct mail as landfill fodder. Some direct marketers (Eddie Bauer, L.L. Bean) print parts of their catalogs on recycled paper, and now new de-inking facilities will make more catalogs recyclable.

- **Antispam laws.** The CAN-SPAM Act and similar laws impose many requirements, making it more difficult for marketers to electronically send prospective clients unsolicited marketing materials.

ficient resources on developing a rich database of customer and prospect information and profiles. There are several ways a company can build its own house list.

Consumer product companies like General Electric gather customer data by enclosing an owner registration form with their products. On the mail-in form, purchasers give their name, address, phone number, birth date, occupation, income range, home ownership status, and number of children. They also indicate their hobbies and interests (such as golf, foreign travel, photography, or bowling). Companies use this information for their own mailings and sell it to other direct-mail advertisers.

Mail-response lists The advertiser's second most important prospects are people who respond to direct-mail pieces from other companies—especially those with complementary products or services. **Mail-response lists** are the house lists of other direct-mail advertisers, and they can be rented with a wide variety of demographic breakdowns.

Compiled lists The most readily available lists are those that some entity compiles for a different reason and then rents or sells—for example, lists of car owners, new-home purchasers, business owners, and so on. **Compiled lists**

Commercial Break 13–B

Developing Effective Direct-Mail Packages

Good direct-mail campaigns help build relationships between advertisers and customers. As with an ad, the effectiveness of a direct-mail campaign relies strongly on both its message and its overall appearance.

Shaping the Message

When Air France wanted to reach valued customers, its agency, Wunderman Cato Johnson, New York, created the direct-mail pieces shown here. The strategy was to emphasize an upscale design style with the *Paris Bistro Cooking* book and *Savoir Faire* newsletter to make the recipient feel like a truly valued Air France customer.

To develop the message element in direct mail, experts suggest several techniques: stress the benefits; repeat your offer more than once; offer an incentive; offer a guarantee; don't be afraid of long copy; don't write copy that is over the reader's head; and give the customer more than one way to respond.

Integrating the Message with the Direct-Mail Pieces

Creating direct mail involves fitting the message with the key physical components of the direct-mail package. As discussed in Chapter 9, the five steps of the creative pyra-

typically offer the lowest response rate, so experts suggest using numerous sources, merging them on computer with mail-response and house lists, and then purging them of duplicate names.[48]

Direct-mail lists can be bought or rented. Purchased lists can be used without limit; rented lists may be used for a single mailing only. List owners plant decoy names in the list to be sure renters don't use it more than once.

Some list owners pay a **list broker** a commission (usually 20 percent) to handle the rental details. The advertiser, in turn, benefits from the broker's knowledge of list quality without having to pay more than the rental cost.

Lists can be tailored to reflect customer location (zip code); demographics such as age, income, and home ownership; or psychographic characteristics such as personality and lifestyle. The SRDS *Direct Mail List Rates and Data* comes in two volumes, *Consumer Lists* and *Business Lists,* and contains more than 48,000 list selections in hundreds of classifications.

Mailing list prices vary according to the accuracy and currency of the data. Rental rates average about $55 per thousand names (or about $50 for 5,000 e-mail addresses) but can be as little as $35 per thousand or as much as $400 per thousand. About half of all catalog companies rent their address lists to other direct mailers; in 2004, revenue from list rental accounted for an average of 2 percent of these companies' total revenues.[49] The more stringent the advertiser's selection criteria, the more expensive the list. An extra $10 per thousand is often well worth the savings in mailers and postage that would otherwise be wasted.

The average mailing list changes more than 40 percent a year as people relocate, change jobs, get married, or die. So mailing lists must be continually updated *(cleaned)* to be sure they're current and correct. Advertisers can also test the validity and accuracy of a given list. They rent or buy every *n*th name and send a mailer to that person. If the results are favorable, they purchase additional names, usually in lots of 1,000.

mid (attention, interest, credibility, desire, and action) may be guidelines for forming the message. Next, this information must be incorporated into all the components of the direct-mail package: the *mailing envelope,* the *sales letter,* the *color piece* or *brochure,* and the *response device.*

Paris Bistro Cooking and *Savoir Faire* attract *attention* with their large type and color. The sales letter's color logo and signature catch the recipient's eye and keep his or her *interest* on the letter and its contents.

The specifics within the letter and the matching travel survey card build *credibility* by providing data useful in the purchase decision. Details include the features and benefits of the product, the deadline and value of the offer, and instructions the recipient should follow.

The cookbook features images suggesting how the airline puts the recipient in touch with the elegance of life, whetting the recipient's *desire* to purchase the product.

In the last step, the postage-free business reply card as well as telephone and fax numbers and Web site address make it easy for the recipient to take *action* to buy the product.

Some Secrets of Direct Mail

Research has revealed countless direct-mail techniques that improve response rates: indent type and set it flush left with a ragged right edge; avoid printing in reverse type; list dollars saved in your offer rather than percentages; use the word *you* in text; provide a reason for sale pricing (almost any will do); and do not paste labels over old addresses—print new materials. And remember that direct-mail advertising is most effective when it arrives on Tuesdays, Wednesdays, and Thursdays.

Applying the Breaks

Locate a direct-mail piece that contains the four components common to most mailings and describe how the elements of the creative pyramid are integrated throughout the components. Review the copywriting in your direct-mail piece and identify how many of the techniques mentioned in this Commercial Break are used or could be improved.

Production and Handling

To create a direct-mail package, the advertiser may use in-house staff, an ad agency, or a freelance designer and writer. Some agencies specialize in direct mail.

The direct-mail piece normally goes through the same production process as any other print piece. The size and shape of the mailing package, as well as the type, illustrations, and colors, all affect printing costs. Special features such as simulated blue-ink signatures, cardboard pop-ups, and die-cutting (the cutting of paper stock into an unusual shape) add to the cost. But the larger the printing volume, or run, the lower the printing cost per unit (see Commercial Break 13–B, "Developing Effective Direct-Mail Packages").

Remaining production and handling tasks can be done by a local **letter shop** (or *mailing house*), or the advertiser can do them internally. On a cost-per-thousand basis, letter shops stuff and seal envelopes, affix labels, calculate postage, and sort, tie, and stack the mailers. Some shops also offer creative services. If the advertiser is using third-class bulk mail, the letter shop separates mailers by zip code and ties them into bundles to qualify for low bulk rates. Then the letter shop delivers the mailers to the post office.

Distribution

Distribution costs are based chiefly on the weight of the mailer and the delivery method. U.S. advertisers can use the U.S. Postal Service, air freight, or private delivery services like UPS and FedEx. The most common, the U.S. Postal Service, offers several types of delivery (for more postal information, see RL 13–1 in the Reference Library on the *Essentials of Contemporary Advertising* Web site).

Chapter Summary

Digital interactive media, which include online database services, the Internet and the World Wide Web, CD-ROM catalogs and magazines, kiosks, and interactive television, represent a revolution in the making. From an advertising standpoint, these media offer an opportunity to develop customer relationships rather than just volume. These media are still in flux, but they're growing at an exponential rate and offer an array of challenges and opportunities for advertising creativity.

The commercialization of the Internet really began with the commercial online services that offered a large subscriber base to potential advertisers. However, the Internet itself dwarfed the online services in potential since it reached so many people around the globe. Once Web browser software became available, it made the Internet user-friendly to computer novices.

Similarly, search engines made sites on the World Wide Web available to PC users with just the click of a mouse. When people began migrating to the Web, so did advertisers.

Web users tend to be upscale, college-educated men and women. This is an ideal target, especially for business-to-business advertisers. This group is rapidly broadening, which will make the Web even more attractive to many mainline advertisers. People currently access the Net through Internet service providers (ISPs). They may connect to their ISP with broadband (cable, satellite, DSL) or narrowband (dial-up) connections.

The most common types of Internet advertising are banners, buttons, sponsorships, interstitials, and classifieds. Like all media, the Internet has many advantages and disadvantages.

Most Internet advertising is priced by CPM. Some, though, is charged for by click-through or results. In some cases, site publishers take a commission on what is sold by their advertisers.

Direct mail attracts nearly 20 percent of all ad dollars. While it has historically been the most expensive major medium on a cost-per-exposure basis, it has also always been the most effective in terms of tangible results. Marketers like direct mail for its targeting ability and accountability. There are many types of direct-mail advertising, from catalogs and brochures to statement stuffers.

One of the great features of direct mail is that it can work in concert with ads in other media. However, direct mail has many drawbacks too—primarily its cost and the junk-mail image.

The two most important things that affect direct-mail success are the mailing list and the creativity used. The direct-mail piece normally goes through the same production process as any other print piece. The size and shape of the mailing package, as well as the type, illustrations, and colors, all affect printing costs.

Key Terms

ad impression, 363
ad networks, 368
adware, 366
affiliate marketing program, 367
antivirus, 366
bandwidth, 357
banner, 358
broadband, 357
broadside, 371
brochures, 371
business reply mail, 371
button, 358
cable modem, 357
catalogs, 372
CD-ROM, 369
classified ad Web site, 360
click rate, 363
click-throughs, 367
compiled lists, 373
cookies, 363, 366
customer relationship management (CRM), 360
digital interactive media, 350

digital subscriber line (DSL), 357
dimensional direct mail, 371
direct-mail advertising, 370
e-mail, 371
e-mail advertising, 360
firewall, 366
folders, 371
freeware, 366
house list, 372
house organs, 372
interactive TV (ITV), 369
Internet, 352
Internet profiling, 366
Internet service provider (ISP), 353
interstitial, 359
keyword, 359, 367
kiosk, 369
landing page, 358
letter shop, 375
list broker, 374
mail-response lists, 373
narrowband, 357

opt-out, 366
pay per click (PPC) advertising, 359
portals, 353
postcards, 371
return path, 369
rich mail, 359
rich-media advertising, 359
sales letters, 371
search engine, 354
search engine optimization, 359
self-mailer, 371
spam, 360
spider, 359
sponsorship, 359
spyware, 366
statement stuffers, 371
viral marketing, 360
Web browser, 353
Web crawler, 359
Web page, 353, 358
Web site, 358
World Wide Web (WWW), 353

Review Questions

1. What types of pages on the Internet generate the greatest amount of advertising revenue? Why?
2. What do we mean when we say a "Web site is really more than an ad; it's an ad-dress"?
3. What are the different ways of advertising online?
4. What are cookies, and what are they used for?
5. What are the different ways Web publishers charge for advertising?
6. How would you describe the advantages the Internet offers advertisers over traditional media?
7. How does audience measurement on the Web differ from that for traditional media?
8. What is the importance of the new interactive media to small advertisers?
9. How could you integrate direct mail into an integrated marketing communications program? Give an example.
10. What factors have the greatest influence on the success of a direct-mail campaign?

Exploring Advertising

1. Try out several search engines (Google, MSN, Yahoo!, etc.). Perform a number of keyword searches. How do the various search engines return the results? Can you determine which results are natural versus paid? Do you get the same results from every engine? If not, why do you suppose you do not? If you were an advertiser, on which search engine would you choose to advertise? Why?
2. Visit several Internet portals (Yahoo!, MSN, iVillage). Click through a few topics and try to find evidence of paid advertising. What forms did they take? Do you think they would be effective if you were in their target audience? Click on some advertisers' links. Did they bring you to a landing page that did a good job drawing you into their product or service?
3. Collect the direct mail that comes to your house for several days. Do any of the pieces stand out? Are some more inviting than others? Why? How do you suppose those advertisers got your name on their mailing lists?
4. Do any of the Web sites or direct-mail pieces you examined above make an effort to connect their graphics or copy to their television or print advertising? What elements cause you to remember seeing other advertising for those products or companies?
5. Despite its junk-mail image, direct mail requires a great deal of creativity. Jones Educational Services, which provides GRE and GMAT preparation, has agreed that a direct-mail campaign may be the best way to increase its market share. Create a direct-mail campaign for Jones, providing specifications for the mailing list and designs for the materials.

chapter fourteen

Out-of-Home, Trade Shows, and Supplementary Media

Objectives

To present the factors advertisers consider when evaluating various out-of-home, trade shows, and supplementary media. Many advertisers use these media to either complement or replace print and electronic media, so it's important to understand how advertisers buy these media and the advantages and disadvantages of each.

After studying this chapter, you will be able to:

* **Discuss** the pros and cons of outdoor advertising.

* **Explain** how to measure exposure to outdoor media.

* **Describe** the types of standard outdoor advertising structures.

* **Detail** the various options available in transit advertising.

* **Identify** the influences on the cost of transit and other out-of-home media.

* **Discuss** the importance of trade shows in a company's marketing mix.

* **Identify** several types of supplementary media.

It was spring in Buffalo, and love was in the air. One Monday morning, as people were driving to work, they suddenly noticed a big new billboard. In large white letters against a siren-red background, it displayed a very personal message:

Angel in Red: Saw You at Garcia's Irish Pub. Love to meet you.—William.

For the next nine weeks, commuters discovered a new message every Monday morning, each more romantic—and more desperate—than the last. "Angel in Red: Still waiting. Garcia's Pub. Friday?—William." "Angel in Red: I'm going broke with these billboards. Garcia's . . . Please!—William."

People started going to Garcia's to see if they could spot Angel, or meet William. Soon a board appeared authored by Frankie warning William that his angel was out of bounds. William responded with a board saying: "Angel in Red: Frankie be damned! I'd risk it all to meet you at Garcia's." Women started calling the local billboard company to see how they could get to meet romantic William.

The story became the talk of the town. And for nine weeks, nobody caught on, not even the employees at Garcia's.

Finally, the board everyone was waiting for appeared: "Dear William: I must be crazy. Garcia's, Friday, 8:30.—Angel."

That night the place was jammed. Garcia's had hired two models to play William and Angel. Yes, William finally found his angel, and they danced to (what else?) "Lady in Red."

The final board appeared the next week. "Angel: Thanks for Friday at Garcia's. I'm in heaven.—Love, William."

The campaign was the brainchild of Crowley Webb & Associates, the ad agency next door to Garcia's. The owner of Garcia's was nervous about a new restaurant chain's plans to open a pub on the lakefront. So he hired Crowley Webb to come up with something really "way out"—for under $20,000.

The agency demonstrated to Garcia's (and the world) that with a little imagination, outdoor advertising is an ideal medium for achieving local reach, frequency, and continuity on a very limited budget.[1]

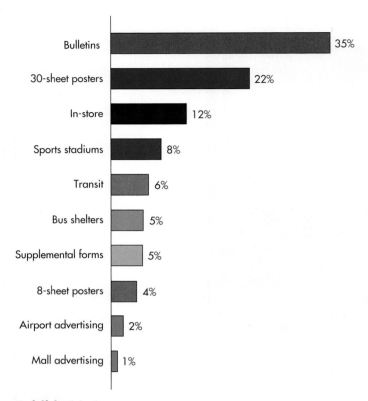

Bulletins	35%
30-sheet posters	22%
In-store	12%
Sports stadiums	8%
Transit	6%
Bus shelters	5%
Supplemental forms	5%
8-sheet posters	4%
Airport advertising	2%
Mall advertising	1%

Exhibit 14–1

Breakdown of out-of-home media.

Out-of-Home Media

Media that reach prospects outside their homes—like outdoor advertising, bus and taxicab advertising, subway posters, and terminal advertising—are part of the broad category of **out-of-home media** (see Exhibit 14–1). Today, there are more than 30 different types of out-of-home media. The most common is *on-premise signage,* which promotes goods and services or identifies a place of business, on the property where the sign is located.[2] The golden arches at McDonald's franchises are a good example. On-premise signage is important for helping us find a place of business, but it doesn't provide any kind of market coverage, and it isn't an organized medium like, for instance, the standardized outdoor advertising business.

In the past three chapters, we've looked at the traditional mass media forms as well as some of the interesting new media vehicles that have burst upon the advertising scene in recent years. Now, to round out our discussion of advertising media, we'll present in this chapter some of the other vehicles that advertisers use today.

We'll start with the last major media category: the organized out-of-home media. These include standardized outdoor and transit advertising. We'll also briefly discuss some other out-of-home vehicles that are gaining in popularity: mobile billboards, electronic signs and displays, and even the ads that are now cropping up on phone booths and parking meters. Then we'll discuss the role that trade shows play in corporate promotion plans and the keys to a successful exhibition.

Finally, we'll examine some of the media that advertisers typically consider supplementary to their other advertising activities—things like promotional products (specialty advertising), directories, and Yellow Pages—as well as some of the emerging media that are beginning to gain advertiser interest.

Outdoor Advertising

As a national and global medium, outdoor advertising has achieved great success. It was probably the first advertising medium ever used, dating back more than 5,000 years to when hieroglyphics on obelisks directed travelers. In the Middle Ages, bill posting was an accepted form of advertising in Europe. And in the nineteenth century, it evolved into a serious art form, thanks to the poster paintings of both Manet and Toulouse-Lautrec.[3]

Today, from Africa to Asia to Europe to South America, both local and global marketers use outdoor media for the same reasons as Garcia's Irish Pub: to communicate a succinct message or image to a mass audience quickly and frequently at the lowest cost per thousand of any major medium.

In 2004, U.S. advertisers spent a total of $5.8 billion in outdoor advertising, a 6 percent increase over 2003 figures.[4] This growth is expected to continue as advertisers seek alternatives to the declining audiences and ad clutter of other mass media forms. Now that TV viewers can choose from more than 100 channels, it has become increasingly difficult for national advertisers to tell their story to mass audiences. But there's still one medium that can carry their message 24 hours a day, seven days a week, without interruption. It's never turned

One of the most common forms of out-of-home advertising is the billboard. Compared to other major media, billboards offer the lowest cost per thousand. This creative example for the Museum of Flight (www.museumofflight.com) is actually a painted bulletin with a 3-D extension added—the take-off ramp for the boy and his wagon.

off, zipped, zapped, put aside, or left unopened. And it's big. That's outdoor. For that reason, some experts refer to billboards as the last mass medium.[5]

Outdoor advertising may be used for a variety of purposes. For example, nothing beats outdoor as a directional medium for motorists. It can reach a large percentage of a market, with high frequency, at a very reasonable cost. Of course, outdoor cannot communicate with the same depth as other media, but in an integrated marketing program, outdoor greatly enhances awareness of or reinforces the advertiser's core message.

Standardization of the Outdoor Advertising Business

Standardized **outdoor advertising** uses scientifically located structures to deliver an advertiser's message to markets around the world.

In the United States, there are approximately 400,000 outdoor ad structures owned and maintained by some 3,000 outdoor advertising companies, known as *plants*.[6] Plant operators find suitable locations (usually concentrated in commercial and business areas), lease or buy the property, acquire the necessary legal permits, erect the structures in conformance with local building codes, contract with advertisers for poster rentals, and post the panels or paint the bulletins. Plant operators also maintain the structures and keep the surrounding areas clean and attractive.

The plant operator may have its own art staff to supply creative services for local advertisers; ad agencies usually do the creative work for national advertisers. The biggest outdoor advertisers are traditionally in the entertainment, amusement, and hospitality categories (see Exhibit 14–2). The next largest category is local retail. Typically, the smaller the market, the larger the percentage of local advertisers.

Exhibit 14–2

Top 10 outdoor advertising categories (based on 2004 year-end outdoor expenditures).

Rank	Industry categories
1	Local services & amusements
2	Media entertainment & advertising
3	Public transportation, hotels, & resorts
4	Retail
5	Insurance & real estate
6	Financial services
7	Automotive dealers & services
8	Restaurants
9	Automotive, accessories, & equipment
10	Telecommunications

Checklist

The Pros and Cons of Outdoor Advertising

The Pros

- **Accessibility.** Outdoor carries the message 24 hours per day and cannot be fast-forwarded, put aside, zapped, or turned off.

- **Reach.** For the same dollars, outdoor reaches over 86 percent compared with spot TV (76 percent), radio (72 percent), and newspaper (72 percent) of the same target audience in the same city. The audience is mostly young, educated, affluent, and mobile—an attractive target to many national advertisers.

- **Frequency.** Most people reached with outdoor advertising see it daily.

- **Geographic flexibility.** Outdoor advertisers can place their advertising where they want it nationally, regionally, or locally in more than 9,000 markets across North America.

- **Demographic flexibility.** Messages can be concentrated in areas frequented or traversed by young people, upper-income people, or people of specific ethnic backgrounds. With computerization, it's possible to characterize outdoor audiences by age, sex, income, and lifestyle down to the block level.

- **Cost.** Outdoor offers the lowest cost per exposure of any major advertising medium. Rates vary depending on market size and concentration, but the GRP system makes cost comparisons possible from market to market.

- **Impact.** Because advertisers can build up GRPs very fast, outdoor is the ideal medium for those with a short, simple, and authoritative message.

- **Creative flexibility.** Outdoor offers a large display and the spectacular features of lights, animation, and brilliant color. New fiber optics, giant video screens, and backlit display technologies offer even more creative options.

- **Location.** Outdoor can target consumers by activity, reaching shoppers on their way to the store, business-people on their way to work, or travelers on their way to the airport, thereby influencing consumers just before they make a purchase decision.

The Cons

- **Fleeting message.** Customers pass quickly, so outdoor advertising must be intrusive to be effective. The design and copy must tell a story briefly and crisply, and the words must sell.

- **Environmental influence.** Outdoor messages are influenced by their environment. Placement in a run-down area can detract from a product's image.

- **Audience measurement.** Audience demographics are difficult to measure. Not every passerby sees or reads the ad, so some media buyers distrust audience estimates.

- **Control.** Unlike print and broadcast ads, it's difficult to physically inspect each outdoor poster panel.

- **Planning and costs.** Outdoor messages usually require six to eight weeks of lead time for printing and posting. High initial preparation cost may discourage local use. And for national advertisers, buying outdoor is complex. As many as 30 companies may sell ad space in a single market.

- **Availability of locations.** Outdoor is so popular that demand for good locations now exceeds the supply.

- **Visual pollution.** Some people object to outdoor advertising as visual pollution. They may have a negative reaction to advertisers who use it.

Types of Outdoor Advertising

To buy outdoor advertising effectively, the media planner must understand its advantages and disadvantages and the types of structures available (see the Checklist, "The Pros and Cons of Outdoor Advertising"). Standardized structures come in three basic forms: *bulletins, 30-sheet poster panels,* and *eight-sheet posters.* For extra impact, some companies may use the nonstandard *spectacular.*

Bulletins

Where traffic is heavy and visibility is good, advertisers find that largest **bulletin structures** work best, especially for long-term use. Bulletins measure 14 by 48 feet, plus any extensions, and may carry either painted or printed messages. They are created in sections in the plant's shop and then brought to the site, where they are assembled and hung on the billboard structure.

Commercial Break 14–A

How to Use Type and Color in Outdoor Advertising

Outdoor advertising is generally viewed from 100 to 500 feet away by people in motion. So it must be simple, brief, and easy to discern. Large illustrations, bold colors, simple backgrounds, clear product identification, and easy-to-read lettering are essential for consumer comprehension.

Type Weight and Spacing
The recommended maximum for outdoor copy is seven words. Very bold typefaces appear blurred and thin ones seem faded. Ornate typefaces are too complicated. Simple sans serifs are the most effective. Spacing between letters and words (kerning) should be increased to improve readability.

Color Contrast and Value
In outdoor advertising, a full range of colors can be vividly and faithfully reproduced. A huge poster or bulletin alive with brilliant reds, greens, yellows, and blues produces an effect unmatched by any other medium.

In choosing colors for outdoor, the designer should seek high contrast in both hue (the color itself, such as red, green, yellow) and value (the color's lightness or darkness) to make it more readable. Contrasting colors work well at outdoor-viewing distances; colors lacking contrast blend together and obscure the message.

The Color Wheel demonstrates the relationships between colors. Colors that are across from each other are complementary or opposites. These colors contrast with each other in the most extreme way possible. For example, green and red are opposite each other on the wheel and are therefore complementary colors. They contrast well in hues—but when their values are similar, they can create an annoying visual vibration. The same is true of a blue and orange combination.

Blue and green, and orange and red, are especially poor combinations to use because they are generally so similar in both hue and value.

Most readable	Least readable
Upper & Lower Case	ALL UPPER CASE
Regular Kerning	Tight Kerning
Bold Face	Light Face
Uniform Thicknesses	**Too Thick & Thin**

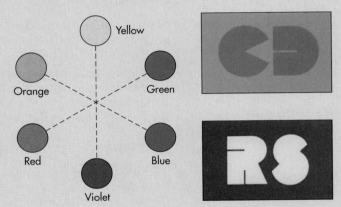

Yellow and violet (dissimilar in both hue and value) provide a strong, effective contrast for outdoor.

White goes well with any dark-value color, while black is good with colors of light value.

Applying the Breaks
Observe several examples of outdoor advertising and signs. Which ones are easy to read and which ones are not? What is it about the style or color of the text and graphics that causes this?

Painted displays are normally lighted and are repainted several times each year (color is very important for readability; see Commercial Break 14–A). Some bulletins are three-dimensional or embellished by extensions (or cutouts) that stretch beyond the frames of the structure. Variations include cutout letters, backlighting, moving messages, and electronic time and temperature units called *jump clocks.*

Painted bulletins are very costly, but some advertisers overcome this expense by rotating them to different choice locations in the market every 60 or 90 days. Over time, this gives the impression of wider coverage than the advertiser is actually paying for. As Garcia's Pub found out, the dominating effect of bulletins frequently make them well worth the extra cost—especially in small markets.

Poster Panels

A poster consists of blank panels with a standardized size and border. Its message is first printed at a lithography or screen plant on large sheets of paper or vinyl and then mounted by hand on the panel. Poster sizes are referred to in terms of *sheets*. This term originated in the days when printing presses were much smaller and it required many sheets to cover a poster panel.

The **30-sheet poster panel** *(standard billboard)* is the most widely used form of outdoor advertising. It is far less costly per unit than the bulletin. The poster sheets are mounted on a board with a total surface of 12 by 25 feet and are usually changed every 30 days. The majority of them are illuminated.

Some local advertisers get high-quality outdoor advertising at reduced cost by using **stock posters.** These ready-made, 30-sheet posters are available in any quantity and often feature the work of first-class artists and lithographers. Local florists, dairies, banks, or bakeries simply place their name in the appropriate spot.

Eight-Sheet Posters

Manufacturers of grocery products, as well as many local advertisers, use smaller poster sizes. Called **eight-sheet posters** (or *junior panels*), these offer a 5- by 11-foot printing area on a panel surface 6 feet high by 12 feet wide. They are typically concentrated in urban areas, where they can reach pedestrian as well as vehicular traffic. Space costs roughly half that of a 30-sheet poster and production costs are significantly lower. They are an excellent medium for advertising close to the point of purchase.

Spectaculars

Times Square in New York is well known for its **spectaculars**—giant electronic signs that usually incorporate movement, color, and flashy graphics to grab attention in high-traffic areas. Spectaculars are very expensive to produce and are found primarily in the world's largest cities, such as Tokyo, London, New York, Los Angeles, and, of course, Las Vegas (see the Portfolio Review, "Out-of-Home Advertising" on the *Essentials of Contemporary Advertising* Web site). A variation on the spectacular is the *wall mural,* a painted or vinyl mural that might cover an entire building.

Spectaculars are expensive, elaborate, animated signs found primarily in the heart of large cities. They incorporate movement, color, and flashy graphics to grab attention in high-traffic areas. Times Square in New York City is a gallery of large electric advertisements for major brands. The confluence of Broadway and 7th Avenue creates a wealth of acute angles and signage opportunities.

Buying Outdoor Advertising

Advertisers use outdoor advertising for a variety of purposes. For example, to introduce a new product or announce a change in package design, an advertiser might want to saturate the market rapidly. For a small portion of its total media budget, for example, Saturn was able to buy 400 billboards and dominate the outdoor medium in the important California market, contributing significantly to the success of the car's introduction. California is the state with the most import car owners, Saturn's key competitive target.[7]

The basic unit of sale for billboards, or posters, is *100 gross rating points daily,* or a **100 showing.** One rating point equals 1 percent of a particular market's population. Buying 100 gross rating points does not mean the message will appear on 100 posters; it means the message will appear as many places as needed to provide a daily exposure theoretically equal to 100 percent of the market's total population.

For less saturation, a company can purchase 75, 50, or 25 gross rating points (GRPs), equivalent to 75 percent, 50 percent, or 25 percent of the market's population. For example, if a showing provides 750,000 total impression opportunities daily in a market with a population of 1 million, it delivers 75 GRPs (75 percent of the population) daily. Over a period of 30 days, the showing would earn 2,250 GRPs (30 × 75).

Location, Location, Location

As in real estate, location is everything in outdoor advertising. Advertisers that want more saturation can increase the number of posters or purchase better locations to achieve 200 or 300 GRPs per day. The map in Exhibit 14–3 shows the billboard locations in Baton Rouge, Louisiana, that together would total 100 or more GRPs per day. To achieve a 100 showing in Baton Rouge, Lamar Outdoor Advertising would place 30-sheet posters along all major traffic arteries, facing in both directions. Rates vary considerably from market to market due to variations in property prices, labor costs, and market size. As you would expect, Exhibit 14–4 shows that locations in larger markets with high traffic volume have higher rates. However, as a rule of thumb, a standard billboard costs around $500–$600 per month. At that rate, billboards still offer the lowest cost per thousand (an average of $1.45 for a 30-sheet poster) of any major mass medium.[8]

Technology in Outdoor Advertising

In the past it was always a problem for a media buyer in New York to adequately supervise the selection of outdoor boards in Peoria, Illinois. A buyer can't just jump on a plane and travel to all the cities where the client's boards are posted to verify the value of the locations. Fortunately, though, new technology has helped solve this dilemma and has thus made outdoor an even more attractive medium to national advertisers. Today, outdoor companies can use sophisticated **global positioning systems (GPS)** to give the exact latitude and longitude of particular boards using satellite technology. Media buyers, equipped with sophisticated new software on their desktop computers, can then integrate this information with demographic market characteristics and traffic counts to determine the best locations for their boards.[9]

Some outdoor companies even provide digitized videos of their locations so the buyer can see the actual boards and the environment in which they are located. Other new

Exhibit 14–3

Typical billboard locations in Baton Rouge that would achieve at least 100 GRPs daily when posted for 30 days. The red semicircles indicate which way the boards face.

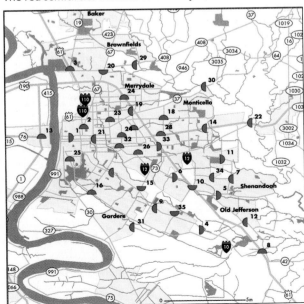

Market	Adult population	25 daily GRPs		50 daily GRPs		100 daily GRPs		Average cost per billboard
		Number	Cost	Number	Cost	Number	Cost	
Baton Rouge metro area	405,500	10	$ 7,300	20	$14,200	40	$25,400	$677
Boise	183,800	85	4,070	8	6,512	14	11,396	814
Buffalo metro area	787,800	25	19,329	49	36,004	97	65,358	706
Cincinnati metro area	1,186,000	23	15,885	47	31,753	93	60,207	649
Chicago suburbs	1,180,246	16	12,800	32	24,800	63	60,844	750
Las Vegas metro area	1,216,158	9	5,400	18	10,260	n/a	n/a	535*
Los Angeles (North County)	525,140	12	6,000	24	12,000	48	24,000	500
Omaha	575,000	8	4,960	18	10,874	34	19,102	588
Pittsburgh metro area	1,941,531	43	52,214	85	91,071	169	160,952	1,016
Savannah metro area	294,700	6	4,050	12	8,100	24	16,200	675

Note: Costs are for space only, based on a 30-day posting period; they do not include production.
*Approximation based on 75 GRPs.

Exhibit 14–4

Monthly rates for standard 30-sheet posters (approximately 12 by 25 feet) in selected metropolitan markets, October 2004.

developments include bar coding of materials so they can be tracked, posted, and authenticated, all by computer. Computerized painting on flexible vinyl is another recent breakthrough that guarantees a high-quality, high-resolution, faithful reproduction of the advertiser's message regardless of the market.[10] Some day, traditional outdoor boards may be replaced by giant video screens, capable of receiving satellite-distributed digital images, that can be changed on a whim.

One exciting new technology may change the future of how we "see" outdoor and other out-of-home ads. Hologrex, a Japanese computer software development company, has created a revolutionary program that can produce 3-D images on translucent film. When backlit, the 3-D image is visible to the naked eye, with no need for special glasses. Imagine a bulletin-size structure on the highway, advertising the latest *Jurassic Park* sequel, with a larger-than-life T-Rex coming at you in 3-D. Thrilling possibilities—especially now that they're working on animating these images.

Regulation of Outdoor Advertising

The Highway Beautification Act of 1965 controls outdoor advertising on U.S. interstate highways and other federally subsidized highways. It was enacted partly in response to consumer complaints that outdoor advertising was spoiling the environment. Over 700,000 billboards were removed by 1991, the year Congress banned the construction of new billboards on all scenic portions of interstate highways.[11] Since that time, the image of outdoor advertising has improved dramatically. Today, most people polled say they like billboards, believe they promote business, and find they provide useful travel information for drivers.[12]

Each state also regulates, administers, and enforces outdoor advertising permit programs through its department of transportation. Some states (Maine, Vermont,

Ethical Issues

Does Spillover Need Mopping Up?

While numerous laws and self-regulatory efforts have banished products like tobacco and hard liquor from the airwaves, it is virtually impossible to keep minors from being exposed to such advertising due to the spillover nature of some media. The ethical issues involved with spillover media are complex, including the kind of advertising appeals used to target audiences.

Take outdoor advertising, for example. It is the most public mass medium. It cannot be turned off like television, radio, or the Internet, and it's displayed 24 hours a day for all to see—even children.

The trend in outdoor advertising today is toward eye-catching, sexually explicit ads, seen especially in densely populated urban areas. Most outdoor advertising regulations have focused on the location of billboards, not the content. The Outdoor Advertising Association of America's (OAAA) Code of Principles says that they "support the right to reject advertising that is misleading, offensive, or otherwise incompatible with community standards." But it is unknown how often this clause is invoked. Communities, therefore, have taken it upon themselves to regulate the placement and content of outdoor advertising, rather than relying on self-regulation by the advertising industry. In 1998, for example, the Los Angeles City Council passed an ordinance that prohibited alcoholic beverage advertising on virtually all publicly visible sites, even store windows. The OAAA and other local Los Angeles trade association members filed a federal civil rights action, claiming that the ordinance violates the right to free speech.

As technology advances, so do the venues for advertising. Advertisers have found ways to work around billboard restrictions. Taxicabs and buses have carried ads for years; however, now appearing on Boston cabs are electronic billboards that have the ability to change their message minute by minute—depending on a few desired variables. The full-color ads change depending on the time of day and location of the cab. Different neighborhoods will see different ads and, if appropriate, in different languages. The taxi's location is monitored by a GPS tracking system. This new technology is inexpensive for advertisers and may become a common feature on taxicabs across America. However, this raises legal and ethical questions. Should mobile billboards be subjected to the same restrictions as stationary billboards? Neighborhoods and schools may be protected from unwanted billboard advertising, but can concerned parents protect their children from advertising that travels on taxis?

Spillover also reaches children in other media vehicles besides out-of-home. The movies, for example, consistently show people smoking. And if the smoker is a celebrity, an impressionable child might interpret that as an endorsement. In a study conducted by Dartmouth Medical School, researchers concluded that actor endorsements of tobacco brands jumped tenfold in the 1990s. The study also found that 87 percent of popular movies contain tobacco use and about one-third display identifiable brand-name logos. Minors make up a large percentage of moviegoers and through movies they may be getting more exposure to smoking endorsements than in real life. Young people who look up to sport stars and movie celebrities may be vulnerable to intentional and unintentional endorsements. Benedict Carey of the *Los Angeles Times* calls today's movies "almost as smoke-laden as the stock car racing circuit."

Many people feel that ads are not to blame for the rise of teen sexual activity and tobacco and alcohol use. Others feel that advertisers have a greater responsibility to separate youth from the adult world of unhealthy and explicit activity. Regardless of who is right, advertisers, agencies, and media companies must be sensitive to public opinion and seek creative solutions to protect impressionable children. Otherwise, the industry will risk severe restriction and regulation for having failed to responsibly and conscientiously assert firm ethical standards itself.

Questions

1. Do you believe the goal of protecting children justifies banning the advertising of legal products or their glorification in movies? Which products specifically?

2. Should ads in spillover media be censored for sexually explicit content? If so, who should the censors be and what specifically should they prohibit?

3. What alternatives might be available to fight teenage smoking, drinking, and sexual promiscuity besides banning advertising for legal adult products?

Hawaii, and Alaska) prohibit outdoor advertising altogether. Ironically, though, some of these states use outdoor advertising themselves in other states to promote tourism.

The Ethical Issue: "Does Spillover Need Mopping Up?" discusses some of the problems inherent in the very public nature of outdoor advertising and whether regulation will be needed here too.

Explain how the unique elements of outdoor advertising enhance the media mix. What are the downsides?

CONCEPT CHECK

Checklist

The Pros and Cons of Transit Advertising

The Pros

- **Long exposure.** The average transit ride is 25 minutes.
- **Repetitive value.** Many people take the same routes day after day.
- **Eagerly read messages.** Riders get bored, so readership is high and ad recall averages 55 percent.
- **Low cost.** Transit ads cost less than any other medium.
- **Creative flexibility.** Special constructions and color effects are available at relatively low cost.
- **Need satisfying.** Transit can target the needs of riders—with ads for cool drinks in summer, for example. Food ads do well as evening riders contemplate dinner.

- **Environmentally sensitive.** As social pressure to use public transportation increases, transit is well positioned as a medium of the future.

The Cons

- **Status.** Transit lacks the status of the major advertising media, like print and broadcast.
- **Crowded environment.** Rush-hour crowding limits the opportunity and ease of reading. The vehicle itself, if dirty, may tarnish the product's image.
- **Limited selectivity.** Transit reaches a nonselective audience, which may not meet the needs of some advertisers.
- **Clutter.** Cards are so numerous and look so similar they may be confusing or hard to remember.
- **Location.** With outlying shopping malls, fewer suburbanites make trips downtown.
- **Creative restrictions.** Although transit cards may carry longer messages than billboards, copy is still limited.

Transit Advertising

Back in 1910, Campbell Soup started advertising. The company spent its first $5,000 placing ads on one-third of the buses in New York City for one year. The ads were so successful that after only six months, Campbell enlarged the contract to include all surface vehicles in the city. People started buying more Campbell's soup and soon sales were up 100 percent. For the next 12 years, transit advertising was the only medium Campbell employed. Today, Campbell is still a major user of transit advertising.

Transit advertising is a category of out-of-home media that includes bus and taxicab advertising as well as posters on transit shelters, terminals, and subways. Although transit is not considered a major medium by most advertising practitioners, standardization, better research, more statistical data, and measured circulation have made transit advertising more attractive to national advertisers. National marketers of designer apparel and movies, for example, are two of the many categories of advertisers spending dramatically more in this medium, replacing the traditional transit advertising leaders such as petroleum products, financial services, and proprietary medicines.[13]

Transit advertising is especially suitable for reaching middle- to lower-income urban consumers and providing supplemental coverage of these groups. Patrick Media and Gannett Outdoor Group are using innovative marketing strategies to promote both outdoor boards and transit ads in Hispanic communities, catering to marketers' increasing desire to tap into the $700 billion Hispanic market. Today, marketers like McDonald's, Miller Beer, and Coca-Cola spend more than $65 million a year on out-of-home ads aimed at Hispanic consumers.[14]

Transit advertising is equally popular with local advertisers. Retailers can expand their reach inexpensively and often receive co-op support from national marketers, which thrive on the local exposure[15] (see the Checklist, "The Pros and Cons of Transit Advertising").

Types of Transit Advertising

Transit advertising targets the millions of people who use commercial transportation (buses, subways, elevated trains, commuter trains, trolleys, and airlines), plus pedestrians and car passengers, with a variety of formats: transit shelters; station, platform, and terminal posters; inside cards and outside posters on buses; and taxi exteriors.

Transit Shelters

In cities with mass-transit systems, advertisers can buy space on bus shelters and on the backs of bus-stop benches. **Transit shelter advertising** is a relatively new out-of-home form enjoying great success. It reaches virtually everyone who is outdoors: auto passengers, pedestrians, bus riders, motorcyclists, bicyclists, and more. It is extremely inexpensive and available in many communities that restrict billboard advertising in business or residential areas. In fact, shelter advertising is sometimes the only form of outdoor advertising permitted. It's also an excellent complement to outdoor posters and bulletins, enabling total market coverage in a comprehensive outdoor program.

Terminal Posters

In many bus, subway, and commuter train stations, space is sold for one-, two-, and three-sheet **terminal posters.** Major train and airline terminals offer such special advertising forms as floor displays, island showcases, illuminated cards, dioramas (3-D scenes), and clocks with special lighting and moving messages.

In Paris, Nike made a splash at the French Open tennis tournament even though a competitor had locked up advertising rights within the stadium. Nike covered the city by buying space on some 2,500 buses during the tournament. As the coup de grace, it bought up every bit of signage space at the Porte d'Auteuil metro (subway) station close to the stadium and turned it into a Nike gallery of terminal posters featuring famous tennis players from around the world.[16]

Inside and Outside Cards and Posters

The **inside card** is placed in a wall rack above the vehicle windows. Cost-conscious advertisers print both sides of the card so it can periodically be reversed to change the message, saving on paper and shipping charges. Inside **car-end posters** (in bulkhead positions) are usually larger than inside cards, but sizes vary.

Outside posters are printed on high-grade cardboard and often varnished for weather resistance. The most widely used outside posters are on the side, rear,

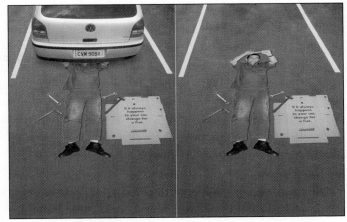

Outdoor advertising doesn't consist of billboards only. Customers entering the parking lot to fetch their cars are met with this inventive ad for Fiat, which employs photographic adhesives to create a lifelike image. The copy reads, "If it always happens to your car, change for a Fiat." Can you imagine the effect this might have on a person whose car is in fact in need of work? The ingenuity of this ad won it a Bronze Lion at Cannes.

This clever transit ad makes it appear that the passenger is receiving an injection. The headline reads, "Doesn't hurt at all." It's promoting a competitively priced health insurance plan in Hong Kong.

and front of a bus. (See RL 14–1 in the Reference Library on the *Essentials of Contemporary Advertising* Web site for common sizes and placement of inside cards and outside transit posters.)

Advertisers may also buy space on **taxicab exteriors,** generally for periods of 30 days, to display internally illuminated, two-sided posters positioned on the roofs. Some advertising also appears on the doors or rear of taxicabs. In Southern California, advertisers can rent cards mounted on the tops of cabs that travel throughout Los Angeles, Orange, and San Diego counties, serving major airports and traveling the busiest freeways in the country. Costing from $110 to $130 per month per cab, this is a very cost-effective way to reach the mobile public.

Buying Transit Advertising

The unit of purchase for transit advertising is a **showing,** also known as a *run* or *service.* A **full showing** (or *No. 100 showing*) means that one card will appear on each vehicle in the system. Space may also be purchased as a *half* (No. 50) or *quarter* (No. 25) *showing.*

Rates are usually quoted for 30-day showings, with discounts for 3-, 6-, 9-, and 12-month contracts. Advertisers supply the cards at their own expense, but the transit company can help with design and production.

The Transit Advertising Association is the national trade organization and promotion arm of the industry. It performs research and supplies advertising rates and industry data on the number of vehicles, trends, and rider demographics.

Special Inside Buys

In some cities, advertisers gain complete domination by buying the **basic bus**—all the inside space on a group of buses. For an extra charge, pads of business reply cards or coupons (called **take-ones**) can be affixed to interior ads for passengers to request more detailed information, send in application blanks, or receive some other benefit.

Special Outside Buys

Some transit companies offer **bus-o-rama signs,** jumbo full-color transparencies backlighted by fluorescent tubes and running the length of the bus. A bus has two bus-o-rama positions, one on each side. A single advertiser may also buy a **total bus**—all the exterior space, including the front, rear, sides, and top.

For years, New York subways have been running **brand trains,** which include all the subway cars in a particular corridor. However, with the July 2004 opening of its monorail system, the city of Las Vegas has taken the concept further. The glitz of the city's strip extends to its public transportation: Each of the nine monorail trains and seven stations has a corporate sponsor, and many feature elaborate immersive advertising themes. **Immersive advertising** describes the integration of advertising into the message delivery mecha-

Unique and resourceful use of transit advertising is on display in this Bronze Lion award-winning bus design from the National Geographic Channel. The clever illusion created by the opening and closing of the bus doors is a concept that was sure to get people talking.

nism so effectively that the product is being promoted while the audience is being entertained. The result is that the prospect becomes totally immersed in the message and the brand.

Las Vegas city officials banked on the monorail system, which is entirely funded by passenger fares instead of tax dollars, to generate at least $6.5 million annually in advertising revenue. However, with the help of ad agency Promethean Partners, ad revenues are now expected to be at least three times that amount. Consider the deal that the city struck with Nextel, estimated at $50 million. The company has signed on for a 12-year sponsorship of one train and the system's "crown jewel," the main station at the Las Vegas Convention Center, which more than 1 million annual visitors are expected to pass through each year.[17] Motorola, Bacardi, Coca-Cola, and General Motors are also negotiating train and station sponsorship deals.

> CONCEPT CHECK
>
> Explain how the unique elements of transit advertising enhance the media mix. What are the downsides?

Other Out-of-Home Media

As mentioned earlier, there are many forms of out-of-home media. Some are so new that they are still unproven. However, several seem to be gaining in popularity, and they demonstrate how far advertisers will go to get their messages seen by the consuming public.

Mobile Billboards

The **mobile billboard,** a cross between traditional billboards and transit advertising, was conceived as advertising on the sides of tractor-trailer trucks. Today in some large cities, specially designed flatbed trucks carry long billboards up and down busy thoroughfares. Local routes for mobile ads are also available on delivery trucks in several cities.

Electronic Signs and Display Panels

Electronic signs display text and graphic messages much like the big screens in sports stadiums. The signs transmit commercial messages to retail stores, where shoppers see them. The stores pay nothing for the signs and receive 25 percent of the advertising revenue. In Montreal, Telecite used its new visual communication network (VCN) technology to install electronic display panels on subway cars. Advertisers got a powerful, inexpensive, and flexible medium with a large, captive audience; the transit authority got a modern, self-financed emergency and public information system; and passengers got something to watch while they ride.[18] Telecite is negotiating with

Clever out-of-home buys can give public exposure and cut through advertising clutter in a spectacular way. The Firm, a workout studio in Minneapolis, came up with this creative way to get attention and people's hearts racing.

numerous U.S. and European cities to install the systems in their subway and metro cars.

Parking Meters, Public Phones, and More

Thanks to a couple of enterprising companies, American Parking Meter Advertising and American Telephone Advertising (ATA), marketers can now advertise on parking meters and public phones. ATA offers 20 market segments, such as hotels, restaurants, airports, college campuses, and convenience stores.

Where will it end? It seems that any blank space is an invitation to advertise. Ads have appeared on bathroom stalls, urinal walls, sandy beaches, city sidewalks, football fields, and construction barriers. If consumers might see it, advertisers will try it out.

Trade Shows

Every major industry sponsors annual **trade shows**—exhibitions where manufacturers, dealers, and buyers get together for demonstrations and discussions. More than 9,000 industrial, scientific, and medical shows are held in the United States each year, and many companies exhibit at more than one show. Trade shows are also very important for global marketers, because they may be the only place where an advertiser can meet the company's major international prospects at one time. Moreover, some of the world's largest trade shows are held overseas.

The construction of trade-show **booths** and **exhibits** has become a major factor in sales promotion plans. To stop traffic, a booth must be impactful and attractive and have good lighting and a large visual. It should also provide a comfortable atmosphere to promote conversation between salespeople and prospects. Many trade-show exhibitors use state-of-the-art technology, such as holograms, fiber optics, and interactive computer systems, to attract and hold the attention of visitors.

When establishing an exhibit booth program, managers must consider planning, budgeting, promotion, people, and productivity.[19]

Planning

Planning pivots on four major areas: the budget, the image of the company or brand, the frequency of the shows, and the flexibility of the booth configuration.[20] In planning the actual exhibits or trade-show booths, advertisers need to consider numerous factors: size and location of the space; desired image or impression of the exhibit; complexities of shipping, installing, and dismantling; number of products to be displayed; need for storage and distribution of literature; use of preshow advertising and promotion; and the cost of all these factors.

Budgeting

Trade shows are expensive, and costs have increased substantially in the last decade. A large company may spend $1 million or more on a booth for one trade show. With staffers' travel, living, and salary expenses and pre-show promotion added to booth costs, the cost per visitor reached rises to more than $185.[21] Despite

Trade shows are an important component in the marketing mix. They provide a unique opportunity for advertisers to meet with a large number of prospects. Over half of trade-show visitors make buying plans as a result of visiting a show.

the expense, trade shows can still be a cost-effective way to reach sales prospects, less expensive than a sales call.

Budgeting for trade shows and a booth may require an extensive review of more than 60 factors (see RL 14–3, "Trade-Show Budgeting Checklist," in the Reference Library on the *Essentials of Contemporary Advertising* Web site).

Promotion

To build traffic for a trade-show booth or exhibit, marketers send out personal invitations, conduct direct-mail campaigns, place ads in trade publications, issue news releases, and perform telemarketing. The pie chart in Exhibit 14–5 portrays how customers typically learn about the trade shows they attend.[22]

At the show itself, activities at the booth and promotional materials (handouts, brochures, giveaway specialty items, raffles) can stimulate customer interest and improve product exposure. 3M's Telcomm Products Division mailed 6,000 potential show attendees a Pony Express theme folder that invited them to pick up a trail map at the booth. The map guided the visitors (Pony Express riders) through a series of stations shared by seven product groups within the huge booth. Once the visitors' maps had been stamped at each station, they were given a "pay envelope" containing replicas of 1850 coins and vouchers redeemable for merchandise awards.[23]

31%
23%
8%
1%
17%
20%

■ Show producer direct mail
■ Association mailing
■ Not notified
■ Trade publication ad
■ Exhibitor announcement
■ Business associate

Exhibit 14–5
How do customers learn about trade shows?

People

The company representatives staffing the booth personify the kind of service the customer can expect to receive. They should be articulate, people-oriented, enthusiastic, knowledgeable about the product, and empathetic listeners.[24]

The primary goal of a trade-show booth is to meet with qualified prospects face to face. Ideally, 80 percent of the salesperson's time should be spent listening and 20 percent talking.[25]

Productivity

A company's trade-show effort may be wasted if prospects' names are not collected and organized properly. Each lead should be evaluated as to the prospect's readiness to receive another contact (A = now; B = 2 weeks; C = 6 months; D = never).[26] The resulting lead list is the link to future sales and augments the company's prospect database. Follow-up contacts are key to extracting the maximum value from trade shows.

Supplementary Media

Many promotional media are difficult to classify because they are tailored to individual needs. Such supplementary media include specialty advertising, directories and Yellow Pages, and a variety of emerging alternative media vehicles.

Specialty Advertising

The Promotional Products Association International (PPAI) defines an **advertising specialty** as a promotional product, usually imprinted with an advertiser's name, message, or logo, that is distributed free as part of a marketing

Almost every business uses advertising specialties, and almost any specialty item can be imprinted with a company's advertising message and logo.

communications program.[27] Today, nearly every business uses advertising specialties of some sort. As many as 15,000 different specialty items, ranging from coffee mugs to ballpoint pens, key chains, and T-shirts, represent an annual volume of more than $6 billion.[28]

An advertising specialty is different from a premium. **Premiums** are also promotional products; they are typically more valuable and usually bear no advertising message. However, to get a premium, recipients must buy a product, send in a coupon, witness a demonstration, or perform some other action advantageous to the advertiser. An advertising specialty, on the other hand, is always given free as a goodwill item. Some specialty items may be kept for years and serve as continuous, friendly reminders of the advertiser's business.

Consumer Specialties

Consumers associate the quality of a specialty item with the organization providing it, so companies tend to lean toward more expensive gifts. Items costing $3 to $5 have become the norm, as opposed to cheap key rings and pencils. Specialties work best when they are integrated into a broader marketing program or service strategy.

Business-to-Business Specialties

In the business-to-business arena, companies use more structured specialty promotions to improve their goodwill standing over competitors. In one case, including an ad specialty with a thank-you letter improved customer attitude by 34 percent compared to sending a thank-you letter alone. At the same time, customers' general feelings about the company and its sales reps improved 52 percent.[29]

In one test, a group of Realtors received a $1.49 ballpoint pen imprinted with a mortgage company's name, a second group received a $10 sports bag (also imprinted), and a third group got nothing. In a follow-up questionnaire, Realtors who received nothing were least inclined to recommend the product, but both the sports bag and ballpoint groups responded equally positively. Evidently, gift recipients felt obliged to reciprocate, but the value of the gift was not crucial. So the $1.49 pen offered the better return on investment.[30]

Inappropriate specialty items can backfire no matter what the cost. A recipient may perceive an overly expensive gift as a form of bribery, yet a cheap trinket could make a quality-conscious business look cheap. Finally, marketers should realize that the value and nature of gifts may raise ethical issues.

Directories and Yellow Pages

Thousands of **directories** are published each year by phone companies, trade associations, industrial groups, and others. They mainly serve as locators, buying guides, and mailing lists, but they also carry advertising aimed at specialized fields. When Yellow Pages advertising is combined with other media, reach increases significantly, as illustrated in Exhibit 14–6. In Yellow Pages ads, content is most important. The ad should tell people how to make the purchase, not why. As with most advertising media, the larger the ad, the more attention it attracts.[31] Most businesses find that advertising in the Yellow Pages is very expensive, but many of them would no longer be in business without it.

The United States has about 6,000 local telephone directories with a combined circulation of 350 million. Since deregulation of the phone industry and the 1984 breakup of AT&T, the Yellow Pages business has boomed, with ad revenues reaching over $14 billion in 2004.[32] In fact, the Yellow Pages is now the

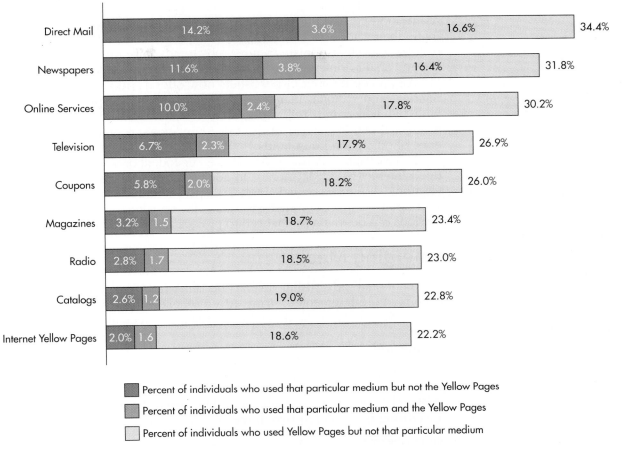

Percent of individuals who used that particular medium but not the Yellow Pages

Percent of individuals who used that particular medium and the Yellow Pages

Percent of individuals who used Yellow Pages but not that particular medium

Exhibit 14–6

Percent of consumers who used various media prior to a decision to purchase; 20.2 percent of consumers consult the Yellow Pages prior to a purchase decision, more than any other medium. Since there is little overlap with other media, the Yellow Pages can significantly extend their reach.

fourth-largest medium, ahead of radio, magazines, and outdoor. The five largest publishers (see Exhibit 14–7) account for more than 90 percent of the industry's revenues.[33] However, competition is possible because the Yellow Pages name and walking fingers logo are not trademarked. Some 250 independent publishers produce Yellow Pages directories, and market share for these companies is steadily increasing.

Stiff competition has forced phone and directory companies to differentiate their Yellow Pages with more user-friendly directories containing supplemental general-interest information, such as local maps and information on parks, events, community services, transportation, coupons, and shopping. Some phone directories offer free interactive voice services (*audiotext*) that link the telephone with a host computer to allow the easy retrieval of helpful information.

In addition, highly specialized directories aim at particular audiences, such as the Chinese-language Yellow Pages in San Francisco and the *Paginas Amarillas* in the border states.

Yellow Pages are often the sole advertising medium for local businesses, and nearly 85 percent of Yellow Pages revenue is derived from local advertisers.[34] But Yellow Pages directories can be an important medium for national advertisers, too. For example, U-Haul spends

Exhibit 14–7

Top Yellow Pages directory publishers by revenue, 2003.

Rank	Publisher	Revenues ($ billions)
1	SBC Communications	$4.478
2	Verizon Communications	4.114
3	BellSouth Corp.	1.906
4	Dex Media (formerly QWest Dex)	1.631
5	Yellow Book USA (Yell Group)	1.023

more than $20 million a year on Yellow Pages ads. The Yellow Pages Publishers Association created the BrandSell program to allow national advertisers to promote their products or services under complementary headings. BrandSell enables a toothpaste manufacturer, say, to advertise under the "Dentists" heading and a soft drink brand to advertise in the "Pizza" section.

A growing number of publishers now offer a "ride-along" program that lets regional and national marketers deliver coupons and product samples along with the white and Yellow Pages directories. The ride-along program now reaches about 75 percent of the top 300 markets, resulting in a potential audience of 60 million households.[35]

Yellow Pages publishers as well as independent organizations have also developed Internet-based directories. In addition to an effective search feature, these electronic directories provide photos, maps, and links to additional resources such as coupons or special promotions. Unlike the traditional Yellow Pages, the Internet versions can be routinely changed to provide updated information.

Emerging Media

As traditional advertising media become more expensive and audiences become more fragmented, many advertisers seek new ways to reach their customers. Several types of alternative media are potentially viable options.

Videotapes

People rent millions of videos every week. However, commercials on movie videos are controversial and have not achieved much success. In a less intrusive approach, ads are placed on the videocassette boxes. A third type of video advertising is the **video brochure,** a video infomercial which advertisers produce and mail to prospects.

Cinema Advertising

Advertising in movie theaters **(cinema advertising)** is a growing but controversial practice. Some audiences boo and hiss during commercials, but studies show that 77 percent of viewers recall theater ads the following day, compared with 20 percent for TV ads.[36] Cinema advertising grew to a $315 million industry in 2003, up 48 percent from 2002.[37] Nonetheless, some movie theater chains prohibit such advertising for fear of offending their audience. Walt Disney Studios no longer allows U.S. theaters to run commercials before any of its movies.

Product Placement

Another way to reach movie and television audiences is to pay a fee to have your product written into the movie or pro-

Product placement, where brands are woven into the content of shows, is turning up in more TV shows and movies as advertisers seek new ways to get their products noticed. Fox Television's *American Idol* judges, Randy Jackson, Paula Abdul, and Simon Cowell, were always seen with their Coca-Cola cups prominently displayed.

gram. Such **product placement** (also referred to as **brand integration**) is another good example of immersive advertising. Launched into the mainstream by the appearance of Reese's Pieces in the 1982 movie "E.T.," product placement is becoming more common—and more controversial. Notice the number of identifiable products in the next television show or movie you see.

Increasingly, product placement in the multibillion-dollar movie industry has become an important advertising medium. By getting their brands appearances, and sometimes roles, in movies, companies benefit from the association with top films and big-name actors. Nokia has had great success with this technique: Its phones were so prominent in the 1999 film *The Matrix* that 31 percent of moviegoers thought that characters in 2003's *The Matrix Reloaded* sequel were still using Nokia phones, when in fact they had switched to Samsung.[38]

Constantly fretting about viewers' newfound ability to avoid commercials by using TiVo, advertisers are also embedding their products more frequently in television programs. Ford and Coca-Cola both had high-profile presences on *American Idol*—judges drank from red cups with the Coca-Cola logo and contestants performed in Ford vehicles. This is but one example in the emerging "brand casting" trend, worth an estimated $300 million in 2003.[39]

However, controversy surrounds some product placement categories. In response to severe new laws prohibiting most forms of tobacco advertising, the Canadian Tobacco Manufacturers' Council withdrew all product placements in films, videotapes, TV programs, and computer games.

An increasing number of ATMs are equipped with video screens, which display advertising messages while the machines are processing transactions. These Wells Fargo ATMs also provide Internet connectivity, offering the potential for additional interactivity between the customer and the bank or other advertisers.

ATMs and Gas Pumps

These days it seems you can't travel one city block without running into the omnipresent automated teller machine (ATM), a fact that marketers are well aware of. With so many thousands of money devices in service, it's only natural that the captive audience of this medium be targeted for creative promotional tactics.

Fleet Financial Group has capitalized on ATM technology by printing retailer coupons on the back of ATM receipts. The coupons, which were initially redeemable at Bruegger's Bagels, Firestone, Great Cuts, Oil Doctor, and Pizza Hut, provided advertising that customers were likely to carry around in their wallets or cars.

The newest ATM innovation, developed by Electronic Data Systems Corp., puts full-motion video ads on the machine's screen as customers wait for their transaction to be processed. The 15-second ads, which debuted in 7-Eleven stores in San Diego, replace the "Transaction being processed" or "Please wait" messages that appeared on the screen. The original ads promoted Fox Searchlight Pictures' films *The Ice Storm* and *The Full Monty*. Motorists filling their fuel tanks may see similar ads displayed on the gas pumps at their local service stations.

Other Media

Technology has spawned a host of new advertising media that can confound even the most knowledgeable media planner and buyer. Advertising appears on videocassettes and computer disks. Computers dial telephones and deliver messages by simulating speech or playing a prerecorded message. Computers also put callers on hold and play prerecorded sales messages until a customer service rep answers. Business presentations are created on computer and copied to CDs that are mailed to prospective customers. As progress continues, so will the proliferation of new media and the opportunities for those seeking careers (or fortunes) in the media.

Why is it important to consider supplementary media as part of an advertiser's media mix?

CONCEPT CHECK

Chapter Summary

Media that reach prospects outside their homes are called out-of-home media. They include outdoor advertising, transit advertising, and exotic alternatives like electronic signs and parking meters. Of the major advertising media, outdoor advertising is the least expensive per message delivered. It also offers other attractive features: instant broad coverage (reach), very high frequency, great flexibility, and high impact. Drawbacks include the limitations of brief messages, long lead times, high initial production costs, and the difficulty of physically inspecting each billboard.

The standardized outdoor advertising industry consists of about 3,000 local and regional plant operators. National advertising makes up the bulk of outdoor business. The three most common forms of outdoor advertising structures are the 30-sheet poster, the eight-sheet poster, and the bulletin. A form of outdoor available in some cities is the spectacular, an expensive electronic display. The basic unit of sale for outdoor advertising is the 100 showing, or 100 GRPs, which means the message will appear on enough panels to provide a daily exposure equal to the market's total population.

Transit advertising includes transit shelters; station, platform, and terminal posters; inside cards and outside posters on buses; and taxi exteriors. This medium offers high reach, frequency, exposure, and attention values at very low cost. It gives long exposure to the advertiser's message and offers repetitive value and geographic flexibility. In addition, advertisers have a wide choice in the size of space used.

But transit advertising does not cover some segments of society. Also, it reaches a nonselective audience, it lacks prestige, and copy is still somewhat limited. Transit advertising is also sold on the basis of a showing, but here a 100 showing means that one ad will appear on each vehicle in that market's system.

Other out-of-home media include mobile billboards, electronic signs and display panels, parking meters, and public phones.

Trade shows are quite expensive undertakings, but they provide a unique opportunity to meet with a large number of prospects in one place and generate future business leads.

Supplementary media include specialty advertising, Yellow Pages directories, and emerging media like videotapes, movie theaters, product placements, and ATMs. Product placement involves integrating branded products into films, videos, computer games, and the Internet.

ATMs and gas pumps provide several means of exposure, from printed ads on receipts to full-motion video to promotions. The media options are endless and continue to increase as technology advances.

Key Terms

advertising specialty, 393
basic bus, 390
booths, 392
brand integration, 397
brand trains, 390
bulletin structures, 382
bus-o-rama sign, 390
car-end posters, 389
cinema advertising, 396
directories, 394
eight-sheet posters, 384
electronic sign, 391

exhibits, 392
full showing, 390
global positioning system (GPS), 385
immersive advertising, 390
inside card, 389
mobile billboard, 391
100 showing, 385
outdoor advertising, 381
out-of-home media, 380
outside posters, 389
premium, 394
product placement, 397

showing, 390
spectaculars, 384
stock posters, 384
take-ones, 390
taxicab exteriors, 390
terminal posters, 389
30-sheet poster panel, 384
total bus, 390
trade shows, 392
transit advertising, 388
transit shelter advertising, 389
video brochure, 396

Review Questions

1. What is the difference between out-of-home media and outdoor advertising?

2. Why is outdoor advertising sometimes referred to as the last mass medium?

3. Which advertising objectives are the outdoor media most suitable for?

4. Is outdoor an effective advertising medium for a local political candidate? Why?

5. How do gross rating points for outdoor media differ from GRPs for electronic media?

6. What are the principal categories of transit advertising?

7. What is a brand train and what advantages does it offer over less expensive forms of transit advertising?

8. Why are the Yellow Pages such an important medium for local businesses?

9. What instructions would you give to an employee who was assigned to staff your company's trade show booth?

10. How does specialty advertising differ from premiums? How could a local computer store use these media, and which would be better for the store to use?

Exploring Advertising

1. Pay attention to outdoor and transit advertising when you are out walking or driving. What formats do you see? Select three examples. Are the creative executions eye-catching? Can you comprehend the messages in a few seconds? Are the boards in good locations for what they are selling and to whom?

2. Thumb through a few pages in a Yellow Pages directory in various subject areas. Which ads do you find the most effective? Are they always the biggest ads? Why do you think some advertisers purchased such large (and expensive) ads? What characteristics make you notice an ad or might make you inclined to use that advertiser?

3. Upshaw Books, the largest independent bookstore in the area, wants to advertise on billboards along the area's main commuter route. Create a series of three standard billboards that would grab commuters' attention and motivate them to visit the store.

4. There appears to be no limit to the places that advertising can appear. What are some additional nontraditional advertising media that you have seen (or expect to see some day) that were not touched on in this text?

chapter fifteen

Media Planning and Buying

Objectives

To show how communications media help advertisers achieve marketing and advertising objectives. To get their messages to the right people in the right place at the right time, media planners follow the same procedures as marketing and advertising planners: setting objectives, formulating strategies, and devising tactics. To make sound decisions, media planners must possess marketing savvy, analytical skill, and creativity.

After studying this chapter, you will be able to:

* **Describe** how a media plan helps accomplish a company's marketing and advertising objectives.

* **Explain** the importance of creativity in media planning.

* **Define** reach and frequency and debate the issues surrounding the concept of effective frequency.

* **Discuss** how reach, frequency, and continuity are related.

* **Calculate** gross rating points and cost per thousand.

* **Identify** the factors that influence media strategy and tactics.

* **Describe** different types of advertising schedules and the purpose for each.

* **Explain** the role of the media buyer.

SONY

When Sony introduced its new Street Style Headphones, its first notion was to market them primarily on college campuses. That may not have been a bad idea since the headphones, which wrap around the back of the head, were the ultimate cool, gotta-have-it accessory. But the following year, Sony appointed a new media agency, and the mavens there had a more radical scheme. They saw an opportunity to go after the much broader 12- to 24-year-old Generation Y segment with a street-level guerrilla marketing campaign. Best of all, they thought they could do it on Sony's modest $600,000 budget.[1]

The Media Edge, as the agency is known, recommended targeting urban youth first because African-American and Hispanic inner-city kids tend to be trendsetters—they're the key youth influencers. And once they adopt and popularize a new product, the trend spreads to the suburbs.

"We do a lot of research on the teen market," says Kim Canfield, VP/planning director at The Media Edge, "and the constants we came up with were basketball and music. If you look at all the admired athletes, they're all from basketball.

"Plus," she says, "it's participatory. If you want to find urban youth in the summer in Manhattan, they're on the courts in Harlem or on West 4th Street. And rap and hip-hop is the music they like."

The Media Edge (TME) spent half its budget in the first summer of the campaign on a van program that took the campaign to inner-city streets.

The brightly graphic vans visited hot spots in five top markets—New York, Los Angeles, Chicago, Atlanta, and Detroit—all of which scored high for urban youth, basketball, and music. During daytime hours they went to basketball courts; at night they appeared outside popular dance clubs. The idea wasn't to sell headphones from the vans, but to offer listening stations where kids could check them out as well as other Sony gear such as MiniDiscs. They also passed out free premiums such as Street Style keychains. The whole purpose was simply to get the product and the creative advertising to work face-to-face with the target market. Sony reps working the vans gave out coupons that, when mailed in with proof of purchase of the headphones, were good for a free CD featuring up-and-coming rap acts such as Nas, Mobb Deep, and Big Pun. Over the course of the campaign, the company moved more than 35,000 CDs.

During the fall back-to-school period, the campaign went national. The Media Edge broadened the target to include high school and college students and used rather unconventional media vehicles to reach them. Through Cover Concepts, they distributed more than a half million Street Style book covers. M@x Racks placed free Street Style postcards in bars and restaurants on 100 college campuses. And Beyond the Wall, a catalog company that sells posters of advertising images to college students, moved about 1,500 Street Style posters—its third biggest seller after Volkswagen and James Bond.

The final phase of the campaign was a holiday shopping effort in which they distributed postcards and plastic shopping bags with the Street Style logo to more than 350 independent music retailers in 65 markets across the country.

"The key to the campaign," Canfield says, "was being able to reach these kids wherever they are. In the summer, we caught them outside playing ball or at the clubs; in the fall we got them at school with the book covers; and during the holidays it was when they were shopping for music as gifts. It was an organic, word-of-mouth message that went from trendsetters to the rest."

The client was pleased. During the van program, Street Style's share of the highly fragmented headphone market jumped 50 percent. During the holiday season, market share tripled. "It was a different way of approaching these kids and impacting them with this product, but it really resonated with them at the grass-roots level," says Bob Gruder, Sony's senior manager, Marketing Communications.

It's this kind of innovative, out-of-the-box thinking, though, that has contributed to the incredible growth and success of The Media Edge.

Media Planning: Integrating Science with Creativity in Advertising

In today's over-communicated society, advertising media planners need to be as analytically competent as top financial officers and as creative as senior art directors and copywriters. Since most money in advertising is spent on media, solid media decisions are critical to the success of the overall marketing communications plan.

The purpose of **media planning** is to conceive, analyze, and creatively select channels of communication that will direct advertising messages to the right people in the right place at the right time. The Media Edge believes that

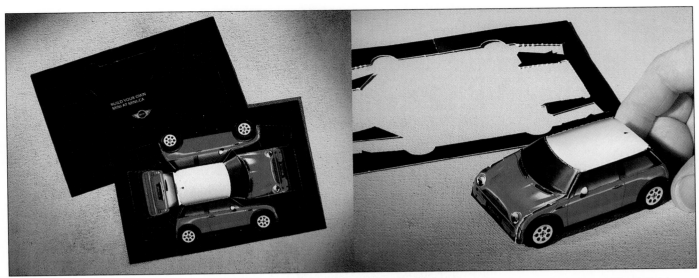

The launch of the MINI Cooper was a global phenomenon that strategically integrated every medium and marketing vehicle available—from TV to print and co-op ads, to massive in-store promotions, public relations, and publicity stunts. This ad shows the little MINI cutouts that the company used to get people excited about the reintroduction of the original European automobile. MINI successfully demonstrated how a well-planned media campaign can generate enormous positive publicity.

"anything you put your message on is media." As we saw, that might even include shopping bags, book covers, and parking meters. As a result, media planning today involves many decisions. For example,

- Where should we advertise? (In what countries, states, or parts of town?)
- Which media vehicles should we use?
- When during the year should we concentrate our advertising?
- How often should we run the advertising?
- What opportunities are there to integrate our media advertising with other communication tools?

Some of these decisions require hard scientific research and detailed mathematical analysis, aided by sophisticated computer software programs. But understanding and interpreting what all the numbers really mean, and then conceiving and implementing a truly masterful media plan like the launch of Sony's Street Style Headphones, demand human intelligence and creativity.[2]

The Challenge

Historically, the people who plan and buy media have enjoyed relative anonymity compared to the "stars" in the creative and account service departments. As evidence of this, witness the fact that entry-level media positions are still among the lowest-paid jobs in the business. This may be due to two facts. First, lower-ranking media jobs are still fairly routine and uncreative, so they don't require employees with high levels of training and competence. They are a good entry point for young people in the business, however, and those with superior skill or ability can move up quickly. Second, in many agencies and companies, conventional media planning is still relatively archaic, based on a bygone era when just a few spots on prime-time network television would easily reach the majority of an advertiser's target audience. These dinosaur media-planning organizations have been able to grind along with their obsolete systems for some time, but this situation is now changing rapidly due to the pressures of competition.

The fact is that today the media planner's assignment is just as critical as the creative director's: One media planner can be responsible for millions of client dollars. The planner's work attests to an agency's strategic ability to negotiate the best prices and use effectively the incredible array of media choices available today. Jack Klues, the senior VP/director of U.S. media services for Leo Burnett USA, says, "Our mission is to buy and plan media so effectively that our clients obtain an unfair advantage versus their competitors."[3]

In the 1990s, the media department suddenly gained new prominence. Clients started taking an a la carte approach to agency services, and agencies began competing for media planning and buying assignments separately from the creative business.[4] By the early 2000s, media wins had become big news: Universal McCann won the $150 million Nestlé account; Gillette awarded its $600 million media account to Mindshare; and Kraft consolidated its $800 million media business at Starcom MediaVest Group.[5]

As the complexity of the field increases, media decisions become more critical and clients more demanding. Advertisers want agencies to be more than efficient. They want accountability and information, particularly about media options. And they want creative buys.

What makes media planning today so much more complicated and challenging than it was just a few years ago?

Increasing Media Options

With the advent of modern electronic technology and the natural maturation of the marketplace, there are many more media to choose from today, and each offers more choices. As we mentioned earlier, it wasn't long ago that major advertisers could ensure a big audience by simply advertising on TV. Not anymore. Today it's much more difficult to reach a big audience. As Stacey Lippman, director of corporate media at TBWA Chiat/Day, says, "There's too much to keep track of and too many things to explore."[6]

TV is now fragmented into network, syndicated, spot, and local television, as well as network and local cable. Specialized magazines now aim at every possible population and business segment. Even national magazines publish editions for particular regions or demographic groups. Finally, the incredible growth of the Internet over the last 10 years has brought with it a host of new media options. But it has also added to the complexity of media work as planners face the challenge of staying current with the constantly expanding technology and mastering a whole new lexicon of associated terminology. Exhibit 15–1 shows the breakdown of total (local and national) advertising expenditures by traditional media in the United States.

As we saw in the previous chapter, nontraditional media—from videotape and cinema advertising to product placement and even restrooms—also expand the menu of choices. In addition, many companies spend a considerable portion of their marketing budgets on specialized communications like direct marketing, sales promotion, public relations activities, and personal selling, topics we'll discuss in the next two chapters. In fact, these "below-the-line" (noncommissionable) activities are the fastest-growing segments at some of the large agency holding companies, like WPP and Interpublic.[7]

Duncan and Moriarty point out that for companies practicing integrated marketing communications, their "media menu" needs to include everything that carries a message to

Exhibit 15–1

U.S. ad spending by medium.

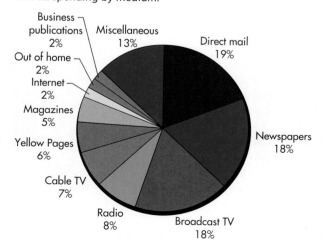

Business publications 2%
Miscellaneous 13%
Out of home 2%
Internet 2%
Magazines 5%
Yellow Pages 6%
Cable TV 7%
Radio 8%
Broadcast TV 18%
Direct mail 19%
Newspapers 18%

and/or from customers and other stakeholders. The proliferation of toll-free phone numbers, e-mail, and Internet Web sites makes it easy and cost-effective to facilitate customer feedback. The result is that advertisers can be very creative in designing systems for both sending and receiving messages. That means that companies and agencies need to think in terms of message handling, being as responsible for receiving messages as for sending them. Mark Goldstein, the president of integrated marketing at Fallon McElligott in Minneapolis, says, "Media is no longer planned and bought; instead it's created, aggregated, and partnered." Perhaps, as Duncan and Moriarty say, the media department of the future will be called the *connect department*.[8]

Increasing Fragmentation of the Audience

Further evidence of the maturing marketplace is the fragmentation of the media audience. This also complicates the media planner's job. Readers and viewers have scattered to all the new media options, selectively reading only parts of magazines or newspapers, watching only segments of programs, and listening to many different radio stations. This makes it very difficult to find the prospect in the marketplace. Consumers are spending more time with media than ever before—an average of over 3,570 hours per year—but an increasing proportion of that time is spent with less traditional media vehicles.[9] (See Exhibit 15–2.)

Increasing Costs

At the same time that there are more media choices, the number of messages that need to be communicated has also grown—so much so, in fact, that they have outstripped the ability of consumers to process them. People can cope with only so many messages, so the media have to restrict the number of ads they sell. As a result, the cost of reaching target audiences is increasing for almost all media. In the last decade, the cost of exposing 1,000 people to each of the major media (cost per thousand) rose faster than inflation. Shows that can deliver a big audience are sold at a premium. To run a 30-second spot on *American Idol,* for instance, now costs over $700,000.[10] Rising costs make media planning more challenging than ever, especially for advertisers with small budgets. Clients want proof that planners are squeezing the most they can out of every media dollar.

Increasing Complexity in Media Buying and Selling

As the process of buying media has become more complex, so has the process of selling media. In the battle for additional sales, many print and broadcast

Exhibit 15–2

Time spent with media.

Category	Hours per person per year						1998–2003 percent change	2003–2008 percent change
	1998	Percent share	2003	Percent share	Forecast 2008	Percent share		
Media with significant advertiser support*	2,112	63.6%	2,064	56.4%	2,194	54.1%	−2.2%	+6.3%
Media supported predominantly by consumers†	1,210	36.4	1,598	43.6	1,865	45.9	+32.1	+16.7

*Broadcast television, broadcast and satellite radio, daily newspapers, and consumer magazines.
†Cable and satellite television, box office, recorded music, consumer books, interactive television, home video, consumer Internet, and video games.

The sports fan's perennial heckle "Come on, ref, do you need glasses?" has finally been answered. Specsavers, a Scottish optical care provider and retailer, has begun to sponsor soccer referees. In addition to providing eye exams and optical eyewear for referees, the company outfits them and advertises in stadiums. The media mix for the campaign, which won a Cannes Media Lion for Mediaedge:cia's London office, combined the clever sponsorship with point-of-sale advertising and newspaper-friendly press releases. As the 22 percent increase in sales shows, Specsavers has positioned itself squarely in Scottish men's field of vision.

media companies developed "value-added" programs to provide extra benefits. Besides selling space or time, these companies now offer reprints, merchandising services, special sections, event sponsorships, and mailing lists. To get a bigger share of the advertiser's budget, larger media companies are bundling the various stations, publications, or properties they own and offering them in integrated combinations as further incentives.

The Discovery Networks, for example, which include the Travel Channel, TLC, Animal Planet, and Discovery, offers its advertisers "multiplatform convergence content sponsorships." What this unwieldy name means is that each advertiser gets a major Internet/TV sponsorship with four or five commercials in a special-event Discovery show and Webcast. Specially created TV spots promote the program and the Webcast, as well as Discovery's Web site and even the advertiser's Web site. Moreover, advertisers get additional off-air exposure in hundreds of Discovery Network retail stores nationwide, which also run in-store videos promoting the shows and the sponsors.[11]

Value-added packages often employ communications vehicles outside traditional media planning, such as public relations activities, sales promotions, and direct marketing. With BMW, for instance, *Yachting* magazine sponsors sailing weeks in various markets and displays the advertiser's cars on site. So people who can afford expensive sailboats are also exposed to the cars, to BMW signage at the event, and to any premium giveaways the sponsors might offer.[12] Integrated events like these help advertisers build relationships with their customers and prospects, and that's a major goal today. But placing a value on these deals is difficult because the nonmedia elements are hard to quantify.

The trend toward integrated marketing communications and relationship marketing is creating a new breed of media planner: younger, computer literate, and schooled in marketing disciplines beyond traditional media. The good media specialist today is actually a real advertising generalist. And with many of the biggest client changes happening in media-only agency reviews, it's apparent that the media professionals have finally come into their own.

Increasing Competition

The final element making media planning more challenging today is the competitive environment, which in just a few years has completely changed the structure of the advertising business. In the 1980s and early 1990s, as clients sought greater efficiency with their media dollars, independent media buying services came into the fore, attracting some of the best and brightest talent in the business to compete with agencies for what was once their private domain. Initially, the independents bought advertising space and time at lower bulk rates and then sold it at a higher rate or for a handling commission to advertisers or ad agencies that didn't have a fully staffed media department. As the media specialists grew, though, clients came to realize the virtues of scale, and financial clout emerged as a potent weapon in negotiating media buys.[13] By 2004, the independents handled 16.4 percent of all national media (advertising and marketing) accounts.[14]

To respond to the competitive pressure, ad agencies started unbundling their own media departments, setting them up as separate media specialist subsidiaries like The Media Edge. These companies could compete with the independents as well as with other agencies for media-only accounts. Over time, all these firms became quite expert at the media function. With the rapid increase in billings, they were able to pour a substantial amount of money into the development of new research tools, which was critical given the continued fragmentation of the mass media into smaller and smaller niches.

Closed-Circuit Programming

Dan is a middle-aged man recovering at his local hospital from a recent stroke. Bedridden and immobile, he spends a lot of time watching television. In a boredom-induced daze, he half-wittedly flips through the channels and stumbles across a show featuring a man in a blue plaid shirt sitting in a doctor's office. A voice chimes in: "Daniel Sorby had no idea that he had high cholesterol—until he suffered from a stroke." Immediately Dan's attention perks up.

For the next half-hour, a discussion ensues on the difference between "good" and "bad" cholesterol, revealing their potential role in heart attacks and strokes. The program ends. Then comes a short commercial break.

The spot is for Plavix—"a prescription pill that can help protect you from a heart attack or stroke if you've recently had one," says a friendly grandmother, as the camera rolls to pictures of her playing with her grandkids.

This is the scene played out every day in roughly 1,000 hospitals nationwide due to the introduction of the Patient Channel—a 24-hour network piped directly into patient and waiting rooms at no cost to the hospital or patient.

Founded in September of 2002 by General Electric Co., the Patient Channel is one of a growing number of closed-circuit programming channels providing news and educational programs to hospitals, schools, and fitness centers across the country. Yet it is not the programs that are making the national headlines. Rather, it is the advertising that pays for the service, such as the Plavix spot, which has stirred much recent debate.

Proponents for the network are principally the pharmaceutical companies that now suddenly have direct advertising access to over 22 million patients. Never before have the drug manufacturers been able to "directly associate their products with a particular condition within a hospital setting." By achieving such a full measure of direct-to-consumer advertising, the pharmaceuticals will likely generate enormous revenues on their new drugs.

Opponents of the network are led by a consumer advocacy group called Commercial Alert, which feels the Patient Channel's ads "pitch drugs at a time when [patients] are most worried about disease, in a way that carries the implicit authority and endorsement of the hospital and its doctors." Furthermore, the group feels the channel unfairly exploits a "captive audience at a time of maximum vulnerability and emotional distress."

Refuting such claims, proponents point to the educational content the network provides. Federal requirements state that hospitals must provide a certain amount of patient education. General Electric, the pharmaceutical advertisers, and some within the medical profession have argued that the channel helps hospitals address this patient education requirement while freeing up already overworked nurses.

Hospitals are not the only venues subject to closed-circuit TV programming. For over 12 years, Channel One has broadcast news and current events to American middle, junior, and high school classrooms. Each day, 8 million students view a 12-minute newscast featuring interesting stories on breaking news events and teen topics, supported, of course, by advertising.

In the process, Channel One keeps teens aware of and involved in a multitude of issues by presenting them in a manner that can easily be absorbed and understood. Channel One further enhances classroom learning by providing a Web site for teens to visit to learn more about the news, find out about the latest teen crazes, offer opinions, play games, take quizzes, and learn about the dangers of alcohol and drug abuse. Plus, for the 400,000 teachers that use Channel One in the classroom, ChannelOneTeacher.com provides ideas and lesson plans—everything they need to teach the news.

However, once again the advertisements have captured the controversial spotlight. As with the Patient Channel, the cost of providing the much-needed free TVs and VCRs to classrooms is offset by the ads that accompany the news segment—typically for junk-food products. Some students and parents have raised their voices in an effort to remove the programs, stating that teens should not be the victims of deceptive advertising campaigns. One parent said he is opposed to Channel One because it creates a slippery slope that could open schools up to even more commercial interests. He said that he would hate to "live in a district where the kids run on the Pepsi track or work out in the Nike gym." The overall concern is that children of this age are highly impressionable, and that makes the junk-food advertisements seen on Channel One unethically exploitative.

In this debate, both the pros and cons seem to have good arguments, making it difficult to craft a policy that would resolve the issue entirely. The future of this medium will depend on how advertisers attempt to use it and how consumers in turn react, as closed circuit programming becomes more prevalent in the years to come.

Questions

1. Is the value of the educational programming provided to hospitals and schools worth the price of the commercial messages that accompany it?

2. Do you feel it's unethical for advertisers to pitch products to patients and students in this fashion?

At this point, the big multinational advertisers realized that they could receive greater impact from their ad dollars by consolidating their media budgets within a single large shop. Procter & Gamble, for instance, pooled $1.2 billion at TeleVest. As the big media shops started winning the big accounts, the large agency holding companies went on an acquisition binge, buying up the largest of the independent media agencies and sometimes merging them with their own subsidiaries and then, as in the case of TME, relaunching them as global media firms. By 2000 the process had gone full circle. For the most part, the agencies were again back in control of the media budgets—albeit at arm's length.[15] And while the structure was different, so was the compensation. They were no longer getting 15 percent of the media budget. In fact, 2 to 3 percent was the norm. But the volume was so high that the business could still be quite profitable.[16]

CONCEPT CHECK

Explain why media planning is so much more critical, complicated, and challenging today than it was just a few years ago.

The Role of Media in the Marketing Framework

As we've discussed in previous chapters, the key to successful advertising is proper planning. Thus, before media planning begins—indeed, before advertising is even considered—companies must first establish their overall marketing and advertising plans for their products.

As we saw in Chapter 7, the top-down marketing plan defines the market need and the company's sales objectives and details strategies for attaining those objectives. Exhibit 15–3 shows how objectives and strategies of a marketing plan result from the marketing situation (or SWOT) analysis, which defines the company's strengths and weaknesses and uncovers any marketplace opportunities and threats. The objectives and strategies of an advertising plan unfold from the marketing plan. But advertising objectives focus on communication goals.

Media objectives and strategies flow from the advertising plan. They determine how the communications goals will be accomplished through the selection of media. The media department's job is to make sure the advertising message (developed by the creative department) gets to the correct target audience (established by the marketing managers and account executives) in an effective manner (as measured by the research department).

The Media Planning Framework

Development of a media plan involves the same process as marketing and advertising planning. First, review the marketing and advertising objectives and strategies and set relevant, measurable objectives that are both realistic and achievable by the media. Next, try to devise an ingenious strategy for achieving these objectives. Finally, develop the specific tactical details of media selection and scheduling.

Defining Media Objectives

Media objectives translate the advertising strategy into goals that media can accomplish. Exhibit 15–4 shows general media objectives for a hypothetical new food product. They explain who the target audience is and why, where messages will be delivered and when, and how much advertising weight needs to be delivered over what period of time.

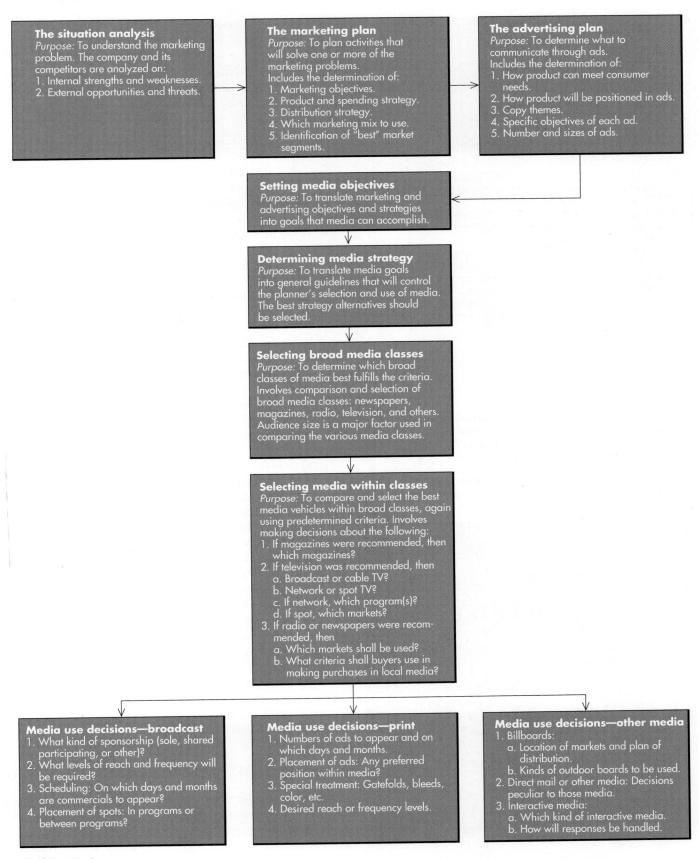

The situation analysis
Purpose: To understand the marketing problem. The company and its competitors are analyzed on:
1. Internal strengths and weaknesses.
2. External opportunities and threats.

The marketing plan
Purpose: To plan activities that will solve one or more of the marketing problems.
Includes the determination of:
1. Marketing objectives.
2. Product and spending strategy.
3. Distribution strategy.
4. Which marketing mix to use.
5. Identification of "best" market segments.

The advertising plan
Purpose: To determine what to communicate through ads.
Includes the determination of:
1. How product can meet consumer needs.
2. How product will be positioned in ads.
3. Copy themes.
4. Specific objectives of each ad.
5. Number and sizes of ads.

Setting media objectives
Purpose: To translate marketing and advertising objectives and strategies into goals that media can accomplish.

Determining media strategy
Purpose: To translate media goals into general guidelines that will control the planner's selection and use of media. The best strategy alternatives should be selected.

Selecting broad media classes
Purpose: To determine which broad classes of media best fulfills the criteria. Involves comparison and selection of broad media classes: newspapers, magazines, radio, television, and others. Audience size is a major factor used in comparing the various media classes.

Selecting media within classes
Purpose: To compare and select the best media vehicles within broad classes, again using predetermined criteria. Involves making decisions about the following:
1. If magazines were recommended, then which magazines?
2. If television was recommended, then
   a. Broadcast or cable TV?
   b. Network or spot TV?
   c. If network, which program(s)?
   d. If spot, which markets?
3. If radio or newspapers were recommended, then
   a. Which markets shall be used?
   b. What criteria shall buyers use in making purchases in local media?

Media use decisions—broadcast
1. What kind of sponsorship (sole, shared participating, or other)?
2. What levels of reach and frequency will be required?
3. Scheduling: On which days and months are commercials to appear?
4. Placement of spots: In programs or between programs?

Media use decisions—print
1. Numbers of ads to appear and on which days and months.
2. Placement of ads: Any preferred position within media?
3. Special treatment: Gatefolds, bleeds, color, etc.
4. Desired reach or frequency levels.

Media use decisions—other media
1. Billboards:
   a. Location of markets and plan of distribution.
   b. Kinds of outdoor boards to be used.
2. Direct mail or other media: Decisions peculiar to those media.
3. Interactive media:
   a. Which kind of interactive media.
   b. How will responses be handled.

Exhibit 15–3

This diagram shows how media objectives, strategies, and plans result from the marketing and advertising plans.

ACME Advertising

Client: Econo Foods

Product/Brand: Chirpee's Cheap Chips

Project: Media plan, first year introduction

Media Objectives

1. To target large families with emphasis on the family's food purchaser.

2. To concentrate the greatest weight of advertising in urban areas where prepared foods traditionally have greater sales and where new ideas normally gain quicker acceptance.

3. To provide extra weight during the introductory period and then continuity throughout the year with a fairly consistent level of advertising impressions.

4. To deliver advertising impressions to every region in relation to regional food store sales.

5. To use media that will reinforce the copy strategy's emphasis on convenience, ease of preparation, taste, and economy.

6. To attain the highest advertising frequency possible once the need for broad coverage and the demands of the copy platform have been met.

Exhibit 15–4

How media objectives are expressed.

Market research helps advertisers determine specific characteristics of media audiences. The audience for the *Economist* (www.economist.com) magazine is highly educated and would be described as upper income. In this clever ad, which won a Bronze Lion at Cannes, the *Economist* promotes the intelligence of its readership by folding issues of the magazine and arranging them to look like a human brain.

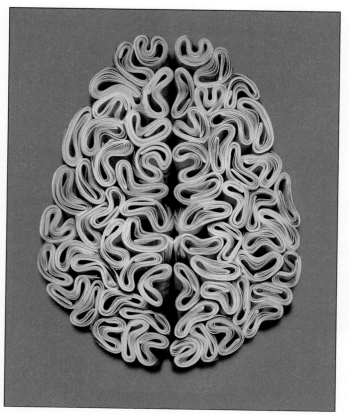

Media objectives have two major components: audience objectives and message-distribution objectives.

Audience Objectives

Audience objectives define the specific types of people the advertiser wants to reach. Media planners typically use geodemographic classifications to define their target audiences. In Exhibit 15–4, for example, the target audience is food purchasers for large families who live in urban areas across the country. The target audience may consist of people in a specific income, educational, occupational, or social group—any of the segments we discussed in Chapter 4.

Media planners rely heavily on secondary research sources, such as Arbitron and Nielsen Media Research, which provide basic demographic characteristics of media audiences. Other sources, such as Simmons Market Research Bureau (SMRB) and Mediamark Research, Inc. (MRI), describe media audiences based on purchase tendencies. These syndicated reports give demographic profiles of heavy and light users of various products and help planners define the target audience. The reports also specify which TV programs or magazines heavy and light users watch and read, which helps planners select media with large audiences of heavy users. Planners can then select **media vehicles**—particular magazines or shows—according to how well they "deliver" or expose the message to the media audience that most closely resembles the desired target consumer.

Unfortunately, due to cost restraints, most media research does not provide the specificity that marketers would really like. Most radio, TV, newspaper, and outdoor audience reports, for example, are limited to age and gender. So media planners often have to rely on their judgment and experience to select the right media vehicles.[17] This is especially problematic with new media such as the Internet where the media planner's experience may be too limited to enable a good estimate of how many clicks to expect from advertising on a given site.

Message-Distribution Objectives

Distribution objectives define where, when, and how often advertising should appear. To answer these questions, a media planner must understand a number of terms, including *message weight, reach, frequency,* and *continuity.*

Audience Size and Message Weight

Marketers are naturally interested in having their messages exposed to as many customers and prospects as they can afford. So they are also logically most interested in those media opportunities that offer the largest audiences.[18] The basic way to express audience size is simply to count the number of people in a medium's audience. This is what media research firms like Nielsen and Arbitron do for the broadcast media, typically using a statistical sample to project the total audience size. For print media, firms like the Audit Bureau of Circulations actually count and verify the number of subscribers (the **circulation**) and then multiply by the estimated number of **readers per copy (RPC)** to determine the total audience. RPC factors in the **pass-along rate**, the number of people who read a magazine without actually buying it.

Media planners often define media objectives by the schedule's **message weight**, the total size of the audience for a set of ads or an entire campaign, because it gives some indication of the scope of the campaign in a given market. There are two ways to express message weight: *gross impressions* and *gross rating points*.

If planners know the audience size, they can easily calculate the number of advertising impressions in a media schedule. An **advertising impression** is a possible exposure of the advertising message to one audience member. It is sometimes referred to as an **opportunity to see (OTS).** By multiplying a medium's total audience size by the number of times an advertising message is used during the period, planners arrive at the **gross impressions,** or potential exposures, possible in that medium. Then, by summing the gross impressions for each medium used, they know the total gross impressions for the schedule (see Exhibit 15–5).

With large media schedules, though, gross impressions can run into the millions and become very awkward to handle, so that's where the concept of ratings came from. The **rating** is simply the percentage of homes exposed to an advertising medium. Percentages are not only simpler numbers to deal with, they are also more useful in making comparisons. Thus, one rating point is equal to 1 percent of a given population group. When we hear that a particular TV show garnered a 20 rating, it means 20 percent of the households with TV sets (expressed as **television households** or **TVHH**) were tuned in to that show. The higher a program's rating, the more people are watching.[19] This definition applies to many media forms, but it is most commonly used for radio and TV.

By adding the ratings of several media vehicles (as we did for gross impressions) we can determine the message weight of a given advertising schedule, only now it's expressed as **gross rating points (GRPs)** (see Exhibit 15–6). When we say a schedule delivered 180 GRPs, that means the gross impressions generated by our schedule equaled 180 percent of the target market population. For broadcast media, GRPs are often calculated for a week or a four-week period. In print media, they're calculated for the number of ads in a campaign. For outdoor advertising, they're calculated on the basis of daily exposure.

In the calculation of message weight, advertisers ignore the fact that there is overlap or duplication. As a result, certain individuals within

Media vehicle	Target audience*	Messages used	Gross impressions
TV-Ch. 6 News	140,000	15	2,100,000
Daily newspaper	250,000	7	1,750,000
Spot radio	10,000	55	550,000
Total gross impressions			4,400,000

*Average.

Exhibit 15–5

Gross impressions analysis for Brand X in the second quarter, 2005.

Exhibit 15–6

Gross rating points analysis for Alpha brand in the second quarter, 2005.

Media vehicle	Adult rating*	Messages used	Gross rating points
TV-Ch. 6 News	14	15	210
Daily newspaper	25	7	175
Spot radio	1	55	55
Total gross rating points			440

*Assumes market size of 1 million people.

the audience may see the message several times while others don't see it at all. While message weight gives an indication of audience size, it does not reveal much about who is in the audience or how often they are reached. This fact necessitated the development of other media objectives, namely reach, frequency, and continuity.

Audience Accumulation and Reach

The term **reach** refers to the total number of *different* people or households exposed, at least once, to a medium during a given period of time, usually four weeks.[20] For example, if 40 percent of 100,000 people in a target market tune in to radio station WKKO at least once during a four-week period, the reach is 40,000 people. Reach should not be confused with the number of people who will actually be exposed to and consume the *advertising,* though. It is just the number of people who are exposed to the *medium* and therefore have an *opportunity* to see or hear the ad or commercial.

An advertiser may accumulate reach in two ways: by using the same media vehicle continuously or by combining two or more media vehicles.[21] Naturally, as more media are used, some duplication occurs. Exhibit 15–7 is a statistical table that estimates how unduplicated reach builds as additional media are added.

Exposure Frequency

To express the number of times the same person or household has an opportunity to see a message—a radio spot, for example—in a specified time span, media people use the term *frequency.* Whereas reach measures the *breadth,* **frequency** measures the *intensity* of a media schedule, based on repeated exposures to the medium or the program. Frequency is important because repetition is the key to memory.

Frequency is calculated as the *average* number of times individuals or homes are exposed to the medium during a specific period of time. For instance, suppose in our hypothetical 100,000-person market that 20,000 people

Exhibit 15–7

Random combination table. Find the reach of the first medium on the horizontal axis. Find the reach of the second medium on the vertical axis. The point of intersection shows the combined reach of the two media. If three or more media forms are combined, use the same procedure, finding the combined reach of the first two media on the horizontal axis and reading down to the intersection with the reach of the third medium.

						Reach of first medium									
		25	30	35	40	45	50	55	60	65	70	75	80	85	90	95
Reach of second medium	25	46	47	51	55	59	62	66	70	74	77	81	85	89	92	95
	30	—	51	54	58	61	65	68	72	75	79	82	86	90	93	95
	35	—	—	58	61	64	67	71	74	77	80	84	87	90	93	95
	40	—	—	—	64	67	70	73	76	79	82	85	88	91	94	95
	45	—	—	—	—	70	72	75	78	81	83	86	89	92	94	95
	50	—	—	—	—	—	75	77	80	82	85	87	90	92	95	95
	55	—	—	—	—	—	—	80	82	84	86	89	91	93	95	95
	60	—	—	—	—	—	—	—	84	86	88	90	92	94	95	95
	65	—	—	—	—	—	—	—	—	88	89	91	93	95	95	95
	70	—	—	—	—	—	—	—	—	—	91	92	94	95	95	95
	75	—	—	—	—	—	—	—	—	—	—	94	95	95	95	95
	80	—	—	—	—	—	—	—	—	—	—	—	95	95	95	95
	85	—	—	—	—	—	—	—	—	—	—	—	—	95	95	95
	90	—	—	—	—	—	—	—	—	—	—	—	—	—	95	95
	95	—	—	—	—	—	—	—	—	—	—	—	—	—	—	95

tune in to WKKO and have three OTSs during a four-week period, and another 20,000 have five OTSs. To calculate the average frequency, divide the total number of exposures by the total reach:

$$
\begin{aligned}
\text{Average frequency} &= \text{Total exposures} \div \text{Audience reach} \\
&= [(20{,}000 \times 3) + (20{,}000 \times 5)] \div 40{,}000 \\
&= 160{,}000 \div 40{,}000 \\
&= 4.0
\end{aligned}
$$

For the 40,000 listeners reached, the average frequency, or number of exposures, was four.

Once we understand reach and frequency, we have another, simple way to determine the message weight. To calculate gross rating points, just multiply a show's reach (expressed as a rating percentage) by the average frequency. In our radio example, 40 percent of the radio households (a 40 rating) had the opportunity to hear the commercial an average of four times during the four-week period:

$$
\begin{aligned}
\text{Reach} \times \text{Frequency} &= \text{GRPs} \\
40 \times 4 &= 160 \text{ GRPs}
\end{aligned}
$$

Thus, the message weight of this radio campaign would be equal to 160 percent of the total market—or 160,000 gross impressions.

Continuity

Media planners refer to the duration of an advertising message or campaign over a given period of time as **continuity.** Few companies spread their marketing efforts evenly throughout the year. They typically *heavy up* before prime selling seasons and slow down during the off-season. Likewise, to save money, a media planner for a new product might decide that after a heavy introduction period of, say, four weeks, a radio campaign needs to maintain *continuity* for an additional 16 weeks but on fewer stations. We'll discuss some common scheduling patterns in the section on media tactics.

While frequency is important to create memory, continuity is important to *sustain* it. Moreover, as people come into and out of the market for goods and services every day, continuity provides a means of having the message there when it's most needed. Ads that can be scheduled to hit targets during purchase cycles are more effective and require less frequency.[22]

Optimizing Reach, Frequency, and Continuity: The Art of Media Planning

Good media planning is both an art and a science. The media planner must get the most effective exposure on a limited budget. As Exhibit 15–8 shows, the objectives of reach, frequency, and continuity have inverse relationships to each other. To achieve greater reach on a limited budget, some frequency and/or continuity has to be sacrificed, and so on. Research shows that all three are critical. But since all budgets are limited, which is most critical? This has always been the subject of hot debate in advertising circles.

Effective Reach

One of the problems with reach is that, by itself, the measurement doesn't take into account the *effectiveness* of the exposures. Some people exposed to the medium still won't be aware of the message. So, on the

Exhibit 15–8

Reach, frequency, and continuity have an inverse relationship to one another. For instance, in the example below, an advertiser can reach 6,000 people once, 3,000 people approximately 5.5 times, or 1,000 people 9 times for the same budget. However, to achieve continuity over time, the advertiser might have to sacrifice some reach and/or frequency.

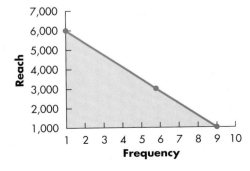

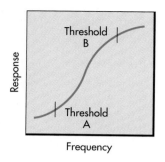

Exhibit 15–9

The S-shaped response curve suggests that a minimum threshold (A) of advertising frequency must be crossed before a meaningful response is achieved. At some level of frequency, another threshold (B) is crossed and the response begins to level off or even decline due to overexposure.

surface, reach doesn't seem to be the best measure of media success. Media people use the term **effective reach** to describe the *quality* of exposure. It measures the number or percentage of the audience who receive enough exposures to truly receive the message. That brings us to effective frequency.

Effective Frequency

Similar to the concept of effective reach is **effective frequency,** defined as the average number of times a person must see or hear a message before it becomes effective. In theory, effective frequency falls somewhere between a minimum level that achieves message awareness and a maximum level that becomes overexposure, which leads to **wearout** (starts to irritate consumers).

The S-shaped **advertising response curve** in Exhibit 15–9 suggests that at a low frequency there is little response. This is because the intensity of advertising is below a threshold where most of the target audience would notice it. Once that threshold is crossed, there is a dramatic response to increasing levels of advertising. Eventually though, the target market becomes saturated and, while advertising frequency continues to increase, the market response levels off or may even decline. The challenge to media planners is to determine the frequency of advertising that will exceed threshold A but remain below threshold B. To complicate matters further, different products or different advertising campaigns may generate different advertising response curves.

Following the publication of Michael Naples's classic book *Effective Frequency* in 1979, most of the industry fell in love with his claim that, in most cases, effective frequency could be achieved by an average frequency of three over a four-week period. Here was a nice, simple conclusion that all media planners could use.

However this assumes that all exposures are equal. If that's the case, then where does advertising creativity come in? And what about the environment in which the advertising appears? Doesn't that have some effect on the quality of exposure? There is no simple solution to this problem.

Once the media objectives have been determined— that is, the optimum levels of message weight, reach, frequency, and continuity—the media planner can develop the strategy for achieving them.

CONCEPT CHECK

Why are message weight, reach, frequency, and continuity all important measures of media delivery?

Developing a Media Strategy: The Media Mix

The media strategy describes how the advertiser will achieve the stated media objectives: which media will be used, where, how often, and when. Just as marketers determine marketing strategy by blending elements of the marketing mix, media planners can develop media strategies by blending the elements of the media mix.

Factors in the Media Strategy: The Five Ms

Many factors go into developing an effective media strategy. For simplicity and ease of memory, we have sorted them into five categories and given them the alliterative moniker of the **five Ms:** *markets, money, media, mechanics,* and *methodology.*

Markets refers to the various targets of a media plan: trade and consumer audiences; global, national, or regional audiences; ethnic and socioeconomic groups; or other stakeholders. In an integrated marketing communications plan, the media planner wants to understand the reasons and motivations for the prospect's purchase and usage patterns and then create a media plan based on those findings.[23]

Using intuition, marketing savvy, and analytical skill, the media planner determines the second element, **money**—how much to budget and where to allocate it. How much for print media, how much in TV, how much to nontraditional or supplemental media, how much to each geographic area?

Media includes *all* communications vehicles available to a marketer—anything you can put your name on. This includes radio, TV, newspapers, magazines, outdoor, the Internet, and direct mail, plus sales promotion, direct marketing, public relations activities and publicity, special events, brochures, and even shopping bags. Good media planners champion the integration of all marketing communications to help achieve their companies' marketing and advertising objectives. They look at the media element both analytically and creatively.

This ad for Kinko's (www.fedex.com) exemplifies three of the five Ms of the media mix. Addressing business owners and executives (market), this ad ran in trade publications such as *Fast Company* magazine (media). The two-page spread (mechanics) is intended to make a big impression on the reader. Methodology refers to the relationship of this ad to the overall media plan, and money determines and is affected by the four other elements.

The media planner also has to deal with the complex **mechanics** of advertising media and messages. Radio and TV commercials come in a variety of time units, and print ads are created in a variety of sizes and styles. The myriad media options now available offer exciting, creative ways to enhance consumer acceptance of the advertiser's message and offer the consumer a relevant purchase incentive.

The **methodology** element refers to the overall strategy of selecting and scheduling media vehicles to achieve the desired message weight, reach, frequency, and continuity objectives. It offers the opportunity for creativity in planning, negotiating, and buying.

Factors That Influence Media Strategy Decisions

Media decisions are greatly influenced by factors over which the media planner has little or no control. These include the scope of the media plan, sales potential of different markets, competitive strategies and budget considerations, availability of different media vehicles, nature of the medium, mood of the message, message size and length, and buyer purchase patterns.

Scope of the Media Plan

The location and makeup of the target audience strongly influence the scope of the media plan, thereby affecting decisions regarding the market, the money, and the media elements.

Domestic markets A media planner normally limits advertising to areas where the product is available. If a store serves only one town, or if a city has been chosen to test-market a new product, then the advertiser will use a *local* plan.

The Arab world is watching, tell them something!

mbc TV puts your brands in the picture

Reaching international markets presents unique challenges to advertisers. There are many unknown variables in regulations, viewers, potential audience, and language and cultural barriers. This ad claims to solve these problems as MBC TV will take the guesswork out of media planning and ad preparation when targeting Arabic audiences.

A *regional* plan may cover several adjoining metropolitan areas, an entire state or province, or several neighboring states. Regional plans typically employ a combination of local media, regional editions of national magazines, spot TV and radio, and the Internet.

Advertisers who want to reach several regions or an entire country use a *national* plan. This may call for network TV and radio, full-circulation national magazines and newspapers, nationally syndicated Sunday newspaper supplements, and the Web.

International markets As we discussed in Chapter 3, foreign media can be a challenge for U.S. advertisers. While many broadcast stations are being privatized in countries as diverse as Israel and Russia, governments around the world still control many broadcast media, and some still do not permit commercials. Others limit advertising to a certain number of minutes per hour or per day.

In countries that do allow TV advertising, advertisers face other problems: how many people own TV sets, who they are, and what channels do they receive. While this is not an issue in Europe and is becoming less so in Latin America, it is still a problem in many of the less-developed nations of Africa and Asia.

Most marketers develop an international media plan by formulating individual national plans first. But it's not as simple as it sounds. Depending on the country, precise media information may not be available, circulation figures may not be audited, audience demographics may be sketchy, and even ad rates may be unreliable. Finally, the methodology used in media research may be considerably different from one market to another, making comparisons virtually impossible.

Because of the media variations from country to country, most international and global advertisers entrust national media plans to in-country foreign media specialists or the local foreign branches of global media agencies such as MindShare, OMD Worldwide, The Media Edge, or Carat, rather than risk faulty centralized media planning.[24]

Sales Potential of Different Markets

The market and money elements of the media mix also depend on the sales potential of each area. National advertisers use this factor to determine where to allocate their advertising dollars. Planners can determine an area's sales potential in several ways.

The brand development index The **brand development index (BDI)** indicates the sales strength of a particular brand in a specific market area. It compares the percentage of the brand's total U.S. sales in an area to the percentage of the total U.S. population in that area. The larger the brand's sales relative to the area's percentage of U.S. population, the higher the BDI and the greater the brand's sales development. BDI is calculated as

$$BDI = \frac{\text{Percent of the brand's total U.S. sales in the area}}{\text{Percent of total U.S. population in the area}} \times 100$$

Suppose sales of a brand in Los Angeles are 1.58 percent of the brand's total U.S. sales and the population of Los Angeles is 2 percent of the U.S. total. The BDI for Los Angeles is

$$BDI = \frac{1.58}{2} \times 100 = 79$$

An index number of 100 means the brand's performance is in balance with the size of the area's population. A BDI index number below 100 indicates poor development of the brand in that market.

	Low BDI	High BDI
High CDI	Low market share *but* Good market potential	High market share *and* Good market potential
Low CDI	Low market share *and* Poor market potential	High market share *but* Poor market potential

Exhibit 15–10

Media buyers compare the brand development index with the category development index for their products to better understand which markets will respond best to advertising. Advertising can be expected to work well when BDI and CDI are both high, but probably not when both are low.

The category development index To determine the strength of the whole product category, media planners use the **category development index (CDI),** which works on the same concept as the BDI and is calculated in much the same way:

$$CDI = \frac{\text{Percent of the product category's total U.S. sales in the area}}{\text{Percent of total U.S. population in the area}} \times 100$$

If category sales in Los Angeles are 4.92 percent of total U.S. category sales, the CDI in Los Angeles is

$$CDI = \frac{4.92}{2} \times 100 = 246$$

The combination of BDI and CDI can help the planner determine a media strategy for the market (see Exhibit 15–10). In our example, a low BDI (under 100) and a high CDI (over 100) in Los Angeles indicate that the product category offers great potential but the brand is not selling well. This may represent a problem or an opportunity. If the brand has been on the market for some time, the low BDI raises a red flag; some problem is standing in the way of brand sales. But if the brand is new, the low BDI may be a positive sign. The high CDI may indicate the brand can grow substantially, given more time and greater media and marketing support. At this point, the media planner should assess the company's share of voice (discussed in Chapter 7) and budget accordingly.

Competitive Strategies and Budget Considerations

Advertisers always consider what competitors are doing, particularly those that have larger advertising budgets. This affects the *media, mechanics,* and *methodology* elements of the media mix. Several services, like Competitive Media Reports, detail competitive advertising expenditures in the different media. By knowing the size of competitors' budgets, what media they're using, the regionality or seasonality of their sales, and any new-product tests and introductions, advertisers can better plan a counterstrategy.

Again, the media planner should analyze the company's share of voice in the marketplace. If an advertiser's budget is much smaller than the competition's, the brand could get lost in the shuffle. Advertisers should bypass media that competitors dominate and choose other media in which they can achieve a strong position.

When Anne Myers, media director of Palmer Jarvis DDB, Toronto, had to develop a media plan for Panasonic Canada's Power Activator batteries, she didn't have the budget of Energizer or Duracell to work with. So she didn't want to place her ads where theirs were. Myers and her team creatively fashioned a guerrilla media plan that targeted a cynical, hard-to-reach

When a product's share of market is less than the competition's, competitive strategies can provide enormous marketing leverage. Here, Fujitsu (www.fcpa.com) advertises its portable data drive as the cheaper and superior alternative to the industry standard Zip and Jaz drives, manufactured by Iomega.

audience, 15- to 22-year-olds, right where they lived—in the clubs, on the street, and on the Internet. The campaign included posters in the dance clubs; sponsorship of popular DJs and VJs; free Power Activator T-shirts, hats, posters, and stickers; an eight-week run of television spots on popular music shows tied to a month-long cross-promotion with a new CD release; and a special contest run on a micro Web site that was linked to Panasonic's home page. The response was excellent: Sales were up 136 percent over the previous year, and the contest promotion generated more than 16,300 entries on the Web site with a click-through rate of 35 percent.[25]

It sometimes makes sense to use media similar to the competition's if the target audiences are the same or if the competitors are not using their media effectively.

Media Availability and Economics: The Global Marketer's Headache

North American advertisers are blessed—or cursed—with an incredible array of media choices, locally and nationally. Such is not always the case in other areas of the world, which is one reason their per capita advertising expenditures are so much lower than in the United States.

Every country has communications media, but they are not always available for commercial use (especially radio and television) and coverage may be limited. Lower literacy rates and education levels in some countries restrict the coverage of print media. Where income levels are low, TV ownership is also low.

To reach lower-income markets, radio is often the medium of choice, as both Coke and Pepsi have demonstrated successfully for years. Auto manufacturers make good use of TV and magazine advertising to reach the upper class. And movie advertising can reach whole urban populations where TV ownership is low because motion picture attendance in such countries is very high.

Some companies are attempting to become true global marketers of their brands with centralized control of media and standardized creative. As a group, global media are growing, which is good news for global marketers.[26] However, there are still few true global media. So these major advertisers must continue to use local foreign media in the countries where they do business and localize their campaigns for language and cultural differences.

Nature of the Medium and Mood of the Message

An important influence on the *media* element of the mix is how well a medium works with the style or mood of the particular message.

Advertising messages differ in many ways. Some are simple messages: "Just do it" (Nike). Others make emotional or sensual appeals to people's needs and wants: "The great taste of fruit squared" (Jolly Rancher candies). Many advertisers use a reason-why approach to explain their product's advantages: "Twice the room. Twice the comfort. Twice the value. Embassy Suites. Twice the hotel."

Complex messages, such as ads announcing a new product or concept, require more space or time for explanation. Each circumstance affects the media selection as well as the *methodology* of the media mix.

A new or highly complex message may require greater frequency and exposure to be understood and remembered. A

The language and imagery of this Godiva chocolate (www.godiva.com) ad exudes a sense of elegance that suits the audience of the medium selected. Godiva placed the ad in magazines such as *Architectural Digest* to reach a target audience of affluent, well-educated individuals. The photo, type, and layout elements reflect the nature of the magazine, the advertiser, and even the audience.

ONE FOR ME, AND ONE FOR ME.

What could make your taste buds happier than one of our wondrous medleys of fresh pecans, hazelnuts or cashews wrapped in caramel and chocolate? Partake of these caramel nut bonchées, and your sweet tooth will positively swoon.

1-800-9-GODIVA   www.godiva.com   AOL (keyword: GODIVA)

New York   Paris   GODIVA   Tokyo   Brussels
                      Chocolatier

dogmatic message like Nike's may require a surge at the beginning, then low frequency and greater reach, plus continuity.

Once consumers understand reason-why messages, pulsing advertising exposures at irregular intervals is often sufficient. Emotionally oriented messages are usually more effective when spaced at regular intervals to create enduring feelings about the product. We discuss these scheduling methods further in the next section, which is on media tactics.

Message Size, Length, and Position Considerations

The particular characteristics of different media affect the mechanics element of the media mix. For example, in print, a full-page ad attracts more attention than a quarter-page ad and a full-color ad more than a black-and-white one (see Exhibit 15–11).

Should a small advertiser run a full-page ad once a month or a quarter-page ad once a week? Is it better to use a few 60-second commercials or many 15- and 30-second ones? The planner has to consider the nature of the advertising message; some simply require more time and space to explain. Competitive activity often dictates more message units. The product itself may demand the prestige of a full page or full color. However, it's often better to run small ads consistently rather than one large ad occasionally. Unfortunately, space and time units may be determined by someone other than the media planner—creative or account management, for example—in which case the planner's options are limited.

The position of an ad is another consideration. Preferred positions for magazine ads are front and back covers; for TV, sponsorship of prime-time shows. Special positions and sponsorships cost more, so the media planner must decide whether the increased readership is worth the higher costs.

As we can see, the nature of the creative work has the potential to greatly affect the media strategy. This means that media planners have to be flexible, since the initial media plan may well have been determined prior to beginning the creative work.

Buyer Purchase Patterns

Finally, the customer's product purchasing behavior affects every element of the media mix. The media planner must consider how, when, and where the product is typically purchased and repurchased. Products with short purchase cycles (convenience foods and paper towels) require more constant levels of advertising than products purchased infrequently (refrigerators and furniture). For a practical checklist of these points, see RL 15–1 on the *Essentials of Contemporary Advertising* Web site.

Exhibit 15–11

Effect of size and color on ad readership (total ads studied = 107,506).

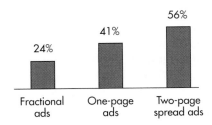

a. Size—as size increases so does readership.

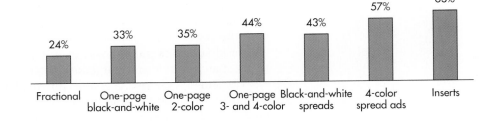

b. Size and color—advertising readership increases with size and the use of color.

Stating the Media Strategy

A written rationale for the media strategy is an integral part of any media plan. Without one, it's difficult for client and agency management to analyze the logic and consistency of the recommended media schedule.

Generally, the strategy statement begins with a brief definition of target audiences (the market element) and the priorities for weighting them. It explains the nature of the message and indicates which media types will be used and why (the media element). It outlines specific reach, frequency, and continuity goals and how they are to be achieved (the methodology element). It provides a budget for each medium (the money element), including the cost of production and any collateral materials. Finally, it states the intended size of message units, and any position or timing considerations (the mechanics element).

Once the strategy is delineated, the plan details the tactics to be employed, the subject of the next section.

CONCEPT CHECK

Describe the important factors that must be considered when developing a media strategy. Why are they important?

Media Tactics: Selecting and Scheduling Media Vehicles

Once the general media strategy is determined, the media planner can select and schedule particular media vehicles. The planner usually considers each medium's value on a set of specific criteria. Commercial Break 15–A summarizes many of the media advantages discussed in Chapters 11–14.

Criteria for Selecting Individual Media Vehicles

In evaluating specific media vehicles, the planner considers several factors: overall campaign objectives and strategy; size and characteristics of each medium's audience; attention, exposure, and motivational value of each medium; and cost efficiency.

Overall Campaign Objectives and Strategy

The media planner's first job is to review the nature of the product or service, the objectives and strategies, and the primary and secondary target markets and audiences. The characteristics of the product often suggest a suitable media choice. A product with a distinct personality or image, such as a fine perfume, might be advertised in media that reinforce this image. The media planner considers how consumers regard various magazines and TV programs—feminine or masculine, highbrow or lowbrow, serious or frivolous—and determines whether they're appropriate for the brand.

The content and editorial policy of the media vehicle and its compatibility with the product are important considerations. *Tennis* magazine is a poor vehicle for cigarette or alcohol ads even though its demographic profile and image might match the desired target audience.

Consumers choose a particular media vehicle because they gain some "reward": self-improvement, financial advice, career guidance, or simply news and entertainment. Advertising is most effective when it positions a product as part of the solution that consumers seek. Otherwise, they may see it as an intrusion.[27]

Commercial Break 15–A

Media Selection: Quick List of Advantages

Medium	Advantages
Newspapers	Many ad sizes available. Quick placement. Local targeting. Audience interest.
Magazines	High-quality graphics/reproduction. Prestige factor. Color. Selective targeting.
TV	Combines sight, sound, movement. A single message. Demonstration. Social dominance.
Radio	Intimacy. Loyal following. Ability to change message quickly. Repetition and frequency.
Internet	Immediate response. Interactive. Highly selective targeting. Global. Fastest growing medium.
Direct mail	Measurable. Graphics, color. 3-D. Highly personal. Adaptable message length.
Outdoor/Transit	Local targeting. Graphics, color. Simple message. Larger than life. Repetition.

Applying the Breaks
What creative advantages can you add to the list?

If the marketing objective is to gain greater product distribution, the planner should select media that might also influence potential dealers. If the goal is to stimulate sales of a nationally distributed product in isolated markets, ads should be placed in local and regional media that penetrate those markets. Pricing strategy influences media choices too. A premium-priced product should use prestigious or classy media to support its market image.

Characteristics of Media Audiences

An **audience** is the total number of people or households exposed to a medium. The planner needs to know how closely the medium's audience matches the profile of the target market and how interested prospective customers are in the publication or program. A product intended for a Latino audience, for example, would likely appear in specific media directed toward Hispanics. Simmons Market Research Bureau (SMRB) provides research data on age, income, occupational status, and other characteristics of magazine readers. Simmons also publishes demographic and psychographic data on product usage of consumers. Likewise, Nielsen provides audience statistics for television programs and Arbitron for radio stations.

The *content* of the medium usually determines the type of people in the audience. Some radio stations emphasize in-depth news or sports; others feature jazz, rock, or classical music. Each type of programming attracts a different audience.

Exposure, Attention, and Motivation Value of Media Vehicles

The media planner has to select media that will not only achieve the desired *exposure* to the target audience, but also attract *attention* and *motivate* people to act.

Exposure As we discussed earlier, just because someone reads a particular magazine or watches a certain program doesn't mean he or she sees the ads. Some people read only one article, set the magazine aside, and never pick it up again. Many people change channels during commercial breaks or leave to get a snack. Comparing the **exposure value** of different media vehicles, therefore, is very difficult. Without statistics, media planners have to use their best judgment based on experience.

Five factors affect the probability of ad exposure:

1. The senses used to perceive messages from the medium (for example, scratch-and-sniff ads really improve the exposure value of magazines).

2. How much and what kind of attention the medium requires (higher involvement suggests greater ad exposure).

3. Whether the medium is an information source or a diversion (for example, radio news programs offer greater ad exposure than elevator music).

4. Whether the medium or program aims at a general or a specialized audience (exposure value will be higher with specialized audiences).

5. The placement of the ad in the vehicle (placement within broadcast programs gives greater exposure than placement between programs; ads placed next to editorial material get greater exposure than ads placed next to other print ads).

Attention Degree of attention is another consideration. As we discussed in Chapter 5, consumers with no interest in motorcycles or cosmetics won't remember ads for those products. For a variety of reasons, they fail to penetrate the viewer's perceptual screens. But someone in the market for a new car tends to notice every car ad.

This ad for Crownline boats will get more exposure and receive more attention in *Lakeland Boating* magazine than in a general-interest publication. Readers will have nautical activities on their minds and may be very motivated if they are actively seeking product information.

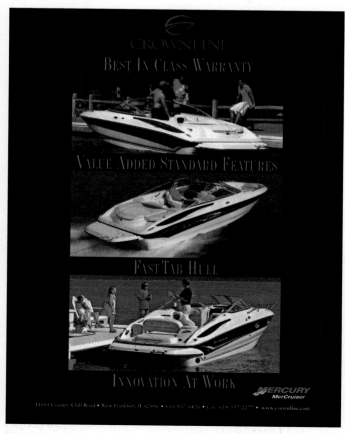

Exposure value relates only to the medium; **attention value** concerns the advertising message and copy, as well as the medium. Special-interest media, such as boating magazines, can offer good attention value to a marine product. But what kind of attention value can the daily newspaper offer such a product? Do sailors think about boats while reading the newspaper? Much research still needs to be done, but six factors are known to increase attention value:[28]

1. Audience involvement with editorial content or program material.

2. Specialization of audience interest or identification.

3. Number of competitive advertisers (the fewer, the better).

4. Audience familiarity with the advertiser's campaign.

5. Quality of advertising reproduction.

6. Timeliness of advertising exposure.

Motivation These same factors affect a medium's **motivation value,** but in different ways. Familiarity with the advertiser's campaign may affect attention significantly but motivation very little. The attention factors of quality reproduction and timeliness can motivate someone, however.

Media planners analyze these values by assigning numerical ratings to their judgments of a medium's strengths and weaknesses. Then, using a weighting formula, they add them up. Planners use similar weighting methods to evaluate other factors, such as the relative importance of age versus income.

Cost Efficiency of Media Vehicles

Finally, media planners analyze the cost efficiency of each medium. A common term used in media planning and buying is **cost per thousand,** or **CPM** (M is the Roman numeral for 1,000). If a daily newspaper has 300,000 subscribers and charges $5,000 for a full-page ad, the cost per thousand is the cost divided by the number of thousands of people in the audience. Since there are 300 *thousands* of subscribers, you divide $5,000 by 300:

$$\text{CPM} = \frac{\$5,000}{300,000 \div 1,000} = \frac{\$5,000}{300} = \$16.67 \text{ per thousand}$$

However, media planners are more interested in **cost efficiency**—the cost of exposing the message to the *target audience* rather than to the total circulation. Let's say the target audience is males ages 18 to 49, and 40 percent of a magazine's subscriber base of 250,000 fits this category. If the magazine charges $3,000 for a full-page ad, the **target CPM (TCPM)** is computed as follows:

$$\text{Target audience} = 0.40 \times 250,000 = 100,000$$

$$\text{TCPM} = \frac{\$3,000}{100,000 \div 1,000} = \$30 \text{ per thousand}$$

The more costly (on an absolute basis) daily newspaper might turn out to be more cost efficient than the magazine if 60 percent of its readers (180,000) belong to the target audience:

$$\text{TCPM} = \frac{\$5,000}{180,000 \div 1,000} = \$27.78 \text{ per thousand}$$

The media planner may also want to compare the **cost per point (CPP)** of different broadcast programs. This is done the same way as cost per thousand, except you divide the cost by the rating points instead of the gross impressions.

Comparing different media by CPM or CPP is important but does not take into account each medium's other advantages and disadvantages. The media planner must evaluate all the criteria to determine

1. How much of each medium's audience matches the product's target audience.

2. How each medium satisfies the campaign's objectives and strategy.

3. How well each medium offers attention, exposure, and motivation.

> In evaluating specific media vehicles, what factors must media planners consider and why are they important?
>
> CONCEPT CHECK

The Synergy of Mixed Media

A combination of media is called a **mixed-media approach.** There are numerous reasons for using mixed media:

- To reach people who are unavailable through only one medium.

- To provide repeat exposure in a less expensive secondary medium after attaining optimum reach in the first.

- To use the intrinsic value of an additional medium to extend the creative effectiveness of the ad campaign (such as music on radio along with long copy in print media).

- To deliver coupons in print media when the primary vehicle is broadcast.

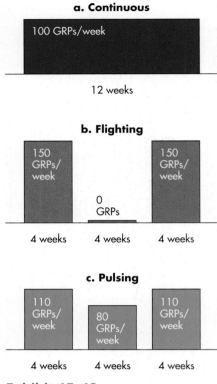

Exhibit 15–12

Three ways to schedule the same number of total gross rating points: continuous, flighting, and pulsing.

- To produce **synergy,** where the total effect is greater than the sum of its parts.

Newspapers, for example, can be used to introduce a new product and give immediacy to the message. Magazine ads can then follow up for greater detail, image enhancement, longevity, and memory improvement.

A mixed-media campaign was effective for General Electric's lighting products. The promotion used a combination of network TV spots, print advertising, Sunday supplement inserts, in-store displays in more than 150,000 stores, and a highly creative publicity program. By using an integrated, mixed-media approach, the campaign produced "unprecedented" consumer awareness and dealer support. It achieved synergy.[29]

Methods for Scheduling Media

After selecting the appropriate media vehicles, the media planner decides how many space or time units to buy of each vehicle and schedules them for release over a period of time when consumers are most apt to be in the market for the product.

Continuous, Flighting, and Pulsing Schedules

To build continuity in a campaign, planners use three principal scheduling tactics: *continuous, flighting,* and *pulsing* (see Exhibit 15–12).

In a **continuous schedule,** advertising runs steadily and varies little over the campaign period. It's the best way to build continuity. Advertisers use this scheduling pattern for products consumers purchase regularly.

Flighting alternates periods of advertising with periods of no advertising. This intermittent schedule makes sense for products and services that experience large fluctuations in demand throughout the year (tax services, lawn-care products, cold remedies). The advertiser might introduce the product with a four-week flight and then schedule three additional four-week flights to run during seasonal periods later in the year. Flighting is also often used by products and services to stretch limited budgets.

The third alternative, **pulsing,** mixes continuous and flighting strategies. The advertiser maintains a low level of advertising all year but uses periodic pulses to heavy up during peak selling periods. This strategy is appropriate for products like soft drinks, which are consumed all year but more heavily in the summer.

Additional Scheduling Patterns

For high-ticket items that require careful consideration, **bursting**—running the same commercial every half hour on the same network during prime time—can be effective. A variation is **roadblocking,** buying air time on all three networks simultaneously. Chrysler used this technique to give viewers the impression that the advertiser was everywhere, even if the ad showed for only a few nights. Digital Equipment used a scheduling tactic called **blinking** to stretch its slim ad budget. To reach business executives, it flooded the airwaves on Sundays (on both cable and network TV channels) to make it virtually impossible to miss the ads.[30]

Once the scheduling criteria are determined, the media planner creates a flowchart of the plan. The flowchart is a graphic presentation of the total campaign to let the creative department, media department, account services, and the client see the pattern

CONCEPT CHECK

What determines the selection of a scheduling pattern for a specific product or service?

of media events that will occur throughout the campaign, usually one year (see Exhibit 15–13).

Computers in Media Selection and Scheduling

The last decade has seen a profusion of new desktop computer software to assist media planners. Computers perform the tedious number crunching needed to compute GRPs, CPMs, reach, frequency, and the like. They also save time and money. One agency found it could plan the entire TV, radio, and print co-op budgets for one of its largest clients in two days with only three people and one software package. Previously, that task required 70 staffers working manually for a week and a half.

Established in 1968, Telmar was the first independent supplier of computerized media planning systems. Today, it is the world's leading supplier of Windows and Internet-based media planning software and support services. More than 3,500 users in 100 countries, including 95 percent of the world's top agencies, use Telmar systems for media and marketing decision making.[31]

Telmar's software suite is designed to help media planners, buyers, research analysts, and sellers work more efficiently and to help them make better judgments in the evaluation or sales process. The software allows advertising executives to estimate the effectiveness of multifaceted marketing plans that use various combinations of media including print, broadcast, in-store, special promotions, special events, PR, and other "new media." Its flexibility permits the user to analyze the potential effectiveness of any and every marketing tool used to reach the consumer.

Similarly, Interactive Market Systems (IMS) has introduced its PowerHouse software, which provides access to more than 600 syndicated and proprietary databases including MRI, Simmons, PMB, Arbitron, PRIZM, Scarborough, J.D. Power and Associates, or the advertiser's own proprietary data.[32]

A second IMS product, *PowerFlow,* is a powerful flowcharting system. *PowerFlow,* on its own, enables planners to produce sophisticated media flowcharts quickly, but its real "power" is derived from its integration with individual planning modules (national, broadcast, magazines, newspaper) and expenditure data.

Even with all the technological timesavers and shortcuts, though, it's still up to the media planner to know the product, the market, and the media, and to then make the call. Computers can't decide which medium or environment is best for the message. They can't evaluate the content of a magazine or the image of a TV program. They can't judge whether the numbers they're fed are valid or reliable, and they can't interpret the meaning of the results. What they can do is help the process along.

Exhibit 15–13

A media plan flowchart like this computerized printout of Telmar's FlowMaster gives a bird's-eye view of the major media purchases and where and when they will appear over a specified period of time.

The advent of computer software has taken some of the more grueling, laborious work out of media planning. Planners can now crunch numbers, track results, and compute GRPs and CPMs right at their desktops. This saves an enormous amount of time and money. The SRDS Media Planning System (www.srds.com) shown here is an example of one of the many programs available.

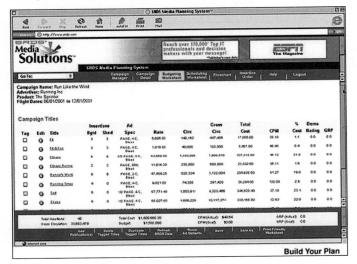

The Role of the Media Buyer

Planning is only the first stage in the media process. Once the media plans are developed, they must be executed. The person in charge of negotiating and contracting with the media is called a **media buyer.** Media buyers often specialize in one medium or another, so there are print media buyers, spot TV media buyers, network media buyers, and so on. The degree of specialization depends on the size of the advertiser or the agency. In small agencies, for example, media buyers frequently don't specialize. They do it all.

Media buying is a complicated process. Buyers must perform several functions in the process of converting a media plan into a successful buy. Placing an ad is not as easy as it may seem, especially when there are hundreds of television and radio stations, newspapers, and magazines around the country with different deadlines, different requirements, and different rates. To say the least, the job can be very tedious and time-consuming.

Fortunately, thanks to technology, media buyers now have a variety of software programs available to assist them. STRATA Marketing, Inc., for example, has developed media buying software for each form of media. It offers media buyers various ways to keep track of orders, clients, and rate information, while providing a large variety of formats for generating reports.

These programs, and others similar in function, save media buyers a lot of time, thereby increasing productivity and efficiency. More time can be spent analyzing information, evaluating various vehicles, and exercising creativity.

The most successful media buyers have developed key skills in the following areas:

Knowing the marketplace. Media buyers have frequent contact with media representatives. As a result, they often gain advance knowledge of trends or opportunities. Some of the best media buys are the result of an alert buyer taking advantage of an opportunity or anticipating a problem.

Negotiating the buy. Media vehicles have published rate cards, but everything is negotiable. Media buyers can often bargain for special rates on volume buys, uncover last-minute deals, negotiate preferred positions, or garner promotional support.

Monitoring performance. The media buyer is responsible for assuring that what was purchased was delivered. Did the advertising appear where and when it was scheduled? Was the size of the audience what was promised? If not, payments must be adjusted or *makegoods* must be negotiated. Whatever the outcome, the client expects to see a *post-buy report* on what audience was actually delivered.

Chapter Summary

Media planning directs the advertising message to the right people at the right time. It involves many decisions: where to advertise and when, which media to use, and how often to use them. Media planners need both analytical skills and creativity. Like good art and copy ideas, media decisions should be based on sound marketing principles and research.

The task of media planners has become more complicated and competitive in recent years due to the dramatic increase in media options, the continuing fragmentation of audiences, the rising cost of space and time, and the increasing complexity in the way media buys are made. But this has also given the professionals who work in media departments new prominence.

The media function involves two basic processes: planning media strategy and selecting media vehicles. Media planning begins with defining audience objectives—the specific types of people to whom the advertising message will be directed—and then setting the goals for communicating with those audiences. The target audience is often determined from the marketer's past experience, through special research studies, or through secondary research sources such as Simmons Market Research Bureau and Mediamark Research. Once the target audience is determined, the planner sets the message-distribution objectives. These specify where, when, and how often the advertising should appear. They may be expressed in terms of message weight, reach, frequency, and continuity. In this process, the planner considers the amount of advertising needed to achieve effectiveness.

To create the appropriate media strategy, the planner considers the five Ms: markets, money, media, mechanics, and methodology. The planner must also consider many uncontrollable variables: the scope of the media plan, which is determined by the location and makeup of the target audience; the sales potential of different markets for both the brand and the product category; competitive strategies and budget considerations; media availability and economics; the nature of the medium and the mood of the message; the size, length, and position of the message in the selected media; and buyer purchase patterns.

For international markets, media planners have to consider the availability and cost structure of foreign media and the differing cultural markets they serve. Some advertisers attempt to standardize their messages through the use of global media, but these media are still quite limited.

After the media strategy is developed, the planner selects specific media vehicles. Both the quantitative and qualitative criteria used to make this decision are important in the evaluation process. Factors that influence the selection process include campaign objectives and strategy; the size and characteristics of each medium's audience; geographic coverage; the exposure, attention, and motivation value of each medium; cost efficiency; and the advisability of a mixed-media approach.

Once media vehicles are selected, the media planner decides on scheduling—how many of each medium's space or time units to buy over what period of time. A media campaign can run continuously or in pulses. These decisions are affected by consumer purchase patterns, the product's seasonality, and the balance of reach, frequency, and continuity that meets the planner's media objectives and budget.

The media planner must spend money wisely to maximize the campaign's effectiveness. To that end, many computer models have been developed, both in the United States and overseas, to help planners determine optimum levels of expenditure or compare alternative media schedules.

The media buyer is responsible for executing the media plan, a very complex process. The buyer's job involves staying current with the market, negotiating the best deals, monitoring the execution of the plan, and reporting on what was actually delivered.

Key Terms

advertising impression, 411

advertising response curve, 414

attention value, 422

audience, 421

audience objectives, 410

blinking, 424

brand development index (BDI), 416

bursting, 424

category development index (CDI), 417

circulation, 411

continuity, 413

continuous schedule, 424

cost efficiency, 423

cost per point (CPP), 423

cost per thousand (CPM), 423

distribution objectives, 410

effective frequency, 414

effective reach, 414

exposure value, 421

five Ms, 414

flighting, 424

frequency, 412

gross impressions, 411

gross rating points (GRP), 411

markets, 414

mechanics, 415

media, 415

media buyer, 426

media planning, 402

media vehicles, 410

message weight, 411

methodology, 415

mixed-media approach, 423

money, 415

motivation value, 422

opportunity to see (OTS), 411

pass-along rate, 411

pulsing, 424

rating, 411

reach, 412

readers per copy (RPC), 411

roadblocking, 424

synergy, 424

target CPM (TCPM), 423

television households (TVHH), 411

wearout, 414

Review Questions

1. Why might a media planning or buying job be a good way to gain entry into the advertising industry?

2. What is meant by "increasing fragmentation of the audience" and why has that trend made a media planner's job more difficult?

3. What caused the unbundling of media departments? Did it benefit advertisers?

4. What secondary research sources are available to planners?

5. What are the "right" reach and frequency for a given message?

6. How are GRPs and CPMs calculated?

7. What are the five Ms that must be factored into media strategy development, and how are they determined?

8. What is the difference between CPM and target CPM and which is more meaningful?

9. Why might an advertiser use a mixed-media approach?

10. What skills are required of a media buyer?

Exploring Advertising

1. Consider products that you commonly purchase in the following categories: athletic shoes, backpacks, sweatshirts, sodas, music, and restaurant food. For each of these products, evaluate:

   a. What media might you select, based on finding the appropriate audience, environment, and mood for that product?

   b. What length or format ads would you use, given the type of message you need to communicate?

   c. How might you schedule the advertising, considering the purchase cycle of the product and the type of message you would be likely to deliver?

2. For the products you selected in #1, if you were the media planner, what questions would you ask of the client, the account planners, and the creatives to provide you with the information you need to develop the most effective media plan?

3. As a media buyer working on behalf of a large toy company, it is your job to buy media space for the launch of the Kitchi Kiss doll, which all advertising research shows will be a tremendous profit maker for the company. Using Exhibit 15–13 as an example, create a flowchart for a year's advertising for Kitchi Kiss. Explain your decisions about the types of media used, when to use which types, and for how long each type should run.

chapter sixteen

Relationship Building: Direct Marketing, Personal Selling, and Sales Promotion

Objectives

To emphasize the importance of relationship marketing in today's high-tech, over-communicated world and to demonstrate how various forms of marketing communications can be integrated with advertising to manage an organization's relations with its various stakeholders. Relationship marketing and IMC are two of the most important trends in marketing and advertising today. Direct marketing, personal selling, and sales promotion play different but often overlapping roles that are vitally important to IMC programs. Each offers many opportunities but also has limitations that advertisers should be aware of.

After studying this chapter, you will be able to:

* **Discuss** the importance of relationship marketing and IMC.

* **Define** direct marketing and discuss its role in IMC.

* **Explain** the importance of databases to direct marketers.

* **Discuss** the role of personal selling in an IMC program.

* **Describe** the advantages and drawbacks of personal selling.

* **Define** sales promotion and discuss its importance as a communications tool.

* **Identify** the benefits and drawbacks of sales promotion.

* **Explain** the difference between push and pull strategies and give some examples of each.

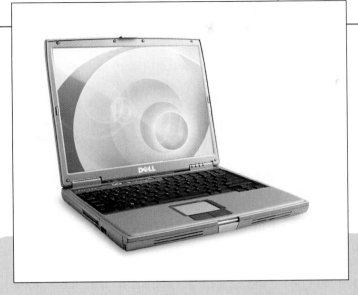

"Dude, you're getting some dough."[1]

That was the opening line from one of the commercials aimed at the burgeoning Generation Y market. It was the summer of 2002, and Dell Computer wanted to increase consumer awareness of its Web site and boost demand for its computers. Rather than just running a big schedule of ads, the company decided it could make a bigger hit by using sales promotion—in this case a sweepstakes. But then, instead of going for a single, Dell decided to go for a triple. And in the process, it hit a home run.

Dell launched the campaign by announcing a $50,000-a-Day Giveaway for the month of July and encouraged people to visit the company's Web site for more information. Once there, people could browse the site and shop for Dell products. While no purchase was necessary to enter, anybody who did purchase a Dell desktop or notebook computer was automatically entered in the national Back-to-School sweepstakes, with a chance to win the daily grand prize of $50,000 in cash. The first segment of the sweepstakes was highly successful. Hundreds of thousands of people actually ended up purchasing a Dell computer, and 30 of them won $50,000 each.[2]

Then came the trip to second base, running from August 1 to 29, but this time it was a Trip-a-Day Giveaway. Similar to the first phase, every day Dell gave away $50,000 in travel and cash. By month's end, 29 lucky customers had received $30,000 in travel and another $20,000 in cash.[3]

In September, Dell decided to complete the triple with a BMW-a-Day Giveaway. Customers who purchased a Dell during this final period were automatically given a chance to "go to class with class" and drive to school in a brand-new BMW 330i, valued at more than $41,000. By the end of September, 32 more people were enjoying "the ultimate driving machine."[4]

What is the incentive for an already highly regarded company to spend more than $4 million on giveaways over a three-month period? In Dell's case, the goal was to entice potential consumers to visit and browse Dell's only storefront—its Web site. But what the company got in exchange for investing in these costly promotions was even better. Dell earned the number-one ranking in terms of global market share; it became the number-one PC maker for consumers and small businesses; and it became the industry leader in a host of other categories as well.[5]

You might ask why such a large and successful company would choose to have a Web site as its only storefront. The answer lies in the very foundation of the company itself—a corporate mission based on direct marketing and personal selling.

Back in 1984, a 19-year-old, pre-med freshman named Michael Dell decided to start a company and base it on a simple premise: By selling computer systems directly to customers, he could better understand their needs and efficiently provide the most effective computing solutions to meet those needs.[6] The net effect of this idea was to eliminate the retailer, who knew less about the product, added unnecessary time and cost to the distribution process, and diluted Dell's own understanding of customer expectations. By dealing directly with its own customers, the company embodied the very essence of relationship building, and hence its slogan, "Be Direct."[7]

Adhering to Michael Dell's philosophy, the company offers its products directly to consumers via the telephone or the Internet, allowing each customer to examine, configure, and price systems within Dell's entire product line; order systems directly; and track orders from the manufacturing stage through the shipping stage. This not only allows consumers to get exactly what they want at competitive prices, but also lets Dell stay in touch with the ever-changing wants and needs of its customers.

The sales model was revolutionary and so were the results. In the 2002 *Fortune* 500, Dell ranked 53rd.[8] During the second quarter of 2002, amid an industrywide sales decline of 10 percent, Dell's profits jumped 11 percent. And after launching its Back-to-School sweepstakes, the company's market share jumped from 13.5 percent to 15 percent—in just one month.[9]

To further its focus on and dedication to the customer, Dell engages in a number of activities aimed at putting customer satisfaction and interaction at the top of the priority list. While many competitors advertise the latest software and hardware inventions, Dell's ads focus on customer service and support.

What Dell has done so successfully is to employ a wide variety of communication tools that consistently reinforce its main goals: serving customers' needs and growing the customer database. Maybe that's why Dell continues to outperform its rivals in the hypercompetitive PC market.[10]

By selling computers directly to customers, Dell (www.dell.com) can stay in touch with their needs and provide the best solutions to meet those needs. This direct relationship with its customers allows Dell to integrate all of its corporate resources to provide a consistently high level of product quality and service, at a competitive price.

The Importance of Relationship Marketing and IMC

In Chapter 7, we pointed out that due to a variety of environmental factors, the key to building brand equity in the twenty-first century is the development of interdependent, mutually satisfying relationships with customers and other stakeholders. Further, to manage these relationships, companies need to consciously (and conscientiously) integrate their marketing communications activities with all their other company functions so that all the messages the marketplace receives about the company are consistent.

However, this is a lot easier said than done, since everything a company does (and doesn't do) sends a message. Seamless, consistent communication—from every corner of the company—is how a firm earns a good reputation. And that is the principal objective of IMC—Integrated Marketing Communications.

Dell is a good example of how IMC works. To attract prospects and initiate the relationship building process, Dell integrates its advertising efforts with a host of other marketing communication tools—direct marketing, sales promotion, personal selling, and even certain public relations activities. These are then integrated with other company functions—product design, manufacturing, assembly, inventory control, and shipping—to reduce errors and assure a consistently high level of quality and service. The result of all this is a happier, more satisfied customer, one whose expectations have not just been met, but exceeded. That contributes to Dell's glowing reputation. In a 2004 Harris Poll, Dell was selected as one of the most popular brands in the United States, ranking third after only Sony and Coca-Cola.[11]

A simple adage: Advertising can create an image, but a reputation must be earned.

While the integration of marketing with other company functions is beyond the scope of an advertising textbook, it is important for advertising people to understand how to integrate the various tools of marketing communications. As they plan a campaign, advertising practitioners need a basic understanding of what other communications tools are available to them and how they can best be used in the overall marketing communications mix. In this chapter, we will discuss the interactive, one-to-one communication tools of direct marketing and personal selling. We'll also look at sales promotion, which might be called the "value-added" tool. In the next chapter, we'll address the "credibility" tools companies use to enhance their reputations. These include various public relations activities, sponsorships, and corporate advertising.

Understanding Direct Marketing

There is a lot of confusion surrounding the term *direct marketing,* even among the experts. In fact, Lester Wunderman, the man who coined the term more than 40 years ago, now thinks it may be due for a change.

The Direct Marketing Association (DMA) not long ago updated its definition of **direct marketing** to include "*any direct communication* to a consumer or business recipient that is designed to generate a response in the form of an order (direct order), a request for further information (lead generation), and/or a visit to a store or other place of business for the purchase of a specific product(s) or service(s) (traffic generation)."[12]

Direct Marketing magazine goes even further: "Direct marketing is a measurable system of marketing that uses one or more advertising media to effect a measurable response and/or transaction at any location, with this activity stored in a database." From this definition a virtually synonymous

Direct marketing is an interactive system in which buyers and sellers participate in a dialogue. Its intent is to stimulate a response in the form of a request for information, an actual purchase, or a visit. This poster by Britain's National Society for the Prevention of Cruelty to Children (NSPCC), which won a Gold Lion at Cannes, prompted calls from abused teenagers to jump 124 percent in just six weeks. The number of Web site visitors also increased, from 4,000 to more than 32,000.

term has emerged: **database marketing.** Database marketers build and maintain a pool of data on current and prospective customers (and other stakeholders) and communicate with them using a variety of media (from personal contact to direct mail to mass media). Database marketing is one of the fastest-growing marketing methods because it has proven to be a cost-efficient method for increasing sales. A good **database** enables marketers to target, segment, and grade customers. It helps them to know who their customers and prospects are, what and when they purchase, and how to contact them. That, of course, leads to the possibility of a relationship. So today, database marketing is a major component of most integrated marketing communications programs.

What we see from these various definitions is that, first and foremost, direct marketing is a *system of marketing* and it is *interactive,* meaning buyers and sellers can exchange information with each other directly. In fact, Joan Throckmorton, a prominent direct marketing consultant and writer, has urged that the term direct marketing be dropped completely and replaced with *interactive marketing.*[13]

A second important part of the definition of direct marketing is the concept of *one or more advertising media.* Part of the confusion with the name is its similarity to *direct mail.* While direct mail is often used in direct marketing, it is just one of the many media that direct marketers use.

In the Dell story, for instance, we saw how the company used a mass media form—newspapers—as well as direct mail in the form of e-mail, to elicit responses from people who might be interested in Dell. In fact, experienced direct marketers have known for years that using more than one medium tends to be far more productive than using a single medium.[14]

The third key point of the direct marketing definition is a *measurable response.* In fact, the kind of advertising direct marketers use is called **direct-response advertising.** This is because direct marketing efforts are always aimed at stimulating some action or response on the part of the customer or prospect. It may be in the form of a request for information, a store visit, or an actual purchase. Because these responses can be tallied and analyzed, direct marketing becomes accountable. And that, more than any other reason, explains the tremendous growth of direct marketing in recent years. Managers like it because they can see what they got for their money.

The final point most of the definitions make is that the response can be at any location. In other words, direct marketing is not restricted to mail order or catalog sales. Customers may respond by telephone, via mail-in coupons, over the Internet, at a retail store or other place of business, or even at a kiosk.

CONCEPT CHECK

What key components are found in the various definitions of direct marketing?

The Role of Direct Marketing in IMC

Today, sophisticated companies use the skills developed by direct marketers to establish, nourish, and maintain relationships, not just with customers, but with all stakeholders.

Dell, for instance, uses magazine and TV advertising as **linkage media**—media that help prospects and customers link up with a company—to inform prospects how to inquire about its products. Next, it uses these responses to build its database of names, addresses, and e-mail addresses. Then it uses the database to communicate with prospects, open a dialogue, and establish a relationship. It may send a catalog with ordering information or direct people to its Web site to enable prospects to further connect with Dell directly.

The Evolution of Direct Marketing

Direct marketing is the oldest marketing method, and today it is growing incredibly fast, propelled by the major social and technological changes of recent decades. Over 65 percent of American women now work outside the home.[15] So while families have more income, they have less time to spend shopping, thus making the convenience of telephones and the Internet an important factor in direct marketing.

Likewise, the expanding use of credit cards has revolutionized the way consumers buy goods and services. Electronic, cashless transactions make products easier and faster to purchase. And now, with advances in credit card security technology, more and more people are shopping right from their computers.

Companies are expected to spend more than $161 billion on direct marketing in the United States in 2005. (Exhibit 16–1 shows the largest direct-response agencies in the United States.) Those expenditures are expected to generate $1.85 trillion in sales in 2005, or 7 percent of total sales in the U.S. economy. Direct marketing–driven sales are forecast to grow by 6.4 percent through 2009, faster than the 4.8 percent growth rate in overall U.S. sales.

Direct marketing advertising expenditures accounted for 47.9 percent of total advertising in 2004, up from 46.9 percent in 1999. The most popular channels in 2005 continued to be direct mail and telemarketing. But direct marketing is poised to become more Internet-oriented in the next five years, as expenditures in Internet marketing and commercial e-mail are predicted to grow three times faster than expenditures in other media.[16]

The boom in telecommunications and computer technology is spurring the growth of direct marketing worldwide. In the mid-1990s, for instance, European spending on direct marketing jumped by more than 23 percent to $46 billion. Today, Germany is by far the largest national market in Europe, spending more than $25 billion on direct marketing efforts annually. Britain comes in second at more than $17 billion, followed closely by France. Interestingly, outside the United States, Japan is by far the number-one market for direct marketing, with estimated annual spending close to $70 billion.[17]

However, certain challenges in foreign markets have limited the growth of direct marketing efforts. There are, of course, a wide variety of legal and regulatory environments to contend with. Likewise, payment and postal systems in different countries vary considerably, as do conventions for addressing mail. And finally, cultural nuances and language can get in the way.

Web sites are an example of linkage media because they provide a way for consumers to hook up with companies. An integrated campaign of radio, print, e-mail, and pop-up ads for Procter and Gamble products like Tampax and Always instructed girls to visit www.beinggirl.com to register for a sweepstakes. Photography by Lauren Greenfield, who specializes in "girl culture," and questions from real girls heightened the impact of the print ads. The Leo Burnett (Chicago) campaign was a critical and commercial success; it resulted in 200,000 Web site visits in a four-week period and won a Cannes Gold Lion.

Exhibit 16–1

Largest direct-response agencies in the United States.

Rank	Agencies	U.S. revenue ($ millions)
1	Draft Worldwide	$ 240,882
2	Rapp Collins	202,241
3	Wunderman	173,039
4	Ogilvy One	135,000
5	McCann Relationship Marketing	105,000
6	Brann	98,570
7	Grey Direct	88,000
8	Targetbase Marketing	56,917
9	Devon Direct	38,800
10	Protocol Marketing Services	32,793

```
Microsoft Access - [Customers : Table]
File  Edit  View  Insert  Format  Records  Tools  Window  Help  Show Me
```

Company Name	Contact Name	Contact Title
Alfreds Futterkiste	Maria Anders	Sales Representative
Ana Trujillo Emparedados y helados	Ana Trujillo	Owner
Antonio Moreno Taquería	Antonio Moreno	Owner
Around the Horn	Thomas Hardy	Sales Representative
Berglunds snabbköp	Christina Berglund	Order Administrator
Blauer See Delikatessen	Hanna Moos	Sales Representative
Blondel père et fils	Frédérique Citeaux	Marketing Manager
Bólido Comidas preparadas	Martín Sommer	Owner
Bon app'	Laurence Lebihan	Owner
Bottom-Dollar Markets	Elizabeth Lincoln	Accounting Manager
B's Beverages	Victoria Ashworth	Sales Representative
Cactus Comidas para llevar	Patricio Simpson	Sales Agent
Centro comercial Moctezuma	Francisco Chang	Marketing Manager
Chop-suey Chinese	Yang Wang	Owner
Comércio Mineiro	Pedro Afonso	Sales Associate
Consolidated Holdings	Elizabeth Brown	Sales Representative
Drachenblut Delikatessen	Sven Ottlieb	Order Administrator
Du monde entier	Janine Labrune	Owner
Eastern Connection	Ann Devon	Sales Agent
Ernst Handel	Roland Mendel	Sales Manager
Familia Arquibaldo	Aria Cruz	Marketing Assistant
FISSA Fabrica Inter. Salchichas S.A.	Diego Roel	Accounting Manager

```
Record:  |◀  ◀       3  ▶ |▶| |▶*|  of 91       ◀
Datasheet View
```

Database marketing was much more difficult before the development of personal computers because of the intense data management requirements. Today, with the cost of personal computers under $1,000, even the smallest companies can engage in complex database building and marketing strategies.

The Impact of Databases on Direct Marketing

Modern computer technology enables marketers to compile and analyze important customer information in unprecedented ways. Pitney Bowes, for instance, was the dominant company in the postal meter business. However, its growth rate and profitability were flattening. So the company used its database to identify its best customers, their value to the organization, and their needs and buying behavior. From this, Pitney Bowes created a **customer lifetime value (LTV)** model based on the customer's historical and potential worth. Computing and ranking the lifetime value of all of its 1.2 million customers showed that more than two-thirds of the customer base value resided in fewer than 10 percent of the customers. The company also found it had a major retention problem within its low-volume, low-cost accounts. Cancellation rates were running as high as 40 percent per year in some segments. This analysis led Pitney Bowes to develop a distinct direct marketing strategy for both its best and its worst customers. It began a sophisticated *loyalty program* for its best customers and a *retention program* for its problem accounts. By the end of the first year, the program had reduced attrition by 20 percent, and the reduction in cost of sales alone paid back the entire direct marketing investment.[18] In another situation, a company might determine from its LTV analysis that its best course of action is simply to drop the most unprofitable customers.

Loyalty (or **continuity**) **programs** are designed to reward customers for their continued business. Most loyalty programs compensate consumers for frequent and continuous patronage. The frequent flyer club, introduced by American Airlines in 1981, is the model for today's continuity programs. Consumer purchases are tabulated on a company's database and discounts, free products, or services are awarded when specific levels are reached. The database can also provide the company with a demographic profile and purchase history for each customer.

The database is the key to direct marketing success. It enables marketers to target, segment, and grade customers. It is the corporate memory of all important customer information. It should record every transaction across all points of contact. The company that understands its customers' needs and wants better than any of its competitors, and consequently retains more of its best customers, will create a sustainable competitive advantage.

The database also lets the company measure the efficiency of its direct-response advertising efforts to determine, for instance, which radio or TV commercials, or which mailing lists, perform the best.

Working with a marketing database requires two processes: database management and database query. **Database management** is the process of gathering, consolidating, updating, and enhancing the information about customers and prospects that resides in the database. For most companies of any significant size, this requires a sophisticated computer system due to the complexity and volume of the processes involved.

Most important, the database enables marketers to make **database queries** to manipulate, analyze, and rank all the information to make better marketing decisions. Thanks to new software, this can now be accomplished on relatively inexpensive, Windows-based desktop PCs sometimes networked to database servers.

Account number	Month of purchase	Recency points	No. of purchases	Frequency points	Dollar purchases	Monetary points	Total points	Carryover points	Cumulative points
701	7	12	1	4	37.45	3.75	19.75		
701	10	24	2	8	17.86	1.79	33.79	16	69.54
702	6	6	2	8	25.43	2.54	16.54	4	20.54
703	4	6	1	4	33.22	3.32	13.32		
703	8	12	2	8	42.34	4.23	24.23		
703	11	24	1	4	18.95	1.90	29.90	7	74.45
704	9	12	1	4	109.45	9.00	25.00	23	48.00
705	5	6	2	8	37.65	3.77	17.77		
705	7	12	3	12	49.63	4.96	28.96	0	46.73
706							0.00	43	43.00

Notes:
- Points assigned by recency of purchase: current quarter—24 points; last 6 months—12 points; last 9 months—6 points; and last 12 months—3 points.
- Frequency points: number of purchases × 4.
- Monetary points: 10 percent of dollar purchase, with a ceiling of 9 points.
- Carryover points: Points carried over from previous calendar year.
- Cumulative total points: Total account points plus carryover from previous calendar year.

The RFM formula is a mathematical model that provides marketers with a method for determining the most valuable customers in a company's database, according to *recency, frequency,* and *monetary* variables. The cumulative points total is a measure of relative customer importance to the company—the larger the value, the more likely a customer is to make additional purchases of significant value. The higher-value customers, such as account numbers 701 and 703, are likely prospects for targeted mailings and special offers.

Exhibit 16–2

RFM (recency, frequency, monetary) analysis of accounts, December 2004.

In the same vein, direct marketing expert Bob Stone recommends using an **RFM formula** *(recency, frequency, monetary)* to identify the best customers—the ones most likely to buy again (see Exhibit 16–2). The best customers have bought recently, they buy frequently, and they spend the most money. Customers may be further ranked by the type of merchandise or services they buy, information that becomes very useful in the effort to cross-sell other merchandise.[19]

A company may simply purchase a mailing list as its initial database. There are typically three types of data available for purchase: demographic, lifestyle (leisure interests), and behavioristics (purchase habits).[20]

The Importance of Direct Marketing to IMC

Perhaps the greatest reason for direct marketing's current growth is that marketers and agencies realize they can't do the job with just one medium anymore. As the mass audience fragmented and companies began to integrate their marketing communications, customer databases became key to retaining and growing customers.

Direct marketing is the best way to develop a good database. The database enables the marketer to build a relationship by learning about customers in-depth: their nuances, what and where they buy, what they're interested in, and what they need. With a database, companies can choose the prospects they can serve most effectively and profitably—the purpose of all marketing. "You don't want a relationship with every customer," says Philip Kotler. "In fact, there are some bad customers out there."[21]

People like to see themselves as unique, not part of some 100-million-member mass market. Through direct marketing, especially addressable electronic media, companies can send discrete messages to individual customers and prospects. With different types of sales promotion (discussed in the last part of this chapter), a company can encourage individuals, not masses, to respond and can develop a relationship with each person. By responding, the prospect self-selects, in effect giving the marketer permission to begin a relationship.[22] The direct marketing database, then, becomes the company's primary tool to initiate, build, cultivate, and measure the effectiveness of its loyalty efforts.[23]

By providing a tangible response, direct marketing offers accountability. Marketers can count the responses and determine the cost per response. They can also judge the effectiveness of the medium they're using and test different creative executions.

Direct marketing offers convenience to time-sensitive consumers, and it offers precision and flexibility to cost-sensitive marketers. For example, to reach small B2B markets, there is no more cost-effective method than the database-driven, direct-response media.

Also, the economics of direct marketing are becoming more favorable. It used to be easy for big companies to spend a few million dollars for prime-time network TV spots when everybody was home watching and the average cost was only a penny to 10 cents per person. But those days are over. Everybody's not home today. And if they are, they're watching 150 different channels or a video. They have a remote control to mute ads. Further, network TV advertising is far more expensive than it used to be. Thus, targeted, direct-response media (magazines, cable TV, direct mail, e-mail, kiosks) are more cost-competitive than ever before.

Finally, unlike the public mass media, direct-response media can be more private. A company can conduct a sales letter campaign without the competition ever knowing about it.

Drawbacks to Direct Marketing

At the same time, direct marketing still faces some challenges. In the past, direct marketers were sales oriented, not relationship oriented. This gave direct marketing a bad reputation in the minds of many consumers. Some people also enjoy the experience of visiting retail stores and shopping. They like to see and feel the goods personally, and they are hesitant to buy goods sight unseen. This is why the objective of many direct marketing campaigns is now to help drive traffic to retail locations.

Direct marketing efforts often have to stand on their own without the content support of the media that advertising enjoys. They don't always get the prestigious affiliation offered by some media. This makes it more difficult (and costly) to build image for the product, something mass-media advertising is particularly good at.

Direct marketing also suffers from clutter. People are deluged with mail from commercial sponsors and drum-beating politicians. Cable channels are filled with infomercials for food processors. And telemarketing pitches for insurance plans intrude on consumers at home and at work.

Many consumers are also concerned with privacy. They don't like having their names sold by list vendors. At one national forum of direct marketers, attendees were told they must self-regulate, give consumers more control, and treat privacy like a customer service issue—or risk legislation restricting access to the information they desperately need.[24] Wise marketers have heeded these warnings and developed methods for responsible direct marketing.

CONCEPT CHECK

Explain why direct marketing is such an important component of IMC. What challenges does direct marketing continue to face?

Types of Direct Marketing Activities

All direct marketers face two basic strategy decisions: the extent to which they will use *direct sales* and the extent to which they will use *direct-response advertising*. They can use either or both.

Direct Sales

In a **direct-sales** strategy, marketers' representatives sell to customers directly, either at home or at work, rather than through a retail establishment or some other intermediary. Direct sales feature *personal* (face-to-face) *direct selling* or *telemarketing*.

Personal Direct Selling

Professors Robert Peterson and Thomas Wotruba define **direct selling** as face-to-face selling away from a fixed retail location. In this sense, direct selling usually refers to a method of marketing consumer goods—everything from encyclopedias and insurance to cosmetics and nutritional products.[25] Companies such as Avon, Amway, Herbalife, Mary Kay Cosmetics, World Book, and Tupperware have achieved very high levels of success in direct sales. In personal direct selling, the representative introduces the product to the customer, convinces the customer of the product's value, and, if successful, completes the sale. There are two main forms of personal selling: person-to-person and group sales. In some *network marketing* (or multilevel marketing—MLM) organizations such as Amway, Nikken, and Shaklee, the direct salespeople are both distributors (sellers) and end users. They often do very little actual retailing of the products. Their primary effort is usually to recruit new distributors who will buy the products at wholesale and consume them personally.

The Peterson–Wotruba definition of direct selling could also apply to business-to-business marketing, since it typically occurs "away from a fixed retail location." However, the common term for this is simply *personal selling*. And since it is so important to B2B marketers, we will deal with that subject more completely in the next section of this chapter.

Each year telemarketing generates more than \$700 billion in sales in the United States. It is cited as the direct marketing medium of choice, providing elements of direct personal sales yet at a substantially lower cost. Telemarketing also integrates easily into database management campaigns for gathering new data and for utilizing the collected data.

Telemarketing

As a method of direct sales, telemarketing has been used for decades, but the term is relatively new. **Telemarketing** includes selling and prospecting by telephone, answering phone inquiries, and providing sales-related services to callers. The information collected is also used to update the company's customer database. Telemarketing is the major source of income for some companies and organizations, such as nonprofit and charitable causes, political candidates, and home-study courses. In 2002, marketers spent 39 percent of all their direct marketing media expenditures, or an estimated \$80.3 billion, on outbound telemarketing calls to both consumers and businesses. This generated an estimated \$719.5 billion in total sales.[26]

The reasons for this are economics and consumers' acceptance of teleculture. First, telemarketing costs a lot less money than personal selling. Second, people have come to accept the idea of shopping by phone. It's convenient, hassle-free, and inexpensive. In the United States, the toll-free telephone business is booming. In any given week, 30,000 to 50,000 toll-free numbers are added across North America. Heavy demand caused the pool of 800 numbers to run dry in 1996. Soon thereafter, concern grew that

even the 888 numbers faced depletion, leading to limits on their allocation. Then 877 and 866 numbers were introduced, with other numbers to be added for toll-free use as needed.[27]

Telemarketing is the next best thing to a face-to-face, personal sales call. In the business-to-business arena, for example, good telemarketers can develop strong, lasting relationships with customers they have never met but with whom they speak every week. Stand Out Designs in San Diego employs highly skilled telemarketers who call on zoos, museums, and boutique retailers all across the country to get them to order and stock the company's unique line of silk-screened T-shirts. The telemarketers don't just take orders; they counsel the dealers with display and promotion suggestions, offer advertising tips, and arrange for special imprints on the shirts when appropriate.

When combined with other direct-response media, telemarketing becomes even more effective. For example, experience shows that when telemarketing is combined with direct mail, there is usually at least a 10 percent increase in responses—often a lot more.

Direct-Response Advertising

Advertising that asks the reader, viewer, or listener to provide feedback straight to the sender is called **direct-response advertising.** Any medium can be used for direct response, but the most common are direct mail, catalogs, magazines, and TV.

Direct Mail

Next to personal selling and telemarketing, direct mail is the most effective method for closing a sale or generating inquiries. It's very useful to direct marketers seeking an immediate response. In 2002, marketers spent approximately $49.1 billion on direct-mail advertising, or 23.8 percent of all direct marketing expenditures. Sales directly attributed to direct-mail advertising reached $246 billion in the B2B category and $390.7 billion in the consumer segment.[28]

As we discussed in Chapter 13, direct mail is an important medium to many advertisers.

Catalogs, such as this one from Lands' End (www.landsend.com), display a company's products and enable customers to order at their convenience via mail, phone, fax, or Internet. J. Crew, Victoria's Secret, the Sharper Image, and Lands' End are just a few of the multitude of consumer catalogs available today.

Catalog Sales

The largest direct marketers are the catalog companies. **Catalogs** are reference books (and now also CD-ROMs) that list, describe, and usually picture the products sold by a manufacturer, wholesaler, jobber, or retailer. With more high-income families shopping at home, specialized catalogs are becoming very popular. Some catalog retailers prosper with specialized approaches like outdoor clothing and equipment (L.L. Bean, Lands' End), electronic gadgets (Sharper Image), and gourmet foods (Balducci's).

Catalogs are big business. In 2001, the catalog industry spent some $14.3 billion in advertising and generated more than $125.9 billion in both B2B and consumer sales. The top 10 catalog companies did over $71.4 billion in business in 2003. And in that year, Dell, the leading catalog marketer, alone sold more than $35 *billion* worth of merchandise.[29]

To increase readership and stand out from the glut of other catalogs, some marketers have added editorial and slick photography, all designed to sell a certain image. Abercrombie & Fitch, for instance, publishes its *A&F Magazine* (which replaced the thicker, glossier *A&F Quarterly* magalog in December 2003). The magazine supplements the clothing line with advice on how to attain a "cool" lifestyle beyond what you wear. By selling the Abercrombie lifestyle, A&F hopes to bring more people into the stores.[30] At the same time, though, A&F has stirred up a lot of controversy by using its catalog to parade a host of nude and seminude models, often in very suggestive poses.

Direct-Response Print Advertising

Newspaper ads and inserts featuring coupons or listing toll-free phone numbers can be very effective at stimulating customer responses. Today, the same is true with magazines. Moreover, in magazines, advertisers can devote most of the space to image-building, thus maximizing the medium's power. We discussed the use of print media in Chapter 11.

Direct-Response Broadcast Advertising

Television is a powerful instrument for direct marketers like Total Gym because of its mass coverage and the ability to display and demonstrate the product with sound and full color right before the customers' eyes.

Direct marketers' use of TV and radio has increased dramatically in recent years. Total Gym, whose products are normally sold through health care and physical fitness professionals, worked with American Telecast to develop a 30-minute infomercial featuring TV star Chuck Norris and supermodel Christie Brinkley. The campaign exceeded their wildest expectations, producing more than $100 million in sales the first year and continuing to generate similar returns for the next four years.[31] As Exhibit 16–3 shows, relatively young and affluent people are watching infomercials and buying the advertised products.

For many years, radio commentator Paul Harvey was very successful pitching a wide variety of products to his loyal audience. Likewise, talk jocks Howard Stern and Rush Limbaugh made Snapple an overnight success by drinking the product and touting its good taste on the air. Still, until fairly recently, radio has rarely been the medium of choice for direct-response advertising. Radio industry executives now expect to see a dramatic increase in the number of direct-response ads on radio. We discussed radio, TV, and infomercials in Chapter 12.

> Describe the two basic strategic alternatives available to direct marketers.

CONCEPT CHECK

Interactive Media

Interactive media systems allow customers and prospects to control both the content and the pace of presentations and to order merchandise directly from the system. The most popular interactive media currently are online personal computers. Although still in the development stage, interactive TV may allow viewers to respond to questions during a commercial, giving advertisers a wealth of demographic information for future promotions. The use of the new digital interactive media was explored in depth in Chapter 13. Now let's take a brief look at the ultimate interactive communication tool, personal selling.

Exhibit 16–3

Who watches (and buys from) infomercials.

	Total viewers	Total buyers
Primary gender	Female, 53.2%	Female, 51.7%
Mean age	41.2	45.9
Primary ethnicity	Caucasian	Caucasian
Primary employment	Full-time	Full-time
Marital status	Married, 49.3%	Married, 60.3%
Children present	Yes, 40.1%	Yes, 43.1%
Residence	Suburban	Suburban
Mean household income	$56,000	$55,000

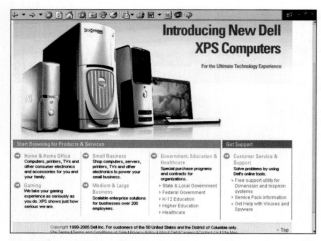

Many companies make their products easily available online. By visiting a comprehensive Web site like Dell's, whose only storefront is, in fact, the Web site, customers can purchase practically everything they previously might buy through a catalog or over the phone. Customers can also check on the status of their orders or get support on products they may already have.

This pharmaceutical sales representative is engaging in missionary selling when she presents the benefits of her products to a doctor. The representative understands that the doctor will not place an order, but she is attempting to get the doctor to prescribe the pharmaceutical for his patients so her company will get an order from the patient's drugstore.

Personal Selling: The Human Medium

Personal selling is the best marketing communication tool for relationship building because the sales rep and the customer are face to face. It's the ultimate one-to-one medium. It's also the most expensive medium. For most companies, personal selling expenditures far exceed expenditures for advertising. And in many companies, the primary role of advertising is to lend support to the sales force either directly by producing leads or indirectly by creating a positive atmosphere for the sales call.

Personal selling can be defined in a number of ways, depending on the orientation of the company using it. For our purposes we define **personal selling** as the *interpersonal communication* process by which a seller ascertains and then satisfies the needs of a buyer, to the mutual, long-term benefit of both parties.[32]

Thus, the task of personal selling is a lot more than just making a sale. The objective of personal selling should be to build a relationship, a partnership, that will provide long-term benefits to both buyer and seller (a win-win situation). The salesperson discovers the buyer's needs by helping the customer identify problems, offers information about potential solutions, assists the buyer in making decisions, and provides after-sale service to ensure long-term satisfaction. Influence and persuasion are only one part of selling. The major part is problem solving.

Types of Personal Selling

Everyone sells, at one time or another. Children sell lemonade, magazine subscriptions, and Girl Scout cookies. Students sell prom tickets, yearbook ads, and term papers. Doctors sell diets to unwilling patients. Lawyers sell pleas to skeptical juries. And cops sell traffic safety to nervous motorists.

The fact is that everything has to be sold, by someone to somebody. A retail clerk may sell you a pocket calculator. Behind that clerk is a virtual army of other salespeople who sold raw materials to the manufacturer, capital equipment for use in the manufacturing process, business services such as human resources and accounting, plant and office furniture, vehicles, advertising services, media space and time, and insurance. Then the manufacturer's salespeople sold the calculator to a wholesaler who, of course, had to buy transportation services and warehousing from other salespeople. And then the wholesaler's sales reps sold the calculator to the retail outlet where you bought it.

As this scenario shows, people in sales work for a wide variety of organizations and call on an equally wide variety of customers. They may call on other businesses to sell products or services used in the manufacture of other products. They may call on resellers—people who buy the product, add value, and resell it. Or they may sell to consumers, either in a retail store or, as we discussed earlier, in a direct selling situation away from a fixed retail location.

Because advertising is basically designed to support and reinforce a company's sales efforts, advertising people (whether in the company or at an agency) have to understand the selling environment their companies or clients deal in. Many companies have their advertising people make calls with the sales force for this very reason. The advertising person can experience firsthand what questions prospects ask, how customers view the company (and its competitors), how people use the company's product, and what information (in either an ad or a piece of sales material) might help the salesperson communicate better with the prospect.

Advantages of Personal Selling

The greatest strength of personal selling is its personal nature. Nothing is as persuasive as personal communication. A skilled salesperson can observe a prospect's body language and read between the lines to detect what's troubling the customer. The rep can ask questions and answer queries as they arise. The face-to-face situation facilitates instant feedback. And the rep has the flexibility to adjust the presentation, tailoring it specifically to the needs and interests of the particular prospect. Not only that, the salesperson can demonstrate the product live. And the rep can negotiate, finding those terms that best suit the buyer's needs.

Time is on the rep's side, too. The sale doesn't have to be made today. The relationship has to be established, though, and a human being is better at doing that than any nonpersonal medium.

One of the major jobs of personal selling is to gain distribution for new products—a task no other communication tool can do as well. In fact, in many trade and industrial situations, personal contact may be vital to closing the sale. This is also true for certain high-ticket or technical consumer products such as camcorders, health care, and estate planning. In these cases, personal selling is well worth its high cost—because it gets the job done.

Drawbacks of Personal Selling

Personal selling is very labor intensive. That's why it's the most costly way to communicate with prospects. This is its single biggest weakness. A business-to-business sales call today costs well in excess of $300. Not only that, it's very time-consuming. Because it is basically a one-on-one medium, there are few economies of scale.

This is why one important role of advertising is to reduce the cost of sales by communicating as much relevant information as possible about the company and its products to prospects and customers before the salesperson even calls. That information may be functional (specifically about the product) or symbolic (building image and credibility for the company).

Another drawback is the poor reputation of personal selling with many people. Decades of "suede shoe" salesmen employing high-pressure tactics, have dishonored the profession. Thus the common jibe: "Would you buy a used car from that man?" Salespeople are frequently given fancier titles such as marketing associate, marketing representative, or account manager in an attempt to reduce guilt or the rejection associated with personal selling.[33]

There's an old saw about one bad apple ruining a barrel. Imagine spending millions of dollars on a nationwide advertising campaign to communicate your expertise and good customer service and then sending an unprofessional sales force out that is improperly groomed or, worse, ignorant of product features and benefits and lacking empathy for customer needs. Unfortunately, it happens all the time. The salesperson has incredible power to either make or break a delicate relationship. As a result, sophisticated firms go to great lengths to screen sales applicants to find the right personality

> **What are the key advantages and potential drawbacks associated with personal selling?**

CONCEPT CHECK

Personal selling is one of the most important facets of an IMC strategy because of the personal nature of the contact. Skilled salespeople can use their creativity to identify customer needs and problems and find solutions that are profitable for both the customer and the company.

attributes and then invest heavily in training. Of course, this goes both ways. A tasteless advertising campaign can hurt a company's national reputation more than one bad salesperson. As always, it's the responsibility of marketing management to ensure consistency among what the advertising presents, what the sales force promises, and what the company actually delivers.

The Role of Personal Selling in IMC

Salespeople are the company's communicators. In fact, to the customer who doesn't know anybody else at the company, the salesperson doesn't just represent the firm. He or she is the firm. The customer's impression of the salesperson, therefore, will frequently govern his or her perception of the company. Again, this makes the sales rep a very important person.

In an integrated marketing communications program, personal selling can play a very important role. Salespeople provide four distinct communications functions: information gathering, information providing, order fulfillment, and relationship building. We'll discuss each of these briefly.

Gathering Information

Sales reps often serve as the eyes and ears of the company. Because they are out in the field talking to customers or attending trade shows, they have access to information and they can see trends. For example, salespeople provide information on who's new in the business, how customers are reacting to new products or styles, what the competition is doing, and where new sales opportunities might exist. Generally, information gathering by the sales force relates to three areas: prospecting; determining customer wants, needs, and abilities; and monitoring the competition.

Providing Information

Salespeople not only gather information, they deliver it. In fact, the stereotype (both negative and positive) of a good salesperson is someone who is a good talker, articulate and persuasive. In truth, a superior salesperson is a good listener first and a good talker second. Salespeople impart information both upstream and downstream within their organization. They deliver information to customers about the company and its products, they recommend solutions to problems, and they use information to communicate value and to build relationships and trust.

Personal selling incorporates all three legs of the IMC integration triangle we learned about in Chapter 7—say → do → confirm—because what the rep says and does will either confirm or contradict the company's other messages. The rep's skill, therefore, will definitely color the relationship between the company and the customer. It's critically important that the salesperson's performance be consistent with the firm's positioning and reinforce its other marketing communications.

Fulfilling Orders

There comes a time in every relationship when someone has to make a commitment. Asking for that commitment can be very difficult if the preceding steps have not been handled well. The inevitable tasks of personal selling are to motivate the customer to action, close the sale, and then make sure the goods and services are delivered correctly.

An important part of personal selling is following up after the sale, making sure the goods or services are delivered in a timely fashion, and seeing to it that the customer is completely satisfied. This is a combination of the "do" and "confirm" steps, and it's critical to continued relationship building.

This is also where cross-functional management and open communication come back into play. If there is any kind of manufacturing glitch or delay in shipping, the salesperson needs to notify the customer immediately. But to do that, the salesperson must be informed. Similarly, goods need to be protected and shipped with care. Salespeople hate to receive calls from new customers saying their first shipment arrived with damaged goods. All employees, including those in the warehouse, need to understand the impact of their actions.

Building Relationships

A company's sales staff should be the ultimate relationship marketers. People naturally want to buy from the salesperson they like and trust. Salespeople build relationships by paying attention to three simple things: keeping commitments, servicing their accounts, and solving problems. Interestingly, those are also probably the three basic requirements for any company's success.

Here again, advertising people can help. When a company advertises, it is making a commitment to its customers and prospects. It is very difficult for a salesperson to keep those commitments if the advertising has overpromised. So puffery should be avoided wherever possible, since by its very nature, it tends to overpromise.

Likewise, it's difficult for salespeople to adequately service their accounts if every time people call customer service they get a busy signal. This happened to the giant telephone utility U.S. West when it downsized and reengineered the company. It continued running ads touting its great service, but nobody could get through to them. Not smart. Advertising people have to know what's going on in the company, and sometimes they need to recommend that advertising be stopped.

Finally, advertising as well as salespeople should be concerned with solving problems. If the sales staff uncovers a problem that customers frequently encounter, and the company's product can help solve that problem, then that should become the focus of some planned communications—advertising, publicity, or company-sponsored events.

> **CONCEPT CHECK**
>
> Describe the roles salespeople can play in an IMC program.

The Role of Sales Promotion in IMC

Imagine walking into the fresh-fruit section of your local grocery store, picking up a big, juicy mango, and discovering a sticker on it stating: "Now available in Snapple. Mango Madness." You turn around and suddenly notice that there, right next to the fresh-fruit bin, stands a big display of, you guessed it, Snapple Mango Madness.

It actually happened. New York agency Kirshenbaum, Bond & Partners launched Snapple's new Mango Madness drink nationally with stickers on 30 million pieces of fruit.[34] Talk about out-of-the-box thinking and creative media planning! Moreover, it was an outstanding example of how sales promotion can be perfectly integrated with a company's positioning, in this case Snapple's "100% natural" message strategy.

The term *sales promotion* is often misunderstood or confused with advertising or publicity. This may be because sales promotion activities often occur simultaneously and use both advertising and publicity as part of the process. In truth, though, it is a very specific marketing communications activity.

Sales promotion is a direct inducement that offers extra incentives anywhere along the marketing route to enhance or accelerate the product's movement from producer to consumer. Within this definition, there are three important elements to consider. Sales promotion

- May be used anywhere in the marketing channel: from manufacturer to wholesaler, wholesaler to dealer, dealer to customer, or manufacturer to customer.

- Normally involves a direct inducement (such as money, prizes, extra products, gifts, or specialized information) that provides extra incentives to buy now or buy more, visit a store, request literature, display a product, or take some other action.

- Is designed to change the timing of a purchase or to shift inventory to others in the channel.

Let's see how this definition applies to Snapple. In an interesting combination of both consumer advertising and *trade promotion* (sales promotion aimed at members of the distribution channel), Snapple used the fresh mangoes as an unusual new advertising medium to introduce its Mango Madness to consumers and to stimulate initial demand for the drink. The magnitude of that media effort (30 million pieces of fruit) served as a huge incentive to retailers to grant Snapple extra floor space (very expensive real estate, by the way) to display Mango Madness right next to the fresh-fruit stand. The result: Snapple sold a lot more Mango Madness a lot faster, and for a lot less money, than they would have if they had just placed some expensive ads in consumer magazines or on TV. Moreover, by creatively integrating different forms of marketing communications, Snapple simultaneously bolstered its positioning strategy and enhanced its relationship with the retail trade—its primary customer.

Some marketers consider sales promotion supplementary to advertising and personal selling because it binds the two together, making both more effective. In reality, however, sales promotion is far more than supplementary. One study showed marketers spend 54 percent of their advertising/promotion budget on sales promotion compared to only 46 percent for advertising.[35] We'll see why shortly.

Sales promotion is expensive. But it's also effective. Unfortunately, it has serious drawbacks, which lead to furious battles in marketing circles between proponents of sales promotion and proponents of advertising. Each approach has an important role to play, but advertisers must consider the positives and negatives and get the balance right.

Snapple's clever promotion of its Mango Madness flavor demonstrates an ingenious integration of sales promotion and product positioning. By placing a sticker ad on actual mangoes in the fresh-fruit section, Snapple reinforced its slogan of "100% natural" and grabbed the attention of customers not necessarily looking to buy the beverage. The marketing strategy was supported by placing bottles of Mango Madness in close proximity to the fruit.

The Positive Effect of Sales Promotion on Brand Volume

Effective sales promotion accomplishes a number of things. First of all, it adds tangible, immediate, extra value to the brand. Snapple's creative media buy suddenly made Mango Madness more valuable to the retail trade. This induced retailers to stock up on the new product and display it prominently. Similarly, when Dell Computers runs a million-dollar sweepstakes, it's adding instant value to the products it sells. This is why we refer to sales promotion as the *value-added tool.*

Second, by adding immediate value, sale promotion *maximizes* sales volume. A short-term price cut or rebate, for instance, may be very effective

Checklist

Creating Effective Sales Promotions

- **Set specific objectives.** Undisciplined, undirected creative work is a waste of time and resources.
- **Set a theme that is relevant.** Start with a strategy, preferably from a unified marketing or advertising plan. Stay on track: A promotion for the telephone giant NYNEX reinforced its "If it's out there, it's in here" campaign with a sweepstakes asking consumers to look up the "heading of the day" in the phone book and note the page.
- **Involve the trade.** Build relationships. Carrier Air Conditioning sponsored the Junior Olympics in key markets, sharing sponsorship with its dealer in each city.
- **Coordinate promotional efforts with other marketing plans.** Be sure to coordinate schedules and plans. A consumer promotion should occur simultaneously with a trade promotion; a free sample promotion should be timed to the introduction of a new line.
- **Know how basic promotion techniques work.** A sweepstakes shouldn't be used to encourage multiple purchases. A price-off deal can't reverse a brand's downward sales trend.
- **Use simple, attention-getting copy.** Most promotions are built around a simple idea: "Save 75 cents." Emphasize the idea and don't try to be cute.
- **Use contemporary, easy-to-read graphics.** Don't expect to fit 500 words and 20 illustrations into a quarter-page freestanding insert.
- **Clearly communicate the concept.** Words and graphics must work together to get the message across.
- **Add advertising when you need measurable responses.** When part of a promotion, advertising directed at too broad an audience is usually wasted. However, trial-building promotions designed to attract new users, for example, can be helped by targeted advertising.
- **Reinforce the brand's advertising message.** Tie promotions to the brand's ad campaign.
- **Support the brand's positioning and image.** This is especially important for image-sensitive brands and categories, like family-oriented Kraft.
- **Know the media you work through.** Determine which media will work best. Should samples be distributed in stores, door to door, or through direct mail? Does the promotion need newspaper or magazine support?
- **Pretest promotions.** Pretesting doesn't have to be expensive. For packaged goods, small samplings in a few stores can reveal how to maximize coupon redemption rates by testing various values, creative approaches, and delivery methods.

at boosting sales. While advertising helps develop and reinforce a quality, differentiated brand reputation, and build long-term market value, sales promotion helps build short-term *market volume*. To become a market leader, therefore, a brand needs both advertising and sales promotion.

Finally, when all brands appear to be equal, sales promotion can be more effective than advertising in motivating customers to try a new brand or to select one brand over another. It can also motivate some customers who might be unmoved by advertising efforts. And sales promotions often generate a more immediate, measurable payoff than traditional advertising campaigns. This is why we might also refer to sales promotion as the "sales accelerator."

To succeed, sales promotions should be creative and hard to imitate. Kirshenbaum, Bond & Partners certainly demonstrated that with their Snapple labels. The Checklist, "Creating Effective Sales Promotions" outlines some basic ideas to consider in designing promotions.

The Negative Effect of Sales Promotion on Brand Value

Advertisers need to understand the negative effects of sales promotion, too. For instance, excessive sales promotion at the expense of advertising can reduce profitability. Some marketers believe a proper expenditure balance for consumer packaged-good products is approximately 60 percent for trade and consumer promotion, 40 percent for advertising.

A high level of trade sales promotion relative to advertising and consumer sales promotion has a positive effect on short-term market share but may have a negative effect on brand attitudes and long-term market share. Without an effective advertising effort to emphasize brand image and quality, customers become deal-prone rather than brand loyal. And overemphasis on price (whether in advertising or sales promotion) eventually destroys brand equity.[36]

Another drawback of sales promotion is its high cost. One analysis showed that only 16 percent of sales promotions were profitable. In other words, some manufacturers spent more than $1 to generate an extra $1 of profits.[37]

Finally, overly aggressive sales promotion or advertising can draw competitors into a price war, which leads to reduced sales and profits for everyone.

Thus, if too much of the marketing mix is allocated to advertising, the brand may gain a high-quality, differentiated image but not enough volume to be a market leader. On the other hand, as Larry Light, McDonald's chief global marketing officer says, "Too much [sales] promotion, and the brand will have high volume but low profitability. Market leadership can be bought through bribes, but enduring profitable market leadership must be earned through building both brand value as well as volume."[38]

CONCEPT CHECK

What positive contributions can sales promotion make to a brand's performance? What are the potential downsides?

Sales Promotion Strategies and Tactics

To move their products through the distribution channel from the point of manufacture to the point of consumption, marketers employ two types of strategies: push and pull. **Push strategies** are primarily designed to secure the cooperation of retailers. **Trade promotions**—sales promotions aimed at members of the distribution channel—are one of the principal tactics marketers use to push products through the distribution pipeline and gain shelf space. We'll discuss some of these tactics in the next section. Marketers may also use **trade advertising** (advertising in publications read by members of the trade) as a push tactic.

Pull strategies, on the other hand, are designed to attract customers and increase demand for the product (see Exhibit 16–4). Consumer advertising and **consumer sales promotions** are examples of pull strategies because they are designed to induce consumers to seek out or ask for the product, in effect pulling the product through the pipeline. Today, some national advertisers spend more dollars on trade sales promotions than on either consumer sales promotions or media advertising. But that is often the price they have to pay to gain and maintain distribution, without which they cannot make any sales.

Exhibit 16–4

Two marketing communications approaches.

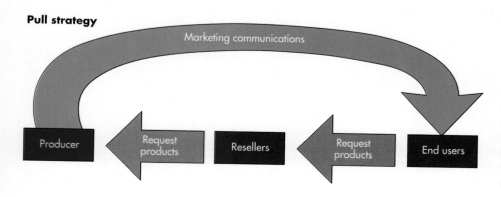

Push strategy

Producer → Marketing communications → Resellers → Marketing communications → End users

Pull strategy

Marketing communications

Producer ← Request products ← Resellers ← Request products ← End users

Giving Brands a Push with Trade Promotions

In supermarkets today, shelf space and floor space are hard to come by. To maintain their own images, department stores set standards for manufacturers' displays. This means that retailers often won't use the special racks, sales aids, and promotional literature supplied by manufacturers.

These are minor problems; major ones have to do with control of the marketplace. **Trade concentration**—more products going through fewer retailers—gives greater control to the retailers and less to the manufacturers. Increased competition for shelf space gives retailers even more power, enabling them to exact hefty deals and allowances. As a result, manufacturers of national brands often don't have enough money left to integrate consumer advertising or sales promotions.[39]

Despite these problems, many manufacturers still implement effective push strategies. And the smart ones safeguard enough money for consumer advertising. Trade tactics include slotting allowances, trade deals, display allowances, buyback allowances, advertising allowances, cooperative advertising and advertising materials, dealer premiums and contests, push money, and company conventions and dealer meetings.

Slotting Allowances

In response to the glut of new products, some retailers charge manufacturers **slotting allowances**—fees ranging from $15,000 to $40,000 or more for the privilege of obtaining shelf or floor space for a new product. The practice is controversial because some manufacturers think they're being forced to subsidize the retailer's cost of doing business. Smaller manufacturers complain that the allowances shut out all but the largest suppliers. The Federal Trade Commission and Small Business Administration are considering taking steps to limit the use of slotting allowances because they reduce competition.

Trade Deals

Manufacturers make **trade deals** with retailers by offering short-term discounts or other dollar inducements. To comply with the Robinson-Patman Act, trade deals must be offered proportionally to all dealers. Dealers usually pass the savings on to customers through short-term sale prices, or "specials."

Excessive trade deals threaten brand loyalty because they encourage customers to buy whatever brand is on sale. Furthermore, marketers who use trade discounts extensively find themselves in a vicious circle: If they cut back on the promotions, they may lose shelf space and then market share.

In addition, some retailers capitalize on trade discounts by engaging in forward buying and diverting. With **forward buying,** a retailer stocks up on a product when it is on discount and buys smaller amounts when it sells at regular price. **Diverting** means using the promotional

Trade promotions are business-to-business incentive programs that are strategically aimed at increasing distribution. This Rapala (www.rapala.com) ad aimed at manufacturers suggests that, for a "catchier" promotion, they should try putting their logo on Rapala's legendary lures.

You could put your logo on a golf ball, but then you'd have to play golf.

For a catchier promotion, put your logo on the legendary Rapala. Minimum order 300. Call 1-800-874-4451. **Rapala**

Manufacturers like DeWalt often pay a display allowance for their in-store exhibits, banners, and shelf signs. These fees benefit retailers like Home Depot by compensating them for the space occupied by the displays. And the manufacturer benefits from the increased exposure.

discount to purchase large quantities of an item in one region, then shipping portions of the buy to areas where the discount isn't offered.

Display Allowances

More and more stores charge manufacturers **display allowances**—fees to make room for and set up displays. In-store displays include counter stands, floor stands, shelf signs, and special racks that give the retailer ready-made, professionally designed vehicles for selling more of the featured products.

Buyback Allowances

When introducing a new product, manufacturers sometimes offer retailers a **buyback allowance** for the old product that hasn't sold. To persuade retailers to take on their product line, some manufacturers even offer a buyback allowance for a competitor's leftover stock.

Advertising Allowances

Manufacturers often offer **advertising allowances** as either a percentage of purchases or a flat fee paid to the retailer. Advertising allowances are more common for consumer than industrial products. They are offered primarily by large companies, but some smaller firms give them to high-volume customers. The purpose of these allowances is to encourage retailers to advertise the manufacturer's products, but compliance is not always enforced.

Co-op Advertising and Advertising Materials

With **cooperative (co-op) advertising,** national manufacturers reimburse their dealers for advertising the manufacturer's products or logos in their trading area. The manufacturer usually pays 50 to 100 percent of the dealer's advertising costs based on a percentage of the dealer's sales. Special co-op deals are used to introduce new products, advertise certain lines, or combat competitors.

Unlike advertising allowances, co-op programs typically require the dealer to submit invoices and proof of the advertising (*tearsheets* from the newspaper or affidavits of performance from radio or TV stations). Many manufacturers also give their dealers prepared advertising materials: ads, glossy photos, sample radio commercials, and so on. To control the image of their products, some advertisers insist that dealers use these materials to qualify for the co-op advertising money.

Dealer Premiums, Contests, and Push Money

To encourage retail dealers and salespeople to reach specific sales goals or push certain products, manufacturers may offer special prizes, gifts, or financial incentives. One inducement is cash payments made directly to the sales staff, called **push money (PM),** or **spiffs.** For example, a shoe salesperson may suggest shoe polish or some other high-profit extra; for each item sold, the salesperson receives a 25- to 50-cent spiff. Some retailers believe that manufacturer's incentives are a potential source of conflict, causing salespeople to serve their own self-interests rather than the interests of their employers. Ethics can also be an issue when dealers and salespeople push certain products on consumers solely for their personal gain.

Company Conventions and Dealer Meetings

Most major manufacturers hold **company conventions** and **dealer meetings** to introduce new products, announce sales promotion programs, or show new advertising campaigns. They may also conduct sales and service training sessions. Meetings can be a dynamic sales promotion tool for the manufacturer.

Push strategies are virtually invisible to consumers. Yet successful inducements mean the product gets more shelf space, a special display, or extra interest and enthusiasm from salespeople. And extra sales interest can spell the difference between failure and success.

Using Consumer Promotions to Pull Brands Through

One reason for today's increased focus on consumer sales promotions is the change in TV viewing habits. With cable TV, VCRs, and DVDs, fewer people watch any one program. Advertising audiences are more fragmented, and major manufacturers must turn to new methods to reach these moving targets.

Common consumer sales promotions include point-of-purchase materials, coupons, electronic coupons and convenience cards, cents-off promotions, refunds, rebates, premiums, sampling, combination offers, contests, and sweepstakes. A successful IMC campaign may integrate several of these techniques along with media advertising, product publicity, and direct marketing. Commercial Break 16–A offers the opportunity to apply what you've learned about push and pull strategies to the marketing of textbooks.

Consumer sales promotions expose potential customers to a product and induce them to seek it out. While trade promotions push products through distribution channels, consumer sales promotions are intended to pull the product through due to customer demand. This Nokia (www.nokia.com) point-of-purchase display can serve as both a trade and consumer promotional tool.

Point-of-Purchase (POP) Materials

Walk into any store and notice the number of display materials and advertising-like devices that are designed to build traffic, exhibit and advertise the product, and promote impulse buying. Collectively, these are all referred to as **point-of-purchase (POP) materials.**

POP works best when used with other forms of advertising. For example, by advertising its gum and candy, one marketer increased sales by about 150 percent. But when POP was added to the same program, the purchase rate jumped 550 percent.[40]

In one poll, 56 percent of mass-merchandise shoppers and 62 percent of grocery shoppers said they noticed point-of-purchase materials. More than half reported noticing signs and displays, 18 percent remembered coupon dispensers, and 14 percent could recall samplings and demonstrations.[41]

Today's consumers make their decisions in the store 66 percent of the time and make unplanned (impulse) purchases 53 percent of the time, so POP can often be the major factor in stimulating purchases.[42]

Commercial Break 16–A

Applying Push/Pull Strategies to Sales Promotion

Moving a product from the manufacturer to the consumer is not a simple task. Goods often have to go through four or five separate steps: from the manufacturer to an agent or broker, then to the wholesaler, to the retailer, and finally it gets to the consumer. Communicating messages along this same path can also be torturous. Something's bound to get lost along the way. This is why push and pull promotions are so important.

By offering incentives in the form of money, prizes, trips, and promotional materials to "push" products into the distribution pipeline, the marketer can also obtain invaluable middleman assistance. Pushing is when a com-

pany uses any form of marketing communication (personal selling, advertising, or sales promotion) to the trade for the purpose of gaining shelf space and cooperation. Reversing the process, the company can also use consumer advertising or offer rebates, coupons, two-for-one deals, or some other incentive directly to the customer. By stimulating demand, that form of communication helps "pull" products through the pipeline.

Applying the Breaks
If you were working for McGraw-Hill/Irwin (the publisher of this textbook), how would you suggest using push and/or pull strategies to increase the sales of the company's textbooks? Which strategy do you think would be more effective?

POP materials may also include window displays, counter displays, floor and wall racks to hold the merchandise, streamers, and posters. Often, the product's shipping cartons are designed to double as display units. A complete information center may even provide literature, samples, product photos, or an interactive computer in a kiosk.

The trend toward self-service retailing has increased the importance of POP materials. With fewer and less knowledgeable salespeople available to help them, customers are forced to make purchasing decisions on their own. Eye-catching, informative displays can give them the nudge they need. Even in well-staffed stores, display materials can offer extra selling information and make the product stand out from the competition.

The proliferation of POP displays has led retailers to be more discriminating in what they actually use. Most are beginning to insist on well-designed, attractive materials that will blend harmoniously with their store atmosphere.

The emphasis on POP has led to a variety of new approaches, including ads on shopping carts, "talking" antacid boxes, beverage jingles activated when in-store refrigerator doors are opened, and interactive computers for selecting everything from shoe styles to floor coverings. Digital technology has led to Hallmark Cards' Touch-Screen Greetings interactive kiosks, which print a customer's personal message onto any card.[43] To send it, look for one of the new Automated Postal Centers rolled out by the U.S. Postal Service. The kiosks allow customers to weigh materials to be mailed, buy postage, and even look up zip codes.[44]

Coupons

A **coupon** is a certificate with a stated value presented to the retail store for a price reduction on a specified item. Consumer packaged goods companies in the United States distributed more than 170 billion coupons in 2002, but only about 1.9 billion were ever redeemed.[45]

Coupons may be distributed in newspapers or magazines, door to door, on packages, in stores, and by direct mail. Many reach consumers through colorful preprinted newspaper ads called **freestanding inserts (FSIs).**

Most coupons reach consumers through newspaper freestanding inserts (FSIs), which have a higher redemption rate than regular newspaper or magazine coupons.

FSIs have a higher redemption rate than regular newspaper and magazine coupons; coupons in or on packages have the highest redemption levels of all.[46]

Manufacturers lose hundreds of millions of dollars annually on fraudulent coupon submissions. Some coupons are counterfeited; others are submitted for products that were never purchased. To fight this problem, some companies have developed computerized systems to detect fraudulent submissions and charge them back to the retailers who made them.

Electronic Coupons and Convenience Cards

High-tech **electronic coupons** work like paper coupons in that they entitle the shopper to a discount, but their method of distribution is entirely different. Interactive touch-screen videos at the point of purchase and coupon printers at checkout counters generate instant discounts, rebates, and offers to try new brands. Electronic coupons are spreading quickly in the nation's supermarkets, though they still represent only a small percentage of the total coupons distributed annually.

Kiosks like these VIP stations use a consumer's membership card to issue a list of manufacturer discounts and to track customer purchase patterns.

Nonetheless, all the nation's top brand marketers are currently involved in tests being conducted by the two leaders in the field, Catalina Marketing and Advanced Promotion Technologies. Catalina's system is installed in more than 21,000 supermarkets across the country and reaches some 250 million shoppers per week.[47]

Electronic couponing targets consumers with specific offers in ways that would not be possible with paper coupons. Many supermarket chains now issue customers **convenience cards** entitling them to discounts at the checkout counter. Consumers often provide detailed information about themselves when they apply for these cards. When customers use a card, a record of their purchases is sent to a database. The card saves customers the hassle of clipping paper coupons, it allows retailers to better understand its customers' purchasing behaviors, and it provides consumers with targeted offers.

Similar systems are used in Europe. Multipoints is an interactive system that lets customers collect points for visiting stores or watching commercials on TV. The points can be redeemed for prizes and discounts on various products at participating stores. Quick Burger, France's second-largest restaurant chain, noticed a significant increase in traffic after joining Multipoints, even when the system was less than a year old.[48]

Cents-off Promotions, Refunds, and Rebates

Cents-off promotions are short-term reductions in the price of a product in the form of cents-off packages, one-cent sales, free offers, and box top refunds. Some packages bear a special cents-off sticker, which the clerk removes and credits at the checkout counter.

Some companies offer *refunds* in the form of cash or coupons that can be applied to future purchases of the product. To obtain the refund, the consumer must mail in a proof of purchase, such as three box tops.

Rebates are larger cash refunds on items from cars to household appliances. Large rebates (like those given on cars) are handled by the seller. For small rebates (like those given for coffeemakers), the consumer sends in a certificate.

Research indicates that many people purchase a product because of an advertised rebate but never collect the rebate because of the inconvenience.[49] This is a phenomenon called **slippage.** Consumers Union estimates that 60 percent of all rebates go unfilled.[50]

THE GOLD'S GYM
3-APPLE
A DAY PLAN

IT MAY BE THE MOST
ECONOMICAL, SIMPLE
AND QUICK
LIFESTYLE CHANGE
YOU'VE EVER MADE.

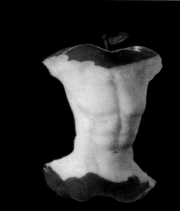

ENTER THE GOLD'S GYM
$500,000 CHALLENGE
AT 3APPLEPLAN.COM

Not too long ago in Wenatchee, Washington, our training experts made a discovery while creating diets for their clients. Eating just one apple before each meal proved to be a perfect supplement for weight loss. And, being in the heart of Washington Apple country, it wasn't a drastic change to anyone's regular meals. The drastic change happened when clients of the fat-loss plan got on the scales. Participants at this small Gold's Gym® in the Pacific Northwest lost tons — literally, three tons of weight.* It turned enough heads for Gold's to declare Washington Apples the official diet pill of Gold's Gym International. That's quite a distinction. It's time you found out more. And to help you get started, we're offering $500,000 to the winners of the Gold's Gym Challenge. Go to www.3appleplan.com to find out more today. Just a Washington Apple before each meal, and you're on your way.

*You don't need to be a Gold's Gym member to participate; this contest is open to anyone 18 years or older. Results may not be typical. See Gold's Gym for complete 3-Apple Plan.

Sometimes a marketer will share the cost of a consumer promotion with comarketing partners as in this creative effort by Gold's Gym and Washington Apples. Eat a Washington Apple before each meal as part of your diet and exercise plan, and you'll be on your way to a leaner you. You might even win cash. Everybody benefits and the cost of the promotion is reduced.

Premiums

A **premium** is an item offered free or at a bargain price to encourage the consumer to buy an advertised product. Premiums affect purchase behavior the same way as rebates but tend to be more effective at getting consumers to buy a product they didn't really need (see Exhibit 16–5). Premiums are intended to improve the product's image, gain goodwill, broaden the customer base, and produce quick sales.

A premium should have strong appeal and value and should be useful or unusual. It may be included in the product's package *(in-pack premium),* on the package *(on-pack premium),* mailed free or for a nominal sum on receipt of proof of purchase (boxtop or label), or given with the product at the time of purchase. Cosmetics companies often hold department store promotions in which scarves, purses, and cosmetic samplers are given free or for a low price with a purchase.

The purchased cosmetics sampler is an example of a *self-liquidating* premium: The consumer pays enough that the seller breaks even but doesn't make a profit. A variation is the *continuity premium,* given weekly to customers who frequent the same store. With a minimum dollar purchase of other items, the customer receives a dish or book each week to complete a set.

Sampling

Sampling is the most costly of all sales promotions. It is also one of the most effective for new products, because it offers consumers a free trial in hopes of converting them to habitual use. Sampling should be supported by advertising and must involve a product available in small sizes and purchased frequently. Successful sampling depends heavily on the product's merits. It offers the greatest credibility and can turn a nonuser into a loyal customer instantly—if the product lives up to its promise.

Samples may be distributed by mail, door to door, via coupon advertising, or by a person in the store. They may be given free or for a small charge. Sometimes samples are distributed with related items, but this limits their distribution to those who buy the other product. In **polybagging,** samples are delivered in plastic bags with the daily newspaper or a monthly magazine. This enables distribution to targeted readers and lets publications give their subscribers added value at no cost.[51]

In-store sampling is very popular. Most in-store sampling programs are tied to a coupon campaign. Depending on the nature of the product, samples can be used as either a push strategy or a pull strategy.

Combination Offers

Food and drug marketers use **combination offers,** such as a razor and a package of blades or a toothbrush with a tube of toothpaste, at a reduced price for the two. For best results, the items should be related. Sometimes a combination offer introduces a new product by tying its purchase to an established product at a special price.

Contests and Sweepstakes

A **contest** offers prizes based on entrants' skill. A **sweepstakes** offers prizes based on a chance drawing of entrants' names. A **game** has the chance element

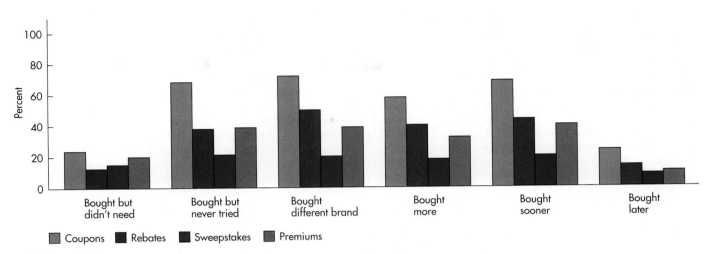

Exhibit 16–5

Next to coupons, premiums are one of the most effective sales promotion techniques for changing consumer behavior.

of a sweepstakes but is conducted over a longer time (like bingo-type games designed to build store traffic). A game's big marketing advantage is that customers must make repeat visits to the dealer to continue playing.

Both contests and sweepstakes encourage consumption of the product by creating consumer involvement. These devices pull millions of entries. Usually contest entrants must send in some proof of purchase, such as a boxtop or label. For more expensive products, consumers may only have to visit the dealer or take a test drive to pick up an entry blank.

To encourage entries, sponsors try to keep their contests as simple as possible. The prize structure must be clearly stated and all the rules listed. National contests and sweepstakes are handled and judged by independent professional contest firms.

Sweepstakes and games are now more popular than contests because they are much easier to enter and take less time. Sweepstakes require careful planning by the advertiser. Companies cannot require a purchase as a condition for entry or the sweepstakes becomes a lottery and therefore illegal. Marketers must obey all local and postal laws. If they run the sweepstakes in Canada, they may have to pay a percentage of the prizes to the Quebec government.

Contests and sweepstakes must be promoted and advertised to be successful, and this can be expensive. And sales promotions need dealer support. To ensure dealer cooperation, many contests and sweepstakes require the entrant to name the product's local dealer. They may also award prizes to the dealer who made the sale.

> **CONCEPT CHECK**
> Contrast the goals of pull and push strategies. Describe several examples of the implementation of each strategy.

Chapter Summary

The key to building brand equity in the twenty-first century is to develop interdependent, mutually satisfying relationships with customers and other stakeholders. To manage these rela-

tionships, companies will need to consciously integrate their marketing communications activities with all their other company functions so that all the messages the marketplace receives about the company are consistent. The idea is to not just meet customer expectations but to exceed them.

As part of this process, it is important for advertising people to understand how to integrate the various tools of marketing communications. Advertising practitioners need to have a basic understanding of what other tools are available to them and how they can best be used in the overall communications mix.

In direct marketing, the marketer builds and maintains a database of customers and prospects and uses anything from personal contact to mass media to communicate with them directly in the effort to generate a response, a transaction, or a visit to a retail location.

The database is the key to direct marketing success, especially in an IMC program. Databases let marketers target, segment, and grade customers. This allows them to identify their best customers, their value to the organization, and their needs and buying behavior. They can then calculate the customers' lifetime value. The database is the corporate memory of all important customer information. It should record every transaction across all points of contact with both channel members and customers. The database also enables the company to measure the efficiency of its direct-response advertising efforts. Working with a marketing database requires two processes: data management and data access.

Advertisers and agencies now realize they can't do the job with one medium. Databases let companies choose the prospects they can serve most effectively and profitably. By providing a tangible response, direct marketing offers accountability. Direct marketing offers convenience to time-sensitive consumers and precision and flexibility to cost-sensitive marketers.

Direct marketing is a rapidly growing industry, but it still suffers from problems of cost, clutter, and image.

Direct marketers use a variety of activities, from direct sales (personal selling and telemarketing) to direct-response advertising. Telemarketing, followed by direct mail, is the medium of choice for most direct marketers, but more are beginning to use other media, especially the Internet and TV infomercials. Interactive TV may be the direct marketing medium of the future.

Personal selling is actually the ultimate interactive medium. It is the interpersonal communication process by which a seller ascertains and then satisfies the needs of a buyer, to the mutual, long-term benefit of both parties.

There are many types of personal selling: retail, business-to-business, and direct selling. Since advertising is a support service for a company's sales efforts, advertising people have to understand the selling environment their companies deal in.

The greatest strength of personal selling is its personal nature. Nothing is as persuasive as personal communication. The one-to-one situation facilitates instant feedback. And the rep has the flexibility to adjust the presentation, tailoring it specifically to the needs and interests of the particular prospect.

Like all communications tools, personal selling also has some drawbacks. It is very labor intensive and therefore very expensive. One important role of advertising is to reduce the cost of sales by communicating as much relevant information as possible about the company and its products before the salesperson even calls. The salesperson has incredible power to either make or break a delicate relationship. So one of the risks is that one bad apple can ruin a previously unblemished association.

Salespeople provide four communications functions: information gathering, information providing, order fulfillment, and relationship building.

Sales promotion complements advertising and personal selling by stimulating sales. It includes direct inducements (such as money, prizes, or gifts) aimed at salespeople, distributors, retailers, consumers, and industrial buyers.

Marketers must balance sales promotion with advertising. Advertising creates market value for a brand; promotion creates market volume. Advertising has a positive effect on profits; promotion can have a negative effect. Sales promotion techniques are used with the trade to push products through the distribution channels and with consumers to pull them through.

Manufacturers use many sales promotion techniques with dealers: slotting allowances, trade deals, display allowances, buyback allowances, advertising allowances, co-op advertising and advertising materials, dealer premiums and contests, push money, and company conventions and dealer meetings. Sales promotions aimed at the ultimate purchaser include point-of-purchase materials, coupons, electronic coupons and convenience cards, cents-off promotions, refunds, rebates, premiums, sampling, combination offers, contests, and sweepstakes.

Key Terms

advertising allowance, 450

buyback allowance, 450

catalogs, 440

cents-off promotion, 453

combination offers, 454

company conventions, 451

consumer sales promotions, 448

contest, 454

convenience cards, 453

cooperative (co-op) advertising, 450

coupon, 452

customer lifetime value (LTV), 436

database, 434

database management, 436

database marketing, 434

database queries, 436

dealer meetings, 451

direct marketing, 433

direct-response advertising, 434, 440

direct sales, 439

direct selling, 439

Review Questions

1. Why is a good marketing database so important to marketers?
2. What is the difference between direct marketing and direct mail?
3. What factors are driving (or hindering) the growth of direct marketing in the United States and internationally?
4. Who are a company's best prospects for additional sales and profits? Why?
5. How can an advertiser use a newspaper for direct-response advertising?
6. What are the three things salespeople must do to build relationships?
7. What are the main purposes of sales promotion?
8. Why is trade promotion controversial?
9. What are the most common pull strategies? Which would you use to launch a new soft drink?
10. Why is there a trend away from push strategies and toward pull strategies?

Exploring Advertising

1. Advertisers commonly use both push and pull techniques. Explore a company of your choice, identifying its pull and push techniques. Push techniques might be more difficult to find; look for indicators of trade promotions such as retailer ads, promotional prices, and in-store displays (with lots of merchandise). Analyze the company's overall sales promotion strategy and discuss why you think one area might be emphasized over another.
2. Develop a direct marketing program for a product that is normally sold only in stores. Describe the target audience, your objectives, and the direct marketing activities you would use and explain why. Create a mockup of a campaign piece. Explain how you would generate and utilize a marketing database.
3. Look at the recruitment advertisements for sales representatives in your local newspaper. What personal characteristics and past work experience are most companies looking for?
4. Find a print ad for a product, service, or retailer. Design a sales promotion that would complement the advertising campaign. Describe ways in which the advertising, sales promotion, and other relationship-building activities could be effectively integrated.

chapter seventeen

Relationship Building: Public Relations, Sponsorship, and Corporate Advertising

Objectives

To explain the role of public relations, sponsorships, and corporate advertising in relationship marketing and integrated marketing communications. By integrating public relations, event sponsorships, and institutional advertising with its general advertising activities, a company can improve the overall effectiveness of its marketing efforts.

After studying this chapter, you will be able to:

* **Distinguish** between advertising and public relations.

* **Discuss** the key elements of crisis communications.

* **Describe** the difference between public relations and publicity.

* **Identify** the tools public relations practitioners use.

* **Explain** how event sponsorships can fit into an IMC plan.

* **Describe** the types of sponsorship advertising and their benefits.

* **Define** advocacy advertising and debate its role in a free society.

* **Explain** the role of corporate identity advertising.

We all know the names: Cherry Garcia, Chunky Monkey, New York Super Fudge Chunk. If some of Ben & Jerry's product names are lovable, the company's customers would say that its premium ice cream is irresistible. With annual sales now topping $200 million, the rise of "Vermont's Finest" has been fine indeed since the company's modest beginnings in a renovated gas station. But the socially conscious outfit has always said that it's not just about the ice cream.

Like its frozen treats, Ben & Jerry's mission statement is quite a mouthful. It details the company's product mission, pledging "a continued commitment to incorporating wholesome, natural ingredients and promoting business practices that respect the Earth and the Environment"; economic mission, promising financial sustainability, value for stakeholders, and opportunity for employees; and social mission, acknowledging "the central role that business plays in society by initiating innovative ways to improve the quality of life locally, nationally, and internationally."[1] Promoting causes as diverse as family farms, solar energy, and child welfare, the company has a long record of incorporating liberal activism into its public relations efforts.

Of course, Ben & Jerry's isn't alone in using its business clout to champion progressive issues. But the breadth of its involvement sets it apart from other would-be corporate philanthropists. Established in 1985, the Ben & Jerry's Foundation offers competitive grants for small-scale grass-roots social programs throughout the United States. In 2003, awardees received grants of up to $15,000 in order to combat homelessness, clean up old mines, and monitor federal land management practices, to cite only a few examples.[2]

Getting back to the ice cream, a portion of the profits from certain Ben & Jerry's flavors is directed toward its social mission. The causes can be local or global: its Primary Berry Graham flavor was developed to encourage voting in the 2004 New Hampshire primary; in 2002, its One Sweet Whirled campaign partnered with the Dave Matthews Band to fight global warming.[3] The company has also touted its use of environment-friendly packaging and encouragement of energy-conserving refrigeration methods.[4]

Sometimes it takes the expression "giving back to the community" very literally. Its Scoop Shops offer an annual Free Cone Day, and Ben & Jerry's Cowmobile delivered free scoops nationwide in the 1980s. Some would argue that the giveaways are as much a marketing tool as an act of generosity, but either way they represent a lot of ice cream: Advance estimates for the 25th Annual Free Cone Day in 2003 predicted that more than 1 million cones would be given away worldwide.[5]

Ben & Jerry's earnestness has always had its share of detractors, who find its image contrived and insincere, but skepticism about its social role has grown since its acquisition in 2000 by Dutch multinational Unilever. How could the brand preserve its home-grown, quirky image as part of a massive conglomerate? Would its activism be diluted, or even eliminated completely? Under pressure from its shareholders to approve the deal, even the company's founders expressed misgivings in announcing its completion: "While we and others certainly would have preferred to pursue our mission as an independent enterprise, we hope that, as part of Unilever, Ben & Jerry's will continue to expand its role in society."[6]

Under Unilever's control, Ben & Jerry's has dramatically increased its product offerings and overseas presence and continues to sponsor politically flavored promotional events. With the subsidiary's ability to retain its proudly liberal voice still an open question, Ben & Jerry's ice cream now, in some ways, has to speak for itself. But the positive public relations fostered by its many years of community involvement, along with the product's popularity, will help to further solidify the brand's worldwide fan base.

The Role of Public Relations

The primary role of public relations is to manage a company's reputation and help build public support for its activities. Today's business environment has become so competitive that public support can no longer be assumed; it must be earned continuously.[7]

The term *public relations* is widely misunderstood and misused. Part of the confusion is due to the fact that public relations covers a very broad area. Depending on the context and one's point of view, it can be a concept, a profession, a management function, or a practice. For our purposes, we define **public relations (PR)** as the management function that focuses on the relationships and communications that individuals and organizations have with other groups (called publics) for the purpose of creating mutual goodwill.

As we've already discussed, every company, organization, or government body has relationships with groups of people who are affected by what it does or says. They may be employees, customers, stockholders, competitors, suppliers, legislators, or the community in which the organization resides. Marketing professionals refer to these people as *stakeholders* because they all have some vested interest in the company's actions. In PR terminology, each of these groups is considered one of the organization's **publics,** and the goal of PR is to develop and maintain goodwill with most, if not all, of its publics. Failure

Certain public relations activities can add great value to the perception of a product. Here, a poet autographs a copy of his book after doing a reading. Book signings are a common form of public relations used by the publishing industry around the world.

to do so may mean loss of customers and revenues, time lost dealing with complaints or lawsuits, and loss of respect (which weakens the organization's brand equity as well as its ability to secure financing, make sales, and expand).

A company's publics change constantly. After being acquired by Unilever, Ben & Jerry's encountered previously silent, content publics. Criticism of the company appears to have increased after the acquisition. The Center for Science in the Public Interest (CSPI) accused Ben & Jerry's of misleading the public by claiming that some of its products were "all-natural" when they in fact contained hydrogenated oils and artificial flavors. CSPI called upon the FDA to take action against the company.[8] Ben & Jerry's hedged response was that the term "all-natural" had various definitions in the food industry, but that it would work with natural food organizations on the issue.[9] In 2003, the company voluntarily recalled pints of its Karamel Sutra ice cream that contained peanuts not mentioned on the label. After receiving one illness complaint about this common food allergen, the recall went forward, with CEO Yves Couette stating that "Our primary concern is always for the health and safety of our consumers."[10]

Because of the powerful effect of public opinion, companies and organizations must consider the breadth of the impact of their actions. This is especially true in times of crisis, emergency, or disaster. But it also holds true for major policy decisions: changes in management or pricing, labor negotiations, the introduction of new products, or changes in distribution methods. Each decision affects different groups in different ways. Effective public relations can channel groups' opinions toward mutual understanding and positive outcomes.

In short, the goals of public relations are to improve public opinion, build goodwill, and establish and maintain a satisfactory reputation for the organization. PR efforts may rally public support, obtain public understanding, or simply respond to inquiries. Well-executed public relations is an ongoing process that molds good long-term relationships and plays an important role in relationship marketing and integrated communications.[11]

The Difference between Advertising and Public Relations

Since they both use the media to create awareness or to influence markets or publics, advertising and public relations are similar—but they're not the same. Advertising reaches its audience through media the advertiser pays for. It appears just as the advertiser designed it, with the advertiser's bias built in. Knowing this, the public views ads with some skepticism or ignores them outright. So, in an integrated marketing communications program, advertising is rarely the best vehicle for building credibility.

Many public relations communications, like publicity, are not openly sponsored or paid for. People receive these communications in the form of news articles, editorial interviews, or feature stories after the messages have been reviewed and edited—filtered—by the media. Since the public thinks such messages are coming from the medium rather than a company, it trusts them more readily. For building credibility, therefore, public relations is usually the better approach. Ben & Jerry's, for example, relies heavily on press coverage of its ice-cream giveaways during events it helps sponsor.

However, while advertising is carefully placed to gain particular reach and frequency objectives, PR is less precise. Public relations objectives are not as easy to quantify. In fact, the results gained from public relations activities depend greatly on the experience and skill of the people executing them and the relationship they have with the press. But PR can go only so far. Editors won't run the same story over and over. An ad's memorability, however, comes from repetition. While PR activities may offer greater credibility, advertising offers precision and control.

Advertising and PR in the Eyes of Practitioners

Another major difference between public relations and advertising is the orientation of professional practitioners. Advertising professionals see *marketing* as the umbrella process companies use to determine what products and services the market needs and how to distribute and sell them. To advertising professionals, advertising and public relations are "good news" marketing tools used to promote sales.

Public relations professionals take a different view. With their background often in journalism rather than marketing, they believe *public relations* should be the umbrella process. They think companies should use PR to maintain relationships with all publics, including consumers. As *Inside PR* magazine says, "Public relations is a management discipline that encompasses a wide range of activities, from *marketing and advertising* to investor relations and government affairs."[12] To PR professionals, public relations should be integrated "corporate" communications, which is certainly broader than what most people consider integrated "marketing" communications.

To date, though, few companies are structured with a public relations orientation; most are still marketing oriented, perhaps due to marketing's bottom-line focus. But today's marketing people would be well advised to adopt the multiple-stakeholder approach and relationship consciousness that PR people bring to the table. Moreover, in times of crisis, the candid, open-information orientation of PR is invariably the better perspective to adopt. Fortunately, with the growing interest in relationship marketing, two-way interactivity, and IMC, companies are finally beginning to embrace a public relations philosophy.

When PR activities are used for marketing purposes, the term **marketing public relations (MPR)** is often used. In support of marketing, public relations activities can raise awareness, inform and educate, improve understanding, build trust, make friends, give people reasons or permission to buy, and create a climate of consumer acceptance—usually better than advertising.[13] Marketing strategists Al and Laura Ries believe the best way to build a brand is through publicity—a PR activity. They cite numerous examples of leading companies that achieved their cachet with relatively little advertising but extensive publicity: Starbucks, The Body Shop, Wal-Mart, to name a few.[14]

In an integrated marketing communications program, advertising and MPR need to be closely coordinated. Many ad agencies now have PR departments for this very purpose. And many companies now have communications departments that manage both advertising and PR.

CONCEPT CHECK

What is the primary role of public relations?

The Public Relations Job

The public relations job comprises a variety of activities, from crisis communications to fundraising. And PR practitioners use many tools besides press conferences and news releases.

PR Planning and Research

The first function of a PR practitioner is to plan and execute the public relations program. Part of this task may be integrated with the company's marketing efforts (for instance, product publicity), but the PR person typically takes a broader view.

Because public opinion is so important, the PR person must constantly monitor, measure, and analyze changes in attitudes among a variety of publics. A common form of public relations research is **opinion sampling** using techniques discussed in Chapter 6: shopping center or phone interviews, focus groups, analysis of incoming mail, and field reports. Some advertisers set up toll-free phone lines and invite consumer feedback.

The PR practitioner analyzes the organization's relationships with its publics; evaluates people's attitudes and opinions toward the organization; assesses how company policies and actions relate to different publics; determines PR objectives and strategies; develops and implements a mix of PR activities, integrating them whenever possible with the firm's other communications; and solicits feedback to evaluate effectiveness.

Sony to pull controversial CDs, offer swap

Copy-protection program raised PC privacy fears

By Jefferson Graham
USA TODAY

LOS ANGELES — Sony BMG Music Entertainment said Monday it will pull some of its most popular CDs from stores in response to backlash over copy-protection software on the discs.

Media

Sony also said it will offer exchanges for consumers who purchased the discs, which contain hidden files that leave them vulnerable to computer viruses when played on a PC.

"Sony BMG deeply regrets any inconvenience to our customers and remains committed to providing an enjoyable and safe music experience," the company said. Sony says more than 20 titles have been released with the XCP copy-protection software, and of those CDs, over 4 million have been manufactured, and 2.1 million sold.

Details about how long it will take to replace the XCP CDs and about its consumer exchange program will come later in the week, Sony said.

For now, pulling the CDs off shelves "could go a long way toward making a consumer feel comfortable that the CD they just purchased isn't going to mess up their computer," says record store owner John Kunz of Waterloo Records in Austin.

Country-rockers Van Zant's *Get Right with the Man* kicked off the firestorm when a blogger traced a hidden, spyware-type file on his computer to the CD. Other XCP copy-protected CDs include new releases by Neil Diamond, Celine Dion, Cyndi Lauper and Burt Bacharach.

Before Sony's announcement, Van Zant manager Ross Schilling urged the label to recall all the CDs. "I said we've got to be proactive, or it could destroy the business model," Schilling says. "Sony should be in the artist business, promoting and selling records. This type of issue sheds a negative light on their ability to do that."

Sony began adding copy-protection to its CDs in June 2004 with the release of a record by the band Velvet Revolver, saying it was taking a step against unauthorized online file-sharing and CD burning.

The label says it will issue all major releases with copy-protection in 2006, as will rival label EMI. The other major labels, Universal Music and Warner, have yet to release copy-protected CDs.

Sony also issues copy-protected CDs using software from digital rights management company SunnComm. But those, which include releases by the Foo Fighters and the Dave Matthews Band, haven't come under the same kind of attack.

However, many artists have spoken out about all forms of copy-protected CDs, including Matthews, the Foo Fighters and Christian rock band Switchfoot. Bela Fleck and the Flecktones are set to release a new album on Sony in January, and it will not be copy protected, says Fleck's manager, David Bendett.

Frustrated when he bought a copy-protected Dave Matthews release and couldn't copy it to his Apple iPod, Fleck insisted that Sony not release his new album with such restrictions, Bendett says.

Sony says its copy-protected CDs are clearly marked, but the front labels don't identify whether they use the XCP software. That information is included in small print on the back of the CD, which reads "?cp.sonybmg.com/xcp".

Companies often use publicity to enhance or defend their firm's reputation. In this case, Sony BMG (www.sonybmg.com) used the press to achieve some damage control in a crisis situation. Attempting to strengthen copy protection on its music CDs, Sony added XCP software to 49 titles, producing some 4.7 million discs. Consumers later found out that the CDs installed a hidden program on their computers, making their PCs vulnerable to hackers and viruses. The publicity campaign allowed Sony to apologize to the public and to announce a CD replacement policy.

Reputation Management

One of the principal tasks of public relations is to manage the standing of the firm with various publics. **Reputation management** is the name of this long-term strategic process.[15] PR practitioners employ a number of strategies and tactics to help them manage their firm's or client's reputation, including publicity and press agentry, crisis communications management, and community involvement.

Publicity and Press Agentry

For many public relations professionals, their primary task is to generate news and get it placed in the media for their companies or clients. A major activity of public relations, **publicity** is the generation of news about a person, product, or service that appears in print or electronic media. Companies employ this activity either for marketing purposes or to enhance the firm's reputation.

Some people think of publicity as "free" because the media don't charge firms to run it (they also don't guarantee they'll use it). This is a misconception, though. Someone still gets paid to write the release and coordinate with the press. However, as a marketing communications vehicle, publicity often offers a considerably greater return on money invested than other communications activities. A large ad campaign might require an investment of 5 to 20 percent of sales; a major publicity program, only 1 to 2 percent.

To be picked up by the media, publicity must be *newsworthy*. Typical publicity opportunities include new-product introductions, awards, company sales and earnings, major new contracts, mergers, retirements, and speeches by company executives. Sometimes publicity is unfavorable and accrues unintentionally, such as when peanuts were found in Ben & Jerry's ice cream. And since publicity can originate from any source, it may be difficult—or impossible—to control. In IMC terms, unintentional publicity is an *unplanned message.*

The planning and staging of events to generate publicity is called **press agentry.** Most PR people engage in press agentry to bring attention to new products or services or to portray their organizations favorably. For print media, the publicity person deals with editors and feature writers. For broadcast media, he or she deals with program directors, assignment editors, or news editors. Successful PR practitioners develop and maintain close, cordial relations with their editorial contacts. An MPR professional practicing IMC sees the press as an important *public,* and writers and editors as important *stakeholders.*

Crisis Communications Management

One of the most important public relations tasks for any corporation is **crisis management.** Brand value can be quickly destroyed if "damage control" is not swift and thorough.

The classic case of exemplary crisis communication management was Johnson & Johnson's handling of a product-tampering episode in 1982. Several people died when a criminal laced bottles of J&J's Extra-Strength Tylenol with cyanide on retail shelves. The moment they received the news, management strategists at J&J and McNeil Products (the J&J subsidiary that markets Tylenol) formulated three stages of action:

1. Identify the problem and take immediate corrective action. J&J strategists got information from the police, FBI, FDA, and press; identified the geographic area affected; corrected rumors; and immediately withdrew the product from the marketplace.

2. Actively cooperate with authorities in the investigation. Johnson & Johnson was proactive. It helped the FBI and other law enforcement agencies generate leads and investigate security at its plants, and it offered a $100,000 reward.

3. Quickly rebuild the Tylenol name and capsule line, including Regular Strength capsules, which were recalled, too. Although J&J believed the poisoning had taken place at the retail end of the chain, it first made sure that the tampering hadn't occurred at McNeil. The company's two capsule production lines were shut down, and dog teams were brought in to search for cyanide.

The insatiable appetite of the news media plus a flood of inquiries from anxious consumers put J&J's PR people under enormous pressure. All communications between the media and the company were channeled through the corporate communications department. All customer, trade, and government communications were coordinated within the company. This way, J&J maintained open, clear, consistent, legal, and credible communications and avoided rumors, political backbiting, and corporate defensiveness.

In the first 48 hours after the news broke, phone calls to Johnson & Johnson and McNeil were nonstop. In the basement at McNeil, a bank of phones usually used for sales was staffed by employees who were briefed on what to say, what not to say, and where to refer tough questions.

The social mission sections of Ben & Jerry's country-specific Web sites reflect both global concerns and local initiatives. Each site shows the company's support for world peace, hormone-free dairy products, and blood donation drives. In Spain, the company also sponsors a homeless shelter for the mentally ill and a group that fights pet abandonment. The Ben & Jerry's Web site for Sweden links to a Swedish organization devoted to child welfare in Benin, West Africa.

At the same time, management and employees had to be informed, authorities contacted, and many others notified. J&J and McNeil public relations managers and staff had to plan, coordinate, and supervise this enormous task.

As infrequent as disasters are, there is no more important activity for PR professionals and public information officers than crisis communications management—especially those in highly sensitive fields such as airlines, government agencies, the military, law enforcement, chemical and oil companies, and public utilities.

Since the Tylenol incident, many companies in normally nonsensitive industries have prepared crisis management plans. The manner in which a company handles communications during emergencies or catastrophes will determine to a great extent how the public responds to the news. When corporations have no plans for coping with crisis, the resulting press coverage can be disastrous. Experts on crisis management encourage all companies to follow J&J's example by being open and candid. Withholding information or evading questions inevitably backfires, as many politicians have learned.

Community Involvement

The goal of **community involvement** is to develop a dialogue between the company and the community.[16] This is best done by having company officers, management, and employees contribute to the community's social and economic development. Every community offers opportunities for corporate involvement: civic and youth groups, charitable fundraising drives, cultural or recreational activities, and so on. A company should ideally adopt one program relevant to its expertise and focus its *mission marketing* activities. The PR department may help set up such programs and publicize them to the community.

Other Public Relations Activities

In addition to planning and reputation management, public relations professionals are often involved in activities such as public affairs and lobbying, speechwriting, fundraising and membership drives, creation of publications, and special-events management.

Public Affairs and Lobbying

Organizations often need to deal with elected officials, regulatory and legislative bodies, and various community groups—the realm of **public affairs.** Public affairs usually requires a specialist. Many experts think PR and public affairs should become more integrated to combine the skills and policy expertise of the specialist with the PR person's media and community relations savvy.

Lobbying refers to informing government officials and persuading them to support or thwart administrative action or legislation in the interests of some client. Every organization is affected by the government, so lobbying is big business.

Speechwriting

Because company officials often have to speak at stockholder meetings, conferences, or conventions, PR practitioners often engage in **speechwriting.** They are also frequently responsible for making all the arrangements for speaking opportunities and developing answers for questions company representatives are likely to be asked. Since public relations people may sometimes represent their employers at special events, press conferences, and interviews, they too should be articulate public speakers.

466 part 6 Integrating Marketing Communications Elements

To meet demanding operating budgets, nonprofit organizations often devote a significant portion of their advertising to raising funds. The Canadian Paraplegic Association (www.canparaplegic.org) ran this creative ad to drum up financial support for its goal of curing spinal cord injuries.

Fundraising and Membership Drives

A public relations person may be responsible for soliciting money for a nonprofit organization or for a cause the company deems worthwhile, such as the United Way or a political action committee (PAC).

Charitable organizations, labor unions, professional societies, trade associations, and other groups rely on membership fees or contributions. The PR specialist must communicate to potential contributors or members the goals of the organization and may integrate promotional tie-ins to publicize the drive or encourage participation. In the process, the company PR people may work closely with the advertising department or agency to create ads promoting the particular cause or to publicize the company's involvement with the cause in product ads.

Publications

Public relations people prepare many of a company's communications materials: news releases and media kits; booklets, leaflets, pamphlets, brochures, manuals, and books; letters, inserts, and enclosures; annual reports; posters, bulletin boards, and exhibits; audiovisual materials; and position papers. Here again, they may work with the advertising department or the agency to produce these materials. The advertising people need to keep the company's overall positioning strategy in mind while trying to help accomplish the particular PR objectives.

Special-Events Management

The sponsorship and management of special events is a rapidly growing field. In fact, it has become such an important topic that we devote the next major section of this chapter to it, following our discussion of PR tools.

Public Relations Tools

The communications tools at the PR person's disposal vary widely, from news releases and photos to audiovisual materials and even advertising. We'll discuss some of the more common ones briefly.

News Releases and Press Kits

A **news release** (or **press release**), the most widely used PR tool, consists of one or more typed sheets of information (usually 8 ½ by 11 inches) issued to generate publicity or shed light on a subject of interest. News releases cover time-sensitive hard news. Topics may include the announcement of a new product, promotion of an executive, an unusual contest, landing of a major con-

The McGraw·Hill Companies

Media Contact:
April Hattori, (212) 904-2078
april_hattori@mcgraw-hill.com

FOR IMMEDIATE RELEASE

MCGRAW-HILL HIGHER EDUCATION
INTRODUCES NEW PAPERBACK ADVERTISING TEXT

NEW YORK (March 10, 2006)—McGraw-Hill Higher Education today announced the release of *Essentials of Contemporary Advertising*, a shorter, more concise version of William Arens' best-selling text, *Contemporary Advertising*. The new paperback text is written by William F. Arens, a veteran of the advertising industry, and David H. Schaefer, a professor of business and marketing at Sacramento City College.

The new text incorporates all of the core concepts for a Principles of Advertising course in a briefer form. *Essentials of Contemporary Advertising* fully covers the advertising process, starting with strategy formulation through the creative execution of ads for print, television, and digital media, as well as research, media planning, and integrated marketing communications. The authors' combined industry and teaching experience results in the text's perfect balance of real-world application and academic concepts.

For a review copy, please contact your McGraw-Hill sales rep at www.mhhe.com.

# # #

McGraw-Hill Higher Education is a unit of McGraw-Hill Education, the premier provider of teaching and learning solutions for the pre-kindergarten through 12th grade, post-secondary, higher education, and professional markets. It is a division of The McGraw-Hill Companies, a global information services provider meeting worldwide needs in the financial services, education, and business information markets. Additional information is available at www.mheducation.com

A news release is used to announce the important events of a company including new products, grand openings, responses to crises, or changes in leadership. This example of a news release might have been used to publicize the publication of this textbook. News releases are sent to the press in the hope that the information will be used to generate a story in trade publications, in local or national newspapers or magazines, or even on radio or television. Companies can even place their news releases online, using services like the PR Newswire to communicate their messages across the country and around the world.

tract, or establishment of a scholarship fund. For pointers in preparing releases, see the Checklist, "How to Write a News Release."

A **press kit** (or **media kit**) supports the publicity of special events such as press conferences, grand openings, and trade shows. It includes a basic fact sheet of information about the event, a program or schedule of activities, and a list of the participants and their biographical data. The kit also contains a news story about the event for the broadcast media, news and feature stories for the print media, and any pertinent photos and brochures.

Photos

Photos of events, products in use, new equipment, or newly promoted executives can lend credence or interest to a dull news story. In fact, a photo tells the story faster. Photos should be high quality and need little or no explanation. Typed captions should describe the photo and accurately identify the people shown.

Feature Articles

Many publications, especially trade journals, run **feature articles** (soft news) about companies, products, or services. They may be written by a PR person, the publication's staff, or a third party (such as a freelance business writer). As an MPR tool, feature articles can give the company or product great credibility. Editors like them because they have no immediate deadline and can be published at the editor's convenience or when space is available.

Features may be case histories, how-to's (such as how to use the company's product), problem-solving scenarios (how one customer uses the company's product to increase production), or state-of-the-art technology updates. Other formats include roundups of what's happening in a specific industry and editorials (such as a speech or essay by a company executive on a current issue).

Checklist

How to Write a News Release

The Role of the News Release

The news release is an effective tool for publicizing information for several reasons. It helps to protect the publicist and the client from being misquoted. It permanently records the preferred word usage, specific terms, key phrasing, and unique details.

Its standardized format also speeds up the process. It eliminates debate over how to format the information, highlights the data most needed by the recipient (contact person's name and telephone, date, etc.), and spells out the source and topic of the story.

The news release also simplifies dissemination by providing a form that is easily reproduced and transferred (e-mail, fax, postal mail, etc.) and by assuring that all recipients receive the same message.

Preparing the News Release

The news release follows a format generally accepted throughout the news industry.

- **Double-space the text and use wide margins.**
- **At the top of the page (left or right side) place the name and phone number of your contact person.** If your page is not preprinted with your company's name and address, add it below the contact person. Finally, write FOR IMMEDIATE RELEASE or TO BE RELEASED AFTER [date].
- **Write a headline that signals the key fact or issue of the story.** For example, TECHCO PRESIDENT SPEAKS TO BAY CITY LIONS CLUB THURSDAY.
- **Place the most important information first.** The editors may shorten your news release by cutting from the bottom.

- **Lead sentence.** The lead sentence is the most important. Keep it focused strictly on who, what, where, when, why, and how. For example, "Techco President Ralph J. Talk will address the Bay City Lions Club at 8 p.m., Thursday, September 16, 2004."
- **Body text.** Add directly related support information. "Mr. Talk's speech will be 'Technology in Albania.' Mr. Talk served five years as assistant to the president of the Albania Travel Association."
- **Final text.** Fill in background details. "Mr. Talk was born on April 30, 1956, and is married to Alice Johnson of Bay City. They have two children. Mr. Talk is a board member of the Bay City Little League."
- **Keep the text as factual, direct, and short as possible.**
- **Carefully proof your copy.**

Etiquette

- **Don't call to see whether the editor received your release.** Editors don't like to be pressured. Don't ask for tearsheets. An editor has little time to send you a copy. Don't promise you'll advertise if the item is published; the editor will be offended at the suggestion that news can be bought. If the article is run, send a thank-you letter to the editor.

Mailing List

- **Prepare a list of local publications.** You may want to group them so that you mail out appropriate news releases to publications that are likely to use that type of information. Refrain from sending mass mailings. Update your list regularly, because editors change and offices move.
- **Ascertain in advance if the editors on your list prefer to have news releases sent by e-mail or postal mail.**

Printed Materials

Printed materials are the most popular tools used by public relations professionals.[17] They may be brochures or pamphlets about the company or its products, letters to customers, inserts or enclosures that accompany monthly statements, the annual report to stockholders, other reports, or house organs.

A **house organ** is a publication about happenings and policies at the company. An internal house organ is for employees only. External house publications go to company-connected people (customers, stockholders, suppliers, and dealers) or to the general public. They may take the form of a newsletter, tabloid-size newspaper, magazine, or even a periodic **e-zine** (a magazine published online or sent by e-mail). Their purpose is to promote goodwill, increase sales, or influence public opinion. A well-produced house organ can do a great deal to motivate employees and appeal to customers. However, writing, printing, and distributing can be expensive—and very time-consuming.

Posters, Exhibits, and Bulletin Boards

Posters can be used internally to stress safety, security, reduction of waste, and courtesy. Externally, they can impart product information, corporate philosophy, or other news of interest to consumers.

Companies use **exhibits** to describe the organization's history, present new products, show how products are made, or explain future plans. Exhibits are often prepared for local fairs, colleges and universities, and trade shows.

Internally, the public relations staff often uses **bulletin boards** to announce new equipment, new products, meetings, promotions, construction plans, and recreation news to employees. Thanks to the new technology, many companies now maintain an **intranet** site where they can post their internal bulletin boards.

Audiovisual Materials

Slides, films, filmstrips, CDs, and videocassettes are all forms of **audiovisual materials** and may be used for training, sales, or public relations. Considered a form of *corporate advertising,* nontheatrical or sponsored films (developed for public relations reasons) are often furnished without charge to movie theaters, organizations, and special groups, particularly schools and colleges. Classic examples include *Why Man Creates,* produced for Kaiser Aluminum, and Mobil Oil's *A Fable,* starring the famous French mime Marcel Marceau.

Many PR departments provide **video news releases (VNRs)**—news or feature stories prepared by a company and offered free to TV stations, which may use the whole video or just segments. Video news releases are somewhat controversial. Critics see them as subtle commercials or even propaganda and object when stations run the stories without disclosing that they came from a public relations firm, not the station's news staff.

House organs may be sent to customers to promote goodwill, increase sales, or influence public opinion. SMUD, a Sacramento, California, energy provider, encloses this two-page newsletter in its monthly mailings. It provides public interest stories, important news, and energy-saving ideas in an appealing and easy-to-read format.

Sponsorships and Events

> What are the key functions of public relations practitioners and what tools do they have at their disposal?
>
> CONCEPT CHECK

In 1984, the owner of a large bicycle shop in the upper Midwest sent some of his mechanics to a local bicycle race sponsored by a national charity. At the time, his store was doing about $200,000 per year in retail sales, and he wanted to help out the charity while finding out what the racers thought of his and his competitors' businesses.

An unexpected benefit of the company's presence at the race was that participants started showing up in his store. Encouraged by these results, the company now supports more than 100 bicycle events each year and sends staff members to dozens of such events. It has hired a full-time representative to coordinate company involvement in special bicycle events that have the potential of increasing its exposure and business revenue.

In 20 years, the company has gone from a low-key presence at bicycling events, donating a few water bottles embossed with the company's name, to large-scale sponsorship, participating in event registration, providing event participants with workshops on bicycle maintenance, and offering in-store discounts to event participants. Within a week of one event, 30 participants had visited his store. Even better news for the company was that nearly half of the more than 5,000 riders reported purchasing goods from it.

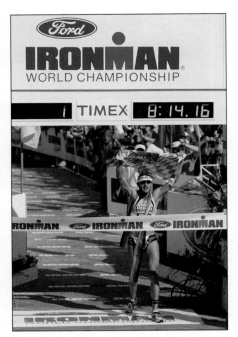

Companies sponsor events or organizations by providing money or other resources that are of value to the sponsored event. This is usually in return for advertising space at the event or as part of the publicity of the event. In 2005, Ford (www.ford.com) became the title sponsor of the Ford Ironman Triathlon events (www.ironmanlive.com) in the United States for three years. Ford SUVs will serve as pace and chase vehicles during each event, and Ford will add $100,000 to the prize purse.

By 1996, the company had revenues of $3 million. The owner attributes much of his success to his sponsorship of bicycle events. In his words, "I support them, and they support us."[18]

The Growth of Sponsorship

Advertising and public relations people get involved in sponsoring many kinds of special events. In fact, sponsorship may be the fastest-growing form of marketing today. It actually embraces two disciplines: sales promotion and public relations. Some sponsorships are designed to create publicity, others to improve public relations through personal contact and affiliation with a worthy cause, and others to immediately improve the sales and bottom line.

A **sponsorship** is a cash or in-kind fee paid to a property (which may be a sports, entertainment, or nonprofit event or organization) in return for access to the exploitable commercial potential associated with that property.[19] In other words, just as advertisers pay a fee to sponsor a program on radio or TV, they may also sign on to sponsor a bike race, an art show or chamber music festival, a fair or exhibition, or the Olympics. The sponsorship fee may be paid in cash or **in kind** (that is, through a donation of goods and services). For instance, if a local TV station signs on as a sponsor of a 10K run, it will typically pay for some part of its sponsorship by providing advertising time for the event.

Cause marketing, a related strategy, is a partnership between a for-profit company and a nonprofit organization, which increases the company's sales while raising money and visibility for the organization's cause. Typically, a portion of the proceeds from the sale of certain products is donated to the cause. For example, Yoplait yogurt's *Save Lids to Save Lives* campaign urges consumers to buy pink-lidded cups of yogurt and mail the lids back. For each lid mailed in, Yoplait donates ten cents to the Susan G. Komen Foundation.

While the sponsored event or organization may be nonprofit, sponsorship is not the same as philanthropy. **Philanthropy** is support of a cause without any commercial incentive. Sponsorship is used to achieve commercial objectives. Mediaedge:cia's MediaLab reports that global spending on sponsorships has increased by 220 percent over the past 10 years and now accounts for $25 billion in marketing expenditures worldwide.[20]

The reasons for this phenomenal growth relate to the economics of marketing we discussed earlier: the escalating costs of traditional advertising media, the fragmentation of media audiences, the growing diversity in leisure activities, and the ability to reach targeted groups of people economically. Initial growth probably came from the tobacco and alcohol companies, which many governments banned from broadcast advertising. Recent legislation in the United Kingdom, Canada, and the United States threatens to end tobacco sponsorships altogether, but their success at sponsoring sports and other events has shown the way for mainstream advertisers, who are rapidly picking up the slack.

Today, there is greater media coverage of sponsored events—everything from beach volleyball to grand prix horse shows to Xtreme games to cultural events. This provides a highly desirable venue for advertisers seeking young, upwardly mobile, educated consumers. Likewise, for transnational marketers, there is growing interest in global events such as World Cup soccer, the Olympics, and the America's Cup yacht race. Even traditional business-to-business marketers, such as Sweden's Ericsson Corp., are making a play for greater brand awareness in the United States by sponsoring the World Championships of Beach Volleyball, which is staged and marketed by Nike.[21]

Benefits of Sponsorship

In the past, for marketers with limited media alternatives (such as tobacco and alcohol companies), sponsorship simply offered a means of communication with customers and prospects. Today, the many benefits of sponsorship are well documented and more far-reaching.

Certainly one benefit of sponsorship is that the public approves of it. One study by Roper Starch Worldwide reported that 80 percent of Americans believe corporate sponsorship is an important source of money for professional sports. This is a far higher approval rating than most companies would get for their advertising programs.

More than almost any other marketing communications tool, sponsorships and events have the ability to involve customers, prospects, and other stakeholders. Events are also highly self-selective of their target audience. So marketers that define their audiences tightly can select just those sponsorships that offer the closest fit. A significant benefit is the opportunity to enhance the company's public image or merchandise its positioning through affiliation with an appropriate event. Of course, marketers that sponsor an event simply because it has a large audience are misusing this tool.[22]

Unlike advertising, sponsorships and events can provide face-to-face access to current and potential customers. Depending on the venue, this access can be relatively clean and uncluttered by competition. Sponsoring a seminar, for instance, creates an opportunity for both customer education and brand involvement. In some cases, it even enables product demonstrations and the opportunity to give a personal sales pitch to multiple prospects at a time when they are open to new information.[23] This is especially good for business-to-business marketers.

Also important, but often overlooked, is the effect sponsorship can have on employees. Affiliating with a dynamic event can really boost the morale and pride of the troops in the trenches. And many companies offer attendance at the event (Super Bowl, Olympics, etc.) as an incentive to their sales staff.[24]

Some marketers have discovered that sponsorships can rapidly convert fan loyalty into sales. For example, 74 percent of stock-car racing fans report that they often buy products they see promoted at the racetrack. This is also true for other sports: 58 percent for baseball, 52 percent for tennis, 47 percent for golf. Finally, sponsorships can be very cost-efficient. Volvo International believes the media exposure it gets from its $3 million sponsorship of local tennis tournaments is equivalent to $25 million worth of advertising time and space.[25]

Drawbacks of Sponsorship

Like all marketing communications tools, sponsorship has some drawbacks. First, it can be very costly, especially when the event is solely sponsored. For this reason, most companies participate in cosponsored events, which spreads the cost among several participants.

The problem with cosponsored events is clutter. Some events have so many sponsors that getting one marketer's message through is extremely difficult. Look again at stock-car racing. How many logos do those cars sport?

Finally, evaluating the effectiveness of a particular sponsorship can be tricky at best—especially since it rarely happens in a vacuum. The problem is in separating the effects of a sponsorship from the effects of other concurrent marketing activities. We'll deal with these issues shortly.

Types of Sponsorship

While there are many, many avenues and events available for sponsorship, IEG Inc. groups most of them into six categories: sports; entertainment, tours, and attractions; causes; the arts; festivals, fairs, and annual events; and associations and membership organizations (see Exhibit 17–1).[26]

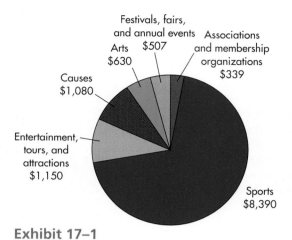

Exhibit 17–1

Annual sponsorship spending in North America ($ millions; 2005 projections).

Cause marketing is a partnership between a for-profit company and a nonprofit organization. In this ad, Campbell promotes its connection to the city letter carriers' union (www.nalc.org) annual food drive. In 2005, Campbell helped sponsor 112 million postcards sent to promote the event; a record 71.3 million pounds of food were donated. In 2006, Campbell will link this effort to its Labels for Education program (www.labelsforeducation.com), raising student awareness about hunger in America and possibly encouraging the sale of more products with Campbell's labels.

Sports Marketing

North American corporations spent an estimated $8.39 billion in 2005 on sports marketing sponsorships. The most popular of these are motorsports and golf.[27] In fact, the vast majority of sponsorship money, approximately 69 percent, is spent on sports events. This includes everything from the Olympics to NASCAR racing to professional athletic leagues. And as we saw from the bicycle shop story, companies don't have to be big multinationals to reap rich rewards from sponsorships—if they do it properly. But without a concerted effort to tie an event to other marketing communications activities like a currently running ad campaign, the money spent on sponsorships is generally wasted.[28]

Controversy often swirls around big sports sponsorships. The most controversial practice is **ambush marketing,** a promotional strategy nonsponsors use to capitalize on the popularity or prestige of an event or property by giving the false impression that they are sponsors. Ambush marketing techniques, like buying up all the billboard space around an athletic stadium, are often employed by the competitors of the property's official sponsor. Fuji did this to Kodak in Nagano. One of the reasons this works is because people are often confused about who the official sponsors actually are—again, the problem is clutter. Just because a company advertises on the Olympic broadcast, for instance, does not mean it is an official sponsor. Ambush marketers take advantage of this.[29]

Entertainment

After sports marketing, the largest area of sponsorship is entertainment, which includes things like concert tours, attractions, and theme parks. For instance, numerous attractions at Disneyland and Disney World are sponsored by major corporations such as GE, AT&T, ARCO, Kodak, and Carnation. In 2005, U.S. companies spent an estimated $1.15 billion on this category.

Causes

Sponsorship of charity events and educational institutions is a tried-and-true PR activity that often fits with the IMC strategy of mission marketing. A number of large corporations (including Chevrolet, AT&T, American Airlines, Pepsi, and Kodak) cosponsored the Live Aid concerts, for instance. In 2005, marketers spent an estimated $1.08 billion in cause-related sponsorships.

The vice president for corporate relations at Philip Morris, the nation's largest event sponsor, refers to mission marketing activities as "enlightened self-interest." People appreciate the fact that businesses do not really get anything tangible out of them to put in the bank.[30]

Arts

Symphony orchestras, chamber music groups, art museums, and theater companies are always in desperate need of funding. In 2005, sponsors spent an estimated $630 million to support the arts—one of the least funded of the major sponsorship categories. What this means is that this is still a relatively untapped area, and it provides outstanding sponsorship and underwriting opportunities for both national and local firms interested in audiences on the highest end of the income scale.

Festivals, Fairs, and Annual Events

In 1997, IEG surveyed 1,000 members of the International Association of Fairs and Expositions. The findings revealed a very healthy, growing environment. The average yearly sponsorship increased a whopping 20 percent over the previous four years, with the biggest growth (30 percent) occurring between 1996 and 1997. Moreover, renewal rates averaged 88 percent! By 2005, sponsorship revenue increased to an estimated $507 million.

One of the largest annual events in the state of Michigan is the National Cherry Festival in Traverse City. Held every year around the Fourth of July, it boasts an impressive lineup of events and promotional activities that drives both attendance and sponsor visibility. Events include band parades, races, concerts, tournaments, an antiques show, an air show, Native American exhibits, and much more. Among the official sponsors are Pepsi, Ford, Toyota, Intel, BankOne, and Sony.

A hot form of sponsorship today is venue marketing, in which corporations pay money to associate their name with a sports arena, theater, or civic center. Often, these companies will invest money into desperately needed repairs or improvements to existing facilities, as Qualcomm (www.qualcomm.com) did with San Diego's former Jack Murphy Stadium. The company saved the city $18 million in stadium renovations and received the right to name the venue Qualcomm Stadium for the next 20 years.

Associations and Membership Organizations

This sponsorship category was added by IEG in 2004. These sponsorships were previously considered a part of festivals, fairs, and annual events because most associations sponsored annual conventions. But that is no longer the case, as sponsors are now more likely to sign year-round partnerships with trade groups, professional membership organizations, and other associations. Those sponsors will spend an estimated $339 million in this category in 2005.

Venue Marketing

Finally, an area not covered by IEG's report is **venue marketing,** a form of sponsorship that links a sponsor to a physical site such as a stadium, arena, auditorium, or racetrack. In 1997, for instance, the cellular technology company Qualcomm made a good name for itself by offering the city of San Diego $18 million to help it meet its shortfall on construction funds for its football stadium. All Qualcomm wanted was the name changed for 20 years. The city agreed—and the San Diego Chargers now play at Qualcomm Stadium. Likewise, Denver has Coors Field, and Charlotte, North Carolina, has Ericsson Stadium. Candlestick Park in San Francisco is now Monster Park. And SBC has put its name on San Francisco's baseball park.

Venue marketing is changing the economics of professional sports. Sponsorships help pay for stadium renovations and upgrades and may assist the home team in defraying high operational costs. Many teams keep the money from their stadium luxury suites, stadium advertising, naming rights, and food and beverage concessions. Under the new economic rules, big stadium revenues are essential to signing big-name players and staying competitive.[31]

Checklist

How to Select Events for Sponsorship

- Can the sponsorship be an exclusive one?
- The demographics of the mass media audience and event participants should match, as closely as possible, the demographics of the target consumer.
- The event should in some way demonstrate, evoke, or represent a key attribute of the product or service (for example, a luxury product sponsoring a thoroughbred racing event—"the sport of kings").
- The value to the sponsored event of the company's association should be no greater than the benefit to the company from the additional mass media exposure from the sponsorship. (This has to do with who is leveraging whom.)
- The participation should promise sufficient (and appropriate) mass media exposure to offset any costs associated with the sponsorship.
- The association of the product with the event should ideally offer or suggest a meaningful sales campaign or theme to be run concurrently with sponsorship.
- Did the company initiate the negotiation or was the company solicited by the event promoters?
- How much financial support is required?

Methods of Sponsorship

Companies interested in sponsorship have two choices: buy into an existing event or create their own. Event marketing specialist Paul Stanley predicts that many corporate event sponsorships will become "sponsownerships," where the sponsor owns and controls the entire event. This would allow more control and would likely be more cost-effective. It would also help the company achieve its marketing objectives.[32]

For most companies, though, it's easier to buy into an existing event, either as the sole sponsor (the Buick Tournament of Champions) or as one of many cosponsors. What's most important is to get a good fit between the sponsor and the event.

In his book *Aftermarketing*, Terry Vavra suggests several guidelines for selecting the right sponsorship opportunity or event. See the Checklist, "How to Select Events for Sponsorship."

Measuring Sponsorship Results

One of the problems with event sponsorship (as with public relations activities in general) has historically been how to evaluate results. Experts suggest there are really only three ways to do this:

1. Measure changes in awareness or image through pre- and postsponsorship research surveys.

2. Measure spending equivalencies between free media exposure and comparable advertising space or time.

3. Measure changes in sales revenue with a tracking device such as coupons.

Unfortunately, none of these methods covers all the reasons for sponsoring. For example, how do you measure the effect on employee morale? What if the sponsorship is aimed at rewarding current customers or enhancing relationships within the trade? These are important possible objectives, but they are very difficult to measure.

Still, most companies are very concerned about the bottom line and look for a substantial return on investment for their sponsorship dollars. Delta Airlines, for example, is said to require $12 in new revenue for every dollar it spends on sponsorship—a ratio the airline claims to have achieved during its Olympic sponsorship.[33]

The International Events Group (IEG) suggests the following pointers for measuring the value of event sponsorships:[34]

- Have clear goals and narrowly defined objectives.

- Set a measurable goal.

- Measure against a benchmark.

- Do not change other marketing variables during the sponsorship.

- Incorporate an evaluation program into the overall sponsorship and associated marketing program.

- At the outset establish a budget for measuring results.

CONCEPT CHECK

Why is sponsorship becoming such a popular form of marketing?

Corporate Advertising

When a company wants to communicate a PR message and control its content, it may use a form of *corporate advertising*. In an integrated marketing communications program, corporate advertising can set the tone for all of a company's public communications. **Corporate advertising** covers the broad area of nonproduct advertising, including public relations advertising, institutional advertising, corporate identity advertising, and recruitment advertising.

Public Relations Advertising

To direct a controlled public relations message to one of its important publics, a company uses **public relations advertising.** PR ads may be used to improve the company's relations with labor, government, customers, suppliers, and even voters.

When companies sponsor art events, programs on public television, or charitable activities, they frequently place public relations ads in other media to promote the programs and their sponsorship, enhance their community citizenship, and create public goodwill. If the public relations people don't have advertising experience, they will typically turn to the firm's advertising department or agency for help.

Corporate/Institutional Advertising

In recent years, the term *corporate advertising* has come to denote a particular type of nonproduct advertising aimed at increasing awareness of the company and enhancing its image. The traditional term for this is **institutional advertising.** These ad campaigns may serve a variety of purposes: to report company accomplishments, position the company competitively in the market, reflect a change in corporate personality, shore up stock prices, improve employee morale, or avoid communications problems with agents, dealers, suppliers, or customers.

Historically, companies and even professional ad people have questioned, or misunderstood, the effectiveness of corporate advertising. Retailers in particular cling to the idea that institutional advertising, although attractive and nice, "doesn't make the cash register ring." A series of marketing research studies, however, offered dramatic evidence to the contrary. Companies using corporate advertising registered significantly better awareness, familiarity, and overall impression than those using only product advertising. Five corporate advertisers in the study drew higher ratings in every one of 16 characteristics measured,

Commercial Break 17–A

David Ogilvy on Corporate Advertising

David Ogilvy, the late founder and former creative director of Ogilvy & Mather, worked with Shell, Sears, IBM, International Paper, Merrill Lynch, General Dynamics, Standard Oil of New Jersey, and other successful corporations.

According to Ogilvy, big corporations are increasingly under attack from consumer groups, environmentalists, governments, and antitrust prosecutors who try their cases in the newspapers. If a corporation does not take the time to cultivate its reputation, it loses by default.

"If it were possible, it would be better for corporations to rely on public relations (that is, favorable news stories and editorials) rather than paid advertising. But the media are too niggardly about disseminating favorable information about corporations. That is why an increasing number of public relations directors have come to use paid advertising as their main channel of communication. It is the only one they can control with respect to content, with respect to timing, and with respect to noise level. And it is the only one which enables them to select their own battleground," he said.

"So I guess that corporate advertising is here to stay. Why is most of it a flop?"

First, because corporations don't define the purpose of their corporate campaigns.

Second, because they don't measure the results. In a survey conducted by *The Gallagher Report,* only one in four U.S. corporate advertisers said it measured changes in attitude brought about by its corporate campaigns. "The majority fly blind," said Ogilvy.

Third, because so little is known about what works and what doesn't work. The marketing departments and their agencies know what works in brand advertising, but when it comes to corporate advertising they are amateurs.

Fourth, very few advertising agencies know much about corporate advertising. It is only a small part of their business. "Their creative people know how to write chewing-gum jingles for kids and how to sell beer to blue-collar workers. But corporate advertising requires copywriters who are at home in the world of big business. There aren't many of them," believed Ogilvy.

"I am appalled by the humbug in corporate advertising. The pomposity. The vague generalities and the fatuous platitudes. Corporate advertising should not insult the intelligence of the public."

Unlike product advertising, Ogilvy said, a corporate campaign is the voice of the chief executive and his or her board of directors. It should not be delegated.

What can good corporate advertising hope to achieve? Ogilvy thought at least one of four objectives:

1. **It can build awareness of the company.** Opinion Research Corp. states, "The invisibility and remoteness of most companies is the main handicap. People who feel they know a company well are five times more likely to have a highly favorable opinion of the company than those who have little familiarity."

2. **Corporate advertising can make a good impression on the financial community,** enabling you to raise capital at lower cost—and make more acquisitions.

3. **It can motivate your present employees and attract better recruits.** "Good public relations begins at home," Ogilvy said. "If your employees understand your policies and feel proud of your company, they will be your best ambassadors."

4. **Corporate advertising can influence public opinion on specific issues.** Abraham Lincoln said, "With public opinion against it, nothing can succeed. With public opinion on its side, nothing can fail."

"Stop and go is the typical pattern of corporate advertising. What a waste of money. It takes years for corporate advertising to do a job. It doesn't work overnight. Only a few companies have kept it going long enough to achieve measurable results," Ogilvy concluded.

Applying the Breaks
Find and discuss a corporate ad that demonstrates what Ogilvy referred to as the humbug in corporate advertising, the pomposity, vague generalities, and fatuous platitudes.

including being known for quality products, having competent management, and paying higher dividends.[35] Ironically, the companies in the study that did no corporate advertising spent far more in total advertising for their products than the corporate advertisers did. Yet, despite the higher expenditures, they scored significantly lower across the board.

David Ogilvy, the late founder and creative head of Ogilvy & Mather, was an outspoken advocate of corporate advertising, but he was appalled by some corporate ads. For more on Ogilvy's views, see Commercial Break 17–A.

Responding to such criticisms and to marketplace forces, corporations now design their corporate advertising to achieve specific objectives: develop awareness of the company and its activities, attract investors, improve a tarnished image, attract quality employees, tie together a diverse product line, or take a stand on important public issues. The primary media used for corporate advertising are consumer business magazines and network TV.

A variation on corporate advertising is **advocacy advertising.** Companies use it to communicate their views on issues that affect their business (to protect their position in the marketplace), to promote their philosophy, or to make a political or social statement. Such ads are frequently referred to as **advertorials** since they are basically editorials paid for by an advertiser.

Corporate advertising can also build a foundation for future sales, traditionally the realm of product advertising. Many advertisers use **umbrella advertising** campaigns to simultaneously communicate messages about the products and the company.

While corporate advertising is an excellent vehicle for promoting the company's desired image, it cannot succeed if the image doesn't fit. If a big tobacco company, for example, tried to project a wholesome, fitness image, it would not be very credible.

Corporate Identity Advertising

Companies take pride in their logos and corporate signatures. The graphic designs that identify corporate names and products are valuable assets, and companies take great pains to protect their individuality and ownership. How does a company increase consumer awareness or enhance its image? What does a company do when it changes its name, logos, or trademarks, as when it merges with another company? This is the job of **corporate identity advertising.**

Familiar corporate name changes include the switch from Datsun to Nissan, the change from Consolidated Foods to Sara Lee Corp., and the creation of Unisys to replace the premerger identities of Burroughs and Sperry.

Recruitment Advertising

Companies use **recruitment advertising** to attract new employees. Most recruitment advertising appears in the classified help-wanted sections of daily newspapers or, increasingly more frequently, on the Internet and is placed by the human resources department rather than the advertising department. But many ad agencies now employ recruitment specialists, and some agencies even specialize in recruitment advertising.

Chapter Summary

Public relations is a process used to manage an organization's relationships with its various publics, including employees, customers, stockholders, competitors, and the general public. The term public relations can describe a concept, a profession, a management function, and a practice. Many PR activities involve media communi-

nications. However, unlike product advertising, many of these communications are not openly sponsored or paid for.

Public relations activities include planning and research, reputation management (publicity and press agentry, crisis management, and community involvement), public affairs and lobbying, speechwriting, fundraising and membership drives, publication preparation, and special-events management.

The tools used in public relations include news releases and press kits, photos, feature articles, all sorts of printed materials, posters and exhibits, and audiovisual materials.

Sponsorship is one of the fastest-growing forms of marketing today. It actually embraces two disciplines: sales promotion and public relations. A sponsorship is a cash or in-kind fee paid to a property (which may be a sports, entertainment, or non-profit event or organization) in return for access to the exploitable commercial potential of that property. It should not be confused with philanthropy.

Sponsorship offers many benefits. It meets with public approval. It has the ability to involve customers, prospects, and other stakeholders. Most events are highly self-selective of their target audience. Sponsorships and events can provide face-to-face access to current and potential customers. They can enhance the company's public image or reinforce its posi-

tioning through affiliation with an appropriate event. And they can boost employee morale.

However, sponsorships can be very costly, and they are also subject to clutter, which reduces their effectiveness.

Types of sponsorships include: sports marketing; entertainment; causes; the arts; festivals, fairs, and annual events; associations and membership organizations; and venue marketing. Sports marketing is by far the largest category, consuming over two-thirds of all sponsorship dollars.

Companies may either buy into an existing event or start their own. One problem with sponsorship is evaluating the results. Three methods include measuring changes in awareness, measuring spending equivalencies with advertising, and measuring changes in sales revenue.

To help create a favorable reputation in the marketplace, companies use various types of corporate advertising, including public relations advertising, institutional advertising, corporate identity advertising, and recruitment advertising.

Key Terms

advertorials, 477
advocacy advertising, 477
ambush marketing, 472
audiovisual materials, 469
bulletin boards, 469
cause marketing, 470
community involvement, 465
corporate advertising, 475
corporate identity advertising, 477
crisis management, 464
exhibits, 469
e-zine, 468
feature article, 467

house organ, 468
in kind, 470
institutional advertising, 475
intranet, 469
lobbying, 465
marketing public relations (MPR), 462
news (press) release, 466
opinion sampling, 463
philanthropy, 470
posters, 469
press agentry, 464
press (media) kit, 467

public affairs, 465
publicity, 463
public relations (PR), 460
public relations advertising, 475
publics, 460
recruitment advertising, 477
reputation management, 463
speechwriting, 465
sponsorship, 470
umbrella advertising, 477
venue marketing, 473
video news releases (VNRs), 469

Review Questions

1. How does public relations differ from advertising?
2. How is the perspective of advertising practitioners different from that of PR professionals? How is marketing public relations used?
3. What is the role of public relations in relationship marketing and integrated marketing communications?
4. What are some activities used in reputation management?
5. Why is it important to establish a crisis management plan? What types of companies are most likely to need one?

6. What types of sponsorship activities are available to marketers today?
7. Which sponsorships are likely to offer the best return on investment, and how can that be measured?
8. What are the various types of corporate advertising? Describe them.
9. What is the purpose of corporate identity advertising?
10. What is the purpose of recruitment advertising? Why is it under the domain of corporate advertising and public relations?

Exploring Advertising

1. You have been put in charge of public relations for a large metropolitan hospital. Make a list of all of your possible objectives in this position and describe examples of programs you might initiate over the next 12 months to help achieve those objectives.
2. Kid Specs is a new brand of eyeglasses designed for children under the age of 12. It comes in a variety of fashionable materials and styles. As the brand manager, you don't have a large advertising budget, but you've heard that sponsorships can be a very cost-effective tool for gaining awareness and brand loyalty. Develop and describe several sponsorship ideas that could benefit Kid Specs.

3. Find an advertisement for a local event or an article about a local company. Imagine that you are the public relations manager for the event sponsor or the local company. Write a news release that might result in a favorable article. Follow the format suggested in the Checklist: "How to Write a News Release." Where would you send the release? Are there any other materials you might include?
4. Every company wants the best and brightest employees. Look at five recruitment advertisements and evaluate them. Which one seems to be the most effective? What makes it superior? Then look at the one you feel is the least effective. Consider what could be done to improve it, and then redesign the ad to make it more attractive to the most qualified candidates.

Glossary

abundance principle States that an economy produces more goods and services than can be consumed. In such an economy, advertising serves two important purposes: It keeps consumers informed of their alternatives, and it allows companies to compete more effectively for consumer dollars.

account executive (AE) The liaison between the agency and the client. The account executive is responsible both for managing all the agency's services for the benefit of the client and for representing the agency's point of view to the client.

account planner The individual at an advertising agency primarily responsible for account planning.

account planning A hybrid discipline that bridges the gap between traditional research, account management, and creative direction whereby agency people represent the view of the consumer in order to better define and plan the client's advertising program.

account supervisor See *management supervisor*.

action programs See *tactics*.

added value The increase in worth of a product or service as a result of a particular activity. In the context of advertising, the added value is provided by the communication of benefits over and above those offered by the product itself.

ad impression A possible exposure of the advertising message to one audience member; see *opportunities to see (OTS)*.

ad networks The Internet equivalent of a media rep firm, *ad networks* act as brokers for advertisers and Web sites. Ad networks pool hundreds or even thousands of Web pages together and facilitate advertising across these pages, thereby allowing advertisers to gain maximum exposure by covering even the small sites.

ad request When an ad is requested from a Web server. This happens when someone visits a Web page that contains an advertisement and the surfer's browser asks the server to deliver the ad.

advertiser A company that sponsors advertising for itself and its products.

advertising The structured and composed nonpersonal communication of information, usually paid for and usually persuasive in nature, about products (goods and services) or ideas by identified sponsors through various media.

advertising agency An independent organization of creative people and businesspeople who specialize in developing and preparing advertising plans, advertisements, and other promotional tools for advertisers. The agency also arranges for or contracts for purchase of space and time in various media.

advertising allowance Either a percentage of gross purchases or a flat fee paid to the retailer for advertising the manufacturer's product.

advertising message An element of the creative mix comprising what the company plans to say in its advertisements and how it plans to say it—verbally or nonverbally.

advertising objective A specific communication task an advertising campaign should accomplish for a specific target audience.

advertising plan The plan that directs the company's advertising effort. A natural outgrowth of the marketing plan, it analyzes the situation, sets advertising objectives, and lays out a specific strategy from which ads and campaigns are created.

advertising research The systematic gathering and analysis of information specifically to facilitate the development or evaluation of advertising strategies, ads and commercials, and media campaigns.

advertising response curve A graphical representation of the relationship between advertising levels and sales results. Most curves suggest that at low levels of advertising, increases in spending have a small, but growing incremental impact on sales. However, at some level, the incremental response to increased spending actually diminishes.

advertising specialty A promotional product, usually imprinted with an advertiser's name, message, or logo, that is distributed free as part of a marketing communications program.

advertising strategy The advertising objective declares what the advertiser wants to achieve with respect to consumer awareness, attitude, and preference; the advertising strategy describes how to get there. Advertising strategy consists of two substrategies: the creative strategy and the media strategy. See also *creative strategy* and *media strategy*.

advertising strategy research Used to help define the product concept or to assist in the selection of target markets, advertising messages, or media vehicles.

advertorial An ad that is half advertising, half editorial, aimed at swaying public opinion rather than selling products.

advocacy advertising Advertising used to communicate an organization's views on issues that affect society or business.

adware A software application that displays advertising banners or pop-up windows. Such ad delivery systems are often integrated into free software as a way for developers to recover costs or generate revenue. They are installed, usually with the user's permission, at the same time as shareware or similar programs.

affidavit of performance A signed and notarized form sent by a television station to an advertiser or agency indicating what spots ran and when. It is the station's legal proof that the advertiser got what was paid for.

affiliate marketing program A contractual advertising program, often used in e-commerce, under which a seller pays a manufacturer, marketer, or other business a percentage of the sale price of an item sold. This payment is compensation for services or cooperation in making the sale. For example, a site devoted to music reviews may have a banner link to an online music retailer. When consumers use that link to buy music, the music seller pays the owner of the music review site a percentage of the sale as consideration for the banner link.

affirmative disclosure Advertisers must make known their product's limitations or deficiencies.

ambush marketing A promotional strategy utilized by nonsponsors to capitalize on the popularity or prestige of an event or property by giving the false impression that they are sponsors, such as by buying up all the billboard space around an athletic stadium. Often employed by the competitors of the property's official sponsor.

analog proof See *Chromalin proof.*

animatic A rough television commercial produced by photographing storyboard sketches on a film strip or video with the audio portion synchronized on tape. It is used primarily for testing purposes.

animation The use of cartoons, puppet characters, or demonstrations of inanimate characters come to life in television commercials; often used for communicating difficult messages or for reaching specialized markets, such as children.

answer print The final print of a filmed commercial, along with all the required optical effects and titles, used for review and approval before duplicating.

antivirus Computer programs that attempt to identify, thwart, and eliminate computer viruses and other malicious software.

art The whole visual presentation of a commercial or advertisement—the body language of an ad. Art also refers to the style of photography or illustration employed, the way color is used, and the arrangement of elements in an ad so that they relate to one another in size and proportion.

art direction The act or process of managing the visual presentation of an ad or commercial.

art director Along with graphic designers and production artists, determines how the ad's verbal and visual symbols will fit together.

Artist role A role in the creative process that experiments and plays with a variety of approaches, looking for an original idea.

art studio Company that designs and produces artwork and illustrations for advertisements, brochures, and other communication devices.

attention value A consideration in selecting media based on the degree of attention paid to ads in particular media by those exposed to them. Attention value relates to the advertising message and copy just as much as to the medium.

attitude The acquired mental position—positive or negative—regarding some idea or object.

attitude test A type of posttest that usually seeks to measure the effectiveness of an advertising campaign in creating a favorable image for a company, its brand, or its products.

audience The total number of people exposed to a particular medium.

audience composition The distribution of an audience into demographic or other categories.

audience objectives Definitions of the specific types of people the advertiser wants to reach.

audience share The percentage of homes with TV sets in use (HUT) tuned to a specific program.

audio The sound portion of a commercial. Also, the right side of a script for a television commercial, indicating spoken copy, sound effects, and music.

audio console In a sound studio control room, the board that channels sound to the appropriate recording devices and that blends both live and prerecorded sounds for immediate or delayed broadcast.

audiovisual materials Slides, films, filmstrips, and videocassettes that may be used for training, sales, or public relations activities.

Audit Bureau of Circulations (ABC) An organization supported by advertising agencies, advertisers, and publishers that verifies circulation and other marketing data on newspapers and magazines for the benefit of its members.

avails An abbreviated term referring to the TV time slots that are *available* to an advertiser.

average quarter-hour audience (AQH persons) A radio term referring to the average number of people who are listening to a specific station for at least 5 minutes during a 15-minute period of any given daypart.

average quarter-hour rating The average quarter-hour persons estimate expressed as a percentage of the estimated population.

average quarter-hour share The radio station's audience (AQH persons) expressed as a percentage of the total radio listening audience in the area.

Ayer No. 1 See *poster-style format.*

bandwidth A measure of the capacity of a communications system. The higher a system's bandwidth, the more information it can carry.

banner Little billboards of various sizes that pop up when a visitor lands on a particular Web page.

barter syndication Marketing of first-run television programs to local stations free or for a reduced rate because some of the ad space has been presold to national advertisers.

base art The first image on an artboard on which an overlay may be placed.

basic bus In transit advertising, all the inside space on a group of buses, which thereby gives the advertiser complete domination.

behavioristic segmentation Method of determining market segments by grouping consumers into product-related groups based on their purchase behavior.

benefit headline Type of headline that makes a direct promise to the reader.

benefits The particular product attributes offered to customers, such as high quality, low price, status, speed, sex appeal, good taste, and so on.

benefit segmentation Method of segmenting consumers based on the benefits being sought.

benefit statement Describes what a product or service does to provide a benefit to the consumer. Whenever possible, benefit statements should focus on an important, single-minded promise.

big idea The flash of creative insight—the bold advertising initiative—that captures the essence of the strategy in an imaginative, involving way and brings the subject to life to make the reader stop, look, and listen.

bleeds Colors, type, or visuals that run all the way to the edge of the page.

blinking A scheduling technique in which the advertiser floods the airwaves for one day on both cable and network channels to make it virtually impossible to miss the ads.

blueline A proof created by shining light through the negatives and exposing a light-sensitive paper that turns from white to blue; it helps reveal scratches and flaws in the negatives.

body copy The text of an advertisement that tells the complete story and attempts to close the sale. It is a logical continuation of the headline and subheads and is usually set in a smaller type size than headlines or subheads.

boldface Heavier type.

booths At trade shows, a major factor in sales promotion plans. To stop traffic, it must be simple and attractive and have good lighting and a large visual.

bottom-up marketing The opposite of standard, top-down marketing planning, bottom-up marketing focuses on one specific tactic and develops it into an overall strategy.

brainstorming A process in which two or more people get together to generate new ideas; often a source of sudden inspiration.

brand That combination of name, words, symbols, or design that identifies the product and its source and distinguishes it from competing products—the fundamental differentiating device for all products.

brand development index (BDI) The percentage of a brand's total sales in an area divided by the total population in the area; it indicates the sales potential of a particular brand in a specific market area.

brand equity The totality of what consumers, distributors, dealers, and competitors feel and think about a brand over an extended period of time; in short, it is the value of the brand's capital.

branding A marketing function that identifies products and their source and differentiates them from all other products.

brand integration See *product placement.*

brand interest An individual's openness or curiosity about a brand.

brand loyalty The consumer's conscious or unconscious decision—expressed through intention or behavior—to repurchase a brand continually. This occurs because the consumer perceives that the brand has the right product features, image, quality, or relationship at the right price.

brand manager The individual within the advertiser's company who is assigned the authority and responsibility for the successful marketing of a particular brand.

brand personality Describes a brand in terms of human characteristics. A significant component in effective branding is imparting personality to a brand, reflecting its reputation, attitudes, and behavior.

brand trains An advertising program under which all the advertising in and on a train is from a single advertiser. This advertising concept was first used in subway trains in New York City and is being used on the Las Vegas monorail.

broadband A type of digital data transmission that enables a single wire to carry multiple signals simultaneously. Examples of broadband transmission include cable and DSL.

broadcast standards department A department at a TV network that reviews all programs and commercials to be broadcast to see that they meet all applicable standards.

broadcast TV Television sent over airwaves as opposed to over cables.

broadside A form of direct-mail advertisement, larger than a folder and sometimes used as a window display or wall poster in stores. It can be folded to a compact size and fitted into a mailer.

brochures Sales materials printed on heavier paper and featuring color photographs, illustrations, typography. See also *folders*.

bulk discounts Newspapers offer advertisers decreasing rates (calculated by multiplying the number of inches by the cost per inch) as they use more inches.

bulletin boards An internal public relations means for announcing new equipment, meetings, promotions, new products, construction plans, and recreation news.

bulletin structures Types of outdoor advertising meant for long-term use and that work best where traffic is heavy and visibility is good. They carry printed or painted messages, are created in sections, and are brought to the site where they are assembled and hung on the billboard structure.

bursting A media scheduling method for promoting high-ticket items that require careful consideration, such as running the same commercial every half-hour on the same network in prime time.

business magazines The largest category of magazines, they target business readers and include: *trade publications* for retailers, wholesalers, and other distributors; *industrial magazines* for businesspeople involved in manufacturing and services; and *professional journals* for lawyers, physicians, architects, and other professionals.

business markets Organizations that buy natural resources, component products, and services that they resell, use to conduct their business, or use to manufacture another product.

business reply mail A type of mail that enables the recipient of direct-mail advertising to respond without paying postage.

business-to-business agency Represents clients that market products to other businesses; also called high-tech agency.

bus-o-rama sign In transit advertising, a jumbo roof sign, which is actually a full-color transparency backlighted by fluorescent tubes, running the length of the bus.

button In Internet advertising, buttons are small versions of a banner and sometimes look like an icon, and they usually provide a link to an advertiser's home page. Because buttons take up less space than banners, they also cost less.

buyback allowance A manufacturer's offer to pay for an old product so that it will be taken off the shelf to make room for a new product.

cable modem A system of connecting with the Internet that offers high-speed data transfer direct to the computer. Only available from those cable TV companies that offer one of the new cable-modem services such as Roadrunner or @Home.

cable TV Television signals carried to households by cable and paid by subscription.

camera-ready art A finished ad that is ready for the printer's camera to shoot—to make negatives or plates—according to the publication's specifications.

car-end posters Transit advertisements of varying sizes, positioned in the bulkhead.

catalogs Reference books mailed to prospective customers that list, describe, and often picture the products sold by a manufacturer, wholesaler, jobber, or retailer.

category development index (CDI) The percent of a product category's total U.S. sales in an area divided by the percent of total U.S. population in the area.

cause marketing A promotion in which a portion of the proceeds from certain for-profit products are donated to a nonprofit cause. The goal is usually to increase sales for the products while raising money and visibility for the cause.

CD-ROM Acronym for compact disk-read only memory; computer storage disk that offers a large amount of storage space.

cease-and-desist order May be issued by the FTC if an advertiser won't sign a consent decree; prohibits further use of an ad.

centralized advertising department A staff of employees, usually located at corporate headquarters, responsible for all the organization's advertising. The department is often structured by product, advertising subfunction, end user, media, or geography.

central location test A type of pretest in which videotapes of test commercials are shown to respondents on a one-to-one basis, usually in shopping center locations.

central route to persuasion One of two ways communication can persuade consumers. When a consumer's level of involvement is high, the central route to persuasion is more likely. In the central route to persuasion, consumers are motivated to pay attention to the central, product-related information, such as product attributes and benefits. Because of their high involvement, they tend to learn cognitively and comprehend the ad-delivered information at deeper, more elaborate levels. See also *elaboration likelihood model* and *peripheral route to persuasion.*

cents-off promotion A short-term reduction in the price of a product designed to induce trial and usage. Cents-off promotions take various forms, including basic cents-off packages, one-cent sales, free offers, and box-top refunds.

channel Any medium through which an encoded message is sent to a receiver, including oral communication, print media, television, and the Internet.

Chromalin proof This proof uses a series of four very thin plastic sheets pressed together; each layer's light-sensitive emulsion turns one of the process colors when exposed to certain wavelengths of light.

cinema advertising Advertising in movie theaters.

circulation A statistical measure of a print medium's audience; includes subscription and vendor sales and primary and secondary readership.

circulation audit Thorough analysis of circulation procedures, distribution outlets, and other distribution factors by a company such as the Audit Bureau of Circulations (ABC).

classified ads Newspaper, magazine, and now Internet advertisements usually arranged under subheads that describe the class of goods or the need the ads seek to satisfy. Rates are based on the number of lines the ad occupies. Most employment, housing, and automotive advertising is in the form of classified advertising.

classified advertising Used to locate and recruit new employees, offer services, or sell or lease new and used merchandise.

classified ad Web site Web sites that specialize in providing classified advertisements, often provided for free. Many classified ad Web sites are supported by ad banners of other advertisers.

classified display ads Ads that run in the classified section of the newspaper but have larger-size type, photos, art borders, abundant white space, and sometimes color.

click rate In Internet advertising, the number of "clicks" on an advertisement divided by the number of ad requests. A method by which marketers can measure the frequency with which users try to obtain additional information about a product by clicking on an advertisement. Also called *click-through rate.*

click-through A term used in reference to when a World Wide Web user clicks on an ad banner to visit the advertiser's site. Some Web publishers charge advertisers according to the number of click-throughs on a given ad banner.

close That part of an advertisement or commercial that asks customers to do something and tells them how to do it—the action step in the ad's copy.

closing date A publication's final deadline for supplying printing material for an advertisement.

clutter tests Method of pretesting in which commercials are grouped with noncompetitive control commercials and shown to prospective customers to measure their effectiveness in gaining attention, increasing brand awareness and comprehension, and causing attitude shifts.

cognition The point of awareness and comprehension of a stimulus.

cognitive dissonance See *theory of cognitive dissonance.*

cognitive theory An approach that views learning as a mental process of memory, thinking, and the rational application of knowledge to practical problem solving.

color key A color proof that is a less-expensive form of the Chromalin, with thicker plastic sheets that can be lifted up.

color separations Four separate continuous-tone negatives produced by photographing artwork through color filters that eliminate all the colors but one. The negatives are used to make four printing plates—one each for yellow, magenta, cyan, and black—for reproducing the color artwork.

color strip Samples of eye shadow, blush, lipstick, and other makeup inserted into magazines.

column inch The basic unit by which publishers bill for advertising. It is one vertical inch of a column. Today, most newspapers—and virtually all dailies—have converted to the SAU system. A SAU column inch is 2-$\frac{1}{16}$ inches wide by 1 inch deep.

combination offers A sales promotion device in which two related products are packaged together at a special price, such as a razor and a package of blades. Sometimes a combination offer may be used to introduce a new product by tying its purchase to an established product at a special price.

combination rates Special newspaper advertising rates offered for placing a given ad in (1) morning and evening editions of the same newspaper; (2) two or more newspapers owned by the same publisher; or (3) two or more newspapers affiliated in a syndicate or newspaper group.

command headline A type of headline that orders the reader to do something.

community involvement A local public relations activity in which companies sponsor or participate in a local activity or supply a location for an event.

company conventions Meetings held by companies with their employees, sales representatives, and/or customers to announce new products, policies, and marketing programs.

comparative advertising Advertising that claims superiority to competitors in some aspect.

compiled list A type of direct-mail list that has been compiled by another source, such as lists of automobile owners, new home purchasers, business owners, union members, and so forth. It is the most readily available type of list but offers the lowest response expectation.

comprehensive layout (comp) A facsimile of a finished ad with copy set in type and pasted into position along with proposed illustrations. The "comp" is prepared so the advertiser can gauge the effect of the final ad.

conceptualization See *visualization.*

conditioning theory The theory that learning is a trial-and-error process. Also called *stimulus-response theory.*

consent decree A document advertisers sign, without admitting any wrongdoing, in which they agree to stop objectionable advertising.

consumer advocates Individuals and groups who actively work to protect consumer rights often by investigating advertising complaints received from the public and those that grow out of their own research.

consumer behavior The activities, actions, and influences of people who purchase and use goods and services to satisfy their personal or household needs and wants.

consumer decision process The series of steps a consumer goes through in deciding to make a purchase.

consumerism Social action designed to dramatize the rights of the buying public.

consumer magazines Information- or entertainment-oriented periodicals directed toward people who buy products for their own consumption.

consumer packaged goods Everyday-use consumer products packaged by manufacturers and sold through retail outlets. Generally these are goods such as food and beverages, health and beauty care, cleaning products, and detergents that get used up and have to be replaced frequently.

consumer sales promotions Marketing, advertising, and sales promotion activities aimed at inducing trial, purchase, and repurchase by the consumer. Also called *pull strategy.*

consumers, consumer market People who buy products and services for their own, or someone else's, personal use.

contest A sales promotion device for creating consumer involvement in which prizes are offered based on the skill of the entrants.

continuity The duration of an advertising message or campaign over a given period of time.

continuous schedule A method of scheduling media in which advertising runs steadily with little variation.

continuous tone Normal photographic paper produces images in black and white with shades of gray in between.

contract rate A special rate for newspaper advertising usually offered to local advertisers who sign an annual contract for frequent or bulk-space purchases.

controlled circulation A free publication mailed to a select list of individuals the publisher feels are in a unique position to influence the purchase of advertised products.

control room In a recording studio, the place where the producer, director, and sound engineer sit, monitoring and controlling all the sounds generated in the sound studio.

convenience cards Cards issued by retailers that allow them to track their customers' purchasing habits and demographic profiles. This information allows manufacturers and merchants to more effectively target promotions. Retailers often provide discounts at the checkout to encourage customers to use their cards for every transaction.

cookies Small pieces of information that get stored on your computer when you download certain Web sites. These cookies can keep track of whether a certain user has ever before visited a specific site. This allows the Web site to identify returning users and to customize the information based on past browsing or purchase behavior.

cooperative (co-op) advertising The sharing of advertising costs by the manufacturer and the distributor or retailer. The manufacturer may repay 50 or 100 percent of the dealer's advertising costs or some other amount based on sales. See also *horizontal cooperative advertising, vertical cooperative advertising.*

copy The words that make up the headline and message of an advertisement or commercial.

copy platform See *creative strategy.*

copy points Copywriting themes in a product's advertising.

copyright An exclusive right granted by the Copyright Act to authors and artists to protect their original work from being plagiarized, sold, or used by another without their express consent.

copy strategy See *creative strategy.*

copywriters People who create the words and concepts for ads and commercials.

corporate advertising The broad area of nonproduct advertising aimed specifically at enhancing a company's image and increasing lagging awareness.

corporate identity advertising Advertising a corporation creates to familiarize the public with its name, logos, trademarks, or corporate signatures, especially after any of these elements are changed.

corporate objectives Goals of the company stated in terms of profit or return on investment. Objectives may also be stated in terms of net worth, earnings ratios, growth, or corporate reputation.

corrective advertising May be required by the FTC for a period of time to explain and correct offending ads.

cost efficiency The cost of reaching the target audience through a particular medium as opposed to the cost of reaching the medium's total circulation.

cost per point (CPP) A simple computation used by media buyers to determine which broadcast programs are the most efficient in relation to the target audience. The CPP is determined by dividing the cost of the show by the show's expected rating against the target audience.

cost per thousand (CPM) A common term describing the cost of reaching 1,000 people in a medium's audience. It is used by media planners to compare the cost of various media vehicles.

coupon A certificate with a stated value that is presented to a retail store for a price reduction on a specified item.

cover date The date printed on the cover of a publication.

cover position Advertising space on the front inside, back inside, and back cover pages of a publication that is usually sold at a premium price.

CPM See *cost per thousand.*

creative boutique An organization of creative specialists (such as art directors, designers, and copywriters) who work for advertisers and occasionally advertising agencies to develop creative concepts, advertising messages, and specialized art. A boutique performs only the creative work.

creative brief See *creative strategy.*

creative director Heads a creative team of agency copywriters and artists that is assigned to a client's business; is ultimately responsible for the creative product—the form the final ad takes.

creative mix Those advertising elements the company controls to achieve its advertising objectives, including the target audience, the product concept, the communications media, and the advertising message. See also *advertising strategy.*

creative process The step-by-step procedure used to discover original ideas and reorganize existing concepts in new ways.

creative pyramid A five-step model to help the creative team convert advertising strategy and the big idea into the actual physical ad or commercial. The five elements are: attention, interest, credibility, desire, and action.

creatives The people who work in the creative department, regardless of their specialty.

creative strategy A written statement that serves as the creative team's guide for writing and producing an ad. It describes the most important issues that should be considered in the development of the ad (the who, what, where, when, and why), including the objective of the advertising; a definition and description of the target audience; the key benefit to be promised; the product features that support that promise; the style, approach, or tone to be used; and, generally, what the copy should communicate.

creativity Involves combining two or more previously unconnected objects or ideas into something new.

crisis management A company's plan for handling news and public relations during crises.

culture A homogeneous group's whole set of beliefs, attitudes, and ways of doing things, typically handed down from generation to generation.

cume persons The total number of different people listening to a radio station for at least one 15-minute segment over the course of a given week, day, or daypart.

cume rating The estimated number of cume persons expressed as a percentage of the total market population.

customer lifetime value (LTV) See *lifetime customer value (LTV).*

customer relationship management (CRM) A promotional program that focuses on existing clients rather than prospecting for new clients.

CYMK printing See *four-color process.*

daily newspapers Often called *dailies,* these newspapers are published at least five times a week, in either morning or evening editions.

database The corporate memory of all important customer information: name and address, telephone number, NAIC code (if a business firm), source of inquiry, cost of inquiry, history of purchases, and so on. It should record every transaction across all points of contact with both channel members and customers.

database management The process of gathering, consolidating, updating, and enhancing the information about customers and prospects that resides in a company's database.

database marketing Tracking and analyzing the purchasing patterns of specific customers in a computer database and then targeting advertising to their needs.

database queries Inquiries that are performed against a database to extract and analyze information for the purpose of making marketing decisions.

daypart mix A media scheduling strategy based on the TV usage levels reported by the rating services.

dealer meetings　Meetings held by companies with their authorized brokers, distributors, and/or retailers to announce new products, policies, and marketing programs.

decentralized system　The establishment of advertising departments by products or brands or in various divisions, subsidiaries, countries, regions, or other categories that suit the firm's needs, which operate with a major degree of independence.

deceptive advertising　According to the FTC, any ad in which there is a misrepresentation, omission, or other practice that can mislead a significant number of reasonable consumers to their detriment.

decline stage　The stage in the product life cycle when sales begin to decline due to obsolescence, new technology, or changing consumer tastes.

decoding　The interpretation of a message by the receiver.

demarketing　Term coined during the energy shortage of the 1970s and 1980s when advertising was used to slow the demand for products.

demographic editions　Magazines that reach readers who share a demographic trait, such as age, income level, or professional status.

demographic segmentation　Based on a population's statistical characteristics such as sex, age, ethnicity, education, occupation, income, or other quantifiable factors.

demonstration　A type of TV commercial in which the product is shown in use.

departmental system　The organization of an ad agency into departments based on function: account services, creative services, marketing services, and administration.

design　Visual pattern or composition of artistic elements chosen and structured by the graphic artist.

designated market areas (DMAs)　The geographical areas in which TV stations attract most of their viewers.

device copy　Advertising copy that relies on wordplay, humor, poetry, rhymes, great exaggeration, gags, and other tricks or gimmicks.

dialogue/monologue copy　A type of body copy in which the characters illustrated in the advertisement do the selling in their own words either through a quasi-testimonial technique or through a comic strip panel.

digital interactive media　Electronic channels of communication—including online databases, the Internet, CD-ROMs, and stand-alone kiosks—with which the audience can participate actively and immediately.

digital media　Channels of communication that join the logic of multimedia formats with the electronic system capabilities and controls of modern telephone, television, and computer technologies.

digital proof　A prepress proof that uses inkjet technology and offers fairly accurate reliability as well as lower cost and faster turn-around time. Also called an *Iris*.

digital subscriber line (DSL)　Technology that transforms a traditional telephone line into a high-speed digital link to provide homes and small businesses with always-on, broadband Internet access.

digital video effects (DVE)　Visual effects that are created using a computer, resulting in interesting transitions from one scene to another, including fades, wipes, zooms, and flips.

digital video recorder (DVR)　A device (such as TiVo) that is similar to a VCR, but records programs on a hard drive in digital format, providing high-quality image and sound and the ability to "pause live TV."

dimensional direct mail　Direct-mail advertising that utilizes three-dimensional shapes and unusual materials.

direct distribution　The method of marketing in which the manufacturer sells directly to customers without the use of retailers.

direct-mail advertising　All forms of advertising sent directly to prospective customers without using one of the commercial media forms.

direct marketing　A system of marketing in which companies build their own database of customers and use a variety of media to communicate with them directly such as through ads and catalogs.

director　The director supervises preproduction, production, and postproduction of radio and television commercials.

directories　Listings, often in booklet form, that serve as locators, buying guides, and mailing lists.

direct questioning　A method of pretesting designed to elicit a full range of responses to the advertising. It is especially effective for testing alternative advertisements in the early stages of development.

direct-response advertising　An advertising message that asks the reader, listener, or viewer to provide feedback straight to the sender. Direct-response advertising can take the form of direct mail, or it can use a wide range of other media, from matchbook covers or magazines to radio, TV, or billboards.

direct sales　Selling to customers directly, at home or at work, rather than through a retail establishment or other intermediary.

direct selling　Face-to-face selling away from a fixed retail location. Usually refers to a method of marketing consumer goods—everything from encyclopedias and insurance to cosmetics and nutritional products.

display advertising   Type of newspaper advertising that includes copy, illustrations or photographs, headlines, coupons, and other visual components.

display allowances   Fees paid to retailers to make room for and set up manufacturers' displays.

display type   A style of typeface used in advertising that is larger and heavier than normal text type. Display type is often used in headlines, subheads, logos, and addresses, and for emphasis.

distribution channel   The network of all the firms and individuals that take title, or assist in taking title, to the product as it moves from the producer to the consumer.

distribution objectives   Where, when, and how advertising should appear.

diverting   Purchasing large quantities of an item at a regional promotional discount and shipping portions to areas of the country where the discount isn't being offered.

drive times   Radio use Monday through Friday at 6–10 a.m. and 3–7 p.m.

DSL   See *digital subscriber line*.

dubs   Duplicates of radio commercials made from the master tape and sent to stations for broadcast.

dummy   A three-dimensional, hand-made layout of a brochure or other multipage advertising piece put together, page for page, just like the finished product will eventually appear.

dupes   Copies of a finished television commercial that are delivered to the networks or TV stations for airing.

early adopter   Prospects who are most willing to try new products and services.

earned rate   A discount applied retroactively as the volume of advertising increases through the year.

effective frequency   The average number of times a person must see or hear a message before it becomes effective.

effective reach   Term used to describe the quality of exposure. It measures the number or percentage of the audience who receive enough exposures for the message to truly be received.

eight-sheet posters   A type of outdoor advertising offering a 5-foot by 11-foot printing area on a panel surface 6 feet tall by 12 feet wide.

elaboration likelihood model   A theory of how persuasion occurs due to promotion communication. It proposes that the method of persuasion depends on the consumer's level of involvement with the product and the message. See also *central route to persuasion* and *peripheral route to persuasion*.

electronic coupons   Offer benefits similar to paper coupons, but they are distributed at the point of purchase, based on customer information stored in an electronic database. This allows manufacturers and retailers to target discounts, rebates, and other offers to the most receptive customers.

electronic production   The process of converting a script or storyboard into a finished commercial for use on radio, TV, or digital media.

electronic sign   Large displays that provide text and graphic messages, similar to those found in sports stadiums.

e-mail   Electronic mail-messages transmitted electronically between computers.

e-mail advertising   Has become one of the fastest growing and most effective ways to provide direct mail.

endcap promotion   A merchandizing method that uses special displays on shelving at the end of aisles in a store. Endcap promotions usually highlight sale merchandise or new products. Such promotions are often one part of a large promotion program that includes coupons, discounts, or other enticements.

encoding   Translating an idea or message into words, symbols, and illustrations.

endorsement   See *testimonial*.

ethical advertising   Doing what the advertiser and the advertiser's peers believe is morally right in a given situation.

evaluation of alternatives   Choosing among brands, sizes, styles, and colors.

evaluative criteria   The standards a consumer uses for judging the features and benefits of alternative products.

evoked set   The particular group of alternative goods or services a consumer considers when making a buying decision.

exchange   The trading of one thing of value for another thing of value.

exclusive distribution   The strategy of limiting the number of wholesalers or retailers who can sell a product in order to gain a prestige image, maintain premium prices, or protect other dealers in a geographic region.

exhibits   A marketing or public relations approach that involves preparing displays that tell about an organization or its products; exhibits may be used at fairs, colleges and universities, or trade shows.

experimental method   A method of scientific investigation in which a researcher alters the stimulus received by a test group or groups and compares the results with those of a control group that did not receive the altered stimulus.

Explorer role   A role in the creative process that searches for new information, paying attention to unusual patterns.

exposure value The value of a medium determined by how well it exposes an ad to the target audience. In other words, how many people an ad "sees" rather than the other way around.

externalities Benefit or harm caused by the sale or consumption of products to people who are not involved in the transaction and didn't pay for the product.

e-zine A magazine published online or sent by e-mail.

fact-based thinking A style of thinking that tends to fragment concepts into components and to analyze situations to discover the one best solution.

family brand The marketing of various products under the same umbrella name.

farm publications Magazines directed to farmers and their families or to companies that manufacture or sell agricultural equipment, supplies, and services.

FCB grid A two-dimensional model that categorizes consumer products into four quadrants based on "high involvement" or "low involvement," and "think" or "feel." By positioning brands in the grid, an agency can determine the type of advertising that would be most appropriate.

feature article Soft news about companies, products, or services that may be written by a PR person, the publication's staff, or a third party.

fee-commission combination A pricing system in which an advertising agency charges the client a basic monthly fee for its services and also retains any media commissions earned.

feedback A message that acknowledges or responds to an initial message.

firewall Hardware or software designed to secure a computer or network from unauthorized access over an outside network, especially the Internet.

first-run syndication Programs produced specifically for the syndication market.

five Ms The elements of the media mix that include markets, money, media, mechanics, and methodology.

flat rate A standard newspaper advertising rate with no discount allowance for large or repeated space buys.

flats Opaque plastic sheets that film negatives are mounted on in perfect registration; light passes through only where lines and dots are to appear on the printing plate.

flighting An intermittent media scheduling pattern in which periods of advertising are alternated with periods of no advertising at all.

focus group A qualitative method of research in which four or more people, typical of the target market, are invited to a group session to discuss the product, the service, or the marketing situation for an hour or more.

folders Large, heavy-stock fliers, often folded and sent out as self-mailers.

font A uniquely designed set of capital, small capital, and lowercase letters, usually including numerals and punctuation marks.

foreign media The local media of each country used by advertisers for campaigns targeted to consumers or businesses within a single country.

formal research Collecting primary data directly from the marketplace using qualitative or quantitative methods.

forward buying A retailer's stocking up on a product when it is discounted and buying smaller amounts when it is at list price.

four-color process The method for printing color advertisements with tonal values, such as photographs and paintings. This process is based on the principle that all colors can be printed by combining the three primary colors—yellow, magenta (red), and cyan (blue)—plus black.

four Ps (4Ps) See *marketing mix.*

fragrance strips Perfume samples included in sealed inserts in magazines.

freestanding inserts (FSIs) Coupons distributed through inserts in newspapers.

freeware Programs and applications that can be downloaded from the Internet and used for free.

frequency The number of times the same person or household is exposed to a vehicle in a specified time span. Across a total audience, frequency is calculated as the average number of times individuals or homes are exposed to the vehicle.

frequency discounts In newspapers, advertisers earn this discount by running an ad repeatedly in a specific time period.

full position In newspaper advertising, the preferred position near the top of a page or on the top of a column next to reading matter. It is usually surrounded by editorial text and may cost the advertiser 25 to 50 percent more than ROP rates.

full-service advertising agency An agency equipped to serve its clients in all areas of communication and promotion. Its advertising services include planning, creating, and producing advertisements as well as performing research and media selection services. Nonadvertising functions include producing sales promotion materials, publicity articles, annual reports, trade show exhibits, and sales training materials.

full showing A unit of purchase in transit advertising where one card will appear in each vehicle in the system.

game A sales promotion activity in which prizes are offered based on chance. The big marketing advantage of games is that customers must make repeat visits to the dealer to continue playing.

gatefold   A magazine cover or page extended and folded over to fit into the magazine. The gatefold may be a fraction of a page or two or more pages, and it is always sold at a premium.

general consumer agency   An agency that represents the widest variety of accounts, but it concentrates on companies that make goods purchased chiefly by consumers.

geodemographic segmentation   Combining demographics with geographic segmentation to select target markets in advertising.

geographic editions   Magazines that target geographic markets and have different rates for ads.

geographic segmentation   A method of segmenting markets by geographic regions based on the shared characteristics, needs, or wants of people within the region.

global marketers   Multinationals that use a standardized approach to marketing and advertising in all countries.

global positioning system (GPS)   New satellite-based system whereby outdoor advertising companies give their customers the exact latitude and longitude of particular boards. Media buyers, equipped with sophisticated new software on their desktop computers, can then integrate this information with demographic market characteristics and traffic counts to determine the best locations for their boards without ever leaving the office.

goods   Tangible products such as suits, soap, and soft drinks.

gross impressions   The total of all the audiences delivered by a media plan.

gross rating points (GRPs)   The total audience delivery or weight of a specific media schedule. One rating point equals 1 percent of a particular market's population.

group system   System in which an ad agency is divided into a number of little agencies or groups, each composed of an account supervisor, account executives, copywriters, art directors, a media director, and any other specialists required to meet the needs of the particular clients being served by the group.

growth stage   The period in a product life cycle that is marked by market expansion as more and more customers make their first purchases while others are already making their second and third purchases.

GRPs   See *gross rating points*.

guaranteed circulation   The number of copies of a magazine that the publisher expects to sell. If this figure is not reached, the publisher must give a refund to advertisers.

habit   An acquired or developed behavior pattern that has become nearly or completely involuntary.

halftone   The process of converting continuous-tone artwork, such as a photograph, into a pattern of different size dots that simulate shades of gray. When printed, the dots merge to give an illusion of continuous tone to the naked eye.

halo effect   In ad pretesting, the fact that consumers are likely to rate the one or two ads that make the best first impression as the highest in all categories.

headline   The words in the leading position of an advertisement—the words that will be read first or that are positioned to draw the most attention.

hidden differences   Imperceptible but existing differences that may greatly affect the desirability of a product.

hierarchy of needs   Maslow's theory that the lower biological or survival needs are dominant in human behavior and must be satisfied before higher, socially acquired needs become meaningful.

horizontal cooperative advertising   Joint advertising effort of related businesses (car dealers, realtors, etc.) to create traffic for their type of business.

horizontal publications   Business publications targeted at people with particular job functions that cut across industry lines, such as *Purchasing* magazine.

households using TV (HUT)   The percentage of homes in a given area that have one or more TV sets tuned on at any particular time. If 1,000 TV sets are in the survey area and 500 are turned on, the HUT figure is 50 percent.

house list   A company's most important and valuable direct-mail list, which may contain current, recent, and long-past customers or future prospects.

house organs   Internal and external publications produced by business organizations, including stockholder reports, newsletters, consumer magazines, and dealer publications. Most are produced by a company's advertising or public relations department or by its agency.

icon   A pictorial image that represents an idea or thing.

ideas   Economic, political, religious, or social viewpoints that advertising may attempt to sell.

illustrators   The artists who paint, sketch, or draw the pictures we see in advertising.

imagery transfer   When advertisers run a schedule on TV and then convert the audio portion to radio commercials, fully 75 percent of consumers replay the video in their minds when they hear the radio spot.

immersive advertising   Proprietary technique developed by Neopets.com for integrating an advertiser's products or services into the Web site experience.

incentive system   A form of compensation in which the agency shares in the client's success when a campaign attains specific, agreed-upon goals.

in-depth interview An intensive interview technique that uses carefully planned but loosely structured questions to probe respondents' deeper feelings.

individual brand Assigning a unique name to each product a manufacturer produces.

induced differences Distinguishing characteristics of products effected through unique branding, packaging, distribution, merchandising, and advertising.

industrial age A historical period covering approximately the first 70 years of the twentieth century. This period was marked by tremendous growth and maturation of the U.S. industrial base. It saw the development of new, often inexpensive brands of the luxury and convenience goods we now classify as consumer packaged goods.

industrializing age The period of time from the mid-1700s through the end of World War I when manufacturers were principally concerned with production.

infomercial A long TV commercial that gives consumers detailed information about a product or service; see also *program-length advertisement.*

informal research The second step in the research process, designed to explore a problem by reviewing secondary data and interviewing a few key people with the most information to share. Also called *exploratory research.*

informational Promising benefits that will offer relief from an undesirable situation or condition. Informational ads tend to address *negatively originated purchase motives,* such as problem removal or avoidance, in an attempt to provide solutions to those problems.

informational motives The negatively originated motives, such as problem removal or problem avoidance, that are the most common energizers of consumer behavior.

in-house agency Agency wholly owned by an advertiser and set up and staffed to do all the work of an independent full-service agency.

in kind The donation of goods and services as payment for some service such as a sponsorship.

inquiry test A form of test in which consumer responses to an ad for information or free samples are tabulated.

insert An ad or brochure which the advertiser prints and ships to the publisher for insertion into a magazine or newspaper.

insertion order A form submitted to a newspaper or magazine when an advertiser wants to run an advertisement. This form states the date(s) on which the ad is to run, its size, the requested position, and the rate.

inside card A transit advertisement, normally 11 by 28 inches, placed in a wall rack above the windows of a bus.

institutional advertising A type of advertising that attempts to obtain favorable attention for the business as a whole, not for a specific product or service the store or business sells. The effects of institutional advertising are intended to be long term rather than short range.

institutional copy A type of body copy in which the advertiser tries to sell an idea or the merits of the organization or service rather than the sales features of a particular product.

in-store sampling The handing out of free product samples to passing shoppers.

integrated commercial A straight radio announcement, usually delivered by one person, woven into a show or tailored to a given program to avoid any perceptible interruption.

integrated marketing communications (IMC) The process of building and reinforcing mutually profitable relationships with employees, customers, other stakeholders, and the general public by developing and coordinating a strategic communications program that enables them to make constructive contact with the company/brand through a variety of media.

intellectual property Something produced by the mind, such as original works of authorship including literary, dramatic, musical, artistic, and certain other "intellectual" works, which may be legally protected by copyright, patent, or trademark.

intensive distribution A distribution strategy based on making the product available to consumers at every possible location so that consumers can buy with a minimum of effort.

intensive techniques Qualitative research aimed at probing the deepest feelings, attitudes, and beliefs of respondents through direct questioning. Typical methods include in-depth interviews and focus groups.

interactive agency An advertising agency that specializes in the creation of ads for a digital interactive medium such as Web pages, CD-ROMs, or electronic kiosks.

interactive media Media such as the Internet and interactive television that permits consumers to give instantaneous, real-time feedback on the same channel used by the original message sender.

interactive TV (ITV) A personal audience venue where people can personally guide TV programming through a remote control box while watching TV.

interior paragraphs Text within the body copy of an ad where the credibility and desire steps of the message are presented.

international agency An advertising agency that has offices or affiliates in major communication centers around the world and can help its clients market internationally or globally.

international media Media serving several countries, usually without change, that is available to an international audience.

Internet   A worldwide network of computer systems that facilitates global electronic communications via e-mail, the World Wide Web, ftp, and other data protocols.

Internet profiling   The gathering of personal information on customers for the purpose of better targeting advertising and marketing.

Internet service provider (ISP)   Companies that offer consumer and business access to the Internet.

interpersonal influences   Social influences on the consumer decision-making process, including family, society, and cultural environment.

interstitial   Animated screens, often advertisements, which pop up momentarily as the computer searches for and downloads information for a requested Web page. Also known as *splash pages*.

intranet   A restricted-access computer network, based on Internet technology, that is designed to meet the internal needs for sharing information within a single organization or company. Such information might include organization policies and procedures, announcements, or information about new products.

introductory phase   The initial phase of the product life cycle (also called the *pioneering phase*) when a new product is introduced, costs are highest, and profits are lowest.

inventory   Commercial time for advertisers.

island half   A half-page of magazine space that is surrounded on two or more sides by editorial matter. This type of ad is designed to dominate a page and is therefore sold at a premium price.

italic   A style of printing type with letters that generally slant to the right.

jingle   A musical commercial, usually sung with the sales message in the verse.

job jacket   In the preproduction phase, a place to store the various pieces of artwork and ideas that will be generated throughout the process.

Judge role   A role in the creative process that evaluates the results of experimentation and decides which approach is more practical.

junior unit   A large magazine advertisement (60 percent of the page) placed in the middle of a page and surrounded by editorial matter.

kerning   The measurement of the space between individual letters of text.

key benefit   The most important benefit offered to consumers by a product or service. The benefit should describe the value provided to the consumer, rather than just the features or attributes of the product.

keyword   A single word that a user inputs into an Internet search engine to request information that is similar in subject matter to that word. Advertisers may buy keywords from search engines so that their advertisements appear when a user inputs the purchased word.

kicker   A subhead that appears above the headline.

Kim-Lord grid   A variation of the FCB grid which allows for the fact that the level of consumer involvement in a product does not have to be high "think" and low "feel" (or vice versa) but can be high (or low) in both categories.

kiosks   Interactive computers in a stand-alone cabinet that make information available 24 hours a day even in remote areas.

landing page   The Web page that a person reaches when clicking on a search engine listing or ad. For best results, these pages are highly targeted for the reader and specific to the referring ad.

layout   An orderly formation of all the parts of an advertisement. In print, it refers to the arrangement of the headline, subheads, visuals, copy, picture captions, trademarks, slogans, and signature. In television, it refers to the placement of characters, props, scenery, and product elements, the location and angle of the camera, and the use of lighting. See also *design*.

leading   The measurement of the space between separate lines of text (pronounced *ledding*).

lead-in paragraph   In print ads, a bridge between the headlines, the subheads, and the sales ideas presented in the text. It transfers reader interest to product interest.

learning   A relatively permanent change in thought processes or behavior that occurs as a result of reinforced experience.

letter shop   A firm that stuffs envelopes, affixes labels, calculates postage, sorts pieces into stacks or bundles, and otherwise prepares items for mailing.

licensed brands   Brand names that other companies can buy the right to use.

lifestyle technique   Type of commercial in which the user is presented rather than the product. Typically used by clothing and soft drink advertisers to affiliate their brands with the trendy lifestyles of their consumers.

lifetime customer value (LTV)   The total sales or profit value of a customer to a marketer over the course of that customer's lifetime.

limen   Our threshold of perception.

line art   Any artwork or type that is comprised of a solid color. There are no continuous tones—shades of gray or any other color.

linkage media   In direct marketing, media that help prospects and customers link up with a company.

list broker An intermediary who handles rental of mailing lists for list owners on a commission basis.

live action The basic production technique in television that portrays real people and settings, as opposed to animation.

lobbying Informing government officials and persuading them to support or thwart administrative action or legislation in the interests of some client.

local advertising Advertising by businesses within a city or county directed toward customers within the same geographical area.

local agency Advertising agencies that specialize in creating advertising for local businesses.

local city magazine Most major U.S. cities have one of these publications. Typical readership is upscale, professional people interested in local arts, fashion, and business.

local time Radio spots purchased by a local advertiser.

location Shooting away from the studio. Location shooting adds realism but can also be a technical and logistical nightmare, often adding cost and many other potential problems.

logotype (logo) Special design of the advertiser's name (or product name) that appears in all advertisements. Also called a *signature cut,* it is like a trademark because it gives the advertiser individuality and provides quick recognition at the point of purchase.

loyalty (continuity) program Program that rewards customers with discounts and free products in return for frequent and continuous patronage. Consumer purchases are tracked on a company's database.

mail-response list A type of direct-mail list, composed of people who have responded to the direct-mail solicitations of other companies, especially those whose efforts are complementary to the advertiser's.

makegoods TV spots that are aired to compensate for spots that were missed or run incorrectly.

management (account) supervisors Managers who supervise account executives and who report to the agency's director of account services.

mandatories The address, phone number, Web address, etc., that the advertiser usually insists be included within an ad to give the consumer adequate information.

market A group of potential customers who share a common interest, need, or desire; who can use the offered good or service to some advantage; and who can afford or are willing to pay the purchase price. Also, an element of the media mix referring to the various targets of a media plan.

marketing An organizational function and a set of processes for creating, communicating and delivering value to customers and for managing customer relationships in ways that benefit the organization and its stakeholders.

marketing communications The various efforts and tools companies use to initiate and maintain communication with customers and prospects, including solicitation letters, newspaper ads, event sponsorships, publicity, telemarketing, statement stuffers, and coupons, to mention just a few.

marketing information system (MIS) A set of procedures for generating an orderly flow of pertinent information for use in making marketing decisions.

marketing mix Four elements, called the 4Ps (product, price, place, and promotion), that every company has the option of adding, subtracting, or modifying in order to create a desired marketing strategy.

marketing objectives Goals of the marketing effort that may be expressed in terms of the needs of specific target markets and specific sales objectives.

marketing plan The plan that directs the company's marketing effort. First, it assembles all the pertinent facts about the organization, the markets it serves, and its products, services, customers, and competition. Second, it forces the functional managers within the company to work together—product development, production, selling, advertising, credit, transportation—to focus efficiently on the customer. Third, it sets goals and objectives to be attained within specified periods of time and lays out the precise strategies that will be used to achieve them.

marketing public relations (MPR) The use of public relations activities as a marketing tool.

marketing research The systematic gathering, recording, and analysis of information to help managers make marketing decisions.

marketing strategy The statement of how the company is going to accomplish its marketing objectives. The strategy is the total directional thrust of the company, that is, the how-to of the marketing plan, and is determined by the particular blend of the marketing mix elements (the 4Ps) which the company can control.

market segmentation Strategy of identifying groups of people or organizations with certain shared needs and characteristics within the broad markets for consumer or business products and aggregating these groups into larger market segments according to their mutual interest in the product's utility.

markup A source of agency income gained by adding some amount to a supplier's bill, usually 17.65 percent.

mass audience venue One category of digital media based on audience size, where hundreds of people are in the live audience and millions more are watching at home.

mass media Print or broadcast media that reach very large audiences. Mass media include radio, television, newspapers, magazines, and billboards.

master tape   The final recording of a radio commercial, with all the music, sound, and vocals mixed, from which dubs (duplicates) are recorded and sent to radio stations for broadcast.

maturity stage   That point in the product life cycle when the market has become saturated with products, the number of new customers has dwindled, and competition is most intense.

mechanical   The set type and illustrations or photographs pasted into the exact position in which they will appear in the final ad. Also called a *pasteup,* this is then used as the basis for the next step in the reproduction process.

mechanics   One of the five Ms of the media mix; dealing creatively with the available advertising media options.

media   A plural form of *medium,* referring to communications vehicles paid to present an advertisement to its target audience. Most often used to refer to radio and television networks, stations that have news reporters, and publications that carry news and advertising.

media buyer   Person responsible for negotiating and contracting the purchase of advertisement space and time in various media.

media-buying service   An organization that specializes in purchasing and packaging radio and television time.

media commission   Compensation paid by a medium to recognized advertising agencies, usually 15 percent ($16\,^2/_3$ percent for outdoor), for advertising placed with it.

media planning   The process that directs advertising messages to the right people in the right place at the right time.

media research   The systematic gathering and analysis of information on the reach and effectiveness of media vehicles.

media strategy   A document that helps media planners determine how messages will be delivered to consumers. It defines the target audience, the communication objectives that must be achieved, and the characteristics of the media that will be used for delivery of the messages.

media vehicles   Particular media programs or publications.

medium   An instrument or communications vehicle that carries or helps transfer a message from the sender to the receiver. Plural is media. See also *media.*

mental files   Stored memories in the consumer's mind.

message   In oral communication, the idea formulated and encoded by the source and sent to the receiver.

message strategy   A simple description and explanation of an ad campaign's overall creative approach—the main idea, details about how the idea will be executed, and a rationale. The elements of a message strategy include

verbal, nonverbal, and technical components. Also called a *copy platform.*

message weight   The total size of the audience for a set of ads or an entire campaign.

methodology   The overall strategy of selecting and scheduling media vehicles to achieve the desired reach, frequency, and continuity objectives.

mixed interlock   The edited version of a filmed television commercial mixed with the finished sound track. Used for initial review and approval prior to being duplicated for airing.

mixed-media approach   Using a combination of advertising media vehicles in a single advertising campaign.

mnemonic device   A gimmick used to dramatize the product benefit and make it memorable, such as the Imperial Margarine crown or the Avon doorbell.

mobile billboard   A cross between traditional billboards and transit advertising; some specially designed flatbed trucks carry long billboards up and down busy thoroughfares.

money   In media planning, one of the five elements in the media mix.

motivation   The underlying drives that stem from the conscious or unconscious needs of the consumer and contribute to the individual consumer's purchasing actions.

motivation value   A consideration in selecting media based on the medium's ability to motivate people to act. Positive factors include prestige, good quality reproduction, timeliness, and editorial relevance.

multimedia presentation   Presenting information or entertainment using several communications media simultaneously.

multinational corporations   Corporations operating and investing throughout many countries and making decisions based on availabilities worldwide.

musical commercial   See *jingle.*

NAICS   See *North American Industry Classification System.*

narrative copy   A type of body copy that tells a story. It sets up a problem and then creates a solution using the particular sales features of the product or service as the key to the solution.

narrowband   A type of digital data transmission in which wires carry only one signal (channel) at a time. Examples of narrowband transmission include many telephone calls and most transmissions between computers and peripheral devices such as printers.

narrowcasting   Delivering programming to a specific group defined by demographics and/or program content, rather than mass appeal. Usually used to describe cable networks. The opposite of broadcasting.

national advertisers Companies which advertise in several geographic regions or throughout the country.

national agency Advertising agencies that produce and place the quality of advertising suitable for national campaigns.

national brands Product brands that are marketed in several regions of the country.

national magazines Magazines that are distributed throughout a country.

national rate A newspaper advertising rate that is higher, attributed to the added costs of serving national advertisers.

needs The basic, often instinctive, human forces that motivate us to do something.

need-satisfying objectives A marketing objective that shifts management's view of the organization from a producer of products or services to a satisfier of target market needs.

negatively originated motives Consumer purchase and usage based on problem removal or problem avoidance. To relieve such feelings, consumers actively seek a new or replacement product.

network marketing A method of direct distribution in which individuals act as independent distributors for a manufacturer or private-label marketer.

networks Any of the national television or radio broadcasting chains or companies such as ABC, CBS, NBC, or Fox. Networks offer the large advertiser convenience and efficiency because the message can be broadcast simultaneously throughout the country.

news/information headline A type of headline that includes many of the "how-to" headlines as well as headlines that seek to gain identification for their sponsors by announcing some news or providing some promise of information.

Newspaper Association of America (NAA) The promotional arm of the American Newspaper Publishers Association and the nation's newspaper industry.

news release A typewritten sheet of information (usually 8 ½ by 11 inches) issued to print and broadcast outlets to generate publicity or shed light on a subject of interest. Also called a *press release*.

noise The sender's advertising message competing daily with hundreds of other commercial and noncommercial messages.

nonpersonal channels Means of communication that rule out interpersonal contact between the sender and the receiver. Examples would include advertising, public relations, and sales promotion.

nonpersonal influences Factors influencing the consumer decision-making process that are often out of the consumer's control, such as time, place, and environment.

nonprobability samples Research samples that do not provide every unit in the population with an equal chance of being included. As a result, there is no guarantee that the sample will be representative.

North American Industry Classification System (NAICS) codes Method used by the U.S. Department of Commerce to classify all businesses. The NAICS codes are based on broad industry groups, subgroups, and detailed groups of firms in similar lines of business.

objective/task method A method of determining advertising allocations, also referred to as the *budget-buildup method,* that defines objectives and how advertising is to be used to accomplish them. It has three steps: defining the objectives, determining strategy, and estimating the cost.

observation method A method of research used when researchers actually monitor people's actions.

off-network syndication The availability of programs that originally appeared on networks to individual stations for rebroadcast.

on camera Actually seen by the camera, as an announcer, a spokesperson, or actor playing out a scene.

100 showing The basic unit of sale for billboards or posters is 100 gross rating points daily. One rating point equals 1 percent of a particular market's population.

online advertising Advertising on Internet Web sites.

on-sale date The date a magazine is actually issued.

open rate The highest rate for a one-time insertion in a newspaper.

opinion leader Someone whose beliefs or attitudes are respected by people who share an interest in some specific activity.

opinion sampling A form of public relations research in which consumers provide feedback via interviews, toll-free phone lines, focus groups, and similar methods.

opportunities to see (OTS) A possible exposure of an advertising message to one audience member. Also called an *ad impression*.

opt-out An option whereby consumers may choose to prevent personally identifiable information from being used by a particular Web site or shared with third parties.

outdoor advertising An out-of-home medium in the form of billboards.

out-of-home media Media such as outdoor advertising (billboards) and transit advertising (bus and car cards) that reach prospects outside their homes.

outside posters The variety of transit advertisements appearing on the outside of buses, including king size, queen size, traveling display, rear of bus, and front of bus.

overlay　On a pasteup, a piece of clear plastic containing a second image from which a second printing plate can be made for color printing.

paid circulation　The total number of copies of an average issue of a newspaper or magazine that is distributed through subscriptions and newsstand sales.

PANTONE Matching System® (PMS)　A collection of colors that are premixed according to a formula and given a specific color number. PANTONE® swatch books feature over 100 colors in solid and screened blocks printed on different paper finishes.

participation　Several advertisers share the sponsorship of a television program. A "participating" advertiser has no control of the program content. Partnership commitment is usually limited to a relatively short period.

pass-along rate　The number of people who read a magazine without actually buying it.

pasteup　See *mechanical*.

patent　A grant made by the government that confers upon the creator of an invention the sole right to make, use, and sell that invention for a set period of time.

pay per click (PPC) advertising　A type of advertising price structure where the advertiser pays based on the number of times a published ad is clicked on. Search engines often base search result rankings on the dollar amount paid for each click. The highest ranking goes to the highest bidder.

percentage-of-sales method　A method of advertising budget allocation based on a percentage of the previous year's sales, the anticipated sales for the next year, or a combination of the two.

perceptible differences　Differences between products that are visibly apparent to the consumer.

perception　Our personalized way of sensing and comprehending stimuli.

perceptual screens　The physiological or psychological perceptual filters that messages must pass through.

peripheral route to persuasion　One of two ways communication can persuade consumers. When consumers have low involvement with a product or message, they have little reason to pay attention to or comprehend the central message of the ad. However, these consumers might attend to some peripheral aspects of an ad for its entertainment value. Consistent with stimulus-response theory, consumers may respond to the message at a later date, when a purchase occasion arises. See also *elaboration likelihood model* and *central route to persuasion*.

personal audience venue　A category of digital media based on audience size; where one person in front of a personal computer can receive multimedia information.

personal channels　Means of communication that involve direct contact between the parties, such as personal selling.

personal processes　The three internal, human operations—perception, learning, and motivation—that govern the way consumers discern raw data (stimuli) and translate them into feelings, thoughts, beliefs, and actions.

personal selling　A sales method based on person-to-person contact, such as by a salesperson at a retail establishment or by a telephone solicitor.

personal video recorders　Consumer electronics devices that record television shows to a hard disk in digital format. They allow viewers to pause, fast-forward, and rewind live TV, store programming, and skip commercials.

persuasion　A change in thought process or behavior that occurs when the change in belief, attitude, or behavioral intention is caused by promotion communication (such as advertising or personal selling).

philanthropy　Support for a cause without any commercial incentive.

photographers　The artists who use cameras to create visuals for advertisements.

physiological screens　The perceptual screens that use the five senses—sight, hearing, touch, taste, and smell—to detect incoming data and measure the dimension and intensity of the physical stimulus.

picture-caption copy　A type of body copy in which the story is told through a series of illustrations and captions rather than through the use of a copy block alone.

picture-window layout　Layout that employs a single, dominant visual that occupies between 60 and 70 percent of an advertisement's total area. Also known as *poster-style format* or *Ayer No. 1*.

place (distribution) element　How and where customers will buy a company's product; either direct or indirect distribution.

planned messages　Traditional marketing communications messages, including advertising, sales promotion, publicity, and personal selling. These messages have the least impact because they are seen as self-serving.

point　In retailing, the place of business. In typography, the measurement of the size and height of a text character. There are 72 points to an inch.

point-of-purchase (POP) materials　Materials set up at a retail location to build traffic, advertise the product, and promote impulse buying. Materials may include window displays, counter displays, floor and wall displays, streamers, and posters.

polybagging　Samples are delivered in plastic bags with the daily newspaper or a monthly magazine.

pop-up ad　A three-dimensional magazine ad.

portals Web pages that provide starting points or gateways to other resources on the Internet.

position The way in which a product is ranked in the consumer's mind by the benefits it offers, by the way it is classified or differentiated from the competition, or by its relationship to certain target markets.

positioning The association of a brand's features and benefits with a particular set of customer needs, clearly differentiating it from the competition in the mind of the customer.

positively originated motives Consumer's motivation to purchase and use a product based on a positive bonus that the product promises, such as sensory gratification, intellectual stimulation, or social approval.

postcards Cards sent by advertisers to announce sales, offer discounts, or otherwise generate consumer traffic.

posters For public relations purposes, signs that impart product information or other news of interest to consumers, or that are aimed at employee behavior, such as safety, courtesy, or waste reduction.

poster-style format Layout that employs a single, dominant visual that occupies between 60 and 70 percent of an advertisement's total area. Also known as *picture-window layout* and *Ayer No. 1*.

postindustrial age Period of cataclysmic change, starting in about 1980, when people first became truly aware of the sensitivity of the environment in which we live.

postproduction phase The finishing phase in commercial production—the period after recording and shooting when a radio or TV commercial is edited and sweetened with music and sound effects.

postpurchase evaluation Determining whether a purchase has been a satisfactory or unsatisfactory one.

posttesting Testing the effectiveness of an advertisement after it has been run.

preemption rates Lower TV advertising rates that stations charge when the advertiser agrees to allow the station to sell its time to another advertiser willing to pay a higher rate.

preferred position rate A choice position for a newspaper or magazine ad for which a higher rate is charged.

preindustrial age Period of time between the beginning of written history and roughly the start of the nineteenth century, during which the invention of paper and the printing press and increased literacy gave rise to the first forms of written advertising.

premium An item offered free or at a bargain price to encourage the consumer to buy an advertised product.

prepress phase The process of converting page art and visuals into materials (generally film negatives and color separations) needed for printing.

preprinted inserts Newspaper advertisements printed in advance by the advertiser and then delivered to the newspaper plant to be inserted into a specific edition. Preprints are inserted into the fold of the newspaper and look like a separate, smaller section of the paper.

preproduction phase The period of time before the actual recording or shooting of a commercial—the planning phase in commercial production.

presenter commercial A commercial format in which one person or character presents the product and sales message.

press agentry The planning of activities and the staging of events to attract attention to new products or services and to generate publicity about the company or organization that will be of interest to the media.

press kit A package of publicity materials used to give information to the press at staged events such as press conferences or open houses. Also, a package of sales material promoting a specific media vehicle. Also called a *media kit*.

press release See *news release*.

press proof A test printing prior to the final production run. Used as a last-minute quality check of alignment and color before the entire job is printed.

pretesting Testing the effectiveness of an advertisement for gaps or flaws in message content before recommending it to clients, often conducted through focus groups.

price element In the marketing mix, the amount charged for the good or service—including deals, discounts, terms, warranties, and so on. The factors affecting price are market demand, cost of production and distribution, competition, and corporate objectives.

primary circulation The number of people who receive a publication, whether through direct purchase or subscription.

primary data Research information gained directly from the marketplace.

primary demand Consumer demand for a whole product category. See also *selective demand*.

primary motivation The pattern of attitudes and activities that help people reinforce, sustain, or modify their social and self-image. An understanding of the primary motivation of individuals helps advertisers promote and sell goods and services.

prime time Highest level of TV viewing (8 p.m. to 11 p.m. EST).

printer Business that employs or contracts with highly trained specialists who prepare artwork for reproduction, operate digital scanning machines to make color separations and plates, operate presses and collating machines, and run binderies.

print production   The systematic process an approved design goes through from concept to final production in a printed medium, such as magazines, newspapers, or collateral materials.

print production manager   Manager who oversees the entire production process, including reproduction of visuals in full color, shooting and editing of scenes, precise specification and placement of type, and the checking, approving, duplicating, and shipping of final art, negatives, tape, or film to the communication media.

print production process   The systematic process a layout for an ad or a brochure goes through from concept to final printing. The four major phases are preproduction, production, prepress, and printing and distribution.

privacy rights   Of or pertaining to an individual's right to prohibit personal information from being divulged to the public.

private audience venue   A category of digital media based on audience size; where meetings, conferences, and seminars use computer-driven multimedia presentations to inform, persuade, remind, and entertain people.

private labels   Personalized brands applied by distributors or dealers to products supplied by manufacturers. Private brands are typically sold at lower prices in large retail chain stores.

probability samples   A research sample in which all members of the target population have an equal and independent chance of being selected for the study. Also called a random sample.

problem the advertising must solve   What you want the advertising to do. The specific challenge that marketing communications must overcome to meet the marketing objectives.

producer   For electronic media, the person responsible for keeping the project moving smoothly and under budget, while maintaining the required level of quality through every step of the production process.

product   The particular good or service a company sells. See also *product concept*.

product advertising   Advertising intended to promote goods and services; also a functional classification of advertising.

product concept   The consumer's perception of a product as a "bundle" of utilitarian and symbolic values that satisfy functional, social, psychological, and other wants and needs. Also, as an element of the creative mix used by advertisers to develop advertising strategy, it is the bundle of product values the advertiser presents to the consumer.

product differentiation   Manufacturers portraying their brands as different from and better than similar competitive products through advertising, packaging, or physical product differences.

product element   The most important element of the marketing mix: the good or service being offered and the values associated with it—including the way the product is designed and classified, positioned, branded, and packaged.

production department   The department in an advertising agency that is responsible for managing the steps that transform creative concepts into finished advertisements and collateral materials.

production house   Companies that specialize in film or video production.

production phase   An element of creative strategy. The whole physical process of producing ads and commercials; also the particular phase in the process when the recording and shooting of commercials is done.

product life cycle   Progressive stages in the life of a product—including introduction, growth, maturity, and decline—that affect the way a product is marketed and advertised.

product messages   Messages communicated by a product, its packaging, price, or distribution elements.

product placement   Paying a fee to have a product prominently displayed in a movie or TV show.

product samples   Small quantities of a product offered for free in stores, by direct mail, inserted in printed publications such as magazines or newspapers, or by other means of delivery, for the purpose of encouraging trial.

program-length advertisement (PLA)   A long-form television commercial that may run as long as an hour; also called an *infomercial*.

programming format   The genre of music or other programming style that characterizes and differentiates radio stations from each other (i.e., contemporary hit radio, country, rock, etc.).

program rating   The percentage of TV households in an area that are tuned in to a specific program.

projective techniques   In marketing research, asking indirect questions or otherwise involving consumers in a situation where they can express feelings about the problem or product. The purpose is to get an understanding of people's underlying or subconscious feelings, attitudes, opinions, needs, and motives.

promotion (communication) element   Includes all market-related communications between the seller and the buyer.

proof copy   A copy of the completed advertisement that is used to check for final errors and corrections.

provocative headline   A type of headline written to provoke the reader's curiosity so that, to learn more, the reader will read the body copy.

psychographics   The grouping of consumers into market segments on the basis of psychological makeup—values, attitudes, personality, and lifestyle.

psychographic segmentation Method of defining consumer markets based on psychological variables including values, attitudes, personality, and lifestyle.

psychological pricing Using price as a means of influencing a consumer's behavior or perceptions; for example, using high prices to reinforce a quality image, or selling at $2.99 instead of $3.00 to make a product appear less expensive.

psychological screens The perceptual screens consumers use to evaluate, filter, and personalize information according to subjective standards, primarily emotions and personality.

public affairs All activities related to the community citizenship of an organization, including dealing with community officials and working with regulatory bodies and legislative groups.

publicity The generation of news about a person, product, or service that appears in broadcast or print media.

public notices For a nominal fee, newspapers carry these legal changes in business, personal relationships, public governmental reports, notices by private citizens and organizations, and financial reports.

public relations (PR) The management function that focuses on the relationships and communications that individuals and organizations have with other groups (called *publics*) for the purpose of creating mutual goodwill. The primary role of public relations is to manage a company's reputation and help build public consent for its enterprises.

public relations advertising Advertising that attempts to improve a company's relationship with its publics (labor, government, customers, suppliers, etc.).

publics In PR terminology, employees, customers, stockholders, competitors, suppliers, or general population of customers are all considered one of the organization's publics.

public service announcement (PSA) An advertisement serving the public interest, often for a nonprofit organization, carried by the media at no charge.

puffery Exaggerated, subjective claims that can't be proven true or false such as "the best," "premier," or "the only way to fly."

pull strategy Marketing, advertising, and sales promotion activities aimed at inducing trial purchase and repurchase by consumers.

pulsing Mixing continuity and flighting strategies in media scheduling.

purchase occasion A method of segmenting markets on the basis of *when* consumers buy and use a good or service.

push money (PM) A monetary inducement for retail salespeople to push the sale of particular products. Also called *spiffs*.

push strategy Marketing, advertising, and sales promotion activities aimed at getting products into the dealer pipeline and accelerating sales by offering inducements to dealers, retailers, and salespeople.

qualitative research Research that tries to determine market variables according to unquantifiable criteria such as attitudes, beliefs, and lifestyle.

quantitative research Research that tries to determine market variables according to reliable, hard statistics about specific market conditions or situations.

question headline A type of headline that asks the reader a question.

radio personality A disk jockey or talk show host.

rate base With magazines, the circulation figure on which the publisher bases its rates.

rate card A printed information form listing a publication's advertising rates, mechanical and copy requirements, advertising deadlines, and other information the advertiser needs to know before placing an order.

rating The percentage of homes or individuals exposed to an advertising medium.

rating services These services measure the program audiences of TV and radio stations for advertisers and broadcasters by picking a representative sample of the market and furnishing data on the size and characteristics of the viewers or listeners.

reach The total number of *different* people or households exposed to an advertising schedule during a given time, usually four weeks. Reach measures the *unduplicated* extent of audience exposure to a media vehicle and may be expressed either as a percentage of the total market or as a raw number.

readers per copy (RPC) Variable used to determine the total reach of a given print medium. RPC is multiplied by the number of vendor and subscription sales to determine the total audience size.

reading notice A variation of a display ad designed to look like editorial matter. It is sometimes charged at a higher space rate than normal display advertising, and the law requires that the word *advertisement* appear at the top.

rebates Larger cash refunds on items from cars to household appliances.

recall tests Posttesting methods used to determine the extent to which an advertisement and its message have been noticed, read, or watched.

receiver In oral communication, this party decodes the message to understand it and responds by formulating a new idea, encodes it, and sends it back.

recruitment advertising A special type of advertising, most frequently found in the classified sections of daily newspapers and typically the responsibility of a personnel department aimed at attracting employment applications.

reference groups People we try to emulate or whose approval concerns us.

regional advertiser Companies that operate in one part of the country and market exclusively to that region.

regional agency Advertising agency that focuses on the production and placement of advertising suitable for regional campaigns.

regional publications Magazines targeted to a specific area of the country, such as the West or the South.

relationship marketing Creating, maintaining, and enhancing long-term relationships with customers and other stakeholders that result in exchanges of information and other things of mutual value.

reliability An important characteristic of research test results. For a test to be reliable, it must be repeatable, producing the same result each time it is administered.

reputation management In public relations, the name of the long-term strategic process to manage the standing of the firm with various publics.

research supplier Companies that conduct and analyze marketing research.

resellers Businesses that buy products from manufacturers or wholesalers and then resell the merchandise to consumers or other buyers; also called *middlemen*. The most common examples of resellers are retail stores and catalog retailers.

residual fee Payment to the talent if the commercial is extended beyond its initially contracted run.

resources axis A term in the Values and Lifestyles (VALS) typology relating to the range of psychological, physical, demographic, and material capacities that consumers can draw upon. The resource axis includes education, income, self-confidence, health, eagerness to buy, and energy level.

retainer method See *straight-fee method.*

return path A communication channel that a user can employ to send data back to a broadcaster. It might be a modem that's connected to a telephone line, a satellite connection, a cable box, the Internet, or some other network.

reverse knockout Area within a field of printed color on a page that is free of ink and allows the paper's surface to show.

RFM formula The RFM formula is a mathematical model that provides marketers with a method to determine the most reliable customers in a company's database, according to Recency, Frequency, and Monetary variables.

rich mail Technology that allows graphics, video, and audio to be included in an e-mail message.

rich-media advertising Internet advertising that utilizes full motion and animated technology such as Flash, Java applets, streaming video, and interactivity.

roadblocking Buying simultaneous airtime on all four television networks.

ROP advertising rates Run of paper. A term referring to a newspaper's normal discretionary right to place a given ad on any page or in any position it desires—in other words, where space permits. Most newspapers make an effort to place an ad in the position requested by the advertiser.

rough Penciled sketch of a proposed design or layout.

run-of-paper advertising rates See *ROP advertising rates.*

run of station (ROS) Leaving placement of radio spots up to the station in order to achieve a lower ad rate.

sale advertising A type of retail advertising designed to stimulate the movement of particular merchandise or generally increase store traffic by placing the emphasis on special reduced prices.

sales letters The most common form of direct mail. Sales letters may be typewritten, typeset and printed, printed with a computer insert (such as your name), or fully computer typed.

sales promotion A direct inducement offering extra incentives all along the marketing route—from manufacturers through distribution channels to customers—to accelerate the movement of the product from the producer to the consumer.

sales promotion department In larger agencies, a staff to produce dealer ads, window posters, point-of-purchase displays, and dealer sales material.

sales-target objectives Marketing objectives that relate to a company's sales. They may be expressed in terms of total sales volume; sales by product, market segment, or customer type; market share; growth rate of sales volume; or gross profit.

sales test A useful measure of advertising effectiveness when advertising is the dominant element, or the only variable, in the company's marketing plan. Sales tests are more suited for gauging the effectiveness of campaigns than of individual ads or components of ads.

sample A portion of the population selected by market researchers to represent the appropriate targeted population. Also, a free trial of a product.

sampling Offering consumers a free trial of the product, hoping to convert them to habitual use.

sans serif A type group that is characterized by a lack of serifs.

SAU See *standard advertising unit*.

scale The regular charge for talent and music agreed to in the union contract.

script Format for radio and television copywriting resembling a two-column list showing dialogue and/or visuals.

seal A type of certification mark offered by such organizations as the Good Housekeeping Institute and Underwriters' Laboratories when a product meets standards established by these institutions. Seals provide an independent, valued endorsement for the advertised product.

search engine Web sites that are devoted to finding and retrieving requested information from the World Wide Web. Because search engines are the gatekeepers to information on the Internet they are extremely popular with advertisers.

search engine optimization The process of optimizing Web pages to achieve high rankings in the search results of spider-based search engines.

secondary data Information that has previously been collected or published.

secondary (pass-along) readership The number of people who read a publication in addition to the primary purchasers.

selective demand Consumer demand for the particular advantages of one brand over another. See also *primary demand*.

selective distribution Strategy of limiting the distribution of a product to select outlets in order to reduce distribution and promotion costs.

selective perception The ability of humans to select from the many sensations bombarding their central processing unit those sensations that fit well with their current or previous experiences, needs, desires, attitudes, and beliefs, focusing attention on some things and ignoring others.

self-concept The images we carry in our minds of the type of person we are and who we desire to be.

self-mailer Any type of direct-mail piece that can travel by mail without an envelope. Usually folded and secured by a staple or a seal, self-mailers have a special blank space for the prospect's name and address.

semiotics The study of how humans use words, gestures, signs, and symbols to convey feelings, thoughts, ideas, and ideologies.

serif The most popular type group that is distinguished by smaller lines or tails called serifs that finish the ends of the main character strokes and by variations in the thickness of the strokes.

service messages Messages resulting from employee interactions with customers. These messages typically have greater impact than planned messages.

services A bundle of benefits that may or may not be physical, that are temporary in nature, and that come from the completion of a task.

session The time when the recording and mixing of a radio commercial takes place.

share-of-market/share-of-voice method A method of allocating advertising funds based on determining the firm's goals for a certain share of the market and then applying a slightly higher percentage of industry advertising dollars to the firm's budget.

shoppers Free publications, delivered by hand or direct mail or in supermarket racks, consisting almost entirely of local advertising. Consumers tend to use these publications to find dealers and to make price comparisons.

short rate The rate charged to advertisers who, during the year, fail to fulfill the amount of space for which they have contracted. This is computed by determining the difference between the standard rate for the lines run and the discount rate contracted.

showing A traditional term referring to the relative number of outdoor posters used during a contract period, indicating the intensity of market coverage. For example, a 100 showing provides an even and thorough coverage of the entire market.

signature A product's or company's primary graphic identity. A signature may be comprised of some combination of a graphic symbol, a logotype, and a slogan.

situation analysis A factual statement of the organization's current situation and how it got there. It includes relevant facts about the company's history, growth, products and services, sales volume, share of market, competitive status, market served, distribution system, past advertising programs, results of market research studies, company capabilities, and strengths and weaknesses.

slice of life A type of commercial consisting of a dramatization of a real-life situation in which the product is tried and becomes the solution to a problem.

slippage Rebate offers that are never redeemed and coupons that are never submitted because people forget, find them inconvenient, or don't follow the instructions. However, many consumers still purchase the promoted products as a result of having seen the offers.

slogan A standard company statement (also called a *tagline* or a *themeline*) for advertisements, salespeople, and company employees. Slogans have two basic purposes: to provide continuity for a campaign and to reduce a key theme or idea to a brief, memorable positioning statement.

slotting allowances   Fees that manufacturers pay to retailers for the privilege of obtaining shelf or floor space for a new product.

social classes   Traditional divisions in societies by sociologists—upper, upper-middle, lower-middle, and so on—who believed that people in the same social class tended toward similar attitudes, status symbols, and spending patterns.

social responsibility   Acting in accordance to what society views as best for the welfare of people in general or for a specific community of people.

sound effects (SFX)   Sounds other than music or dialogue used in radio and television.

source   In oral communication, this party formulates the idea, encodes it as a message, and sends it via some channel to the receiver.

spam   Unsolicited, mass e-mail advertising for a product or service that is sent by an unknown entity to a purchased mailing list or newsgroup.

special effects   Unusual visual effects created for commercials.

special requirements   Unique characteristics of the advertiser, brand, target audience, media, competition, budget, etc., that should be considered during the creative development process.

spectaculars   Giant electronic signs that usually incorporate movement, color, and flashy graphics to grab the attention of viewers in high-traffic areas.

speculative presentation   An agency's presentation of the advertisement it proposes using in the event it is hired. It is usually made at the request of a prospective client and is often not paid for by the client.

speechwriting   Function of a public relations practitioner to write speeches for stockholder meetings, conferences, conventions, etc.

spider   A program that follows Web site links, seeking documents to be indexed in a database that can then be examined for matches by search engines.

spiff   See *push money.*

split runs   A feature of many newspapers (and magazines) that allows advertisers to test the comparative effectiveness of two different advertising approaches by running two different ads of identical size, but different content, in the same or different press runs on the same day.

sponsorship   The presentation of a radio or TV program, or an event, or even a Web site by a sole advertiser. The advertiser is often responsible for the program content and the cost of production as well as the advertising. This is generally so costly that single sponsorships are usually limited to TV specials.

spot announcements   An individual commercial message run between programs but having no relationship to either. Spots may be sold nationally or locally. They must be purchased by contacting individual stations directly.

spot radio   National advertisers' purchase of airtime on individual stations. Buying spot radio affords advertisers great flexibility in their choice of markets, stations, airtime, and copy.

spots   Another name for a radio commercial.

spyware   Software that covertly gathers user information through the user's Internet connection without his or her knowledge or consent, usually for advertising purposes. Spyware applications are typically bundled as a hidden component of freeware or shareware programs that can be downloaded from the Internet. Spyware is potentially more dangerous than adware because it can record keystrokes, history, passwords, and other confidential and private information and transmit that information to a third party.

stakeholders   In relationship marketing, customers, employees, centers of influence, stockholders, the financial community, and the press. Different stakeholders require different types of relationships.

standard advertising unit (SAU)   A system of standardized newspaper advertisement sizes that can be accepted by all standard-sized newspapers without consideration of their precise format or page size. This system allows advertisers to prepare one advertisement in a particular size or SAU and place it in various newspapers regardless of the format.

standard-size newspaper   The standard newspaper size, measures approximately 22 inches deep and 13 inches wide and is divided into six columns.

statement stuffers   Advertisements enclosed in the monthly customer statements mailed by department stores, banks, utilities, or oil companies.

stereotypes   Negative or limiting preconceived beliefs about a type of person or a group of people that do not take into account individual differences.

stimulus   Physical data that can be received through the senses.

stimulus-response theory   Also called *conditioning theory.* Some stimulus triggers a consumer's need or want, and this in turn creates a need to respond.

stock music   Existing music that can be purchased for a specific use.

stock posters   A type of outdoor advertising consisting of ready-made 30-sheet posters, available in any quantity and often featuring the work of first-class artists and lithographers.

storyboard   A sheet preprinted with a series of 8 to 20 blank frames in the shape of TV screens, which includes text of the commercial, sound effects, and camera views.

storyboard roughs   A rough layout of a television commercial in storyboard form.

straight announcement   The oldest type of radio or television commercial, in which an announcer delivers a sales message directly into the microphone or on-camera or does so off-screen while a slide or film is shown on-screen.

straight-fee (retainer) method   A method of compensation for ad agency services in which a straight fee, or *retainer*, is based on a cost-plus-fixed-fees formula. Under this system, the agency estimates the amount of personnel time required by the client, determines the cost of that personnel, and multiplies by some factor.

straight-sell copy   A type of body copy in which the text immediately explains or develops the headline and visual in a straightforward attempt to sell the product.

stripping   Assembling line and halftone negatives into one single negative, which is then used to produce a combination plate.

studio lot   Outdoor space at a film studio, shielded from undesirable noises. It provides large spaces, scenery, and natural lighting, without the added cost and logistics of location shooting.

subculture   A segment within a culture that shares a set of meanings, values, or activities that differ in certain respects from those of the overall culture.

subhead   Secondary headline in advertisements that may appear above or below the headline or in the text of the ad. Subheads are usually set in a type size smaller than the headline but larger than the body copy or text type size. They may also appear in boldface type or in a different ink color.

subliminal advertising   Advertisements with messages (often sexual) supposedly embedded in illustrations just below the threshold of perception.

substantiation   Evidence that backs up cited survey findings or scientific studies that the FTC may request from a suspected advertising violator.

Sunday supplement   A newspaper-distributed Sunday magazine. Sunday supplements are distinct from other sections of the newspaper since they are printed by rotogravure on smoother paper stock.

supers   Words superimposed on the picture in a television commercial.

suppliers   People and organizations that assist both advertisers and agencies in the preparation of advertising materials, such as photography, illustration, printing, and production.

support statement   Provides information about the product or service that will convince the target audience that the *key benefit* is true.

survey   A basic method of quantitative research. To get people's opinions, surveys may be conducted in person, by mail, on the telephone, or via the Internet.

sweeps   The four, month-long periods each year when rating services measure all TV markets for station viewing habits and demographic information for the purpose of setting advertising rates. Sweep months are February, May, July, and November.

sweepstakes   A sales promotion activity in which prizes are offered based on a chance drawing of entrants' names. The purpose is to encourage consumption of the product by creating consumer involvement.

SWOT analysis   An acronym for internal *strengths* and *weaknesses* and external *opportunities* and *threats*, which represent the four categories used by advertising managers when reviewing a marketing plan.

synergy   An effect achieved when the sum of the parts is greater than that expected from simply adding together the individual components.

tabloid newspaper   A newspaper size generally about half as deep as a standard-sized newspaper; it is usually about 14 inches deep and 11 inches wide.

tactics   The precise details of a company's marketing strategy that determine the specific short-term actions that will be used to achieve its marketing objectives.

tagline   See *slogan.*

take-ones   In transit advertising, pads of business reply cards or coupons, affixed to interior advertisements for an extra charge, that allow passengers to request more detailed information, send in application blanks, or receive some other product benefit.

talent   The actors in commercials.

target audience   The specific group of individuals to whom the advertising message is directed.

target CPM (TCPM)   The *cost per thousand* to expose a message to the *target audience* rather than to the total circulation.

target market   The market segment or group within the market segment toward which all marketing activities will be directed.

target marketing   The process by which an advertiser focuses its marketing efforts on a target market.

taxicab exteriors   In transit advertising, internally illuminated, two-sided posters positioned on the roofs of taxis. Some advertising also appears on the doors or rear.

tearsheets   The printed ad cut out and sent by the publisher to the advertiser as a proof of the ad's print quality and that it was published.

telemarketing Selling products and services by using the telephone to contact prospective customers.

television households (TVHH) Households with TV sets.

terminal posters One-sheet, two-sheet, and three-sheet posters in many bus, subway, and commuter train stations as well as in major train and airline terminals. They are usually custom designed and include such attention getters as floor displays, island showcases, illuminated signs, dioramas (three-dimensional scenes), and clocks with special lighting and moving messages.

testimonial The use of satisfied customers and celebrities to endorse a product in advertising.

test market An isolated geographic area used to introduce and test the effectiveness of a product, ad campaign, or promotional campaign, prior to a national rollout.

text See *body copy.*

text type The smaller type used in the body copy of an advertisement.

themeline See *slogan.*

theory of cognitive dissonance The theory that people try to justify their behavior by reducing the degree to which their impressions or beliefs are inconsistent with reality.

30-sheet poster panel The basic outdoor advertising structure; it consists of blank panels with a standardized size and border. Its message is first printed on large sheets of paper and then mounted by hand on the panel.

3-D ads Magazine ads requiring the use of 3-D glasses.

thumbnail A rough, rapidly produced pencil sketch that is used for trying out ideas.

top-down marketing The traditional planning process with four main elements: situation analysis, marketing objectives, marketing strategy, and tactics or action programs.

total audience The total number of homes reached by some portion of a TV program. This figure is normally broken down to determine the distribution of audience into demographic categories.

total audience plan (TAP) A radio advertising package rate that guarantees a certain percentage of spots in the better dayparts.

total bus A special transit advertising buy that covers the entire exterior of a bus, including the front, rear, sides, and top.

trade advertising The advertising of goods and services to middlemen to stimulate wholesalers and retailers to buy goods for resale to their customers or for use in their own businesses.

trade concentration More products being sold by fewer retailers.

trade deals Short-term dealer discounts on the cost of a product or other dollar inducements to sell a product.

trademark Any word, name, symbol, device, or any combination thereof adopted and used by manufacturers or merchants to identify their goods and distinguish them from those manufactured or sold by others.

trade promotions See *push strategy.*

trade shows Exhibitions where manufacturers, dealers, and buyers of an industry's products can get together for demonstrations and discussion; expose new products, literature, and samples to customers; and meet potential new dealers for their products.

traffic department The department in an advertising agency that coordinates all phases of production and makes sure everything is completed before the deadline.

transformational Promising benefits that will reward consumers. Transformational ads tend to address *positively originated purchase motives,* such as sensory gratification, intellectual stimulation, or social approval, in an attempt to make people feel happier.

transformational motives Positively originated motives that promise to "transform" the consumer through sensory gratification, intellectual stimulation, and social approval. Also called *reward motives.*

transit advertising An out-of-home medium that actually includes three separate media forms: inside cards; outside posters; and station, platform, and terminal posters.

transit shelter advertising A newer form of out-of-home media, where advertisers can buy space on bus shelters and on the backs of bus-stop seats.

trap Where, in the printing process, one color overlays the edge of another to keep the paper from showing through.

trial close In ad copy, requests for the order that are made before the close in the ad.

TV households (TVHH) The number of households in a market area that own television sets.

type families Related typefaces in which the basic design remains the same but in which variations occur in the proportion, weight, and slant of the characters. Variations commonly include light, medium, bold, extra bold, condensed, extended, and italic.

typography The art of selecting, setting, and arranging type.

umbrella advertising Advertising campaigns intended to simultaneously communicate messages about a company and its products.

unfair advertising According to the FTC, advertising that causes a consumer to be "unjustifiably injured" or that violates public policy.

unique selling proposition (USP) The distinctive benefits that make a product different than any other. The reason marketers believe consumers will buy a product even though it may seem no different from many others just like it.

Universal Product Code (UPC) An identifying series of vertical bars with a 12-digit number that adorns every consumer packaged good.

universe An entire target population.

unplanned messages Messages that emanate from gossip, unsought news stories, rumors, or major disasters. Companies have little control over unplanned messages, but the messages can dramatically affect customers' attitudes.

usage rates The extent to which consumers use a product: light, medium, or heavy.

user status Six categories into which consumers can be placed, which reflect varying degrees of loyalties to certain brands and products. The categories are *sole users, semisole users, discount users, aware nontriers, trial/rejectors,* and *repertoire users.*

utility A product's ability to provide both symbolic or psychological want satisfaction and functional satisfaction. A product's problem-solving potential may include form, time, place, or possession utility.

validity An important characteristic of a research test. For a test to be valid, it must reflect the true status of the market.

value The ratio of perceived benefits to the price of the product.

value-based thinking A style of thinking where decisions are based on intuition, values, and ethical judgments.

venue marketing A form of sponsorship that links a sponsor to a physical site such as a stadium, arena, auditorium, or racetrack.

vertical cooperative advertising Co-op advertising in which the manufacturer provides the ad and pays a percentage of the cost of placement.

vertical publications Business publications aimed at people within a specific industry; for example, Restaurants & Institutions.

video brochure A type of video advertising which advertises the product and is mailed to customers and prospects.

video news release (VNR) A news or feature story prepared in video form and offered free to TV stations.

viral marketing The Internet version of word-of-mouth advertising e-mail.

visualization The creative point in advertising where the search for the "big idea" takes place. It includes the task of analyzing the problem, assembling any and all pertinent information, and developing some verbal or visual concept of how to communicate what needs to be said.

visuals All of the picture elements that are placed into an advertisement.

voice-over In television advertising, the spoken copy or dialogue delivered by an announcer who is not seen but whose voice is heard.

volume discount Discounts given to advertisers for purchasing print space or broadcast time in bulk quantities.

volume segmentation Defining consumers as light, medium, or heavy users of products.

wants Needs learned during a person's lifetime.

Warrior role A role in the creative process that overcomes excuses, idea killers, setbacks, and obstacles to bring a creative concept to realization.

wearout The point at which an advertising message has been seen or heard so often that it starts to irritate consumers and therefore loses its effectiveness.

Web browser Computer program that provides computer users with a graphical interface to the Internet.

Web crawler See *spider.*

Web design house Art/computer studios that employ specialists who understand the intricacies of HTML and Java programming languages and can design ads and Internet Web pages that are both effective and cost efficient.

Web page A document or file, written in HTML, that is stored on a Web server and can be viewed over the Internet using a Web browser.

Web site A collection of Web pages on the World Wide Web that are linked together and maintained by a company, organization, or individual.

weekly newspapers Newspapers that are published once a week and characteristically serve readers in small urban or suburban areas or farm communities with exclusive emphasis on local news and advertising.

word of mouth (WOM) advertising The passing of information, especially product recommendations, by verbal communication, in an informal, unpaid, person-to-person manner, rather than by advertising or other forms of traditional marketing.

work plan See *creative strategy.*

work print The first visual portion of a filmed commercial assembled without the extra effects or dissolves, titles, or supers. At this time, scenes may be substituted, music and sound effects added, or other changes made.

World Wide Web (WWW) Information available on the Internet that can be easily accessed with software called a *browser.* It is named the *Web* because it is made up of many sites linked together; users can travel from one site to another by clicking on *hyperlinks.*

Endnotes

Chapter One

1. www.altoids.com.
2. Altoids case study.
3. Ibid.
4. R. Craig Endicott, "100 Leading National Advertisers," *Advertising Age,* special report, June 28, 2004, pp. S1–S21.
5. "Advertising: The Way Great Brands Get to Be Great Brands" (retrieved from www.aaf.org).
6. John McDonough, "FCB: From One-Man Fiefdom to Global Powerhouse," *Advertising Age,* Commemorative Section: "FCB at 120," December 13, 1993, p. F4.
7. "AMA Adopts New Definition of Marketing," (retrieved from www.marketingpower.com, December 19, 2005).
8. William M. O'Barr, Culture and the Ad, excerpted at www2.uwsuper.edu/hps/mjohnson/intro/obarr.htm.
9. www.kodak.com.
10. Some material in this section has been adapted from Hugh M. Cannon, Course Packet for Advertising Management, Fall 1996, Wayne State University.
11. William O'Barr, address to the Council on Advertising History, Duke University, March 12, 1993, reported in *Advertising in America: Using Its Past, Enriching Its Future* (Washington, DC: Center for Advertising History of the National Museum of American History, 1994), p. 6.
12. Leonard L. Bartlett, "Three Giants—Leo Burnett, David Ogilvy, William Bernbach: An Exploration of the Impact of the Founders' Written Communications on the Destinies of Their Advertising Agencies," paper presented to the annual meeting of the Association for Education in Journalism and Mass Communication, Kansas City, August 13, 1993.
13. Schwarz, "A Brief History of Ad Time."
14. Cannon, Course Packet for Advertising Management.
15. Warren Berger, "Chaos on Madison Avenue," *Los Angeles Times Magazine,* June 5, 1994, p. 14.
16. William F. Arens and Jack J. Whidden, "La Publicité aux Etats-Unis: Les Symptômes et les Stratégies d'une Industrie Surpeuplée," *L'Industrie de la Publicité au Québec* (Montreal: Le Publicité Club de Montréal, 1992), pp. 383–84.
17. Berger, "Chaos on Madison Avenue," pp. 12, 14.
18. Bob Coen, "Bob Coen's Insider's Report," December 2002, McCann-Erickson WorldGroup, www.universalmccann.com/ourview.html.
19. Judann Pollock, "Marketing Put on Hold," *Advertising Age,* September 17, 2001, pp. 1, 25.
20. Coen, "Bob Coen's Insider's Report."
21. R. Craig Endicott, "100 Leading National Advertisers," *Advertising Age,* special report, June 28, 2004, pp. S1–S21.
22. Tom Cuniff, "The Second Creative Revolution," *Advertising Age,* December 6, 1993, p. 22.
23. John McManus, "Cable Proves It's Media's Live Wire," *Advertising Age,* November 26, 1990, p. S6; "Media & Measurement Technologies (Part 1)," *Direct Marketing,* March 1991, pp. 21–27, 79.
24. Tobi Elkin, "Analysts Predict iTV Growth in 2002," December 10, 2001, www.adage.com.
25. Clinton Wilder, "Interactive Ads," *Information Week,* October 3, 1994, p. 25.
26. Tom Cuniff, "The Second Creative Revolution," *Advertising Age,* December 6, 1993, p. 22.
27. Brad Lynch, address to the Council on Advertising History, Duke University, March 12, 1993, reported in *Advertising in America: Using Its Past, Enriching Its Future* (Washington, DC: Center for Advertising History of the National Museum of American History, 1994), p. 3.

Chapter Two

1. Sean Collins, "Quarterly Concern: The Boycott of Abercrombie & Fitch," Disinformation online, July 29, 2001, www.disinfo.com/archive/pages/dossier/id1439/pag1.
2. "National Coalition Requests Written Statement from Abercrombie & Fitch before Calling Off Boycott," National Coalition for the Protection of Children and Families Online, December 10, 2003, http://php.eos.net/nationalcoalition/index.phtml.
3. John O'Toole, *The Trouble with Advertising* (New York: Times Books, 1985), pp. 7–14.
4. Marcel Bleustein-Blanchet, *La Rage de Convaincre* (Paris: Editions Robert Laffont, 1970), p. 25.
5. Ernest Dichter, *Handbook of Consumer Motivations* (New York: McGraw-Hill, 1964), pp. 6, 422–31.
6. Richard E. Kihlstrom and Michael H. Riordan, "Advertising as a Signal," *Journal of Political Economy,* June 1984, pp. 427–50.
7. Ivan Preston, *The Tangled Web They Weave* (Madison: University of Wisconsin Press, 1994), pp. 94–95.
8. John Kenneth Galbraith, "Economics and Advertising: Exercise in Denial," *Advertising Age,* November 9, 1988, pp. 80–84.
9. Fabiana Giacomotti, "European Marketers Keep Up Ad Budgets," *Adweek,* January 24, 1994, pp. 16–17.
10. Ivan Preston, "A New Conception of Deceptiveness," paper presented to the Advertising Division of the Association for Education in Journalism and Mass Communication, August 12, 1993.
11. "Pizza Hut Files Suit against Pizza Rival," *Advertising Age,* August 13, 1998; "Papa John's Ordered to Move 'Better' Slogan," *Advertising Age,* January 5, 2000 (retrieved from http://adage.com).
12. Stuart C. Rogers, "Subliminal Advertising: Grand Scam of the 20th Century," paper presented to the Annual Conference of the American Academy of Advertising, April 10, 1994.
13. Ibid.; Martha Rogers and Kirk H. Smith, "Public Perceptions of Subliminal Advertising," *Journal of Advertising Research,* March/April 1993, p. 10.
14. Andrew Jaffe, "Advertiser, Regulate Thyself," *Adweek,* August 2, 1993, p. 38.

15. Ibid.

16. Preston, *The Tangled Web They Weave,* p. 164.

17. Kevin Downey, "TV Ad Clutter Worsens, and Buyers Grouse," *Media Life Magazine,* February 15, 2002 (retrieved from **www.medialifemagazine.com**).

18. Joe Flint, "Meredith Cuts 'Clutter' and Boosts Ratings," *The Wall Street Journal,* January 4, 2000, p. B8.

19. "The Public and Broadcasting," *FCC Mass Media Bureau,* June 1999 (retrieved from **www.fcc.gov/mb/audio/includes/ 45-public_and_broadcasting.htm**).

20. "French May Get Second Break," *Advertising Age International,* October 11, 1993, p. I-6.

21. Shelly Garcia, "What's Wrong with Being Politically Correct?" *Adweek,* November 15, 1993, p. 62.

22. Adrienne Ward, "What Role Do Ads Play in Racial Tension?" *Advertising Age,* August 10, 1992, pp. 1, 35.

23. U.S. Census Bureau, *Statistical Abstract of the United States: 2001* (Washington, DC: U.S. Department of Commerce, 2001; retrieved from **www.census.gov**).

24. John B. Ford and Michael S. LaTour, "Differing Reactions to Female Role Portrayals in Advertising," *Journal of Advertising Research,* September/October 1993, pp. 43–52.

25. Michael L. Klassen, Cynthia R. Jasper, and Anne M. Schwartz, "Men and Women: Images of Their Relationships in Magazine Advertisements," *Journal of Advertising Research,* March/April 1993, pp. 30–39.

26. "Revealing Abercrombie Catalog Sparks a Boycott," *The Cincinnati Enquirer,* June 26, 2001 (retrieved from **www. enquirer.com/editions/2001/06/26/tem_revealing.htm**).

27. Mark Schone, "Rubbered Out," *Adweek,* July 18, 1994, p. 22.

28. Laurel Wentz and Geoffrey Lee Martin, "Cheaply Made Gore Scores," *Advertising Age,* July 4, 1994, p. 38.

29. Matt Warren, "Are You Ready for This?" *The Scotsman,* Edinburgh (UK), October 6, 2000, p. 9 (retrieved from Lexis-Nexis Academic Universe).

30. Gary Levin, "More Nudity, but Less Sex," *Advertising Age,* November 8, 1993, p. 37.

31. Caity Olson, "Ad Boycott Concern Is Real," *Advertising Age,* June 13, 1994, p. 3.

32. Preston, "A New Conception of Deceptiveness."

33. Robert W. McChesney, *Corporate Media and the Threat to Democracy* (New York: Seven Stories Press, 1997), p. 23.

34. Preston, *The Tangled Web They Weave,* pp. 94, 127–31.

35. James R. Maxeiner, "United States," in Maxeiner and Schotthoffer, eds., *Advertising Law in Europe and North America,* p. 321; see also *Virginia State Board of Pharmacy v. Virginia Citizens Consumer Council,* 425 U.S. 748 (1976).

36. See *Central Hudson Gas & Electric Corp. v. Public Service Commission of New York,* 447 U.S. 557 (1980).

37. Kartik Pashupati, "The Camel Controversy: Same Beast, Different Viewpoints," paper presented to the annual conference of the Association for Education in Journalism and Mass Communication, Kansas City, MO, August 11, 1993; Maxeiner, "United States," pp. 321–22.

38. Steven W. Colford, "Big Win for Commercial Speech," *Advertising Age,* March 29, 1993, pp. 1, 47.

39. "Tobacco Settlement Agreement at a Glance," National Association of Attorneys General Web site: (**www.naag.org**), October 2000.

40. John Malmo, "Restricting Commercial Speech Isn't Justifiable," *The Commercial Appeal,* Memphis, TN, July 5, 1999, p. B3;

John Malmo, "Banning Tobacco Ads Spells Monopoly," *The Commercial Appeal,* Memphis, TN, August 9, 1999, p. B4 (retrieved from ProQuest).

41. "Self-Regulatory Guidelines for Children's Advertising," The Children's Advertising Review Unit (CARU), Copyright 2000 Council of Better Business Bureaus (retrieved from **http://216.46.241.4/advertising/caruguid.asp**); "CARU Issues Breakthrough Advertising Guidelines to Protect Children on the Internet," Better Business Bureau Press Release, April 21, 1997 (retrieved from **www.caru.org/ guidelines/index.asp**).

42. "A Spoonful of Sugar: Television Food Advertising Aimed at Children: An International Comparative Survey," *Consumers International.*

43. Eric Gross and Susan Vogt, "Canada," in Maxeiner and Schotthoffer, eds., *Advertising Law in Europe and North America,* pp. 39, 41.

44. Federal Trade Commission, "Vision, Mission, and Goals," 1997.

45. Minette E. Drumwright, "Ethical Issues in Advertising and Sales Promotion," in N. Craig Smith and John A. Quelch, eds., *Ethics in Marketing* (Burr Ridge, IL: Richard D. Irwin, 1993), p. 610.

46. Ann Carrns, "FTC Settles with Office Depot, Buy.com, Value America over 'Low Cost' PC Ads," *The Wall Street Journal,* June 30, 2000, p. B4.

47. "Exxon Settles FTC Charges; Ground-Breaking Educational Ad Campaign Ordered," FTC news release, June 24, 1997.

48. Dean Keith Fueroghne, *But the People in Legal Said . . .* (Burr Ridge, IL: Professional Publishing, 1989), p. 14.

49. Christy Fisher, "How Congress Broke Unfair Ad Impasse," *Advertising Age,* August 22, 1994, p. 34.

50. "Editorial: A Fair FTC Pact?" *Advertising Age,* March 21, 1994, p. 22.

51. "Arizona Trade Association Agrees to Settle FTC Charges. It Urged Members to Restrain Competitive Advertising," FTC News Release, February 25, 1994 (retrieved from **www.ftc. gov/opa/predawn/F95/azautodealers.htm**).

52. "Comparative Advertising," *ADLAW,* copyright 2000 Hall Dickler Kent Goldstein & Wood (retrieved from **www.adlaw. com/rc/handbk/rf_comparative.html**).

53. "Crackdown on Testimonials," *The Wall Street Journal,* July 13, 1993, p. B7.

54. Drumwright, "Ethical Issues in Advertising and Sales Promotion," pp. 615–16.

55. Ira Teinowitz, "Doan's Decision Sets Precedent for Corrective Ads," *Advertising Age,* September 4, 2000, p. 57.

56. Gross and Vogt, "Canada," pp. 50, 67.

57. "The Food and Drug Administration: An Overview," **www. eduneering.com/fda/courses/fdatour/welcome.html**.

58. "The Growing Brouhaha over Drug Advertisements," *The New York Times,* May 14, 1989, p. F8.

59. "FDA to Review Standards for All Direct-to-Consumer Rx Drug Promotion," FDA news release, August 8, 1997.

60. Steven W. Colford, "Labels Lose the Fat," *Advertising Age,* June 10, 1991, pp. 3, 54; Steven W. Colford and Julie Liesse, "FDA Label Plans under Attack," *Advertising Age,* February 24, 1992, pp. 1, 50; John E. Calfee, "FDA's Ugly Package: Proposed Label Rules Call for Vast Changes," *Advertising Age,* March 16, 1992, p. 25; and Pauline M. Ippolito and Alan D. Mathios, "New Food Labeling Regulations and the Flow of Nutrition Information to Consumers," *Journal of Public Policy & Marketing,* Fall 1993, pp. 188–205.

61. John Carey, "The FDA Is Swinging a Sufficiently Large Two-by-Four," *BusinessWeek,* May 27, 1991, p. 44; Steven W. Colford, "FDA Getting Tougher: Seizure of Citrus Hill Is Signal to Marketers," *Advertising Age,* April 29, 1991, pp. 1, 53.

62. *U.S. Constitution,* Article 1, Section 8.

62a. U.S. Copyright Office, Library of Congress, 1997.

62b. Howard Schlossberg, "Marketers Say State Laws Hurt Their 'Green' Efforts," *Marketing News,* November 11, 1991, pp. 8–9.

63. Frank Phillips, "Mass. in Court to Defend Curbs on Tobacco Ads," *The Boston Globe,* April 7, 2000, p. A1; Gaylord Shaw, "Smoking Ads a Smoldering Issue: High Court May Review City's Ban on Tobacco Displays," *Newsday,* Long Island, NY, March 18, 2000, p. A31.

64. E. J. Gong, "Fraud Complaints on the Rise, Reports D.A.," *Los Angeles Times,* February 13, 1994, p. B1.

65. "Closet Factory to Pay Penalty for Misleading Advertising," Orange County District Attorney press release, June 24, 2002.

66. Felix H. Kent, "Control of Ads by Private Sector," *New York Law Journal,* December 27, 1985; reprinted in Kent and Stone, eds., *Legal and Business Aspects of the Advertising Industry,* 1986, pp. 20–79.

67. "NAD Pilots Successful Resolution Between Neil Cooper and Avirex," Better Business Bureau News Release, August 11, 2000 (retrieved from **www.nadreview.org/casereports. asp**).

68. Public Relations Department, KLBJ, Austin, TX, 1991.

69. Public Relations Department, KDWB, Minneapolis/St. Paul, MN, 1991.

70. Public Relations Department, KSDO, San Diego, CA, 1991.

71. Kevin Goldman, "From Witches to Anorexics, Critical Eyes Scrutinize Ads for Political Correctness," *The Wall Street Journal,* May 19, 1994, p. B1.

72. Garcia, "What's Wrong with Being Politically Correct?" p. 62.

73. Ibid.

74. James Maxeiner and Peter Schotthoffer, eds., *Advertising Law in Europe and North America* (Deventer, The Netherlands: Kluwer Law and Taxation Publishers, 1992), p. v; Rein Rijkens, *European Advertising Strategies* (London: Cassell, 1992), pp. 201–2.

75. Keith Boyfield, "Business Europe: When Advertising Is against the Law," *The Wall Street Journal,* European edition, March 6, 2000, p. 11 (retrieved from Lexis-Nexis Academic Universe).

76. Karly Preslmayer, "Austria," in Maxeiner and Schotthoffer, eds., *Advertising Law in Europe and North America.*

77. Peter Schotthoffer, "European Community," in Maxeiner and Schotthoffer, eds., *Advertising Law in Europe and North America,* p. 89.

78. Jaffe, "Advertiser, Regulate Thyself," p. 38.

79. Federal Trade Commission, 1991.

Chapter Three

1. **www.bajagrill.com.**

2. Henry A. Laskey, J. A. F. Nicholls, and Sydney Roslow, "The Enigma of Cooperative Advertising," *Journal of Business and Industrial Marketing,* vol. 8, no. 2 (1993), pp. 70–79.

3. Riccardo A. Davis, "Retailers Open Doors Wide for Co-op," *Advertising Age,* August 1, 1994, p. 30.

4. Tobi Elkin, "Intel Set to Revamp $800 Million War Chest," *Advertising Age,* November 8, 1999, p. 1 (retrieved from **http://webgate.sdsu.edu**).

5. "100 Leading National Advertisers," *Advertising Age,* September 28, 1999 (retrieved from **http://adage.com**).

6. *Standard Directory of Advertisers* (New Providence, NJ: National Register Publishing Company, 2000), p. 616.

7. **www.pg.com.**

8. R. Craig Endicott, "100 Leading National Advertisers."

9. E. Jerome McCarthy and William D. Perreault Jr., *Basic Marketing,* 11th ed. (Burr Ridge, IL: Richard D. Irwin, 1993), p. 593.

10. "U.S. Firms with the Biggest Foreign Revenues," *Forbes,* July 23, 1990, p. 362.

11. Eric N. Berkowitz, Roger A. Kerin, Steven W. Hartley, and William Rudelius, *Marketing,* 3rd ed. (Burr Ridge, IL: Richard D. Irwin, 1992), p. 609.

12. Anne Cooper, "Cosmetics: Changing Looks for Changing Attitudes," *Adweek,* February 22, 1993, pp. 30–36.

13. James E. Ellis, "Why Overseas? 'Cause That's Where the Sales Are," *BusinessWeek,* January 10, 1994, p. 63; "How CAA Bottled Coca-Cola," *Fortune,* November 15, 1993, p. 156; Deborah Hauss, "Global Communications Come of Age," *Public Relations Journal,* August 1993, pp. 22–23; Sally Solo, "How to Listen to Consumers," *Fortune,* January 11, 1993, pp. 77–78; Jennifer Lawrence, "Delta Gears Up for Global Fight," *Advertising Age,* August 19, 1991, pp. 3, 44; Charles Hennessy, "Globaldegook," *BusinessLondon,* March 1990, p. 131; Raymond Serafin, "W. B. Doner Hits a Gusher," *Advertising Age,* June 6, 1988, p. 43.

14. Jim Patterson, "Viewpoint: Global Communication Requires a Global Understanding," *Adweek,* October 31, 1994, p. 46; "Efficacy of Global Ad Prospects Is Questioned in Firm's Survey," *The Wall Street Journal,* September 13, 1984, p. 29.

15. Patterson, "Viewpoint: Global Communication Requires a Global Understanding."

16. Amy Dockser Markus, "Advertising Breezes along the Nile River with Signs for Sale," *The Wall Street Journal,* July 18, 1997, p. A1.

17. Frederick R. Gamble, *What Advertising Agencies Are—What They Do and How They Do It,* 7th ed. (New York: American Association of Advertising Agencies, 1970), p. 4.

18. "Brands on Trial," *Adweek,* May 24, 1993, pp. 24–31.

19. Melanie Wells, "The Interactive Edge—Part II: Desperately Seeking the Super Highway," *Advertising Age,* August 22, 1994, pp. 14–19.

20. Jennifer Gilbert, "Gotham Gathers Interactive under Hinkaty," *Advertising Age,* July 31, 2000, p. 42 (retrieved from **http://webgate.sdsu.edu**).

21. *Standard Directory of Advertisers,* pp. 245–46.

22. "Casting a Broader Net," *The Washington Post,* August 17, 2002 (retrieved from **http://pqasb.pqarchiver.com/washingtonpost/search.html**).

23. Beth Snyder, "True North Unites Modem, Poppe into Digital Force," *Advertising Age,* May 1998 (retrieved from Articles & Opinions, **http://adage.com**); Kate Maddox, "Agency Pitch Heats Up Camp Interactive Show," *Advertising Age,* August 1998 (retrieved from Articles & Opinions, **http://adage.com**); "Think New Ideas Takes AnswerThink Moniker," *Advertising Age,* April 3, 2000 (retrieved from Interactive Daily, **http://adage.com**).

24. Kevin Goldman, "IBM—Account Fight Lifts Planner Profile," *The Wall Street Journal,* October 26, 1993, p. B8.

25. William F. Arens and Jack J. Whidden, "La Publicité aux Etats-Unis: Les Symptômes et les Stratégies d'une Industrie

Surpleuplée," *L'Industrie de la Publicité au Québec* (Montreal: Le Publicité-Club de Montréal, 1992), pp. 383–84.

26. Jon Lafayette and Cleveland Horton, "Shops to Clients: Pay Up—4A's Members Call for an End to Free Services," *Advertising Age,* March 19, 1990, pp. 1, 66.

27. Andrew Jaffe, "Has Leo Burnett Come to the End of the 'Free Overservice' Era?" *Adweek,* December 6, 1993, p. 46; Melanie Wells and Laurel Wentz, "Coke Trims Commissions," *Advertising Age,* January 31, 1994, p. 2.

28. John Micklethwait, "Cut the Ribbon," *The Economist,* June 9, 1990, pp. S16–S17; Tom Eisenhart, "Guaranteed Results' Plan May Suit Business Marketers," *Business Marketing,* July 1990, p. 32; Jim Kirk, "Miller Sets Free Rates," *Adweek,* January 24, 1994, p. 4.

29. James R. Willis, Jr., "Winning New Business: An Analysis of Advertising Agency Activities," *Journal of Advertising Research,* September/October 1992, pp. 10–16.

30. Andrew Jaffe, "The Fine Art of Keeping Clients Happy While Chasing New Business," *Adweek,* May 9, 1994, p. 38.

31. Melanie Wells, "Courtship by Consultant," *Advertising Age,* January 31, 1994, pp. 10–11; "Accounts on the Move," *Advertising Age,* June 2, 1997 (retrieved from **http://adage. com**); "H&R Block Review Down to 3," *Advertising Age,* May 17, 2000 (retrieved from Daily Deadline, **http://adage.com**); "Monster, L.L. Bean Open Account Review," *Advertising Age,* July 12, 2000 (retrieved from Daily Deadline, **http://adage. com**); "Deutsch Tunes in $70 mil DirecTV Account," *Advertising Age,* August 18, 2000 (retrieved from Daily Deadline, **http://adage.com**).

32. Thorolf Helgesen, "Advertising Awards and Advertising Agency Performance," *Journal of Advertising Research,* July/August 1994, pp. 43–53.

33. Paul C. Katz, "Getting the Most of Your Advertising Dollars: How to Select and Evaluate an Ad Agency," *Bottomline,* March 1987, pp. 35–38.

34. Steven Raye, "Agencies, Clients: It's Mutual Contribution for Mutual Gain," *Brandweek,* September 12, 1994, p. 20; Ed Moser, "Inside Information," *Adweek,* January 24, 1994, p. 22; Mat Toor, "Fear and Favour in Adland," *Marketing* (UK), November 15, 1990, pp. 30–32.

35. Paul C. N. Mitchell, Harold Cataquet, and Stephen Hague, "Establishing the Causes of Disaffection in Agency-Client Relations," *Journal of Advertising Research,* March/April 1992, pp. 41–48.

36. Isabelle T. D. Szmigin, "Managing Quality in Business-to-Business Services," *European Journal of Marketing,* vol. 27, no. 1 (1993), pp. 5–21.

37. Ron Jackson, "If You Hire a Vendor, You Get a Vendor Mindset," *Marketing News,* April 25, 1991, pp. 13–14.

38. Steven A. Meyerowitz, "Ad Agency Conflicts: The Law and Common Sense," *Business Marketing,* June 1987, p. 16.

39. Andrew Jaffe, "For Agencies, Conflict Taboo Seems Strong as Ever," *Adweek,* January 24, 1994, p. 46.

40. Betsy Sharkey, "New Suit," *Adweek,* June 20, 1994, p. 20.

Chapter Four

1. Gregg Cebrzynski, "Hardee's: Thickburger Ads Help Chain Beef Up Same-Store Sales," *Nation's Restaurant News,* August 4, 2003 (retrieved from **www.findarticles.com**, August 1, 2004).

2. Bruce Horovitz, "Fast-Food Battle Escalates into Whopper of a Price War," *USA Today,* December 2, 2002 (retrieved from **www.usatoday.com**, August 1, 2004).

3. Hardee's, Inc., press release, "Hardee's Breaks Rank from Competition," January 21, 2003 (retrieved from **www.hardees.com**, July 31, 2004).

4. American Family Association Online (retrieved from **www.afa.net/activism/IssueDetail.asp?id=134**, accessed November 10, 2004).

5. Hardee's, Inc., press release, "Hardee's Introduces the Lettuce-Wrapped Low Carb Thickburger," December 15, 2003 (retrieved from **www.hardees.com**, July 30, 2004); Dave Marino-Nachison, "The Health of Hardee's," *The Motley Fool,* June 23, 2004 (retrieved from **www.fool.com**, July 29, 2004).

6. E. Jerome McCarthy and William D. Perreault Jr., *Basic Marketing: A Global-Managerial Approach,* 11th ed. (Burr Ridge, IL: Richard D. Irwin, 1993), pp. 5–6; Eric N. Berkowitz, Roger A. Kerin, Steven W. Hartley, and William Rudelius, *Marketing,* 3rd ed. (Burr Ridge, IL: Richard D. Irwin, 1992), p. 27.

7. Chart #649, U.S. Census Bureau, *Statistical Abstract of the United States: 2004–2005,* 124th ed. (Washington, DC: U.S. Department of Commerce, 2005).

8. Chart #728, U.S. Census Bureau, *Statistical Abstract of the United States: 2005.*

9. S. Kent Stephan and Barry L. Tannenholz, "The Real Reason for Brand Switching," *Advertising Age,* June 13, 1994, p. 31, and "Six Categories That Hold Elusive Consumers," *Advertising Age,* June 20, 1994, p. 32.

10. Quoted in Al Stewart, "Edgy Ads, Burgers Drive CKE," *Orange County Business Journal* 27, no. 30 (July 26, 2004): 5.

11. "Descriptive Materials for the VALS2 Segmentation System," *Values and Lifestyles Program* (Menlo Park, CA: SRI International, 1989).

12. "Weather or Not to Sell," *Personal Selling Power,* September 1994, p. 79.

12b. "Hispanic Media and Marketing Factoids," Association of Hispanic Advertising Agencies Media Room (retrieved from **www.ahaa.org/media/Finalfacts03.htm**, August 23, 2004).

13. Leon E. Wynter, "Business and Race: JCPenney Launches Diahann Carroll Line," *The Wall Street Journal,* July 2, 1997, p. B1.

14. Jennifer Foote, "Shhh, It's a Secret: Buick Discovers Untapped Market of Mature Singles," *Chicago Tribune,* May 5, 1994, sec. 6, p. 4.

15. Jean Halliday, "The Coming Generation Y Car-Buying Boom: And How Population Racial Shifts Impact Auto Advertising," AdAge.Com (retrieved from **www.adage.com/news. cms?newsId=35462**, July 15, 2002).

16. Eric Schlosser, "Meat & Potatoes," *Rolling Stone* 800 (November 26, 1998); accessed November 9, 2004, via EBSCO.

17. Eric Schlosser, "The True Cost of America's Diet," *Rolling Stone* 794 (September 3, 1998); accessed November 9, 2004, via EBSCO.

18. Kathleen Barnes, "Changing Demographics: Middle Class," *Advertising Age International,* October 17, 1994, pp. 1–11, 1–16.

19. Kevin Goldman, "U.S. Brands Trail Japanese in China Study," *The Wall Street Journal,* February 16, 1995, p. B8.

20. Henry Assael and David F. Poltrack, "Can Demographic Profiles of Heavy Users Serve as a Surrogate for Purchase Behavior in Selecting TV Programs?" *Journal of Advertising Research,* January/February 1994, p. 11.

21. Emanuel H. Demby, "Psychographics Revisited: The Birth of a Technique," *Marketing Research: A Magazine of Management & Applications,* Spring 1994, pp. 26–29.

22. SRI Consulting Business Intelligence, "Welcome to VALS" (**www.sri-bi.com/vals**).

23. Ibid.

24. Ibid.

25. Judith Waldrop, "Markets with Attitude," *American Demographics,* July 1994, pp. 22–32.

26. Lewis C. Winters, "International Psychographics," *Marketing Research: A Magazine of Management & Application,* September 1992, pp. 48–49.

27. James Hutton, "A Theoretical Framework for the Study of Brand Equity and a Test of Brand Sensitivity in an Organizational Buying Context," dissertation, University of Texas, Austin, 1993.

28. William D. Perreault Jr. and E. Jerome McCarthy, *Basic Marketing,* 12th ed. (Burr Ridge, IL: Irwin, 1996), p. 261.

29. *New Data for a New Economy,* U.S. Bureau of the Census, Economic Classification Policy Committee (Washington, DC: U.S. Department of Commerce, 1998).

30. U.S. Bureau of the Census, *Statistical Abstract of the United States: 1999,* 119th ed. (Washington, DC: U.S. Department of Commerce, 1999), pp. 741–42, 744.

31. Michael Schrage, "Think Big," *Adweek,* October 11, 1993, p. 25.

32. Perreault and McCarthy, *Basic Marketing,* pp. 48–49, 91–112.

33. Walter van Waterschoot and Christophe Van den Bulte, "The 4P Classification of the Marketing Mix Revisited," *Journal of Marketing,* October 1992, pp. 83–93.

34. The now widely popularized conceptual model of the 4Ps was developed by E. J. McCarthy, *Basic Marketing* (Homewood, IL: Richard D. Irwin, 1960); the usage of the marketing mix derived from Neil H. Borden, "The Concept of the Marketing Mix," *Journal of Advertising Research,* June 1964, p. 27.

35. Perreault and McCarthy, *Basic Marketing,* pp. 310–21.

36. "Use of Cellular Phones Trends Upward, Survey Shows," press release, Decision Analyst, Inc., July 24, 1998; Matthew Klein, "More Callers Unleashed," *Forecast,* September 1998 (**www.demographics.com**).

37. Brian Wansink, "Making Old Brands New," *American Demographics,* December 1997 (**www.demographics.com**).

38. Adrienne Ward Fawcett, "In Glut of New Products, 'Different' Becomes Key," *Advertising Age,* December 13, 1993, p. 28.

39. "On the Pavement, 'Corporate Graffiti' to Sell Fruit Juice," *The New York Times,* May 19, 2002.

40. Haim Oren, "Branding Financial Services Helps Consumers Find Order in Chaos," *Marketing News,* March 29, 1993, p. 6.

41. Frank Bilorsky, "Grocers Labels Offer a New Kind of Branding," *Rochester Democrat and Chronicle,* July 11, 2004 (**www.rochesterdandc.com**).

42. "The Best Global Brands; BusinessWeek and Interbrand Tell You What They're Worth," *BusinessWeek Special Report,* August 5, 2002 (retrieved from **www.businessweek.com**).

43. "Billion Dollar Brand," *Financial Times,* July 17, 2000 (retrieved from **http://news.fr.com**).

44. C. Manly Molpus, "Brands Follow New Shopping Patterns," *Advertising Age,* February 14, 1994, p. 22.

45. Stephan and Tannenholz, "The Real Reason for Brand Switching," p. 31.

46. Annetta Miller, "The Millenial Mind-Set," *American Demographics,* January 1999 (**www.demographics.com/publications/AD/99_ad/9901_ad/ad990102a.htm**).

47. Andrew Jaffe, "A Compass Point Out of Dead Calm: 'Brand Stewardship,'" *Adweek,* February 7, 1994, p. 38.

48. Perreault and McCarthy, *Basic Marketing,* p. 16.

Chapter Five

1. Matthew A. Debellis, "VCs Patronize HomeGrocer.com," Red Herring online, November 3, 1999 (retrieved from **www.redherring.com**).

2. Monica Soto, "HomeGrocer Fortunes Steadily Decline after Merger with Rival," Dow Jones Publications Library, May 6, 2001.

3. Ibid.

4. "HomeGrocer/Webvan Group: Deceased," Seattle Dot Economy. Discussion group, February 22, 2002 (retrieved from **http://pub86.ezboard.com/bseattledoteconomy**).

5. Communication process adapted from J. Paul Peter and Jerry C. Olsen, *Understanding Consumer Behavior* (Burr Ridge, IL: Richard D. Irwin, 1994), p. 184.

6. Martin Ryder, "Semiotics: Language and Culture," *Encyclopedia of Science, Technology, and Ethics* (Macmillan Reference USA, July, 2005).

7. William O. Bearden, Thomas N. Ingram, and Raymond W. LaForge, *Marketing Principles and Perspectives,* 2nd ed. (Burr Ridge, IL: Irwin/McGraw-Hill, 1997) p. 99.

8. S. Kent Stephan and Barry L. Tannenholz, "The Real Reason for Brand Switching," *Advertising Age,* June 13, 1994, p. 31.

9. "Ad Nauseum," *Advertising Age,* July 10, 2000.

10. Kellaris, Cox, and Cox, "The Effect of Background Music on Ad Processing," p. 123.

11. Michael J. McCarthy, "Mind Probe—What Makes an Ad Memorable? Recent Brain Research Yields Surprising Answers," *The Wall Street Journal,* March 22, 1991, p. B3.

12. Al Ries and Jack Trout, *Positioning: The Battle for Your Mind,* rev. ed. (New York: McGraw-Hill, 1986), pp. 30–32.

13. Stephan and Tannenholz, "The Real Reason for Brand Switching."

14. J. Paul Peter and Jerry C. Olson, *Consumer Behavior and Marketing Strategy,* 4th ed. (Burr Ridge, IL: Richard D. Irwin, 1996), p. 554.

15. R. E. Petty, J. T. Cacioppo, and D. Schumann, "Central and Peripheral Routes to Advertising Effectiveness: The Moderating Role of Involvement," *Journal of Consumer Research,* vol. 10, no. 2 (1983), pp. 135–46.

16. This section and the model are adapted from Peter and Olson, *Consumer Behavior and Marketing Strategy,* pp. 554–55.

17. Ibid., pp. 556–57.

18. Yumiko Ono, "Overcoming the Stigma of Dishwashers in Japan," *The Wall Street Journal,* May 19, 2000, p. B2.

19. Karen A. Machleit, Chris T. Allen, and Thomas J. Madden, "The Mature Brand and Brand Interest: An Alternative Consequence of Ad-Evoked Affect," *Journal of Marketing,* October 1993, pp. 72–82.

20. Ibid.

21. Peter and Olson, *Consumer Behavior and Marketing Strategy,* p. 513.

22. Ken Dychtwald and Greg Gable, "Portrait of a Changing Consumer," *Business Horizons,* January/February 1990, pp.

62–74; Larry Light, "Trust Marketing: The Brand Relationship Marketing Mandate for the 90s," address to the American Association of Advertising Agencies annual meeting, Laguna Niguel, CA, April 23, 1993.

23. Colin McDonald, "Point of View: The Key Is to Understand Consumer Response," *Journal of Advertising Research,* September/October 1993, pp. 63–69.

24. McCarthy and Perreault, *Basic Marketing,* p. 204.

25. Vanessa O'Connell, "Nabisco Portrays Cookies as Boost to Women's Self-Esteem," *The Wall Street Journal,* July 10, 1998, p. B7.

26. John R. Rossiter and Larry Percy, *Advertising Communications and Promotion Management,* 2nd ed. (New York: McGraw-Hill, 1997), pp. 120–22.

27. Ibid., p. 121.

28. Ken Bryson and Lynne M. Casper, "Current Population Reports, Household and Family Characteristics: March 1997 and March 1998," U.S. Bureau of the Census; Laura Zinn, "Move Over, Boomers, the Busters Are Here—And They're Angry," *BusinessWeek,* December 14, 1992, pp. 74–82; Jeffrey Zaslow, "Children's Search for Values Leading to Shopping Malls," *The Wall Street Journal,* March 13, 1987.

29. "The Worth of the Cool: Asking Teenagers to Identify the Coolest Brands," *Adweek,* May 9, 1994, p. 18.

30. Greg Farrell, "Star Search," *Adweek,* December 6, 1993, p. 26.

31. Wayne Friedman, "Jordan the Star Athlete Retires, Jordan the Brand Comes to Life," *Advertising Age,* January 18, 1999, p. 3.

32. McCarthy and Perreault, *Basic Marketing,* p. 131; Peter and Olson, *Consumer Behavior and Marketing Strategy,* p. 368.

33. Carolyn A. Lin, "Cultural Differences in Message Strategies: A Comparison between American and Japanese TV Commercials," *Journal of Advertising Research,* July/August 1993, pp. 40–48.

34. Ibid.

35. Peter and Olson, *Consumer Behavior and Marketing Strategy,* p. 413.

36. U.S. Census Bureau, *Statistical Abstract of the United States: 2004–2005* (Washington, DC: U.S. Department of Commerce, 2004), Table 15.

37. **www.adage.com**.

38. Rebecca Purto, "Global Psychographics," *American Demographics,* December 1990, p. 8.

39. The classic studies on cognitive dissonance were initiated by Leon Festinger, *A Theory of Cognitive Dissonance* (Evanston, IL: Row, Peterson, 1957), p. 83; for more recent views, see Hugh Murray, "Advertising's Effect on Sales—Proven or Just Assumed?" *International Journal of Advertising* (UK), vol. 5, no. 1 (1986), pp. 15–36; Delbert Hawkins, Roger Best, and Kenneth Coney, *Consumer Behavior,* 7th ed. (Burr Ridge, IL: McGraw-Hill/Irwin, 1998), pp. 609–10; Ronald E. Milliman and Phillip J. Decker, "The Use of Post-Purchase Communication to Reduce Dissonance and Improve Direct Marketing Effectiveness," *Journal of Business Communication,* Spring 1990, pp. 159–70.

40. Larry Light, "Advertising's Role in Building Brand Equity," speech to annual meeting of the American Association of Advertising Agencies, April 21, 1993.

41. Johan C. Yssel and Mark W. Walchle, "Using the FCB Grid to Write Advertising Strategy," paper presented to the Annual Conference of the Association for Education in Journalism and Mass Communication, 1992.

42. Chung K. Kim and Kenneth R. Lord, "A New FCB Grid and Its Strategic Implications for Advertising," in *Proceedings of the Annual Conference of the Administrative Sciences Association of Canada (Marketing),* Tony Schellinck, ed. (Niagara Falls, Ontario: Administrative Sciences Association of Canada, 1991), pp. 51–60.

Chapter Six

1. John Martin, "Playing for Keeps: How to Build a Lasting Partnership," *Agency,* Summer 1997, pp. 16–18.

2. Beth Rilee-Kelley, personal interview, November 1997.

3. Martin, "Playing for Keeps," p. 18; Rilee-Kelley interview.

4. Jon Steel, *Truth, Lies and Advertising: The Art of Account Planning* (New York: Wiley, 1998), p. 5.

5. Ibid., p. 37.

6. Ibid., p. 53.

7. Media kits: **www.businessweek.com** and **www.forbes.com,** October 2000; Chad Rubel, "Some Cute Super Spots Now Just a Memory," *Marketing News,* March 13, 1995, p. 15.

8. Rilee-Kelley interview.

9. Jerry W. Thomas, "Media Advertising Is an Unfulfilled Promise," *Marketing News,* September 23, 1996, p. 28.

10. Ibid.

11. Story adapted from "Cheese, Please!" *American Demographics,* March 2000, pp. S6–S8. (Copyright Primedia Intertec March 2000.)

12. Ibid.

13. Pat Sloan, "DDB Boosts Planning by Hiring Brit Expert," *Advertising Age,* September 21, 1992, pp. 3, 53.

14. Perreault and McCarthy, *Basic Marketing,* p. 153.

15. Paul Conner, "Defining the 'Decision Purpose' of Research," *Marketing News,* September 23, 1996, p. 18.

16. Michael L. Garee and Thomas R. Schori, "Focus Groups Illuminate Quantitative Research," *Marketing News,* September 23, 1996, p. 41.

17. Robert West, Schering Canada, personal interview, May 17, 1993.

18. William Weylock, "Focus: Hocus Pocus?" *Marketing Tools,* July/August 1994, pp. 12–16; Thomas L. Greenbaum, "Focus Groups Can Play a Part in Evaluating Ad Copy," *Marketing News,* September 13, 1993, pp. 24–25.

19. Pat Sloan and Julie Liesse, "New Agency Weapon to Win Clients: Research," *Advertising Age,* August 30, 1993, p. 37.

20. Gloria F. Mazzella, "Show-and-Tell Focus Groups Reveal Core Boomer Values," *Marketing News,* September 23, 1996, p. 9.

21. Jack Honomichl, "The Honomichl 50," *Marketing News,* June 10, 2002, p. H2; Don E. Schultz, Stanley I. Tannenbaum, and Robert F. Lauterborn, *Integrated Marketing Communications: Putting It Together and Making It Work* (Lincolnwood, IL: NTC Business Books, 1993), pp. 149–50.

22. Leah Rickard, "Helping Put Data in Focus," *Advertising Age,* July 11, 1994, p. 18.

23. François Descarie, director, Impact Research, personal interview, May 17, 1993.

24. Richard Gibson, "Marketers' Mantra: Reap More with Less," *The Wall Street Journal,* March 22, 1991, p. B1.

25. Pamela L. Alreck and Robert B. Settle, *The Survey Research Handbook,* 2nd ed. (Burr Ridge, IL: Richard D. Irwin, 1995), pp. 56–59.

26. Ibid., p. 40.

27. Perreault and McCarthy, *Basic Marketing,* p. 173.

28. Alreck and Settle, *The Survey Research Handbook,* pp. 88–90.

29. MINITAB software for IBM-PC, for Microsoft Windows, and for academic use in an inexpensive student edition through Addison-Wesley Publishing Co., Reading, MA.

30. George S. Fabian, panelist, "Globalization: Challenges for Marketing and Research," *Marketing Review,* February 1993, p. 23.

31. Maureen R. Marston, panelist, "Globalization: Challenges for Marketing and Research," pp. 20–21.

32. Michael Brizz, "How to Learn What Japanese Buyers Really Want," *Business Marketing,* January 1987, p. 72.

33. Thomas L. Greenbaum, "Understanding Focus Group Research Abroad," *Marketing News,* June 3, 1996, pp. H14, H36.

34. Deborah Szynal, "Big Bytes," *Marketing News,* March 18, 2002, p. 3.

Chapter Seven

1. Undated promo sheet and letter from BBDO-NY (1995).

2. Theresa Howard, "Brand Builders: Being True to Dew," *Brandweek,* April 24, 2000, p. 28.

3. Ibid., p. 30.

4. William O. Bearden, Thomas N. Ingram, and Raymond W. LaForge, *Marketing Principles & Perspectives,* 2nd ed. (Burr Ridge, IL: Richard D. Irwin, 1998), pp. 75–76.

5. *Advertising Age,* Ad Age Dataplace—September 27, 1999: "Top 10 Soft Drink Brands" (retrieved from **www.adage.com/dataplace/archives/dp364.html**).

6. "Market Analysis—Defining the Market," Tutor2u, retrieved from **www.tutor2u.net/business/marketing,** February 26, 2003).

7. Greg Farrell, "Dew Poses Real Pepsi Challenge to Coke Ads for Soft-Drink Brand Gain in Teen Popularity," *USA Today,* July 10, 2000, p. B2.

8. Sergio Zyman, *The End of Marketing As We Know It.* (New York: HarperBusiness, 1999).

9. "Saturn SC1 and the Young, College-Educated Import Intenders," *1993 Case Study, NSAC: AAF College World Series of Advertising,* pp. 2, 11, 23.

10. Kate MacArthur and Hillary Chura, "Urban Youth," *Advertising Age,* September 4, 2000, pp. 16–17.

11. Private interview with Scott Moffitt, Director of Marketing, Pepsi-Cola Company, December 2000.

12. Automation Marketing Strategies, "The Art of Market Positioning," Strategic Advantage Newsletter, January 2000 (retrieved from **www.automationmarketing.com,** February 2003).

13. Ernest Martin, "Target Marketing: Summary and Unit Learning Outcomes," Course Syllabus CADV 213 (retrieved from **www.campbell.edu/faculty/martine/index.htm,** February 26, 2003).

14. Raju Narisetti, "Xerox Aims to Imprint High-Tech Image," *The Wall Street Journal,* October 6, 1998, p. B8.

15. Farrell, "Dew Poses Real Pepsi Challenge to Coke," p. B2.

16. Adapted from Al Ries and Jack Trout, *Bottom-Up Marketing* (New York: McGraw-Hill, 1989), p. 8.

17. Frederick E. Webster, Jr., "Executing the New Marketing Concept," *Marketing Management* 3, no. 1 (1994), pp. 8–16.

18. Philip Kotler and Gary Armstrong, *Principles of Marketing* (Englewood Cliffs, NJ: Prentice Hall, 1994), p. 560; Don E. Schultz, Stanley I. Tannenbaum, and Robert F. Lauterborn, *Integrated Marketing Communications: Putting It Together &*

Making It Work (Lincolnwood, IL: NTC Business Books, 1993), p. 52.

19. Frederick E. Webster, Jr., "Defining the New Marketing Concept (Part I)," *Marketing Management* 2, no. 4 (1994), pp. 22–31.

20. Frederick E. Webster, Jr., "The Changing Role of Marketing in the Corporation," *Journal of Marketing,* October 1992, pp. 1–17, 22–31.

21. Ibid.

22. Ibid.

23. Kotler and Armstrong, *Principles of Marketing,* p. 559.

24. Ibid., p. 560.

25. Stan Rapp and Thomas L. Collins, "Nestlè Banks on Databases," *Advertising Age,* October 25, 1993, pp. 16, S–7.

26. Denison Hatch, "The Media Mix: How to Reach the Right Person with the Right Message in the Right Environment," *Target Marketing,* July 1994, pp. 8–10; and Kenneth Wylie, "Direct Response: Database Development Shows Strong Growth as Shops Gain 16.9% in U.S.," *Advertising Age,* July 12, 1993, p. S8.

27. Gary Levin, "Wunderman: 'Personalized' Marketing Will Gain Dominance," *Advertising Age,* October 25, 1993, p. S1.

28. Kotler and Armstrong, *Principles of Marketing,* p. 560.

29. Glen Nowak and Joseph Phelps, "Conceptualizing the Integrated Marketing Communications Phenomenon: An Examination of Its Impact on Advertising Practices and Its Implications for Advertising Research," *Journal of Current Issues and Research in Advertising,* Spring 1994, pp. 49–66.

30. Thomas R. Duncan and Sandra E. Moriarty, *Driving Brand Value: Using Integrated Marketing to Manage Stakeholder Relationships* (New York: McGraw-Hill, 1997), p. 42.

31. Adapted from Kotler and Armstrong, *Principles of Marketing,* pp. 560–61.

32. Arthur M. Hughes, "Can This Relationship Work?" *Marketing Tools,* July/August 1994, p. 4.

33. Hillary Chura and Kate MacArthur, "Flat Colas Anxiously Watch Gen Yers Switch," *Advertising Age,* September 25, 2000; and Howard, "Brand Builders," p. 30.

34. Kotler and Armstrong, *Principles of Marketing,* p. 561.

35. Schultz, Tannenbaum, and Lauterborn, *Integrated Marketing Communications,* p. 52.

36. Regis McKenna, "Marketing Is Everything," *Harvard Business Review,* January/February 1991, p. 65.

37. Tom Duncan, "Integrated Marketing? It's Synergy," *Advertising Age,* March 8, 1993, p. 22.

38. Duncan and Moriarty, *Driving Brand Value,* pp. 3–6.

39. Karlene Lukovitz, "Get Ready for One-on-One Marketing," *Folio: The Magazine for Magazine Management,* October 1, 1991, pp. 64–70.

40. Don E. Schultz, "Four Basic Rules Lay Groundwork for Integration," *Marketing News,* August 16, 1993, p. 5.

41. William F. Arens and Jack J. Whidden, "La Publicité aux Etats-Unis, 1992; Les Symptomes et les Stratégies d'une Industrie Surpeuplée," *L'industrie de la Publicité au Québec 1991–1992* (Montreal: Le Publicité-Club de Montréal, October 1992), pp. 365–99.

42. Regis McKenna, "Marketing in an Age of Diversity," *Harvard Business Review,* September/October 1988, p. 88; Schultz, Tannenbaum, and Lauterborn, *Integrated Marketing Communications,* p. 21.

43. Duncan and Moriarty, *Driving Brand Value,* pp. 78–90.

44. Ibid., p. 90.

45. Adapted from Tom Duncan, "A Macro Model of Integrated Marketing Communication," paper presented to the annual conference of the American Academy of Advertising, Norfolk, VA, March 23–24, 1995, pp. 7–10.

46. Don E. Schultz, "The Next Step in IMC?" *Marketing News,* August 15, 1994, pp. 8–9.

47. Rapp and Collins, "Nestlé Banks on Databases," pp. 16, S7.

48. Don E. Schultz, "Trying to Determine ROI for IMC," *Marketing News,* January 3, 1994, p. 18; Don E. Schultz, "Spreadsheet Approach to Measuring ROI for IMC," *Marketing News,* February 28, 1994, p. 12; and Matthew P. Gonring, "Putting Integrated Marketing Communications to Work Today," *Public Relations Quarterly,* Fall 1994, p. 45.

49. Don E. Schultz, "Integration Helps You Plan Communications from Outside-In," *Marketing News,* March 15, 1993, p. 12.

50. McKenna, "Marketing Is Everything."

51. Schultz, Tannenbaum, and Lauterborn, *Integrated Marketing Communications,* pp. 55–58.

52. Wayne Henderson, "The IMC Scale: A Tool for Evaluating IMC Usage," *Integrated Marketing Communications Research Journal,* vol. 3, no. 1 (Spring 1997), pp. 11–17.

53. Ibid; Cyndee Miller, "Everyone Loves 'IMC,' but . . . ," *Marketing News,* August 16, 1993, pp. 1, 6.

54. Don E. Schultz and Paul Wang, "Real World Results," *Marketing Tools,* premier issue, May 1994, pp. 40–47.

55. Ibid.

56. Don E. Schultz, "Integrated Marketing Communications: A Competitive Weapon in Today's Marketplace," *Marketing Review,* July 1993, pp. 10–11, 29.

57. Gregg Ambach and Mike Hess, "Measuring Long-Term Effects in Marketing," *Marketing Research: A Magazine of Management and Applications,* American Marketing Association, Summer 2000, pp. 23–30.

58. Robert D. Buzzell and Frederick D. Wiersema, "Successful Share-Building Strategies," *Harvard Business Review,* January/February 1981, p. 135; Siva K. Balasubramanian and V. Kumar, "Analyzing Variations in Advertising and Promotional Expenditures: Key Correlated in Consumer, Industrial, and Service Markets," *Journal of Marketing,* April 1990, pp. 57–68.

59. Bernard Ryan Jr., *Advertising in a Recession: The Best Defense Is a Good Offense* (New York: American Association of Advertising Agencies, 1991), pp. 13–29; Priscilla C. Brown, "Surviving with a Splash," *Business Marketing,* January 1991, p. 14; Edmund O. Lawler, "A Window of Opportunity," *Business Marketing,* January 1991, p. 16; Rebecca Colwell Quarles, "Marketing Research Turns Recession into Business Opportunity," *Marketing News,* January 7, 1991, pp. 27, 29.

60. Fabiana Giacomotti, "European Marketers Keep Up Ad Budgets," *Adweek,* January 24, 1994, pp. 16–17.

61. Leo Bogart, *Strategy in Advertising,* 2nd ed. (Chicago: Crain Books, 1984), pp. 45–47.

62. John Philip Jones, "Ad Spending: Maintaining Market Share," *Harvard Business Review,* January/February 1990, pp. 38–42; James C. Schroer, "Ad Spending: Growing Market Share," *Harvard Business Review,* January/February 1990, pp. 44–49.

63. Peter Breen, "Seeds of Change," Promo Sourcebook Supplement, Copyright 2000, INTERTEC, p. 18 (retrieved from **www.lexisnexis.com**).

Chapter Eight

1. Gary Levin, "VitroRobertson Lets Success Do the Talking," *Advertising Age,* August 29, 1994, p. 29; Ken Mendelbaum, "I Wish I'd Done That Ad," for Magazine Publishers of America, *Adweek,* September 19, 1994, p. 29; private correspondence and interviews with Taylor Guitar and VitroRobertson, February 1995.

2. Kevin Goldman, "Leap Partnership Touts All-Creative Shop," *The Wall Street Journal,* December 23, 1993, p. B3.

3. Adapted from interviews and private correspondence with Hugh G. Cannon, Wayne State University, 1997.

4. Adapted from Bruce Bendinger, *The Copy Workshop Workbook* (Chicago: The Copy Workshop, 1993), pp. 128–47.

5. Hank Seiden, *Advertising Pure and Simple* (New York: AMACOM, 1990), pp. 23–340.

6. Nancy A. Mitchell, Diane M. Badzinski, and Donna R. Pawlowski, "The Use of Metaphors as Vivid Stimuli to Enhance Comprehension and Recall of Print Advertisements," in Karen Whitehill King, ed., *Proceedings of the 1994 Conference of the American Academy of Advertising* (Athens, GA: Henry W. Grady College of Journalism and Mass Communication, the University of Georgia, 1994), p. 199.

7. Ibid.

8. Sandra Moriarty and Shay Sayre, "An Interpretive Study of Visual Cues in Advertising," paper presented to the annual convention of the Association for Education in Journalism and Mass Communication, Montreal, August 1992, p. 5.

9. Sal Randazzo, *The Mythmakers: How Advertisers Apply the Power of Classic Myths and Symbols to Create Modern Day Legends* (Chicago: Probus Publishing, 1995), pp. 28–51.

10. Barry A. Hollander, "Infomation Graphics and the Bandwagon Effect: Does the Visual Display of Opinion Aid in Persuasion?" paper presented to the annual convention of the Association for Education in Journalism and Mass Communication, Montreal, August 1992, p. 21.

11. Kevin Goldman, "Nike, H-P Gamble on New Sales Pitches," *The Wall Street Journal,* April 8, 1994, p. B8.

12. Allen F. Harrison and Robert M. Bramson, *The Art of Thinking* (New York: Berkley Books, 1984), pp. 26, 34, 181.

13. Ibid.

14. Roger von Oech, *A Kick in the Seat of the Pants* (New York: HarperPerennial, 1986), p. 12.

15. John O'Toole, *The Trouble with Advertising,* 2nd ed. (New York: Random House, 1985), p. 132; Fred Danzig, "The Big Idea," *Advertising Age,* November 9, 1988, pp. 16, 138–40.

16. O'Toole, *The Trouble with Advertising,* pp. 132–33.

17. Adapted with permission from von Oech, *A Kick in the Seat of the Pants,* pp. 55–87.

18. Bob Garfield, "Lovestruck Praying Mantis Is Hooked on Fila," *Advertising Age,* February 13, 1995, p. 3.

19. William D. Perreault Jr. and E. Jerome McCarthy, *Basic Marketing,* 14th ed. (Burr Ridge, IL: Richard D. Irwin, 2002), p. 467.

20. Adapted with permission from von Oech, *A Kick in the Seat of the Pants,* pp. 89–111.

21. Bendinger, *The Copy Workshop Workbook,* pp. 170–74.

22. David Ogilvy, *Ogilvy on Advertising* (New York: Random House, 1985), pp. 17–18.

Chapter Nine

1. U.S. FTC and Synovate Research, Identity Theft Survey Report (September 2003), 4–7, accessed October 28, 2004, at **www.ftc.gov/os/2003/09/synovatereport.pdf.**

2. U.S. FTC, Overview of the Identity Theft Program (September 2003), 8, accessed October 28, 2004, at **www.ftc.gov/os/2003/09/timelinereport.pdf.**

3. Quoted in Eleftheria Parpis, "Campaign of the Year: Citibank," *Adweek* 45, no. 6 (February 9, 2004): 30, accessed October 28, 2004, at **www.proquest.com.**

4. Ibid.

5. Mae Anderson, "Creative Best Spots: April," *Adweek* 45, no. 20 (May 17, 2004): 26–27, accessed October 28, 2004, at **www.proquest.com.** See also Lance Ulanoff, "Opting into Identity Theft," *PC Magazine* online (July 21, 2004), accessed October 29, 2004, at **www.pcmag.com.**

6. Sue Chastain, ed., "Types of Graphics Software, Part 3," About.com, October 5, 1999, **http://graphicssoft.about.com/library/weekly/aa051099.htm.**

7. Jeremy Sindair, "Why I Think It's Time for a New Kind of Advertising," *Campaign* (UK), September 8, 2000 (retrieved from Lexis-Nexis Academic Universe **http://web.lexis-nexis.com/universe/printdoc,** January 2001).

8. Glenn Mohrman and Jeffrey E. Scott, "Truth(s) in Advertising? Part II," *Medical Marketing & Media,* October 1, 1988, pp. 28–32.

9. A. Jerome Jeweler and Bonnie L. Drewniany, *Creative Strategy in Advertising* (Belmont, CA: Wadsworth Publishing, 1998), p. 139.

10. Roy Paul Nelson, *The Design of Advertising* (Dubuque, IA: Brown & Benchmark, 1994), p. 107; J. Douglas Johnson, *Advertising Today* (Chicago: Science Research Associates, 1978).

11. John O'Toole, *The Trouble with Advertising,* 2nd ed. (New York: Random House, 1985), p. 149.

12. Axel Andersson and Denison Hatch, "How to Create Headlines That Get Results," *Target Marketing,* March 1994, pp. 28–35.

13. Murray Raphel and Neil Raphel, "A New Look at Newspaper Ads," *Progressive Grocer,* November 1993, pp. 13–14; David Ogilvy, *Ogilvy on Advertising* (New York: Random House, 1985), pp. 88–89.

14. Philip Ward Burton, *Advertising Copywriting,* 6th ed. (Lincolnwood, IL: NTC Business Books, 1991), pp. 65–66, 70.

15. Nelson, *The Design of Advertising,* p. 91.

16. Jeweler and Drewniany, *Creative Strategy in Advertising,* p. 115; Burton, *Advertising Copywriting,* p. 188; Julia M. Collins, "Image and Advertising," *Harvard Business Review,* January/February 1989, pp. 93–97.

17. Neil Raphel and Murray Raphel, "Rules to Advertise By," *Progressive Grocer,* December 1993, pp. 13–14; Murray Raphel, "How to Get A-head in Direct Mail," *Direct Marketing,* January 1990, pp. 30–32, 52.

18. Ogilvy, *Ogilvy on Advertising,* p. 71.

19. Raphel and Raphel, "A New Look at Newspaper Ads," pp. 13–14.

20. James H. Leigh, "The Use of Figures of Speech in Print Ad Headlines," *Journal of Advertising Research,* June 1994, pp. 17–33.

21. Ogilvy, *Ogilvy on Advertising,* pp. 10–11.

22. Andersson and Hatch, "How to Create Headlines That Get Results," pp. 28–35.

23. Burton, *Advertising Copywriting,* p. 54; Arthur J. Kover and William J. James, "When Do Advertising 'Power Words' Work? An Examination of Congruence and Satiation," *Journal of Advertising Research,* July/August 1993, pp. 32–38.

24. Burton, *Advertising Copywriting,* p. 58.

25. Raphel and Raphel, "A New Look at Newspaper Ads," pp. 13–14.

26. Burton, *Advertising Copywriting,* p. 54.

27. Burton, *Advertising Copywriting,* p. 12.

28. Raphel and Raphel, "Rules to Advertise By," pp. 13–14.

29. Bendinger, *The Copy Workshop Workbook,* p. 192.

30. Burton, *Advertising Copywriting,* p. 74.

31. Ogilvy, *Ogilvy on Advertising,* p. 119.

32. Burton, *Advertising Copywriting,* p. 79.

33. Leigh, "The Use of Figures of Speech in Print Ad Headlines," pp. 17–33.

34. Burton, *Advertising Copywriting,* p. 90; Marjorie Zieff-Finn, "It's No Laughing Matter," *Direct Marketing,* September 1992, pp. 38–40.

35. O'Toole, *The Trouble with Advertising,* p. 149.

36. Levinson, *Guerrilla Advertising,* p. 203; Burton, *Advertising Copywriting,* pp. 221–22.

37. Herschell Gordon Lewis, "Radio Copywriting—Not as Easy as You May Think," *Direct Marketing,* July 1992, pp. 17–18.

38. Ogilvy, *Ogilvy on Advertising,* p. 109.

39. Ibid., pp. 103–13.

40. Bendinger, *The Copy Workshop Workbook,* p. 284.

41. "Corporate Advertising Study," Burson-Marsteller, October 13, 2003, **www.efluentials.com/documents/pr_101303.pdf.**

42. John Morkes and Jakob Nielsen, "Concise, SCANNABLE, and Objective: How to Write for the Web," 1997 (**www.useit.com/papers/webwriting/writing.html**).

43. Richard N. Weltz, "How Do You Say, 'Ooops!'" *Business Marketing,* October 1990, pp. 52–53.

44. Lennie Copeland, "Foreign Markets: Not for the Amateur," *Business Marketing,* July 1984, pp. 112–18.

45. John Freiralds, "Navigating the Minefields of Multilingual Marketing," *Pharmaceutical Executive,* September 1994, pp. 74–78.

Chapter Ten

1. Saatchi & Saatchi Los Angeles and Toyota Motor Sales, personal correspondence and interviews, January 2001.

2. Personal interview, Lorraine Alper Kramer, Saatchi & Saatchi Los Angeles, January 2001.

3. "Amid Media Price Inflation, TV Production Costs Also Soar, Pose Threat to Addressability," *Media Daily News* (MediaPost Communications), October 13, 2004 (retrieved from **http://publications.mediapost.com,** September 18, 2005).

4. Kenneth Roman and Jane Maas, *How to Advertise* (New York: St. Martin's Press, 1992), pp. 26–28; Miner Raymond, "How to Cut Commercial Production Costs without Anyone Knowing You've Done It," *Sales & Marketing Management in Canada,* December 1987, pp. 20–22; "Marketing Guide 19: Advertising Production," *Marketing* (UK), February 7, 1991, pp. 21–24.

5. Cleveland Horton, "Spots: Cheaper Is More Effective," *Advertising Age,* July 4, 1994, p. 6.

6. "Button Pushers: Ordering Kiosks Boost Sales and Speed of Service but Don't Necessarily Cut Labor Costs," *Chain Leader* 9, no. 1 (January 2004), p. 54 (retrieved from www.lexisnexis.com, August 26, 2004).

7. Personal interview, Dean Van Eimeren, Saatchi & Saatchi Los Angeles, January 2001.

8. PANTONE® is a registered trademark of PANTONE, Inc.

9. Kathleen Lewis, "Printing: Teach Your Boss a Lesson," *In-House Graphics,* February 1990, p. 89.

10. Dave Zwang, "Proof of What? (New Technologies in Proofing Operations)," *American Printer,* October 1, 1996, pp. 40–44.

11. Jonathan Bond and Richard Kirshenbaum, *Under the Radar: Talking to Today's Cynical Consumer* (New York: John Wiley & Sons, 1998), p. 154.

12. Adapted from Greg Hofman, "Splash Graphics That Say 'Gotcha,'" *Step-by-Step Graphics,* May/June 1991, p. 40.

13. David Ogilvy, *Ogilvy on Advertising* (New York: Random House, 1985), pp. 113–16.

14. Tom Cuniff, "The Second Creative Revolution," *Advertising Age,* December 6, 1993, p. 22.

Chapter Eleven

1. National Institutes of Health.

2. "Milk Mustache Campaign Moves into Second Phase," *DQA Quest,* August 1996.

3. "Magazines by Circulation for 6 Mos. Ended 12/31/2002," AdAge.com Data Center (retrieved from www.adage.com, March 2003).

4. Shu-Fen Li, John C. Schweitzer, and Benjamin J. Bates, "Effectiveness of Trade Magazine Advertising," paper presented to the annual conference of the Association for Education in Journalism and Mass Communication, Montreal, Quebec, August 1992.

5. Gene Willhoft, "Is 'Added Value' Valuable?" *Advertising Age,* March 1, 1993, p. 18.

6. Answers: *Car & Driver* is $103.83 CPM, *Car & Driver* media kit (www.caranddriver.com); *Road & Track* is $112.42 CPM, *Road & Track* media kit (www.roadandtrack.com).

7. "CorePrint 2.2 Stewardship," COREMedia Systems, Inc. (retrieved from www.coremedia-systems.com, April 16, 2001); "STRATA's Media Buying," STRATA Marketing, Inc. (retrieved from www.stratag.com, April 16, 2001); rate data from *SRDS Consumer Magazine Advertising Source* 85, no. 4 (April 2003).

8. Joyce Rutter Kaye, *Print Casebooks 10/The Best in Advertising,* 1994–95 ed. (Rockville, MD: RC Publications, 1994), pp. 63–65; Tony Case, "Getting Personal," *Editor & Publisher,* February 1, 1992, pp. 16, 31; Ann Cooper, "Creatives: Magazines—Believers in the Power of Print," *Adweek* (Eastern ed.), April 12, 1993, pp. 34–39.

9. "Facts about Newspapers," Newspaper Association of America (retrieved from www.naa.org/info/facts04, October 8, 2004).

10. Ibid.

11. Ibid.

12. Ronald Redfern, "What Readers Want from Newspapers," *Advertising Age,* January 23, 1995, p. 25.

13. "Facts about Newspapers."

14. "Newspaper Circulation Volume," Newspaper Association of America (retrieved from www.naa.org, October 8, 2004).

15. "General Facts on *Parade*" (retrieved from www.parade.com/mediarelations, October 9, 2004).

16. "Top 100 Daily Newspapers in the United States," *Infoplease Arts & Entertainment Almanac* (retrieved from www.infoplease.com/ipea, October 8, 2004).

17. *Newspaper Rate Differentials* (New York: American Association of Advertising Agencies, 1990); Christy Fisher, "NAA Readies National Ad-Buy Plan," *Advertising Age,* March 1, 1993, p. 12.

18. "Facts about Newspapers."

19. John Flinn, "State of the National Buy," *Adweek,* June 26, 1995, p. 56.

20. Christy Fisher, "Chrysler's One-Stop Ad Buys Boost Ailing Newspapers," *Advertising Age,* March 7, 1994, p. 49.

21. Dorothy Giobbe, "One Order/One Bill System Gets a Dress Rehearsal," *Editor & Publisher,* March 12, 1994, pp. 26, 46.

22. Fisher, "Chrysler's One-Stop Ad Buys Boost Ailing Newspapers," p. 49; ibid.

23. Sally D. Goll, "Ignoring the Masses, *Avenue* Magazine Launches an Edition for China's Elite," *The Wall Street Journal,* September 28, 1994, p. B1.

24. Stephen Barr, "Moving Ahead," *Adweek,* January 31, 1994, p. 26.

Chapter Twelve

1. Paula Mergenhagen. "How 'Got Milk?' Got Sales," *American Demographics,* September 1996.

2. Ibid.

3. "Trends in Advertising Volume" (retrieved from www.tvb.org, November 15, 2005).

4. "U.S. Advertising Expenditures—All Media," Newspaper Association of America (retrieved from www.naa.org, August 26, 2004).

5. "TV Basics: Commercial Television Stations" (retrieved from www.tvb.org, August 26, 2004).

6. "TV Basics: Reach-Broadcast vs. Cable" (retrieved from www.tvb.org, November 15, 2005).

7. "Time Spent Viewing—Households," Television Bureau of Advertising, Inc. (retrieved from www.tvb.org, April 11, 2001); "Time Spent Viewing—Persons," Television Bureau of Advertising, Inc. (retrieved from www.tvb.org, April 11, 2001); "Consumer Media Usage," Television Bureau of Advertising, Inc. (retrieved from www.tvb.org, April 11, 2001).

8. "TV Basics: Channels—Receivable vs. Viewed," Television Bureau of Advertising, Inc. (retrieved from www.tvb.org, August 26, 2004).

9. "Ad-Supported Cable Networks" (retrieved from www.onetvworld.org, October 2, 2005).

10. "Media Comparisons Study 2003," TVB Research Central (retrieved from www.tvb.org/mediacomparisons, October 11, 2004).

11. "Time Spent Viewing by TV Source in Hrs:Mins per Week (2000/01)" (retrieved from www.cabletvadbureau.com, March 24, 2003).

12. "Basic Cable—Biggest Gains," *Cable Advertising*, CableSCAN, a division of Tapscan, Inc., December 1997 (**www.cableads. com**); *Marketer's Guide to Media*, Fall/Winter 1992–93, p. 50.

13. Retrieved from **www.mediainfocenter.org**, November 15, 2005.

14. "Local Cable Ad Revenues on the Rise," December 10, 2004 (retrieved from **www.reclaimthemedia.org**, November 15, 2005).

15. Thomas R. Duncan and Sandra E. Moriarty, *Driving Brand Value: Using Integrated Marketing to Manage Stakeholder Relationships* (New York: McGraw-Hill, 1997), pp. 101–2.

16. Ibid.

17. "How Cable Stacks up against the Competition," Cabletelevision Advertising Bureau (retrieved from **www.cabletvadbureau.com**, August 26, 2004).

18. Kathy Haley, "Spot TV Is Power Tool," *The Power of Spot TV*, supplement to *Advertising Age*, September 29, 1993, p. T3.

19. Michael Burgi, "Welcome to the 500 Club," p. 45; Christopher Stern, "Advertisers Hear Promise of Smooth Spot Cable Buys," *Broadcasting & Cable*, April 26, 1993, pp. 56, 58.

20. R. Craig Endicott, "100 Leading National Advertisers," *Advertising Age*, June 28, 2004, p. S21.

21. "What Is Syndication?" *1994 Guide to Advertiser-Supported Syndication*, supplement to *Advertising Age* (New York: Advertiser Syndicated Television Association, 1994), p. A6; David Tobenkin, "Action Escalates for Syndicators," *Broadcasting & Cable*, August 29, 1994, pp. 29–35.

22. "Syndication Showcase," *Broadcasting & Cable*, January 24, 1994, pp. 82–86.

23. Kathy Haley, "The Infomercial Begins a New Era as a Marketing Tool for Top Brands," *Advertising Age*, January 25, 1993, p. M3.

24. Nancy Coltun Webster, "Marketers Look to Cable for Direct-Response Ads," *Advertising Age Special Report: Cable TV*, December 8, 1997, p. S8.

25. Kevin Goldman, "CBS to Push Videotaping of Infomercials," *The Wall Street Journal*, November 15, 1993, p. B7.

26. Ibid.; Tom Burke, "Program-Length Commercials Can Bring These Six Benefits to a Major Brand Campaign," *Advertising Age*, January 25, 1993, p. M5.

27. "2003 infomercials—out with the new, return to the old" (retrieved from **www.shfwire.com**, November 15, 2005).

28. Bill Carter, "Television: A Monopoly Once More, Nielsen Is Still Unloved," *The New York Times*, September 7, 1992, p. 19; Jim Cooper, "Arbitron Exit Sparks Concern about Lack of Competition," *Broadcasting & Cable*, October 25, 1993, p. 45.

29. Will Workman, "ADcom's Cable Meter: A Revolution in the Making," *Cable World*, March 17, 1997 (**www.mediacentral. com**).

30. Ibid.

31. Kevin Goldman, "CBS Pays Price for Losing Bet on Ratings," *The Wall Street Journal*, November 30, 1993, p. B4; Kevin Goldman, "CBS Again Must Offer Make-Good Ads," *The Wall Street Journal*, October 27, 1994, p. B6; Kevin Goldman, "'Scarlett' Make-Goods," *The Wall Street Journal*, November 21, 1994, p. B8.

32. Joanne Lipman, "Video Renters Watch the Ads, Zapping Conventional Wisdom," *The Wall Street Journal*, April 28, 1989, p. B1.

33. Wei-Na Lee and Helen Katz, "New Media, New Messages: An Initial Inquiry into Audience Reactions to Advertising on Videocassettes," *Journal of Advertising Research*, January/February 1993, pp. 74–85.

34. *Radio Marketing Guide & Fact Book for Advertisers 2000–2001 Edition*, Radio Advertising Bureau, pp. 5, 6, 9 (retrieved from **www.rab.com**, April 11, 2001).

35. "Radio Is Cost-Effective," *1997 Radio Marketing Guide & Fact Book for Advertisers*.

36. "Radio's Personalities Help Find Snapple's Sales Targets," *The Power of Radio*, special advertising supplement to *Advertising Age*, October 18, 1993, p. R3.

37. "Media Comparisons," *1997 Radio Marketing Guide and Fact Book for Advertisers*; Imagery Transfer Study (New York: Network Radio Association, 1993).

38. Ibid.; *Media Facts: The Complete Guide to Maximizing Your Advertising* (New York: Radio Advertising Bureau, 1994), pp. 8–9.

39. "Maximize Your Marketing Message with Radio," *1997 Radio Marketing Guide and Fact Book for Advertisers; Radio Marketing Guide and Factbook for Advertisers: 1993–1994*, pp. 29–33.

40. "There's a Radio Format for Everybody," *1997 Radio Marketing Guide and Fact Book for Advertisers*.

41. Network Radio: *Targeting the National Consumer*, supplement to *Advertising Age*, September 6, 1993, pp. R2, R4; *Marketer's Guide to Media*, Fall/Winter 1992–93, pp. 69–70.

42. **AdAge.com**, April 22, 2005.

43. Janet Stilson, "Radio Scraps for Its Ad Share," *Advertising Age*, February 2, 2004, p. 22 (retrieved from **www.lexisnexis. com**, October 12, 2004).

44. Scott MacDonald, "Cable, Satellite TV Fuel Top 100," from "100 Leading Media Companies," *Advertising Age*, August 25, 2004, p. S2 (retrieved from **www.lexisnexis.com**, October 12, 2004).

45. Ibid.

Chapter Thirteen

1. Meeting with Rik Kinney and Stephanie Yost Cameron at NeoPets office in Glendale, California, March 25, 2003; "NeoPets Online Presskit" (retrieved from **http://info.neopets.com/presskit**, September 2, 2004).

2. Thom Forbes, "Ads in Cyberspace: Light Your Beacon, but Don't Get Flamed," *Agency*, Winter 1995, p. 32.

3. "December Shopping Up from Last Year in Spite of Rough Economy, According to the Forrester Research Online Retail Index," January 24, 2002 (retrieved from **www.forrester.com**).

4. "Ad Spending in the US: Online & Offline," August, 2004 (retrieved from **www.emarketer.com**).

5. "GartnerGroup Says Business-to-Business E-Commerce Transactions Becoming More Global," February 16, 2000 (retrieved from **www.europe.gartner.com**, November 17, 2005).

6. Kevin Goldman, "Shopping Comes to Cyberspace with Launch of On-Line Catalogs," *The Wall Street Journal*, November 18, 1994, p. B7.

7. "Web Characterization," Online Computer Library Center, Inc., Office of Research (retrieved from **http://wcp.ock.org**, September 2, 2004).

8. "Top 25 Websites for October Announced," *Relevant Knowledge*, 1997 (**www.relevantknowledge.com**); "Media

Metrix Top 50 U.S. Web & Digital Media Properties for November 2000" (http://us.mediametrix.com).

9. "Media Metrix Top 50 U.S. Web & Digital Media Properties for April 2004" (retrieved from www.comscore.com, September 2, 2004).

10. "How Many Online?" Nua Internet Surveys, September 2002 (retrieved from www.nua.com/surveys/how_many_online/n_america.html); "United States: Average Web Usage, July 2004," Nielsen//NetRatings (retrieved from www.nielsen-netratings.com, September 3, 2004).

11. "Countries with Highest Internet Penetration Rate," *Internet World Stats,* September 1, 2004 (retrieved from www.internetworldstats.com, September 3, 2004).

12. Mary Kuntz, "Burma Shave Signs on the I-Way," *BusinessWeek* via America Online, April 17, 1995.

13. Marissa Gluck, "Online Advertising through 2005: Flourishing in the Dot-com Decline," *Vision Report,* Jupiter Research, August 16, 2000 (retrieved January 2001 from www.jup.com); "IAB Advertising ABC's," Internet Advertising Bureau, 1997 (www.iab.net); Kate Fitzgerald, "Debate Grows over Net Data," *Advertising Age,* March 15, 2004 (retrieved from www.adage.com, September 3, 2004).

14. Susannah Fox, principal researcher, Older Americans and the Internet, Pew Internet and American Life Project, pp. 2–3, March 25, 2004 (retrieved from www.pewinternet.org/pdfs/PIP_Seniors_Online_2004.pdf, September 1, 2004).

15. Tom Spooner, principal researcher, Internet Use by Region in the United States, Pew Internet and American Life Project, August 27, 2003 (retrieved from www.pewinternet.org/pdfs/PIP_Regional_Report_Aug_2003.pdf, September 1, 2004).

16. U.S. Census Bureau, "Table No. 1156 Internet Access and Usage and Online Service Usage: 2003," *Statistical Abstract of the U.S. 2003,* p. 735 (retrieved from www.census.gov/prod/2004pubs/03statab/inforcomm.pdf, September 1, 2004).

17. Ibid.

18. Tobi Elkin and Jack Neff, "Dove Soap Study Documents Branding Impact of Online Ads: Analyzed a Six-Week Integrated Campaign," Ad Age.com, February 20, 2002 (retrieved from www.adage.com/news).

19. "Baseband Transmission," Webopedia (retrieved January 2001 from http://webopedia.internet.com).

20. "Broadband Transmission," Webopedia (retrieved January 2001 from http://webopedia.internet.com).

21. Tobi Elkin, "51% of U.S. Online Time Now Broadband," AdAge.com, March 5, 2002 (retrieved from www.adage.com/news); "Broadband Access Grows 59 Percent, while Narrowband Use Declines, According to Nielsen//NetRatings," Nielsen//NetRatings press release, January 15, 2003 (retrieved from www.nielsennetratings.com); "U.S. Broadband Connections Reach Critical Mass," Nielsen//NetRatings press release, August 18, 2004 (retrieved from www.nielsennetratings.com/pr/pr_040818.pdf, September 3, 2004).

22. Greg Holden, "DSL vs. Cable: The Truth about Cable," CNET Internet (retrieved January 2001 from www.cnet.com).

23. Greg Holden, "DSL vs. Cable: The Straight Dope about DSL," CNET Internet (retrieved January 2001 from www.cnet.com).

24. "DSL Beats Cable Modem in Prime-Time Internet Performance Duel," press release from Keynote Systems, May 17, 1999 (retrieved January 2001 from www.keynote.com/news/announcements/pr051799.html).

25. Netlingo Dictionary, 1997 (www.netlingo.com).

26. "IAB Announces Final Interactive Universal Ad Package," Interactive Advertising Bureau Press Release, April 28, 2003 (retrieved from http://www.iab.net/news).

27. Charles Waltner, "Going Beyond the Banner with Web Ads," *Advertising Age,* March 4, 1996, p. 22.

28. Claudia Kuehl, "Spam's Good Twin: If E-mail Is Done Just Right, People Will Want to Receive It. Really," The DMA Interactive, Library White Papers, May 2000 (retrieved January 2001 from www.the-dma.org/library/whitepapers/spamsgoodtwin.shtml).

29. Bart Lazar, "CAN-SPAM Creates Quandary, Opportunities," *Marketing News,* June 15, 2004 (retrieved from www.lexis-nexis.com, September 1, 2004); William Jackson, "FTC Files First CAN-SPAM Cases," *Newsbytes,* April 29, 2004 (retrieved from www.lexis-nexis.com, September 1, 2004).

30. David Gikandi, "Find and Keep: Sticky and Viral Site Marketing," Web Developer's Journal, Internet.com (retrieved January 2001 from www.webdevelopersjournal.com).

31. Amanda Beeler, "Word-of-Mouth Pitches Mutate into New Forms on the Internet," *Advertising Age,* April 2000 (retrieved January 2001 from www.adage.com).

32. *The Wall Street Journal* (Eastern edition). New York, June 27, 2005, p. B.1

33. Ibid.

34. "Interactive Audience Measurement and Advertising Campaign Reporting and Audit Guidelines," Interactive Advertising Bureau, September 2004.

35. "Ratings That Know What You're Looking At, and When," June 7, 2000 (retrieved from www.newyorktimes.com).

36. "Net rankings vex dot-coms," June 20, 2000 (retrieved from www.usatoday.com).

37. Ibid.

38. Kate Maddox, "ANA Study Finds Marketers Triple Net Ad Budgets," *Advertising Age,* May 1998 (retrieved from www.adage.com).

39. "U.S. Online Marketing Forecast: $26 billion by 2010," May 3, 2005 (retrieved from http://blogs.forrester.com/charleneli/2005/05/US_online_marke.html).

40. Alicia Orr, "The Lowdown on High Tech," *Target Marketing,* January 1995, pp. 8–10.

41. Ibid.

42. "New Media Envision Multimedia Awards," *New Media,* August 1994, pp. S16, S19.

43. Orr, "The Lowdown on High Tech."

44. *Business 2.0,* November, 2004, p. 120.

45. R. Craig Endicott, "100 Leading National Advertisers," *Advertising Age,* June 28, 2004.

46. "Catalog Tracker: Volume Steady, Offers Rising," June 1, 2005 (retrieved from http://multichannelmerchant.com, November 18, 2005).

47. Ibid.

48. Robert H. Hallowell III, "The Selling Points of Direct Mail," *Trusts & Estates,* December 1994, pp. 39–41.

49. Sherry Chiger, "Benchmark 2004: Lists," *Catalog Age* 21, no. 8 (August 1, 2004) pp. 34–38 (retrieved from www.proquest.com, October 15, 2004).

Chapter Fourteen

1. Mary Yeung, *Print Casebooks 9: The Best in Advertising* (Rockville, MD: R. C. Publications, 1991), pp. 19–20.

2. "Introduce Yourself to Outdoor Advertising," Outdoor Advertising Association of America, Inc. (retrieved from **www.oaaa.org**, October 8, 2004).

3. *Billboard Basics* (New York: Outdoor Advertising Association of America, 1994), p. 5.

4. **www.oaaa.org** (retrieved November 19, 2005).

5. Mary Jo Haskey, "The Last Mass Medium," *Mediaweek,* December 6, 1993, p. 17.

6. Ibid., pp. 11, 21; Kevin Goldman, "Billboards Gain Respect as Spending Increases," *The Wall Street Journal,* June 27, 1994, p. B5.

7. Riccardo A. Davis, "Apparel, Movies Orchestrate an Outdoor Rebirth," *Advertising Age,* November 22, 1993, p. S2.

8. "Facts and Figures," OAAA about Outdoor (retrieved from **www.oaaa.org/outdoor/facts/cpmcomparison.asp**, October 11, 2004).

9. "Technology Standards," Outdoor Advertising Association of America, 1997 (**www.oaaa.org/Tech**).

10. Ibid.

11. Cyndee Miller, "Outdoor Advertising Weathers Repeated Attempts to Kill It," *Marketing News,* March 16, 1992, pp. 1, 9; *Billboard Basics,* pp. 15–16.

12. "Surveys Show Americans Like Their Billboards," Outdoor Advertising Association of America, 1997 (**www.oaaa.org**).

13. Davis, "Apparel, Movies Orchestrate an Outdoor Rebirth," p. S1.

14. "2002 Media Markets Report," *Hispanic Business Magazine,* December 2002 (retrieved from **www.hispanicbusiness.com**, November 19, 2005).

15. Riccardo A. Davis, "Retailers Open Doors Wide for Co-op," *Advertising Age,* August 1, 1994, p. 30.

16. "Advertising That Imitates Art," *Adweek,* June 20, 1994, p. 18.

17. Fara Warner, "DKNY Takes Upscale Ads Underground," *The Wall Street Journal,* October 6, 1994, p. B4; "Nextel, Las Vegas Link Brands in Monorail Deal," *Los Angeles Times,* November 17, 2003 (retrieved from **www.lvmonorail.com/about_01_news_detail.asp**, September 9, 2004).

18. James Ferrier, "Spotlight on Technology—Telecite," *Advertising Age,* November 22, 1993, p. SS10.

19. Susan A. Friedmann, *Exhibiting at Trade Shows* (Menlo Park, CA: Crisp Publications, 1992), p. V.

20. Ibid., p. 16.

21. Helen Berman, "The Advertising/Trade Show Partnership," *Folio: The Magazine for Magazine Management,* May 1, 1995, pp. 44–47.

22. Friedmann, *Exhibiting at Trade Shows,* p. 24.

23. Ibid., pp. 34–39.

24. Ibid., p. 44.

25. Ibid., pp. 70–71.

26. Ibid., p. 90.

27. "Promotional Products Fact Sheet," Promotional Products Association International, Irving, TX, 1995.

28. "1993 Estimate of Promotional Products Distributor Sales," Promotional Products Association International, Irving, TX, 1994.

29. *How Specialty Advertising Affects Goodwill* (Irving, TX: Specialty Advertising Association International, 1993).

30. Avraham Shama and Jack K. Thompson, "Promotion Gifts: Help or Hindrance?" *Mortgage Banking,* February 1989, pp. 49–51.

31. *Yellow Pages Industry Facts Booklet,* 1994–95 edition (Troy, MI: Yellow Pages Publishers Association, 1994), p. 32.

32. "Independent Yellow Pages Publishers' Revenues to Increase 16.7% to $2.8 Billion in 2004," PR Newswire, July 19, 2004 (retrieved from **www.lexisnexis.com**, September 9, 2004).

33. "100 Leading Media Companies," *Advertising Age Special Report,* August 23, 2004, p. S7.

34. Bradley Johnson, "Yellow-Pages Deals Red Hot as Telecom Industry Regroups," *Advertising Age,* January 6, 2003 (retrieved from **www.proquest.com**, May 12, 2003).

35. Randall Crosby, "Is Ride-Along the Right Track?" *Link,* February 1995, pp. 17–23.

36. Kevin Goldman, "Capital Cities Builds New Media Sales Unit," *The Wall Street Journal,* January 24, 1994, p. B7.

37. Nicole Sperling, "Cinema Advertising Exhibits Growth," *The Hollywood Reporter,* June 14, 2004 (retrieved from **www.lexisnexis.com**, September 9, 2004).

38. Emma Hall, "Young Consumers Receptive to Movie Product Placement," *Advertising Age,* March 29, 2004 (retrieved from **www.lexisnexis.com**, September 9, 2004).

39. Michael McCarthy, "Also Starring (Your Product Name Here)," *USA Today,* August 12, 2004 (retrieved from **www.lexisnexis.com**, September 9, 2004).

Chapter Fifteen

1. Sony story adapted from Eric Schmuckler, "Best Campaign Spending $1 Million or Less (Tie): Media Edge/Y&R," *Mediaweek,* June 19, 2000, pp. S50–S54.

2. Laurie Freeman, "Experience Worth More than Byte," *Advertising Age,* July 23, 1996, p. S15.

3. Julie Liesse, "Inside Burnett's Vaunted Buying Machine," *Advertising Age,* July 25, 1994, p. S6.

4. Yumiko Ono, "Cordiant Puts Hamilton in Key U.S. Post," *Advertising Age,* July 18, 1997, p. B2.

5. Stephanie Thompson, "Universal McCann Gets $150 Million Nestlé Account," AdAge.com, April 12, 2002; Richard Linnett and Jack Neff, "Mindshare Wins $600 Million Gillette Media Account," AdAge.com, September 26, 2002 (retrieved from **www.adage.com**).

6. Jon Lafayette, "Agency Media Staffs Gain Clout," *Advertising Age,* March 4, 1991, p. 12; Peter J. Danaher and Roland T. Rust, "Determining the Optimal Level of Media Spending," *Journal of Advertising Research,* January/February 1994, p. 28.

7. "Business: Hi Ho, Hi Ho, Down the Data Mine We Go," *The Economist,* August 23, 1997, pp. 47–48.

8. Tom Duncan and Sandra Moriarty, *Driving Brand Value* (New York: McGraw-Hill, 1997), p. 100.

9. Veronis Suhler Stevenson, 16th Annual Communications Industry Forecast, August 5, 2002 (retrieved from **www.veronissuhler.com**).

10. "Fox Breaks Prime-Time Pricing Record," September 12, 2005 (retrieved from **www.adweek.com**).

11. Wayne Friedman, "Discovery Pitches Ad Convergence," *Advertising Age,* March 2000 (retrieved from **www.adage. com**, December 2000).

12. Dorothy Giobbe, "Newspapers Urged to Be More Creative," *Editor & Publisher,* July 2, 1994, p. 38.

13. Christina Merrill, "Media Rising," *Adweek,* November 9, 1998 (retrieved from **http://members.adweek.com/archive**).

14. R. Craig Endicott and Kenneth Wylie, "Special Report: Agency Report," *Advertising Age,* May 2, 2005, p. S–1 and p. S–12.

15. Winston Fletcher, "Independents May Have Had Their Day: Media Buying Is Returning to the Full-Service Fold, But This Time Only at Arm's Length," *Financial Times,* July 27, 1999, p. 15.

16. Christina Merrill, "Media Agencies: What's in a Name? Lots!" *Adweek,* August 24, 1998 (retrieved from **http://members. adweek.com/archive**).

17. Adapted from Donald W. Jugenheimer, Arnold M. Barban, and Peter B. Turk, *Advertising Media: Strategy and Tactics* (Dubuque, IA: Brown & Benchmark, 1992), p. 131.

18. Ibid., pp. 131–33.

19. Jim Surmanek, *Introduction to Advertising Media: Research, Planning, and Buying* (Chicago: NTC Business Books, 1993), p. 54.

20. Adapted from Surmanek, *Introduction to Advertising Media,* p. 106.

21. Jugenheimer, Barban, and Turk, *Advertising Media: Strategy and Tactics,* p. 135.

22. Joe Mandese, "Revisiting Ad Reach, Frequency," *Advertising Age,* November 27, 1995, p. 46.

23. Schultz, Tannenbaum, and Lauterborn, *Integrated Marketing Communications: Putting It Together & Making It Work,* pp. 116–22, 132–33; Julie Liesse, "Buying by the Numbers? Hardly," *Advertising Age,* July 25, 1994, p. S16.

24. Rein Rijkens, *European Advertising Strategies* (London: Cassell, 1992), pp. 86–87.

25. Special Report: Best Media Plan Competition, "Guerrilla Tactics Get Panasonic Noticed," *Strategy* (Canada), March 27, 2000, p. BMP10.

26. Todd Pruzan, "Global Media: Distribution Slows, but Rates Climb," *Advertising Age International,* January 16, 1995, p. I19.

27. Neil Kelliher, "Magazine Media Planning for 'Effectiveness': Getting the People Back into the Process," *Journal of Consumer Marketing,* Summer 1990, pp. 47–55.

28. Kenneth Longman, *Advertising* (New York: Harcourt Brace Jovanovich, 1971), pp. 211–12.

29. "The Power of Partnership," *NBC Marketing Supplement, Advertising Age,* November 16, 1992, p. 13.

30. Kevin Goldman, "Digital Warms Couch Potatoes with Only-on-Sunday TV Ads," *The Wall Street Journal,* November 22, 1994, p. B8.

31. Telmar Web site, July 2004 (**www.telmar.com**).

32. Interactive Market Systems Web site, December 2000 (**www.imsusa.com/products-applications.html**).

Chapter Sixteen

1. "Dell Kicks Off Back-to-School Season with a '$50,000-a-Day Giveaway,'" July 2, 2002 (retrieved from **www.dell.com**).

2. Ibid.

3. "Dell's Back-to-School Sweepstakes Takes to the Skies," August 1, 2002 (retrieved from **www.dell.com**).

4. "Dell's 'BMW-a-Day Giveaway' Puts Customers in Driver's Seat," August 29, 2002 (retrieved from **www.dell.com**).

5. "Dell Says Making Customers No. 1 Accounts for Return to Global Market-Share Leadership," October 17, 2002 (retrieved from **www.dell.com**).

6. "Dell at a Glance" (retrieved from **www.dell.com**).

7. Todd Wasserman, "Grand Marketer; The 'Dude' You May Not Know; One of the Few Firms to Survive the Tech Crash; Dell Won Over Consumer Market with a Savvy Business Model and Its Ads' Unlikely Teen Hero," October 14, 2002 (retrieved from **www.lexis-nexus.com**).

8. The 2002 *Fortune* 500 (retrieved from **www.fortune.com**).

9. Wasserman, "Grand Marketer."

10. Shelly Solheim, "Dell Reclaims PC Crown," April 16, 2004 (retrieved from **www.eweek.com**, August 7, 2004).

11. "Sony Tops the List in Annual 'Best Brands' Survey for Fifth Consecutive Year," The Harris Poll 50, July 7, 2004 (retrieved from **www.harrisinteractive.com/harris_poll/index. asp?PID=479**, August 12, 2004).

12. "1999 Economic Impact: U.S. Direct Marketing Today," The WEFA Group and The Direct Marketing Association, 2000 (retrieved from **www.the-dma.org**, December 2000).

13. Joan Throckmorton, "We Are Interactive—Repeat—We Are Interactive," *Direct,* November 1997.

14. Bob Stone, *Successful Direct Marketing Methods,* 4th ed. (Chicago: NTC Business Books, 1988), p. 3.

15. "Civilian Labor Force and Participation Rates with Projections: 1980 to 2008," *Statistical Abstract of the United States: 2001,* Table 568 (Washington DC: U.S. Census Bureau, 2001).

16. Direct Marketing Association, "Growth Trends Continue for Direct Marketing," September 29, 2005 (retrieved from **www.the-dma.org**, November 25, 2005).

17. "Economic Impact: U.S. Direct Marketing Today Executive Summary; International Direct Marketing Expenditures in All Markets (Ranked by Level of 2001 Forecast)" (retrieved from **www.the-dma.org**).

18. Peppers and Rogers Group, Marketing 1 to 1 (**www.m1to1. com/success_stories**).

19. Stone, *Successful Direct Marketing Methods,* pp. 29–33.

20. Jackson, "Database Doctor."

21. Thomas E. Caruso, "Kotler: Future Marketers Will Focus on Customer Data Base to Compete Globally," *Marketing News,* June 8, 1992, pp. 21–22.

22. Seth Godin, "GUEST COLUMNIST: Permission Key to Successful Marketing," *Advertising Age,* November 1997 (**http://adage.com**).

23. Poulos, "Customer Loyalty and the Marketing Database," pp. 32–35.

24. Mollie Neal, "Marketers Looking Ahead in Chicago," *Direct Marketing,* March 1993, pp. 9–11.

25. Robert A. Peterson and Thomas R. Wotruba, "What Is Direct Selling?—Definition, Perspectives, and Research Agenda," *Journal of Personal Selling and Sales Management,* 16, no. 4 (Fall 1996), pp. 1–16.

26. "Economic Impact: U.S. Direct & Interactive Marketing Today Executive Summary 2002."

27. "Brief History of Toll-Free Numbers" (retrieved from **www.tollfreenumbers.com**, August 7, 2004).

28. "Economic Impact: U.S. Direct & Interactive Marketing Today Executive Summary 2002."

29. "The Catalog Age 100: Ranking 1–50," *Catalog Age*, August 1, 2003 (retrieved from **www.catalogagemag.com**).

30. Laura Bird, "Beyond Mail Order: Catalogs Now Sell Image, Advice," *The Wall Street Journal*, July 29, 1997, pp. B1, 2.

31. Personal Interview with Tom Campanaro, President, Total Gym Inc., December 2000.

32. Adapted from Barton A. Weitz, Stephen B. Castleberry, and John F. Tanner Jr., *Selling: Building Partnerships* (Burr Ridge, IL: Richard D. Irwin, Inc., 1992), p. 5.

33. Edwin Klewer, Robert Shaffer, and Bonnie Binnig, "Sales Is an Investment, Attrition an Expense," *Journal of Health Care Marketing*, September 1995, p. 12.

34. "Excerpt: Under the Radar," *Brandweek*, December 8, 1997 (**http://members.adweek.com/archive/adweek/current/brandweek**).

35. Peter Breen, "Seeds of Change," *Promo Sourcebook Supplement*, October 2000, p. 18.

36. Larry Light, "Trustmarketing: The Brand Relationship Marketing Mandate for the 90s," address to American Association of Advertising Agencies annual meeting, Laguna Niguel, CA, April 23, 1993.

37. Magid M. Abraham and Leonard M. Lodish, "Getting the Most Out of Advertising and Promotion," *Harvard Business Review*, May/June 1990, p. 51.

38. Light, "Trustmarketing."

39. Larry Light, "At the Center of It All Is the Brand," *Advertising Age*, March 29, 1993, p. 22.

40. *The Point of Purchase Advertising Industry Fact Book* (Washington, DC: POPAI, 1997), p. 51.

41. Kelly Shermach, "Study: Most Shoppers Notice P-O-P Material," *Marketing News*, January 1995, p. 27.

42. *The Point of Purchase Advertising Industry Fact Book*, p. 39.

43. Kelly Shermach, "Great Strides Made in P-O-P Technology," *Marketing News*, January 2, 1995, pp. 8–9.

44. Angela Lawson, "The End of the Line," June 18, 2004 (retrieved from **www.kioskmarketplace.com**, August 8, 2004).

45. Kathleen M. Joyce, "Fast Clip," *Promo Magazine*, April 1, 2003; "CPG Coupon Volume on the Rise: NCH Study," *Promo Magazine*, April 11, 2003 (retrieved from **http://promomagazine.com**).

46. The 16th Annual Survey of Promotional Practices, Donnelley Marketing Inc., 1994.

47. "About Us," *Catalina Marketing* (retrieved from **www.catalinamarketing.com/our_advantage/index.html**, August 8, 2004).

48. Bruce Crumley, "Multipoints Adds Up for Quick Burger," *Advertising Age*, November 29, 1993, p. 14.

49. Stephanie Moore, "Rebate Madness: How to Defend Yourself against Ruthless Rebate Scams" (retrieved from **www.consumeraffairs.com**, August 8, 2004).

50. *Washington Post*, Tuesday, February 1, 2005; Page C10, washingtonpost.com, **www.washingtonpost.com/wp-dyn/articles/A52798-2005Jan31.html**.

51. Lorraine Calvacca, "Polybagging Products to Pick Up Customers," *Folio: The Magazine for Magazine Management*, January 1993, p. 26.

Chapter Seventeen

1. **www.benjerry.com** (retrieved August 4, 2004).

2. Ibid.

3. Ben & Jerry's Homemade, Inc., press release, "Fight Global Warming with Ice Cream, Music and Activism: Dave Matthews Band, Ben & Jerry's and Environmental Leaders Launch One Sweet Whirled Campaign," April 2, 2002 (retrieved from **www.benjerry.com**, August 5, 2004).

4. Ben & Jerry's Homemade, Inc., press release, "Turn It Up to Cool It Down! This Earth Day, Ben & Jerry's Introduces Thermoacoustic Refrigeration—An Environmentally Friendly Way to Chill Out," April 15, 2004 (retrieved from **www.benjerry.com**, August 5, 2004).

5. Ben & Jerry's Homemade, Inc., press release, "Happiness Is . . . Free Ice Cream! Ben & Jerry's Celebrates 25th Annual Free Cone Day," April 22, 2003 (retrieved from **www.benjerry.com**, August 5, 2004).

6. Ben & Jerry's Homemade, Inc., press release, "Ben & Jerry's and Unilever to Join Forces," April 12, 2000 (retrieved from **www.benjerry.com**, August 5, 2004).

7. Jim Osborne, "Getting Full Value from Public Relations," *Public Relations Journal*, October/November 1994, p. 64.

8. CSPI Newsroom, "Ben & Jerry's Fudging the Truth, Says CSPI: Nothing 'All-Natural' about Ingredients," July 30, 2002 (retrieved from **www.cspinet.org/new/200207301.html**, August 8, 2004).

9. Ben & Jerry's Homemade, Inc., press release, "Ben & Jerry's Response to CSPI Concerns," July 31, 2002 (retrieved from **www.benjerry.com**, August 8, 2004).

10. Ben & Jerry's Homemade, Inc., press release, "Ben & Jerry's Voluntarily Initiates the Recall of Pints of Karamel Sutra Ice Cream with Code 02/14/04," March 28, 2003 (retrieved from **www.benjerry.com**, August 8, 2004).

11. Sandra Moriarty, "PR and IMC: The Benefits of Integration," *Public Relations Quarterly*, Fall 1994, pp. 38–44.

12. Publisher's Statement, *Inside PR*, March 1993, p. 3.

13. Thomas L. Harris, "PR Gets Personal," *Direct Marketing*, April 1994, pp. 29–32.

14. Al Ries and Laura Ries, *The 22 Immutable Laws of Branding* (New York: HarperCollins, 1998), pp. 25–31.

15. Bill Patterson, "Crisis Impact on Reputation Management," *Public Relations Journal*, November 1993, p. 48.

16. Dennis L. Wilcox, *Public Relations Strategies and Tactics* (New York: HarperCollins, 1994), p. 381.

17. "What's Your Best Marketing Tool?" *Public Relations Journal*, February 1994, p. 12.

18. Adapted from Stephanie Gruner, "Event Marketing: Making the Most of Sponsorship Dollars," *Inc.*, August 1996, p. 88.

19. IEG FAQ:"What Is Sponsorship?" IEG Network 1998 (**www.sponsorship.com**).

20. "Cause Marketing's Power Shown in MediaLab Study," Mediaedge:cia; MediaLab, 2004 (**www.causemarketingforum.com**). Retrieved November 25, 2005.

21. "Telco Ericsson Calls on James Bond, Volleyball," *Advertising Age,* June 1997 (**www.adage.com**).

22. Thomas R. Duncan and Sandra E. Moriarty, *Driving Brand Value: Using Integrated Marketing to Manage Stakeholder Relationships* (New York: McGraw-Hill, 1997), p. 203.

23. Ibid.; Terry G. Vavra, *Aftermarketing: How to Keep Customers for Life Through Relationship Marketing* (Burr Ridge, IL: Irwin Professional Publishing, 1992), p. 190.

24. Vavra, *Aftermarketing,* p. 192.

25. Ibid.

26. "Sponsorship Spending to See Biggest Rise in Five Years," IEG Sponsorship Report, December 27, 2004 (**www. sponsorship.com**).

27. "Where the Dollars Go," IEG Sponsorship Report 2003 (**www.sponsorship.com/learn/wheredollarsgo.asp**).

28. Junu Bryan Kim, "Most Sponsorships Waste Money: Exec," *Advertising Age,* June 21, 1993, pp. S2, S4.

29. Lesa Ukman, "Assertions," IEG Sponsorship Report, February 23, 1998 (**www.sponsorship.com**).

30. Wilcox, *Public Relations Strategies and Tactics,* p. 384.

31. John Karolefski, "The Sport of Naming," Brand Channel.com, May 13, 2002 (**www.brandchannel.com**).

32. Paul Stanley, "Sponsownership: Sponsorships Will Become Standard for Events," *Potentials in Marketing,* June 1990, p. 64.

33. Lesa Ukman, "Assertions," IEG Sponsorship Report, January 26, 1998 (**www.sponsorship.com**).

34. Vavra, *Aftermarketing,* p. 191.

35. "Corporate Advertising/Phase II, An Expanded Study of Corporate Advertising Effectiveness," conducted for *Time* magazine by Yankelovich, Skelly & White, undated.

Credits and Acknowledgments

Chapter One

Photos/Ads

p. 3, Used with permission of Callard & Bowser-Souchard, Inc.; Agency: Leo Burnett/Chicago   **p. 5,** Courtesy International Advertising Festival, Ltd.   **p. 9,** Colonial Williamsburg Foundation   **p. 12 (top),** Courtesy NW Ayer Agency   **p. 12 (bottom),** Stock Montage, Inc.   **p. 13,** Stock Montage, Inc.   **p. 15,** These ads have been copyrighted and are reproduced with the permission of Volkswagen of America   **p. 16,** Courtesy International Advertising Festival, Ltd.   **p. 17,** Courtesy Team One Advertising/El Segundo, California; Photographer: Scott Downing   **p. 18 (top),** Courtesy The Coca-Cola Company   **p. 28 (bottom),** Courtesy TiVo, Inc.   **p. 19,** ©2005 Dell Computer Corp. All Rights Reserved.

Chapter Two

Photos/Ads

p. 25, Photo by Tim Boyle/Getty Images   **p. 26,** Concept: O. Toscani. Courtesy of United Colors of Benetton   **p. 30,** Courtesy DocuSystems   **p. 31,** Stock Montage   **p. 32,** Courtesy International Advertising Festival, Ltd.   **p. 33,** Courtesy Devito Verdi   **p. 37,** Courtesy Saturn Corporation   **p. 38,** Agency: OgilvyOne Worldwide/Bangkok; Client: **www.abccookingstudio.com**   **p. 39 (top),** Courtesy DDB Needham/NY   **p. 39 (bottom),** Courtesy CLM/BBDP Paris   **p. 44,** **www.gala-marketlaw.com**   **p. 46 (top),** Courtesy Meyer & Wallis   **p. 46 (bottom),** ©The Procter & Gamble Company. Used by permission   **p. 48,** Courtesy Pfizer Animal Health   **p. 49,** Courtesy The Coca-Cola Company   **p. 53,** Courtesy Heat-N-Glo.

Exhibits/Checklists/Commercial Breaks/Ethical Issues

Exhibit 2–1: Per capita ad spending around the world, 2005, **Datamonitor.com.**

Ethical Issues: Truth in Advertising: Fluffing and Puffing. "Advertising Puffery: Current Status," Reed Smith Hall Dickler, 2004 (retrieved from **www.adlaw.com**); Lane Jennings, "Hype, Spin, Puffery and Lies: Should We Be Scared? Media Mythmakers Keep the Public Ill Informed," *The Futurist,* January/February 2004 (retrieved from InfoTrac); Perry Haan and Cal Berkey, "A Study of the Believability of the Forms of Puffery," *Journal of Marketing Communications,* December 2002, p. 248; Thomas Morrison, "How a Seemingly Innocuous Slogan Led to the Pizza Wars," Spring 2002 (retrieved from **www.pbwt.com/Resources/index-newsletter.html**); and Ivan Preston, "A Problem Ignored: Dilution and Negation of Consumer Information by Antifactual Content," *Journal of Consumer Affairs,* December 22, 2002 (retrieved from InfoTrac).

Exhibit 2–3: Reprinted with permission of the Council of Better Business Bureaus, Inc., copyright 2003. Council of Better Business Bureaus, Inc., 4200 Wilson Blvd., Arlington, VA 22203. World Wide Web: **www.bbb.org.**

Exhibit 2–4: American Association of Advertising Agencies Guidelines. Reprinted by permission of the American Association of Advertising Agencies, **www.aaaa.org/.**

Exhibit 2–5: Advertising Principles of American Business of the American Advertising Federation (AAF). Reprinted by permission.

Chapter Three

Photos/Ads

p. 59, Courtesy Honda North America; Agency: Muse Cordero Chen/San Francisco   **p. 61 (top),** Courtesy Florin Glass & Screens   **p. 62,** Courtesy Michaels Stores, Inc.   **p. 63,** ©Sears Brands, LLC   **p. 66,** Courtesy of Dunkin' Donuts, Inc. and Hill, Holliday, Connors, Cosmopulos, Inc.   **p. 68,** Courtesy Leo Burnett/Copenhagen   **p. 69,** Courtesy Hewlett-Packard/Canada; Agency: Publicis Hal Riney   **p. 71,** Courtesy Mad Dogs & Englishmen; Writer: Deacon Webster; Art Director: Nick Cohen   **p. 73,** Courtesy DHL   **p. 74,** Courtesy International Festival, Ltd.   **p. 76,** Courtesy Honda North America; Agency: Muse Cordero Chen; Photo by John Thoeming   **p. 78,** Courtesy Callison Architecture, Inc.   **p. 80,** Concept: O. Toscani; Courtesy of United Colors of Benetton   **p. 84,** Courtesy of Fallon McElligott   **p. 85,** Courtesy of Kinetic Interactive (Singapore) PTE Ltd.. (**www.kinetic.com.**)

Exhibits/Checklists/Commercial Breaks/Ethical Issues

Exhibit 3–1: Top ten advertisers ranked by total U.S. advertising, 2005. *Advertising Age* magazine, June 27, 2005, S-1 and S-2,

Exhibit 3–2: Co-op dollars as a percent of ad budget.

Exhibit 3–3: Reprinted with permission from June 27, 2005, issue of *Advertising Age.* Copyright Crain Communications Inc., 2005.

Ethical Issues: Accounting for Account Reviews. "The Bond between an Advertiser and His Client Is Changing," *Escalate,* April 20, 2004 (retrieved from **www.escalate.ca**); Douglas LaBahn, "Advertiser Perceptions of Fair Compensation, Confidentiality and Rapport: The Influence of Advertising Agency Cooperativeness and Diligence" (retrieved from **www.highbeam.com/library/index. asp?refid=ae_org_1**); Mark Gleason, "MIA on Madison Ave.: Agency, Client Loyalty," *Advertising Age,* January 27, 1997 (retrieved from: **www.adage.com**); Alice Z. Cuneo, "Agencies Feel Business Pinch, Eye More Cuts," *Advertising Age,* January 29, 2001 (retrieved from: **www.adage.com**); Michael Marsak, "Conducting an Effective Advertising Agency Review," Effective Marketing Strategies, Inc. (retrieved from **www.effectivemarketing.com**).

Exhibit 3–8: Top media companies in 2004. Retrieved from **www.adage.com,** August 22, 2005.

Chapter Four

Photos/Ads

p. 91, Chris Hunt/The Atlanta Journal-Constitution   **p. 92,** Courtesy Honda North America   **p. 94,** Courtesy Audi of America, Inc.; Agency: McKinney & Silver/Raleigh   **p. 96,** Courtesy David Yang   **p. 98,** Courtesy Crate & Barrel   **p. 99 (top),** Courtesy Hardee's Food Systems, Inc.   **p. 99 (bottom),** Courtesy Columbia Sportswear Company   **p. 102 (top),** Courtesy International Advertising Festival, Ltd.   **p. 102 (bottom),** Courtesy Adidas America, Inc.   **p. 104,** Courtesy Sybase, Inc.   **p. 107,** Courtesy TBWA Hunt Lascaris/Capetown, South Africa   **p. 110,** Made by Telstar Interactive Corporation/Cincinnati, OH   **p. 112,** Courtesy BBDO/Toronto   **p. 113 (top),** Courtesy Braun, Inc.   **p. 113 (bottom),** ©M. Hruby   **p. 114,** Courtesy Cusido Comella/Barcelona, Spain; Creative Director: Josep Cusidó and Jordi Comella; Copywriter: Ricardo Quemades   **p. 117,** ©1995–2001. FedEx All Rights Reserved   **p. 118,** Courtesy Catalina Marketing.

Exhibits/Checklists/Commercial Breaks/Ethical Issues

Exhibit 4–1: Methods for segmenting consumer markets. Data used with permission from Mediamark Research, Inc., 2000.

Exhibit 4–2: Source: MediaMark Research, Inc., 2000 data.

Ethical Issues: Brand Niching. "White House to End Drugs and Terror Ads," AdAge.com, April 1, 2003 (www.adage.com); "Bush Administration's Controversial New Anti-Drug Campaign to Be Target of Upcoming Roll Call Ad by Drug Policy Alliance," February 25, 2002 (www.drugpolicy.org/news/pressroom/pressrelease/pr_february25_02b.cfm); Human Rights Campaign Foundation, "Mainstream Marketing—John Hancock Financial Services," 2004 (www.hrc.org); Kimberly Alcantara, "Let the Games Begin . . . " Pattishall, McCauliffe newsletter, Winter 2002 (www.pattishall.com/pdfs/winter_2002.pdf); Sonya Brathwaite, "Denny's: A Diversity Success Story," International Franchise Association, August 2002 (www.franchise.org/news/fw/aug2002b.asp).

Exhibit 4–3: Reprinted with permission from the July 11, 2005, issue of *Advertising Age*. Copyright Crain Communications, Inc., 2005.

Exhibit 4–5: Source: SRI Consulting Business Intelligence, www.sric-bi.com/VALS/. All rights reserved.

Exhibit 4–7: Source: Claritas, Inc.

Exhibit 4–8: Adapted from Ben M. Ennis, *Marketing Principles* (Santa Monica, CA: Good Year Publishing, 1980), 351.

Exhibit 4–10: Reprinted with permission from the March 13, 1997, issue of *Advertising Age*. Copyright, Crain Communications, Inc., 1997.

Exhibit 4–11: *BusinessWeek*, August 2, 2004, page 64.

Commercial Breaks 4–B, 4–C, and 4–D: Sources: Diane Brady et al., "Cult Brands," *BusinessWeek* 3958 (August 9, 2004): 58; Starbucks "Annual Report 2004," part I; "Corporate Social Responsibility Annual Report 2003"; and "Timeline and History," all accessed at www.starbucks.com/aboutus/.

Chapter Five

Photos/Ads

p. 125, ©2004 Great Brands of Europe, Inc. **p. 126,** Tracy Swedlow's InteractiveTV Today [itvt] http://www.itvt.com **p. 127,** By Fallon-McElligott/Rolling Stone **p. 130,** Courtesy Tibor Nemeth **p. 131,** Courtesy International Advertising Festival Ltd. **p. 134,** Courtesy Stride Rite Corporation **p. 135,** Courtesy Southwest Airlines; Agency: GSD&M/Austin **p. 136,** PORSCHE, BOXSTER, the Porsche Crest are registered trademarks and the distinctive shapes of Porsche automobiles are trademarks of Dr. Ing. h.c.F Porsche AG. Used with permission of Porsche Cars North America, Inc. Copyrighted by Porsche Cars North America, Inc. **p. 138 (top),** Courtesy of BDDP-GGT Advertising/London **p. 138 (bottom),** Courtesy The Coca-Cola Company **p. 139,** Courtesy A.T. Cross Company **p. 142,** Ogilvy & Mather/Singapore **p. 143,** Army Reserves Materials courtesy of the U.S. Government, as represented by the Secretary of the Army **p. 144,** Courtesy Jenn-Air; Agency: Leo Burnett **p. 145,** Courtesy Leonard/Monahan Providence.

Exhibits/Checklists/Commercial Breaks/Ethical Issues

Exhibit 5–5: Rossiter, John R., and Larry Percy, *Advertising Communications and Promotion Management*, 2nd ed. (McGraw-Hill, 1977). Reprinted with permission from the McGraw-Hill Companies.

Exhibit 5–7: Rossiter and Percy.

Ethical Issues: Is It Marketing or Is It Exploitation? John Berthelsen, "China's Consumer Era Takes Hold," Asia Times online, August 6, 2003 (retrieved from www.atimes.com/atimes/china/EH06Ad01.html); G. Edmonson, J. Ewing, and C. Passariello, "Has Benetton Stopped Unraveling?" BusinessWeek online, June 23, 2003

(retrieved from www.businessweek.com/magazine/content/03_25/b2828134_mz034.htm); Patrick Goodenough, "Children Harmed by Too Much TV, Exploitative Advertising, Report Says," CNSNews.com, May 19, 2004 (retrieved from www.cnsnews.com); Catherine Seipp, "Marketing the Mouse," National Review online, July 7, 2004 (retrieved from www.nationalreview.com).

Exhibit 5–8: Source: Claritas, Inc.

Exhibit 5–9: Used by permission of Foote, Cone & Belding.

Exhibit 5–10: Kim, Chung K., and Kenneth R. Lord (1991), "A New FCB Grid and Its Strategic Implications for Advertising," in *Proceedings of the Annual Conference of the Administrative Sciences Association of Canada, Marketing Division,* Vol. 12, Part 6, T. Schellinck, ed., Niagara Falls, Ontario: Administrative Sciences Association of Canada, 51–60. Used by permission.

Chapter Six

Photos/Ads

p. 151, Courtesy Healthtex; Agency: The Martin Agency **p. 152,** Courtesy National Fluid Milk Processor Promotion Board; Agency: Lowe Worldwide, Inc. **p. 154 (top),** ©2002 Nielsen/NetRatings **p. 154 (bottom),** Courtesy Healthtex; Agency: The Martin Agency **p. 156,** Courtesy Healthtex; Agency: The Martin Agency **p. 158 (top),** Courtesy Interactive Art Services, Inc. **p. 158 (bottom),** Courtesy Bissell **p. 160,** www.edgar-online.com **p. 163,** Courtesy Nordhaus Research, Inc./Southfield, MI **p. 164 (bottom),** Courtesy Envirosell, Inc. **p. 165,** Bob Daemmrich/Stock Boston LLC **p. 173,** Courtesy International Advertising Festival, Ltd..

Exhibits/Checklists/Commercial Breaks/Ethical Issues

Exhibit 6–1: Categories of research. Adapted with permission from Edmund J. Faison, *Advertising: A Behavioral Approach for Managers* (New York: John Wiley, 1980), 664.

Ethical Issues: Research Statistics Can Be Friends or Foes. ABC News [When Good Drugs Go Bad, Rose Pike] (http://more.abcnews.go.com/sections/newsuse/fenfollow/); ABC News [Fen-Phen Articles Questioned, Associated Press] (http://abcnews.go.com/sections/living/DailyNews/fenphenghostwriters990523.html); ABC News [Report Faults Drug Maker, Associated Press] (http://abcnews.go.com/sections/living/DailyNews/fenphen990921.html); ABC News [Fen-Phen Settlement Clouded, Associated Press] (http://more abcnews,go,com/sections/living/DailyNews/fenphen991222.html); CBS News [Medical Journals Tighten Rules, Associated Press] (www.cbsnews.com/stories/2001/09/10/national/main310621.shtml); "KFC Launches Campaign to Change High-Fat Image," Advertising Age online, October 28, 2003 (retrieved from www.adage.com, August 3, 2003); "KFC's Claims That Fried Chicken Is a Way to 'Eat Better,' Don't Fly," FTC for the Consumer online, June 3, 2004 (retrieved from www.ftc.gov/opa/2004/06/kfccorp.htm, August 4, 2004); Rob Walker, "Chicken-Fried Bull," MSN Slate online, November 10, 2003 (retrieved from http://slate.msn.com/id/2090861, August 4, 2004); Letter to the FTC, November 6, 2003, Center for Science in the Public Interest (retrieved from http://cspinet.org/new/pdf/letter_to_ftc.pdf, August 4, 2003); "KFC Responds to Resolution of Advertising Inquiry," KFC online press release, June 3, 2004 (retrieved from www.kfc.com/about/pr/060304.htm, August 4, 2004).

Exhibit 6–6: The reliability/validity diagram. Adapted from Pamela Alreck and Robert Settle, *The Survey Research Handbook* (Burr Ridge, IL: McGraw-Hill/Irwin, 1995), 32.

Checklist: Developing an Effective Questionnaire. Adapted from Don E. Schultz and Dennis G. Martin, *Strategic Advertising Campaigns* (Chicago: Crain Books, 1979).

Chapter Seven

Photos/Ads

p. 177, Courtesy Pepsi Cola Company   **p. 178,** Courtesy Pepsi Cola Company   **p. 180,** ©British Airways plc 2005   **p. 182 (top),** Courtesy Saturn Corporation   **p. 182 (bottom),** ©The Procter & Gamble Company. Used by permission   **p. 183,** Courtesy BMW of North America   **p. 186,** ©Microsoft Corporation   **p. 187,** Courtesy Marriott International, Inc.   **p. 188,** Courtesy Promotion Marketing Association, Inc.   **p. 190,** Concept: O. Toscani. Courtesy of United Colors of Benetton   **p. 193,** Courtesy International Advertising Festival, Ltd.   **p. 194,** Courtesy of Oneida, Ltd.   **p. 195,** Courtesy Pepsi Cola Company   **p. 196,** Courtesy Seattle Chocolate Company **p. 197,** School: The Creative Circus; Copywriter: Dave Laskarzewski.

Exhibits/Checklists/Commercial Breaks/Ethical Issues

Commercial Break 7–A: The Strategies of Marketing Warfare. Adapted from Al Ries and Jack Trout, *Marketing Warfare* (New York: McGraw-Hill, 1986).

Ethical Issues: A War of Comparisons. Francesca Barigozzi, Paolo G. Garella, and Martin Peitz, "With a Little Help from My Enemy: Comparative Advertising," June 2002 (**www.dse.unibo.it/wp/441.pdf**); "Duracell Bunny Races again after Appeal Victory," B&T, July 30, 2002 (**www.bandt.com.au/news/a1/0c00f7a1.asp**); "10 Advertising Legal Issues for 2004," *Advertising Age,* December 22, 2003 (**www.adage.com**); Rich Thomaselli, "Industry Wrestles with Comparative Ads," *Advertising Age,* October 27, 2003 (**www.adage.com**); Daniel Bereskin and Jennifer McKenzie, "Comparative Advertising: Canada and the United States" (**www.bereskinparr.com/publications/pdf/Mrktg%20Compare%20Bereskin.pdf**); Advertising Education Forum, "United Kingdom: Self-Regulatory Organisations" (**www.aeforum.org/european/United_Kingdom.html**); The Business Research Lab, "Danger—Comparative Advertising" (**www.busreslab.com/tips/tip8.htm**); Reed Smith Hall Dicker, "Comparative Advertising" (**www.adlaw.com/rc/handbk/rf_comparative.html**).

Exhibit 7–3: Adapted from Philip Kotler and Gary Armstrong, *Principles of Marketing* (Englewood Cliffs, NJ: Prentice-Hall, 1994), p. 561.

Exhibit 7–7: Used with permission from *Marketing Tools* magazine. Copyright 1994.

Commercial Break 7–B: The Economic Effect of Advertising on Sales. Adapted from William J. Baumol and Alan S. Blinder, *Economics: Principles and Policy,* 3rd ed. (New York: Harcourt Brace Jovanovich, 1985), p. 386.

Exhibit 7–8: Reprinted with permission from the June 27, 2005, issue of *Advertising Age.* Copyright Crain Communications, Inc., 2005.

Chapter Eight

Photos/Ads

p. 205, Ad Agency: Franklin Stoorza; Creative Directors: John Vitro, John Robertson; Art Director: John Vitro; Copywriter: John Robertson; Photographers: Art Wolfe, Marshall Harrington   **p. 207,** Courtesy Lowe Worldwide   **p. 208,** Agency: Frank Stoorza; Creative Directors: John Vitro, John Robertson; Art Director: John Vitro; Copywriter: John Robertson; Photographer: Art Wolfe   **p. 209,** Courtesy of California Department of Health Services   **p. 212,** Courtesy The Coca-Cola Company; Agency: Fitzgerald + Co.; Photographer: Doug Rosa   **p. 213,** Courtesy Capital One Financial Corporation   **p. 215,** Courtesy International Advertising Festival Ltd. **p. 216 (top),** Courtesy Allianz AG   **p. 216 (bottom),** Courtesy Pepsi-Cola Company   **p. 218,** Photo by: Betsie Van Der Meer/Taxi/Getty Images   **p. 219,** Courtesy International Advertising Festival Ltd.   **p. 220,** Agency: Frank Stoorza; Creative Directors: John Vitro,

John Robertson; Art Director: John Vitro; Copywriter: John Robertson; Photographers: Art Wolfe, Marshall Harrington   **p. 223,** Courtesy K2 Skis   **p. 227,** Courtesy A.G. Edwards & Sons, Inc.   **p. 228,** Courtesy Sara Lee Bakery Group.

Exhibits/Checklists/Commercial Breaks/Ethical Issues

Ethical Issues: Does Sex Appeal? Erin Cooksley, "Sex Sells, Ethics Absent from Advertising Industry," *The Daily Skiff,* February 11, 2004 (retrieved from **www.skiff.tcu.edu/2004/spring/issues/02/11/sex.html**); Florence Kennel, "Burgundy Ads Banned for Sexual Innuendo," January 23, 2004 (retrieved from **www.decanter.com**); Nikki Katz, "Sex Sells—Using Sex in Advertising," (retrieved from **http://womensissues.about.com/cs/bodyimage/a/aasexsells.htm**); Robynn Tysver, "Family Group Protests 'Sexualized' Ads at Stores in Lincoln Mall," *Omaha World-Herald,* February 12, 2003; Deborah Alexander, "Family Group Ends Protest after Shop Changes Displays," *Omaha World-Herald,* February 21, 2003 (both retrieved from **www.nexis.com**); Rance Crain, "Relevance Is Operative Word in 'Catfight' or Chip-Dip Ads," *Advertising Age,* January 27, 2003; Basem Boshra, "Un, Can You Say Appallingly Sexist?" *Montreal Gazette,* February 1, 2003 (retrieved from **www.nexis.com**); Julie Dunn, "The Light Stuff. Coors Loves the Young Male Demographic—and Twins!" *Denver Westword,* January 23, 2003 (retrieved from **www.nexis.com**); Tom Daykin, "Miller Gets Down and Dirty with Lite Ad; Reaction Mixed, but Commercial Is Being Noticed," *Milwaukee Journal Sentinel,* January 26, 2003 (retrieved from **www.nexis.com**).

Chapter Nine

Photos/Ads

p. 233, Courtesy CIT Group, Inc.   **p. 234,** Courtesy CIT Group, Inc.   **p. 235,** Courtesy Ogilvy & Mather/Capetown   **p. 238,** Courtesy Ogilvy & Mather Advertising/Bangalore, India   **p. 239,** Courtesy Tom Michael; Market Design/Encinatas, CA   **p. 240,** Courtesy Tom Michael; Market Design/Encinatas, CA   **p. 241,** Courtesy Tom Michael; Market Design/Encinatas, CA   **p. 243,** Courtesy International Advertising Festival Ltd.   **p. 246 (top),** Courtesy The Allstate Insurance Company   **p. 246 (bottom),** Courtesy of Campbell Soup Company   **p. 247 (top),** Courtesy The Florida Department of Citrus **p. 247 (bottom),** Courtesy International Advertising Festival Ltd.   **p. 252,** Courtesy McCann-Erickson Worldwide   **p. 254,** Courtesy Ford Motor Company   **p. 255,** Courtesy Jack In The Box, Inc.   **p. 257,** Courtesy Mastercard   **p. 258,** Courtesy Saatchi & Saatchi/Los Angeles **p. 259,** Courtesy GEICO   **p. 260,** Courtesy Korean Air. Agency: Ogilvy & Mather/Hong Kong.

Exhibits/Checklists/Commercial Breaks/Ethical Issues

Ethical Issues: Imitation, Plagiarism, or Flattery? Richard A. Posner, "On Plagiarism," *The Atlantic Online,* April 2002 (retrieved from **www.theatlantic.com/doc/prem/200204/posner**); "Plagiarism," *Copyright—CopySense,* August 1, 2003 (retrieved from **http://stellarone.com/copyrightcopysense/plagiarism.htm**); "Grey Rejects Plagiarism Claims," June 19, 2003 (retrieved from **www.bandt.com.au/default.asp**); "Plagiarism," *Screen & Media Studies,* May 20, 2004 (retrieved from **www.waikato.ac.nz/film/handbook/plagiarism.html**); David Greer, "Imitation: The Smartest Form of Flattery" (retrieved from **http://www.home-based-business-opportunities.com/library/online106-imitation.shtml**); "What Is Plagiarism?" December 5, 2003 (retrieved from **www.abc.net.au/**); Hans Kullin, "More Plagiarism in Scandinavian Media," *Media Culpa,* August 2, 2004 (retrieved from **www.kullin.net**); David Benady, "Crunch Time for Copycats," *Marketing Week,* February 13, 2002, p. 24.

Checklist: Writing Effective Copy. Sources: David L. Malickson and John W. Nason, *Advertising: How to Write the Kind that Works* (Charles Scribner's Sons, 1982), p. 74; Jay Conrad Levinson, *Guerilla Advertising* (New York: Houghton Mifflin, 1994), pp. 174–75; Neil

Raphel and Murray Raphel, "Rules to Advertise By," *Progressive Grocer,* December 1993, pp. 13–14; William H. Motes et al., "Language, Sentence, and Structural Variations in Print Advertising," *Journal of Advertising Research,* September/October 1992, pp. 63–77; and "Copy Chaser Criteria," *Business Marketing,* January 1991, p. 33.

Checklist: Creating Effective Radio Commercials. Source: Peter Hochstein, "Ten Rules for Making Better Radio Commercials," *Viewpoint III,* 1981.

Checklist: Creating Effective TV Commercials. Sources: Bruce Bendinger, *The Copy Workshop* (Chicago: The Copy Workshop, 1993), pp. 286–92; and David Ogilvy, *Oglivy on Advertising* (New York: Random House, 1985).

Chapter Ten

Photos/Ads

p. 267, Courtesy Saatchi & Saatchi/Los Angeles   **p. 268,** Courtesy Saatchi & Saatchi/Los Angeles   **p. 273,** ©M. Hruby   **p. 273,** ©M. Hruby   **p. 276,** Courtesy Elena Ramirez   **p. 278,** ©2005 Oldemark, LLC. Reprinted with permission   **p. 282,** Digital Vision/Getty Images   **p. 287,** Courtesy Saatchi & Saatchi/Los Angeles   **p. 288,** Courtesy Saatchi & Saatchi/Los Angeles   **p. 290,** Courtesy Saatchi & Saatchi/Los Angeles.

Exhibits/Checklists/Commercial Breaks/Ethical Issues

Exhibit 10–5: Adapted from William M. Wellbacher, *Advertising* (Free Press, 1962), p. 273. Copyright Macmillan Publishing Co., Inc.

Chapter Eleven

Photos/Ads

p. 295, Courtesy National Fluid Milk Processor Promotion Board; Agency: Lowe Worldwide, Inc.   **p. 300,** Courtesy Colgate Palmolive Company   **p. 301,** Courtesy Chicago Magazine   **p. 303,** Reprinted with permission from the February 10, 2003 issue of *Advertising Age.* Copyright Crain Communications, Inc. 2003   **p. 306,** Agency: Mad Dog & Englishman; Writer: Mikal Reich; Art Directors: Carol Holsinger, Gina Fortunato, David Cook; Creative Directors: Nick Cohen & David Cook   **p. 309,** Courtesy BBDO/Atlanta; Creative Director: Leo Dayvault   **p. 312,** Courtesy Dallas Morning News   **p. 314,** Reprinted with permission of the Newspaper Association of America.

Exhibits/Checklists/Commercial Breaks/Ethical Issues

Exhibit 11–1: Reprinted with permission from *Advertising Age.* Copyright Crain Communications, Inc., 2005.

Exhibit 11–2: Adapted with permission from Magazine Publishers Association, *Magazine Newsletter of Research* 8, no. 1.

Exhibit 11–3: Map courtesy of the Reader's Digest Association.

Exhibit 11–4: Reprinted with permission from *Advertising Age.* Copyright Crain Communications, Inc., 2005.

Exhibit 11–5: Reprinted with permission from *Advertising Age.* Copyright Crain Communications, Inc., 2005.

Ethical Issues: What's at Stake with Sweepstakes? **www.crimesof-persuasion.com/Crimes/Telemarketing/Outbound/Major/Sweepstakes/sweepstakes.htm**; "Sweepstakes Advertising: A Consumer's Guide," *Consumers: A Helpful Guide* (**www.dmaconsumers.org/sweepstakeshelp.html**); "Be Smart Buy Smart," State of California Department of Consumer Affairs (**www.dca.ca.gov/r_r/sweep.pdf**); "Sweepstakes Assistance: A Caregiver's Guide," *Consumers: A Helpful Guide* (**www.dmaconsumers.org/olderconsumers.html**); "Stop Calling Me!" National Consumers League (**www.nclnet.org/privacy/stopcalling2.htm**); "How to Opt Out," Consumer Privacy Guide (**www.consumerprivacyguide.org/howto/optout.shtml**).

Chapter Twelve

Photos/Ads

p. 321, Courtesy California Milk Processor Board   **p. 322,** Courtesy DIRECTV   **p. 328,** Courtesy BBDO/Detroit   **p. 331,** Courtesy Total Gym, Inc.   **p. 334,** Reprinted courtesy of Nielsen Media Research   **p. 336,** Courtesy Nielsen Media.

Exhibits/Checklists/Commercial Breaks/Ethical Issues

Exhibit 12–1: Reprinted with permission *Advertising Age.* Copyright Crain Communications, Inc., 2005.

Exhibit 12–2: Cable Program Investor, May 19, 2005, p. 18, by Kagan Research LLC. Data from company data and estimates (accessed at **www.ncta.com**, October 2, 2005).

Exhibit 12–3: Adapted with permission from "Media Comparisons Study 2003," TVB Research Central, accessed at **www.tvb.org/mediacomparisons**. © Television Bureau of Advertising. Used by permission.

Exhibit 12–4: Forrester Research, Inc., April 2004.

Exhibit 12–5: Reprinted with permission from the June 27, 2005, issue of *Advertising Age.* Copyright Crain Communications, Inc., 2005.

Exhibit 12–6: "Fox Breaks Prime-Time Pricing Record," September 12, 2005 (accessed at **www.adweek.com**).

Exhibit 12–8: WTVM coverage map, **www.wtvm.com**.

Exhibit 12–9: Adaped with permission from R. Craig Endicott, "100 Leading National Advertisers," *Advertising Age,* June 28, 2004, S-20.

Exhibit 12–10: Reprinted with permission *Advertising Age.* Copyright Crain Communications, Inc., 2005.

Ethical Issues: Advertising to Children: Child's Play? "Self-Regulatory Guidelines for Children's Advertising," Children's Advertising Review Unit, 2003 (**www.caru.org/guidelines/index.asp**); "Barraging Kids with Ads," *San Francisco Chronicle,* July 20, 2004 (**http://sfgate.com**); "The Original Chocolate Factory Ad, Broadcast during Children's Programming, Violates CARU Guidelines," CARU news releases, August 12, 2004 (**www.caru.org/news/2004/chocfactory.asp**); "Responsibility and Children's Advertising," Concerned Children's Advertisers (**www.cca-canada.com/ethics**).

Commercial Break 12–A: Where Do These Infamous TV Ratings Come From? Nielsen people meter: Reprinted courtesy of Nielsen Media Research.

Chapter Thirteen

Photos/Ads

p. 349, Courtesy Neopets   **p. 351,** Courtesy **www.barnesandnobel.com**   **p. 359,** Courtesy Millstone Adnet   **p. 363,** ©comScore Media Matrix   **p. 368,** These materials have been reproduced with the permission of eBay Inc. COPYRIGHT ©EBAY INC. ALL RIGHTS RESERVED   **p. 369,** ©David Schaefer   **p. 371,** Courtesy Conversant Relationship Marketing   **p. 374,** Courtesy AirFrance USA; Agency: Wunderman Cato Johnson.

Exhibits/Checklists/Commercial Breaks/Ethical Issues

Exhibit 13–1: Reprinted with permission from *Advertising Age.* Copyright Crain Communications, Inc., 2005.

Exhibit 13–2: Source: ComScore Media Matrix.

Exhibit 13–3: Table adapted from "World Internet Usage and Population Statistics," *Internet World Stats,* September 1, 2004, accessed at **www.internetworldstats.com/stats.html**.

Exhibits 13–4 and 13–5: Data from U.S. Census Bureau, "Table No. 1150: Internet Access and Usage and Online Service Usage: 2004," *Statistical Abstract of the U.S. 2004,* accessed at **www.census.gov/prod/2004pubs/04statab/infocomm.pdf**.

Exhibit 13–6: "Internet Ad Revenues by Advertising Vehicle," IAB Internet Advertising Revenue Report (April 2004), 10. Used by permission.

Commercial Break 13–A: Internet Ratings: The Next Frontier. Sources used with permission and accessed at **www.adage.com**; Kate Fitzgerald, "Debate Grows over Net Data," *Advertising Age,* March 15, 2004; Randall Rothenberg, "Understanding the Audience Knowability Paradox," *Advertising Age,* June 20, 2004; "Ad Buyers, Sellers Rip Online Audience Data Accuracy," *Advertising Age,* November 3, 2003; "Old-Line Marketers Drive New Surge in Online Advertising," *Advertising Age,* March 25, 2004. Copyright Crain Communications, Inc., 2003 and 2004; and **www.nielsen-netratings. com**.

Exhibit 13–7: Reprinted with permission from *Advertising Age.* Copyright Crain Communications, Inc., 2005.

Ethical Issues: Profiling: Would You Take Cookies from a Stranger? Matt Hicks. "E-mail Privacy Debate Heads to Congress," *eWeek,* July 28, 2004 (retrieved from **www.eweek.com/article2/0,1759,1628666,00. asp**); "How Web Servers' Cookies Threaten Your Privacy," *Junk-Busters,* 2002 (retrieved from **www.junkbusters.com/cookies. html**); Christopher Penson, "Rights: The Use of Individual Information" (retrieved from **www.stedwards.edu/newc/capstone/ sp2000/rights/EFFStance.htm**); "Online Tracking FAQ," Center for Democracy & Technology (retrieved from **www.cdt.org/privacy/ guide/start/track.html**).

Exhibit 13–9: Adapted with permission from Sherry Chiger, "Looking Up: The Catalog Age 100," *Catalog Age* 21, no. 9 (August 15, 2004), accessed at **www.proquest.com**.

Chapter Fourteen

Photos/Ads

p. 379, Client: Garcia's Irish Pub; Agency: Crowley/Webb & Associates; Account Executive: Joseph Crowley, Bart Tschamler; Copywriter/Creative Director: Paul Cotter; Art Director: Jean Schweikhard; Media Director: Richard Spears   **p. 381,** Courtesy Wong Doody/Seattle   **p. 384,** ©Alan Schein Photography/CORBIS   **p. 385,** Courtesy Gannett Outdoor of Southern California   **p. 389 (top),** Courtesy International Advertising Festival Ltd.   **p. 389 (bottom),** Courtesy J.Walter Thompson/Hong Kong   **p. 390,** Courtesy International Advertising Festival Ltd.   **p. 391,** Courtesy The Firm   **p. 392,** ©Oscar/Einzig Photography   **p. 394,** Courtesy LCD Exposition Services   **p. 396,** Photo by Kevin Winter/Getty Images   **p. 397,** ©David Schaefer.

Exhibits/Checklists/Commercial Breaks/Ethical Issues

Exhibit 14–1: Outdoor Services, Division of Western Media, New York, NY.

Exhibit 14–2: Reprinted with permission from June 27, 2005 issue of *Advertising Age.* Copyright Crain Communications, Inc., 2005.

Checklist: The Pros and Cons of Outdoor Advertising. *Outdoor Advertising: Guide to Out-of-Home,* Gannett Outdoor Network, U.S., 1992, p. 21; and *Yellow Pages Industry Fact Book,* 1990–1995 Edition (Troy, MI: Yellow Pages Publishers Association, 1994).

Commercial Break 14–A: How to Use Type and Color in Outdoor Advertising. Outdoor Advertising Association of America, 1995.

Exhibit 14–3: Courtesy Gannett Outdoor of Southern California.

Exhibit 14–4: Data courtesy of Lamar Outdoor Advertising, accessed at **www.lamaroutdoor.com/main/rates/**.

Ethical Issues: Does Spillover Need Mopping Up? "Los Angeles Alcoholic Beverage Ban Statement," Outdoor Advertising Association of America, September 30, 1999 (retrieved from **www.oaaa.org**, April 2001); Benedict Carey, "Cigarettes Are Doing Big Box Office," *Los Angeles Times,* January 8, 2001; OAAA Code of Principles (retrieved from **www.oaaa.org/government**); Jon P.

Nelson, "Advertising Bans in the United States," May 21, 2004 (retrieved from **http://econ.la.psu.edu/papers/adbans_critical. pdf**); "Tobacco Menace," Consumer-Voice.org (retrieved from **www.consumer-voice.org/tobacco/tobacco3.htm**); "Beer Advertising Facts," Beer Institute (retrieved from **www.beerinstitute. org/pdfs/beeradfacts.pdf**); David Goetz, "Liquor Industry Gets Stricter on Advertising," *The Courier-Journal,* September 10, 2003 (retrieved from **www.courier-journal.com/business**); "Framework Convention on Tobacco Control," Health Canada, October 2002 (retrieved from **www.hc-sc.gc.ca/english/media/releases/ 2002/2002_66bk.htm**).

Exhibit 14–5: Trade Show Bureau, Denver, Colorado.

Exhibit 14–6: Source: 2005 Media Impact Study, conducted by TNS.

Exhibit 14–7: Reprinted with permission from *Advertising Age.* Copyright Crain Communications, Inc.

Chapter Fifteen

Photos/Ads

p. 401, Courtesy of Sony Electronics, Inc.   **p. 403,** Courtesy BMW Canada Inc.—MINI; Agency: Taxi; Creative Director: Zak Mroueh; Copywriter: Michael Clowater; Art Director: Lance Martin   **p. 406,** Courtesy International Advertising Festival Ltd.   **p. 410,** Courtesy International Advertising Festival Ltd.   **p. 415,** Courtesy Kinko's Inc.   **p. 416,** The Advertising Practice/London   **p. 417,** Courtesy Fujitsu Computer Products of America, Inc.   **p. 418,** Courtesy Godiva Chocolatier, Inc.   **p. 422,** Courtesy Crownline Boats   **p. 425 (top),** Telmar Flomaster, **www.us.telmar.com**   **p. 425 (bottom),** Courtesy SRDS.

Exhibits/Checklists/Commercial Breaks/Ethical Issues

Exhibit 15–1: Adapted with permission from "Total U.S. Spending by Media," *Advertising Age FactPack 2004,* accessed at **www. adage.com**. Copyright, Crain Communications, 2004.

Exhibit 15–2: Communications Industry Forecast, Veronis Suhler Stevenson, August 2004.

Ethical Issues: Closed-Circuit Programming. Sources: Alexandra Marks, "Patient Channel in Hospitals: Healthy Move?" *The Christian Science Monitor,* March 19, 2003 (retrieved from **www.nexis.com**); Suzanne Vranica, "Patient Channel to Blast Ads at Bedridden," *The Wall Street Journal,* September 26, 2002; Stephanie Riesenman, "Critics Object to Drug Ads on Hospital Channel," *Reuters,* February 26, 2003; "Keep Drug-Sponsored 'Patient Channel' Out of Hospitals, Doctors Say," Commercial Alert News Release, February 25, 2003 (retrieved from **www.commercialalert.org**); **www.channelone. com** (home/about channelone.com); **www.channeloneteacher. com**; Mike McWilliams, "Channel One Broadcasts Stir Debate," *Iowa City Press-Citizen,* February 27, 2003 (retrieved from **www.nexis.com**).

Exhibit 15–7: Reprinted with permission of the McGraw-Hill Companies, from Jim Surmanek, *Introduction to Advertising Media Research: Planning and Buying* (Lincolnwood, IL: NTC Business Books, 1993), 119.

Exhibit 15–10: Adapted from Sissors and Bumba, *Advertising Media Planning.*

Exhibit 15–11: "How is Advertising Readership Influenced by Ad Size and Color?" CARR—Cahners Advertising Research Report, September 2, 2005. Used by permission.

Chapter Sixteen

Photos/Ads

p. 431, ©2003 Dell Computer Corp. All rights reserved   **p. 432,** ©2005 Dell Computer Corp. All rights reserved   **p. 433,** Courtesy

International Advertising Festival Ltd. **p. 435,** Courtesy International Advertising Festival Ltd. **p. 436,** Courtesy Microsoft Corporation **p. 439,** ©Charles Gupton/Corbis **p. 440,** ©lands' End, Inc. Used with permission **p. 441,** Courtesy Total Gym **p. 442 (top),** ©2003 Dell Computer Corp. All Rights Reserved **p. 442 (bottom),** Custom Medical Stock Photo **p. 444,** Photo Disc Blue **p. 446,** Courtesy Tri-Arc Beverage Group **p. 449,** Courtesy Carmichael Lynch Advertising **p. 450,** Zigy Kaluzny/Gamma Liaison **p. 451,** Courtesy Nokia Americas **p. 452,** Courtesy Campbell Soup Company **p. 453,** Photo by: John Saller **p. 454,** Courtesy Gold's Gym.

Exhibits/Checklists/Commercial Breaks/Ethical Issues

Exhibit 16–1: R. Craig Endicott and Kenneth Wylie, "Special Report: Agency Report," *Advertising Age,* May 2, 2005, p. S-11.

Exhibit 16–2: Adapted from Bob Stone, *Successful Direct Marketing Methods,* 6th ed. (New York: McGraw-Hill/Contemporary Books, 1996).

Exhibit 16–3: Adaped with permission from "2003 Consumer Expenditure Study (Summary)," Electronic Retailing Association, accessed at **www.retailing.org**.

Exhibit 16–6: Used with permission from "Study: Some Promotions Change Consumer Behavior," *Marketing News,* October 15, 1990, p. 12.

Chapter Seventeen

Photos/Ads

p. 459, ©M. Hruby **p. 460,** Tara Flanagan **p. 466,** Courtesy Butler, Shine & Stern **p. 469,** Courtesy The Sacramento Municipal Utility District **p. 470,** Photo by Marco Garcia/Getty Images **p. 472,** Courtesy Campbell Soup Company **p. 473,** H. Howe/Allsport.

Exhibits/Checklists/Commercial Breaks/Ethical Issues

Exhibit 17–1: Annual Sponsorship Spending in North America, IEG Sponsorship Report. Used by permission.

Checklist: How to Select Events for Sponsorship. From Terry G. Vavra, *Aftermarketing: How to Keep Customers for Life Through Relationship Marketing* (Burr Ridge, IL: Irwin Professional Publishing, 1992).

Commercial Break 17–A: David Ogilvy on Corporate Advertising. Sources: Judann Dagnoll, "Ogilvy at 80," *Advertising Age,* November 4, 1991: 1, 53; David Ogilvy, *Ogilvy on Advertising* (New York: Crown Publishers, 1985), 117–26; and David Ogilvy, "We Sell, Or Else," *A.N.A./The Advertiser,* Summer 1992: 21–25.

Name Index

Company Index

Subject Index